MAKE THE CONNECTION.

WHAT DOES BECOMING A PROFESSIONAL IN EARLY CHILDHOOD EDUCATION MEAN TO YOU?

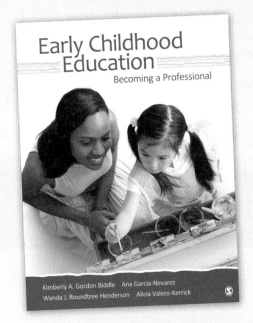

Early Childhood Education: Becoming a Professional is an inspiring introduction to the world of Early Childhood Education, preparing the educators of tomorrow to reach their full potential in their schools and communities. Written by a diverse and experienced author team, this text engages readers to connect the most modern educational and developmental theory and research to developmentally appropriate practices and applications that are easily implemented in the classroom. In response to today's ever-changing educational environment, it provides a greater focus on the importance of taking personal and professional responsibility, and it helps readers understand the importance of diversity— from individual inclusion to broader cultural contexts.

Wanda J. Roundtree Henderson, Ana Garcia-Nevarez,
Kimberly A. Gordon Biddle, Alicia Valero-Kerrick

EARLY CHILDHOOD EDUCATION: BECOMING A PROFESSIONAL

OUR AUTHOR TEAM CONNECTS:

- Theory into Practice for students to take into ECE classrooms

- Professionalism, policy, principles, and standards into the forefront of their professional lives

- Developmentally Appropriate Practice into the classroom with practical sample lesson plans for all age groups

- The importance of diversity in the early childhood classroom from individual inclusion to broader cultural contexts

THE PROFESSIONALISM CONNECTION

This textbook maps its content with the National Association for the Education of Young Children (NAEYC) developmental principles and the professional development standards for programs. Additionally, the five Core Propositions of the National Board for Professional Teaching Standards (NBPTS) are correlated with each chapter. All of these professional principles, standards, and propositions emphasize the child as capable and early childhood educators as professional and highly competent facilitators of their learning.

—*Authors*

"I enjoyed the Professionalism & Policy boxes. They were provocative and . . . they would get my students to think deeply and discuss."

— *Michelle Fryer Hanson, University of Sioux Falls*

"Professionalism is fully developed and integrated throughout the chapters . . . the author(s) actually use(s) the term Professional ECE teacher . . . The policy boxes at the end of the chapters help students understand putting theory and research into practice . . . There is discussion on developmentally appropriate practices throughout the chapters as well."

— *Kimberly K. Sellers, PhD , Pikes Peak Community College*

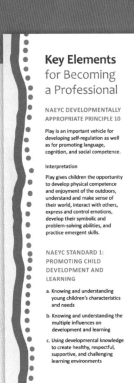

Key Elements
for Becoming
a Professional

NAEYC DEVELOPMENTALLY
APPROPRIATE PRINCIPLE 10

Play is an important vehicle for
developing self-regulation as well
as for promoting language,
cognition, and social competence.

Interpretation

Play gives children the opportunity
to develop physical competence
and enjoyment of the outdoors,
understand and make sense of
their world, interact with others,
express and control emotions,
develop their symbolic and
problem-solving abilities, and
practice emergent skills.

NAEYC STANDARD 1:
PROMOTING CHILD
DEVELOPMENT AND
LEARNING

a. Knowing and understanding
   young children's characteristics
   and needs

b. Knowing and understanding the
   multiple influences on
   development and learning

c. Using developmental knowledge
   to create healthy, respectful,
   supportive, and challenging
   learning environments

◄ *Key Elements for Becoming a Professional*
boxes demonstrate which NAEYC principles and
standards are addressed in each chapter. In addition,
the authors provide students with an interpretation
for the DAP principle.

Professionalism & Policy — Technology in the Classroom

Since the 1970s, technology has become a major part
of today's culture and has found itself in almost every
classroom. Technology brings many benefits to child
development. While children pretend to talk on old
cell phones, they are becoming familiar with how the
phone works. Computer games are not only fun for
young children; they also provide important

eye-hand coordination and an early introduction to
the keyboard (which is necessary for later years in
school and work). Games can also enhance cognitive
development. Television programs such as *Dora the
Explorer* and *Go, Diego, Go!* interact with viewers,
asking them questions and introducing Spanish during
the show.

▲ *Professionalism & Policy* boxes engage students in
examining the impact of policies dealing with issues such
as universal preschool, teacher-child ratios, and care of
mildly ill children.

Reflection, Application, and Analysis Questions

1. Describe and provide two examples of Vygotsky's
   idea of the zone of proximal development as it relates
   to play.

2. Provide examples of the relationship between language
   development and symbolic play.

3. What theoretical view of play do you consider the most
   important for a child's development?

4. Reflect on and discuss with a classmate some of the play
   development issues that teachers must keep in mind
   when planning the environment to promote the play of
   children with a physical disability.

▲ *Reflection, Application, and Analysis
Questions* help students reflect upon and critically
analyze the concepts and examples, and apply it all
to real-world situations.

▼ *Extension Activities* provide students
with additional assignments for observation
and collaboration.

Extension Activities

1. Interview an adult who attended kindergarten prior to
   1960. Observe a kindergarten and compare the two
   types of play experiences.

2. Observe and record young children during play.
   Categorize the play activities using theories of
   play discussed in this chapter (e.g., surplus energy,
   relaxation, pre-exercise, and recapitulation theory).

Additional Readings

The following list of readings will be useful for those who are interested in keeping up with the most current developments.

Broadhead, P., Howard, J., & Wood, E. (2010). *Play and
learning in the early years.* Thousand Oaks, CA: Sage.

This text examines current theoretical perspectives on
play. Examples of recent and innovative play research are
presented from a range of disciplinary and methodological
perspectives. With contributions from leading play
scholars, it brings together theory, research, policy, and
practice in relation to play and learning in early childhood
settings.

Casey, T. (2010). *Inclusive play: Practical strategies for
children from birth to eight* (2nd ed.). Thousand Oaks,
CA: Sage.

This is a practical and child-focused book that gives you
the tools you need to make sure all the children in

your classroom are included and involved in play
opportunities. Inside the second edition, updated content
includes a new chapter on risk and challenge in play, new
case studies, international perspectives, full coverage of the
birth to 8-year age range, and consideration of inclusive play
from a children's rights perspective.

Goncu, A., & Gaskins, S. (2007). *Play and development:
Evolutionary, sociocultural, and functional perspectives.*
Mahwah, NJ: Erlbaum.

The editors of this textbook explore assumptions about play
and its status as a unique and universal activity in humans.
Topics covered in this text include evolutionary foundations and
functions of play, children's play as cultural interpretation, and
the use of imagination in children's play.

On the Web

Circle Time - *http://www.badghill.pair.com/circtime/subpgs/toylinks.htm*
This website provides information about toy safety, as well as annotated links to toy stores and manufacturers. It also offers practical
information for parents on the best books for kids.

Games Kids Play - *http://www.gameskidsplay.net*
This website provides a description of children's games, game rules, the appropriateness of each game for children, and game
safety. It also contains all-time favorite rhymes.

KidSource Online - *http://www.kidsource.com*
This is an informative website for parents and children. Elementary-grade children can get assistance with their homework with
the useful link to Homework Helpers. Parents can read articles on education, health, and safety.

A Parent's Guide to Nature Play: How to Give Your Children More Outdoor Play . . . and Why You Should! -
http://www.greenheartsinc.org/uploads/A_Parents__Guide_to_Nature_Play.pdf
This guide provides parents with information on outdoor play. It gives you a perspective on how childhood has changed from 30
years ago and how you can incorporate outdoor activities in a child's life.

Play, Creativity, and Lifelong Learning: Why Play Matters for Both Kids and Adults - *http://www.helpguide.org/
life/creative_play_fun_games.htm*
This is an article from HelpGuide.org, a nonprofit source for parents and educators. This article presents important information
that was introduced in this chapter about play and its benefits for both children and adults.

▲ *Additional Readings* and *On the Web*
features provide links to resources that help
students develop as lifelong learners in early
childhood education.

THE THEORY TO PRACTICE CONNECTION

"I love all of [the pedagogical features]! Making connections from the text to the 'real world' seems to be the area students struggle in the most—and yet is the most important part."

— *Jody M. Carson, Northern Essex Community College*

Vignette: Let's Make Lunch

Gabriela, a 4-year-old preschooler, is sitting in a playhouse by a table with a plastic plate, cup, and utensils. She calls out, "Do you want to eat lunch? Come on, it's lunchtime!" Aviva, also 4, answers, "Wait." She wraps up a doll in a cloth and comes in and sits opposite Gabriela. Aviva says, "I want to help you make a sandwich." Gabriela says, "OK, let's make lunch." In the playhouse, there are plastic slices of bread, ham, tomato, and lettuce. Each child starts preparing her sandwich, and when they finish, the two girls sit and pretend to eat. Aviva then says, "I am thirsty; can I have some orange juice?" Gabriela says, "Yes, let's have some orange juice." Gabriela pretends to pour orange juice into a cup. Aviva then pretends to drink from the cup. Adam, another 4-year-old, approaches and says, "I want to play." Gabriela tells him, "You have to knock on the door to come in." Adam knocks on the imaginary door, and Gabriela asks, "Who is it?" Adam answers, "It's Adam." Gabriela then pretends to unlock and unbolt the door. Gabriela invites Adam in and asks him, "Do you want some orange juice?" They all sit down together and pretend to drink orange juice.

◀ *Chapter-opening vignettes*—about a teacher, program, child, or family—connect concepts and theories to the realities in and out of the classroom.

▶ *Consider This* boxes offer quotes from teachers, children, and parents that provide a lively, real-life illustration of textbook concepts.

Consider This The Importance of *Play*

Susan is a grandmother who raised her three kids in the mid-1960s. When she was raising her kids, she did not know much about the importance of play and the benefits that play has for children. The research was not as evident, and parents did not know that play forms the foundation for cognitive, creativity, and language development. Susan thought that when her children were playing, they were just having fun and entertaining themselves. She never thought that their play promoted their intellectual and social development. She is glad to

see and read the extensive research people have done in the area of play. Her grown-up daughter has benefitted from reading the research on play because she has exposed her kids, Susan's grandchildren, to quality books and exploratory toys that engage and challenge the mind.

How would you respond if a parent asked why the children in your care were allowed to spend so much time playing or told you that play has no contributions to learning in a child's development?

"Students really depend upon examples to show them what is actually being discussed or defined for them. The author does a great job including practical examples in the chapters to help the reader make the connections."

— *April M. Grace, Madisonville Community College*

"In my experience, many ECE textbooks focus on birth to age 5, but tend to leave out or not place as much emphasis on the early elementary students. I see more information included on this age group within this text."

— *Kimberly K. Sellers, PhD,*
Pikes Peak Community College

▶ **Sample lesson plans** designed for students in three different age groups—infants/toddlers, preschoolers, and early elementary children—are located at the end of each curriculum chapter and on the Student Study Site.

Reviewers agree on the importance of these lesson plans and their coverage of a broad range of ages.

Lesson Plan:
Sensory Exploration

Subject:
Learning through the senses.

Focus:
Use language to describe, explain, and elaborate on children's discoveries.

Overview:
Children will be exploring through the use of their senses.

Purpose:
According to Piaget, children learn through exploration of their environment during the first two years of life. Providing children with opportunities that allow them to exercise their senses is important for young developing minds.

Objective:
To promote language development, thinking, and problem solving. Children will

- Be able to use their senses to learn about their environment.
- Develop a sense of confidence.
- Have the opportunity to socially interact with other children and adults.

Resources and Materials:
None.

Activities and Procedures:
Allow infants and toddlers to explore each of the materials that will engage their various senses. Teachers or other adults can play with children to facilitate their learning.

- Sense of Touch: *Touch a Box*
  - Set out one large box, big enough for a child to crawl into.
  - Line the walls of the box with different textured paper or material. The child will have fun exploring this sensory cave.
- Sense of Hearing: *Sound of Bottles*
  - Collect some small plastic bottles and fill them with items that make a different sound (e.g., salt, beans, paper clips, rice).
  - Let the children shake the bottles to listen to the sounds.

- Caution: Be sure to supervise this game and that the children do not attempt to open the bottles.
- Sense of Smell: *Smelly Cups*
  - Set out two or three paper cups.
  - Place a cotton ball in each cup, upon which you have planted a scent (e.g., coffee, lemon extract, floral perfume).
  - Have the children tell you what each cup smells like. If they do not know the name of the smell, they can tell you if they like the smell or not.
- Sense of Vision: *Color Areas*
  - Set out a red piece of paper.
  - Ask the children to look around the room for small objects that are the same color as the red paper, and have them place the objects on the paper.
  - Continue with other colors, if interest lasts.

Lesson Plan:
The Animal World

Source: http://atozteacherstuff.com/lessonplans/programs/animalColorsShapes

Grade:
Kindergarten to third grade (5- to 8-year-olds).

Objectives and Purpose:
- Understand that animals come in different colors and shapes.
- Describe the purpose of color in the animal world.
- Use different colors and shapes to create pictures of animals.

Resources and Materials:
- Crayons
- White construction paper (1 sheet per student)
- Print images of different animals
- Different-colored construction paper cut into different-sized triangles, circles, squares, and rhomboids
- Glue

Activities and Procedures:
- After reading a book about animals, ask students to share examples of shapes they have seen. What body part of most animals is circular? What animals have triangles?
- Talk about the children's favorite animals. What colors can be found on them? Discuss some of the purposes of color in the animal world. Why are the feathers on most male birds brightly colored, while female birds have gray or brown feathers? How do some animals use color to stay hidden?
- Share print images of animals. Talk about the different colors and shapes of these animals. Tell students that they are going to create pictures of animals with different shapes. They will also draw a picture of their habitat.
- Demonstrate using a print image as an example. Talk about the animal. In what kind of environment would you expect to find this animal? Have students describe where this animal might live. Does it live in a desert or a forest?
- Next, talk about the different shapes students might see on the animal. What shape are its ears? What shape is its body?

- Use different-sized construction paper shapes to create the animal. Arrange the shapes on the background habitat, being sure to tell students that you will not use glue until it looks the way you want it to. Finally, glue the shapes on the background habitat. Demonstrate using crayons to make additional lines that should appear (such as whiskers) on the animal.
- Making sure that students understand what they are supposed to do, give them print images of animals, and tell them to choose one to copy for their picture. Have them first draw the background habitat and then use the paper shapes to make their animal. Check student work before allowing them to glue their animal shapes to the background.
- Once students have finished their pictures, ask volunteers to share them. Talk about the shapes they used. Discuss the colors of the animals. Ask about the animals' habitats. Does the color of the animal help it blend into its habitat? Display the finished pictures in the classroom.

Lesson Plan:
Representational Objects

Subject:
Cognitive and physical development.

Focus:
Promoting critical thinking with an emphasis on fine and gross motor skills.

Overview:
This activity will encourage children to remember prior knowledge and stimulate their curiosity.

Purpose:
Representational toys look like real objects in our society and environment. Many representational toys allow children to project their emotions, process feelings, and develop certain skills.

Objectives:
Encourage children to

- Make logical distinctions.
- Be able to identify, compare, and contrast objects.

Resources and Materials:
- Puzzles for fine motor skills
- Blocks for sensorimotor skills in young children and dramatic play in older children

Activities and Procedures:
Allow preschoolers to explore with the puzzles and blocks that will engage their fine motor skills.

- Teachers/adults can play with children to facilitate their learning.
- Preschoolers need to master their fine motor skills, and puzzles will aid in developing fine motor

coordination. Have preschoolers explore using the blocks. You will observe the process of stacking and knocking over blocks, and you may allow the child to do this multiple times. For older preschoolers, observe the process of building something using the blocks or using the blocks as props (e.g., telephone).

Tying It All Together:
Ask the children if they were able to put the puzzle together. What was challenging about putting the puzzle together? Playing with different types of toys provides children with opportunities to combine spoken language with imagination, to imitate, and to pretend to be someone or something else. It stimulates all areas of children's growth and can in turn affect their success in school.

Visit www.sagepub.com/gordonbiddle to access templates of these lesson plans.

DIVERSITY CONNECTION

MATH, SCIENCE, AND TECHNOLOGY CONNECTION

▶ A unique chapter, *Mathematics, Science, and Technology (Chapter 13),* provides future early childhood educators the tools needed to incorporate these topics into their classroom.

INSTRUCTOR AND STUDENT RESOURCES

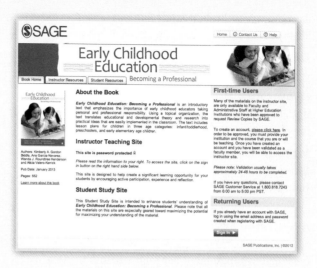

SAGE provides comprehensive and free online resources at **www.sagepub.com/gordonbiddle** designed to support and enhance both instructors' and students' experiences.

PASSWORD-PROTECTED INSTRUCTOR SITE

This password-protected site provides instructors with everything that they need to prepare and teach their introductory course. Included on the site are:

- *Test Bank (Word®):* This Word test bank offers a diverse set of test questions and answers for each chapter of the book. Multiple-choice, true/false, short-answer, and essay questions for every chapter help instructors assess students' progress and understanding.

- *Test Bank (Respondus):* This electronic test bank using Respondus software is available for use with PCs. The test bank offers a diverse set of test questions and answers for each chapter of the book. Multiple-choice, true/false, short-answer, and essay questions for every chapter help instructors assess students' progress and understanding.

- *PowerPoint:* Chapter-specific slide presentations offer assistance with lecture and review preparation by highlighting essential content, features, and artwork from the book.

- *Lecture Notes:* Summaries and outlines of each chapter are posted online for lectures/student handouts.

- *Sample Syllabi:* Sample syllabi for semester and quarter classes provide suggested models for instructors to use when creating the syllabi for their courses.

- *Discussion Questions:* Chapter-specific questions help launch discussion by prompting students to engage with the material and by reinforcing important content.

- *Class Activities:* These lively and stimulating ideas for use in class reinforce active learning. The activities apply to individual or group projects.

- *Tables and Figures:* Tables and figures from the book are available for use in handouts, lectures, or quizzes.

- *Web Resources:* These links to relevant websites direct both instructors and students to additional resources for further research on important chapter topics.

- *SAGE Journal Articles:* This feature provides access to recent, relevant, full-length articles from SAGE's leading research journals.

- *Video Links:* Carefully selected, web-based videos feature relevant interviews, lectures, personal stories, inquiries, and other content for use in independent or classroom-based explorations of key topics.

- *Audio Links:* Each chapter includes links to audio resources, which cover important topics and are designed to supplement key points within the text.

OPEN-ACCESS STUDENT STUDY SITE

Found at **www.sagepub.com/gordonbiddle**

This open-access Student Study Site is intended to enhance students' understanding of the concepts in Early Childhood Education. On this site, students have access to:

- **Quizzes:** Flexible self-quizzes allow you to review the concepts from each chapter.

- **eFlashcards:** These study tools reinforce your understanding of key terms and concepts outlined in the chapters.

- **Video Links:** Carefully selected, web-based videos feature relevant interviews, lectures, personal stories, inquiries, and other content for use in independent or classroom-based explorations of key topics.

- **Audio Links:** Each chapter includes links to audio resources, which cover important topics and are designed to supplement key points within the text.

- **Web Resources:** These links to relevant websites direct both instructors and students to additional resources for further research on important chapter topics.

- **SAGE Journal Articles:** A "Learning From SAGE Journal Articles" feature provides access to recent, relevant full-text articles from SAGE's leading research journals. This feature also provides discussion questions to focus and guide student interpretation.

- **Workshop Formats:** These author-created workshop formats include topic discussions, workshop activities, wrap-up activities, and evaluation questions and activities all of which allow a hands-on approach to exploring topics in the text.

- **Lesson Plans:** Sample lesson plans give you the tools you need to conduct meaningful lessons in the classroom. Plans are provided for different age ranges.

ACKNOWLEDGMENTS

SAGE and our authors would like to thank the numerous outside reviewers who provided many valuable comments and suggestions.

Erin Barton – *University of Colorado, Denver*

Heather Batchelder – *University of Central Florida*

Mary K. Bendixen-Noe – *Ohio State University, Newark*

Mona Bryant-Shanklin – *Norfolk State University*

Jody Carson – *Northern Essex Community College*

Sharon Carter – *Davidson County Community College*

Marilyn Chu – *Western Washington University*

Sabine Gerhardt – *The University of Akron*

April M. Grace – *Madisonville Community College*

Carolyn J. Griess – *Pennsylvania State University, Harrisburg*

Michelle Fryer Hanson – *University of Sioux Falls*

Mary Hynes-Berry – *Erikson Institute*

Celia Billescas Hilber – *Jacksonville State University*

Cheryl J. Hitchcock – *Middle Tennessee State University*

Wendy Jacocks-*Southeastern Louisiana University*

Jennifer A. Kampmann – *South Dakota State University*

Kejing Liu – *Shawnee State University*

Wendy McCarty – *Illinois College*

Nancy Merryman – *Mount Mercy University*

Dawn S. Munson – *Elgin Community College*

Tara Newman – *Stephen F. Austin State University*

Angela Pack-*Hudson County Community College*

Sureshrani Paintal – *Chicago State University*

Barba Aldis Patton – *University of Houston, Victoria*

Deborah J. Ranz-Smith – *College of Mount St. Joseph*

Linda Rivers – *University of Tennessee at Chattanooga*

Dr. Patsy J. Robles-Goodwin – *Texas Wesleyan University*

Cheryl Sanchez – *Southwest Texas Junior College*

Hilary Seitz – *University of Alaska Anchorage*

Kimberly Sellers – *Pikes Peak Community College*

Lois Silvernail – *Spring Hill College*

Ruslan Slutsky – *University of Toledo*

Ranae Stetson – *Texas Christian University*

Ursula Thomas – *University of West Georgia*

Candra D. Thornton – *University of North Carolina, Wilmington*

Leslie Haley Wasserman – *Heidelberg University*

Su-Jeong Wee – *Purdue University Calumet*

James C. Young – *Clark Atlanta University*

Early Childhood Education

Early Childhood Education
Becoming a Professional

Kimberly A. Gordon Biddle
California State University, Sacramento

Ana Garcia-Nevarez
California State University, Sacramento

Wanda J. Roundtree Henderson
California State University, Sacramento

Alicia Valero-Kerrick
California State University, Sacramento

Los Angeles | London | New Delhi
Singapore | Washington DC

Los Angeles | London | New Delhi
Singapore | Washington DC

FOR INFORMATION:

SAGE Publications, Inc.
2455 Teller Road
Thousand Oaks, California 91320
E-mail: order@sagepub.com

SAGE Publications Ltd.
1 Oliver's Yard
55 City Road
London EC1Y 1SP
United Kingdom

SAGE Publications India Pvt. Ltd.
B 1/I 1 Mohan Cooperative Industrial Area
Mathura Road, New Delhi 110 044
India

SAGE Publications Asia-Pacific Pte. Ltd.
3 Church Street
#10-04 Samsung Hub
Singapore 049483

Acquisitions Editor: Diane McDaniel
Associate Editor: Megan Krattli
Associate Editor: Theresa Accomazzo
Assistant Editor: Rachael Leblond
Editorial Assistant: Megan Koraly
Production Editor: Libby Larson
Copy Editor: Melinda Masson
Typesetter: C & M Digitals (P) Ltd.
Proofreader: Scott Oney
Indexer: Michael Ferriera
Cover Designer: Gail Buschman
Marketing Manager: Terra Schultz
Permissions Editor: Adele Hutchinson

Printed in the United States of America

Library of Congress Cataloging-in-Publication Data

Gordon, Kimberly A. (Kimberly Ann), 1965-

Early childhood education: becoming a professional /
Kimberly A. Gordon Biddle, California State University, Sacramento,
Ana Garcia-Nevarez, California State University, Sacramento,
Wanda J. Roundtree Henderson, California State University,
Sacramento, Alicia Valero-Kerrick, California State University,
Sacramento.

pages cm
Includes bibliographical references and index.

ISBN 978-1-4129-7345-8 (pbk.)

1. Early childhood teachers—Training of. 2. Early childhood education—Study and teaching. I. Title.

LB1732.3.G67 2014
372.21—dc23   2012035565

This book is printed on acid-free paper.

SUSTAINABLE FORESTRY INITIATIVE
Certified Chain of Custody
Promoting Sustainable Forestry
www.sfiprogram.org
SFI-01268
SFI label applies to text stock

13 14 15 16 17 10 9 8 7 6 5 4 3 2 1

Brief Contents

Detailed Contents

Preface

We four authors of *Early Childhood Education: Becoming a Professional* each took a different path to becoming higher education instructors of early childhood education, but we were united by a singular motivation: We truly believe education changes lives. We each deeply wanted to help all children, including underserved populations, children with special needs, ethnic and language minorities, and children from low socioeconomic backgrounds to have the chance to reach their full potential. Quality early childhood education (ECE) experiences for young children that are the result of a well-informed, knowledgeable, and skilled workforce afford children the best possible start down the path to lifelong learning. Yet, despite playing such a crucial role in society, in the past early childhood educators have too frequently been dismissed as merely caregivers rather than teachers. However, as early childhood professionals, we have witnessed the beginning of a mammoth change in the field. This change is the transition from early childhood professionals relying on intuition to demanding high-quality instruction and engagement of children that utilizes research to support effective learning and development. Accordingly, we wanted to provide our students and students across the country with an introductory textbook that emphasizes professionalism and the impact quality ECE teachers can have when they embrace the professional responsibilities of their role. It is our hope that *Early Childhood Education: Becoming a Professional* will inspire and inform the next generation of early childhood professionals.

Themes

The purpose of our text is to prepare students to become professionals who will positively impact the lives of young children. We have done this by focusing on five thematic areas that highlight the following:

1. The importance of personal and professional responsibility;

2. The potential for developmentally appropriate practice to promote optimal development and maximize learning;

3. The impact of policy and the social landscape on the field of early childhood education;

4. The need to support and advocate for all children and their families; and

5. The positive outcomes derived by applying theory and research to practical, easy-to-implement ideas.

Our aim is to increase the amount of professional and personal responsibility that early childhood educators assume for their own learning as well as the creation of learning experiences for the children they teach. To that end, we have ensured that this textbook maps its content with the National Association for the Education of Young Children (NAEYC) developmental principles and the professional development standards for programs. Additionally, the Five Core Propositions of the National Board for Professional Teaching Standards (NBPTS) are correlated with each chapter. All of these professional principles, standards, and propositions emphasize high expectations for children and early childhood educators as professional and highly competent facilitators of their learning.

Audience

We recognize that for the majority of students, the intro course and its textbook will be their first introduction to the early childhood profession. Therefore, we have written *Early Childhood Education: Becoming a Professional* in an approachable, personal style using frequent examples, vignettes, and classroom scenarios to help students relate the theory and research therein to their own lives and experiences.

Features

The features throughout the book were developed to reinforce the themes described above.

Chapter-opening vignettes. Each chapter begins with a vignette (a story) about a teacher, program, family worker, child, or family that illustrates how the content of the chapter relates to real situations an early childhood educator may encounter. Frequently, the opening vignette is revisited within the chapter, as a way of making connections between theory, concepts, and reality.

Learning objectives. Each chapter also contains learning objectives formatted as important questions to consider while reading. These correspond with the section headings throughout the chapter and serve as a guide to readers to help them understand the chapter's organization and prepare them for what they will be learning.

Reflection, Application, and Analysis Questions. At the end of each chapter, students are asked to delve a little deeper and reflect on the knowledge they have gained, apply it to real-world situations, and critically analyze the material.

Extension Activities. These activities challenge students to take what they've learned a step further by observing ECE environments, interviewing professionals in the field, or journaling about their own experiences, among other engaging exercises.

Additional Readings and *On the Web.* These end-of-chapter features offer helpful resource lists for students that give readers an expanded perspective on the content of the chapter.

Lesson plans. Each of the curriculum chapters closes with lesson plans developed for three age-groups: infant/toddler, preschool, and early elementary. These concrete activities further demonstrate how the theories, research, and foundational ideas students have just read about can be applied in real early childhood classroom settings.

Additionally, the text features six types of boxes within the chapters that reinforce the book's themes:

Key Elements for Being a Professional. These boxes demonstrate which NAEYC principles and standards are addressed in each chapter.

Consider This. Hypothetical scenarios featuring teachers, children, and parents provide lively illustrations of textbook concepts and challenge students to consider how they would respond.

Professionalism & Policy. These boxes engage students in examining the impact of policies dealing with issues such as universal preschool, teacher-child ratios, and care of mildly ill children.

Best Practices. Professional ECE teachers embrace the responsibility of improving the quality of early childhood education. To invest students with an ethic of professional responsibility, we have incorporated *Best Practices* models in many of the chapters. For students, these boxes create a link between the idea of a best practice and the many examples discussed in the chapter. Some of the best practices highlighted include techniques for guidance of children, motivating professionals to further their education, and advocating for children and families.

Promoting Optimal Development. School readiness is a key result of quality early childhood education. These boxes demonstrate strategies for teaching young children in a developmentally appropriate fashion, which will prepare them to succeed in school as they grow.

The Practice of Research and Theory. These boxes contain a summary of a current article on theory or research and describe a process for incorporating the ideas or study results into early childhood teaching practices. This information helps students understand the process of translating research and theory into practice—a crucial skill for all early childhood professionals.

Ancillaries

Instructor Teaching Site

A password-protected site, available at www.sagepub.com/gordonbiddle, features resources that have been designed to help instructors plan and teach their courses. These resources include an extensive test bank, chapter-specific PowerPoint presentations, lecture notes, sample syllabi for semester and quarter courses, class activities, discussion questions, SAGE journal articles, video links, and web resources.

Student Study Site

An open-access student study site is available at **www.sagepub.com/gordonbiddle**. This site provides access to several study tools including eFlashcards, web quizzes, links to SAGE journal articles, web resources, video resources, lesson plan templates, and more.

Acknowledgments

W e wish to thank the entire editorial and marketing staff at SAGE Publications. We are especially grateful to Diane McDaniel and Megan Krattli, whose support and suggestions greatly improved the content of this textbook. We would also like to recognize the invaluable assistance given to us by Jessica McCollum, Rian Carroll, Alicia Alacron, Vanessa Bentley, Crystal Furhman, Chantaal Eliot, Brittany Nelson, Jennifer Gonzalez, Danielle Walker, Sadat Zarek, Celina Clark, and Lisa Heritage.

We also wish to thank the numerous outside reviewers who provided many valuable comments and suggestions:

Erin Barton, University of Colorado, Denver

Heather Batchelder, University of Central Florida

Mary K. Bendixen-Noe, Ohio State University, Newark

Mona Bryant-Shanklin, Norfolk State University

Jody Carson, Northern Essex Community College

Sharon Carter, Davidson County Community College

Marilyn Chu, Western Washington University

Sabine Gerhardt, The University of Akron

April M. Grace, Madisonville Community College

Carolyn J. Griess, Pennsylvania State University, Harrisburg

Michelle Fryer Hanson, University of Sioux Falls

Mary Hynes-Berry, Erikson Institute

Celia Billescas Hilber, Jacksonville State University

Cheryl J. Hitchcock, Middle Tennessee State University

Jennifer A. Kampmann, South Dakota State University

Kejing Liu, Shawnee State University

Wendy McCarty, Illinois College

Nancy Merryman, Mount Mercy University

Dawn S. Munson, Elgin Community College

Tara Newman, Stephen F. Austin State University

Sureshrani Paintal, Chicago State University

Barba Aldis Patton, University of Houston, Victoria

Deborah J. Ranz-Smith, College of Mount St. Joseph

Linda Rivers, University of Tennessee at Chattanooga

Cheryl Sanchez, Southwest Texas Junior College

Kimberly Sellers, Pikes Peak Community College

Lois Silvernail, Spring Hill College

Ranae Stetson, Texas Christian University

Ursula Thomas, University of West Georgia

Candra D. Thornton, University of North Carolina, Wilmington

Leslie Haley Wasserman, Heidelberg University

Su-Jeong Wee, Purdue University Calumet

James C. Young, Clark Atlanta University

We also have some individual acknowledgments we would like to share.

Dr. Biddle wants to thank her mother, Mary Ann, and her brother, Randy, for their love and support. She also wishes to thank her husband, Chris Biddle, and her son, Emmanuel Biddle, for loving her and being her motivation to complete this project. Special thanks go to Chris Biddle for caring for the household, the family, and their son, Emmanuel, when Dr. Biddle was too busy writing. She also wants to thank God, with whom all things are possible.

Dr. Garcia-Nevarez would like to thank her husband, Dr. Carlos Nevarez, and her two children, Gabriela and Carlitos, for their support, patience, understanding, and love during these past few years of researching and writing this textbook. Further, this textbook is dedicated to her devoted and loving mother, Alma Garcia, and her beloved son, Samuel Nevarez, whose memory will live on forever.

Dr. Roundtree Henderson wishes to first acknowledge the One in whom she lives and moves and has her being, the Christ in her life. It is because of Him that she continues to rise to greater heights. She is eternally indebted to her husband, her one true love and keeper of her heart, Dr. Darryl O'Neal Henderson, and to her identical twin sister and better half, Dr. Gwendolyn R. Evans—both of whom always help her to realize what is possible. Many thanks to her host of nieces and nephews who always provided her with invaluable insight into the nuances of early development and to her West Coast sister-friend, Dalila Rubin, JD candidate, for always believing in her. And last, she is deeply grateful to her very able administrative assistant, Denise Auzenne, for lending her technical talents and support to this project.

Dr. Valero-Kerrick wishes to express her appreciation to her husband, Ken Kerrick, for his love and encouragement, and for entertaining their sons, Kenny and Daniel, while she wrote incessantly. She also wishes to thank Ricanne Roberts, a wonderful and resourceful classroom teacher, who willingly shared her expertise on various educational topics. Special thanks to her mother, Virginia Valero, and to her mother-in-law, Genoveva Kerrick, for being a source of strength and wisdom.

PART I

Foundations of Early Childhood Education

CHAPTER

1

The Early Childhood Teacher

This chapter will help you answer these important questions:

- Who is the early childhood teacher?

- What are the roles of the early childhood teacher?

- What are the requirements for becoming an early childhood teacher?

- What knowledge and skills should early childhood teachers possess?

Vignette: The Decision

Susana, a college senior, is preparing to graduate this semester. After exploring other career options in her junior year, she decided to major in child development—a major that would give her the option of working with children and their parents. Susana's mom is a preschool teacher, and now that Susana is about to graduate, she feels a calling to become an early childhood teacher too. Susana recognizes that she enjoys and has a significant amount of experience working with young children, both as a babysitter and through helping in preschool classrooms. Susana spent time in her mom's classroom in order to fulfill a fieldwork class that required her to volunteer in a preschool setting. Helping her mom in the classroom and watching how her mom interacted with the children was inspiring and motivating for Susana. Based on her experience, her skills, and her enthusiasm to work with children, she decides that she wants to be an early childhood teacher.

In this chapter, you will learn about the most important person in early childhood education—the teacher. We will describe teachers' motivations, their personal and professional characteristics, the different roles they fill, the requirements they must meet, the knowledge and skills they must have, and the challenges male early childhood education (ECE) teachers face.

We present two of the standards that the National Association for the Education of Young Children (NAEYC) has developed. The first is the developmentally appropriate principle that informs the best developmentally appropriate practice in the care and education of young children from birth through age 8. The second is the standards for becoming an early childhood professional. These two key elements are important for the development of young children. Young children benefit from the well-planned curriculum that supports and challenges them. Therefore, a well-trained teacher who uses responsive and intentional strategies will teach to enhance development and learning and plan curriculum aligned with important learning outcomes.

Early childhood education is the education of children from birth through age 8 and includes the programs we separately refer to as nursery school, child care, day care, preschool, kindergarten, first grade, second grade, and third grade. However, early childhood education is also a field of study. Studying early childhood education means learning about

- Children's development—the developmental stages children go through and the general characteristics (e.g., physical, socioemotional, and cognitive) of each stage
- The history and current state of early childhood education—the various theories about children and the different approaches to educating them, past and present

Key Elements for Becoming a Professional

NAEYC DEVELOPMENTALLY APPROPRIATE PRINCIPLE 7

Children develop best when they have secure, consistent relationships with responsive adults and opportunities for positive relationships with peers.

Interpretation

A supporter of this principle is John Bowlby (1969/1982), the first attachment theorist, who described attachment as a "lasting psychological connectedness between human beings" (p. 194). Bowlby believed that the earliest relationships formed by children with their caregivers have a great impact on their relationships that continues throughout life.

NAEYC STANDARD 6: BECOMING A PROFESSIONAL

a. Identifying and involving oneself with the early childhood field

b. Knowing about and upholding ethical standards and other professional guidelines

c. Engaging in continuous, collaborative learning to inform practice

d. Integrating knowledgeable, reflective, and critical perspectives on early education

e. Engaging in informed advocacy for children and the profession

- Basic methods and techniques—how to observe, assess, and evaluate children; how to provide guidance to children; and how to provide children with a safe and educationally productive physical environment
- Parenting techniques—helping parents become aware of the latest educational methods
- Curriculum—the techniques and tools used to help children develop the physical, socioemotional, and cognitive skills required to function in the world
- The latest state and federal policies
- Personal and professional responsibility for improving the quality of early childhood education

WHO IS THE EARLY CHILDHOOD TEACHER?

Teaching at any level is much more than standing in front of a class and controlling students' attention while stating facts. Teachers also have to keep students interested, help them maintain their enthusiasm for learning, and respond creatively to their questions and concerns. They also have to create lessons and activities that stimulate students' thinking. All in all, teaching consists of thousands of everyday "acts of creation"—constructing new activities—that spring from the teacher's knowledge, abilities, and training (C. Phillips, 1994).

Teaching preschoolers is similar to teaching elementary children because, in both cases, teaching is largely aimed at promoting children's general intellectual, linguistic, physical, and socioemotional development. (Teaching elementary school–age children, in contrast, is primarily aimed at helping them acquire specific knowledge and skills.) In addition, the educational curriculum for preschoolers and early elementary children is the same—math, science, history, social studies, art, geography, and language—except that the content and teaching methods must be developmentally appropriate for the age-group.

WHY BECOME AN EARLY CHILDHOOD TEACHER?

You probably have multiple reasons for wanting to become an early childhood teacher. Maybe you enjoy working with and teaching young children, or you developed an interest in the field of early childhood education. Whatever your reasons might be, you have started on the path toward becoming an early childhood teacher.

Characteristics of Good Early Childhood Teachers

There are many characteristics and qualities that make someone a good early childhood teacher. As we will see in the discussions that follow, these qualities include certain personality characteristics, an ability to be self-aware, and an intrinsic motivation to teach. Early childhood teachers are aware of the many ethical issues involved in teaching, an awareness that allows them to make responsible decisions. They develop a philosophy of teaching that lets them function well in the classroom, while allowing them to grow as professionals and as human beings.

Personality and Self-Awareness

Good early childhood teachers need to be patient, energetic, creative, flexible, caring, cheerful, optimistic, encouraging, and enthusiastic. Of course, nobody can be all these things all the time, but striving to be is important since children react to and are influenced by a teacher's personality. A teacher who is patient, caring, and encouraging can help a child with separation anxiety on the first day of preschool. For example, the teacher approaches the child and welcomes him or her by saying his or her name and good morning in a friendly voice and giving the child a hug. Personality characteristics like these will not only have a positive influence on students' growth and development, but will also lead to better relationships with colleagues and parents (Saracho & Spodek, 2007).

Being **self-aware**—understanding your own behavior, motivation, and personality—will help you develop a teaching style that makes you comfortable. For example, an **intentional teaching style**, which involves planning, thinking about the goals of the lesson, and organizing the learning experiences of the children (Epstein, 2007; see next sections for more information on intentional teaching), will make your teaching more effective. You can increase your level of self-awareness by asking yourself what your personality is like. For example:

- Are you generally relaxed or tense, positive or negative?
- Do you get frustrated or anger easily?
- How do you feel when something is difficult or when you make a mistake?
- Do you get along well with people?
- Can you handle negative feedback from others?
- Do you see yourself as a learner? Where does your learning take place—in a classroom setting or in the field, working with children? Do you learn from other teachers? Do you learn from children?

In addition to being self-aware, you need to believe in your own **competence**—to value your abilities and feel justified in aspiring to success—in order to make the best use of your teaching skills and positive aspects of your personality (Harackiewicz, Sansone, & Manderlink, 1985). Believing in your teaching abilities can lead to increased motivation.

Intrinsic Motivation

You probably have multiple reasons for wanting to become an early childhood teacher. Maybe you enjoy working with young children, you just like teaching, or you have developed an interest in the field of early childhood education.

Having **intrinsic motivation** for doing something means that you want to engage in the activity because it gives you internal satisfaction (Wade & Travis, 1990). For example, you may be intrinsically motivated to become a teacher because you find teaching pleasurable, you enjoy the intellectual challenge it offers, or it satisfies your curiosity about children and how they learn (Wade & Travis, 1990). To find out if you are intrinsically motivated to work with young children, ask yourself the following questions:

An intrinsically motivated teacher enjoys the challenge of helping young children participate actively and productively in classroom activities.

- Why do you want to become an early childhood teacher?
- What will make you happy in your job? What will be your sources of interest and pleasure on the job?
- What will make you unhappy in your job? What might make the job unfulfilling or unpleasant?
- Overall, will you be satisfied with your job? Will the positives outweigh the negatives?

Ethics

Ethics are principles that help us make decisions about how to act morally and socially. The more difficult and complex the situation, the more we need ethical principles to guide us. We all follow ethical guidelines; being aware of our own ethical guidelines helps us to stop and think before acting hastily.

Teachers are role models for children, parents, and members of the community, so it is especially important that they behave ethically. As a teacher, you will inevitably face difficult situations, ones in which you will have to make ethical choices. Some schools offer in-service classes to discuss ethical issues. All schools have codes of ethics for their employees, so teachers can become familiar with what is expected of them.

Recognizing the importance of ethics, the NAEYC has developed a document called the Code of Ethical Conduct and Statement of Commitment, which provides guidelines for early childhood educators (see Appendix A). The four sections in the code spell out educators' responsibilities to children, families, colleagues, the community, and society. The detailed guidelines in the NAEYC (2005) code are based on a list of "core values that are deeply rooted in the history of the field of early childhood care and education." These values should lead early childhood educators to make a commitment to the following NAEYC principles:

- Appreciate childhood as a unique and valuable stage of the human life cycle.
- Base your work on knowledge of how children develop and learn.
- Appreciate and support the bond between the child and family.
- Recognize that children are best understood and supported in the context of family, culture,[1] community, and society.
- Respect the dignity, worth, and uniqueness of each individual (child, family member, and colleague).
- Respect diversity in children, families, and colleagues.
- Recognize that children and adults achieve their full potential in the context of relationships that are based on trust and respect.

Philosophy of Teaching

Your philosophy of teaching—your approach to and beliefs about teaching—reflects your values, knowledge, education, and experience. The following things come together to compose your philosophy of teaching: what you know and believe about yourself, schools, children, colleagues, and so on; what you have studied and learned; and what you have experienced in school, on the job, and in your personal life. Clearly, your philosophy of teaching will change and develop over time as you gain knowledge and experience and grow as a person and as a professional.

When you go for a job interview, school administrators will ask you to explain your teaching practices and your philosophy of teaching. This will be a challenge if you haven't thought about the question beforehand. You also need to understand that this isn't an offhand question—your teaching philosophy will guide your daily teaching practices in the classroom, and administrators are well aware of that fact. For example, if your philosophy of teaching is that children's development of knowledge and understanding occurs through experimentation, active exploration, and questioning, then this philosophy will guide your teaching practices and assist you with the organization and activities of the classroom environment.

As you think about and develop your philosophy of teaching, keep in mind the special importance of understanding children's different needs, interests, and learning styles, both in general and individually. This kind of understanding—gained from your studies and from your practical classroom experiences—will enrich your teaching philosophy. At a practical level, it will also help you select materials and activities that are developmentally appropriate for your students as a group and for each student individually.

Intentional Teaching

There are many examples of teaching philosophies, but the one example provided here is intentional teaching. Intentional teachers are those who plan with a goal in mind, and who teach to accomplish that goal (Epstein, 2007). These teachers use their knowledge to think about all aspects of the learning environment, such as arranging the classroom and the delivery of instruction, prior to accomplishing their goal.

REWARDS OF BEING AN EARLY CHILDHOOD TEACHER

As an early childhood teacher, you will get pleasure from helping children refine their understanding of the world, make appropriate choices, and make connections with other children. You will also treasure the opportunity to influence children's lives by providing motivation and guidance that can open up possibilities and help children achieve happiness and success. Then there are the smaller daily satisfactions: assisting children with specific tasks, soothing them when they're upset, resolving conflicts, and talking with them about their work. For someone who loves teaching, these interactions provide the rewarding satisfaction of making a child feel secure and productive. Each of these experiences is a teaching opportunity, and no two are the same. Teachers who can keep both the big and the little rewards in mind day to day and minute to minute will be happier in their work and will find it easier to overcome difficulties in the classroom (Ghazvini & Mullis, 2002). For example, when asked, "What was the most rewarding aspect of being an early childhood teacher?" Mickey Eichenhofer (personal communication, October 3, 2011), a preschool teacher, said, "The most rewarding thing for me is when I know that I've made a difference in a child's life. This could be when a child tells me a simple 'thank you' or when a child achieves beyond his or her expectations."

People who choose teaching as their career stay in the profession because their daily routine is not the same every day. Teaching is not a desk job. Daily variations of activities and routines can be a motivator and rewarding. This, in effect, can foster your enjoyment of the job and retention in the profession.

Making a Contribution

Some teachers find teaching students from urban settings and who are English language learners to be satisfying because it offers them self-fulfillment and makes them feel that they are making an important contribution to society. Research suggests that teachers of color or teachers who know a second language are very much interested in serving urban communities and enjoy working with minority students (Liu, Kardos, Kauffman, Peske, & Johnson, 2000). One such example is Alma Ponce (personal communication, November 13, 2011), a preschool teacher, who said, "I like working with a diverse student population, especially English language learners. I feel needed, and I can communicate with the children in their native language [Spanish]."

Other research studies propose that the most competent teachers for diverse learners possess knowledge of students' "cultural and linguistic norms" (Gandara, Rumberger, Maxwell-Jolly, & Callahan, 2003, p. 17). Wong-Fillmore and Snow (2000) note that teachers' understanding of English language learners' native language, in both structure and usage, is important. Working with minority students provides meaningful and fulfilling work experience.

A teacher's reward is helping children learn, grow, and be happy.

Teaching as Career Choice

As a teacher, you must possess a strong commitment to a career in preschool and the public school sector as well as have a deep commitment to being involved in the communities where you will be teaching. Most preservice teachers enter their college programs with already high levels of commitment to the profession (Gomez, Garcia-Nevarez, Knutson Miller, & Strage, 2006; Root, Callahan, & Sepanski, 2002). Many are drawn to the profession because a family member is a teacher, they enjoy working with children, or the prospect of having summers off and the opportunity to obtain tenure is attractive (Liu et al., 2000). Despite this initial high level of dedication, some preservice teachers have reported a decrease in career commitment; these results may represent a developing appreciation of the realities of teaching's challenges rather than a change of career goals (Gomez et al., 2006; Malone, Jones, & Stallings, 2002).

A CHALLENGE FACED BY EARLY CHILDHOOD TEACHERS

Teaching young children isn't easy. You, as teachers, need to be knowledgeable, skillful, alert, and flexible; in addition, you need to be able to take constructive criticism and learn from your mistakes. Beyond the personal challenges of the profession, the field of early childhood education itself also poses a serious professional challenge. The challenges that will be discussed in the following sections are teacher shortages, turnover rate, and burnout.

Teacher Shortages

Many early childhood teachers face challenges due to the problem of teacher shortages. The shortage in the number of teachers is mainly due to retirement, the lack of qualified teachers, poor salaries and benefits, the increased need for child care, employee turnover, and teacher burnout. Obviously, there are many challenges in any profession, but because early childhood teaching deals with young children and the type of education they are getting outside of their home, this issue of teacher shortages becomes very important to parents and society.

The retirement of the "baby boomers" generation and a lack of qualified teachers to replace them is a contributing factor to the teacher shortage. A new study by First 5 California and the University of California, Berkeley (2006) found that one quarter of preschool teachers with a bachelor's degree are close to retirement age. This creates a challenge for the profession since there are not enough young, qualified teachers to replace those who will be retiring (Miranda, 2006). Not only is there a shortage of teachers, but early childhood education has a much bigger issue—the lack of qualified teachers, especially ones who are linguistically diverse. The inability of a teaching staff to communicate with parents and children due to language barriers has become a concern in many child care centers (Chang, Muckelroy, & Pulido-Tobiassen, 1996; Chang & Sakai, 1993; D. Phillips, 1996). Directors of preschools and child care centers are hiring staff who are bilingual to assist with this language barrier and to try to integrate non-English-speaking parents into their child's education.

Another reason for the teacher shortage is the low salaries and poor benefits that teachers receive (Torquati, Raikes, & Huddleston-Casas, 2007). Not only early childhood teachers, but also teachers in general (elementary, middle, and high school), are underpaid when compared with other people who have just graduated from college. For example, an individual with a bachelor's degree in business who has a similar amount of work experience as a teacher with a bachelor's degree will tend to start a new job with a higher salary and better benefits than the teacher. Private businesses tend to pay their employees much higher salaries than most state governments pay their teachers. Therefore, the teacher salaries grow at a significantly slower rate than the salaries paid by private employers. Nevertheless, early childhood teachers choose this profession not because of the monetary rewards but for the love of working with young children and the satisfaction they receive from everyday interactions.

While the number of teachers is expected to drop, the number of children entering preschool nationwide is growing and is expected to continue growing at a significant rate (U.S. Bureau of Labor Statistics, 2000). Demographic changes in the United States, including an increase in the proportion of women entering the workforce, have had a significant impact on the demand for child care services (U.S. Bureau of Labor Statistics, 2000). In 1999, 73% of children under age 5 with an employed parent were in a child care program for all or part of the day (Sonenstein, Gates, Schmidt, & Bolshun, 2002). This high demand for child care also comes from parents who want their children to experience the educational and socioemotional enrichment provided by child care centers. All of this growth creates a high demand for teachers.

Not only has a teacher shortage been a concern, but so has the teacher **turnover rate**—the percentage of teachers who leave their jobs in a given period of time. The relatively high turnover rate reflects the fact that the early child care workforce is unstable. Significant turnover rates in ECE are a result of the low salaries and benefits teachers receive. A study conducted by Whitebook, Sakai, Gerber, and Howes (2001) followed a group of teachers, assistants, and directors at child care centers over three points in time (1994, 1996, and 2000). This longitudinal study was conducted in the same child care centers in three California communities with 117 teaching staff: 71% teachers, 17% assistants, and 12% directors.

Through observations and interviews with teachers, assistants, and directors, the study summarizes the major reasons why these staff members stayed with or left the child care centers (Whitebook et al., 2001). The major reasons why teachers left their jobs were for better pay and benefits, to seek better work relationships, and because of high turnover rates among coworkers and directors. The primary reason why directors left their jobs was the high level of teacher turnover. Directors faced the challenge of running a program without trained teaching staff, and many directors had to be in the classroom, which kept them from being able to do their administrative work. Others reported that better pay or funding would have made a difference in their staying (Holochwost, DeMott, Buell, Yannetta, & Amsden, 2009; Whitebook et al., 2001). Reasons why directors stayed in the field included gratification obtained from their work, the respect that comes with the job, and the flexibility of working part- or full-time (see Chapter 16 for more information on supporting early childhood educators in the workplace).

Teacher turnover results in teacher shortages and in turn discourages the consistent relationship between children and teachers. An inconsistent teacher-child relationship can affect children's socioemotional and language development. If teachers are constantly leaving, children may feel insecure with their caretakers, not knowing whom they can trust. This lack of trust can create a less interactive environment that causes children not to communicate with their caretakers.

For example, classrooms with higher turnover were characterized by an environment that is less developmentally appropriate and includes fewer developmentally appropriate activities, and the teaching staff in these programs interacted with less sensitivity toward the children (Whitebook et al., 2001). The overall result is that the high turnover rate affects the quality of care the program is able to provide.

Many early childhood teachers experience burnout at some point during their career. **Burnout** has been defined as "physical, emotional, and attitudinal exhaustion" (Hendrickson, 1979).

Typically, burnout begins with a feeling of uneasiness that becomes increasingly hard to bear as job satisfaction decreases. The specific symptoms of burnout are different for each person, but they generally consist of feelings of lacking or having lost something (McGee-Cooper, Trammel, & Lau, 1990), such as energy, enthusiasm, satisfaction, motivation, interest, concentration, self-confidence, or humor. Factors that contribute to teacher burnout can include low salaries, inadequate benefits, long working hours, lack of breaks, and high child-teacher ratios (Whitebook et al., 2001). In some cases, burnout results in teacher turnover.

There are many factors causing the teacher shortage. The problem of poor salary and benefits is relatively minor when compared with the other factors mentioned earlier (retirement, the increased number of children in day care, job instability, and burnout). Despite these stresses, many early childhood teachers, whether or not they continue in their job as teachers, report much satisfaction from working with young children (Whitebook et al., 2001). This satisfaction comes from the pure enjoyment of working with children and believing in the work that they do.

DEVELOPMENTAL STAGES OF EARLY CHILDHOOD TEACHERS

As teachers, most of you will go through a certain sequence of steps over the first few years of your careers, which the renowned educator Lilian Katz calls **developmental stages**. Each of the four stages is described in Table 1.1 and involves distinctive developmentally appropriate assignments and training needs. Overall, at each developmental stage, you, as a teacher, will expand and progress in your career, your classroom responsibilities, and your interactions with children, parents, and colleagues.

Her first year teaching preschool, Karla experienced several challenges that made her feel unprepared to be in the classroom. She was able to obtain some guidance by Mary, who advised her in basic classroom routines and behavioral problems. During her second year, she reached the "consolidation" stage—she assimilated her knowledge gained that first year and began to focus on the students' learning. In her third and fourth years, Karla reached the "maturity" stage and was able to ask more profound and abstract questions that made an impact on the community in which she was working.

Consider This The First Year

This is Karla's first year teaching at a preschool. She was trying to keep afloat with managing classroom behavior, preparing thematic lessons, and attending to daily classroom routines. She felt overwhelmed by simple things such as dealing with behavioral problems. One day, she decided to partner up with Mary (another preschool teacher), who guided and assisted her with the basic survival skills that she needed her first year. Mary mentored Karla through the process of daily classroom routines, such as transitioning the children from one activity to the next and keeping them engaged in the activity. In Karla's second year, she felt much more comfortable with her teaching practices and focused on her student learning by assisting individual children with classroom routines and lessons. Her third and fourth year, she was able to handle classroom behavioral problems and thematic lessons all by herself. She was able to move beyond classroom routines and look at other related organizations to be involved in, such as the National Association for the Education of Young Children.

Do you believe that all teachers experience the four developmental stages (survival, consolidation, renewal, and maturity)?

Table 1.1	Developmental Stages of Teachers

STAGE	DEVELOPMENTAL TASKS	TRAINING NEEDS
1. Survival	• Survive daily challenges of being responsible for whole groups of young children. • Anticipate successes and classroom realities that may intensify feelings of inadequacy and unpreparedness.	• Receive support, understanding, encouragement, reassurance, comfort, and guidance. • Receive direct, timely, onsite help with specific skills and insight into complex causes of children's behavior.
2. Consolidation	• Consolidate overall gains made during first stage and differentiate specific tasks and skills to be mastered next. • Begin to focus on individual children and problem situations.	• Receive onsite training. • Become familiar with a wider range of resources, such as psychologists and social workers. • Exchange ideas with more experienced colleagues. • Share feelings with other teachers in same stage.
3. Renewal	• Remember that repeating tasks and activities with each new class may be insufficiently interesting. • Ask questions about new developments in the field.	• Meet colleagues from different programs. • Attend conferences and workshops; become active in professional associations. • Widen scope of reading; view films and videotapes; use Internet as source of ideas. • Watch video recordings of own classroom teaching.
4. Maturity	• Having reached a comfortable level of self-confidence, teacher now asks deeper questions, such as these: What is the nature of growth and learning? How are educational decisions made? Can schools change societies?	• Continue to participate in conferences and seminars. • Work toward advanced degree. • Read widely; interact with educators working on many different problem areas.

Source: Adapted from Katz (1999).

WHAT ARE THE ROLES OF THE EARLY CHILDHOOD TEACHER?

Teachers play crucial roles in the lives of young children. They are responsible for educating children and are accountable for what happens to them during school hours. Early childhood teachers function in many different roles, such as nurturer, instructor, facilitator, advocate, secretary, counselor, custodian, storyteller, and whatever else may be needed in the moment-to-moment life of the classroom. But the most important role they play is that of a friend, someone who listens to, cares about, and interacts with children every day in many different ways (Saracho & Spodek, 2007).

Teacher as Nurturer

Teachers serve as second parents to young children in school, giving them comfort, support, and love and taking responsibility for their health, safety, and learning. Teachers must take on these nurturing roles in the place of parents who work and must depend on the teachers to provide quality

Maslow ✓

child care. Children who are hungry, sick, frightened, or uncomfortable won't be able to learn or participate in activities. As a teacher of young children, you will often have to go beyond teaching and take on basic care and nurturing responsibilities.

Teacher as Instructor or Facilitator

Originally, day care centers were designed simply to provide basic care to young children. Today, however, teachers at day care centers prepare lessons and follow a curriculum—they are responsible for conveying knowledge to their students. Knowledge can be transmitted through either direct or indirect instruction. With **direct instruction**, also known as *programmed instruction,* the teacher determines what to teach and what students should learn (Skinner, 1986; Somerville & Leach, 1988). Based on students' responses to the teacher's instruction, the teacher then decides how to proceed with the lesson, as well as how to control and modify the flow of information. This contrasts with **indirect instruction**, which focuses on the students as active learners with the teacher acting as more of a facilitator than an instructor. Children are encouraged to ask questions that make them think in order to test their perceptions of reality. This method of instruction emphasizes children's creativity, brings depth and breadth to their learning experiences, and helps them develop problem-solving skills (Somerville & Leach, 1988).

When they are responsible for very young children, teachers are nurturers, instructors, nurses, facilitators, advocates, secretaries, counselors, custodians, and storytellers.

To see the differences between direct and indirect instruction, it is helpful to look at a sample activity. In direct instruction, a teacher might plan a writing activity to make an open house invitation for students' parents. She prepares the required materials (paper, pencils, crayons, scissors, and markers) and sets up the writing center by creating workstations for each child. She provides direct instruction by creating a model invitation and shows the students what they need to do. Students will need to follow the instructions provided by the teacher; they will create and write invitations similar to what she created. With indirect instruction for a writing activity, on the other hand, the teacher will plan multiple writing activities and set up multiple writing centers. Students will have the flexibility of choosing a different writing activity at each center, such as making an alphabet book, tracing magnetic letters, interacting with a computer alphabet program that identifies key letters, and writing a storybook. Children will choose the writing center with the activity of their liking. Teachers will assist with the children's work.

These two methods of instruction allow teachers to be either instructors or facilitators, depending on what is required at that particular time or in response to particular student needs. Whichever method is used, it will provide children the knowledge necessary to learn.

Teacher as Advocate

One of the reasons people choose the field of early childhood education is that they love children and care deeply about their welfare. These feelings make many teachers want to be **advocates** for children (and their families)—to take action and speak out on their behalf. Children and families in need of advocates often include children who suffer from poor health, have been abused or neglected, or live in poverty.

As a teacher, when you encounter students and families facing issues like these, you should be aware that such problems are usually complex and not easy to solve. Because each child and each family is different, the effects of poverty and ill health, for example, are never exactly the same from one family to the next. Some children in these situations may be sad and withdrawn, but others may have learning or social difficulties. Understanding the parent-child relationship is crucial in order to better help a child with problems. Also, families are often sensitive about discussing difficulties, and these sensitivities can take very different forms according to each family's cultural, socioeconomic, and personal characteristics. A successful advocate attempts to understand differences in order to handle these complex situations. The following are tips to help you learn how to be a successful advocate:

- Become informed about the problems and issues that children and families in need face by reading the newspaper or subscribing to local child welfare newsletters from groups that support children and families.
- Get involved in activities that support children and their families, such as becoming an active participant in local organizations or events that support child and family wellness.
- Continue your education throughout your professional career, beyond obtaining a degree or certification, because ideas change, and educational theories you learn about in college will undergo modification. Staying on top of developments in your field not only improves your teaching skills but also is essential for your professional growth, including your ability to be an effective advocate (Spodek, 1985).
- Convey your knowledge and expertise to others by getting involved with professional organizations and discussing the issues that your community faces.
- Become informed of the state, federal, and local policies affecting families and children (refer to Chapter 16 for more information on policies).

Teachers and Diversity

Teaching in today's society means working with a diverse student population. Student **diversity** refers to differences in students' ethnic, linguistic, and religious backgrounds as well as differences in their experiences, knowledge, and abilities. Throughout the United States, experienced teachers report that their classes are more diverse now than in the past, which reflects the fact that ethnic minority populations are growing in most parts of the country and now compose more than one third of the school population. Demographic data on immigration and birthrates show that by the year 2020 there will be a nationwide increase in an ethnically and linguistically diverse student population (National Center for Public Policy and Higher Education, 2005). Hispanics and Asian groups are expected to surpass other ethnic minority groups, and by 2050 Whites are estimated to compose 53% of the U.S. population (Smelser, Wilson, & Mitchell, 2001). Thus, you as a teacher will find yourself learning to understand and appreciate the variety of characteristics from the diverse ethnicities, languages, cultures, religions, political backgrounds, and economic statuses that each student brings into the classroom.

As a teacher, you are expected to embrace diversity in the classroom, but this can be overwhelming if you are not properly prepared. Preparation includes gaining an understanding of the differences among children and being trained to work effectively with diverse student populations. To help teachers acquire the knowledge and skills needed to manage a diverse classroom, many day care centers and preschools offer training sessions, workshops, conferences, and onsite assistance and mentoring.

In addition to striving to understand and work effectively with student diversity, you, as a teacher, must understand that diversity also applies to you and can affect your teaching style and way of interacting and communicating with others. You, too, have your own ethnic, linguistic, and religious background, as well as your own group and individual experiences, knowledge, and abilities. Before we can understand, teach, and work with a diverse student population, we must recognize and understand our own differences and special characteristics. Embracing diversity often begins with seeing how we ourselves think, what we believe, how we behave, and how we are seen by others who may think, believe, and behave differently than we do (Nieto & Bode, 2011).

To provide the different types of learning opportunities that a diverse student population requires, it will be increasingly important to have a diverse group of teachers—ideally, teacher diversity that matches students' diversity. When teachers share the cultural background knowledge of the students, they can connect the students' background knowledge with the classroom lessons. The cultural background knowledge provides guidance to teachers in incorporating the cultures of the minority students in ways that enable them to succeed. Research indicates that greater teacher diversity promotes a more culturally sensitive environment for children (Horm-Wingerd & Hyson, 2000). In such an environment, teachers learn to recognize, appreciate, and respond in positive, productive ways to the special characteristics of different groups of children. Having diverse colleagues who intuitively understand how factors such as gender, culture, language, temperament, and socioeconomic status influence the behavior of different groups of children helps teachers see that children aren't deficient or at risk simply because they behave differently (Horm-Wingerd & Hyson, 2000). This knowledge makes it possible for each of us to play a constructive role in building

a culturally sensitive environment. For example, when a Chinese or Hispanic child doesn't look the teacher in the eye when he or she is talking, this can be viewed as a bad behavior. But in these cultures, children are taught that making eye contact with an adult is disrespectful. Once the teacher becomes aware of this cultural practice, he or she would not require the child to do something contrary to what he or she has already learned. In many Asian cultures, children are taught to value silence and to avoid overt displays of emotion, which a teacher may interpret as being shy and withdrawn. In order for teachers to support such a child's behavior, they may want to provide a variety of avenues to assist with the expression of the child's feelings, such as art, dramatic play, and literature. Providing experiences that allow all children to make the most of their educational experience helps support diversity.

Learning about the cultures and background of students takes time but allows teachers to acknowledge the differences in children and support them accordingly.

Teachers and Parents

Because children are shaped by how parents behave, parents are a child's first teachers (Baldwin Dancy, 2000). Preschool and elementary school teachers become the subsequent teachers in a child's life. What happens at home impacts what happens at school; it is therefore crucial that teachers involve parents in a child's education and that parents involve the teacher. However, teachers vary widely in their views about parents' roles in their children's education. At one extreme, some teachers take the position that family background holds little or no importance in the education of children and even exclude parents from school life or activities. At the opposite extreme, other teachers believe that parents entirely shape their children; these teachers tend to include parents and get

BEST

Practices   NAEYC Recommendations for Supporting Diversity

The National Association for the Education of Young Children (1995/2009c) has developed the following set of recommendations for early childhood educators to create a welcoming environment that will support linguistically and culturally diverse children and their families.

Working With Young Children

- Ensure that children remain cognitively, linguistically, and emotionally connected to their home language and culture.

- Encourage literacy development in children's native language, knowing that this contributes to their ability to acquire English language proficiency.

- Help develop essential concepts using cultural contexts and the children's first language.

- Support and preserve home-language usage.

- Develop and provide innovative, alternative strategies to promote all children's participation and learning.

- Provide children with a variety of ways to show what they know and can do. *Differentiated Instr. – Assessment.*

Working With Families

- Actively involve families in the early learning program.

- Help all families realize the cognitive advantages of knowing more than one language, and provide them with strategies to support, maintain, and preserve home-language learning.

- Convince families that their home's cultural values and norms are honored at school.

Preparing Early Childhood Professionals

- Provide professional preparation and development in the areas of culture, language, and diversity.

- Recruit and support educators who are trained in languages other than English.

them extensively involved in the classroom. Most early childhood teachers, however, take a middle ground and believe that an understanding of a child's home background is necessary to fully understand the child and that some involvement of parents in the child's education is necessary (Saracho & Spodek, 2007; Spodek, 1985). Such teachers believe that information on family backgrounds allows them to communicate with and educate children more effectively (Nieto & Bode, 2011). They tend to interact with parents in regular, defined ways and to involve parents to some extent with what goes on at school.

The teacher-parent relationship is a reciprocal one. Teachers should keep parents informed about their children's progress, and parents should inform teachers about how the child is doing at home. For instance, the mother of a boy who is being potty trained might let the teacher know how her son is doing at home, and in return the teacher might inform the boy's mother of how things go during the day. This exchange of information allows teachers and parents to jointly solve children's problems. Beyond sharing information about individual children, teachers and parents can improve teaching and parenting overall by working together. Teachers can help parents organize parent meetings, develop parent education programs, and arrange for parents' participation in the classroom. While teachers can provide professional consultation for parent policy-making groups, parents can be extremely effective advocates for teachers and the profession of early childhood education. Although teachers generally are not formally trained to function as parent counselors or parent educators, their position allows them to serve parents in important ways, and parents are likewise often able to make unique contributions to school life.

WHAT ARE THE REQUIREMENTS FOR BECOMING AN EARLY CHILDHOOD TEACHER?

States vary widely in their requirements for becoming an early childhood teacher at a preschool or a day care center. In many states, a high school diploma is the only requirement; however, many of those states may now require that early childhood teachers have a Child Development Associate (CDA) Credential or an academic degree from a 2-year or 4-year college in order to perform certain teaching responsibilities. In states requiring more than a high school diploma, different positions or teaching levels have varying requirements.

In addition to inconsistencies in the requirements for teachers, their educational backgrounds vary by the type of program they work for, as shown in Table 1.2. As you can see in the table, 87% of those who work in a public school

Getting parents involved in their children's education should be a priority.

have at least a bachelor's degree, whereas in most other settings this figure is less than 50%. Nineteen percent have a CDA Credential. With regard to nonacademic training, 62% have attended workshops in early childhood education, and less than 1% of early childhood education teachers have no specialized training (Saluja, Early, & Clifford, 2002). This information indicates that early childhood teachers are required to have some educational training in the field; however, teachers working in public schools are more educated than those in other settings. In their research study, Saluja et al. (2002) reported that many states are attempting to reform their policies to create a more highly educated early childhood workforce.

The following section will more thoroughly explain some of the requirements for becoming an early childhood teacher by reviewing the teaching levels defined by the NAEYC, describing some of the requirements for each, and describing the CDA Credential, academic degrees, and licensing. (See also the discussion of the NBPTS Early Childhood/Generalist certificate later in this chapter.)

NAEYC Teaching Levels

At each teaching level, the early childhood education professional is authorized to take on different responsibilities, and each level has different educational requirements. Table 1.3 illustrates how one state (California) defines these levels, responsibilities, and requirements (information on the educational requirements of other states is presented on the ancillary website, www.sagepub.com/gordonbiddle).

CDA Credentialing

The Child Development Associate (CDA) National Credentialing Program was established in 1971 to assess early childhood professionals and provide qualified individuals with a credential. Applicants must meet certain course requirements and demonstrate competency in six areas in order to earn the credential (see Table 1.4). There are typically four required courses to receive a Child Development Associate Credential—Introduction to Early Childhood Education, Child Development, CDA

Table 1.2 **Educational Backgrounds of Early Childhood Teachers**

EDUCATIONAL BACKGROUND	ECE TEACHERS OVERALL	PUBLIC SCHOOL	HEAD START	OTHER PUBLIC AGENCY OR INDEPENDENT NONPROFIT	CHURCH	FOR-PROFIT
High school graduation or below	8.6%	0.1%	6.0%	7.4%	7.7%	14.5%
Vocational training or some college	26.8%	4.0%	33.2%	20.4%	28.6%	36.0%
Associate's degree	14.7%	8.9%	17.7%	17.7%	17.9%	10.8%
Bachelor's degree or higher	49.9%	87.0%	40.4%	54.5%	45.8%	38.6%

Source: Adapted from Saluja, Early, and Clifford (2002).

Credential Preparation, and CDA Credential Preparation II—and these can also be applied toward an associate's degree program in early childhood education.

Early childhood professionals working with various age-groups (e.g., preschoolers or infants/toddlers) can obtain the CDA Credential. Candidates for a CDA Credential should apply to the Council for Professional Recognition. The Council for Professional Recognition administers the CDA National Credentialing Program and regulates the policies and procedures for assessment and credentialing. The organization is also responsible for publishing the Competency Standards and other related materials used for CDA credentialing.

Forty-six states (all states except Idaho, Indiana, Virginia, Wyoming, and the District of Columbia) list the CDA Credential in their child care licensing regulations. Because states have the power to establish qualifications for staffs that work in licensed child care centers, some states require that the holder of a CDA Credential also have additional work experience and/or academic courses in order to fill certain positions. For example, in Pennsylvania, a person can become a preschool teacher if he or she holds a CDA Credential and has taken additional courses in college.

Academic Degrees

As we have seen, states vary widely in whether they require a person to hold an academic degree to fill certain positions in child care centers. Some states, like California (see Table 1.3), use NAEYC teaching levels to define their requirements and require a person to have an associate's degree to be a **master teacher** and a master's degree to be a director. However, other states that also use the NAEYC teaching levels might have quite different requirements. For example, North Dakota requires that teachers have a CDA Credential but not a degree, whereas New York allows someone with only a bachelor's degree to be a director (Pianta, 2012).

The Associate's Degree

Typically, an associate's degree is awarded after a 2-year course of study at an institution such as a community or junior college. This degree, with appropriate course work in early childhood education, provides the qualifications for various positions at child care and development centers. It may also meet the requirements for work as an instructional assistant in kindergarten and primary-grade classrooms in public schools or as a teacher or a teacher's assistant in private schools. The course

Table 1.3   California Child Development Permits—Levels, Responsibilities, and Requirements

LEVEL	AUTHORIZED RESPONSIBILITIES	REQUIREMENTS
Assistant	• To care for and assist in the development and instruction of children in a child care and development program under the supervision of an associate teacher, a teacher, a master teacher, a site supervisor, or a program director	• 6 semester units of early childhood education or child development course work
Associate Teacher	• To provide service in the care, development, and instruction of children in a child care and development program • To supervise an assistant and an aide	• A CDA Credential
Teacher	• To provide service in the care, development, and instruction of children in a child care and development program • To supervise an associate teacher, an assistant, and an aide	• An associate's degree (AA) or higher in early childhood education or child development or a related field • 3 semester units of supervised field experience in an early childhood education setting
Master Teacher	• To provide service in the care, development, and instruction of children in a child care and development program • To supervise a teacher, an associate teacher, an assistant, and an aide • To serve as a coordinator of curriculum and staff development in a child care and development program	• A bachelor's degree (BA) or higher • 12 semester units of early childhood education or child development course work • 3 semester units of supervised field experience in an early childhood education or school-age setting
Site Supervisor	• To supervise a child care and development program operating at a single site • To provide service in the care, development, and instruction of children in a child care and development program • To serve as a coordinator of curriculum and staff development in a child care and development program	• A bachelor's degree (BA) or higher • 12 semester units of early childhood education or child development course work • 3 semester units of supervised field experience in an early childhood education setting
Director	• To supervise a child care and development program operated in a single site or multiple sites • To provide service in the care, development, and instruction of children in a child care and development program • To serve as coordinator of curriculum and staff development in a child care and development program	• A master's degree (MA) or higher in early childhood education, child/human development, or a closely related field

Note: The educational requirements listed in this table are abbreviated.

Source: To see the complete requirements and possible alternatives, go to http://www.ctc.ca.gov.

Table 1.4	Course Requirements and Competency Standards for the CDA Credential

COURSE REQUIREMENTS	COMPETENCY STANDARDS
• Introduction to Early Childhood Education • Child or Infant/Toddler Growth and Development • Supervised fieldwork hours or credential preparation	1. Establish and maintain a safe and healthy learning environment. 2. Advance physical and intellectual competence. 3. Support socioemotional development and provide positive guidance. 4. Establish positive and productive relationships with families. 5. Ensure a well-run, purposeful program responsive to participant needs. 6. Maintain a commitment to professionalism.

Note: States vary on the title and number of courses needed.

Source: Council for Professional Recognition (2010).

work required to qualify for these types of positions would also be relevant for becoming a foster parent or a family social worker. In addition, the associate's degree provides a strong foundation for those who plan to complete a 4-year degree in child development and then teach in a public elementary school.

The Bachelor's Degree

A bachelor's degree, or baccalaureate, is awarded after a 4-year course of study at a college or university. Currently, most states don't require teachers in preschool programs to have a bachelor's degree. However, as mentioned earlier, some states are now moving toward this requirement. The course of study for prospective teachers at 4-year schools has traditionally focused on preparing elementary and secondary school teachers. Due to the need to define appropriate course work for those interested in teaching younger children, the NAEYC has developed professional preparation standards for people completing a 4-year degree (see Table 1.5 for a more detailed description of the standards).

The Master's Degree

People who already have a bachelor's degree in early childhood education and want to extend their education or qualify for higher-level positions can pursue a master's degree (and then, perhaps, earn an even more advanced degree such as a doctorate in philosophy [PhD] or a doctorate in education [EdD]). Some elementary school teachers who earn a master's degree might elect to stay in the classroom, while others might seek positions as program administrators, curriculum specialists and coordinators, or community college instructors.

LICENSING REQUIREMENTS FOR CHILD CARE PROGRAMS

In order for an early child care program to operate, it must obtain a state license that is administered by state government, and the program must set a baseline of requirements to follow. The license

STANDARD	COMPETENCIES: WHAT WELL-PREPARED EARLY CHILDHOOD PROFESSIONALS SHOULD KNOW AND BE ABLE TO DO
1. Promoting child development and learning	• Understand what young children are like. • Understand what influences children's development. • Use this understanding to create environments where all children can thrive.
2. Building family and community relationships	• Understand and value diverse children's families and communities. • Create respectful, reciprocal relationships. • Involve families in their children's development and learning.
3. Observing, documenting, and assessing to support young children and their families	• Understand the purposes of assessment. • Use effective assessment strategies. • Use assessment responsibly, in partnership with families and other professionals, to positively influence children's development and learning.
4. Using developmentally effective approaches to connect with children and families	• Build close relationships with children and families. • Understand effective strategies and tools. • Use developmentally appropriate teaching and learning strategies. • Combine all of these to give children experiences that promote positive outcomes.
5. Using content knowledge to build meaningful curriculum	• Understand the academic disciplines and content areas. • Have sound knowledge of central concepts, inquiry tools, and structures of academic discipline and content areas. • Apply knowledge to design, implement, and evaluate meaningful and challenging curriculum.
6. Growing as a professional	• Identify with the early childhood profession. • Be guided by ethical and other professional standards. • Be a continuous, collaborative learner. • Think reflectively and critically. • Advocate for children, families, and the profession.
7. Early childhood field experience	• Have opportunities to observe and practice in at least two of the three early childhood age-groups. • Have opportunities to observe and practice in at least two of the three main types of early education settings (early school grades, child care centers and homes, Head Start programs).

Source: National Association for the Education of Young Children (http://www.naeyc.org/accreditation).

necessitates that early childhood teachers meet certain requirements and obtain a certification or credential in order to teach in a child care center. Such requirements might include preservice training and might also require teachers to work a minimum number of hours yearly (annual ongoing hours) in order to retain their certification. States may also have different licensing requirements for different roles at child care centers. Most of the states with master teachers require a high school diploma or a general equivalency diploma (GED).

A next step after licensing is **accreditation**. Accreditation is when early childhood programs voluntarily apply to attain national recognition for their high-quality program.

NAEYC ACCREDITATION OF EARLY CHILDHOOD EDUCATION PROGRAMS

In 1985, the NAEYC established standards for early childhood programs to receive NAEYC accreditation. The accreditation process encourages programs to make ongoing improvements, and gaining accreditation is a stamp of approval that indicates to parents (and society in general) that a program offers children high-quality education and a rich array of early experiences that can help prepare them for kindergarten and beyond.

The NAEYC's accreditation standards have evolved over time. Table 1.6 summarizes the 10 most recent standards, which took effect in 2006.

Table 1.6   **NAEYC Early Childhood Program Standards**

STANDARD	DESCRIPTION
1. Relationships	The program promotes positive relationships among all children and adults to encourage each child's sense of individual worth, to facilitate each child's being part of a community, and to foster each child's ability to contribute as a responsible community member.
2. Curriculum	The program implements a curriculum that is consistent with its goals for children and promotes learning and development in each of the following areas: socioemotional, physical, linguistic, and cognitive.
3. Teaching	The program uses developmentally, culturally, and linguistically appropriate and effective teaching approaches that enhance each child's learning and development within the context of the program's curriculum goals.
4. Assessment of Child Progress	The program is informed by ongoing, systematic formal and informal assessment approaches that provide information on children's learning and development. These assessments occur within the context of reciprocal communications with families and with sensitivity to the cultural contexts in which children develop. Assessment results inform sound decisions about children, teaching, and program improvement and, thus, benefit children.
5. Health	The program promotes the nutrition and health of children and protects children and staff from illness and injury.
6. Teachers	The program employs and supports a teaching staff that has the educational qualifications, knowledge, and professional commitment necessary to promote children's learning and development and to support families' diverse needs and interests.
7. Families	The program establishes and maintains collaborative relationships with each child's family to foster children's development in all settings. These relationships are sensitive to family composition, language, and culture.
8. Community Relationships	The program establishes relationships with and uses the resources of the children's communities to support the achievement of program goals.
9. Physical Environment	The program has a safe and healthful environment that provides appropriate and well-maintained indoor and outdoor physical environments. The environment includes facilities, equipment, and materials to facilitate the learning and development of children and staff.
10. Leadership and Management	The program effectively implements policies, procedures, and systems that support stable staff, strong personnel, and appropriate fiscal and program management so all children, families, and staff have high-quality experiences.

Source: National Association for the Education of Young Children (http://www.naeyc.org/accreditation).

WHAT KNOWLEDGE AND SKILLS SHOULD EARLY CHILDHOOD TEACHERS POSSESS?

Early childhood education has come to be regarded as critical in helping children fulfill their potential for success, both during their school years and in their adult lives. Evidence on the effectiveness of early childhood education programs indicates that children who attend preschool will have positive long-term educational success (Feinstein, 2003). Similarly, children who attend a Head Start program will enter kindergarten as well prepared as children who attend a non–Head Start program (Henry, Gordon, & Rickman, 2006). For this reason, legislators and professional organizations have been paying more attention to the professional development of early childhood teachers and are calling for higher standards in teaching and learning. Currently, more than a dozen states have established a set of teacher competencies with the goal of ensuring that all early childhood teachers have the knowledge and skills necessary to meet children's developmental needs. Clearly, the field of early childhood education is changing in ways that will be significant for both teachers and the children they teach.

NAEYC CORE COMPETENCY STANDARDS

In an effort to encourage quality instruction, in 2010 the NAEYC published its latest competency standards for early childhood professionals. **Teacher competencies** define what early childhood teachers need to know and be able to do in their job of educating and caring for young children. These competencies indicate a teacher who is considered to be a well-rounded and well-prepared professional. The NAEYC standards differ in depth and scope depending on the academic degree the person is pursuing, but for all levels there are seven core standards directed at the same types of competencies, as shown in Table 1.5.

These NAEYC standards have not been adopted universally in the United States, but educators and policy makers increasingly agree that teacher competency standards are needed. In California, for example, several policy proposals and legislative efforts within the past few years have called for a comprehensive plan for the professional development of the early childhood care and education workforce, which would include establishing teacher competencies. Other states (Illinois, Kansas and Missouri [developed jointly], Kentucky, Nevada, New Jersey, New Mexico, New York, Pennsylvania, and West Virginia) have already developed similar early childhood teacher competency standards (Center for the Study of Child Care Employment & Institute for Research on Labor and Employment, 2007).

Quality teachers use multiple teaching strategies to support meaningful student learning.

NBPTS EARLY CHILDHOOD/ GENERALIST STANDARDS

The National Board for Professional Teaching Standards (NBPTS) is another organization that is taking steps to increase the preparedness of early childhood teachers. The NBPTS is an independent, nonprofit, nonpartisan organization governed by a board of directors, the majority of whom are classroom teachers. The organization offers an Early Childhood/Generalist certification to early childhood teachers who pass a rigorous, performance-based assessment that typically takes more than a year to complete. Candidates for certification must demonstrate competency and achievement inside and outside the classroom in nine areas defined by the NBPTS's Early Childhood/Generalist Standards (see Table 1.7).

Table 1.7	Early Childhood/Generalist Standards

STANDARD	DESCRIPTION
1. Understanding Young Children	Accomplished early childhood teachers use their knowledge of child development and their relationships with children and families to understand children as individuals and to plan classroom materials and activities in response to their unique needs and potentials.
2. Equity, Fairness, and Diversity	Accomplished early childhood teachers model and teach behaviors appropriate for a diverse society by creating a safe, secure learning environment for all children; by showing appreciation of and respect for the individual differences and unique needs of each member of the learning community; and by empowering children to treat others with, and to expect from others, equity, fairness, and respect.
3. Assessment	Accomplished early childhood teachers recognize strengths and weaknesses of multiple assessment methodologies and know how to use them effectively. Employing a variety of methods, they systematically observe, monitor, and document children's activities and behavior, analyzing, communicating, and using the information they glean to improve their work with children, parents, and others.
4. Promoting Child Development and Learning	Accomplished early childhood teachers promote children's cognitive, socioemotional, physical, and linguistic development by organizing and orchestrating the environment in ways that best facilitate the development and learning of young children.
5. Knowledge of Integrated Curriculum	On the basis of their knowledge of how young children learn, of academic subjects, and of assessment, accomplished early childhood teachers design and implement developmentally appropriate learning experiences that integrate within and across the disciplines.
6. Multiple Teaching Strategies for Meaningful Learning	Accomplished early childhood teachers use a variety of practices and resources to promote individual development, meaningful learning, and social cooperation.
7. Family and Community Partnerships	Accomplished early childhood teachers work with and through families and communities to support children's learning and development.
8. Professional Partnerships	Accomplished early childhood teachers work as leaders and collaborators in the professional community to improve programs and practices for young children and their families.
9. Reflective Practice	Accomplished early childhood teachers regularly analyze, evaluate, and synthesize to strengthen the quality and effectiveness of their work.

Source: Adapted from National Board for Professional Teaching Standards (2012).

Professionalism & Policy

Early Learning Standards

Many states throughout the country are considering the implementation of early learning standards and curriculum guidelines for young children. The National Association for the Education of Young Children (NAEYC) and the National Association of Early Childhood Specialists in the State Departments of Education (NAECS-SDE) take the stance that early learning standards can be an important part of a comprehensive, high-quality system of services and can contribute to the educational experiences and the future success of young children only if such standards do the following:

- Emphasize significant, developmentally appropriate content and outcomes

- Use implementation and assessment strategies that are ethical and appropriate for young children

- Are developed and reviewed through informed, inclusive processes

- Are accompanied by strong support for early childhood programs, professionals, and families (NAEYC & NAECS-SDE, 2002)

These guidelines indicate that early childhood education is becoming part of a standards-based learning environment. More than 25 states have specific outcome standards for young children. The "Child Outcomes Framework" of the Head Start Bureau (2003) describes learning expectations in eight domains (language development, literacy, mathematics, science, creative arts, socioemotional development, approaches to learning, and physical health and development). The National Council of Teachers of Mathematics and the NAEYC have developed content standards in mathematics and literacy (NAEYC & NAECS-SDE, 2002). All of these standards—program standards, content standards, performance standards, and child-outcome standards—are part of a large nationwide effort to develop school readiness by improving teaching and learning in the early years.

A standards-based environment presents risks and benefits for the field of early childhood education. One major risk is that standards will be developed and implemented in rigid, superficial, or culturally and educationally limited ways, driving the curriculum toward a narrow fact- and skill-driven approach that loses depth and coherence. Also, narrowing a teacher's focus to ensuring that children meet the standards could result in the loss of teacher creativity and the setting aside of innovative practices.

In contrast, well-developed and well-implemented early learning standards could contribute to a responsive and effective system of education for all young children, creating significant benefits for children's learning and development (Bredekamp, 2004; Kagan, Rosenkoetter, & Cohen, 1997; Schmoker & Marzano, 1999). If these standards are linked to K–12 expectations, they could also contribute to a more coherent, unified approach for children's overall education. Early learning standards that are clear and developmentally appropriate can bring together content and instruction, helping teachers and families provide appropriate educational opportunities for all children. Standards can help families better understand their children's development, including skills developed through play and exploration in early education settings. A developmental continuum of standards, curriculum, and assessment, extending from the early years into later schooling, can support better transitions from infant-toddler care, through preschool programs, to kindergarten, and into the primary grades. This is because teachers would be working within a consistent framework across educational settings.

Summary

To know if you want to be a teacher, you must understand the many characteristics and qualities that teachers should possess. These qualities include the ability of being self-aware and being intrinsically motivated in teaching. In order to be considered a good early childhood teacher, you must be able to reflect on your own behavior, motivation, and personality. Understanding these characteristics will allow you to make ethical and responsible decisions that may impact children, parents, or the community. A good early childhood professional will also develop a teaching philosophy that will allow him or her to function well in the classroom. Despite the multiple stressors that early childhood teachers face, they have reported much satisfaction from working with children and in the work that they do, and the teaching career can be very rewarding and satisfying.

Key Terms

Accreditation 20

Advocates 12

Burnout 9

Competence 5

Developmental stages 10

Direct instruction 12

Diversity 13

Early childhood education (ECE) 3

Ethics 6

Indirect instruction 12

Intentional teaching style 5

Intrinsic motivation 5

Master teacher 17

Philosophy of teaching 6

Self-awareness 5

Teacher competencies 22

Turnover rate 9

Reflection, Application, and Analysis Questions

1. What are some characteristics of an effective early childhood teacher?

2. Name three strategies for supporting diversity in the classroom.

3. Why is involving parents in the classroom important?

4. Identify two requirements for becoming an early childhood teacher.

Extension Activities

1. Research your local and state policies affecting early childhood education.

2. Interview an early childhood teacher about his or her teaching philosophy.

Additional Readings

Early childhood education is a field that is constantly changing. The following list of readings will be useful for those who are interested in keeping up with the most current developments.

Isenberg, J. P., & Jalongo, M. R. (2003). *Major trends and issues in early childhood education: Challenges, controversies and insights* **(2nd ed.). New York: Teachers College Press.**

This text covers the historical tradition of early childhood education, the controversial issues surrounding the field, its policies, and its professional development.

Jalongo, M. R., & Isenberg, J. P. (1995). *Teachers' stories: From personal narrative to professional insight.* **San Francisco: Jossey-Bass.**

This narrative-style book demonstrates how teachers can use stories based on their professional experiences to express their values and beliefs, reflect on their practices, and understand the decision-making process of teaching.

Klein, M. D., & Chen, D. (2001). *Working with young children from culturally diverse backgrounds.* **Albany, NY: Delmar.**

This book presents a summary of the ways in which cultural differences influence young children's behavior, communication, and learning styles. This book also offers examples of curriculum and instructional revisions that can be used to accommodate children from diverse backgrounds.

Saifer, S. (2003). *Practical solutions to practically every problem: The early childhood teacher's manual* (Rev. ed.). St. Paul, MN: Redleaf Press.

This is a wonderful book that a first-year teacher should have. The book tackles the everyday concerns and questions that a teacher has when working in an early childhood program.

Saracho, O., & Spodek, B. (2003). *Studying teachers in early childhood settings*. Greenwich, CT: Information Age.

The contextual framework of this book is based on theory and research. It also addresses the effect that teachers have on their students when standing in front of the classroom.

On the Web

Center for the Child Care Workforce - *http://www.ccw.org*
The Center for the Child Care Workforce addresses issues of workforce recruitment and compensation. The voice of teachers and providers, it advocates for public policy to reform early child care and the education delivery system of teachers.

Children Now - *http://www.childrennow.org*
Children Now is a national organization that serves the needs of children with a successful combination of research and advocacy.

Children, Youth, and Family Consortium - *http://www.cyfc.umn.edu*
This website provides information on children and their families through partnerships and initiatives that engage people across professional, intellectual, and disciplinary fields. Linked with the University of Minnesota, it connects research, teaching, policy, and community practice.

National Association for the Education of Young Children - *http://naeyc.org*
This website provides important information regarding quality education and developmental services for young children. With nearly 100,000 members, the NAEYC is the world's largest organization working on behalf of young children.

NAEYC's Code of Ethical Conduct and Statement of Commitment - *http://www.naeyc.org/files/naeyc/file/positions/PSETH05.pdf*
The NAEYC provides the Code of Ethical Conduct, a set of guidelines outlining responsible behavior for children and their families in early childhood programs. A Statement of Commitment is also presented that states a personal acknowledgment of an individual's willingness to embrace the distinctive values and moral obligations of the field of early childhood care and education.

National Board for Professional Teaching Standards - *www.nbpts.org*
This organization informs teachers about the quality of teaching and learning. It provides a list of professional standards, information on how to certify teachers who meet those standards, and information on how to integrate certified teachers into educational reform efforts.

Note

1. Culture includes ethnicity, racial identity, economic level, family structure, language, and religious and political beliefs, which profoundly influence each child's development and relationship to the world.

Student Study Site

Visit **www.sagepub.com/gordonbiddle** to access several study tools including eFlashcards, web quizzes, links to SAGE journal articles, web resources, video resources, lesson plan templates, and more.

History

Exploring the Beginnings of Early Childhood Education

This chapter will help you answer these important questions:

- What were the major ideas that influenced early childhood education?
- What contributions have individuals made to the field of early childhood education?
- Who were the major contributors to the kindergarten movement?

Vignette: Émile

It is the mid-1700s. A young lad, assumed to be Émile from Jean-Jacques Rousseau's Émile, ou de l'Education, *resides on an island with an older man, his tutor. The young Émile is being raised on the island, seeing only his tutor. Aside from receiving instruction from his tutor, Émile's education comes largely from his surroundings—his immediate contact with the world of nature, which helps to form his senses and personality. In this vignette, Émile is engaged in kite flying.*

Émile's rearing on a desolate island represents the very essence of Rousseau's educational philosophy. Rousseau believed that children's early learning should be the result of their interactions with the world rather than of their engagement with books. In the case of Émile, a simple kite-flying activity affords him the opportunity to develop his sensibilities relative to his surroundings. While flying a kite, his tutor asks him to determine the kite's relative position by simply looking at the shadow that the kite casts on the sand. Émile does so successfully, a result of his evolved understanding of his physical world.

The above vignette is inspired by Jean-Jacques Rousseau's novel, *Emile, ou de l'Education*. Rousseau, one of early childhood education's earliest philosophers, was clearly ahead of his time. His literary work *Émile*, though written in the form of a novel for the purpose of entertaining, was actually a compendium of wide-ranging aspects of child rearing and education. As depicted above, Rousseau's character, Émile, was raised on an island in isolation. The novel clearly conveyed Rousseau's belief that, until the age of about 12, "education ought to be purely negative. It consists neither in teaching virtue nor truth; but in guarding the heart from vice and the mind from error" (Braun & Edwards, 1972, p. 42). Rousseau contended that by "attempting nothing in the beginning, you might produce a prodigy of education" (Braun & Edwards, 1972, p. 42). Rousseau's novel was one of the first depictions of the first 5 years of life, and it clearly distinguished young children from earlier portrayals of them as miniature adults or embodiments of original sin.

This chapter examines the historical roots of current practice in the field of early childhood education. By examining the people and events from the past that have been instrumental in shaping early childhood educational theory and practice as we know it today, you will develop a deeper understanding of and an enhanced appreciation for this exciting field.

Key Elements for Becoming a Professional

NAEYC DEVELOPMENTALLY APPROPRIATE PRINCIPLE 2

Many aspects of children's learning and development follow well-documented sequences, with later abilities, skills, and knowledge building on those already acquired.

Interpretation

Young children's development is orderly and predictable. The early pioneers of early childhood education discussed in this chapter have made significant contributions to our understanding of children's development over time and what constitutes best practices at every turn in their developmental sequence.

NAEYC STANDARD 1: PROMOTING CHILD DEVELOPMENT AND LEARNING

a. Knowing and understanding young children's characteristics and needs

b. Knowing and understanding the multiple influences on development and learning

c. Using developmental knowledge to create healthy, respectful, supportive, and challenging learning environments

WHAT MAJOR IDEAS INFLUENCED EARLY CHILDHOOD EDUCATION?

From the very beginning, the ideas emanating from key political leaders, teachers, and philosophers have influenced the history of early childhood education. In the subsequent paragraphs, you will acquire an appreciation for the cyclical and transformative aspects of history and their impact on early childhood education.

Ancient Educational Theorists

There is a tendency to think that early childhood education is a relatively recent phenomenon in Western civilization. Actually, today's education practices are much older than you think, dating as far back as antiquity. We can find the remnants of early childhood philosophical thought dated as far back as Athens, Greece, and strands of educational thinking and practice in the written scrolls of ancient Judea. Historically, the need for formal education was twofold: first, to maintain more stable, orderly, and viable communities of men; and second, to assist humankind in its quest of becoming more self-actualized, to experience personal fulfillment, and to be more attuned to God (Braun & Edwards, 1972).

History conveys to us, and it is still the case today, that there exist two competing ideas regarding education at any level: the importance of meeting the needs of the individual versus meeting the needs of society as a whole. As far back as we can go, the politics and curricula of any given era challenged educators' ability to bring the two ideas to fruition simultaneously.

Greek philosophers **Plato** (428–348 B.C.) and **Aristotle** (384–322 B.C.) also struggled with this dilemma. Both Plato and Aristotle upheld Greek intellectual society views, placing a great deal of emphasis on man as inherently good and capable of gaining personal fulfillment by simply adhering to the laws of life within the context of a good society. Plato's educational ideas were lofty and theoretical, with very little connection to the concerns of everyday life. On the other hand, Aristotle was more practical in his thinking, an advocate of a more individualized and diverse educational system. Aristotle believed, unlike his predecessor Plato, that education was the right of ordinary male offspring of the free citizens of the state and not just the right of the upper class, as was the case in Plato's utopian society. Yet, it is important to note that neither Plato nor Aristotle dealt with early childhood education as a separate category. But Plato, a student of the great philosopher Socrates, spoke passionately about youth as a special time of development in his *Republic*: "You know that the beginning is the most important part of any work, especially in the case of a young and tender thing; for that is the time at which the character is being formed and the desired impression is more readily taken" (Braun & Edwards, 1972, p. 13). The appreciation of early childhood education as a special case would come much later in history.

The Dark and Middle Ages

The Romans, on the other hand, did very little to enhance Greek educational thought. But one Roman, **Plutarch** (A.D. 46–120), wrote about the need for a more humane treatment of children during that period, an idea that was not necessarily upheld by the Greeks. After the collapse of the Roman Empire, Europe literally sunk into ruins. It was then that the very notion of childhood was also lost. Not only was there no specific emphasis on early childhood education, but young children wore the garments of adults, assumed adultlike chores, and participated in adult activities. For more than 1,000 years, Europe was school-less and, from a conceptual point of view, childless as well. These were, indeed, the very dark Middle Ages. For several years following the collapse, church doctrine was the focal point, projecting a vastly discrepant image of human nature. Children, therefore, were seen as inherently evil, and bodily punishment was deemed suitable for both body and soul. The innocence and special needs of the young were suspended until the time of Europe's great transformation—a time of great enlightenment, pride, and magnificence known as the Renaissance (Braun & Edwards, 1972; Weber, 1984).

The ancient Greeks' *paideia*, or process of education and child rearing, underscored the dichotomy between the children's world and the world of adults, ushering in altered views of childhood. But medieval society failed to perceive childhood as a distinct period and gave no real thought to the importance of a transitional period. However, it was during the Renaissance that the concept of childhood began to emerge. Philippe Aries's *Centuries of Childhood* (1962) gave rise to a paradigm shift regarding children's place in society. Aries chronicled the changing attitudes toward the very young, which were becoming evident in art, religion, iconography, and literature. By the 16th or 17th century, children were given a special costume to distinguish them from adults—especially male children. Newly written material portrayed the child's sweetness, and adults began to derive pleasure from observing childhood antics (Weber, 1984). Writings of adults engaged in behavior as natural as the "coddling" of children gave rise to the changing view of children as a special case and distinct from adults.

WHAT CONTRIBUTIONS HAVE INDIVIDUALS MADE TO THE FIELD OF EARLY CHILDHOOD EDUCATION?

Plato's *Republic*, often referred to as one of the most significant works analyzing politics and education, has made an indelible imprint on the thinking of early education pioneers for centuries. It has been said that every major philosopher since Plato's time has been heavily influenced by his insights in some shape or form (Braun & Edwards, 1972). The contributions made to education by countless men and women during the post-Plato era cannot be understated. Educational practices and philosophies during the days of old have proven to be reliable—and they have stood the test of time. Such principles still govern our practices in the early childhood classroom today.

Professionalism & Policy

Who Should Care for America's Children?

The issue of whether or not early childhood education should focus on children's needs or the needs of the state continues to loom large in today's political circles. Conservatives contend that the raising of children should be the exclusive province of parents, and liberals argue that early care and education is the inalienable right of all children—Black, White, rich, and poor. But early care and education as a public entitlement raises concerns relative to the national debt, national security, equity, access, depleting resources, and so on. This great debate is an issue of ideology and challenges government's legitimate role in advancing the growth and well-being of children, promoting a shared culture and human capital for employees, and finally as the great equalizer in society (Zigler, Gilliam, & Barnett, 2011).

Renaissance and Reformation

Needless to say, the Renaissance and Reformation period was a unique and special time in European history. Brave "men of the cloth" like Luther, Erasmus, and others were quite instrumental in using their influence and novel ideas relative to religiosity and faith to usher in a period during which the view of the young child was greatly ameliorated.

European Influences

The upheavals and struggles of European society in the early 16th century were unprecedented. The societal landscape was one of sheer chaos; congregations were against clergy, and peasants were against the ruling classes. It was necessary for members of society to engage in spiritual introspection; men, women, boys, and girls were charged by their religious authorities to move toward a more personal relationship with God. This would require that individuals learn to read the Bible and participate in formal schooling. Religious leaders during this era were instrumental in broadening the purpose of education beyond the religious. In the pages to follow, you will see the significant role that the church (religion) played in the history of early childhood education and the evolution of the concept of childhood.

Martin Luther

Children were often depicted as miniature adults during the Middle Ages.

By the early 16th century, a young religious leader emerged by the name of **Martin Luther** (1483–1546), who proclaimed a type of doctrine that was quite nonconventional; his ideas about education were surprisingly liberal. Born in Germany, Martin Luther was raised in a deeply religious home; his parents were strict disciplinarians who valued hard work (Frost, 1966). Martin Luther studied religion and related subject matter throughout his early years and during his pursuit of higher education, becoming an ordained priest in 1507 and eventually earning a doctorate in theology.

Luther urged nobles, civil leaders, and laypeople to move away from the church and instead focus on a "more personal road to God and salvation" (Braun & Edwards, 1972, p. 25), which got Martin Luther into serious trouble with church authorities. In the year following his excommunication from the church, Martin Luther translated the Bible into High German because he believed that people should read the Bible for themselves in order to come to their own conclusions about what God intended. This effort made the Bible more accessible to the people and freed them from relying solely on priests to interpret God's message (Braun & Edwards, 1972; Frost, 1966).

In his educational writings, Martin Luther proposed three novel ideas about education. First, people needed to find their own way to God by reading the Bible for themselves (Braun & Edwards, 1972). This idea presupposed the need for the population to be literate and led to Luther advocating for the education of the entire population, including girls as well as boys. Second, Martin Luther believed that all towns and villages should have schools (Braun & Edwards, 1972) and that these schools should be governed by the state and not by the church—thereby creating a system that would support the development of morality and increase the stability of the state, simultaneously. Third, while Luther *did* stress the importance of religious instruction in schools, he promoted the idea that in order to ensure that educated people became good citizens, it was also important for schools to support children's intellectual, physical, emotional, and social development (Braun & Edwards, 1972). Martin Luther also advocated for adult continuing education, thereby urging authorities that there was a need for libraries.

Although the ideas that Luther put forth in his educational writings were considered radical for his time, they had an enormous impact on the people in authority who, for the first time, listened and implemented his ideas. People everywhere joined Martin Luther's cause, resulting in Germany having "the most complete public school system to exist in any country before the nineteenth century" (Braun & Edwards, 1972, pp. 25–26).

Erasmus

Erasmus (1466–1536), Martin Luther's contemporary, was instrumental in ushering in a more humanistic way of instructing young children. His doctrine emphasized the "here and now" and was less focused on preparing the soul for eternity; preparation for life in the world became paramount. A professor of divinity at Cambridge University in England, Erasmus was initially regarded as Martin Luther's ally, but soon became his staunch enemy. Erasmus firmly believed that human beings need to develop within the context of culture and proposed that there were three conditions that determined individual progress: (a) nature, (b) training, and (c) practice. Erasmus's thinking laid the groundwork for a very enlightened 18th century; emphasis was on viewing human life from a very humanistic perspective, which emphasizes the "here and now."

John Amos Comenius

Moravian Bishop **John Amos Comenius**'s (1592–1670) contribution to education came during a time of great upheaval and religious reformation in European society. Thanks to him and the religious reformation movement, civil control over education and educational accessibility for all classes of people increased (Weber, 1984). Comenius was born in southeastern Moravia (Czech Republic) to a family who had gained membership in the Moravian Brethren (Frost, 1966). Orphaned at an early age, Comenius went to live with his aunt in Strážnice and attended a "folk school," where he learned some arithmetic, Czech language, and catechism. It was due to Comenius's early personal experiences that he first began to "despise" the teaching methods used in schools. Comenius described the methods as "so severe that schools have been looked on as terrors for boys and slaughterhouses of the mind" (Frost, 1966, p. 221). His next encounter with schooling solidified this thinking; at 16, John Amos Comenius attended a Latin school at Přerov where he was required to study with 6- and 7-year-old boys.

During the 16th century, Martin Luther, single-handedly, ushered in the idea of public education in Europe.

Despite the inadequacies of his early education, at age 20, Comenius decided to attend the college in Nassau, Germany, to become a minister (Frost, 1966, p. 221), where he became interested in educational reform. After pursuing his studies, Comenius returned to Moravia and was ordained a priest in 1616. This was also the period of the Thirty Years' War, which was a vicious war between the Catholics and the Protestants. The defeat of the Protestants led to the religious persecution of all non-Catholics, especially the Moravian Brethren of which Comenius was a member. As a result, Comenius fled from Bohemia in 1626 "to become a schoolmaster, writer, and bishop of the Moravian communities, which had found refuge in Poland" (Braun & Edwards, 1972, p. 30). In 1638, Comenius was asked to come to Sweden to devise a complete educational system, which spanned the early years through young adulthood (the university years). After a brief stint in Europe, Comenius returned to Sweden where he spent several years writing textbooks for the schools. By that time, "Comenius had become the most sought-after educator in all Europe . . . and he was in correspondence with scholars and educators in both Europe and America" (Frost, 1966, p. 222).

Comenius spent the last years of his life in Amsterdam where he died in 1670, leaving a collection of work, books and manuscripts detailing his philosophical approach to education (Braun & Edwards, 1972; Weber, 1984).

Comenius broadened the aim of education beyond religious goals; he believed that in order for children to develop human nature and to be prepared for their life on earth, as well as for eternal life, children needed to be educated. According to Comenius, education should begin at birth and should be made accessible to all children, "rich and poor, male and female, bright and dull" (Braun & Edwards, 1972, p. 30). Comenius's writings offer insight into how young children learn and how they should be taught, including the idea that schools should strive to use methods in "which the teachers teach less and the learners learn more" (Braun & Edwards, 1972, p. 31). His most influential books include *The School of Infancy, Didactica Magna (The Great Didactic),* and *Orbis Sensualium Pictus (The World in Pictures)* (Frost, 1966, pp. 224–225).

In *The School of Infancy,* Comenius introduces the idea that home is "the first school." Comenius believed that it was important for mothers to recognize this so that they could take advantage of the opportunity to "begin their children's education correctly" (Frost, 1966, p. 225). Comenius stressed the importance of allowing young children to learn through experiences and activities that coincided with their interests and level of ability.

In *The Great Didactic,* Comenius offers his thoughts on how children grow and develop as well as how they should be taught in schools (Frost, 1966, p. 224). In this great work, outlined in Table 2.1, Comenius lays out nine important principles for instruction of young children.

The World in Pictures emphasizes Principle 7, which states that learning occurs best when everything is related to the senses. The aim of writing this book was to "make the meaning of the words visual" (Frost, 1966, p. 224). In it, pictures of objects were paired with the word for the object as well as a story about the objects in the picture. Comenius believed that this approach was far more effective than simply asking children to learn the names of objects out of context. Not only did Comenius believe that all senses should be engaged in the educational process; he also contended that the best way to learn anything was by doing it.

Table 2.1	Comenius's Principles of Instruction

1. It must begin early and before the mind is corrupted.

2. The mind must be made ready for it.

3. It must proceed from the general to the particular.

4. It must proceed from the easier to the more difficult.

5. Progress must not be rushed.

6. The minds of individuals must not be forced to do anything but that to which they aspire according to their age and motivation.

7. Everything must be related through sense impression, if possible.

8. Everything must be applied immediately.

9. Everything must be taught consistently according to one and the same method.

Source: Ulich (1954), as quoted in Braun and Edwards (1972, p. 33).

Consider This The Past as Prologue

One crucial area of knowledge needed to become an effective early childhood educator is a firm understanding of the origins of this branch of education. It has been frequently said that "it is impossible to know where you are going unless you know from whence you came." In every aspect of life, progress can become stagnant, and setbacks are likely to recur unless one has a firm grasp of past actions and their results. Effective practice in the field of early childhood education is predicated on teachers' understanding of history and a firm understanding of the interplay among social, political, economic, and educational influences.

How do you think the politics and economics of the past decade are impacting the educational ideology of today? When you consider the historical contributions of Martin Luther, Erasmus, and Comenius to the field of early childhood education, how do you think the education of young children will be influenced by the social and political climate created by today's leaders?

John Locke

Not too long after the death of Comenius, **John Locke** (1632–1704) wrote *Some Thoughts Concerning Education*, which became a popular read in 1693. While Locke's writings have long been associated with the idea of the newborn child as a **tabula rasa** (an earlier held view of the child's mind as a blank slate that is sensitive and responsive to instruction), Locke also had regard for the peculiarities of the individual child. He advised parents and tutors to get to know the child; to investigate his or her interests, innate capacities, and temperament; and to devise an educational plan according to this information.

An Improved View of Childhood

The mid-16th and 17th centuries marked the beginning of an enhanced view of childhood. For the very first time, children were being viewed as a separate and special category in human development. The new lens through which children were viewed began to spur educational practices that were in the best interests of children.

Jean-Jacques Rousseau

Born in Geneva, Switzerland, **Jean-Jacques Rousseau** (1712–1778) was orphaned at a very young age and sent to live with his maternal relatives. After a few failed attempts in apprenticeship training, first as a notary and then as an engraver, Rousseau ran away from Switzerland and ended up in Paris, where he started writing articles for a well-known group called the Encyclopaedists. Over the next several years, Rousseau dedicated his time to writing, and in 1762 published his most famous and influential book regarding educational theory, *Émile*, which is referenced in our opening vignette. The work is a fictional story that provides details of the education of a young boy from upper-class society. *Émiles* focus on education in the early years was a clear departure from conventional educational thought during that time, which was purely religious authoritarianism. Hence, the church eventually attacked its content, and, as a result, the Paris Parliament condemned the book (Weber, 1984, p. 25). Fearing for his safety, Rousseau fled Paris and returned to Switzerland. Upon voicing his criticism of those who disagreed with the ideas put forth in *Émile*, the Swiss government also condemned the book, and once again, fearing for his life, Rousseau fled the country and settled in London in 1765.

   Although Rousseau received very little formal schooling, his ideas about how children should be raised, as put forth in his book *Émile*, have had a significant influence on education. Often labeled

the "father" of modern child psychology, Rousseau believed that all children were born "innately moral" and that their inherited nature determined the progress of their development (Thomas, 2000, p. 44). According to Rousseau, the role of the adult or teacher was (a) to protect children from the "vices" of society and (b) to provide an environment that supported the stage of development that children were in so that they were able to develop to their potential (Frost, 1966, p. 294). Interestingly, though, "Rousseau abandoned his own children to a foundling hospital" (Braun & Edwards, 1972, p. 40).

According to Rousseau, there exist four stages of development through which children progress. However, only the first two stages are applicable to our discussion here (Frost, 1966, p. 295). In the first stage, from birth to age 5, the educational focus should be on motor activity, physical development, sense perception, children's individual development, and abandonment of the idea that children act morally or socially (Frost, 1966). In the second stage, from age 5 to age 12, the focus should be on the child deriving learning from the environment, which is motivated by "the demands of his nature at the time, not by the requirements of others" (Frost, 1966, p. 296).

Rousseau was among the first individuals to acknowledge that young children were not simply "miniature adults" and among the first to introduce the idea of "stages" in development (Braun & Edwards, 1972, p. 43) as well as the idea that children should only learn what they are ready to learn.

The Beginning Point for Early Childhood Education

Thanks to Rousseau's view of childhood as a very distinct period in human development, the beginning point of early childhood education emerged, followed by a wellspring of unique educational approaches and experiences geared specifically toward society's youngest citizens.

Johann Heinrich Pestalozzi

Educator and theorist **Johann Heinrich Pestalozzi** (1746–1827), born in Zurich, Switzerland, did not begin elementary school until he was 9 years old. He did not enjoy school and preferred to spend most of his time with his grandfather, who was a pastor who spent most of his time ministering to the poor. As a result of his early experiences, Pestalozzi developed a strong sense of compassion for the poor as well as a great desire to help others (Frost, 1966). During his early tenure as a minister, Pestalozzi read some of Rousseau's books, becoming a supporter of his educational and political theories (Frost, 1966).

In order to make money for his family, Pestalozzi began writing *Leonard and Gertrude*, which was successful as a novel but not as a "work on education and social uplift" (Frost, 1966, p. 348), which is what Pestalozzi had intended it to be. Nevertheless, Pestalozzi continued his forays into writing in spite of this, eventually becoming a schoolmaster. Pestalozzi expanded the work of Rousseau, and although his methods were criticized, he made significant progress with the children in his role as schoolmaster. Pestalozzi and his friends organized the Society of the Friends of Education to make people aware of his theories and methodologies. In an effort to achieve his life's goal, Pestalozzi wrote "an exposition of his philosophy of education and methodology, which he titled *How Gertrude Teaches Her Children*" (Frost, 1966, p. 350).

"Pestalozzi represents a beginning point for early childhood education [as] he actually taught young children" (Braun & Edwards, 1972, p. 45). Like Rousseau before him, Pestalozzi believed that education should follow the natural development of the child and that instruction should not require more or less than the child is capable of handling (Frost, 1966). Pestalozzi's focus on proceeding from the concrete to the abstract and from the particular to the general was a way of placing instruction in sync with the child's development (Weber, 1984). Only after learning in this concrete way is a child ready to move on to learning more abstract concepts. For example, Pestalozzi believed that in order for children to learn to read, they must start by learning the letters, then syllables, and then words. Once children have mastered these concepts, they can move on to understand that words strung together have meaning (Frost, 1966).

As an early pioneer in the field of early childhood education, Pestalozzi was destined to change the educational thinking and practice of the Western world. To Pestalozzi's everlasting credit, educational equality did not constitute educational uniformity; he believed in education for all yet deeply understood the idiosyncrasies of the individual learner and the unique role that human nature plays in the life of each learner.

Friedrich Froebel

Born in Oberweissbach, a village in East Germany, **Friedrich Froebel**'s (1782–1852) early childhood was one of neglect, frustration, and loneliness (Frost, 1966). He lost his mother at the tender age of 9 months and felt neglected by his father. When his father attempted to indoctrinate Froebel with his teachings, "he found the boy dull and placed Froebel in the girls division of the village school" (Braun & Edwards, 1972, p. 62). At age 10, Froebel went to live with his maternal uncle where he experienced affectionate understanding and was able to catch up academically. Froebel attended several universities, studying a variety of subjects, including architectural design. Later employed by the Frankfurt Model School, Froebel was given the opportunity to study a brief course in Pestalozzi's educational approach. Froebel, like Pestalozzi, respected the dignity of children and wanted to establish an educational program that provided children with emotional stability. But unlike Pestalozzi, Froebel opposed the authoritative and regimented aspects of Pestalozzi's teachings. In 1816, Froebel established the Universal German Educational Institute, a Pestalozzian-type school in a small village called Keilhau, where he remained until 1829. From the period 1831 to 1837, Froebel went on to establish an institute and administered an orphanage and a boarding school in various places in Europe.

In 1837, Froebel returned to Germany to establish a new early childhood school, a type of child's garden for 3- and 4-year-old children, ushering in the **kindergarten** movement, which was not yet named. Incorporating the use of play, games, stories, and activities, the kindergarten was seen as an educational environment in which children could develop in the right direction, according to the divine laws of human growth. Froebel's study of architectural design would serve him well in the design of the gifts and occupations that eventually became a part of the kindergarten curriculum. Froebel's reputation as an early childhood educator grew, and soon kindergartens began to spring up throughout Germany. However, Froebel was soon accused of spreading atheism and socialism by the Prussian minister at the time, and kindergartens were ultimately banned throughout Prussia. Although kindergartens still existed in other German states, they did not return to Prussia until the 1860s, after Froebel's death. But by the late 19th century, kindergartens began to appear throughout Europe and North America.

Froebel's major contributions to the field of early education came during a period in Europe often referred to as the Age of Reason—a time when intellectual curiosity surpassed religious dogma. In Froebel's literary work, *The Education of Man,* which focused on distinct periods of childhood between the ages of 7 and 10, Froebel outlined his premise for education: (a) All existence originates from God; (b) humans possess an inherent spiritual essence, which is the vitalizing force that spurs development; and (c) all humans are connected by their ideas—they are a part of a grand scheme that exists in the universe. Froebel contended that the child, at birth, has an internal spiritual essence that is driven by self-activity, and that development follows a special process of unfolding. According to Froebel, kindergarten should promote self-actualization in children. He claimed that the kindergarten gifts and occupations (described in Figure 2.1) and children's sociocultural experiences, especially play, work together in the life of a child to bring self-actualization to fruition.

Froebel would be the first early childhood educator to place a strong emphasis on the value of play in the life of the young child. Froebel contended that play allowed children to express their innermost needs, desires, and thoughts and was a means by which children sought to imitate adult vocational activities and socializations.

As a part of the kindergarten curriculum, Froebel developed a series of "gifts" and "occupations" for the kindergartener. Figure 2.1 delineates **Froebel's gifts**, each of which had its own physical appearance and symbolic meaning.

The gifts progressed from the simple and undifferentiated to the more complex. Based on the principle of synthesis of opposites, Froebel's cylinders represented the integration of the sphere and cube. The various cubes and their subdivisions were used to assist children in creating geometrical and architectural designs. The sticks and rings provided children practice at exercising their small muscles and coordinating hand-eye movements, and they also provided the basis for early drawing and writing.

The occupations consisted of artifacts such as pencils, wood, sand, clay, straw, and sticks for construction purposes. Kindergarten activities also included a collection of games, songs, and stories designed to promote children's sensory and physical development. Teachers would often present the occupations to groups of children using hand motions and rhythmic songs. This marked the birth of what is now called "circle time" in many of today's early childhood programs. Overall, Froebel's kindergarten was designed to convey basic ideas about the unity of the world to young children (Braun & Edwards, 1972; Lawrence, 1969; Lilley, 1967; Spodek, 1986).

European Women Who Influenced Early Childhood Education

Throughout history, women have played a crucial role in influencing the trajectory of early childhood education. The following pages speak of a few female trailblazers in the field of early childhood education to whom we owe a debt of gratitude.

Margaret McMillan

Margaret McMillan (1860–1931) was born in Westchester County, New York, after her parents had emigrated to the United States in 1840 from Inverness, Scotland. As an adult, Margaret lived in London and worked sporadically as a governess while also being active in the suffrage and socialist movements, along with her sister, Rachel (Braun & Edwards, 1972; see also Chapter 3). In 1893, she was elected to the school board in Bradford, England. It was in this position that McMillan discovered her interests in improving the health problems of children. As a school board member, McMillan pushed for "medical inspection of school children, school baths, and other causes" (Braun & Edwards, 1972, p. 127).

A few years later, Margret and Rachel moved to Deptford and "started a day and night camp school" for children who were sick. They were "appalled by the rickety legs, lice, scabies, and impetigo in children, which they saw as evidence of neglect for the children growing up in Great Britain" (Braun & Edwards, 1972, p. 127). After working with these children, they decided that by the time the children were school-aged, their health problems were too advanced. Believing that they could prevent children from becoming gravely ill, the sisters turned their attention to younger children and opened an "open-air nursery school" (Braun & Edwards, 1972, p. 127). Just 3 years after opening the school, Rachel died. With a strong belief in what they were trying to accomplish, "[Margaret] McMillan continued their work . . . training teachers, promoting nursery schools, and writing political tracts until her own death in 1931" (Braun & Edwards, 1972, p. 127).

| Figure 2.1 | Froebel's Kindergarten Gifts |

Gift 1	• Six soft, colored balls	
Gift 2	• A wooden sphere, cube, and cylinder	
Gift 3	• A large cube divided into 8 smaller cubes	
Gift 4	• A large cube divided into 8 oblong blocks	
Gift 5	• A large cube divided into 21 whole, 6 half, and 12 quarter cubes	
Gift 6	• A large cube divided into 18 whole oblongs: 3 divided lengthwise; 3 divided breadthwise	
Gift 7	• Quadrangle and triangle tablets for arranging figures	
Gift 8	• Splints of various lengths	
Gift 9	• Small points in various materials	
Gift 10	• Sticks for outlining figures, and connectors	

Source: Used by permission of Scott Bultman, Froebel Foundation USA, http://www.froebelfoundation.org

The open-air nursery school had "one side open to the elements in order to let the sun shine in" (Braun & Edwards, 1972, p. 127). It was intended mainly to be an outdoor center where children could play in the sandbox, the gardens, and the "junk heap (piles of coal ashes, old nuts and bolts, etc.)" (Braun & Edwards, 1972, p. 127). The school served children ages 1 to 6 years old. Devoted to the idea of improving the health problems of young children, McMillan ensured that the children were provided with baths, clean clothes, nourishing meals, and medical and dental care. McMillan also believed that it was important to provide children with "cognitive stimulation" as well as to foster their emotional development.

Margaret McMillan discounted the idea that children should be instructed on an individual basis and insisted that children participate in group experiences (Braun & Edwards, 1972). Margaret McMillan also valued children's art; she encouraged drawing because she thought that children's "spontaneous drawings of what had been remembered" provided valuable information to the teacher (Braun & Edwards, 1972, p. 130). It allowed the teacher to obtain an understanding of what a child deemed important enough to remember and what he or she did not, thus providing information about the child's development.

Another important aspect of McMillan's educational philosophy was her emphasis on parent involvement. McMillan held monthly group meetings where mothers could talk about their children and teachers could listen and suggest "child rearing methods and games that the mother might introduce to the child" (Braun & Edwards, 1972, p. 129). She also required that the teachers make home visits so that they could learn more about a family's history and roots. By cultivating strong relationships with families through meetings and home visitation, she hoped that the families would turn to the nursery school in times of crisis and/or illness.

McMillan's emphasis on children's health, small group work, and parent involvement is evident in early childhood programs today. The comprehensive nature of the McMillan sisters' work at the end of the 19th century and in the early 20th century was both intuitive and noteworthy.

Maria Montessori

A late-19th-century Italian feminist and physician, **Maria Montessori** (1870–1952) was way ahead of her time. Growing up during this era, girls had only two career choices—to become a nun or a teacher—and Montessori didn't want to be either. Instead, she was interested in mathematics and science. Montessori was considered to be self-confident, optimistic, and greatly interested in change. After her primary schooling, Montessori began her studies in engineering and later became the first female to graduate from medical school in Italy.

In 1904, the University of Rome offered Montessori a teaching job as a professor of anthropology. She accepted, but in 1906 resigned to work with 60 young children of working families instead.

Working with these young children is where Montessori developed all of her educational methods, which became so successful that even children with learning disabilities began to pass examinations constructed for children who were "normal." Soon thereafter, Montessori started the first "Casa dei Bambini" or "Children's House" in San Lorenzo, Rome. Montessori developed a welcoming environment for the children, which included child-sized furnishings and a child-sized family room (Kramer, 1976). Montessori's pedagogy and approach were undifferentiated from her work with students who were atypically developing. However, she soon realized that children who were "normal" or typically developing did not need the direct instruction, as did the students exhibiting atypical development, to manipulate the materials. Montessori began to notice how the children would absorb knowledge almost effortlessly from their surroundings. She felt the children were teaching

Maria Montessori's methodology encouraged self-regulation and independent learning in young children.

themselves, which helped inspire her lifelong pursuit of educational reform. This realization became a major premise in Montessori's pedagogy—providing children the opportunity to discover and learn by manipulating the objects. Today, this technique is called the "hands-on" approach to learning.

Unlike her predecessor, Margaret McMillan, Montessori discounted the idea that children should be instructed in a group. Montessori believed that children should be given the freedom to work independently once they learned how to use the materials. Montessori gave children the freedom of independence by providing open shelves for children to select materials. Another major revolutionary change that came as a result of the Montessori methodology was her emphasis on materials that induced self-discipline or self-regulation in children. Montessori was also best known for her creation of materials for sense training. According to Montessori, such materials must be simple, inherently interesting, self-correcting, and fully comprehensible to teachers (Braun & Edwards, 1972). Montessori also engaged children in real-life activities (life skills training) like washing hands, buttoning, preparing food, cleaning tables, or polishing shoes. She received worldwide attention by helping to transform an unruly group of young children into happy, calm, self-disciplined, well-behaved children. It is important to note that Montessori classrooms placed very little value on children's art, which was quite a departure from Margaret McMillan's pedagogical approach.

sensory
real-life

Montessori's pedagogy included (a) encouraging teachers to observe and pay attention to children rather than children paying attention to the teacher, (b) allowing children to work at their own pace by providing a stimulating learning environment, (c) providing teaching materials that would allow children to use their imagination, and (d) allowing children to correct their own mistakes. Montessori often reminded teachers in her courses, "When you have solved the problem of controlling the attention of the child, you have solved the entire problem of education" (Kramer, 1976, p. 217).

Montessori published many books based on her observations of children that provide guidance in how to best educate them. An insightful educator during her time, many of her observations uncover the process of how children learn. She reported that children under 6 years of age had an astonishing power of the mind, which she called the absorbent mind. She believed that children's minds resemble a sponge—they have the ability to absorb knowledge from their environments. Montessori also reported that children have sensitive phases of development in which they begin to show an interest in acquiring a particular skill.

Despite Montessori's educational genius in Europe during the 20th century, her influence in the United States was short-lived because, with the range of several emerging psychological and learning theories, some considered her ideas far-fetched. Nonetheless, Montessori schools began to reappear in the mid-1950s (Braun & Edwards, 1972).

Early Childhood Education Constructivists

Effective early childhood education practices are constructivist in nature. The pioneering efforts of theorists like Piaget, Vygotsky, and others have done much to up the ante with regard to quality educational programming for young children.

Jean Piaget

Jean Piaget (1896–1980), born in Neuchâtel, Switzerland, had a father who was a professor at the University of Neuchâtel where he taught medieval classics. Piaget deeply respected his father, and Piaget's mother was a kind person who, sadly, struggled with neuroticism. Piaget adopted his scientific perspective from an early age; he was always engaged in scientific pursuits. Piaget had many interests, including birds, seashells, and mechanics. At age 10, Piaget published his first work when a local natural history journal printed a paper he had written on a partly albino sparrow (Miller, 2002). Later, Piaget's work at a local museum, which consisted of cataloging mollusks, resulted in a series of published papers on mollusks.

Piaget pursued his studies in the natural sciences, receiving his bachelor's degree at the age of 18 and a doctoral degree at the young age of 21. Despite the fact that he had devoted his graduate studies to biology, Piaget found that he did not want to spend his life conducting research in this field. Instead, he decided to pursue postdoctoral studies in psychology. Piaget's later studies in psychology afforded him the opportunity to work in the laboratory of Alfred Binet and Theodore Simon, the developers of the intelligence test. During his testing of children, Piaget began to try out the psychiatric (clinical) interviewing techniques he had learned, and children's responses intrigued him. As Piaget administered the test to the children, and followed up their answers with probing questions, he found their responses to be nothing short of astonishing—magical and unrealistic. Piaget used this technique of posing questions and encouraging children to explain their answers, commonly referred to as the clinical interview method, throughout the remainder of his career.

Because Piaget was among the first to propose a stage model of cognitive development, his perspective on children's learning has had an enduring impact on the way we view children. Piaget proposed four stages of cognitive development: the sensorimotor period (0–2 years old), preoperational period (2–7 years old), concrete operational period (7–12 years old), and formal operational period (12 years old to adulthood).

In addition to the concept of stages, several other important aspects of Piaget's cognitive theory of development have influenced the field of early childhood education. Piaget's theory was often considered a **constructivist** theory because it posits that children need to actively participate (construct their own learning) in the environment in order to learn. His theory also suggests that children do not require outside motivation to do this; rather they have an innate drive to explore and interact with their surroundings. As "little scientists," they will investigate, hypothesize about, and experiment with the materials available to them (Miller, 2002). Piaget believed that teachers need to design the environment to capitalize on the intrinsic motivation that children have to explore and interact with the world around them. According to Piaget, teachers should mainly provide "guidance and resources so that children can teach themselves" (Miller, 2002, p. 73).

Over the course of his life, Piaget is estimated to have written more than 100 articles and more than 40 books on child psychology alone (Miller, 2002), making him one of the world's most prolific modern contributors to children's thinking. Jean Piaget's contribution to the field of early childhood education is unprecedented. Very well respected by his psychology colleagues, Piaget remains one of the most celebrated giants and influential figures in the fields of both early childhood education and psychology. (See Chapter 4 for a more extensive explanation of Jean Piaget's theory of cognitive development.)

Lev Semyonovich Vygotsky

Lev Semyonovich Vygotsky (1896–1934) was born to a large, intellectual Jewish family in Russia. Vygotsky studied law, literature, philosophy, psychology, and social science at universities in Moscow. Vygotsky's early encounter with children with congenital defects such as blindness, deafness, and mental retardation helped to pique his interest in medicine, which led him to undertake several years of medical training (Miller, 2002).

The development of Vygotsky's theory needs to be understood in the historical context of the post-Revolutionary zeal to create novel ways of thinking and living in Russia. Vygotsky and his colleagues set out to construct a new psychology based on **Marxism** (social, political, and economic policies derived from socialist principles and advocated by Karl Marx during the 19th century) following the Russian Revolution. Vygotsky's goal was to link the ideas about the politics and economics of Marx and Engels (a German socialist leader and close associate of Marx) to psychology. Referred to as a sociocultural theorist, Vygotsky asserted that human beings were embedded in the sociocultural context and that it is virtually impossible to explain human cognition or thought independent of the individual's context. Vygotsky recognized that learning takes place within the context of relationships and underscored the vital role that adults and peers play in the development of cognition.

One of the most well-known concepts of Vygotsky's sociocultural theory is the **zone of proximal development (ZPD)**, which can be defined as the difference between what children can do independently and what they can achieve with adult assistance and guidance. Related to the notion of the ZPD is the idea of **scaffolding**, which has often been used to help illustrate this concept. In much the same way as a scaffold extends the work of a builder or a painter, adults and peers extend the growth and learning of children through modeling, encouragement, discussion, joint participation, leading questions, and verbal prompts (Miller, 2002). Vygotsky also emphasized the important link between thinking and language—that language, as a cultural tool, transforms and influences thinking.

Unfortunately, at the end of his career, Vygotsky had fallen victim to political strife and was blacklisted under Stalin's rule (Miller, 2002, p. 371). But Vygotsky remained involved in psychology and education for the remainder of his life, which was cut short at the age of 37 by tuberculosis. However, by that time, Vygotsky had already published more than 180 works, presented extensive lectures to students and colleagues, and compiled extensive data from his research.

The basic tenets of Vygotsky's sociocultural theory—including the notion that children develop within the context of relationships with adults and peers, the idea of the ZPD or the scaffolding of children's development, and the belief that language precedes the development of more advanced thought—have contributed significantly to the practice of early childhood education. (See Chapter 4 for more information on Vygotsky's sociocultural theory of development.)

The Progressive Education Movement

By the early 20th century, educational thought had progressed considerably, and the public schools were confronted with their first great challenge: to educate the streams of immigrant children coming to the shores of America. Sound familiar? The father of progressive education, John Dewey, and his followers were espousing a new type of educational reform—an educational methodology that was grounded in the ideals and principles of democracy. Dewey's educational approach would emphasize growth, interaction, continuity, and unity. He placed a great deal of emphasis on connecting the child to his or her experiences but, more importantly, the school to society.

American Influences

American educational thought, having its antecedents and being well steeped in European society and history, was heavily influenced by the tenor of the times. In the pages to follow, you will learn about the unprecedented work of American educators and their marked influence on the field of early childhood education.

John Dewey

John Dewey (1859–1952) was the third of four sons, born to Archibald and Lucina Dewey, in the town of Burlington, Vermont, on October 20, 1859. Given the prestigious family background of Dewey's mother, Dewey grew up among adults who imposed great expectations on him. Consequently, Dewey graduated from high school at the age of 15 and pursued college, graduating in 1879. Following his graduation from college, Dewey continued to work as a high school teacher for 2 years and, in 1882, pursued graduate study in philosophy and psychology at Johns Hopkins University, graduating in 1884. During his 2 years of study, Dewey worked with G. Stanley Hall in physiological psychology. In the years to follow, Dewey taught philosophy and psychology at institutions of higher education, until securing a teaching position at Columbia University, where he remained until his death in 1952.

During the period of 1880 to 1920, the United States was experiencing a significant increase in immigration, industrialization, and urbanization, giving rise to widespread poverty. These conditions resulted in the progressive education movement, a groundswell of social and educational reforms led by John Dewey and other progressive educators. These educators, who focused on the social consciousness of education, contended that the rich and poor could learn from one another and that the same education opportunities should be available to all.

education for all

Dewey's ideas concerning education were fresh and intriguing to 20th-century educators; his educational philosophy touted the need to get rid of rote memorization in schools and to replace it with a more cooperative, child-centered approach, which stressed each child's individuality, creative

experience) rote memorization

Froebel vs. Dewey

expression, social interaction, discovery learning, and validation of emotions (Cremin, 1965; Graham, 1967). Dewey also believed that a child's family, school, and surrounding community were responsible for supporting his or her education, which is in sync with today's popular cliché "It takes a village to raise a child." Dewey asserted that children learn best when cooperatively engaged in real-life activities with their peers and that experimentation was more conducive to knowledge acquisition than rote memorization (Gargiulo & Kilgo, 2004). Furthermore, Dewey purported that the role of the teacher was not to impose education on children but rather to observe children's activities in order to better understand their unique interests, and to guide their activities to support the process of learning.

Dewey diverged from the traditional perspective of early education as proposed by Froebel and reorganized the structure of the kindergarten classroom to emphasize a cooperative learning environment in which children actively participated in making decisions regarding daily learning activities (Peltzman, 1998). The Froebelian kindergarten, you may remember, focused on symbolism, play, unity, and imitation, while Dewey's approach emphasized experiences and methods that were more relevant to children's everyday existence. Dewey believed that teachers should use creative methods when instructing young children in order to better support children's independent problem-solving capabilities. Dewey's classroom was organized to allow children to direct the sequence of activities, while teachers supported their learning through the provision of learning experiences such as field trips, art, and music. Teachers fostered children's developing social skills through having children interact with their peers. Children's self-initiated activities promoted the internal motivation for them to learn more about formal subjects taught in school, such as reading, writing, and arithmetic.

Dewey's educational dogma focused on bringing the school closer to life. Because his era was a time of educational inequality, Dewey espoused democratizing culture, and the need for a new socialized education system—education for everyone—ideas that remain relevant for today's educational landscape.

Lucy Sprague Mitchell

Lucy Sprague Mitchell (1878–1967), who was born to a wealthy Chicago family, did not attend formal schooling until the age of 16 due to suffering from an uncontrollable nervous condition. Introduced to John Dewey by her influential father as a young teenager, Mitchell was soon active in the social reform of Dewey and his followers, negating her own upper-class status. Mitchell was largely self-educated before college but attended Radcliffe as an undergraduate, graduating with honors in 1900 with a degree in philosophy (Antler, 1987). Mitchell later worked at the University of California, Berkeley, as the first dean of female students.

After marrying and relocating to New York City, Mitchell joined Columbia University. As a devotee of Dewey's philosophy, Mitchell was interested in children and research, which led her to work in conjunction with another colleague, Harriet Johnson, to establish the Bureau of Educational Experiments (known today as the Bank Street College of Education). The bureau was a laboratory for testing progressive education principles and studying children's learning. The bureau also sponsored a teachers' college to promote progressive methods, a workshop for writers of children's literature, and a bulletin to disseminate the collaborators' findings from their research (Antler, 1987). The school that Mitchell founded was considered "developmentally appropriate" and thus served as a model for the design of subsequent early education programs in the country. Later, in the early 20th century, Mitchell

In education, John Dewey is referred to as the Father of the Progressive Movement.

Promoting Optimal Development

Child-Centered Teaching

Dewey was quite child-centered in his approach to education. Today, effective early childhood programs are child-centered, meaning that curricula, assessment, and teaching methodology emanate from the child. Child-centered classrooms provide constructivist learning opportunities for children; provide numerous opportunities for children to engage with their peers and adults; provide a range of learning centers that are accessible, fully equipped, and intriguing to children; provide culturally relevant materials and experiences for children; and are led by teachers who serve as guides/facilitators and use language as a primary medium to scaffold children's development. However, early childhood educators who utilize child-centered approaches when engaging children must also recognize the value of intentional teaching. These teachers use children's leading questions, symbolic play, nonlinguistic representations, interests, and so on, in order to capitalize on a teachable moment.

and other progressives who had developed these once well-received programs for young children were labeled "flamingly radical." However, by the 1950s, these same schools became the standard for the traditional nursery schools.

We remain indebted to Mitchell and her collaborators for their life's work in the study of how children learn. Mitchell and her colleagues professionalized the field of early childhood education, and their legacy lives on in programs like Head Start and the Bank Street College of Education (Antler, 1987).

Abigail Adams Eliot

Abigail Adams Eliot (1892–1992), born in Dorchester, Massachusetts, attended Winsor School, a private secondary school in Boston, and graduated in 1914 from Radcliffe College. Eliot, who began her career as a social worker, became disenchanted with the field and eventually went on to study at Oxford. Eliot studied and worked under McMillan at the Rachel McMillan Nursery School and Children's Centre in London. Eliot's training there and her social work background prepared her aptly to begin a similar school in Boston, the Ruggles Street Nursery School and Training Center, located in Roxbury. Eliot went on to earn a master's degree in education in 1926 and a doctorate in education from Harvard University in 1930.

The nursery school movement—which was closely linked to three fields: home economics, social work, and education—was launched in the United States in the early 20th century. Early nursery training centers emphasized good health and hygiene for children, education for better mothering, and education and habit training through play. Eliot is probably best known as the founder of the 20th-century nursery school movement. One year after Eliot and her cofounder, philanthropist Elizabeth W. Pearson, began the Ruggles Street Nursery School, a group of mothers formed a cooperative called the Cambridge Nursery School. Eliot was very instrumental in this effort, and soon nursery schools were popping up everywhere (Braun & Edwards, 1972). The Cambridge Nursery School later changed its name to the Nursery Training School of Boston, and by 1931, student interns and graduate teachers were being sent for training to 40 schools around the country. The Nursery Training School later became affiliated with Tufts University and bears the name of Eliot-Pearson today.

Practices Addressing the Mental Health Needs of Young Children

In the early part of the 20th century, many educators in the United States deemed the nursery school movement to be a primary venue for addressing the overall health needs of young children. Today, many early childhood programs provide comprehensive care and support to young children, which include addressing the mental health and/or social emotional needs of children. Over the past 20 years, there has been increased emphasis on assessing the mental health status of infants, toddlers, and preschoolers. A range of mental health assessment tools have been devised and are currently used by both lay and mental health practitioners in many programs to determine children's mental health status. These programs recognize the importance of working with both the infant/toddler or preschooler and his or her family in order to ameliorate the child's mental health status.

During the Great Depression, Eliot served as a member of the National Advisory Committee for President Roosevelt's Federal Emergency Relief program, which sponsored emergency nursery schools for needy children. Eliot was also known as a leader in the "National Association for Nursery Schools (1926), the forerunner of the National Association for Nursery Education (1929), now known as the National Association for the Education of Young Children (NAEYC)" (Braun & Edwards, 1972, p. 148).

Erik Homburger Erikson

Erik Erikson (1902–1994) was born near Frankfurt, Germany, an offspring of an extramarital affair. Erikson never knew his biological father and never connected to his stepfather when his mother remarried. This dynamic resulted in great family strife, causing Erikson to often feel like an outsider. As a result of a difficult childhood, Erikson entered elementary school and high school feeling conflicted about his own ethnic, religious, and familial identity, which would greatly impact Erikson's life's work. Erikson struggled with school and, after graduating from high school, attended an art school in hopes of becoming a successful artist. But his dream began to wane due to his restlessness. Erikson traveled extensively throughout Europe and would eventually meet Sigmund Freud's daughter, Anna, upon a visit to Austria. As a young adult, Erikson studied psychoanalysis with Anna Freud and eventually earned certification and membership in the Vienna Psychoanalytic Society. During this same period, Erikson worked at a small school and pursued studies in the Montessori method, eventually earning a certificate.

After marrying an American and fleeing Europe just prior to World War II, Erikson taught at a number of distinctive universities and professional schools in the United States such as the Harvard Medical School, the University of California, Berkeley, and the San Francisco Center for Psychoanalysis, to name a few. He also ran a private practice in psychoanalysis. Upon becoming a U.S. citizen, Erikson changed his last name from Homburger to Erikson. Plagued by his early struggles with personal identity, Erikson's decision to change his name was believed to be an attempt to define himself as a self-made man, thereby resolving his own personal conflict relative to identity.

Erikson's theory of psychosocial development emphasized that individuals confront eight primary internal conflicts throughout the course of development that occur in response to one's maturational level and the demands imposed on oneself by societal expectations. According to Erikson, there are five psychosocial crises or conflicts that children progress through before reaching young adulthood Erikson proposes a total of eight psychological crises that individuals undergo throughout the lifespan.) (a) trust versus mistrust (infancy); (b) autonomy versus shame and doubt (1 to 3 years of age); (c) initiative versus guilt (3 to 6 years of age); (d) industry versus inferiority (ages 6 to 12); and (e) identity versus role confusion (ages 12 to 20) (Shaffer, 2009). Erikson believed that healthy psychosocial development occurs as a result of resolving each psychosocial conflict.

Erikson's theory is significant in that it emphasizes the relationship between the child's biological maturation and the influential nature of the culture in which the child lives. Although each individual develops along the same sequence of developmental stages, each person does so in a culturally specific way (Miller, 2002). Erikson further attested that culture, itself, changes to address and support the changing needs of each consecutive generation. Erikson's perspective on the evolution of individuals' identity emphasizes the continuity of change across the life span (Miller, 2002). Thus, Erikson's emphasis on development occurring across the entire life span decreased the expectation for children to develop fully early on. Rather, Erikson was instrumental in promoting the idea that humans are a continuing work in progress, and that identity formation is achieved through a lifetime of crisis management. Erikson's method of study also encouraged future child development researchers to observe children's natural behaviors and to consider the influence of culture on developing identity within diverse contexts (Miller, 2002). (See Chapter 4 for a more extensive account of Erikson's theory of psychosocial development.)

Abraham Maslow

Abraham Maslow (1908–1970) was born in Manhattan, New York, to a family of Russian-Jewish immigrants. He experienced an unhappy childhood growing up; Maslow was often subjected to gang violence and an abusive mother who used religious superstition to threaten and coax him into behaving appropriately. These conditions, including the fact that Maslow had a distant relationship with his father, greatly impacted his school performance. Although his grades were not as high as those of his peers, Maslow eventually earned acceptance into the City College of New York (CCNY). Initially intrigued with studies in the humanities, Maslow turned his attention toward the field of psychology during his second year at CCNY while reading the works of John B. Watson (Dewsbury, Benjamin, & Wertheimer, 2006). Maslow transferred to the University of Wisconsin to pursue graduate studies in primatology, and while there he worked under his mentor Harry Harlow. Maslow received his doctoral degree in 1934. Upon returning to New York in 1935, Maslow became involved with a conference sponsored by Edward L. Thorndike at the Teachers College at Columbia University where he was eventually offered a postdoctoral fellowship. In 1937, he earned a teaching position at Brooklyn College. With the events of World War II, in 1949, Maslow redefined his interests in dominance and sexuality and turned his focus toward social and abnormal psychology, especially human motivation (Dewsbury et al., 2006).

As a result of his studies in social psychology, Maslow questioned human motivation, which led him to develop his theory on the hierarchy of needs. Maslow hypothesized that humans experience needs on a continual basis, and for every need that is satisfied, another emerges (Dewsbury et al., 2006). Maslow prioritized these human needs within a pyramid graphic. At the base of the pyramid are physiological needs, such as hunger and thirst. Following these basic needs are safety, belongingness, love, esteem, and self-actualization. Maslow's theory posits that individuals will tend to progress through this hierarchy of needs as each level of need is met. Ultimately, if an individual is successful at meeting all of the prior basic needs, he or she will arrive at the stage of self-actualization in which the primary concern is to achieve one's greatest potential.

Guided by his work in self-actualization, Maslow believed in the importance of meeting the biological needs that stem from childhood as a means of moving the individual toward fulfillment of self-actualization (Myers, 1998). Maslow believed that positive early experiences during the period of childhood shaped one's emotional development. Although Maslow later rejected the notion that secure emotional development is necessary in order for an individual to achieve self-actualization, the idea that positive experiences early on in life have the potential to shape one's development over time is still an important consideration for educators today. Many early childhood educators still support Maslow's ideas concerning education and motivation. (See Chapter 4 for further discussion on Maslow's hierarchy of human needs.)

Benjamin Bloom

Benjamin Bloom (1913–1999) was one of five children born to a family of Russian immigrants in Lansford, Pennsylvania (Zimmerman & Schunk, 2003). After graduating from high school with the distinction of valedictorian in 1931, Bloom received a scholarship to attend Pennsylvania State University. Within 4 years, Bloom had succeeded at earning both his bachelor's and master's degrees in psychology. Later, as a doctoral student at the University of Chicago, where he earned his PhD in 1942, Bloom assumed a research assistant position for the office of the university's Board of Examinations. The primary responsibility of the Board of Examinations was to design, administer, and score the examinations upon which degrees were awarded. In 1940, Bloom advanced from his work in research to working directly as a board member, a position Bloom held until 1959.

Bloom was eventually appointed as an instructor of educational psychology and remained at the university for a period of more than 30 years. During this time, Bloom also secured the position of University Examiner. In 1939, the Board of Examination's emphasis on testing factual information using multiple-choice, true-false, and matching formats shifted to measuring students' abilities to reason and problem solve across all disciplines of study (Zimmerman & Schunk, 2003). Bloom's role as University Examiner naturally led him to experiment with different instructional methods and various ways to measure subsequent knowledge. Bloom would later design different methods for measuring problem-solving capabilities and, from 1959 to 1960, Bloom worked at the Center for Advanced Study in the Behavioral Sciences in Stanford, California.

While working at Stanford, Bloom shifted his attention from measurement and instructional methods to examining curriculum and instruction within the framework of human development. In 1956, he published the *Taxonomy of Educational Objectives—Handbook I: The Cognitive Domain*, in which he sought to classify the various goals of education in terms of curriculum and evaluation (Zimmerman & Schunk, 2003). From Bloom's *Taxonomy* came a set of principles that addressed education and instruction (see Figure 2.2). "These principles emphasized students' 'intended learning outcomes,' teachers' distinctions between the different learning objectives, the necessity for consistent and logical objectives while adhering to current theories in psychology, and 'descriptive' educational classifications" (Zimmerman & Schunk, 2003, p. 374). Bloom's publication of *Taxonomy* helped broaden the field of education to encompass numerous educational goals and enabled teachers to develop and enhance curriculum and their methods for measuring educational outcomes.

Bloom's publication of *Stability and Change in Human Characteristics* (1964) emphasized that while there is little evidence that changing one's environment impacts intelligence, marked changes in environment during the early years can have a greater impact on intelligence than the same degree of changes in later periods of development (Braun & Edwards, 1972). Bloom believed that in order to maximize each child's greatest learning potential, educators must begin as early as the preschool years to facilitate children's motivation to achieve and learn. Just before the publication of *Stability and Change*, Bloom utilized the research findings from his book to support the creation of Head Start.

Bloom's work emphasized the necessity for providing optimal learning environments for children at home and in early learning centers. His philosophy of education also focused on the

Figure 2.2　　**Bloom's Revised Taxonomy**

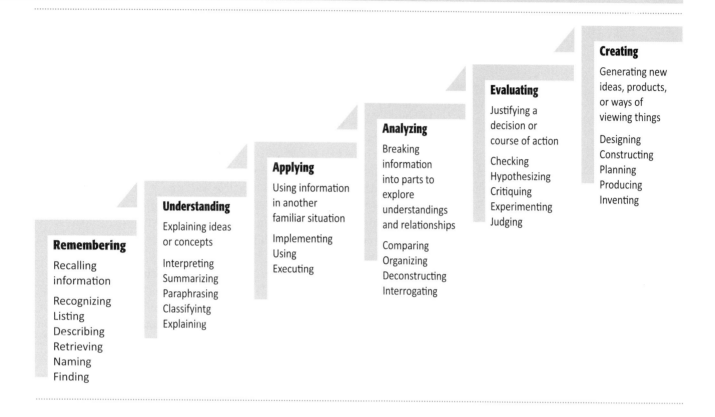

Remembering

Recalling information

Recognizing
Listing
Describing
Retrieving
Naming
Finding

Understanding

Explaining ideas
or concepts

Interpreting
Summarizing
Paraphrasing
Classifyintg
Explaining

Applying

Using information
in another
familiar situation

Implementing
Using
Executing

Analyzing

Breaking
information
into parts to
explore
understandings
and relationships

Comparing
Organizing
Deconstructing
Interrogating

Evaluating

Justifying a
decision or
course of action

Checking
Hypothesizing
Critiquing
Experimenting
Judging

Creating

Generating new
ideas, products,
or ways of
viewing things

Designing
Constructing
Planning
Producing
Inventing

importance of promoting children's problem-solving capabilities and developing the essential foundations for learning that will enable children to move forward—past financial and cultural barriers. According to Bloom, the primary goal of education is to enable students to develop the necessary reasoning skills that can be used across all disciplines, placing far greater emphasis on how knowledge is taught than on the value of knowledge in its factual form.

Jerome Bruner

Jerome Bruner (1915–) was the youngest of four children born to an affluent Jewish, Eastern European family in New York. During his secondary school years, Bruner became interested in subjects like French, mathematics, and history, with surprisingly little interest in the sciences (Bruner, 1983). Bruner entered the field of psychology by chance, having taken courses in comparative psychology and neuropsychology. He earned an undergraduate degree and doctoral degree from Duke and Harvard, respectively. During his doctoral program, Bruner's academic emphasis centered on experimental psychology, examining the subjects of perception, memory, and learning and motivation, including animal behavior. Toward the end of World War II, Bruner accepted a teaching position at Harvard, where he remained for 27 years.

Jerome Bruner's work was an influential source of change for the field of cognitive development. Influenced by the work of Piaget and Vygotsky, Bruner believed that children were active learners and that the act of organizing new information occurs in three phases: enactive, iconic, and symbolic representation. Infants use enactive representation to learn about their environment through active exploration and manipulation (Slee, 2002). Children pass through the stage of enactive representation to iconic representation at about 2 or 3 years of age as they begin to rely less on active manipulation of their environment and more on using mental pictures to create meaning. Around age 7, children enter the stage of symbolic representation, at which time they make use of symbols to represent knowledge. According to Bruner, it is during the stage of symbolic representation that children's language development aids them in the use of symbolic thought, and without it, children would be dependent on enactive and iconic representation to acquire meaning. Bruner believed that it is most effective for the introduction of new material to progress through these three stages.

Bruner is also well known for his advocacy of the spiral curriculum, in which knowledge is presented in the format of a continuous spiral. As children progress in their acquisition of new material, teachers should construct the curriculum in such a way that it provides numerous opportunities for children to revisit the material over time—each time exploring a different aspect of the material—as a means of helping children develop a deeper understanding (Bakhurst & Shanker, 2001). In short, the spiral curriculum allows children an opportunity to revisit basic ideas and concepts repeatedly (Bruner, 1960).

Bruner also emphasized the importance of introducing children to a variety of subject matter very early on in their development. According to him, this helps children to identify their own unique interests and better supports their motivation. Bruner (1960) himself once said, "We begin with the hypothesis that any subject can be taught effectively in some intellectually honest form to any child at any stage of development" (p. 33). Indeed, Bruner's work has assisted educators in the process of reconsidering the approach toward educating young children.

Bruner's ideas on supporting the development of children's individual interests and competencies have moved educators to support learning environments that foster collaborative exploration and problem-solving skills. "To those who know him, Bruner remains the [complete] educator in the flesh" (Gardner, 2001, p. 94).

WHO WERE THE MAJOR CONTRIBUTORS TO THE KINDERGARTEN MOVEMENT?

The kindergarten movement constituted a more formalized approach to the socialization and education of young children. Contributors to the movement championed the spirit of Rousseau's and Froebel's educational philosophy, which was an important beginning point for a movement that would define early childhood education as we know it today.

European Influences

To his everlasting credit, Friedrich Froebel bears the distinction as the sovereign leader of the kindergarten movement. Below you will see how Froebel's disciples helped launch one of the most quintessential movements in Western educational history. Initially, kindergarten would be viewed as the great hope to turn the tide of hopelessness and disillusionment—the only means of eradicating U.S. slums. During the early years, the movement was primarily a philanthropic and religious undertaking. However, over time, its purposes for society would be altered again and again in response to societal needs and concerns.

Friedrich Froebel

As mentioned earlier in this chapter, Friedrich Froebel was, single-handedly, one of the most prolific contributors to the kindergarten movement in the United States. Vestiges from Froebel's 19th-century kindergarten in Germany are still evident today in early childhood classrooms across America. As you will glean from the following paragraphs, Froebel joins the ranks of his U.S. counterparts in making an indelible imprint on the creation of effective kindergartens.

American Influences

Early pioneers of the kindergarten movement captured the attention of esteemed and well-respected educators and philosophers. Although their efforts were often fraught with literal and conceptual misinterpretations of Froebelian philosophy, the movement gained great momentum in the United States. The contributions of these early pioneers to the field of early care and education at large cannot be underestimated.

The Peabody Sisters

Elizabeth Palmer Peabody (1804–1894) and **Mary Tyler Peabody Mann** (1807–1887) were the eldest of seven children born to Nathaniel Peabody and Elizabeth Palmer. Elizabeth Palmer was raised in the Unitarian religion and ran a school that emphasized bringing out the unique excellence in every student, girls included. Primarily due to their mother's influence, these sisters read widely and had a broad range of interests. Elizabeth Peabody's ambition as a young adult was to escape Salem, her native town, in order to experience the cultural riches and theological controversies of Boston. In 1822, she made her move and established a private school for girls in Boston. However, the school failed to attract enough enrollees to survive for much more than a year. Mary Peabody later joined Elizabeth in Boston to embark on a teaching career. In 1825, the sisters opened another girls' school in Brookline, Boston. The school thrived until 1832, when Elizabeth Peabody learned of a partner's misappropriations of school finances.

Elizabeth Peabody's educational philosophy was based on **transcendentalism,** which was anchored in the idea of a just society informed by liberal Christianity. Transcendentalism stressed the need for historical knowledge in order to balance the movement's focus on individual intuition. Peabody soon learned of the German kindergarten movement, which would dovetail nicely with her ideas regarding the education of the very young. Greatly inspired by Friedrich Froebel's work in Germany, Elizabeth and her sister Mary opened the nation's first *formal* kindergarten in Boston in 1860. The sisters worked tirelessly in the school and on promoting their ideas. Eventually, Elizabeth Peabody published a journal on kindergartens, which became her main focus for most of her career. From 1879 to 1884, Elizabeth Peabody was a lecturer at Bronson Alcott's Temple School in Boston. Elizabeth Peabody lived longer than any of her sisters and met her life's goal to institutionalize transcendentalism in a very practical way—by establishing kindergartens in every state of the union.

Margarethe Meyer Schurz

Margarethe Meyer Schurz (1833–1876) was born in Hamburg, Germany, to a prominent family that encouraged her to pursue the arts and education. As a teenager, Schurz was exposed to the teachings of her predecessor and kindergarten advocate Friedrich Froebel. In 1849, Schurz and her sister Bertha met Froebel. Bertha spent the next 2 years opening kindergartens in Germany, and in 1851, Bertha and her husband opened the England Infant Garden in Tavistock Place. Margarethe Schurz taught there before moving to Watertown, Wisconsin, with her husband.

When Schurz arrived in America, she carried Froebel's ideas with her. Schurz was committed to employing Froebel's philosophy while caring for her daughter, Agathe, and four neighbor children. She engaged them in games, songs, and group activities that channeled their energy while, at the same time, preparing them aptly for formal schooling. In 1859, Elizabeth Peabody visited the Schurzes' home and was impressed with Agathe's ability and maturity. Schurz informed her of the Froebelian philosophy, and Elizabeth became an immediate convert, establishing a kindergarten within a year. Other parents were also impressed with the children's progress and urged Schurz to assist them with their own children. Responding to the pressure, Schurz opened a kindergarten in her own home. Actually, Schurz's kindergarten was one of the very first in the United States. Like most of the early kindergartens in the United States, all activities were conducted in German. The kindergarten in Watertown continued until World War I, when it was closed due to the prohibition of the German language. Nevertheless, Schurz's work gained her preeminence and an audience; kindergarten became an accepted and integral part of American education and an accepted course of study for elementary teachers.

Susan Elizabeth Blow

Born in St. Louis, Missouri, **Susan Elizabeth Blow** (1843–1916) was the oldest of six children born to Henry Taylor Blow and Minerva Grimsley Blow. Blow's father was a successful businessman who made his money in the lead industry, and Blow had a very comfortable lifestyle. Blow was tutored by her governesses and attended private school in New Orleans, Louisiana. Blow enjoyed sharing her lessons with her younger brothers and sisters. In 1859, when she was 16, Blow attended a private school in New York City, but her education there was cut short by the Civil War, so she returned to Missouri in 1861.

Blow then traveled to Germany, and there she experienced something that gave the rest of her life direction. She observed kindergarten classrooms inspired by the work of Froebel and decided that children in America should have a similar experience. Once back in the United States, Blow had a ferocious appetite for learning as much as she could about the kindergarten movement and Froebelian philosophy, and she spoke regularly to educators about creating a kindergarten program in America. Capitalizing on her family's social status and connections, Blow recruited her father to ask Dr. William Torrey Harris, superintendent of St. Louis Public Schools, to open an experimental kindergarten. Susan offered to direct it if Dr. Harris provided a room and a paid teacher. In September 1873, Susan Blow opened the first public kindergarten classroom in the United States at the Des Peres School in Carondelet (Braun & Edwards, 1972; Weber, 1984).

While most other classrooms were plain, Blow's kindergarten classroom was bright and cheerful. It had low tables and short benches suitable for small children. The room also contained many plants, books, and toys for children to use. The kindergarten curriculum entailed students learning about color, shapes, and fractions by using simple objects like balls and blocks. Students also learned about hygiene, eating well, and getting regular exercise. Blow taught children in the morning and teachers in the afternoon. And by 1883, every St. Louis public school had a kindergarten, becoming the model for the nation.

Patty Smith Hill

Patty Smith Hill (1868–1946) was born in Kentucky in 1868. Her upbringing was remarkably unique for that period; her father believed in the right of women to receive an education, and her mother believed that children should experience a happy and adventurous childhood (Wolfe, 2002). As a result of the family relocating to Texas and Missouri and then returning to Kentucky, Hill witnessed and experienced firsthand the severe poverty that pervaded the country in the late 1880s.

She was convinced that she wanted to work with children who experienced financial hardship and severe work conditions (Wolfe, 2002). Hill graduated from the Louisville Collegiate Institute at age 18 and later attended the Louisville Training School for Kindergarten, where she completed her training in 1889 (Wolfe, 2002).

In 1905, Hill was hired by Columbia Teachers College (now Teachers College, Columbia University) as a faculty member and was later promoted to the position of professor in 1922 (Osborn, 1980). While there, Hill had assumed the role of director of the Kindergarten Department in 1910. However, as a result of her status in the department and her work with G. Stanley Hall, an American leader in emerging psychological and social thought, Hill began to question her roots in Froebelian philosophy, which later compelled her to modify the kindergarten curriculum. She also worked alongside John Dewey and William Kilpatrick, both of whom further contributed to her evolving perspective on early childhood education during the kindergarten movement (Osborn, 1980). Hill was an avid supporter of the progressive education movement in the late 1800s. Subsequently, she began to incorporate new ideas into her teaching approach that encouraged children to make their own choices and to actively experiment with materials within the context of a flexible daily schedule (Osborn, 1980). Hill promoted democracy in the classroom and mutual respect among the students (Cohen & Rudolph, 1977).

While Hill continued to believe in the utility of Froebel's gifts as a part of the kindergarten curriculum, she rejected the use of his occupations and further modified the curriculum by adding supplemental materials and activities like dolls and dollhouses, games, blocks, music, art, nature, and literature (Osborn, 1980). Hill's kindergarten materials and activities encouraged creativity among children, socialization, and parent involvement. Her transition away from Froebel's educational philosophy and its emphasis on fine motor activities (Cohen & Rudolph, 1977) also included the development of the Hill floor blocks, which promoted children's gross motor development (Wolfe, 2002). Patty Hill was the first educator to join kindergartens with first-grade classes, resulting in cooperative and multiage learning settings (Peltzman, 1998). In addition to reforming the kindergarten curriculum, she was also known for being an elder statesman of nursery school education. Hill established a nursery school on the campus of Columbia's Teachers College in 1921.

In the very beginning of early childhood education in the United States, only a few educators had experience in the field; most of them had varied backgrounds and experiences. Additionally, they were unfamiliar with their respective colleagues. Recognizing this, Hill convened a small group of these educators at Columbia Teachers College. This group became the precursor of what is now the National Association for the Education of Young Children (NAEYC) (Braun & Edwards, 1972). To her everlasting credit, Patty Smith Hill professionalized the field of early childhood education. We remain grateful to her for the endorsement of early childhood teachers as valid professionals, a by-product of her very important work.

Summary

The preceding pages chronicle the rich and diverse history of early childhood education as a special branch of education. One common denominator at every turn in history was the interplay between the demands of society and educational philosophy and practice. Society dictated early childhood educational approaches, and as time progressed, these approaches became more refined and developmentally appropriate. As practitioners in the field, we have benefitted greatly from the trials and tribulations of those who have gone before us. Thanks to the perseverance and insight of our predecessors, our young children, their families, and our preschools are better today. It is now up to us to make our own individual contributions to early childhood education's rich heritage.

Key Terms

Reflection, Application, and Analysis Questions

1. How did the impact of childhood ideology or the concept of childhood influence the history of early childhood education?

2. Describe progressive education and its impact on the kindergarten movement.

3. In your opinion, who are two of the most influential figures in the field of early childhood education and why? Select one key figure from each of the headings "European Influences" and "American Influences."

4. What aspects or elements of the Froebelian kindergarten still exist in today's kindergarten classrooms?

Extension Activities

1. Take a few moments to reflect about the rich history of early childhood education and your specific experiences in the field of early childhood education to date. What has that experience been like for you? More specifically, what aspects of early childhood education methodology, approaches, and ideology (Froebelian, Montessori, Vygotskian, Deweyan, etc.) have you personally experienced or witnessed? Take a few moments to write down your reflective thoughts about the experience.

2. Observe a minimum of three different preschools or early elementary school grades over the course of several weeks. In a journal, detail aspects of the teaching and learning and link them to a particular time in early childhood education history.

Additional Readings

The texts listed below will provide the reader with in-depth information regarding the history of early childhood education and early childhood education approaches and methodologies.

Ariès, P. (1962). *Centuries of childhood: A social history of family life* (R. Baldick, Trans.). New York: Vintage Books.
This volume represents a classic work in the history of childhood. A primary focus for the author was the birth of modern education and the conceptualization of childhood.

Berk, L. E., & Winsler, A. (1995). *Scaffolding children's learning: Vygotsky and early childhood education.* Washington, DC: National Association for the Education of Young Children.
A scholarly and highly palatable read, this text has been found to be quite suitable for early childhood educators, teachers, and students. Vygotsky's theories, which focus on social, cultural, and societal development, as well as practical ideas for transferring theory into practice, are fully explicated in this text. Also included are key discussions on concepts such as play, language, assessment, development, special needs, and other topics.

Brosterman, N. (2002). *Inventing kindergarten.* **New York: Harry N. Adams.**

This text utilizes extraordinary visual materials in an attempt to fully expound on and reconstruct German educator Friedrich Froebel's very successful kindergarten system, which was widely touted throughout the world by the end of the 19th century.

Lascarides, V. C., & Hinitz, B. F. (2000). *History of early childhood education.* **New York & London: Farmer Press, a member of the Taylor & Francis Group.**

Thoroughly and eloquently presented, this book provides a clear description of the history of early childhood education in the United States. The text uniquely combines historical literature and the prominent, influential, and theoretical underpinnings of the time to create a fascinating read. An essential source for every early childhood educator, scholar, and student, this complete and well-written volume captures the profound traditional and creative knowledge base of early care and education.

Weber, E. (1984). *Ideas influencing early childhood education: A theoretical analysis.* **New York: Teachers College Press.**

This book conveys the quintessential concepts and theories that have molded the behavior, prompted the thinking, and awakened the emotions of countless generations of teachers in the field of early childhood education.

On the Web

John Dewey - *http://www.britannica.com/EBchecked/topic/160445/John-Dewey*
http://dewey.pragmatism.org/

These websites provide essential information regarding the outstanding work of John Dewey and are a must-visit for the curious and aspiring educational pragmatist and scholar.

Maria Montessori - *www.webster.edu/~woolflm/montessori.html*
http://en.wikipedia.org/wiki/Maria_Montessori

These websites offer a historical perspective on Maria Montessori and her unique methodology for teaching young children.

Jean Piaget - *http://www.piaget.org/*

Contains comprehensive information on the theories and work of Piaget, including information about related conferences and publications.

Lev Vygotsky - *http://www.marxists.org/archive/vygotsky/*

Provides biological and philosophical information about Lev Semyonovich Vygotsky.

Student Study Site

Visit **www.sagepub.com/gordonbiddle** to access several study tools including eFlashcards, web quizzes, links to SAGE journal articles, web resources, video resources, lesson plan templates, and more.

CHAPTER

3

Types of Programs and Services

This chapter will help you answer these important questions:

- What are the different types of early childhood programs?
- How are early childhood programs financed?
- What are home-based and center-based child care settings?
- Why do child care centers need to be licensed?
- Do home day care centers need to be licensed?

Vignette: Picking a Preschool

Mary and Jonathan are parents of a 2-year-old daughter, Cassie, and a 4-year-old son, Brian. Both parents work, and their children attend the ABC Preschool. In the beginning, Mary and Jonathan were happy with the preschool and program in which their children were enrolled. Brian has attended ABC Preschool since he was 1 year old, and so has Cassie.

The philosophy of the preschool is to provide a nurturing, success-oriented environment for all children. The ABC Preschool provides opportunities for success by viewing each child as an individual with unique developmental needs. The preschool curriculum developed by the teachers and directors closely follows academic standards. The professional child care staff members make the children their primary focus and foster a positive self-concept for each child. Positive self-concept, how one perceives and evaluates oneself, is a strong foundation for future development and learning. Although self-concept is very important for the development of their children, Mary and Jonathan are concerned that too much academic instruction is occurring in the school.

Both Mary and Jonathan are very involved in the educational growth of their children and are raising them to have a love for nature. As the children have gotten older, Mary and Jonathan have felt that the ABC Preschool curriculum has not been providing their children with the critical thinking necessary for educational growth or the important connection to nature. They have decided to enroll their children in a different preschool. After visiting and interviewing different preschools, they found one that uses the Waldorf method of teaching. The Waldorf method is one that focuses upon nurturing the child's self-confidence and self-reliance, while fostering the child's personal integrity and a sense of social and environmental interdependency and responsibility.

There are many types of early childhood programs. Some may be different, but many programs throughout the United States share many similarities. These similarities include anything from particular educational philosophies to the types of services the programs provide for children. Mary and Jonathan found that the philosophy of the Waldorf schools was a good match for their children, and they liked that the curriculum integrated the arts, music, crafts, and the natural world with the regular educational disciplines. Finding a preschool that shares your same philosophy, whether it is home or center based and licensed or not, are some of the topics that we will be discussing throughout this chapter.

Key Elements
for Becoming a Professional

NAEYC DEVELOPMENTALLY APPROPRIATE PRINCIPLE 9

Always mentally active in seeking to understand the world around them, children learn in a variety of ways; a wide range of teaching strategies and interactions are effective in supporting all these kinds of learning.

Interpretation

Jean Piaget, a leader in cognitive development, would argue that children are active learners who construct their understanding from the things around their environment.

NAEYC STANDARD 1: PROMOTING CHILD DEVELOPMENT AND LEARNING

a. Knowing and understanding young children's characteristics and needs

b. Knowing and understanding the multiple influences on development and learning

c. Using developmental knowledge to create healthy, respectful, supportive, and challenging learning environments

WHAT ARE THE DIFFERENT TYPES OF EARLY CHILDHOOD PROGRAMS?

There are many different types of early childhood programs, and each one has its own philosophy, mission, and approach to teaching. Even though there are many differences in the programs, they share some common ideologies. These ideologies are based on the well-being, developmental needs, and capacities of children.

Montessori Programs

Maria Montessori, introduced in Chapter 2, established a school for children living in the poorest conditions in Italy. This first school was a scientific experiment that would lead to her now famous philosophy and method of teaching young children. Today, the Montessori method of teaching is being used with preschool through high school students and now serves primarily middle-class students. Most of the schools that follow the Montessori philosophy are private, though some public schools are using the Montessori teaching method (Chatting-McNichols, 1992). One major difference between Montessori education and other early childhood programs in the United States is Montessori's emphasis on work experiences that children must have with practical tools that have been presented to them as part of the environment rather than playtime. Although some other programs share this concept of work experience, the differences between them and Montessori are significant.

Philosophy and Mission

According to the Montessori philosophy and mission, all children are born with special mental abilities that aid in the work of their own learning. This self-learning develops as they explore their surroundings and their environments. Children are given the freedom to use their inborn mental abilities so that they can develop physically, spiritually, and intellectually. The teacher presents a sense of order and self-discipline to supply certain environmental limits on this freedom.

The Montessori philosophy also emphasizes the importance of sensory awareness. Children are taught to explore by using their senses. The curriculum is designed to develop consciousness of the senses through the use of specially prepared materials. The idea of using these materials to teach children the Montessori skills and concepts has spread throughout the world (Standing, 1984; Watts, 2000).

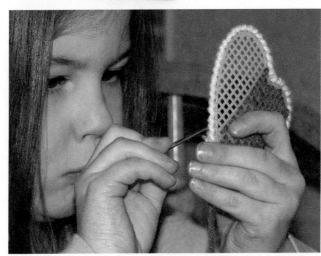

The Cylinder Block and Lacing Frame are examples of Montessori materials.

Role of the Teacher

In Montessori schools, the teacher's role is of primary importance, but it is also very subtle; that is, the teacher serves as a guide rather than instructing the children to do specific tasks (Watts, 2000).

The child's environment is of utmost importance because it serves as an educational tool from which children learn. The role of the child is to be an active explorer, and Montessori schools encourage the children to express themselves within their educational environments. It is important to note that the Montessori philosophy and mission may vary in different schools, states, and countries. Some schools have modified their philosophies or evolved in other directions and no longer fit the standard description of a Montessori school (Watts, 2000).

The Environment

The Montessori approach upholds that society helps to facilitate children in following a natural course of development that progressively moves to a higher level of cooperation, peace, and harmony. According to this philosophy, children have a series of developmental stages. These stages are described as **planes of development**—the child moves to adulthood through a series of developmental periods that are related to the child's physical, mental, and social being. Montessori describes four stages of development. In the first stage, from birth to age 6, children are characterized by their "absorbent minds," absorbing all aspects of their environments, languages, and cultures. In the second stage, from age 6 to age 12, children use a "reasoning mind" to explore the world with abstract thought and imagination. In the third stage, from age 12 to age 18, adolescents have a "humanistic mind" that is eager to understand humanity and the contribution the adolescent can make to society. In the last stage of development, from age 18 to age 24, adults explore the world with a "specialist mind," taking their place in the world by choosing appropriate actions for the self and knowing how to make choices.

The sensory area enables students to classify and describe sensory impressions as they relate to length, width, temperature, mass, color, and pitch.

Reggio Emilia Programs

The **Reggio Emilia programs** were established after World War II when parents from a region in Italy wanted schools that would teach their children collaboration and critical thinking skills necessary for a democratic society. This sense of democratic purpose inspired **Loris Malaguzzi,** an elementary school teacher who dedicated himself to pedagogical activities within the early childhood educational system, to join parents and further develop the Reggio Emilia program.

Philosophy and Mission

The Reggio Emilia approach encompasses and implements the theoretical contributions of Dewey, Piaget, Vygotsky, and Bruner. The curriculum is based on teachers closely observing and documenting the children's ideas and **co-constructing knowledge** (the teacher works with the child who learns by questioning, identifying, and developing an understanding of the curriculum) with them. The teacher gives special roles to the children as they express their ideas with the teacher. Parents continue to be engaged as partners in their child's learning. The environment is a valuable source of learning to inspire, reflect, and promote the work of the children, which is done in small groups. The educational philosophy of the Reggio Emilia schools is to be dedicated to the formation of a learning environment that will improve and assist a child's construction of "his or her own powers of thinking through the combination of all the expressive, communicative, and cognitive languages" (Edwards, Gandini, & Forman, 1993). The Reggio Emilia approach is based on the following principles:

Table 3.1 The Reggio Emilia Approach

THE ROLE OF THE REGGIO EMILIA TEACHER:

- To co-explore the learning experience with the children.
- To stimulate ideas, solve problems, and solve conflicts.
- To receive ideas from the children and return those ideas to them for further exploration.
- To organize the classroom and materials to be aesthetically pleasing.
- To organize materials to help children make thoughtful decisions about the media.
- To document children's progress: visuals, videos, sound recordings, portfolios.
- To help children see the connections between learning and experience.
- To help children express their knowledge through representational work.
- To form a "collective" among other teachers and parents.
- To have a dialogue about the projects with parents and other teachers.
- To foster the connection between home, school, and community.

PROJECTS:

- can emerge from children's ideas and/or interests;
- can be initiated by teachers;
- can be introduced by teachers knowing what is of interest to children: shadows, puddles, tall buildings, construction sites, nature, etc.;
- can be long enough to develop over time, to discuss new ideas, to negotiate over, to induce conflicts, to revisit, to see progress, and to see movement of ideas; and
- can be concrete, personal from real experiences, important to children, "large" enough for diversity of ideas, and rich in interpretive and representational expression.

MATERIALS:

- can have variation in color, texture, and pattern to help children "see" the colors, tones, and hues and help children "feel" the similarities and differences in texture;
- can be presented in an artistic manner that is aesthetically pleasing to look at and that will invite touch, admiration, and inspiration; and
- can be revisited throughout many projects to help children see multiple possibilities (New, 2000).

Source: Roopnarine, Jaipaul; Johnson, James E., *Approaches to Early Childhood Education.* 5th Edition. © 2009. Adapted by permission of Pearson Education, Inc., Upper Saddle River, NJ.

- Emergent Curriculum: An **emergent curriculum** builds upon the interests of children. Topics for study are captured from the talk of children, through community or family events, and from the known interests of children (planets, shadows, dinosaurs, etc.). Team planning is an essential component of the emergent curriculum. Teachers work together to formulate hypotheses about the possible directions of a project, the materials needed, and possible parent and community support and involvement.

- Project Work: Projects, also emergent, are in-depth studies of concepts, ideas, and interests that arise within the children. Considered as an adventure, projects may last one week or could continue throughout the school year. Throughout a project, teachers help children make decisions about the direction of study, or the ways in which the children will research the topic. Teachers will also assist with the representational process that will showcase the topic, and the selection of materials needed to represent the work.

- Representational Development: Consistent with Howard Gardner's (2006) notion of schooling for multiple intelligences (a list of seven intelligences where children are able to solve problems valued in their cultural setting: linguistic, logical-mathematical, musical, bodily-kinesthetic, spatial, interpersonal, and intrapersonal), the Reggio Emilia approach uses the integration of the graphic arts as tools for cognitive, linguistic, and social development. Demonstration and presentation of concepts in multiple forms of illustration—print, art, construction, drama, music, puppetry, and shadow play—are viewed as essential to children's understanding of experience.

- Collaboration: Collaborative group work, both large and small, is considered valuable and necessary to advance cognitive development. Children are encouraged to dialogue, critique, compare, negotiate, hypothesize, and problem solve through group work. Within the Reggio Emilia approach, multiple perspectives promote both a sense of group membership and the uniqueness of self.

Reggio Emilia teachers work together with students and families to promote and stimulate children's thinking and academic success.

- Teachers as Researchers: The teacher's role within the Reggio Emilia approach is multifaceted. The role of the teacher is first and foremost that of a learner alongside the children. The teacher is a teacher-researcher, a resource and guide who lends expertise to children (Edwards et al., 1993). Within such a teacher-researcher role, educators carefully listen, observe, and document children's work and the growth of community in their classroom and are to provoke, co-construct, and stimulate thinking and children's collaboration with peers. Teachers are committed to reflect on their own teaching and learning.

- Documentation and Showcasing: Similar to the development of a portfolio, documentation of children's work in progress is viewed as an important tool in the learning process for children, teachers, and parents. To explicitly represent the dynamics of learning, teachers display pictures of children engaged in experiences; print the children's own words about what they are doing, feeling, and thinking during the learning process; and exhibit the children's visual artwork that reveals their interpretations of their experiences.

- Environment: Within the Reggio Emilia schools, great attention is given to the look and feel of the classroom. The environment is considered the third teacher. Teachers carefully organize space for small and large group projects and small intimate spaces for one, two, or three children. The work, plants, and collections that children have made from former outings are displayed at both the children's and adults' eye level. Common space available to all children in the school includes dramatic play areas and work tables for children from different classrooms to come together (Hewett, 2001; Schroeder Yu, 2008).

Some of the characteristics that make this approach different from other programs or philosophies are the role of the teacher (see Table 3.1), the kinds of projects that engage children, and the kind of materials that are necessary in a child's education.

HighScope Curriculum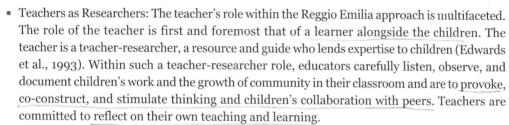

The HighScope curriculum, created during the 1960s, is a model developed from the theories of Jean Piaget that was one of the first intervention programs for disadvantaged children. It is designed to provide a "decision-making framework," in which teachers plan the lessons to reflect the needs and interest of the students (DeVries & Kohlberg, 1987). The curriculum views children as active learners who construct knowledge that helps them make sense of their world. This approach supports the notion that children learn best from activities that they themselves plan, carry out, and reflect upon and that adults both support and challenge.

Philosophy and Mission

There are certain goals that the HighScope curriculum considers to be important in a child's development. These goals are for children to build up an array of skills through active learning in the arts and physical fitness as well as to learn the ability to dramatize, speak, collaborate with others, plan time effectively, make decisions, and review one's own work. This concept to "plan-do-review" allows children to plan and convey their goals, carry them out, and reflect on their learning (Hohmann & Weikart, 1995). The approach also allows children to be involved in problem-solving and decision-making situations and activities throughout the day.

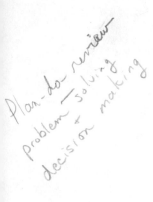

The Role of the Teacher

HighScope's focus on active learning depends on positive teacher-student interactions. The role of the teacher is to assist and support students' decision making and to foster their cognitive abilities. Teachers who use the HighScope preschool approach strive to be supportive as they converse and play with children. Throughout the day, teachers practice positive interaction strategies, such as sharing control with children, forming authentic relationships with children, supporting children's play, and adopting a problem-solving approach to social conflict.

There are four key factors that Roopnarine and Johnson (2000) have identified as important interactions between teacher and student in the HighScope classroom:

1. Teachers as Active Learners: Teachers need to be active learners. They need to model and encourage students in the interest and enthusiasm of learning new things.

2. Careful Observers: Teachers are to make systematic and detailed observations of their students' behaviors and interests in order to understand their learning abilities. HighScope has

BEST
Practices HighScope Curriculum

There are eight key experiences that the HighScope curriculum stresses as important for curriculum implementation (Weikart, Rogers, Adcock, & McClelland, 1971):

1. Active Learning: Children are required to initiate and convey their own tasks in the classroom.

2. Using Language: Children are expected and encouraged to communicate with others through oral and written language about their feelings and experiences.

3. Experiencing and Representing: Children are presented with opportunities to experience through their senses and represent those actions through movement, music, and role-playing.

4. Classification: Children are encouraged to observe the similarities and differences among objects because classification is important in mathematical learning.

5. Seriation: Children learn to order objects from smallest to largest based on their length, width, or weight as this is also vital for mathematics.

6. Number Concept: Children are taught to have an understanding of what numbers represent.

7. Spatial Relationship: Children learn to understand up/down, in/out, and under/over.

8. Time: Children come to understand the concept of time and are encouraged to learn the seasons, the sequence, and the past and future of events.

developed the Child Observation Record (COR) in order to assist teachers with this careful observation process of their students (Schweinhart, 1993).

3. Environmental Planning and Organization: Teachers prepare the classroom to encourage and involve students with daily work and play activities because the environment and physical setting are important aspects for stimulating students' growth and development.

4. Positive Interactions With Children: Teachers maintain a positive interaction and communicate effectively with their students.

The Environment

Organizing the classroom and playground setting is an important aspect of the HighScope curriculum because it has a strong impact on children's behavior. Children's curiosities are organized into areas of interest to support their decision-making process. Examples of children's interest areas are role-playing, drawing, painting, reading and writing, dancing, climbing, counting, and pretend play (Hohmann, 1996). Teachers store materials on low shelves, in clear boxes, and by using picture labels; this allows children to find, use, and return materials independently.

Children's daily routines are an active and engaging sequence of events that helps the children anticipate what will happen next and provides them the control for what they will do during their

day (Hohmann & Weikart, 1995). Teachers encourage the children to work in small and large groups. In the small groups, teachers provide students with new and familiar materials (based on teachers' observations of what students are interested in) for them to explore and experiment with. In large groups, teachers and students begin with a physical activity, such as dance, and then proceed to story time, group discussion, and cooperative play.

Social being linked to intellectual development. Dewey Progressive Movement

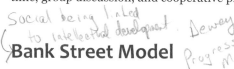

Bank Street Model

Lucy Sprague Mitchell (introduced in Chapter 2) founded the **Bank Street School for Children** (a school that educates the whole child, emphasizing how children learn and how they interact with their environment) in 1916. Mitchell saw children as unique human beings with an avid desire to learn, which, if nurtured, would invigorate a lifetime of learning. Mitchell and her colleague, Harriet Johnson, believed children learn best in environments specifically suited to their ages and stages of development. In addition, they understood the close relationship between learning and the child's development. Mitchell and Johnson were aware that children's emotional lives were inseparable from their learning, interest, and motivation. They considered that in the Bank Street School setting, children would thrive and learn more naturally and happily.

In the HighScope curriculum, children plan, do, and review their daily experiences and become active learners within their environments.

Philosophy and Mission

The philosophy and mission of the Bank Street model have their origins in the **Progressive movement** of the early 20th century, specifically in the work of John Dewey (Kliebard, 1995). This movement was a period of political, societal, economic, and educational change. The Progressives pushed for social justice, equality, and public safety. A major focus of the Progressive movement was child labor and education reform. Many immigrant children were being exploited in factories and at home, and the Progressives encouraged and mandated parents to send their children to public schools.

Lucy Sprague Mitchell and colleagues were strong believers in the Progressive education movement. They wanted to create classrooms and schools that would resemble democratic communities, with no rigid curriculum, students being responsible for their own learning, and mixed-age classrooms. They also saw the classroom as a place to study the development of children with the idea that doing so would lead to social change. The Bank Street model did not support rote learning and memorization practices but rather followed the Progressive philosophy in which children were encouraged to be active learners. The educational Progressives believed that children learned by doing real-world experiences and activities (Kliebard, 1995).

The Role of the Teacher

The role of the teacher in the Bank Street model is that of a facilitator of learning, and students are to be the scientists and researchers; they discuss, debate, and perform hands-on activities on their

Communication, support, and collaboration are the hallmarks of the Bank Street classroom.

assigned work (Mitchell & David, 1992). The Bank Street curriculum has an underlying theme that teachers reinforce throughout the academic year. The premise is for children to develop a sense of community and social responsibility—to broaden their play and classroom activities from a small group, to a larger group, and ultimately to the school community. Teachers encourage children to share and learn from each other's skills and needs. A major part of the teacher's educational goals and the classroom environment is to help children attain a balance between their individual needs and the needs of the group. The ultimate goal is for each child to become a social individual who cares for, respects, and contributes to the welfare of others (Mitchell & David, 1992).

The Environment

The most important principle of the Bank Street model is that in order for children to learn and become lifelong learners, they must interact with their social and physical environments and interpret those experiences. In most of the Bank Street schools today, young children are learning by experimenting with materials. Children are encouraged to organize the Bank Street classroom with attractive furniture and school materials that promote individual and group study and interaction. Teachers use teaching strategies that encourage children to make discoveries and provide them with the time to make meaning out of those discoveries. Children choose fewer topics to learn about compared with a typical public school curriculum, but Bank Street teachers organize and develop their topics thoroughly and in depth. A unit on math, for example, might take one month in public schools while in the Bank Street school the same topic might last as long as three months, the reason being that teachers will spend more time engaged in the exploration process and making meaning.

A key feature of Bank Street is the idea that the child develops as a social being, which is strongly linked to the child's intellectual development. Children work in groups in order to communicate their ideas, share their experiences, pose their questions, and solve their problems. Working in groups allows children to undertake a problem and brainstorm a solution. Group work and learning to solve problems together are a fundamental part of the Bank Street classroom (Mitchell & David, 1992).

Waldorf Model

Rudolf Steiner is considered the founder of **Waldorf education**, which serves students through the 12th grade and functions independently from political and economic restrictions. Steiner's educational and personal background constitute the central focus of Waldorf education today. The central focus is in the understanding of every person's background and place in the world, not as members of any specific nation or race, but as members of humanity and world citizens (Davy, 2006).

Philosophy and Mission

Rudolf Steiner, an educator and a philosopher, was asked to start a school for the children of the workers in a Waldorf factory in Stuttgart, Germany. He described his new school of philosophy as **anthroposophy**: the wisdom of the human being. Anthroposophy, though oriented toward the Christian faith, is primarily concerned with the acknowledgment and development of spirituality in the person and the universe. Anthroposophy forms the philosophical and theoretical basis of the Waldorf teaching methods, which is reflected in the attitudes of its teachers—that is, to explore the nature of the human being as body, soul, and spirit; to seek the deeper meaning of life; to grasp the laws of karma and reincarnation; and to strive to create new forms through practical work and community building. Anthroposophy, however, is not taught as such to students in Waldorf schools worldwide. Focusing on each student's developmental needs, the Waldorf concept integrates the arts, music, movement, crafts, and drama with the disciplines of science, humanities, math, and technology. A unique aspect of Waldorf education is that the same teachers stay with their students from first through eighth grade. A class in a Waldorf school becomes very much like a family; the challenge for the teacher is to master all the subjects in the elementary curriculum.

The Waldorf philosophy educates the whole child by the "head, heart, and hands":

- Head (the academics)—stimulating the mind and cultivating imagination and creativity.
- Heart—engaging the heart with a sense of caring and responsibility for the earth and its inhabitants.
- Hands—encouraging respect for the arts, respect for humanity, and reverence for nature; fostering an enduring love of learning; and creating a close community of students, teachers, and parents (Davy, 2006; Easton, 1997).

The Role of the Teacher

The role of the Waldorf teacher is to guide the students in their daily work of creative play and discovery. Waldorf teachers offer their young students a sense of comfort and security, since young ones are just discovering their place in the world. The teacher encourages the students to widen their imaginations through the process of investigating their surroundings. This investigation process is persuaded by engaging the students in dramatic play. During the preschool and kindergarten years, children learn through "imitation" (Swartz, 1996), and the teacher serves as a role model worthy of imitating. Once the child is in first grade, students start searching for greater influence to assist and lead them with their next discovery. Therefore, the role of the teacher changes to one that is teacher-centered. The teacher will be the primary teacher for the lower-grade classes through eighth grade, serving as the main teacher and the authority figure for the entire elementary education. Teachers present the curriculum in a structural and sequential manner relying on lessons that are not accompanied by textbooks. The students create their own textbooks, by recording what they have learned and creating experiments, poetry, and stories.

Waldorf teachers teach all the important subject areas that conventional schools offer, subjects such as math, reading, and science. Teachers provide the lessons through a process of exploring nature, constructive and creative play, oral (not written) language and storytelling, and song singing.

The lessons are carefully developed for each age, but the timing for teaching them might be different than that of conventional schools because the Waldorf curriculum is designed with the growing child in mind (focusing on aesthetics, spirituality, and interpersonal skills). This makes the lessons naturally relevant and satisfying.

The Environment

The classroom environment is organized to make it pleasing and harmonious to all students. The Waldorf environment takes into consideration the child's own physical body and sensory experience by considering everything that the child sees, hears, and touches. The indoor and outdoor environments provide diverse and nourishing opportunities for the child to experience the senses—touch, balance, lively and joyful movement, and listening. Classroom materials are made out of natural wood, and students use wax to write and color. On a given morning, children might do such things as paint with watercolors, color with beeswax crayons, cook, sing a song, or build with wooden blocks. Rudolf Steiner (1965) would argue that an environment is one that nourishes the senses:

> The essential task of the kindergarten teacher is to create the proper physical environment around the children. "Physical environment" must be understood in the widest sense imaginable. It includes not just what happens around the children in the material sense, but everything that occurs in their environment, everything that can be perceived by their senses, that can work on the inner powers of the children from the surrounding physical space. (p. 24)

Programs Based on a Behaviorist Perspective

A kindergartner coloring a picture using a natural material such as beeswax crayons exemplifies the Waldorf approach.

Behaviorism originated with the work of **John B. Watson**, an American psychologist who claimed that psychology was not concerned with the mind or with human consciousness but instead was concerned only with behavior (Good & Brophy, 1990). Other key players in the development of behaviorist theory were Ivan Pavlov, Edward Lee Thorndike, and Burrhus Frederic Skinner. Today, **behaviorism** (the study of observable behavior) is most closely associated with the name of B. F. Skinner, who made his name by testing and rejecting Watson's theories. In doing so, Skinner formed his own theory that almost exclusively emphasized reflexes and conditioning as the primary forces behind behavior (this research study is discussed in Chapter 4). Skinner would say that people respond to their environment to produce certain consequences.

Philosophy and Mission

According to Watson, humans and animals could be trained to do anything one wanted. This concept set the stage for other researchers to investigate the idea of **cognitive maps**—a type of mental processing by which we can acquire, code, store, recall, and decode information about a specific location, word, idea, or task in our everyday environment. This process of learning new information can shape a learner's behavior through reinforcing the desired behavior. In other words, manipulation of reinforcements can control the behavior of a learner, and reinforcements need to continue in order to maintain the behavior. Skinner believed that children in schools were taught to learn through **aversive stimulation**. An aversive stimulus is something that is unpleasant or a punishment. A behavior followed by an aversive stimulus results in a decreased probability of the behavior occurring in the future. The behaviorists believe the following major principles:

1. Behavior that is positively reinforced will reoccur; intermittent reinforcement is particularly effective.

2. Information should be presented in small amounts so that responses can be reinforced (referred to as "shaping").

3. Reinforcement will generalize across similar stimuli—that is, responding to a stimulus similar to but distinct from the conditioned stimulus (referred to as "stimulus generalization") (Markle, 1969; Skinner, 1968).

The following sections explain the methodologies that educational behaviorists use to teach new behavior to children.

Learning

From a behaviorist perspective, learning is a process of disseminating information from teacher to student. "The teacher must present the student with appropriate behavioral responses to the student's specific stimuli—incentive or motivation—and reinforce those responses through an efficient reinforcement schedule" (Skinner, 1976, p. 161). An efficient reinforcement schedule must consist of a consistent repetition of the material; small, progressive sequences of tasks; and continuous, positive reinforcement. A learned response will become extinct without the positive reinforcement. Students will continue to adjust their behavior until they receive some positive reinforcement (Mook, 2004). Many educators use the behaviorist learning styles to teach students in their classrooms.

Strengths of Behaviorism

Educators who use the behavior model in their teaching do so for the following reasons:

1. A behaviorist lesson plan works well when there is a clear goal, and the learner responds and learns that goal. For example, the skills that require a significant amount of integration between muscle memory and cognitive processing, such as putting a puzzle together or riding a bike, are usually implemented successfully in the behaviorist learning style.

2. The behavior that is observed can be reinforced for it to occur again or punished in order to eliminate it.

Limitations of Behaviorism

Just as there are strengths to the behaviorist model, there are also limitations. Critics of this model have presented the following:

1. Behaviorists believe that learning is an activity independent from the mind; therefore, behaviorism does not account for all means of learning.

2. Behaviorism is not able to explain learning that occurs on its own without reinforcement, such as a child developing new language patterns.

Motivation

Behaviorists explain motivation as "schedules of positive and negative reinforcement" (Magoon & Critchfield, 2008, p. 1). Humans and animals learn positive or negative behavior by the type of reinforcements they receive. If the reinforcement is positive, then the student will be motivated to continue that behavior. For example, if each time a dog catches a ball it receives food, this behavior will teach the dog that a desired connection between a stimulus (food) and an appropriate response (catching the ball) is motivating, and the dog will continue catching the ball. Another example of reinforcement is when toddlers stop wetting their pants and tell their parents that they need to use the restroom. Parents reinforce the practice of using the restroom by praising their child. That verbal praise will motivate the toddler to use the restroom next time.

The Role of the Teacher

The behaviorists claim that the teacher's job is to establish classroom situations that reinforce desired behavior from their students. Behaviorist-based teachers need to predetermine all the skills necessary for their students to learn and then present them in a sequenced manner.

Teachers are constantly using the behaviorist approach to teaching in our educational system. Students are taught certain skills and then are asked to practice what they have learned over and over; this method is referred as "skill and drill" (Conway, 1997). This skill and drill exercise consists of constant recurrence of practice in order to efficiently reinforce a desired behavior. An example of reinforcement is testing students on the degree of their learning using an exam. Another behaviorist instructional method is question and answer, an activity in which questions can be of increasing difficulty and a good source for review of material covered in class. Research shows that teaching with the behaviorist method can be effective in areas where memorization is required and where there is either a correct or an incorrect response. This method of teaching has been successful in teaching structured material (e.g., mathematical formulas and facts, scientific concepts, and vocabulary for foreign language). The effectiveness of behaviorist teaching in comprehension and analytical aptitude, however, has been disputed (Conway, 1997).

Skinner's Operant Conditioning

B. F. Skinner is the best-known psychologist of his generation, and his theory of **operant conditioning** revolutionized the educational system. Operant conditioning is the effect of the consequences of a particular behavior on the future occurrence of that behavior. Skinner described four types of operant conditioning: **positive reinforcement**, **negative reinforcement**, **extinction/nonreinforcement**, and **punishment**. Below are descriptions of the four types of operant conditioning and some examples of how teachers might use operant conditioning in the classroom (Davey & Cullen, 1988).

- Positive Reinforcement: Responses that are rewarded are likely to be repeated. (Verbal praise, smiling, a pat on the back, and candy are reinforcers that motivate a child to do a behavior again.)
- Negative Reinforcement: Responses that allow escape from painful or undesirable situations are likely to be repeated. (Being excused from taking an exam because of good behavior throughout the year will likely motivate a child to continue good behavior.)
- Extinction or Nonreinforcement: Responses that are not reinforced are not likely to be repeated. (Ignoring a child screaming should extinguish that behavior.)
- Punishment: Responses that bring painful or undesirable consequences will be restrained but may reappear if a reinforcement changes. (Penalizing children for not putting their toys away by withdrawing privileges should stop their messiness.)

Child Care Centers and Nursery Schools

Child care, day care centers, and day nurseries existed in the United States long before such services were publicly recognized, regulated, or financed. Child care centers were originally designed to serve

Consider This Shining Stars

Jessica is a second-grade teacher who has been teaching for 4 years. In her classroom, she likes giving shining stars to her students because it rewards them for good behavior. Shining stars are blue slips of paper that describe the good behavior that the child has performed. Such behaviors include *Be Safe, Be Responsible, Be Respectful, Be on Task, and Be Kind*. Multiple behaviors can be marked if a student performed more than one. When students reach 20 shining stars, they get to turn them in to the office to have lunch with the school principal. Shining stars are given to all students who earned them by the end of the week. Shining stars are a reward mechanism that the entire school district has adopted. The district has been using this for a long time, and it has been extremely successful with Jessica's students. What Jessica's students like the most about earning shining stars is having lunch with the principal.

In your classroom, what type of reinforcements would you use to motivate your students' behavior?

as custodial care rather than fulfill an educational need. With the creation of the factory system and the hiring of a large number of females during the Industrial Revolution, there was an increased need for child care. Philanthropic institutions, private individuals, and community service organizations or private homes typically organized these services, and they were funded by parent fees, private contributions, and, in some cases, state funds. The responsibilities of the caregiver were simply to feed the children, clean them, and keep them safe. The need for child care increased as a larger age range of young children were enrolled in child care centers, including infants and toddlers (Gomby, Larner, Stevenson, Lewit, & Behrman, 1995).

Nursery schools were first established in the poorest areas of London, England. Children who attended these schools were children who needed cognitive or physical assistance. Therefore, the schools focused on preventative methods for children's mental and physical illnesses. Nursery school activities varied, with some schools providing educational opportunities while others simply provided basic child care services. Schools that focused on education taught such early social skills as interpersonal interaction, peer relationships, and classroom skills, such as following teacher instructions. **Margaret and Rachel McMillan** developed this educational program because they believed that a nursery education should be one of nurturance (Spodek, 1985).

Philosophy and Mission

The McMillans considered nurturance as teaching the whole child through working with the social, physical, emotional, and intellectual aspects of a child's development. Their nursery school programs taught children the skills involved in caring for oneself, such as tying shoelaces and washing hands. Part of the program taught the students a sense of responsibility through activities such as keeping the school clean or taking care of plants and animals. **Edward Seguin**, who developed activities to improve the sensory education of children with mental retardation (Winzer, 1986), influenced the philosophy of nurturance and helping children learn observational skills through their senses. His influence can be seen today in programs for children with "special needs" and in the Montessori teaching method that emphasizes using the senses. Early nursery schools also emphasized specific activities that included the senses, such as language, music, rhythm, and color activities. Play activities were part of the nurturance approach, allowing young children to work with water, sand, and other nonstructured materials (N. E. Cohen, 1996).

Head Start

Head Start is a preschool program that was developed in 1965 for low-income children and their families. This is a U.S. federally funded program mandated to meet students' social, emotional, health, nutritional, and psychological needs (Vinovskis, 2005). Head Start programs serve preschool children 3 to 5 years of age and their families. It is a comprehensive program in that it stresses all of the child's development domains (social, emotional, language, cognitive, and physical). Head Start also stresses the importance of good health and provides families with the resources needed to meet medical, psychological, dental, and nutritional needs. Because this is a federally funded program, there has been underfunding of the program, and not all children who are entitled to participate do receive these services.

The Benefits of Head Start

Research shows that young children who attend Head Start benefit from its programs. Findings demonstrate that children who have the opportunity to attend Head Start do better in elementary school, have fewer absences, and are less likely to drop out of school, be held back, or be in special education classes (Garces, Thomas, & Currie, 2000).

There are three factors that the National Head Start Association has recognized as important for the development of early childhood programs and programs for low-income children and their families.

1. Quality Early Childhood Programs. The guiding principle for Head Start is that high-quality standards are followed for their educational programs. The central focus of the curriculum is the physical, mental, and emotional aspects of a child's development. Head Start believes that a successful early childhood program will combine a child's developmental knowledge with his or her learning abilities. Allowing children to use their developmental knowledge will benefit their development. Table 3.2 presents the requirements that Head Start programs must follow.

Table 3.2	Head Start Requirements

1. Secure, supportive, nurturing environment.
2. Small class size.
3. Small adult-child ratio.
4. Culturally sensitive curriculum and staff.
5. Staff trained in child development and comprehensive services.
6. Safe environment.
7. Parent involvement in the child's education.
8. Individualized approach that builds on children's strengths and promotes positive self-image.
9. Combination of individual, small group, and large group activities.
10. Child initiated/directed activities.
11. Class not segregated by language, handicap, behavior, etc.
12. Focus on health, cognitive, emotional, social, and physical development.
13. Encouraging social relationships.
14. Balance between children-initiated and teacher-initiated activities.
15. Developmentally appropriate curriculum.
16. Teacher training minimum standard. (This minimum standard will soon be a BA degree.)

Source: © National Head Start Association.

2. A Comprehensive Approach. A comprehensive approach to a child's education consists of providing children and their families with medical, dental, and mental health services as well as proper nutrition. Children need good nutrition and good health care in order to succeed and reach their full potential academically. The program also provides parent education and encourages significant parental involvement. Head Start recognizes that families with young children are prone to higher stress levels, and these stressors are increased for single parents, minority families, young parents, and working parents.

These are some of the services that Head Start programs provide for eligible children and their families:

- Medical/dental screenings and follow-up treatment
- Home visits
- Parent support groups
- Mental health counseling
- Social service information and referral
- Community advocacy
- Meaningful involvement in decision making

3. Parent Involvement. Children whose parents are involved in their education will have long-lasting benefits in their educational future. Parents are considered the child's first and continuing teachers; preschool programs should incorporate parental activities in their curriculum. Head Start programs do a good job in involving and collaborating with parents. There may be differences in the type and level of parental involvement depending on the parents' needs (see Table 3.3).

HOW ARE EARLY CHILDHOOD PROGRAMS FINANCED?

Many of the early childhood programs that have been mentioned in this chapter are financed either by one or multiple owners or by an organization, or are partially supported by the federal system or the state. Early child care programs are financed by different organizations or individuals. This section will introduce you to several organizations that finance childhood centers and their programs.

For-Profit

For-profit businesses are those that produce profit for their owners. The profits are generally from parent fees, which are the sole income for the program. This money is used to pay for teacher salaries, space, housing costs, and expenses for toys and equipment used in the program. Most for-profit programs are locally owned child care centers and family child care homes. The child care teachers may or may not have academic training in early childhood education. Therefore, the quality of the child care center may vary due to discrepancies in academic knowledge and training.

Table 3.3	The Different Types of Parental Involvement

1. Ongoing communication about the child and program.
2. Parent education regarding child development.
3. Parent participation in the program as volunteers, observers, etc.
4. Parent input and decision making in program design and evaluation.
5. Parental access to children's programs at any time.

Source: © National Head Start Association.

Nonprofit

Nonprofit programs do not make a profit from their businesses. In for-profit care centers, after expenses are paid, the remainder is considered profit, and the money goes to the owner. Nonprofit monies are incorporated back into the program or are returned to the sponsoring agency (Mocan, 1995). The reason nonprofit centers are popular is because the sponsoring agencies are not operated for profit. Churches are the most common sponsors of early childhood programs. Other common groups include YMCAs, city recreation departments, hospitals, colleges, and universities.

Parent Cooperative

In parent cooperative programs, parents are responsible for paying for their children's education. Parental involvement is required in order to keep the tuition low. Parents assist teachers and are expected to spend a specific number of hours each month helping out in the classroom. This arrangement works well for both parents and the child care centers because it allows the center to operate with fewer paid adults, and it reduces the financial cost for parents. The increasing trend of a higher number of parents entering the workforce full-time, however, impacts their level of involvement in various school functions.

University- and College-Affiliated Programs

Many early childhood programs throughout the United States are affiliated with universities and community colleges. These child care centers function as laboratories, or training programs, for college students training in early childhood education. The centers also serve as sources of experience for practicum and research and demonstrate the best practices in the field. Other university centers serve primarily as campus child care centers for the young children of students, staff, and faculty. The main aim of this type of campus center is to provide a service to the members of the campus community. The majority of university and community college child care centers combine both research and a fieldwork component.

University and college child care centers operate as affiliates of a campus department, such as a child development, early childhood, or psychology department, or as a university-wide program. These programs are usually considered of high quality because theory and research about child development are integrated within them, and there is high involvement of professional educators. Part of the funding comes from parents, and the other part from the sponsoring university or college.

Professionalism & Policy

Funding Sources

Historically, the federal government has provided funding for child care and early education programs; however, funding has fluctuated in amount and purpose. Today's child care financing system is a confused collection of funding streams with unclear goals, standards, and administrative structure. Public support for child care, for example, has tended to focus on one particular goal of child care, such as promoting school readiness, protecting children from abuse or neglect, or providing opportunities to compensate for disadvantage (A. J. Cohen, 1996). Some administrative decisions and comprehensive child care programs that the federal government has supported have been created with virtually no public discussion about child care. The Lanham Act—passed by Congress in 1940, authorizing federal grants and loans to public or private agencies for the maintenance and operation of public works—was later interpreted to apply only to child care facilities in war-impacted areas and passed without even mentioning child care. Head Start is seen as an educational program and not as child care; therefore it has funding allocation differences.

WHAT ARE HOME-BASED AND CENTER-BASED CHILD CARE SETTINGS?

Home-based and center-based are two different types of child care settings, and depending on their preference, parents are encouraged to make informed decisions about the specific programs that are most appropriate for their children. Ultimately, whatever the choice, parents should consider choosing a high-quality program with a low adult-child ratio and trained teachers who offer an affectionate, caring, and developmentally appropriate curriculum.

Home-Based Care

Caretakers in private households run home-based day care centers. In the United States, it has been estimated that the largest number of children are cared for in family child care homes. Infants and toddlers are most often cared for in such homes because parents typically prefer a more intimate, homelike setting for their young ones. Most states require licensing or registration of family child care homes, although it is estimated that a great majority of homes are unlicensed (Halpern, 1987; Pence & Goelman, 1991). Table 3.4 presents the advantages and disadvantages of home-based programs.

Center-Based Care

Many parents prefer center-based care because they offer a formal, structured environment. All centers must be licensed and comply with appropriate regulations, teachers are supervised (many classrooms

Table 3.4	Advantages and Disadvantages of Home-Based Programs

ADVANTAGES	DISADVANTAGES
1. There is generally a low ratio of children to adults.	1. Not all home-based care providers are licensed.
2. Most day care workers choose this career because they love children.	2. Providers are not required to have background experience in child care.
3. It is generally cheaper than a nanny or a day care center.	3. Not all settings offer an academic program.
4. There are opportunities for socialization with other children.	4. Exposure to extracurricular activities, such as dance and art, may be limited.
5. Child is taken care of by one (or possibly two) provider(s).	5. If there are only one or two other children in the home, there may be times when the child will be the only one in attendance.
6. Hours are generally flexible. Some providers watch children on the weekends as well.	6. Most providers will not take children before a certain time, so if parents have early morning meetings or an early morning work schedule, they may need to find alternative transportation to the home.
7. Often home-based settings do not charge enormous overtime fees when you have to pick up late due to a meeting.	7. The provider may not have the funds to provide the same type of equipment, activities, and learning experiences as a center-based program.
8. A comfortable home setting might be more fitting for some children than a center.	8. If the child care provider is ill, the parent may need to find a backup placement or take a day or more off of work.
	9. Without a contract, home-based providers can stop watching children at any time they wish.

have more than one teacher), and a director oversees the entire operation. Teachers who have taken college units in early childhood education or child development, or who hold a current and valid Child Development Associate Credential, run center-based programs. These centers are located in elementary schools, churches, or other types of child care facilities. Center-based programs usually include larger groups of children than do home-based programs. Centers have clear-cut rules for parents to follow (such as pickup and drop-off times) so they know exactly what is expected of them (Halpern, 1987; Read, 1987). Table 3.5 presents the advantages and disadvantages of center-based programs.

WHY DO CHILD CARE CENTERS NEED TO BE LICENSED?

All states have licensing requirements that define minimum acceptable standards for center-based and home-based centers. Licensing assures that those programs that are licensed have achieved at least the minimum standards required by law to meet the health, educational, and social needs of the children receiving those services. Licensed child care centers protect children's well-being and maintain high standards of service. However, not all center-based and home-based centers have licenses. Many home-based centers get away without one, especially if the provider is taking care of only one or two children. According to the Children's Defense Fund (2011), many states require a background check and some educational training, but only a few states inspect all family child care homes. Some states require nothing more than that the provider mail in a self-certification form or add his or her name to a list. See your state's child care profile from the National Child Care Information Center. Centers that are licensed tend to provide more comprehensive services, as required by state law, to children and their families.

Table 3.5	Advantages and Disadvantages of Center-Based Programs

ADVANTAGES	DISADVANTAGES
1. Caregivers in center-based care may be better educated and may have received more specialized training than caregivers in home-based care, but not always—ask about the educational background of the provider or specific teachers in your child's age-group.	1. Center-based child care often feels and looks institutional and is usually located in large facilities.
2. Center-based programs usually have a substitute pool, so if a teacher is sick or on vacation, a substitute teacher can fill in for the day.	2. May not meet needs of parents with late, early, rotating, or part-time work schedules; usually less able to adjust to changes in parent schedules or emergencies.
3. Children in center-based programs may be exposed to an educationally enriched curriculum that encourages literacy, language development, and social and emotional development, or they may be exposed to a rigid academic curriculum that may be developmentally inappropriate and can add stress and discourage future success.	3. Larger group sizes and instability in staffing may pose a difficulty for some children and families.
4. Dependable schedule; open daily year-round; availability usually not affected by teacher illness or absence.	4. Children attending a full-day center for only part of the day, or for less than a full week, may have more challenges creating friendships or fitting in when most other children attend full-time; they may not have a sense of stability.

Promoting Optimal Development

Licensing and Regulation

In theory, almost all home day cares are required to meet state licensing regulations for health and safety to operate. But in practice, many get away without a license, especially if the provider is taking care of only one or two children besides his or her own. Many states require home day care providers to go through a background check and some training, according to the Children's Defense Fund (2011), but only a few states inspect all family child care homes. Some states require nothing more than that teachers or directors mail in self-certification forms or add their names to a list. A license is not a guarantee of quality child care; but a license shows that the provider takes at least a degree of professional pride in his or her work.

The National Association for the Education of Young Children (1996b) has provided these 10 principles for applying an effective system of early childhood care and education services:

1. Any program providing care and education to children from two or more unrelated families should be regulated; there should be no exemptions from this principle.

2. States should license all facilities that provide services to the public, including all centers, large family or group child care homes, and small family child care homes (i.e., granting permission to operate).

3. In addition to licensing facilities, states should establish complementary processes for professional licensing of individuals as teachers, caregivers, or program administrators (i.e., granting permission to practice).

4. Licensing standards should be clear and reasonable and reflect current research findings related to regulative aspects that will reduce the risk of harm.

5. Regulations should be vigorously and equitably enforced.

6. Licensing agencies should have sufficient staff and resources to effectively implement the regulatory process.

7. Regulatory processes should be coordinated and streamlined to promote greater effectiveness and efficiency.

8. Incentive mechanisms should encourage the achievement of a higher quality of service beyond the basic floor.

9. Consumer and public education should inform families, providers, and the public of the importance of a child's early years and of ways to create environments that promote children's learning and development.

10. States should invest sufficient levels of resources to ensure that children's healthy development and learning are not harmed in early care and education settings.

Certain states require that child care facilities have a license if they provide child care services. Here is an example of the requirements from the state of Connecticut for a child care center to receive licensing:

- Private family day care homes must care for no more than 6 children, including the provider's own children, who are not in school full-time. The hours of caretaking should be no less than 3 and no more than 12 hours in a day. In a regular academic school year, an additional 3 full-time children are allowed to be under the care of the provider, including the provider's own children.
- Group day care homes should care for 7, but no more than 12, children when offering a supplementary day care program.
- A child day care center provides, on a regular basis, services to more than 12 children outside of their home.

There are some child day care programs that are not required to meet the licensing standards requirement and, therefore, are not liable for licensing. Programs that are not liable are those administered by a nanny or family relative, programs where parents stay with their child at a recreation facility, and extracurricular programs limited to 2 hours (Connecticut Department of Public Health, 2011).

Summary

Quality child care programs are essential in today's society. The type of program you choose to teach will depend on its philosophy, mission, environment, and approach to teaching. Montessori programs give children the freedom to use their inborn mental abilities so that they can develop physically, mentally, and spiritually. In the Reggio Emilia programs, the teachers work closely with children to co-construct knowledge and the curriculum. HighScope allows children to be involved in problem solving and decision making; children have to plan, do, and review their goals and reflect on their learning. Bank Street focuses on the developmental stages of the child, in an environment where the child has the opportunity to be an active learner through experimentation. The central focus in Waldorf education is to understand the child as whole and as a member of humanity. Anthroposophy is the theoretical basis underpinning teaching practices. Behaviorist programs are based on the learners' behaviors. Children learn new information through positive or negative reinforcements. Head Start includes programs that provide early education and intervention to low-income children and their families. Many of the programs mentioned above are financed by public or private businesses, agencies, churches, hospitals, recreational departments, and universities.

Key Terms

Anthroposophy 65

Aversive stimulation 67

Bank Street School for Children 63

Behaviorism 66

Co-constructing knowledge 59

Cognitive maps 66

Edward Seguin 69

Emergent curriculum 60

Extinction/nonreinforcement 68

For-profit 71

Head Start 70

John B. Watson 66

Loris Malaguzzi 59

Margaret and Rachel
  McMillan 69

Negative reinforcement 68

Nonprofit 72

Operant conditioning 68

Planes of development 59

Positive reinforcement 68

Positive self-concept 57

Progressive movement 63

Punishment 68

Reggio Emilia program 59

Rudolf Steiner 65

Waldorf education 65

Reflection, Application, and Analysis Questions

1. Reflect back on the Montessori approach to teaching, and describe how this approach fits into your own ideas of teaching young children.

2. Observe a teacher carrying out an activity in any of the early childhood programs described in this chapter, and explain how the activity corresponds to what you have learned. Provide examples to illustrate your observations.

3. Talk to an early childhood teacher and find out what model he or she is familiar with and how the philosophy has influenced his or her practices in the classroom.

4. Identify two advantages and two disadvantages of home-based and center-based programs.

Extension Activities

1. Observe a Montessori, a Waldorf, and a Reggio Emilia program. Compare the similarities and differences in their philosophies and school practices.

2. Find out the necessary requirements for a home day care to be licensed in your state. Compare your state's requirements with those of a neighboring state.

Additional Readings

The following reading list will be useful for those of you interested in learning more about the different educational approaches.

Brunton, P., & Thornton, L. (2005). *Understanding the Reggio approach: Early years education in practice.* **London: David Fulton Publishers.**

This book describes key features of the Reggio Emilia approach to early childhood education and provides examples from infant-toddler to preschool centers. It highlights key ideas that practitioners should consider when reviewing and reflecting on their own practices.

Helm, J. H., & Katz, L. G. (2010). *Young investigators: The project approach in the early years.* **New York: Teachers College, Columbia University.**

This book introduces the project approach and provides step-by-step guidance for conducting meaningful projects. It provides a variety of nature experiences, with examples that show how project work is an excellent way to connect children to the natural world.

Lillard, P. P., & Jessen, L. L. (2003). *Montessori from the start: The child at home, from birth to age three.* **New York: Random House.**

Montessori From the Start is a practical and useful guide to raising calm, competent, and confident children. The authors provide guidance for establishing a beautiful and serviceable environment for babies and very young children.

Petrash, J. (2002). *Understanding Waldorf education: Teaching from the inside out.* **Beltsville, MD: Gryphon House.**

If you want to learn more about Waldorf education, this book contains important views on its philosophy and learning experiences that involves all of the senses.

Taylor, G. R., & MacKenney, L. (2008). *Improving human learning in the classroom.* **Lanham, MD: Rowman & Littlefield.**

This book is written for classroom teachers who may want to learn more about the behaviorists. It is designed to translate the educational psychological theories into practical classroom application.

On the Web

American Montessori Society - *http://www.amshq.org/*

This website is for parents, educators, and all of those who are interested in learning more about the Montessori programs in the United States. This site gives you information on how to find a school, a program, or a regional Montessori group, as well as other important information.

HighScope Educational Research Foundation - *http://www.highscope.org/*

This informative website offers a wealth of information on its curriculum starting from infant and toddler to youth development. It also provides training to those who are interested in teaching the HighScope curriculum and other information about its research and conferences.

International Montessori Society - *http://imsmontessori.org/*

This website provides information about types of Montessori teaching, teaching technology, accreditation, workshops, and more.

National Head Start Association - *http://www.nhsa.org/*

This website keeps its visitors informed of the latest news and conferences affecting Head Start. It also gives information on their services, research, and Head Start membership.

North American Reggio Emilia Alliance - *http://www.reggioalliance.org*

A historical overview of the Reggio Emilia approach is provided, in addition to community and parental support, administrative policies, teachers as learners, the role of the environment, and other important topics.

Student Study Site

Visit **www.sagepub.com/gordonbiddle** to access several study tools including eFlashcards, web quizzes, links to SAGE journal articles, web resources, video resources, lesson plan templates, and more.

PART II

Development and Early Childhood Education

Learning Theories

This chapter will help you answer these important questions:

- How do we define development, learning, and theory?
- What is the constructivist view of learning?
- What is Piaget's theory of cognitive development?
- What is information processing theory?
- What is Vygotsky's sociocultural theory of development?
- What is Bronfenbrenner's bioecological theory of development?
- What is Erikson's theory of psychosocial development?
- What is Maslow's hierarchy of human needs?

Vignette: Let Me Show You How

A mother-child dyad (pair) is engaged in stringing beads of different sizes, shapes, and colors. The child (C), who is 4 years old, must refer to the series of picture cards (each depicting a specific stringing pattern) as she engages in the learning task of stringing beads with her mother (M).

M: (Enlists the child's interest by asking a question and pointing to one of the two cards placed on the table.) "OK, see these? What are these?"

C: "Circles."

M: "And these?" (Points again to another picture card with beads.)

C: "Squares."

M: "Look at them closely."

C: "Oh, triangles!"

M: "OK, and what are these?"

C: "What?" (Looks on very intently.)

M: "What are these?" (Holds up another picture card with beads.)

C: "Triangles."

M: "Are they all the same size?"

C: "Yes." (Points to other shapes on the card.)

M: "That's little, so then not all the . . ."

C: "And that's little, and that's little . . ." (Interrupts the mother, pointing to the beads on the card.)

M: "Yes. What sizes do you see here?"

C: "Big ones."

M: "Uh huh . . ."

C: "And little ones and short ones." (Interrupts again.)

M: "So are they all the same size?"

C: "No."

M: "OK. Now you have to take this little thing here and put it through the center of the shape." (Holds up the string in front of the child.) "What color shape should you use, and what size?" (Moves the card closer to the child and points.)

Key Elements
for Becoming a Professional

NAEYC DEVELOPMENTALLY APPROPRIATE PRINCIPLE 2

Many aspects of children's development follow well-documented sequences, with later abilities, skills, and knowledge building on those already acquired.

Interpretation

When teachers are familiar with the sequences and patterns of children's development, they are better equipped to plan successful learning experiences for children, and they are more adept at intentional teaching.

NAEYC STANDARD 1: PROMOTING CHILD DEVELOPMENT AND LEARNING

a. Understand young children's characteristics and needs from birth to age 8.

b. Understand multiple influences on the child's development.

c. Use developmental knowledge to create healthy, respectful, supportive, and challenging environments for children.

C: "A small blue square?" (Scrambles around in the box, selects a small blue square, and attempts to string it.)

M: "Let me show you how." (Gently takes the string and bead from the child's hand and demonstrates as the child looks on intently.)

C: "I want to try now." (Reviews the picture card.)

M: "Alright. You will need to find a small orange triangle to match the card, OK?" (Hands over the string to the child with the blue bead already on it.)

C: "I like stringing beads." (Successfully places a small orange triangle on the string.) (Roundtree, 2000)

This vignette, as in the case of countless others that you have either experienced or witnessed at some point in your life, demonstrates the very essence of teaching and learning. In every exchange between mother and child, this vignette underscores the crucial role that mothers and other significant caregivers play in bolstering children's (cognitive) development. For a novice in the field of early childhood education, this vignette probably raises countless questions about children's growth and development, and, oftentimes, an answer to one question gives rise to another. While most critical questions have been answered by the various theories of learning and development that we uphold today, some questions still warrant further observation and study of young children. Nevertheless, this chapter seeks to provide the budding early childhood professional with answers to some of the most fundamental questions about how children come to "know" and provides an introduction to what many early childhood educators deem the quintessential theories of learning and development. The theories discussed below are "blueprints" of the human change process and provide a sound basis for our understanding of how and why young children change as they age.

HOW DO WE DEFINE DEVELOPMENT, LEARNING, AND THEORY?

Before we proceed any further, it is important to garner an understanding of three very important terms that we will use quite frequently in this chapter. These terms are *development, learning,* and *theory.*

Development

Development, a term that has its basis in human biology, is the process of change and movement in all domains of a child's existence (i.e., cognitive, linguistic, socioemotional, and physical). Such changes begin from the moment a child is conceived and continue throughout the course of that child's life. Development comes as a result of the individual's ongoing interaction with his or her environment. Therefore, development is never static; it is always dynamic and persistent. Early childhood is a period of unprecedented growth and change, a time when a child masters a range of skills and confronts a plethora of life tasks and challenges in preparation for adulthood.

As humans, our developmental patterns are more alike than different, thanks to the leading role that **genes** play in the drama of human development. Genes, our units of hereditary information, are composed of **DNA** (deoxyribonucleic acid) and are the very foundation of human development. Genes are passed on to us by our parents, and they impact every aspect of human development. Life begins with genes. The DNA carried in the genes provides specific instructions to the egg (zygote) to form the body, brain, and specific heritable traits of a growing fetus. Certainly you discovered a long time ago that the curly locks or brown eyes you inherited were not simply by chance. Genes not only determine one's physical traits; they affect an individual's growth and development over time. Hence, human genetics seems to place most of us on a typical course of development.

However, although genes remain a primary determinant of human development, they alone do not have the final say in what each individual will ultimately become. It is important not to underestimate the impact that culture, experience, and individual differences (i.e., temperament, birth order, socioeconomic status, etc.) have on development. For example, most young children begin to walk at about 12 months of age. However, infants who are firstborn and whose parents often carry them might walk much later than their peers and future siblings. Hence, a child's delay at walking might be due to several factors, i. e., genes, doting, overprotective parents ("helicopter moms"), the child's temperament, which might perpetuate the parents' doting behavior or health concerns of the child. Similarly, a child who experienced a severe ear infection as a toddler might experience significant speech delay during the preschool years, resulting in the need to participate in speech therapy.

Fortunately for our sake, personal traits and environmental experiences very rarely result in delayed or challenged development. In most cases, our genes and personal experiences work together to propel our development, placing us on a very forward-moving trajectory or life course. Consider the case of one of the greatest entertainers of all time, Michael Jackson, the "King of Pop." As a toddler during the late 1950s, Michael Jackson began to synchronize his body movements to the rhythmic sounds of the family's old washing machine while sitting on his mother's lap. This unique ability to hear rhythm and music from a rather uncanny source demonstrated Michael's

As is the case with many child stars, the early nurturing Michael Jackson (middle, above) experienced was a major determinant of his prolific career.

unusual musical genius at a very young age, which was, it seems, genetically based. However, Michael's life circumstances and the range of musical experiences that his family afforded him were very instrumental in cultivating his musical prowess over time. It seems that Michael Jackson's unique personal circumstances (sociocultural experiences, in-home musical instruments, child rearing, etc.) and his unique genetic makeup (temperament, musical talent, kinesthetic abilities, etc.) interacted in such a way as to gain him preeminence in the entertainment world.

Based upon a child's unique experiences and hereditary factors, he or she may be described as either delayed, typically developing, or genius or as demonstrating various degrees of these categories. In the case of Michael Jackson, his musical genius far exceeded that of his siblings, who were also musically gifted and a part of the famous family singing group, the Jackson 5. When it comes to development, young children of the same age can take their respective place anywhere on the developmental continuum. It is our understanding of the general course of development that most children undergo, as well as the individual differences that exist among children, that makes the study of child development so fascinating.

Learning

For the purposes of this chapter, the term **learning** is defined as a relatively fixed or lasting change in the way a child behaves or responds to his or her environment due to experience. Learning consists of adaptations in the child's thinking or cognitive processing abilities as a result of his or her personal experiences—adaptations that are ultimately manifested in the child's observable behavior.

However, it is important to note that not all experience-based cognitive changes are immediately observable in a child's behavior output. Observable changes can be quite unpredictable in the life of the active toddler or growing preschooler because, like adults, young children also need to experience the "aha" reaction in order to solidify their learning. Sometimes evidence of appreciable changes in a child's thinking capacity is seen much later in the child's development, such as when a child finally masters a 12-piece puzzle that he or she has been struggling with for about a month or when a child successfully ties his or her sneaker laces after several trials. Learning is delayed until such time the child's experience affords him or her another opportunity to demonstrate mastery of a particular skill.

Over the course of history, the concept of learning and its related processes have been widely investigated. In fact, we have been engaging in the process of learning for so long that we think about the very process itself. When individuals engage in the process of "thinking about thinking," it is referred to as **metacognition**, a term often used by **developmentalists**, individuals who investigate the changes that people undergo in all aspects of their development throughout the life span. According to Bjorklund (2005), metacognition is "the knowledge of one's cognitive abilities and processes related to thinking" (p. 5).

While metacognition, or one's capacity to "think about learning," doesn't even begin to surface until a child is about 5 or 6 years of age, becoming increasingly better during the elementary school years, children's ability to learn is with them from their very earliest existence. As a matter of fact, there is evidence of some learning occurring while the developing child is in utero (Bjorklund, 2005).

But when it comes to learning and development, which comes first? Does learning precede development, or does development precede learning? Most developmentalists would say neither precedes the other but rather that a reciprocal relationship exists between learning and development— meaning that learning impacts development *and* development, or a child's maturational readiness in any of the domains (cognitive, linguistic, socioemotional, and physical), impacts his or her ability to learn. This reciprocal relationship is like a dance, with development edging one's learning potential right along and learning, simultaneously, doing what it can to advance one's development, or maturation, in a given domain.

Learning is a cumulative process, and qualitative changes in development do not end with childhood. As you read this textbook, we hope that you are acquiring some basic information that will increase your knowledge base and, ultimately, improve your skill set as a professional in the field of early childhood education. Learning continues to be a lifelong process for both the writers and the readers of this textbook.

Theory

According to **Kurt Lewin** (1943), a German American psychologist known for his work in the areas of social/applied psychology, group dynamics, and change theory, nothing is better or more practical for our basic understanding of life and how and why things work than a "theory." Theories uncover mysteries and lead to discoveries, and discoveries lead to further questions—and so the cycle continues (Salkind, 2004). For our purposes here, a **theory** is a systematic statement comprising principles, generalizations, and assumptions that helps to frame our understanding, interpretation, and explanation of learning and development. Theories help us to organize our thinking or mental schemes (structures) around interesting and complex phenomena that are often difficult to explain. Moreover, theories are the result of critical thinking. **Critical thinking** is the process by which individuals evaluate their assertions and claims about an interesting or puzzling phenomenon and provide justifications based on well-documented evidence that has been empirically researched.

All of us have theories, and many of us theorize all day long. In everyday life, these "theories" are usually referred to as gut feelings or hunches (not to be confused with "scientific theories" that are based on empirical research). We have a hunch about what makes a person "tick." We have a gut feeling about the necessary strategies to use in order to maintain a healthy relationship with a loved one. We even possess our very own instincts regarding the best way to raise children, which might be altered somewhat after completing this textbook—even though theories regarding child-rearing practices are usually "hardwired" or firmly ingrained in one's psyche (Greenfield, Keller, Fuligni, & Maynard, 2003).

Adults are not the only ones whose way of life is often determined by the theories they embrace. Very young children have theories, too. For instance, a young toddler, albeit unknowingly, has a theory about how to push or pull a particular toy in order to get certain results. Even infants utilize their early experiences to draw assumptions about how individuals are likely to respond to them. These experiences form a frame of reference that infants tend to tap into as they grow. This frame of reference, referred to as a **working model**, is employed whenever the infant comes in contact with people. For example, infants who receive consistent and responsive care will, invariably, use that working model whenever they meet someone over the duration of their life. Their working model, which is subject to change, is that all people are consistent and quite predictable (Bretherton & Munholland, 1999; Thompson & Raikes, 2003). Recently, **theory theorists**, or researchers who purport that humans are naturally driven to devise theories, have noted that infants and children possess sets of innate theories that they constantly adapt during their childhood years until they arrive at an understanding of the world that is very much in sync with that of the adults belonging to their culture (Spelke & Newport, 1998). Young children tend to use their innate theories in much the same way as scientists do: to predict, interpret, and explain the world around them (Bjorklund, 2005). Researchers have also found that 2- and 3-year-olds seem to be obsessed with asking questions that alleviate their obsession with seeking reasons, causes, and underlying principles for things, especially things that concern them. During the early childhood years, children appear to be driven to construct their own theories about almost everything they see and hear (Gopnik, 2001). In a study involving Mexican children and their mothers, the mothers were asked to maintain a journal detailing their children's "Why?" and "How?" questions and their response to the youngsters for a period of two weeks. For the most part, children's

Children, at any age, can employ the steps of scientific inquiry.

questions centered on the purpose of things and human behavior, and the children were less curious about nonliving objects (Kelemen, Callanan, Casler, & Perez-Granados, 2005). This engagement or interest in scientific reasoning (asking questions, formulating a hypothesis or hypotheses, researching, collecting data, analyzing results, and drawing conclusions) continues throughout the elementary school years and beyond. Hence, an 8-year-old child will patiently employ the various steps of the scientific method in order to witness the metamorphosis of the caterpillar into a beautiful butterfly by either proving or disproving his or her theory at every step in the process.

WHAT IS THE CONSTRUCTIVIST VIEW OF LEARNING?

Most learning and developmental theories underscore the vital role that environment and significant adults (mother, father, teacher, and/or other consistent caregivers) play in the life of a developing child. Young children are constantly interacting with their physical and social worlds; it is how they come to know and understand the people and things around them. Children are active and persistent in their approach to construct their own meaning of their world. They have a natural ability to think about their actions and social interactions. Children's motivation to understand the inner workings of the world around them is the very essence of the constructivist view of learning (see Chapter 2). Structural changes in the way children come to think about their world are a direct result of their myriad experiences. They seem to be always about the business of framing and reframing their mental structures (altering their thought processes) as they derive meaning from their daily experiences and interactions. Children are like "little construction engineers"; in much the same way that construction workers need tools, nails, and steel to build a building, young children need people, places, and things in order to construct their knowledge of their personal world.

Thanks to the seminal ideas of John Dewey (1916), a pragmatic and progressive educator in the late 19th century, we now have an evolved understanding of constructivist learning (see Chapter 2). Dewey, who considered the classroom a small democratic society, rejected the notion of learning as a passive process and emphasized the importance of providing learning experiences for students that were interactive and thoroughly engaging. Dewey's philosophy prompted schools in the late 1800s and early 1900s to adopt deliberate and systematic ways to create learning environments in which children's cognitive gains were the direct result of their classroom encounters and freedom to form relationships. Devotees of Dewey's educational philosophy still exist today. Those who adopt a purist constructivist position would vow that constructing meaning *is* learning—and, therefore, that knowledge does not exist independent of the learner. Knowledge is not simply floating around in space somewhere waiting for someone to come along and grab it; the only *true* knowledge that exists is the knowledge we construct for ourselves. Constructivists believe that knowledge cannot simply be "spoon-fed" to children. Children's learning process must consist of hands-on experiences that engage both their bodies and their minds; children must have the opportunity to experience the world through their many senses as well as to process those sensory data.

Furthermore, constructivists also believe that how young children process information changes with time and experience, as evidenced by their behavior. Children of different developmental ages and, oftentimes, children who are the same age are not likely to perceive the same experience in exactly the same way. This is a result of variations in children's processing (thinking) abilities and differences in their extant (existing) knowledge at any given stage in their development. A 3-year-old, a 5-year-old, and a 7-year-old will have very different perspectives and interpretations of the same event (Bjorklund, 2005). Similarly, an older infant who picks up a crayon and tries to eat it soon learns as a toddler that the crayon can be used to make squiggly lines on a piece of paper or on a wall. It will take several more months before the child realizes that walls are typically excluded as a likely venue to show off artistic abilities.

Early childhood educators who uphold a constructivist view of learning facilitate children's thinking by seeking varied opportunities to engage them. They encourage collaborative and peer learning among children, organize stimulating and challenging classroom environments, and provide numerous opportunities for children to problem solve on their own. These teachers facilitate children's learning by focusing their attention to details, modeling, guiding children's behavior, asking questions, and getting children to think "a head above," or slightly above their developmental capacity.

WHAT IS PIAGET'S THEORY OF COGNITIVE DEVELOPMENT?

Piaget can be credited with making the most appreciable advances in our understanding of children's thought processes, thanks to his thorough investigation into the **epigenesis** of human intelligence—that is, the study of how one's interactions in the environment influence development. According to Piaget, with increase in age comes increase in cognitive abilities; thus adults, unlike children, demonstrate both reasoned and logical thought processes. Some psychologists revere Piaget as the "giant in developmental psychology in the area of cognition" (Weber, 1984, p. 151). Before Piaget introduced his theory, children were considered to be passive beings, molded and shaped by their surroundings (DeVries & Kohlberg, 1987). Much of Piaget's research in child cognition was based on the very meticulous observations of his three children; he spent years watching his three children, carefully observing the use and function of their eyes, ears, arms, and legs during their very early development. A constructivist at heart, Piaget firmly believed that children construct their knowledge of the world by using what they already know to interpret novel experiences and events. Piaget was not as concerned about what children knew as he was about how they processed problems and devised solutions to challenging tasks.

Quality early childhood classrooms provide experiences for children that are constructivist in nature. The 5-year-old in this photo is reconstructing her experiences of visiting community helpers by journaling these events.

According to constructivists such as Piaget, cognitive development constitutes qualitative *and* quantitative changes in the way children reason and think about their worlds. A 3-year-old is not a miniature version of a 10-year-old who simply lacks the experience and knowledge of his or her older peer. Not only are there **quantitative differences**—variations in the *amount* or *degree* of knowledge that each child possesses—but also there are **qualitative differences**, or variations in how children know what they know. There are differences in the *type* and *form* of knowledge that each child possesses (Bjorklund, 2005).

Piaget's work in intelligence testing spurred his interests in children's thought processes. Resultantly, he became interested in the further exploration of children's right or wrong responses. Piaget wanted to know why individual children provided different reasons to justify their response to a particular test item. For example, two children may agree that a tree is alive but offer very different explanations for their response; one child might reply "because the tree moves," and another child might say "because it makes seeds." Piaget's work revealed many surprising ways in which children think (DeVries & Kohlberg, 1987, p. 17). He contended that children's "incorrect" views about the world are subjective—reflecting a very unique personal perspective (DeVries & Kohlberg, 1987). In other words, each child's unique interactions in the world precipitate his or her thoughts and reactions.

A giant in the field of developmental psychology, Piaget made an unprecedented contribution to the study of cognition in children.

Piaget's use of the clinical interview method (see Chapter 2) during intelligence testing provided copious notes describing the reasoning processes underlying children's correct and incorrect responses. One researcher referred to Piaget's particular technique of questioning children as a **semi-clinical interview**—a type of "peculiar play situation" (Russell, 1956, p. 160). As children engaged in a task, Piaget would use a flexible, unstructured questioning technique to determine their thought processes. During these semi-clinical interviews, a child's first response would determine Piaget's line of questioning or the series of subsequent questions.

Piaget is also considered to be a **stage theorist**. He believed that children's cognitive development consists of four distinct stages, with each stage of development to be qualitatively and quantitatively different from the one that preceded it and the one that would follow (see Table 4.1). According to Piaget's theory, all children's cognitive processes proceed in the same sequential manner; it is not possible for a child to miss a stage, nor is it possible for children to regress to an earlier stage of reasoning or cognitive functioning. Changes in children's thought processes and their progression from one stage to the next occur rather abruptly and over relatively brief periods. However, Piaget emphasized that there is evidence of continuity in the development of cognition, which facilitates the child's relatively easy transition from one stage of cognitive development to the next. According to Bjorklund (2005, p. 79), continuity is achieved due to brief "preparatory phases" between stages in which the developing child withstands a dual existence in two qualitatively different cognitive worlds. Thus, a 7-year-old child may demonstrate some aspects of concrete operational thought (e.g., the ability to classify objects and reverse operations) but may, at times, show signs of egocentric thought, which is prevalent at the preoperational stage of development.

Before examining Piaget's stages of cognitive development, it is necessary to explicate key terms that are central to his theory: *schemes, physical knowledge, logico-mathematical knowledge,* and *social* or *conventional knowledge.*

Schemes

People of all ages, including babies, have a tendency to organize knowledge of their environment into what Piaget refers to as schemata, or **schemes**. Schemes consist of physical actions, concepts, and theories that children use to gain information about their world. They are **mental structures** in the brain that underlie an individual's intelligence. For example, young infants have particular schemes for interacting with their favorite rattle; they know how to grab it and thrust it in their mouth. By the same token, an 8-year-old child might possess a particular scheme for writing that includes both print and cursive letters, and a 5-year-old child who has had both urban and suburban experiences might possess a broad scheme that includes knowledge of both domestic animals (cats and dogs) and farm animals (cows and sheep).

Piaget believed that when learning occurs, unobservable changes in an individual's cognition occur as well; a person's schemes are modified and refined. It is logical to assume that the older an individual becomes and the more experiences he or she gains, the more extensive the person's mental structures become. However, it is also important to remember that the schemes of very young children primarily comprise physical actions; children between birth and age 2 learn about the world primarily through their senses and motor abilities. As children develop, their schemes expand to include a range of mental

Table 4.1	Piaget's Theory of Cognitive Development

Developmental Stage/Age Range	Stage Characteristics	Major Milestones
Sensorimotor Birth to 2 Years	Infants' knowledge of the world is derived primarily from their senses and motor abilities.	Infants begin to think through mental actions and acquire the skill of object permanence. People/things still exist even when they are not in the infant's sight.
Preoperational 2 to 6 Years	Children's thinking is primarily egocentric; they tend to view the world from their own perspective.	Imaginative thought, vocabulary, and language explosion lead to young children's self-expression and increased sociability.
Concrete Operational 6 to 11 Years	Children's thinking is limited to concrete experiences, what they can see, hear, touch, and directly experience. They begin the process of applying logical operations and principles to interpret the world.	Children are able to comprehend concepts of conservation, number classification, and scientific theory through the application of logical thought.
Formal Operations 12 Years Through Adulthood	Adults and adolescents enter into the realm of analytical thinking; their reasoning ability is characterized by abstractions, hypothetical ideas/thoughts.	Adults and adolescents think broadly and theorectically about ethical/moral issues and politics.

operations, concepts, and theories that are largely facilitated by language. For instance, children become increasingly more adept at using symbol systems (e.g., language, numbers, sign language) to organize schemes of an abstract and complex nature.

Piaget's Three Types of Knowledge

Children simply do not wait to be instructed in knowledge but are always busy making sense out of every single thing that they encounter. It was Piaget's preoccupation with how children acquire knowledge that led him to distinguish between three types of knowledge: physical knowledge, logico-mathematical knowledge, and social or conventional knowledge.

According to Piaget, **physical knowledge** is knowing the physical properties or attributes of an object, such as the number, size, shape, and color. For example, a young child may know that balls roll but books do not, and an older child might know the properties of a pencil, such as its color and shape. Physical knowledge is best gained by individuals acting on objects, experimenting with objects, and carefully observing reactions.

Logico-mathematical knowledge, on the other hand, entails the mental construction of relationships between things. For example, a 6-year-old child may know that six marbles, which can be observed and counted, are also represented by the word *six* and the numeral *6*. Likewise, a preschooler who observes a blue crayon and a red crayon recognizes the difference between the two crayons when they are placed side by side. Logico-mathematical knowledge is dependent upon physical knowledge for its construction, and vice versa.

Social or conventional knowledge has its roots in social conventions that are created by people. The 26 letters of the alphabet, mathematical words and signs, musical notations, social and moral conventions like taking turns when engaged in a conversation, the creation of chairs to sit on, and designating the second Sunday in May as Mother's Day are all examples of social knowledge. However, social knowledge, for the most part, is arbitrary. For example, some people may celebrate Mother's Day, and others, perhaps due to their particular religious beliefs, may not. Piaget recognized that social or conventional knowledge is partly derived from individuals' encounters with other people; children require input from others in order to build their social knowledge.

Cognitive Equilibrium

The concept of **adaptation**, which is a very important concept in human biology, is also central to Piaget's theory of cognitive development. With regard to human biology, adaptation is the evolutionary or change process whereby an organism becomes better suited or adjusts to its habitat. And in much the same way that our bodies adapt to our immediate environment, our mental structures adapt in order to better represent our external world. Also, through a process referred to as **organization**, children reorder and connect new schemes to other schemes in order to create a more elaborate scheme or cognitive system.

As a cognitive theorist, Piaget believed that individuals are always engaged in the process of achieving some degree of **cognitive equilibrium**, or mental balance. The tendency for people to achieve some balance among their mental structures or schemes is innate, and it is the state of **disequilibrium**, or imbalance, that continuously motivates us to adapt our cognitive structures in order to restore balance. The state of disequilibrium is a most dissatisfying and undesirable mental state. Piaget, therefore, maintains that individuals use two complementary processes to achieve a state of cognitive balance: assimilation and accommodation. Through the process of **assimilation**, children utilize new experiences to fit preexisting schemes. In assimilation, children interpret novel or new experiences through an old lens, so to speak. For example, a young child who has never seen a cow may refer to the cow as a big dog with funny spots. The process of assimilation is not a passive one; the child is earnestly trying to modify or reinterpret the new experience to fit his or her existing mental scheme.

On the other hand, when children encounter a new task or experience that does not fit into their existing scheme, they are compelled to alter their old way of thinking and acting in order to accommodate or fit the new information into an already existing scheme—or they may be forced to create a brand-new scheme. Thus, in the case provided above, children may simply expand their existing scheme to include "cow," or they might create a brand-new scheme (e.g., farm animals) once they figure out that the farm animal is not a dog but a cow. **Accommodation** requires more mental activity and energy than assimilation because new concepts and experiences may not always fit into preexisting cognitive structures. Accommodation can only occur if the new idea or task that the child is confronting is only slightly discrepant with his or her existing mental scheme; an idea or a task that is too discrepant will not be accommodated. Under these circumstances, the child does not have an available mental structure to interpret the new information or experience (Meece & Daniels, 2008). When accommodation does occur, intellectual growth advances, and the child is promoted to the next stage of cognitive development. In short, cognitive equilibrium is the ongoing process of striking a balance between assimilation and accommodation (see Figure 4.1).

Figure 4.1   The Processes of Assimilation and Accommodation

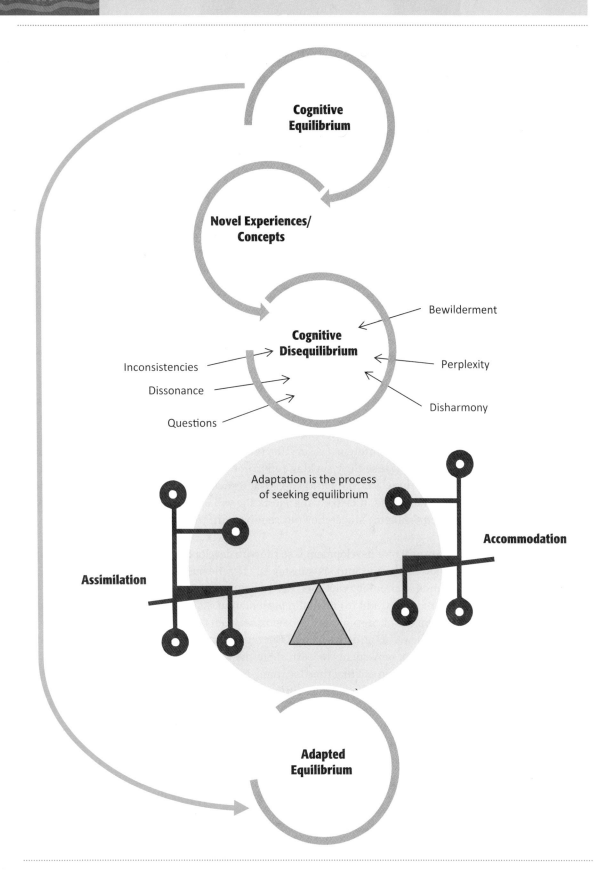

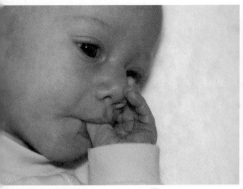

The processes of assimilation and accommodation begin very early in the life of the young infant.

Piaget proposed that cognitive development progresses in a predictable sequence from infancy through adolescence for all human beings. The periods or stages are age-related, and each period promotes a particular way of thinking and behaving (Inhelder & Piaget, 1958; Piaget, 1952). Additionally, children meet important developmental benchmarks at each stage of cognitive development. According to Piaget, there are four stages of cognitive development: (1) sensorimotor, (2) preoperational, (3) concrete operational, and (4) formal operational.

Sensorimotor Stage

The first stage, **sensorimotor**, spans the first 2 years of a child's life (see Table 4.2). This is the period when children's mental structures are developed largely through their senses and motor reflexes. The range of children's reflexive behaviors assists them in building their knowledge and understanding of the world. Infants have an extensive repertoire of reflexes (a total of 18 in all), some of which are absolutely necessary for their survival (e.g., sucking and breathing). Young infants, for example, use their sucking reflex not just for feeding, but to learn about the world. Initially, everything fits the child's existing "suckable scheme." As the child grows and is introduced to table food, it is likely that he or she will need to create a brand-new scheme in order to gain nourishment, since chewing requires different, specific mouth and tongue movements.

The period of sensorimotor development is so rife with developmental changes that Piaget found it necessary to divide the period into six substages: (1) reflexive schemes, (2) primary circular reactions, (3) secondary circular reactions, (4) coordination of secondary circular reactions, (5) tertiary circular reactions, and (6) mental representation. As you can see from Table 4.2, each substage provides evidence of continuous interaction between the child's brain, senses, and motor functions; the child is viewed as an active being. Over time, young infants become increasingly adept at coordinating a variety of movements to learn about the world around them.

The first 24 months are an exciting time for young infants. By the end of children's first year of development, they often appear as amateur little scientists, regularly flirting with the method of trial and error. The older they get, the more abbreviated the process of trial and error; older children at this stage are capable of solving problems more expeditiously in comparison with their younger peers. Also, these children are just beginning to participate in **deferred imitation**, the ability to imitate the behaviors of others who are not present, and **make-believe play**, the process of acting out common, everyday experiences and imaginary activities.

By the end of the sensorimotor period, children achieve two major competencies: (1) goal-directed behavior and (2) object permanence. When young infants engage in **goal-directed behavior**, they are more expansive, creative, and intentional—meaning they are deliberate in their

Table 4.2 **Piaget's Sensorimotor Substages**

THE FIRST TWO YEARS OF LIFE						
Sensorimotor Substage	Reflective Schemes (Birth–1 Month)	Primary Circular Reactions (1–4 Months)	Secondary Circular Reactions (4–8 Months)	Coordination of Secondary Circular Reactions (8–12 Months)	Tertiary Circular Reactions (12–18 Months)	Mental Representation (18 Months–2 Years)
Characteristic Behaviors	Newborn behavior is reflexive in nature—rooting, sucking, grasping, etc.	Limited ability to anticipate events; motorized actions centered on the infant's own body	Motorized actions are repetitious—aimed at interesting effects in the infant's world	Increased anticipation of events; goal-directed behavior; object permanence; imitative behavior	Exploration of the properties of objects; increased imitation of novel behaviors; relentless search for hidden objects—infants will search for an object in many locations	Mental representations of objects and events; deferred imitation; make-believe play; basic problem solving—ability to find an object that was moved while out of the child's sight

coordination of behavioral schemes as a means to an end. They will intentionally and repeatedly use their coordinated schemes (e.g., hand and arm movements) to manipulate a favorite toy, just to hear its interesting sounds and see its blinking lights. Children's goal-directed behavior comes as a result of their awareness of cause and effect, improved memory, and increased understanding of people's intentions (Behne, Carpenter, Call, & Tomasello, 2005; Willatts, 1999). **Object permanence**, on the other hand, which begins to emerge around the time a child is 8 months old, entails children's basic understanding that objects or people still exist even when they can no longer see them. The child who achieves an understanding of object permanence is unlike his or her 8-month-old peer who relates to objects and people in an out-of-sight, out-of-mind fashion. Children around this age will soon cease to search for an object that is out of sight. However, a 22-month-old will intentionally use a number of coordinated schemes to search for a ball that has rolled under the bed until he or she finds it. This type of action conveys both goal-directed behavior and the child's acquisition of object permanence.

Early childhood professionals providing care for infants and toddlers during the sensorimotor stage of development can foster children's learning by playing games like peek-a-boo, pat-a-cake, and hide-and-go-seek with them, and by providing them with wide-open, stimulating, and safe environments that foster active exploration.

Preoperational Stage

Children between the ages of 2 and 6 years are said to possess what Piaget referred to as **preoperational intelligence**. The preoperational stage of development is an exciting period, marked by significant childhood competencies such as increased language facility, **representational thought** (the young child's ability to internalize visual experiences and maintain mental imagery of things not present), and an enhanced ability to engage in both deferred imitation and make-believe play. However, there are also limits to children's thinking during this stage of development. Children tend to be quite **egocentric** (self-centered) with regard to their thinking ability. Egocentric thinking is often defined as children's inability to consider other perspectives. Children at this phase of development will, undoubtedly, focus on a particular aspect of a situation without taking other aspects of the situation under consideration. For example, it is hard for a child at this stage to understand that "Daddy" can be a brother or husband because the child is singularly focused on the role that his or her father plays in his or her life. Children's thinking during this stage is focused on appearance to the exclusion of other factors.

Children also engage in **static reasoning**; they think that nothing ever changes. Therefore, whatever exists today constitutes what it was yesterday and what it will be tomorrow. So, for example, a child might contend that "Mommy" was never a little girl or will never be a grandmother. One final characteristic of preoperational thought is **irreversibility**, the ability to understand that reversing an action or a process restores it to its original state. A 3-year-old child who doesn't like his or her sandwich cut in two will have an absolute fit when he or she sees the two halves. Any attempt to place the two halves closely together on his or her plate in order to create the illusion of wholeness is futile. Preoperational children focus on the one feature: the "divided sandwich." They do not think reversibly or consider the fact that by simply putting the sandwich halves back together again, the sandwich, for all intents and purposes, is whole once again!

In order to test the limitations of children's preoperational thinking, Piaget devised several experiments in **conservation**, the fact that something remains the same regardless of changes in its form or appearance. These classic landmark studies in conservation have greatly enhanced our understanding of children's reasoning abilities during the preoperational stage of development. In one classic experiment, children were shown two identical glasses with the same amount of liquid in each (Piaget, 1952). The liquid of one was poured into a tall narrow glass (see Table 4.3). When children were asked whether one glass contained more liquid than the other or if they both contained the same amount of liquid, children insisted that the tall narrow glass contained more liquid. Children's responses to the questions were all characteristic of preoperational thought. They failed to realize the conservation of liquids by centering their thoughts exclusively on appearance; they attended only to the immediate condition or state (**static reasoning**), and they did not consider the possibility of reversing the process. Children tended to focus solely on the higher level of liquid in the taller, narrower glass.

Nevertheless, children's use of language and symbolic thought processes is a hallmark of the preoperational stage of cognitive development. Teachers who work with children in the preoperational stage of development can best promote their learning by providing numerous opportunities for language development, such as reading, writing, and speaking activities; experiences in exploration;

Imaginary play is the cornerstone of young children's intellectual growth and the very beginning of children being at home in the world. It is through children's imaginary play that they begin to use symbols and words to make sense of their surroundings.

and opportunities in creative art expression and working with a range of manipulative materials.

Concrete Operations Stage

During the **concrete operational period**, which usually occurs between the ages of 6 and 11 years, children tend to use increasingly more mental operations that involve symbols and images, and they are even capable of reversing operations. In other words, at this stage in children's cognitive development, they recognize that things can return to their original state. In the case of the liquid conservation experiment described above, the concrete operational child recognizes that the amount of liquid does not change by one simply pouring the liquid from a shorter,

Young children love singing and finger-plays. Pat-a-cake helps to foster children's language development and social skills.

wider glass into a taller glass. Mentally, children are able to reverse the operation in their head to provide a correct response to the question "Which glass has more?" During this crucial developmental period, children are also less egocentric and are able to apply logical thinking to operations that are concrete, or visible and tangible. One important logical concept that children master during this stage of development is **classification**, the organization of things into some group or class based on a certain characteristic. As children grow older, they are more precise and flexible when engaged in classification tasks. During middle childhood, children use mental categories and subcategories flexibly, inductively, and simultaneously (Hayes & Younger, 2004). Children become adept at using many subcategories when categorizing or classifying. For example, food can be separated into various categories such as fruits, vegetables, meats, and grains.

Some **pedagogical techniques** or teaching methods that teachers can use when instructing children who are in the early stages of concrete operations are experiences in classification that are increasingly more sophisticated, tangible examples to explain complex phenomena, opportunities to engage in the scientific exploration and manipulation of materials, and presentations that are brief and well organized.

Formal Operations

Piaget's fourth and final stage of development, **formal operations**, begins at age 12 years and continues throughout the life span. During this period, adolescents and adults effectively consider abstractions and hypothetical situations and are able to reason analytically—as opposed to children in the stage of concrete operations who reason logically but only about direct experiences and perceptions. This is the stage in which you currently find yourself and where most of your mental operations are executed. All of us, however, at times revert to the use of mental processes that are characteristic of previous stages. For example, adults may use their sensorimotor intelligence (sense of touch) to feel a sweater's fabric in order to determine its suitability for their wardrobe. Still others may engage in concrete operations by using their fingers to count the days remaining in a given month.

Table 4.3   **Piaget's Conservation of Volume, Mass, and Number Tasks**

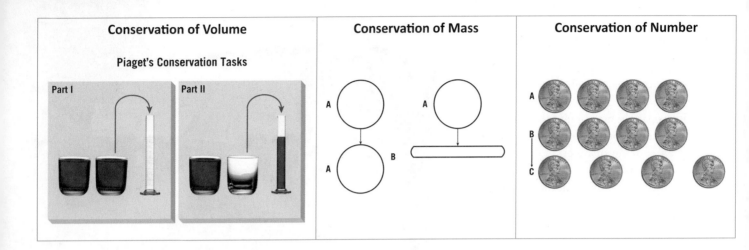

Limitations of Piaget's Theory

Non-Piagetian research has proven that Piaget clearly underestimated the intellectual capabilities of young children, especially infants. Over the years, his work in cognitive development theory has ignited both criticism and praise from developmentalists and other researchers in related fields (education, psychology, etc.) (Bjorklund, 2005). For example, we now know that infantile intelligence is quite significant at birth and that this quality is evident even before infants are capable of moving about, which Piaget found to be an essential ability that leads to increased knowledge. Also, numerous studies have found young children in the preoperational stage of development to demonstrate the ability to think more concretely or to function at the concrete operational stage of development. For instance, children's nonverbal gestures demonstrated their capacity to engage in complex classification tasks during play. Their words demonstrated a deficit in classifying, but their actions showed something entirely different (Halford & Andrews, 2006). Research has found children to be more cognitively competent and capable of being trained to use both concrete and formal operations than Piaget once claimed. Young children can manifest complex cognitive functioning and are generally less homogeneous with regard to their reasoning ability than Piaget originally thought (Bjorklund, 2005). Researchers have also found that children during the preoperational stage of development are not as egocentric in their thinking as Piaget once contended; children can be quite sensitized to the thoughts, wishes, and emotions of other people. Furthermore, we now know that children's knowledge during the preoperational phase of development can be bound by culture. For example, there is evidence of wide variation in the timing of children's acquisition of conservation concepts across cultures, which appears to be linked to the relative weight placed on conservation activities (e.g., children's exposure to conservation activities within society) (Berk & Winsler, 1995).

Perhaps the limitations with regard to Piaget's cognitive development theory were the direct result of his approaches toward studying young children. As mentioned earlier, Piaget based most of his conclusions regarding children's thinking, especially during the sensorimotor period, on what he observed in his own three children. Researchers agree that one major problem with Piaget's

The Practice of **Research** and **Theory**
We All Scream for Ice Cream

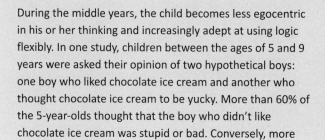

During the middle years, the child becomes less egocentric in his or her thinking and increasingly adept at using logic flexibly. In one study, children between the ages of 5 and 9 years were asked their opinion of two hypothetical boys: one boy who liked chocolate ice cream and another who thought chocolate ice cream to be yucky. More than 60% of the 5-year-olds thought that the boy who didn't like chocolate ice cream was stupid or bad. Conversely, more

than 90% of the 9-year-olds thought that both boys could be right and were less critical of the boy who didn't like chocolate ice cream. As children grow older, they are more willing to accept other people's opinions and individual beliefs.

Source: Wainryb, C., Shaw, L. A., Langley, M., Cottam, K., & Lewis, R. (2004). Children's thinking about diversity of belief in early school years: Judgments of relativism, tolerance, and disagreeing persons. *Child Development, 75,* 687–703.

investigative technique was that it was highly subjective. Additionally, contemporary researchers view his method and very limited sample size (three children) as problematic. Furthermore, there are concerns with regard to the "fidelity and credibility" (Bornstein, Arterberry, & Mash, 2005, p. 287) in collecting data on infants. Modern researchers today employ various statistical methods and appropriate sample sizes, as well as other research techniques (e.g., the use of fMRI [functional magnetic resonance imaging] to measure infants' brain activity) to avert such problems (Berger, 2011; Hartmann & Pelzel, 2005).

Regardless of the limitations to his theory, Piaget's fascination with children's thought processes and their acquisition of knowledge sustained his expansive work in developmental psychology for almost 60 years, giving rise to a very prolific career.

WHAT IS INFORMATION PROCESSING THEORY?

Information processing theory is antithetical to Piaget's theory of cognitive development. Piaget's theory focuses on distinct stages of cognitive development, whereas information processing theory provides a step-by-step description of thought processes occurring at every age. In the past 30 years, information processing theory has become the leading strategy for studying children's cognitive development (Klahr & MacWhinney, 1998). Information processing theory emphasizes how children learn a particular thing; it focuses not on theories but on details of the learning process, such as the sensory data input, connections made in the brain, stored memories, retrieval of information, and output. This theory uses the computer as a model for human thinking in that it assumes data enter the brain through the five senses and are processed, giving rise to some kind of behavioral response, or the data are stored for later retrieval. So, for example, an infant's output might take the form of waving bye-bye, moving a shoe to uncover a toy, or gazing at a large picture that resembles a human face. By the same token, an 8-month-old who is crying because of hunger will cease crying once the child recognizes the mother's familiar actions that signal she is preparing to feed him or her. The people, places, and things in the child's environment afford the infant numerous opportunities to perceive and then act. Eight-year-old children are better at information

Consider This Cultural Transmission

Martin, a teacher in the Children's Center, watched carefully as 4-year-old Kyla Ann entered the preschool classroom, running directly to the dramatic play area. Immediately, she put on an apron and rolled up her sleeves. Kyla Ann then picked up a dishcloth and pretended to wash the plastic dishes in the sink. After washing each dish, she carefully placed each one on the counter adjacent to the sink. Kyla Ann then grabbed a towel and began to dry each dish very meticulously. Kyla Ann's observable behavior was clearly reminiscent of an adult handling expensive china. When we carefully observe children's behavior, it is often indicative of the transmission of culture, whatever their respective culture happens to be. Kyla Ann's handling of the dishes was indicative of a very specific ("dish-drying") technique

that she learned after observing a significant person in her life engaged in the behavior over time. Well-provisioned early childhood classrooms include cultural artifacts, not just in the dramatic play area, but in every area of the early childhood classroom. When we provide cultural tools, instruments, and artifacts that are invariably found in children's homes, local stores, communities, and so on, we provide consistency and relevancy for children as they engage in learning.

What type of artifacts would you consider including in your future classroom? What are your thoughts about the early childhood classroom becoming an extension of children's personal worlds and how best to achieve this in very diverse contexts?

processing; they are better at retrieval strategies and analysis of data than their younger counterparts. Nevertheless, **perception**, defined as the mental processing of sensory data, is an active cognitive process that is highly selective in both children and adults. The brain recognizes a particular sensation, perhaps a result of the individual's past experience.

WHAT IS VYGOTSKY'S SOCIOCULTURAL THEORY OF DEVELOPMENT?

Western educators have only recently embraced Lev Semyonovich Vygotsky's pioneering work from the 1920s and 1930s in the area of sociocultural theory. Over the past 20 years, Vygotsky's theory has been gaining popularity among early childhood educators and researchers alike. Vygotsky's **sociocultural theory** asserts that an individual's development can only be understood in the context of his or her social and cultural experiences; there is always a dynamic interplay between one's sociocultural context and one's personal development (Rogoff, 2003). According to Vygotsky's theory, also referred to as the sociogenesis of cognitive development (Yu & Bain, 1980), knowledge, or how it is that we come to know things, is socially constructed. "What we know is inextricably bound to when and where we know it" (Grave, 1993, p. 2). In other words, cognition, or the development of mental structures, is consummately social in nature.

The Vygotskian sociocultural perspective, which also places emphasis on how children construct knowledge, is distinctly different from Piaget's perspective. Piaget's theory focuses on the individual's attempt to make sense of the world on his or her own; knowledge is always constructed, in part, according to the child's already developed mental structures (Weber, 1984). Vygotsky, however, moves away from Piaget's individualism by placing a great deal of emphasis on the child's sociocultural context. Thus, Piaget is often described as being a cognitive constructivist theorist, and Vygotsky as a theorist of **social constructivism**.

According to Vygotsky, "Any function in the individual's psychological development appears twice, initially on the **interpsychological**, or social plane [between people] and then on the **intrapsychological** plane [within the individual]" (Vygotsky, 1978, p. 57). In other words, learning first occurs between people; it is an externalized social process. Then, the learning is internalized. This process applies across the board in all areas of the child's intellectual functioning, such as voluntary attention, logical memory, and the formulation of concepts.

Zone of Proximal Development

Vygotsky coined the term *zone of proximal development* (ZPD, as introduced in Chapter 2) to further explain the internalization process. The ZPD is the distance between the child's actual developmental level, as determined by what the child is able to do independently, and the child's potential level of development, as determined by what the child can master under adult guidance or in collaboration with a more capable peer (see Figure 4.2). Within the ZPD, intrapsychological functioning represents mental processes that are mature. Such mental processes constitute tasks that children can do independently or concepts that they fully understand. With regard to the interpsychological plane, mental processes are not fully mature but still unfolding. Therefore, children functioning on this psychological or social plane will require adult assistance or guidance in order to fully engage in a task or to acquire an understanding of a particular concept. For example, a 5-year-old who is just learning how to tie his or her sneaker laces will need the assistance of an adult in the process. Children might need to see the adult model the task several times, and/or they may need several practice runs with the adult before they can tie their sneaker laces independently.

According to Vygotsky, cognition is consummately social in nature; information is passed on to children by more *expert* others in their environment.

Figure 4.2	**Zone of Proximal Development Diagram**

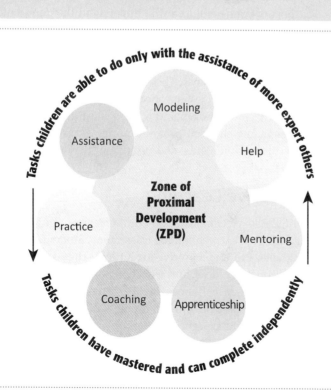

When engaging in tasks like learning to tie laces, both the child and the adult are likely to enter the problem-solving situation with their own subjective thoughts about how to best proceed or approach the task. When engaged in problem-solving tasks or operating in the ZPD, both the child and the more capable other must arrive at a place of **intersubjectivity**, which is a shared understanding or a mutually agreed upon way of approaching a task. Intersubjectivity is evident in this chapter's opening vignette, which describes the parent and child engaged in the joint task of stringing beads of varying shapes and sizes. When a mutual understanding is achieved between the child and a more capable other, learning is facilitated.

The amount of assistance and support that the adult provides the child within the ZPD is always changing because the adult is sensitive to the abilities of the learner and responds accordingly. This changing level of support during a teaching-learning situation is called scaffolding (see Chapter 2). The more capable other provides more assistance and support during the initial phase of the task (when the task is new) and begins to gradually withdraw support as the child becomes increasingly more capable. For example, a father who is teaching his young daughter how to ride a bike will initially assist the child by holding on to the child's handlebars in order to help her maintain her balance. As he provides support by encouraging her to pedal, he begins to roll her along more swiftly.

It may take several trials before he can safely remove his hands from the handlebars altogether. Eventually, the father removes his hands from the handlebars after witnessing his daughter's increased mastery in balancing her weight and pedaling. This process, which may take several trials before the child fully masters the technique of bike riding, requires patience and flexibility on behalf of the more capable or expert other.

In scaffolding, the child is seen as the edifice under construction, and the child's social environment and experiences (more experienced others, teaching tools/materials) scaffold or build the child up so that he or she can achieve new and improved competencies. The term *scaffolding* is also recognized in the research as a **"tutorial intervention"** (Wood, Bruner, & Ross, 1976, p. 89), **guided participation**, and **apprenticeship learning**.

Teachers of young children who understand the importance of scaffolding children's development are warm and responsive to the child's needs and strengths, flexible and willing to allow the child to self-regulate the joint problem-solving task as much as possible, and willing to assume the role as "learner" rather than "teacher" at appropriate times. They assume the role of facilitator or coach; use a range of distancing strategies (questioning techniques) and other techniques, such as gesturing (e.g., prompting, pointing, modeling); and use authentic assessments, including engaging children in group projects, task analysis, and peer group evaluations to assess students' understanding (Berk & Winsler, 1995).

Collaborative Learning

Sociocultural theory emphasizes the importance of **collaborative learning** (group learning) in early childhood classrooms. Students are quite influential at impacting each other's cognitive structures; they support one another and encourage new ways to think, construct ideas, and reflect on novel material. Teachers who engage young elementary school children in collaborative learning experiences must create ideal circumstances that foster children's passion and achievement of a common goal and the various groups' functionality. Cooperation and aspects of the group's culture and diversity are essential elements for successful group learning. The breadth and scope of children's wide-ranging contributions to the group provide a more comprehensive view of the material to be learned, significantly advancing children's knowledge base.

The parent and child engaged in learning how to ride a bike is an example of learning in the Zone of Proximal Development.

Vygotsky's sociocultural theory and its related concepts have made appreciable advances in the early childhood community's understanding of the interconnectedness between children's engagement in legitimate sociocultural activities and their subsequent development.

WHAT IS BRONFENBRENNER'S BIOECOLOGICAL THEORY OF DEVELOPMENT?

Urie Bronfenbrenner, like the theorists before him, was acutely aware of the importance of caring adults in the lives of young children when he developed his theory in the late 1970s. Bronfenbrenner's early experiences working alongside his father at a mental institution for young children provided the seeds for his theory of the **ecology of human behavior** and his later work as a staunch advocate for the obliteration of social and political practices that negatively impact children and families. Recently, Bronfenbrenner's theory has been renamed *bioecological* **systems theory** in order to emphasize the importance of the child's own biology as a primary factor in the interplay between the child and his or her environment, and the environment's crucial role in fueling the child's development (see Figure 4.3).

Bronfenbrenner greatly increased our understanding regarding the impact of the immediate environment and the social landscape on the developing child and his or her family.

One might agree that the popular cliché "It takes a village to raise a child" underscores the very essence of Bronfenbrenner's bioecological systems theory. According to him, educators and developmentalists need to fully consider all of the various systems that surround the development of the child. For instance, a child's ability to read may be just as contingent upon the teacher's pedagogical skills as it is upon the quality of the relationship between the child's school and home. Bronfenbrenner's concept of the various layered environmental systems that make up society can be described as a set of seriated toy cups, like the ones that can be found in most infant/toddler classrooms today. Each cup can be nested neatly in another until all of the cups of various sizes become one large cup—but with many layers. These environmental systems, according to Bronfenbrenner, are constantly unfolding over the course of the child's development, impacting his or her total being, as well the existence of the adults around the child.

BEST
Practices Scaffolding Children's Development: The First Dance

Effective teachers of young children use the technique of scaffolding when engaging young children in a teaching-learning task. Rather than allowing children to accomplish only those tasks that they can do independently—without assistance from a more capable other—intuitive teachers who are also deliberate and intentional in their teaching style recognize that children, invariably, are capable of functioning on a higher developmental plane when they are appropriately challenged and afforded the right degree of assistance and support. Teachers who effectively spur children's thinking prowess are adept at providing just the right amount of support to children when they are engaged in a challenging task. Such teachers provide elevated levels of scaffolding support when children need additional help and shrink back when children begin to demonstrate mastery of a given task. This choreographed interplay is the first of many dances that children will have with a more expert other.

Figure 4.3	Bronfenbrenner's Bioecological System of Development

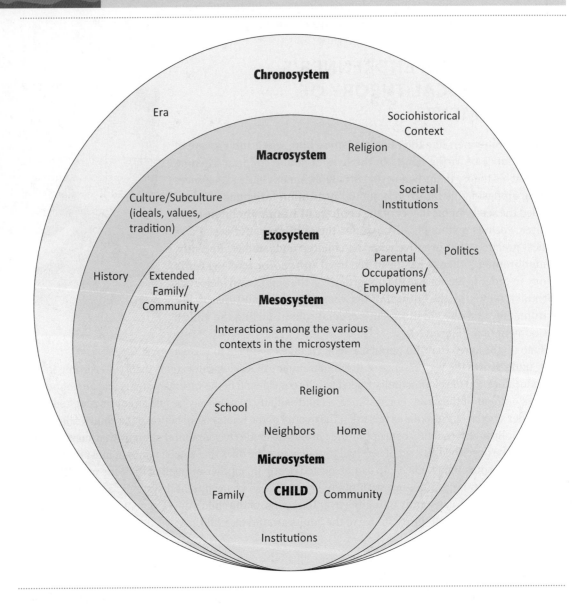

Bronfenbrenner's theory consists of three nested systems: (1) microsystems, (2) exosystems, and (3) macrosystems. The **microsystem** is the innermost level and comprises the child's immediate environment—the child's home, family, peer group, kindergarten classroom, religious institution, and so on. These are the settings in which the child has direct, personal experience. The **mesosystem**, on the other hand, constitutes the interactions or connections between and among the various settings at this and other levels, as well as the interactions between and among the various elements or settings belonging to the three systems. For example, an aggressive 7-year-old might be required by the school psychologist to participate in a special after-school program aimed at averting bullying behavior in young elementary school students. Bullying concerns evident in the larger social context (at the local school) can impact children who may be already primed for aggressive behavior, in one way or another.

The **exosystem** consists of events that might influence the child's development but only indirectly. For instance, a single parent who has recently been laid off might drift into a state of depression, which may ultimately impact his or her parenting skills.

The **macrosystem** represents culture and the subcultures in which the child lives, including the ideals, values, and traditions, as well as regional identity. For example, some children growing up in the infamous town of Juarez, Mexico, today, which has been referred to by many as the "murder capital of the world," might grow to be very indifferent to pain, suffering, and death over time.

Bronfenbrenner recognized that familial interrelationships are modified with the passage of time, and that societal and sociohistorical trends can impact family life. The **chronosystem** recognizes the timing of these adjustments and the relative position of the child during these periods, including the impact of these changes on the developing child (Bronfenbrenner, 2005). For instance, during the housing boom at the turn of the 21st century, many working-class families realized the "American Dream" and were able to buy houses, thereby bolstering the family's socioeconomic status. However, by 2006, the incomes of many families plummeted due to the "Great Recession," and many of these same families lost their homes. Scores of children and their families became homeless for the very first time. When children lack a permanent residence and are forced to double up with other family members and change schools, such major transitions can have a deleterious effect on their growth and development over time. Thus, the child's well-being is closely tied to the various systems of which he or she is a part.

According to Bronfenbrenner, there are many influences that can impact the development of the child; however, being aware of these environmental influences is simply not enough. Careful consideration of the impact of these various systems on the child and his or her family should propel early childhood professionals to work in conjunction with families in creating public policy and practices that lead to the creation of social landscapes that clearly support and protect the sanctity of family life.

WHAT IS ERIKSON'S THEORY OF PSYCHOSOCIAL DEVELOPMENT?

Erik Erikson (1902–1994) contributed significantly to the field of human development (see Chapter 2). Erikson, a follower of **Sigmund Freud**, the father of **psychosexual development** who posited that the child's inner drives, urges, and unconscious wishes are the basis for children's thinking and behavior over their extended life, extended Freud's theory to include children's social context. Erikson viewed the human life span as consisting of various stages, each one involving a psychological crisis or conflict that requires a resolution. And while the crisis at each stage is presented in an either/or fashion, Erikson recognized that the resolution of the crisis at each stage led not necessarily to one extreme or the other but to somewhere in the middle. According to Erikson, there are eight stages of psychosocial development, which begin at birth and end in the twilight years of the adult's life (see Table 4.3). Please note that the chart delineates Erikson's theory in its totality, but for our purposes here, only Erikson's first four stages apply.

The first stage, **trust versus mistrust**, is the period between birth and age 1 year. During this period, children learn to trust their primary caregivers to address their basic needs for nourishment, consolation, warmth, and so on. Infants and toddlers who are not afforded responsive care soon learn to mistrust the care of others over time.

During the second stage, the child, who is usually between the ages of 1 and 3 years, must resolve the conflict of **autonomy versus shame and doubt**. Either children gain a sense of self-efficacy—they begin to feel self-sufficient in many activities like toileting, feeding, walking, and exploring—or they begin to doubt their abilities.

Erik Erikson's theory of psychosocial development consists of eight developmental stages, each presenting a unique challenge to the individual.

Federally Funded Head Start/ Early Head Start

Urie Bronfenbrenner bears the distinction of being a cofounder of the national Head Start program. Head Start, which has been in existence for more than 55 years, was one of the original federally funded War on Poverty programs of the mid-1960s. It was the first and only time that children's access to preschool education became a matter of social policy. Head Start and its later appendage, Early Head Start (which serves infants to children age 2), provide comprehensive services to young children and their families such as early childhood education;

assessment, placement, and educational planning for children who are atypically developing; social services; and mental/physical health and nutrition services that are both responsive and appropriate to each child's and family's developmental, ethnic, and linguistic heritage and experience. Although Congress continues to widely debate the need for continued funding support of the national Head Start and Early Head Start program, the efficacy of the program for families from low-socioeconomic-status backgrounds persists (Zigler & Styfco, 2004).

Children entering Erikson's third stage of psychosocial development, **initiative versus guilt**, are interested in adult activities; they are often interested in engaging in activities that exceed their abilities or the boundaries established by adults. For example, children at this age will put their shoes on the wrong feet, concoct messy sandwiches, make breakfast for "Mommy," or jump into the swimming pool. Children's initiation of tasks at this stage may be a source of pride or failure, with failure leading to guilt.

Erikson's fourth stage of psychosocial development is **industry versus inferiority** and includes children between the ages of about 6 and 11 years. At this stage, the outcome of the prior stage matters greatly. The child will either seek independence, becoming increasingly competent and productive at mastering certain tasks, or experience feelings of inadequacy.

Erikson recognized that the child's resolution of the crisis at each stage of development is predicated on such factors as the child's sociocultural context, the parents' child-rearing practices, and both the child's and the family's temperament.

WHAT IS MASLOW'S HIERARCHY OF HUMAN NEEDS?

Maslow's hierarchy of human needs underscores the importance of tending to basic needs before addressing higher order needs.

Abraham Maslow, introduced in Chapter 2, conceptualized and devised a pyramid scheme to convey a **hierarchy of human needs**, which was prompted by his earlier work with primates (see Figure 4.4). One of the things that stood out for Maslow during his research with monkeys was that certain needs of the monkeys trumped, or took precedent over, others.

At the very basest level of the pyramid are the **needs addressing human survival**. These needs consist of food, water, and sleep. Maslow contended that the individual's primary needs must be met first before the person can even consider the challenges of addressing the needs presented at the next level. Thus, the assumption is that when a young child is hungry, it is impossible for him or her to concentrate in school or to learn effectively. When considering the logic of Maslow's

Table 4.4 **Erikson's Theory of Psychosocial Development**

AGE	PSYCHOSOCIAL STAGE	PSYCHOLOGICAL CONFLICT/DILEMMA
Birth to 1 year	Basic Trust vs. Mistrust	Infants learn to trust others to meet their basic needs **OR** Mistrust develops
1 to 3 years	Autonomy vs. Shame & Doubt	Children learn to make choices and acquire agency **OR** Become uncertain and doubtful about their abilities
3 to 6 years	Initiative vs. Guilt	Children learn to initiate activities and acquire a sense of purpose **OR** They begin to feel guilty about their efforts at independence
6 years to Adolescence	Industry vs. Inferiority	Children are eager and curious **OR** They begin to feel inferior and become disenchanted
Adolescence	Identity vs. Role Confusion	Adolescents begin the process of acquiring their personal identity **OR** They become confused, misguided, and misdirected
Young Adulthood	Intimacy vs. Isolation	Young adults enter into committed relationships **OR** They become isolative and disenfranchised
Middle Adulthood	Generativity vs. Stagnation	Adults proliferate and nurture others **OR** They become self-centered and disengaged
Old Age	Integrity vs. Despair	Older adults engage in introspection about their life and emanate pride **OR** They feel regretful and resentful about how their life has transpired

hierarchy of needs, we can now fully understand why schools should implement free breakfast programs for children from low-socioeconomic-status (LSES) backgrounds. Everywhere today, schools provide a range of nutritional programs for children because these schools recognize that children need nourishment before they can successfully engage in learning activities.

Maslow's second level on the pyramid addresses the human **need for security and safety**. People of all ages need shelter, a sanctuary or home that makes them feel safe. Even infants and toddlers need to feel secure enough to use their range of sensorimotor skills to explore their

Children at Erikson's third stage of psychosocial development need to gain a sense of ambition and responsibility.

immediate environment. As children grow older and become adults, their basic need for safety and security can also become threatened. In the history of this country, there have been many incidences of catastrophic events and natural disasters that have seriously compromised people's sense of security and well-being. In the aftermath of Hurricane Katrina in New Orleans, Louisiana, in 2005, the situation grew even more chaotic as people dealt with the lack of basic shelter and safety. People of all ages and backgrounds committed a number of aberrant acts in a desperate attempt to survive and to achieve a certain degree of sanctity.

Maslow's third level on the pyramid deals with the social needs of people, the **need for belonging and love**. Both children and adults need to know that they matter and that someone cares. Urie Bronfenbrenner once said that children need the irrational involvement of people in their lives in order to become human; somebody has to be crazy about them (Bronfenbrenner, 1971). Children who feel rejected internalize their pain and feelings of worthlessness and begin to act out these emotions in a number of ways. These are the children who later become bullies and juvenile delinquents. In our day-to-day life, we exhibit the need for belonging in our desire to marry, have a family, and become a member of a community, church, fraternity, or bowling league, or even a member of a gang!

The fourth stage of Maslow's hierarchy of needs addresses the **need for achievement and prestige**. In our day-to-day life, the need for achievement and prestige is manifested in a number of ways, such as pursuing an academic degree, purchasing a house, or writing a book. This elevated level of human needs in Maslow's scheme represents our desire for self-respect and the respect of others. The young father who boasts about his recent promotion on the job and the young girl who points out to her mother her "perfect" spelling test pinned to the bulletin board are both experiencing the joys resulting from recognition from others.

At the very top of Maslow's hierarchy of human needs is the **need for self-actualization**. Children and adults who are self-actualized recognize their full potential and are motivated to become the very best that they can be. They have an enhanced sense of self-efficacy and self-worth. These are the children who are typically very excited about learning; they demonstrate what is referred to as **intrinsically motivated scholarship**. In such cases, children across the developmental spectrum learn for learning's sake and begin to rely increasingly less on external reinforcements in order to engage in learning.

While Maslow's theory has become incredibly popular, it has been criticized for its lack of empirical support; the theory was predicated mostly on his observations and intuitions about the human experience (Sheldon, Elliot, Kim, & Kasser, 2001; Smither, 1998). Maslow's theory also yields some discrepant themes throughout in that it *is* plausible for individuals to demonstrate needs from two or more levels simultaneously. Also, people who have had their basic needs met may not care to address their higher needs, and those whose basic needs have gone unmet may not always be destined to act out or to behave poorly. Furthermore, higher needs may, at times, supersede lower ones. For example, people who have dared to climb Mount Everest or who have walked across the country have obviously dismissed their need to be safe at home.

BURRHUS FREDERIC SKINNER

B. F. Skinner referred to his theory of operant conditioning as **radical behaviorism** because he wanted to distinguish it from John B. Watson's behaviorism, known as classical conditioning.

Classical conditioning is the learning process by which a meaningful stimulus (e.g., food) becomes connected to a neutral stimulus (e.g., a bell) again and again, until such time the neutral stimulus (i.e., the bell), alone, triggers the behavior (i.e., salivation in a dog). On the other hand, Skinner's operant conditioning (introduced in Chapter 3) is a type of behaviorism that is best described as a learning process by which a certain action is followed either by something that causes the behavior to be repeated or by something negative, which makes the action less likely to be repeated. This concept constitutes one of the basic laws of learning; that behavior is less likely or more likely depending on the consequences that follow it. Skinner argued that when it comes to behavior, we must focus our attention on the external consequences of an action. In other words, in order to explain behavior, we must first look outside the individual, not inside.

In operant conditioning, pleasant consequences are **rewards**, and unpleasant ones are called punishments (see Chapter 3). But for some people, a punishment might actually be considered a reward, and the converse is also true. For example, for a child who is craving attention, spanking may be welcomed—a means of gaining his parents' attention. On the other hand, withholding dessert from a child who does not eat all of his or her food may not constitute a punishment for the child, because the child might not care for the dessert in the first place. According to Skinner, any consequence that follows a behavior and increases the likelihood of the behavior being repeated is referred to as a **reinforcement**. Operant responses are typically

Skinner's contribution to early childhood stems from his work in operant conditioning.

Figure 4.4	Maslow's Hierarchy of Needs

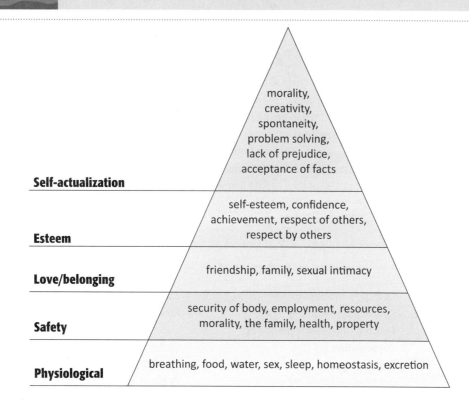

nonreflexive, compared with classical conditioning responses, which are usually reflexive in nature. Operant responses include complex behaviors like riding a skateboard or scooter, writing a letter, or throwing a tantrum.

We witness operant conditioning played out in the grocery store all of the time. A child puts a favorite food in the shopping cart and throws a fit when the mother doesn't buy the item. To avoid further embarrassment, the mother eventually gives in and purchases the item, which causes the child to end his or her tantrum. When the child and mother visit the grocery store again, the same scenario is repeated. The child has obviously learned that crying and throwing a tantrum is instrumental in obtaining the favorite food. (Operant conditioning has also been called **instrumental conditioning**.)

Skinner's contributions to the field of early childhood education stem from his work in operant conditioning. As illustrated in his book *Walden Two*, Skinner (1948/2005) described the idea of using consistent, positive reinforcement to shape the behavior of individuals within society. The book is a well-written treatise on humans living in a carefully controlled society (utopia) and how to establish desirable behavior among them (Weber, 1984). His theories on reinforcing desired behaviors guided parents and teachers, alike, to influence and shape school-age children's behavior by using appropriate environmental reinforcements. The ideas set forth in Skinner's book represent an alternative method for shaping human behavior instead of resorting to the use or threat of punishment. Skinner's landmark research on the effects of reinforcement helped to shift society's focus from restricting undesirable behaviors (punishment) to emphasis on supporting desirable behaviors.

Summary

The variety of major developmental theories discussed in this chapter help to crystallize the early childhood educator's understanding of the role of children's early learning experiences in shaping their growth and development. The theories discussed in this chapter provide a comprehensive view of human development at the very beginning of the life span. It is important for teachers of very young children to have an evolved understanding of the development of children and what the various theorists have to say about learning and the interplay between nature and nurture in the lives of children. An in-depth understanding of children's development translates into effective practices and engagement of young children. Learning theories unlock the secret of how children begin to discover both what they can do and who they can become—in other words, how children begin to develop both their range of abilities and their unique identity as individuals (Bronfenbrenner, 1971).

Key Terms

Accommodation 90

Adaptation 90

Apprenticeship learning 100

Assimilation 90

Autonomy versus shame and doubt 103

Bioecological systems theory 101

Chronosystem 103

Classical conditioning 107

Classification 95

Cognitive equilibrium 90

Collaborative learning 100

Concrete operational period 95

Conservation 94

Critical thinking 85

Deferred imitation 92

Development 82

Developmentalist 84

Disequilibrium 90

DNA 82

Ecology of human behavior 101

Egocentric 94

Epigenesis 87

Exosystem 103

Formal operations 95

Genes 82

Goal-directed behavior 92

Reflection, Application, and Analysis Questions

1. Select two of the developmental theories described in this chapter and discuss the similarities and differences that exist between the two theories.

2. Summarize Piaget's theory of cognitive development and provide examples of *adult* intellectual functioning that are characteristic of each of the four stages of development. Refer to the examples provided in the text for guidance.

3. Visit an early childhood classroom and observe the interactions among the children and between the children and their teachers. Provide a detailed analysis of the scaffolding behaviors that occur.

4. Select one or more of the theories discussed in this chapter and conduct a thorough investigation of two preschool children's portfolios (a compilation of the child's work samples, products, and observational notes). Describe each child's developmental progress in light of the concepts presented in the theory or theories you select.

Extension Activities

1. Take a few moments to reflect about a specific time when you were engaged in apprenticeship learning. What was that experience like for you? Write down your reflective thoughts about the experience.

2. Observe a preschooler and a significant caregiver engaged in a teaching-learning activity, perhaps similar to the one described in the chapter opening vignette. In a journal, detail the series of exchanges, both verbal and behavioral, between the child and the more expert other.

Additional Readings

The recommended readings below will provide students with a comprehensive and deeper understanding of the essentials of human development and learning theory.

Berk, L. E., & Winsler, A. (1995). *Scaffolding children's learning: Vygotsky and early childhood education.* Washington, DC: National Association for the Education of Young Children.

A scholarly and highly palatable read, this text has been found to be quite suitable for early childhood educators, teachers, and students. Vygotsky's theories, which focus on social, cultural, and societal development, as well as practical ideas for transferring theory into practice, are fully explicated in this text. Also included are key discussions on concepts such as play, language, assessment, development, special needs, and other topics.

Bjorklund, D. F. (2005). *Children's thinking: Cognitive development and individual differences.* **Belmont, CA: Wadsworth.**
This book discusses typical patterns of change in thinking observed over time and individual differences in children's thinking in infancy and childhood, and provides a plethora of research evidence relative to children's cognitive development.

Bodrova, E., & Leong, D. (2007). *Tools of the mind: The Vygotskian approach to early childhood education* **(2nd ed.). Upper Saddle River, NJ: Merrill/Prentice Hall.**

This book provides a comprehensive overview of Vygotsky's theory and alternative theories, as well as concrete instructional techniques to foster children's growth and development.

DeVries, R. (2001). *Developing constructivist early curriculum: Practical principles and activities.* **New York: Teachers College Press.**
This book offers a constructivist overview of developmentally appropriate curriculum in early childhood education and practical ideas for classroom activities.

Puckett, M. B., Black, J., Wittmer, D. S., & Petersen, S. H. (2009). *Young children: The development from pre-birth to age 8.* **Upper Saddle River, NJ: Merrill.**
A very easy read, this book is an excellent blend of academic research and practical information.

On the Web

Jean Piaget Society - *www.piaget.org/links.html*
This website contains a collection of essays for the purposes of teacher training.

Resources for the Constructivist Educator - *http://www.constructivistassociation.org/*
This website from the Association for Constructivist Teaching provides a rich, problem-solving arena that encourages the learner's investigation, invention, and inference.

Student Study Site

Visit **www.sagepub.com/gordonbiddle** to access several study tools including eFlashcards, web quizzes, links to SAGE journal articles, web resources, video resources, lesson plan templates, and more.

Child Development and Milestones

This chapter will help you answer these important questions:

- What are the major physical and motor milestones?
- What are the major cognitive milestones?
- What are the major language milestones?
- What are the major emotional and social milestones?
- What are some implications of developmental milestones?

Vignette: A Tale of Twin Boys

Jake was born first weighing in at 4 pounds, which was 10 ounces more than his brother Luke who weighed 3 pounds, 6 ounces. In addition to weighing more, Jake was ahead of his brother in physical and maturational development: He walked at 10 months in comparison to Luke's 12-month solo walking voyage; Jake's pincer grasp (thumb and forefinger) developed 2 weeks before his brother's; Jake was potty trained a month sooner, and he learned to run earlier. This discrepancy in the boys' development would have concerned the twins' parents if it were not for the fact that Luke attained cognitive, linguistic, and social milestones more quickly.

Luke's social smile came first, he said his first word before his brother, and he was the first to categorize concrete objects (objects easily identified by the senses). He also had more developed writing and graphic representation skills. These differences in the twins' milestone development taught their parents that development happens at different times and varies from child to child. These different strengths also prompted them to encourage Jake in sports and Luke in intellectual pursuits.

The above tale of twin boys Jake and Luke demonstrates how the range and averages of developmental milestones are not absolutes, but rather guidelines for what is normal. When teaching young children, we can let these milestones guide our expectations of children's abilities.

Understanding some of the basic child development milestones is important for the early childhood professional. This information is needed as a teacher begins to prepare for instruction. Basic milestones and the impact of brain development are relayed in this chapter, while more in-depth information is supplied in Part III of the textbook.

The first section of the textbook got you excited about your chosen profession and the prospects of becoming a teacher, while it also informed you about the challenges and rewards of being an early child-hood teacher. Here, in Chapter 5, you will be introduced to your student, the young child. This chapter covers some of the major developmental milestones in a brief and fundamental fashion. Consequently, many of the topics covered here will be elaborated in subsequent chapters. What is really unique about the treatment of these topics in this chapter is the inclusion of brain development research and how it impacts milestones. The addition of this new research helps to keep this chapter cutting-edge and current.

Key Elements
for Becoming a Professional

NAEYC DEVELOPMENTALLY APPROPRIATE PRINCIPLE 2

Many aspects of children's learning and development follow well-documented sequences, with later abilities, skills, and knowledge building on those already acquired.

Interpretation

Human development research suggests that relatively stable, predictable sequences of growth and change occur in children during the first 9 years of life. However, there are ranges that accompany the average sequences.

NAEYC STANDARD 5: USING CONTENT KNOWLEDGE TO BUILD MEANINGFUL CURRICULUM

a. Understanding content knowledge and resources in academic disciplines

b. Knowing and using the central concepts, inquiry tools, and structures of content areas or academic disciplines

c. Using knowledge, appropriate early learning standards, and other resources to design, implement, and evaluate developmentally meaningful and challenging curriculum for each child

Implications of developmental milestones include discussions of the following:

- Learning and education of all children
- Children who are gifted and talented
- Children with special needs

This chapter on developmental milestones takes the same general tone as the rest of the text and endeavors not only to pique the reader's interest but to educate and inform the reader. Learning the information in this chapter will help you as a teacher to make better lesson plans, communicate more effectively with staff and parents, and create meaningful interactions with the children.

WHAT ARE THE MAJOR PHYSICAL AND MOTOR MILESTONES?

This chapter delineates the major milestones, stages, or phases of children's growth and development. We begin here with basic physical and motor milestones, topics that will be expanded upon when we discuss curriculum for teaching young children in Chapter 14.

The Physical Development of the Brain

Early childhood educators impact the actual development of children's brains by providing educational experiences. At birth, all of the sections or lobes of the child's brain are differentiated (DeKaban, 1970). This means that the lobes of the brain are all ready for their specialized functions. The brain is composed of **neurons** that are the basic brain cells. These basic brain cells carry and store information. They are protected by **myelin sheaths** that begin covering the neurons before an infant's birth (Spreen, Risser, & Edgell, 1995). These sheaths grow rapidly during infancy and toddlerhood, but growth slows around the fifth year of life. The sheaths determine how fast information is carried from one neuron to another, which is why their optimal growth is important to learning (see Figure 5.1).

| Figure 5.1 | Myelination of a Neuron |

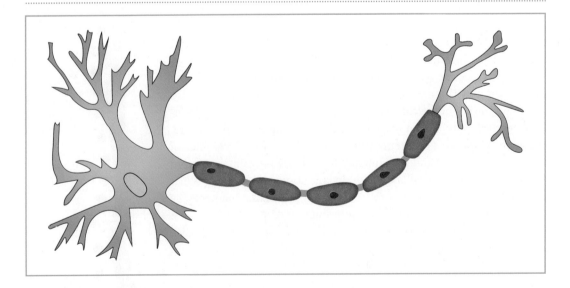

Source: Adapted from http://en.wikipedia.org/wiki/File:Neuron_Hand-tuned.svg.

The neurons come together to form various parts of the brain. The different parts with their own functions come into being with **lateralization** (Kolb & Whishaw, 1990). Lateralization means certain parts of the brain control certain bodily actions and thought processes. However, the brain has a lot of **plasticity**, meaning that it can adapt and recover very well if injured. In other words, one part of the brain can take over the functions of another if that section of the brain is weakened or damaged in some manner (Nash, 1997). The brain's plasticity is significant because it speaks to the vast and wonderful adaptive ability of the brain, which is reflected in the vast and wonderful adaptive abilities of children.

The plasticity and adaptability of the brain are aided as the brain grows and the different neurons are connected, a process called **synaptogenesis** (Kolb, 1999). Basically, synaptogenesis is the connecting of the different brain neurons. These neuron connections are generally referred to as **synapses**. The connections form based on information gathered during environmental experiences. Environmental experiences—on a foundation of genetics, biology, and chemistry—create connections between similar neurons and create pathways through which information can travel within the brain. If environmental experiences do not repeatedly and strongly send information along a specific synapse, then it is possible for the synapse to be erased or eliminated. This process is sometimes called **pruning**. The pruning of synapses is one of the main reasons that the educational nature of the environment created by a child's caregiver is very important. An environment that is organized, responsive, predictable, and information-rich helps to foster synaptic connections that help a child to learn and develop optimally.

Arousal States

Just as an infant's brain begins developing before birth, an infant's **arousal state**, or place or state of being, which includes being asleep or awake, develops a pattern before birth as well. There are

BEST
Practices Facilitating Brain Development

Two of the most important processes or strategies an early childhood teacher can use to facilitate brain development in young children are to create a predictable and emotionally safe classroom and to get in sync with the child's natural rhythms (Perry, 2007a, 2007b). These two strategies help with the creation of synaptic connections. Dr. Bruce Perry gives teachers some tips on how to do both. First, to create an emotionally safe classroom:

- Keep early interactions simple.
- Make interactions predictable.
- Watch for each child's saturation point.
- Make room for quiet time.
- Give optimal challenges and plenty of praise.
- Emphasize nutrition and getting enough sleep.
- Remember just how important you are as a teacher.

Now here are Perry's things to remember for getting in sync with the child's natural rhythms:

- Each child is unique.
- Each child has his or her own strengths, weaknesses, and communication styles.
- Observation of each child in the classroom is important.
- Each child's social category makes him or her more or less comfortable in different social environments.
- Each child's facial expressions are important barometers.
- You have influence as a teacher as you criticize and praise.

Remember that everyday emotional interactions create connections in the brain.

six basic states of arousal that an infant experiences during a typical day (Wolff, 1966). The following is a list of the arousal states, followed by explanations for each state in the paragraphs below:

- Regular sleep
- Irregular sleep
- Drowsiness
- Alert inactivity
- Alert activity
- Crying

The different arousal stages signal appropriate times for meeting the infant's various needs. Not surprisingly, the infant's best time for learning and interaction is alert inactivity, which occurs about 10% of each day in early infancy. During this arousal stage the infant is alert, relaxed, and curious without crying or fussing. Alert inactivity is the best time to interact with the baby and impact his or her brain development. A less optimal time for interaction is the alert activity stage (also about 10% of the day), in which an infant is more active and fussy, but has not yet entered the crying stage. The state of crying, perhaps, needs no introduction or definition. However, it is important to note that very active movement accompanies crying. Also, most amazingly, infants only spend about 5% of the time in this state (Berg, Adkinson, & Strock, 1973; Wolff, 1966).

In addition to the three stages of wakefulness, there are two states of sleep. Sixty-seven percent of the infant's time is spent in one of these sleep states. A majority of the time is spent in regular sleep when the infant is still and relaxed. Less time is spent in irregular sleep when the baby is sleeping, but breathing occurs irregularly and is accompanied by jerky movements and changes in facial expressions. During the last arousal state, drowsiness, the infant is changing from a state of sleep to a state of wakefulness or from a state of wakefulness to one of sleep. While in a state of drowsiness, the infant opens and closes his or her eyes, but breathes regularly. Only 8% of the time is spent in drowsiness. Because of their growth needs, infants spend most of their time in some state of sleep (Berg et al., 1973; Wolff, 1966).

Although they are very basic, sleeping and waking patterns are very important. They signal how the objects and humans in infants' environments can best interact with them to suit their needs at a particular time. These arousal states and the regularity of their patterns are milestones that signal development is occurring well but, if irregular, can also be predictive of infants' risk level for later developmental problems (Myers et al., 1997). Irregular patterns may signal an impaired neurological system, which is related to future problems such as attention difficulties and mental vulnerabilities.

Reflexes

At birth, infants exhibit some inborn, genetic movements or **reflexes** that help them to interact with their world and survive. Reflexes are only elicited by specific environmental stimuli and may be a signal of whether the infant's nervous system is intact and mature (Illingworth, 1991). Some of the more general and basic reflexes are listed here and defined below:

- Rooting
- Sucking
- Grasping
- Stepping

The **rooting** reflex happens when you touch a newborn's cheek. The infant will turn his or her head that way in search of something to suck. The **sucking** reflex occurs in response to something touching his or her mouth or lips, which causes the infant to suck. These two reflexes, rooting and sucking, usually occur together, because both are related to feeding behavior. Also present at birth is the **grasping** reflex, which happens when a small object is placed in a baby's hand. The baby reflexively grasps the object very strongly and tightly to hold on to it. Not long after, at about 3 or 4 months, this reflex is replaced by voluntary and purposeful grasping, which help an infant interact with and explore his or her world. The last important newborn reflex is **stepping**. Whenever an infant's bare feet touch a flat surface, the infant reflexively takes steps forward in a rhythmic fashion. This reflex, a precursor to walking, disappears as a baby's legs grow bigger and heavier (Thelen, 1995).

Motor Skills

There are also a number of motor skills that are acquired in phases during the early childhood period. Some of the skills acquired in infancy and toddlerhood are fine motor, gross motor, and self-help. We begin by discussing the fine motor skills of young children.

Fine Motor Skills

Grasping an object and playing with it may seem fairly simple, but in reality it is a complex function. **Fine motor skills** require voluntary and intentional movement of the fingers, hands, arms, and eyes. **Prereaching**, the first step to acquiring fine motor skills, occurs when infants clumsily reach for or swat at objects in their visual field. This type of "grasping" is visually elicited but not visually guided. In other words, the infants reach for the object because they see it but do not use their vision to guide their hand movements (Bushnell, 1985). Rudimentary forms of this show early, at birth, and change around the age of 6 weeks. During this period of change, infants spend more time looking at their hands (Van Hofsten, 1984; Williams, 1983). Eventually, the infants learn visually guided reaching.

Near the age of 3 months, the second stage manifests, during which **visually directed reaching** begins. While reaching to grasp an object at this stage, infants use their eyes to examine the target object's position and to guide the movement of their hand in an attempt to grasp the object. At 8 months of age this process reaches another level of complexity (Haywood, 1993). Infants use both arms and hands in an independent, yet coordinated, fashion when reaching and grasping for objects. Even with these advances, infants have not reached an adult level of this fine motor skill.

Infants obtain adult-type grasping, **prehension**, around 12 months of age, which can be observed in their ability to use their thumb and forefinger to pick up objects. A preliminary milestone for prehension comes at 9 months when infants' ability to use their thumb greatly improves. For example, at approximately 9 months infants move their thumb in a wider range of motion, and then at about 12 months they can pick up many objects such as a spoon. This new ability to grasp like an adult opens up opportunities for infants to learn about the objects in their world. Infants can now grasp objects, bring them close, and explore them. Grasping and the other fine motor skills listed in Table 5.1 all develop in phases.

Gross Motor Skills

Large muscle control, necessary for using **gross motor skills**, develops in a universal sequence with averages and ranges much like the small muscle control that is required for fine motor skills. Sitting, crawling, and walking all happen in the same general sequence for all infants. Gross motor skills, as a set, begin with head control.

Head control means infants are able to keep their head steady in an upright position and move it voluntarily. The infant's muscles and nervous system must develop appropriately for head control to be possible. Head control is generally achieved at the age of 3 months (Frankenburg et al., 1992) and is usually established before an infant can acquire other gross motor skills.

Table 5.1	Milestones of Fine Motor Development

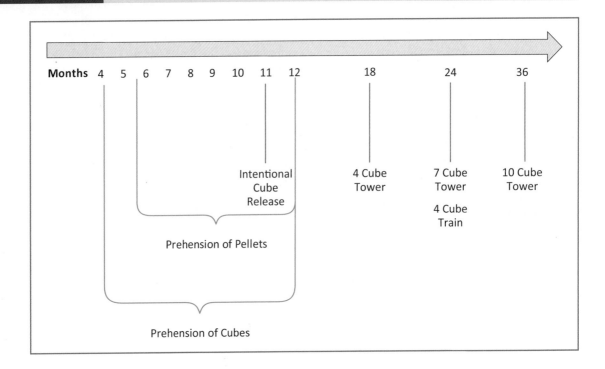

Rolling from side to side is another motor milestone that exhibits large muscle control. By the age of 6 months, infants should be able to roll from their back to their stomach and from their stomach to their back. Rolling becomes more coordinated and smooth as the infant gains strength and control (Frankenburg et al., 1992). Having this ability helps an infant to gain locomotion, or movement.

Infants begin **sitting** on their own at around 7 months. At first, infants lean forward a little. As they gain balance and support, they do not need to lean forward to sit independently (Frankenburg et al., 1992). By 9 months, infants become better at sitting and maneuvering from the sitting position, which leads to creeping.

Creeping, or what the layperson calls crawling, begins around 9 months. However, it can start as early as 5 months or as late as 15 months. The technical definition of creeping is getting around on the hands and knees or the hands and feet. Once an infant begins creeping, caregivers must remain vigilant and think about the child's safety (Gordon Rouse, 1998), as the child does not fully understand the danger possible in some behaviors. This is a time of great development, learning, and possible resilience (Bertenthal, Campos, & Bennett, 1984; Gordon Rouse, 1998). As young children creep through their environment, they encounter people and objects and can explore them more closely and increase competence.

Soon after learning to creep, infants begin pulling themselves up to the standing position. Usually by 10 to 13 months infants are stable enough to stand by themselves and on their own volition. In the standing position, infants can learn more and more about objects and people in their environment because their hands are free to explore.

Learning to walk follows learning to stand, usually around 12 months (Frankenburg et al., 1992). However, walking can emerge as early as 9 or 10 months as demonstrated by the scenario about the young twins at the beginning of this chapter. Children's walking is unstable until about 3 years of age. Furthermore, mature adultlike walking does not occur until the child is approximately 7 years old.

Despite their instability, infants attempt **running** by the age of 18 months. However, their running is not mature, and children have an obvious point where their whole body is in the air (off the ground) until around the age of 2 years. Running continues to develop into the early childhood years and beyond, as movements become more balanced and coordinated (Gallahue, 1982).

Gross motor skill development is important for you, as a teacher, to understand. As with all milestones, you can interact with children much more effectively and have realistic expectations of their abilities and the activities that they can perform. Realistic expectations are important for this next set of motor skills, too.

Self-Help Skills

The next set of skills includes dressing and hand washing and increases children's independence and impacts their resilience or ability to thrive and survive (Gordon Rouse, 1998). These **self-help skills** are sometimes called adaptive behavior, because they help young children adapt to their environment. The times at which these kinds of skills develop depend on environmental experience and exposure to challenging tasks, a child's internal motivation, and pure biological maturation. Part of your job as a caregiver is helping children to become self-sufficient. Knowing when to expect these skills to emerge can help you plan your curriculum and daily routines.

The development of self-help skills allows a young child to develop more independence.

Infants begin to help with **dressing** themselves around 12 months. They start by helping with undressing; perhaps they remove their socks. Help with dressing starts with pushing their hands and feet through shirts and pants. However, it is not until 3 years old or later that they can completely dress themselves. Even at 3 years old, they may still have trouble tying, buttoning, and zipping (Frankenburg et al., 1992). You, as a teacher, need to have realistic expectations of young children's abilities in this area of development. In general, don't push them too fast or hamper their development by helping them when they do not need it.

Self-feeding begins around 7 months, when infants can grasp small pieces of food and place them in their mouths. They can also hold a small spoon. This ability improves around 12 months, again at 18 months, and then again at 24 months, when an infant is fairly proficient with a spoon (Gesell & Ilg, 1937).

Potty training can begin when infants are maturationally able to control elimination, somewhere between 15 and 18 months. However, some believe it is better to wait until 24 months to potty train (Shelov, 1998; White, 1975). This is because a 24-month-old is more biologically and emotionally mature. Most children are potty trained by 3 years of age, but some take longer (Broude, 1995). What is important for a teacher of young children to know is that biological maturation and emotional readiness will signal when each individual child can control his or her elimination.

The Development of Coordinated Movement

Another view of gross motor development, which comes from a Montessori and European perspective, is the development of coordinated movement (Montanaro, 2002). This perspective is introduced in the chapter on types of programs (Chapter 3). According to this viewpoint, coordinated movement develops much as humans have developed through evolution in three stages: slithering, crawling, and walking. Furthermore, this point of view stresses that movement is pleasurable for the young child, which suggests that movement has important implications for psychological development (both cognitive and social). Additionally, this outlook suggests that movement aids in myelinization and other brain developments. Of course, the amount of pleasure and development that the child gains from movement depends on the individual child and the environmental arrangements. This is a point that the parents of our twin Jake from the opening scenario should consider. Jake's parents could have some impact on his abilities to use coordinated movement by the manner in which they arrange his environment. This is also true for the early childhood teachers in Jake's life. More ideas about how to make the most of coordinated movement, a gross motor skill, and more information about the Montessori perspective will be discussed in other areas of the text. Another type of development that is closely related to coordinated movement is perception (see Chapter 4).

Perceptual Development

As stated earlier, **perception** is related to coordinated movement. Perception, or the use of the senses, is important for young children to explore, grow, and develop. A bit of novelty and stimulation to be perceived by the senses is important for brain development and reaching milestones (Nutbrown, 2006). Many senses are developed in a rudimentary manner before birth, and the senses continue to develop and improve throughout early childhood. **Taste**, for instance, is mature at 14 weeks of **gestation** (or 14 weeks after conception). At birth, infants can discriminate between sweet, sour, and bitter tastes. By the age of 2 years, they have a sense of what should and should not be salted. Again, understanding these milestones helps you as a teacher to interact with young children, be aware of their food likes or dislikes, and have more realistic expectations of them. This way you will know what changes and occurrences are to come.

The sense of taste is closely connected to the sense of smell and develops similarly. The organs that allow a baby to **smell** are mature before birth, but research has not shown us whether an infant can smell before birth (Bossey, 1980; Varendi, Porter, & Weinberg, 1997). It is true, though, that infants can smell at birth and discriminate odors (Steiner, 1977). Some researchers, however, disagree (Guillory, Self, & Paden, 1980). If indeed infants can smell at birth, it is important for you as the teacher to create an optimal environment that provides infants with experiences to use their sense of smell.

Touch, which develops first, is sometimes called the mother of all senses (Montagu, 1971). Some embryos can feel beginning at 7 weeks; for others the sense of touch appears when the fetus is 14 weeks. As with all milestones, there is an average development age and a range. Whenever the sense of touch does appear, it develops and matures a bit faster than other senses. At birth touch is one of the most complex senses (Eliot, 1999). After birth and indeed on into early childhood, touch plays an important role in human development and experience (Field, 1995) since it is crucial for brain development, emotional development, and social development. When an infant touches an

Consider This The Challenge of Teaching Infants

When Jordan obtained her degree, she did not want to be an infant teacher. However, she soon found out that infants are quite capable, and their senses are well developed. She found she was really able to teach them as much as she could teach children of other ages. As an added bonus, infants are such a delight. Jordan helped the infants develop their fine and gross motor skills. She taught them self-help skills and developed their senses.

She always tried to remain aware of the fact that infant brains are developing and making connections and tried to avoid overwhelming her students.

What are some strategies that you might use as an infant teacher to stimulate an infant's senses, yet still be developmentally appropriate?

object, brain connections are made. Feelings and emotions arise. Touch is also important for social interactions between human beings. Therefore, touch impacts human development even in infancy.

As is the case with other senses, **hearing** emerges even before birth. When the fetus is 5 or 6 months old, it can hear (Lecaunet, 1998). However, babies do not hear as well as adults. It is not until the age of 2 years that toddlers can hear high-frequency sounds much like an adult can (Werner & Van Den Bos, 1993). Hearing and the structures that support it continue to mature and improve into early childhood. Teachers would be wise to consider this when they interact with young children. That way infant teachers can be more intentional and careful when they make sounds around young children.

At birth, an infant can see, but **vision** is the newborn's least mature sense (Banks & Shannon, 1993). After birth, a series of vision milestones occur. Infants learn to recognize faces soon after birth and can differentiate between their mother and strangers (Bushnell & Sai, 1987). At 2 months, an infant can discriminate between two of the three primary colors (red, yellow, blue). By 6 weeks to 3 months, an infant has depth perception (Bertenthal & Campos, 1990). Visual acuity continues to improve until 4 years of age when adultlike 20/20 vision is attained (Teplin, 1995).

Physical and motor milestones are an appropriate place to begin because they serve as the basis for the development of milestones in other areas. Because these physical and motor milestones in some manner provide the basic living skills for a child, they lay the foundation for cognitive, linguistic, and emotional/social milestones. Some researchers even theorize that the interaction between perception and action is the main theoretical base for a young child's physical, cognitive, and social development (Bower, 1999). We now turn to a brief discussion of cognitive milestones, beginning with a section on how brain development influences cognition.

WHAT ARE THE MAJOR COGNITIVE MILESTONES?

Cognition or intellect is one of the most important areas of development that we will discuss, because it is a developmental area on which early childhood education focuses. However, because it is important to teach the whole child, educators should recognize the relationship between cognition or intellect and other areas of development, such as physical, brain, linguistic, and social, and plan their activities accordingly.

Brain Development

Brain development is quite important for cognitive development since all of a young child's learning is based on physical changes in the brain. In fact, teachers of young children actually change children's brains through education (Perry, 1990; Schiller, 1997). As young children learn and are educated, connections are made in the brain. However, some cognitive advances are not possible until the underlying brain matter supports them (Case, 1985). Therefore, brain development and cognitive development are intimately intertwined, and one could say that the two parallel each other.

A young child's early experiences with the environment (physical environment and human environment) are important for brain development and learning. However, it is important to note that early experiences do not determine what will happen in the future. These experiences just predispose a child to certain types of learning and development (W. Brown, 2000). In other words, early experiences make the child more receptive to certain types and patterns of development and learning. That is partially why our two twins are developing at slightly different rates and why their parents notice strengths and weaknesses and take their cues from their sons. Indeed, the experiences and environments created by parents and early childhood educators are very important because the early childhood years are optimal and active ones in terms of brain and cognitive development (Schiller, 1997).

The Practice of **Research** and **Theory**
Positive Relationships and Brain Development

In 2008 researchers Gilkerson and Klein edited a volume that provided pedagogical resources for teachers of young children. This volume (Gilkerson & Klein, 2008) focuses on current and cutting-edge brain research. The most striking information according to the authors of this textbook is found in the fourth chapter where the importance of positive relationships is discussed. It is obvious that positive relationships impact socioemotional development. However, they also impact brain development, young children's reactions to stress, and young children's academic achievement. How does this information influence the practice of a professional early childhood educator? Gilkerson and Klein (2008) had these suggestions:

- Think about your relationships with children and their parents.

- Think about how you support parent-child and peer relationships.
- Think about the importance of positive emotion in these relationships.
- Think about collaborating with parents, especially when teaching children how to regulate intense emotions.

The authors of the textbook also suggest that teachers of young children do the following:

- Make the learning experiences of the children as emotionally positive as possible.
- Consider young children's individual manner of expressing emotion and respect those individual differences.
- Be an ideal model of relationship building and positive emotional expression.

Perceptual Organization

As children mature, their senses become integrated. In other words, as children develop and their neural systems mature, they begin to be able to taste what they smell and see what they touch (Bahrick & Lickliter, 2000). In fact, they search for sensory integrating experiences (Bahrick & Lickliter, 2000). For example, young children would rather listen to music while watching it being produced by other humans than just hear the music alone. Because sensory experiences help develop children's perceptual systems, it is important for adults, parental figures, and educators to provide children with sensory-rich environmental experiences. These rich environmental experiences help with building neuronal networks and help to organize a child's brain perceptually. This leads to optimally organized brain development, which helps with learning and development in other areas.

Cross-modal perception, the ability to integrate and coordinate information from two or more modalities, or senses, develops and enriches over time. Rudimentary cross-modal perception is present at birth (Mendelson & Haith, 1976). Vision and sound seem to show evidence of being integrated at first (Lewkowicz, 1996). Within the first year of life, infants can coordinate facial movement and vocal sounds (Soken & Pick, 1992). For example, they recognize the facial movements that correspond with the word *hello*. These types of coordination facilitate perceptual organization, brain development, and cognitive development, as well as signal that a child is developing at a normal rate. Early weaknesses or issues in cross-modal perception signal problems with processing information and delays in cognitive development (Sears, 1994).

Cognitive Development

The hallmark theory of cognitive development belongs to Jean Piaget (1952, 1954). Piaget theorized four stages of cognitive development, but only three of these stages occur during the early childhood years (Piaget, 1952, 1954). Even though a few cognitive researchers and theorists have found some weaknesses and inaccuracies in Piaget's theory, his theory is utilized extensively by early childhood educators. Afterward, neo-Piagetians extended and reaffirmed his findings (Case, 1985). The basic premise of Piaget's findings is that children construct their world differently at the various stages of cognitive development. The coverage of Piaget in this chapter gives a general overview of the stages and milestones, but his theory was covered in more depth in Chapter 4.

Piaget's first stage is sensorimotor. During this stage of development, which begins at birth and ends at approximately 18 months, young children come to know their world through their senses and their actions upon it. They construct their world with their senses and motor movements. As a result, their cognitive thoughts consist simply of sensory and motor experiences. To a young child in this stage, an apple is sweet or cold, because a child can sense coldness or sweetness. A child cannot sense whether an apple is alive or dead. There are six substages to the sensorimotor period, which are described in Chapter 4.

Following the sensorimotor stage is the **preoperational** stage. During this stage, approximately 18 months to 6 years of age, children know their world through concrete symbols (concrete objects). The hallmark ability for entry into this stage is object permanence. As described in Chapter 4, obtaining object permanence means a child realizes that an object exists even though he or she does not see it. However, young children cannot yet think logically about concrete or abstract objects or events or ideas. For instance, an apple symbolizes something to eat in the thoughts of children at this stage. They can also begin to learn how to spell and read the word *apple*. However, they can get confused and think that one apple is really two apples if the one apple is cut in half. Children during this stage are also **egocentric**. In other words, as you may recall from Chapter 4, children believe everyone sees the world from their point of view. On a positive note, the **symbolic thought** that happens during this period allows children to enrich their play experiences by allowing an object to symbolize something else. A piece of chalk or a crayon can become a choo-choo train or a car. This use of symbolic thought is indicative of a higher level of cognition.

With the advent of symbolic thought, a higher cognitive level of play is possible.

Piaget's third stage, called concrete operational, spans from approximately 6 to 8 years of age through 11 years (see Chapter 4). When children are in this stage, they can "conserve" and think logically about concrete objects and events. Children at this stage know that an apple cut in half is still one apple. They also know that apples come in several colors, such as green, yellow, and red. Children at this stage are less egocentric as they have begun to realize that more than one vantage point exists. They can also solve simple addition and subtraction problems with concrete objects. Learning about Piaget helps you, as a teacher, plan cognitive (educational) interactions with children and obtain optimal development.

Beyond Piaget

Piaget's theory is utilized extensively in the field of early childhood education (Bredekamp & Copple, 1997). Teachers use his constructivist approach and stages both to create lesson plans and to coordinate lesson plans with developmentally appropriate practice. However, there are a few weaknesses in his theory as discovered by some researchers. Most encouragingly for the professional early childhood educator, new research shows that children accomplish some tasks sooner than the age Piaget identified (Case, 1985; Flavell, 1992). More important, neo-Piagetians have continued

Piaget's work and improved upon it. They have made discoveries that show his stages correspond with major neurological developments in the brain (R. Case, personal communication, May 1990). Below, we will discuss some of the limitations of Piaget's theory, which have led to additional discoveries about cognition.

The Weaknesses in Piaget's Original Theory

These types of math skills require concrete thought.

The main weakness in Piaget's theory was stated above: Children can accomplish some tasks sooner than his stated ages (Case, 1985; Flavell, 1992). Additionally, some cognitive theorists have shown that cognition does not develop in one unitary, qualitative stage. Instead cognition changes in frequency, size, and amount. In other words, thought changes in number and not in type or in stages (Flavell, 1992), according to information processing theorists. Along with these slight flaws in Piaget's theory came the discovery that children's thinking may progress unevenly in different domains. In other words, a child may be at one stage in the domain of mathematics and at another stage in the domain of English. Children's thinking has an element of **domain specificity**. Domain specificity, a discovery of neo-Piagetians, is illustrated quite well by the twins in our opening scenario. Jake has more advanced thought in the domain of physical development whereas his brother, Luke, excels in the academic, intellectual, and creative domains.

The Work of the Neo-Piagetians

Robbie Case, the leading neo-Piagetian before his early passing, conducted research and created theories that integrated the information processing approach to cognition with Piaget's developmental approach. Case (1985) discovered that the mind develops much like a "staircase," which has horizontal and vertical structure. In other words, the brain develops qualitatively and quantitatively in parallel fashion. Therefore, both Piaget and the information processors are correct. The major excitement about the neo-Piagetian discoveries results from the findings of "stage-like" cognitive developments that occur in concert with major neurological shifts in the brain (R. Case, personal communication, May 1990), findings that show the relationship between the information processing approach to cognition and the developmental approach.

Memory

Cognitive researchers known as information processors (Flavell, 1992; Siegler, 1996) study the quantity of the changes that take place in a child's cognition or intellect. These researchers examine how the brain takes in, processes, stores, and puts out information. They also examine brain abilities such as memory: how it works and changes with time. Unlike Piaget and neo-Piagetians, however, information processing researchers do not talk about stages. Instead, their discussion is based on the ways in which brain and cognitive functions change in frequency, quantity, or amount. Their research has found that being able to work with larger amounts of memory helps with information processing as well as cognitive storage and output. In general, humans use memory strategies to remember information. The ability to use these strategies increases with age and experience. The more information in storage, the better and stronger are the synaptic connections. Thus adults would have a greater capacity for memory than children, because they have more experience and more information in storage.

Promoting Optimal Development

Navigating the 5- to 7-Year-Old Shift

The key difference between a 4½-year-old and a 7½-year-old when it comes to learning is that with the 7½-year-old there is more complex thought and a different level of motivation (Sameroff & McDonough, 1994). This does not mean that very young preschool children cannot learn complex skills or that you must wait to teach specific skills until a child is 7 years old. Rather, even preschool children can learn such skills and become ready for more advanced education if the teaching is done appropriately. First, the teacher needs to analyze and simplify the skill. Then he or she should embed the learning of the skill in a meaningful social or cultural context and provide motivational incentives for the child. For instance, the teacher can help students learn addition by using actual pennies that can then be spent to buy something from the "goody" jar. This type of approach to learning helps to optimize the child's cognitive development.

As children grow, develop, and mature, they become cognitively ready for conservation and abstraction, and they can learn for the sake of learning (Sameroff & McDonough, 1994). Hypothetically, an early elementary-aged child does not need a specific context, simplification, or extra motivation to learn any longer. However, all good early childhood educators keep motivation and context in mind. They also remember that the best way to promote optimal development, during the cognitive shift that happens between ages 5 and 7 years, is to keep in mind the child's individual characteristics, have an understanding of the child's home life and culture, and get an idea of the amount and quality of the child's previous experience in group learning settings.

Knowing how the brain processes information is helpful for an early childhood educator in creating lesson plans that accommodate children's memory capacity and strategies, since children are not as sophisticated as adults. However, this accommodation changes with time; once a child obtains **metamemory** between ages 5 and 7 (Janowsky & Carper, 1996), more advanced lesson plans are possible. Metamemory is the ability to think about and control one's own memory. For instance, teaching children who have no memory strategies in their repertoire is different from teaching children who actively use and control their memory strategies. Once children are aware that they have a memory, recognize that it sometimes works better than other times, and know that they can control it, their learning capacity greatly improves. Thus, more complex educational approaches and plans are possible (see Figure 5.2).

WHAT ARE THE MAJOR LANGUAGE MILESTONES?

The stages and milestones of language development mentioned in this section of the chapter serve as a brief introduction to material that will be covered in Chapter 12. Let us begin by exploring how the foundation of **language** (which allows young children to express their needs, emotions, and desires and give and receive information) relies on brain development and by examining the relationship that exists between cognition and language.

Brain Development

As we mentioned in the section on physical milestones, the brain is still developing during early childhood. Indeed it keeps developing on into adulthood (Schiller, 2001). As we saw with cognitive

Figure 5.2 **School Supplies for an Early Elementary Student**

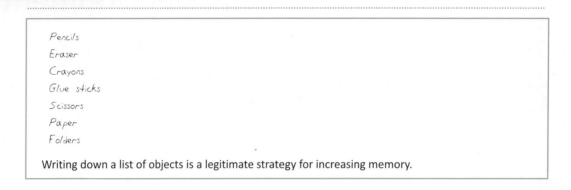

Pencils
Eraser
Crayons
Glue sticks
Scissors
Paper
Folders

Writing down a list of objects is a legitimate strategy for increasing memory.

development and brain development, there is delicate interplay between language development and brain development (Schiller, 1997). Having a safe and rich environment aids in brain development, and in turn as the brain develops it affords a child language (Perry, 2007b). Not surprisingly, there is also a relationship between cognition and language.

Relationship Between Cognition and Language

This relationship between cognition and language led Chomsky (1968) to theorize a "language acquisition device," which some believe is a young child's cognition. This language acquisition device makes early childhood an optimal time for learning one or more languages. Other researchers such as Piaget and the neo-Piagetians (Case, 1985) also recognized a relationship between cognition and language. These researchers posit that a certain level of cognitive development is needed before language can be produced and understood. Even information processing researchers (Flavell, 1992) recognize that most information is processed in the brain with language made up of words and sentences.

The Beginnings of Language

As a child matures, language becomes the major avenue for communication. But communication begins at birth with an infant's cry. An infant's cries vary in intensity and pitch depending on what he or she is trying to communicate (Lester & Boukydis, 1985). The next step in communication comes when infants begin to discern the speech sounds in their environment and attempt to produce them. Infants also come to understand the meanings of the speech sounds around them (Jusczyk & Hohne, 1997). However, they mainly communicate with facial and bodily expressions and gestures until 3 months of age when they produce intentional coos and speech sounds (Lalonde & Werker, 1995).

Phases or Stages of Language Development

In general terms, language develops rapidly during the infant and toddler years as demonstrated by Table 5.2. After the toddler years, language improves in terms of vocabulary size, grammar, syntax (sentence structure), and pragmatics (use) as children grow and develop. Understanding the phases of language development helps you as a teacher to facilitate its growth. The progression toward uttering the first word typically moves in this way:

- At 3 months a baby coos (makes intentional vowel-like speech sounds).
- At 6 months a baby babbles (makes consonant-vowel speech sounds such as *baa-baa*).
- At 9 months a baby produces **echolalia** (makes sounds that approximate words).
- At 12 months a baby produces his or her first word (makes a sound like a real word that actually refers to a person or an object).

Table 5.2   Language Milestones From Birth to 3 Years

AGE	MILESTONE	ASPECT OF LANGUAGE			
		PHONOLOGY	MORPHOLOGY & SEMANTICS	SYNTAX	PRAGMATICS
Birth	Crying	X			X
	Speech perception	X			
	Sound response	X			X
1 to 4 Months	Speaking voice Response and attention	X			X
	Cooing (vowels)	X			
	Vocalizes to social stimulus	X	X		X
5 to 10 Months	Babbles (consonants and vowels)	X			
	Echolalia (sounds that approximate words)	X			
	Understands some words		X		
	Uses and understands gestures		X		X
12 Months	Says first word		X		
	Can't discriminate sounds not in own language	X	X		X
13 to 14 Months	Understands symbols and the naming function		X		X
	Uses elaborate gestures		X		X
	Uses symbolic gesturing		X		X
16 to 24 months	Rapidly expanding vocabulary		X		X
	Uses verbs and adjectives	X	X	X	X
	Two-word utterances telegraphic speech	X	X	X	X

(Continued)

(Continued)

AGE	MILESTONE	ASPECT OF LANGUAGE			
		PHONOLOGY	MORPHOLOGY & SEMANTICS	SYNTAX	PRAGMATICS
	Vocalizes needs	X			X
	Comprehension spurt		X		
	Vocabulary from 250 to 400 words		X		
	Pronouns, prepositions, simple sentences, phrases			X	
	Conversational turn-taking				X
30 to 36 months	Three or more word utterances			X	
	Some grammatical errors			X	
	Expressive language of 1,000 words	X	X		X
	Syntactical errors		X	X	

Source: Adapted from Feldman, Olds, & Papalia, (2007); Snow & McGaha, (2003); Carmichael, L. (Ed.), (1954).

Young children begin with simple utterances and understand more than they can produce. After the first word is produced a child's language development keeps enriching and developing in all language structures, such as grammar, syntax, and pragmatics. By the time children reach 8 years old, they have a more precise vocabulary and use language much more as an adult (Anderson, Clark, & Mullin, 1994; Owens, 1996; Vosniadou, 1987).

As children's language develops, their grammar expands. Roger Brown (1973) uncovered specific stages of grammar expansion, which can be summarized as follows:

- Stage 1 is **two-word utterances/telegraphic speech**. (A young child produces telegraphic speech by saying phrases such as "up mama.")
- Stage 2 involves utterances slightly longer than two words. (Young children produce sentences from approximately three to five words long with the addition of prepositions, articles, case markers, regular past tense, and regular plurals. For instance, a child might say, "I love mama.")
- Stage 3 is exemplified by simple modified sentences. (Young children produce creative negative sentences, make demands, and ask yes/no questions. They also create original sentences and use active and passive voice. (To illustrate, a child may create a sentence such as "I don't like peas.")
- Stages 4 and 5 include complex sentences. (Young children in Stage 4 can use subordinate clauses, compound sentences, and complex sentences and in Stage 5 increasingly come to understand how to use syntax and how to structure sentences. Sentences children use in these stages are ones such as "I want to go with [or without] you.")

Brown (1973) demonstrated in his research that by the age of 8 years a young child has mastered grammar much the same as an adult. Clearly, a majority of language development occurs in the early childhood period, and children's caregivers will play a major role in facilitating this development.

The Development of Speech

Speech specifically involves producing word sounds whereas language refers to a whole system of communication. Speech development usually follows language development because young children can understand more language than they can produce. Since speech involves articulation and coordination of muscles, it can be much more complicated. Speech, however, is the method through which most language development is measured (Hammer, 1998).

The Development of Literacy

Children's speech and language development impact their development of literacy, which is another language milestone. **Literacy** in the early childhood years involves just a basic awareness and understanding of language. Children go through stages in learning to read and write, and these skills go hand in hand with each other (Rosberg, 1995).

During the first stage of reading, **preliteracy**, children learn the reasons for reading and writing and make their first attempts (see Table 5.3). With the next stage, **phonemic awareness**, comes an understanding of the structure of reading and writing. Children at this stage understand how words and sentences are put together and can be broken down into smaller parts. Next, young children become aware of symbolic meanings. In other words, they realize that the pencil marks are representations of some object or person.

Table 5.3	Favorite Books

INFANT/TODDLER BOOKS

Ten Little Fingers and Ten Little Toes by Mem Fox
Mama Cat Has Three Kittens by Denise Fleming

Pat the Bunny by Dorothy Kunhardt

Where's Spot? by Eric Hill

Goodnight Moon by Margaret Wise Brown

Brown Bear, Brown Bear by Bill Martin, Jr.

The Very Hungry Caterpillar by Eric Carle

If You Give a Mouse a Cookie by Laura Numeroff

PRESCHOOL BOOKS

Owl Moon by Joan Yolen

Chika Chika Boom Boom by Bill Martin, Jr.

Wemberly Worried by Kevin Henkes

Blue Chameleon by Emily Gravett

Happy Birthday Moon by Frank Asch

EARLY ELEMENTARY BOOKS

Ling and Tang: Not Exactly the Same by Grace Lin

Miss Brooks Loves Books (and I Don't) by Barbara Bottner

The Willoughbys by Lois Lowry

Bunnicula: A Rabbit Tale of Mystery by Deborah Howe

Source: Adapted from Hammer (1998).

The first stage of writing is called **recurring**. This is where children repeat the same strokes. After this, children learn the **generative principle**. With this awakening they come to understand that there are rules for putting letters and other writing elements together. Next young children learn the **flexibility principle** during the **sign and message stage**. They realize letters can be put together in varied arrangements to produce new words, and words can be used to produce sentences. The final stage of writing is the **constructive stage**, during which children compare and contrast letters and words (Rosberg, 1995).

The development of reading skills and that of writing skills are dependent on one another and occur simultaneously. After acquiring preliteracy skills, children can move on to become literate, actually reading and producing writing. Also developing around this time and related to language development is **storytelling**.

Writing begins very simply but develops into complex, adult-like lettering.

The Development of Storytelling

It is not surprising that the ability to tell stories develops with language. Additionally, allowing children to tell their own stories helps with language development (Marjanovic-Umek, Kranjc, & Fekonja, 2002). The development of storytelling happens roughly in three phases. When 4-year-olds tell a story, it usually has no structure, and the children repeat themselves often. Six-year-olds, on the other hand, tell stories with structured patterns and sequence events temporally. Eight-year-old storytellers can do what the 6-year-olds have accomplished, and they create more elaborate stories by giving more details. Eight-year-olds also relay thoughts and feelings with appropriate connections in their stories, and they understand causal relationships.

These differences in storytelling abilities can be understood by looking at a hypothetical illustration of children telling "Goldilocks" at the different ages. A 4-year-old would say something such as "Goldilocks ate the food. The bear got mad, and Goldilocks went to sleep. The end." In contrast, a 6-year-old might say, "Goldilocks ate the little bear's food and then went to bed. The bears came home and found her in the little bear's bed. Suddenly Goldilocks woke up and went home." An 8-year-old's story might be structured in the same manner as the 6-year-old's story; however, the older child would add phrases such as "Goldilocks was hungry. The bears were mad and Goldilocks was scared." An 8-year-old might say, "Goldilocks ate the bears' food because she was hungry, and then she went to bed. The bears came home and found her in the little bear's bed. This made the bears mad! When Goldilocks woke up, she got scared and ran home." As a child's language develops, her storytelling abilities increase. Knowledge of these developments helps you as a teacher to provide children with preliteracy activities (storytelling and prewriting, for example)

Storytelling abilities develop right along with language.

that help them to meet their full potential, and this knowledge also helps you to better assess children's development.

Language is one of the major avenues of communication, and communicating with others helps young children to be social beings. Becoming aware of and communicating emotions are excellent methods to maintain social relationships. This ability to maintain social relationships can be indicative of how young children are developing socially and emotionally, too. These emotional and social milestones will be outlined in the next section.

WHAT ARE THE MAJOR EMOTIONAL AND SOCIAL MILESTONES?

Brain Development

Emotional and social development are related to brain development in that brain development and growth happen much better in a safe emotional and social environment (Perry, 2007b). When the brain is stressed, it produces the substance **cortisol**, and this interferes with brain functioning, growth, and development. This is just one way that brain development and emotional/social development interact. Brain development, much in the same manner as it influences cognitive and language development, influences and supports emotional/social development and provides a foundation for optimal emotional/social enrichment (Perry, 2007b).

A stressful environment is not conducive to brain development or learning.

Beginning Social Relationships

An infant's first relationships begin within the family, and both mother and father play an important role (Malatesta & Haviland, 1982; Whaley, 1990 [see Table 5.4.]). Infants depend on parents to care for them, play with them, and teach them how to love. The manner in which mothers and fathers care for and play with their infants has a great influence on how infants of every ethnic group develop in the emotional/social realm (Kelley, Smith, Green, Berndt, & Rodgers, 1998; Malatesta & Haviland, 1982; Whaley, 1990).

Stages of Attachment

Attachment is a bond or an emotional tie to another person who plays a special role in the infant's life (Klaus & Kennell, 1982; Maccoby, 1980). Infants' primary caregivers are their first attachment figures or love objects. This is usually the mother, but it can be the father (Lamb & Bornstein, 1987). General characteristics of attachment and the categories of attachment are discussed in Chapter 11, but the stages of attachment are mentioned briefly here since they indicate social and emotional milestones. In a hallmark study, Bowlby (1969) uncovered the stages of attachment, shown in Table 5.5. Earlier, however, Schaffer and Emerson (1964) uncovered similar stages of attachment, also shown in Table 5.5. To summarize and paraphrase the findings, in Stage 1 a child cannot tell the difference between one person and another or one person and inanimate stimuli; in Stage 2 children begin to prefer people and, more specifically, certain people over others; in Stage 3 children are clearly attached to one or two caregivers and use them as a secure base from which to explore their social and physical world; and in Stage 4 the number of people to whom children attach increases, as they begin to realize that their needs may be met by more than one or two people and may even realize that their needs will not always be met as soon as they would like.

Table 5.4   Whaley's Stages of Infant-Adult Social Play

AGE	0–4 MONTHS	4–8 MONTHS	7–13 MONTHS	13–18 MONTHS	18–24 MONTHS
Stage	Complementary/ reciprocal social play	Complementary/ reciprocal play with mutual awareness	Simple social/ simple object play	Object play with mutual regard	Simple parallel play
Interaction	Face-to-face smiles, sounds, and gazes; adult as object	Adult provides objects, observes child, and supports child	Adult is base of support; child obtains own objects; child engages in parallel play with peers	Child focuses on objects and adults simultaneously in games and conversations	Independent play with adults and/ or peers near

Source: Adapted from Snow & McGaha (2003); Whaley (1990).

Table 5.5   Various Stages of Attachment

Bowlby (1969), who identified four stages in the formation of attachment:

1. *Preattachment: Undiscriminating social responsiveness* (birth to 8–12 weeks). During this phase, infants do not typically differentiate one person from another and can be comforted by anyone.

2. *Beginnings of attachment: Discriminating social responsiveness* (3 to 6–8 months). The infant begins to recognize the primary caregiver and a few other familiar people. These preferred adults are usually able to soothe the baby and elicit social responses more quickly than strangers.

3. *Clear-cut attachment: Maintaining proximity* (6–8 months to about 3 years). Around the middle of the first year, infants are typically attached to one specific person. This person is usually the mother, although some infants prefer the father or other caregivers.

4. *Formation of a goal-corrected partnership* (3–4 years and on). This phase begins when children recognize that other people have needs and desires of their own and that the mother has to give priority to other activities at times.

Four Stages of Attachment

1. *Asocial phase* (0–6 weeks). Many kinds of social and/or nonsocial stimuli produce a favorable reaction. At the end of this period infants show a preference for social stimuli, such as a smiling face.

2. *Phase of indiscriminate attachments* (6 weeks to 6–7 months). Infants enjoy human attention in an indiscriminate fashion. They enjoy attention from all humans, including strangers.

3. *Specific attachment phase* (about 7–9 months). A specific attachment to a primary caregiver occurs. Infants want to be close to this primary attachment figure. Infants protest when separated from this attachment figure and greet the attachment figure warmly upon return.

4. *Phase of multiple attachments* (about 7–9 months to 18 months). Soon after the first attachment bond is made, infants become able to attach to other adults and caregivers.

Source: Adapted from Snow & McGaha (2003); Shaffer, (2005).

Attachment is very important for a young child's development in all areas, and most early childhood educators play an important role as attachment figures. The topic of attachment is the subject of contemporary research in early childhood education and will be explored further in Chapter 11. Now let us look briefly at another area of social and emotional development, Erik Erikson's stages of psychosocial development, a topic that was covered in Chapter 4.

Psychosocial Development

Erikson (1963, 1982) delineates a total of eight stages of what he terms psychosocial development. Only four of the stages pertain to the early childhood period: trust versus mistrust, autonomy versus shame and doubt, initiative versus guilt, and industry versus inferiority.

Erikson created these stages based on psychosocial crises that occur in the child's life. In the first stage, infants must come to make sense of and trust their environment. In the second stage, toddlers must come to understand and to control their competencies and their own body. In the third stage, preschoolers come to explore their physical and social world. In the fourth stage, early elementary students begin comparing themselves with their peers and competing with their peers. Obviously, there is more to these stages than what has been briefly relayed here. Chapter 4 further expounded on the ideas and concepts of Erikson's theory as it is a foundational and hallmark theory of early childhood education. During each stage early childhood education teachers, as well as parents, need to be cognizant of how they interact with the young children they encounter, since the children's success in reaching each of these milestones depends on adult interaction to some degree. How well children resolve these crises depends on the adults in their social environment.

Friendships or Peer Relationships

Just as the adults in children's lives are important for their development, their peers play a vital role. Peer relationships make a unique contribution to children's lives above and beyond the contributions made by adults. And most surprisingly, peer relationships (or friendships) begin to develop early.

There are important friendships with peers that occur during the first year of life. These relationships consist of simple and direct behaviors (Eckerman & Whatley, 1977) that begin about the age of 2 months. Infants look at each other, touch each other, and smile at and talk to each other (Field, 1990; Hartup, 1983). Smiling and talking begin around age 6 months. Infants even exhibit turn-taking behavior with each other by 12 months of age (Ross & Lollis, 1987). It is at this point that infants seem to consistently respond to each other's attempts at socializing.

Professionalism & Policy

Child Care and Attachment

The Convention on the Rights of the Child is a policy that has been adopted by all countries but two (Somalia and the United States). Article 18 states that both parents have responsibilities for the upbringing and development of the child. It also states that governments should ensure that children of working parents have the benefit of child care services. These two statements are important for early childhood professionals to know and remember.

This is particularly true for the attachment process. Since children can have multiple attachments, they can attach to both parents and their caregivers in child care. However, all of these relationships are important. Early attachment relationships shape future intimate relationships. Both parents and caregivers of children should work together to ensure that young children have secure attachments.

Between 12 months and 24 months, infant peer relationships become more complex. By 18 months, young children have playmate preferences that are reciprocal (Howes, 1987). This reciprocity means that both children like each other and want to be around each other. Near 24 months, their interactions are reciprocal, cooperative, and repetitive (Asher, Erdley, & Gabriel, 1994). During this period of time, toddlers play games, such as chase, and they exchange objects back and forth (Meltzoff & Moore, 1994; Sinclair, 1994). Researchers have concluded that toddlers' friendships are true relationships where sharing, loyalty, helpfulness, togetherness, mutual interest, preference, and positive affect all take place (Vandell & Mueller, 1980; Whaley & Rubenstein, 1994). Whaley and Rubenstein (1994) also discovered that toddlers feel distress when their friendships are terminated. From birth, peer relationships gradually gain importance in the child's life.

These friendships or peer relationships continue into the early childhood years. Despite the above findings, most researchers believe that infants do not have true friendships, but that real friendships start at age 3 years (Rubin, Bukowski, & Parker, 1998; Snyder, West, Stockemer, Gibbons, & Almquist-Parks, 1996). This fact just represents an area of disagreement that early childhood researchers have. The main point is that the quality of friendships changes at 3 years old. At that age, and indeed throughout early and middle childhood, children spend time with same-gender peers who exhibit similar behaviors and with whom they can play or do activities. During the early childhood years, children focus on concrete traits such as physical appearance and size when choosing friends (Furman & Bierman, 1983).

In the middle childhood years, friendships get more complex and are not based solely on concrete features. Children during this period still want same-gender friendships with peers around their same age, but they also try to find friends of the same ethnicity and friends who share their hobbies. At this stage, friends trust each other, are committed, and believe each other to be equals. Reciprocity is still a major element in friendships at this time (George & Hartmann, 1996; Hartup, 1992, 1996a, 1996b; Newcomb & Bagwell, 1995).

Peer and adult-child relationships, psychosocial stages, and phases of attachment are all important emotional/social milestones for early childhood teachers to understand because teachers play major socialization roles in the lives of young children, roles that can have a lasting impact on a child's social and emotional development.

Friendships at this age are based on characteristics such as loyalty and trust.

WHAT ARE SOME IMPLICATIONS OF DEVELOPMENTAL MILESTONES?

This chapter has briefly covered some of the developmental milestones that occur during a child's first 8 years of life. In later chapters of the text, some of the topics covered here will be revisited in more depth and with coverage of the various implications for early childhood teachers. The implications mentioned in this chapter focus on how milestones impact education and learning as well as how atypical development patterns apply to children who are gifted and those with special needs. In this next portion of the text, we will address how milestones, averages, and ranges, as well as individual differences, should be considered when creating strategies and lesson plans for teaching young children. Let's begin with education and learning.

Implications of Developmental Milestones for Education and Learning of All Young Children

The brain development research mentioned earlier supports several notions that can assist early childhood teachers in performing their duties. First, to provide optimal development for their students, they must try to create an emotionally safe classroom environment that is responsive to the children's interests (Perry, 2007a, 2007b). They must also consider six strategies brought forth by Dodge and Bikart (2000) in order to enrich the many developmental areas of the children they teach. These six strategies are as follows:

- Know the children.
- Create a classroom community.
- Establish a structure.
- Guide children's learning.
- Assess children's learning.
- Build a partnership with families.

All of these strategies are important for effective teaching, and their utilization can be enhanced by knowing developmental milestones. However, the strategy most impacted by developmental milestones is "know the children." Teachers who know the developmental milestones have the potential to know their children very well, which leads them to employ optimal teaching strategies and curricula. Moreover, when it comes to teaching young children, knowing the children may be the most important teaching strategy in order to facilitate learning.

Developmental Milestones and Atypical Development

As much as teachers can use milestones to develop effective environments and curricula, how can an early childhood educator continue to be responsive when teaching children who do not follow the typical developmental milestones? Some children develop faster, or others need more support to reach the typical averages and ranges of milestone development. What follows are some implications and considerations for teaching children who do not fit the typical pattern of development.

Children Who Are Gifted and Talented

Children who are gifted are at risk of losing motivation and becoming underachievers in terms of their overall development during the early years. They become at risk when they are misidentified as slow learners, placed in the wrong grade, or taught the wrong curriculum, or when they try to hide their ability from their peers (Gross, 1999). These problems can be particularly magnified in children who are highly gifted, that is, who have abilities that are beyond those of children who are traditionally gifted. The main solutions are to correctly identify these youngsters and to provide them with educational experiences that correspond to their needs (Gross, 1999).

Identification usually occurs through teachers, but parents can often recognize giftedness in their children as well. Utilization of more scenarios, testimonies, and anecdotes provided by parents can assist and greatly improve identification of young children who are gifted (Robinson, 1993).

Other methods of identifying young children who are gifted are psychometric and intellectual assessments. However, early childhood educators are more reluctant than middle childhood educators to use these methods. Also, the tests themselves may underestimate giftedness simply because of the child's fatigue and for a whole host of other reasons (Gross, 1999; Jackson & Klein, 1997). One way to assess a child who is gifted is by using an individual test with high ceilings (lots of succeeding items) that have been well designed (Gross, 1999). Sometimes multiple tests can be used, especially when assessing children who are ethnic minorities or from poverty (Plucker & Callahan, 2008). More information can be found in Chapters 6 and 7 of this textbook.

After a child has been identified as gifted, placement is also important. The best place for such a child may be the next highest grade level. This placement should occur only if the child is ready emotionally and socially, as well as intellectually and academically. The best determiners of this are the child, his or her parents, and his or her teachers (Gross, 1999).

Children With Special Needs

Another group of children who do not fit the developmental norms are those who need more support to reach their developmental milestones. As an early childhood education teacher, you may have the pleasure of working with children who need more support. This situation can be challenging, yet it brings rewards as you as the teacher observe the child participating in class, learning, and growing.

To best meet such a child's growth and educational needs, a teacher first needs an assessment of the child's developmental level in the area or topic of concern (Greenspan, 2004). A teacher

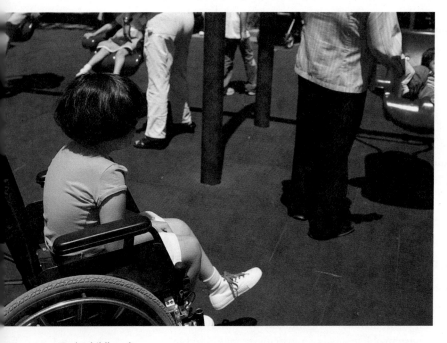

Early childhood educators must work to include all children in the educational interactions of the day.

can determine the child's level of development in mathematics or art, for instance. Assessment can occur formally with standardized tests or informally through teacher observation or portfolio (a collection of relevant work) assessment. After the assessment, a teacher can arrange educational experiences for this child that will help move him or her from the current developmental level to the next developmental level. This may entail devising individual lesson plans for the child and giving him or her more attention and support. When working with a child who has special needs, it is helpful to have a teacher's aide (Greenspan, 2004). Such an arrangement gives the child chances to have one-on-one time, to practice, and to actively engage and interact with a teacher.

If the teacher's interactions have been set at the correct level of development, the child will progress and grow. His or her progress, growth, and development should be observed over a period of approximately two or three months. If the child is learning, then the assessments, teaching strategies, and lesson plans have been appropriate (Greenspan, 2004). If the child is not learning, begin the process again with a more sensitive assessment and specifically focused lesson plans. In other words, early childhood teachers must adjust to the children in their care and must continue to adjust as the children learn to be sure they are making some progress. Teachers should not worry about trying to have the children "catch up" with their peers. Children will reach their own level (Greenspan, 2004). Making progress through the milestones, rather than catching up to their peers, is the most important measure of whether children are continuing to thrive.

Summary

In this chapter, we have examined very briefly some of the developmental milestones of the early childhood period. Exposure to these milestones will help you as a teacher to know the general expectations of all children and will allow you an intimate and dynamic understanding of the children with whom you work. It is important for early childhood teachers to know their children so that they can be more effective teachers.

Key Terms

Arousal states 115
Constructive stage 130
Cortisol 131
Creeping 118
Cross-modal perception 122
Domain specificity 124
Dressing 119
Echolalia 126
Egocentric 123
Fine motor skills 117
Flexibility principle 130
Generative principle 130
Gestation 120
Grasping 117
Gross motor skills 117
Head control 117
Hearing 121
Language 125
Lateralization 115

Literacy 129
Metamemory 125
Myelin sheaths 114
Neurons 114
Perception 120
Phonemic awareness 129
Plasticity 115
Potty training 119
Prehension 117
Preliteracy 129
Preoperational 123
Prereaching 117
Pruning 115
Recurring 130
Reflexes 116
Rolling 118
Rooting 116
Running 119
Self-feeding 119

Self-help skills 119
Sign and message stage 130
Sitting 118
Smell 120
Speech 129
Stepping 117
Storytelling 130
Sucking 116
Symbolic thought 123
Synapses 115
Synaptogenesis 115
Taste 120
Telegraphic speech 128
Touch 120
Two-word
    utterances 128
Vision 121
Visually directed
    reaching 117

Reflection, Application, and Analysis Questions

1. Brain development is important for enriched development in all areas of a child's life. Name and describe five reasons why brain development may be more closely related to emotional and social development than the other areas.

2. The developmental patterns of children who are gifted and children with special needs differ from those of children who exhibit typical development. Name and describe three ways your interactions with the first two groups of children would be the same and three ways your interactions would be different from your interactions with children who are typically developing.

3. Pretend you have a child who is being assessed in the area of language development. Name and describe five types of evidence you could collect as a teacher to present as an assessment of this child.

Extension Activities

1. Take a few minutes to think about your best friend in kindergarten. Reflect or just write in your journal. Was this person of the same or other gender? What did you do together? Was your friend similar to you or different from you? What words best characterize this friendship? Do you still know this person? Are you still best friends?

2. Cognitive development influences language development, and language development influences cognitive development. Take some time and think about how these two areas of development influence each other. Reflect or just write in your journal. Name and describe two ways that cognition influences language. Then name and describe two ways that language influences cognition.

Additional Readings

Interested in finding out more about developmental milestones in children? The readings here are quite informative. They give milestones and strategies for facilitating milestone development in certain domains.

Neuman, S. B., Copple, C., & Bredekamp, S. (2000). *Learning to read and write: Developmentally appropriate practices for young children*. **Washington, DC: National Association for the Education of Young Children.**
This is a great book for early childhood educators. It describes pedagogical strategies for teaching young children to read. It also describes milestones involved in the process of learning to read.

Orion, J. (2002). Independence of the young child from birth to three. *The NAMATA Journal, 27*(1), 67–89.
This journal article is great for teachers, parents, and parent educators. It describes how children develop independence at a young age.

Peth-Pierce, R. (2000). *A good beginning: Sending America's children to school with the social and emotional competence they need to succeed*. **Bethesda, MD: National Institute of Mental Health.**
This publication describes the ever important socioemotional domain of child development. It puts forth methods for helping young children be well-rounded and not just academically prepared for school. Competence in the socioemotional domain is related to success in later life.

On the Web

American Academy of Pediatrics - *http://www.healthychildren.org/English/Pages/default.aspx*
This website focuses on the general health of children and describes milestones of healthy development.

March of Dimes - *www.marchofdimes.com/pnhec/298_10203.asp*
This is a useful website to refer parents to. It contains milestones for helping a young child develop optimally.

National Institute on Deafness and Other Communication Disorders - *www.nidcd.nih.gov*
This is a valuable website for parents and educators that describes speech and language milestones for children with special needs in the area of hearing.

Student Study Site

Visit **www.sagepub.com/gordonbiddle** to access several study tools including eFlashcards, web quizzes, links to SAGE journal articles, web resources, video resources, lesson plan templates, and more.

PART III

The Early Childhood Classroom

CHAPTER 6

Assessment and Evaluation Through Observation

This chapter will help you answer these important questions:

- Why do teachers observe young children?
- How do teachers observe young children?
- How do teachers assess and evaluate young children?
- How do teachers use effective assessment to improve teaching?
- What are some assessment and evaluation concerns?

Vignette: Adapting

Myra is a new teacher, and she wants to do well. The students in her new class are eager and respectful. However, the class presents some challenges because the children's developmental levels are widely varied, and some of the children have obvious special needs. Myra is nervous because her school has educational standards for all children. Nevertheless, Myra begins observing her children carefully and devising teaching strategies based on what she observes.

Eventually, Myra begins the next steps of assessment and evaluation. She documents the progress of her students with pictures and videos. She keeps copies of sample work. She assesses several domains of each child's development such as cognitive, language, and social. She administers some standardized assessments and some teacher-designed assessments. All the while she is adapting her teaching techniques to meet each child's needs.

By the end of the year, all of Myra's children are performing at the appropriate level according to the educational standards of the school where she teaches. Myra believes that her first year of teaching has been a success. She looks forward to the next year when the process will begin anew.

Professionalism and professional responsibility in the area of assessment are controversial. However, as the early childhood field garners more attention and support, assessment and increased accountability are becoming more typical and common. The question is no longer whether we should assess young children and as a result assess their teachers, but how we should assess young children and their teachers. Best practices in assessment today include a team of experts involved in the assessment. These experts may include educational psychologists, occupational therapists, and nurses. Teachers and others in the field are conducting more novel, unique, and authentic assessments including the use of curriculum-based assessment, judicious use of naturalistic observation, and optimal use of videotaping. The authors of this text want this chapter to demonstrate to you as the teacher some of the positive aspects of assessment. We want you to come to understand how assessment can help you with your teaching duties. Some issues and concerns with assessment will also be shared.

The first five chapters of this text have relayed foundational knowledge about the early childhood education field by covering early childhood elements such as theories, milestones, and history. The next section of the text contains four chapters that will help prepare you for instructing children in the early childhood classroom, and guide you in applying the foundational knowledge along with some new information as you prepare to meet and teach the children in your class.

Key Elements for Becoming a Professional

NAEYC DEVELOPMENTALLY APPROPRIATE PRINCIPLE 3

Development and learning proceed at varying rates from child to child, as well as at uneven rates across different areas of a child's individual functioning.

NAEYC DEVELOPMENTALLY APPROPRIATE PRINCIPLE 8

Development and learning occur in and are influenced by multiple social and cultural contexts.

Interpretation

When observing young children for assessment and evaluation purposes, a professional teacher keeps these principles in mind. The stakes are quite high for the children and teacher involved in assessment and evaluation because of accountability measures. Therefore, observation must be done objectively and sensitively.

NAEYC STANDARD 3: OBSERVING, DOCUMENTING, AND ASSESSING TO SUPPORT YOUNG CHILDREN AND FAMILIES

a. Understanding the goals, benefits, and uses of assessment—including its use in development of appropriate goals, curriculum, and teaching strategies for young children

b. Knowing about assessment partnerships with families and with professional colleagues to build effective learning environments

c. Knowing about and using observation, documentation, and other appropriate assessment tools and approaches, including the use of technology in documentation, assessment, and data collection

This chapter, the sixth, focuses on observation, assessment, and evaluation. It addresses why we carry out these important procedures and how to put them into practice. It also discusses common concerns of assessment and evaluation such as the following:

- Psychometrics
- Sensitive, supportive, and inclusive parental communication
- Accountability and high-stakes testing
- Test bias
- Age at assessment
- Environmental assessment

Although observation, assessment, and evaluation can be time-consuming and controversial, these processes are some of the most important in the endeavor of teaching young children. **Observation** is seeing, noting, and recording specific behavioral phenomena. **Assessment** is observation that is more systematic and structured. Additionally, assessment checks to see if goals and objectives are being met and places a value judgment on the behavior being observed. **Evaluation** takes observation even further. Evaluation judges the worth and value of the behavior, event, program, or teaching strategy based on what is observed. If observation, assessment, and evaluation are completed competently and sensitively, they can tremendously enhance the education of young children. You as a teacher can obtain the same satisfaction that Myra experienced with her successful first year teaching young children.

WHY AND HOW DO TEACHERS OBSERVE YOUNG CHILDREN?

Good, detailed observation is the foundation of evaluation and assessment.

Careful and sensitive observation underlies effective teaching, assessment, and evaluation of children. Wise teachers know that in order to observe young children, they have to be aware of their own observational filters, or biases, and endeavor to be as objective as possible. Teachers' observations of their students can impact the children's developmental and educational trajectory. Therefore, it is important to observe objectively, yet to be careful and sensitive as seen in the National Association for the Education of Young Children (NAEYC) position statement in Table 6.1.

One Reason for Observing

The main reason teachers observe young children is to assess their interests, development, educational progress, and behavior. Observational perceptions are then used to interact with the children more effectively in teaching, guiding, and evaluating them. At the beginning of the observational process, it is important to have a certain purpose that is stated as a clear **objective** (Bentzen, 2000; Brandt, 1972), or a specific and practical aim for your observation. This helps you to focus your attention and select the most important behavior and emotional expression to fulfill your reason for observing. Once your reason and objective for observing are clear, you can begin the observation.

Table 6.1 **Excellent Teachers and Assessment**

Excellent teachers should use assessment to	Developmentally appropriate assessment requires attention to	Assessment decisions require partnerships with family members by
1. monitor children's development and learning; 2. guide planning and decision-making; 3. identify children who might benefit from special services and supports; and 4. report and communicate with others (including families).	1. appropriateness for child's age and developmental status; 2. appropriateness for child's individuality; and 3. appropriateness for child's culture.	1. making family members feel welcome in the classroom and inviting their participation in the program; 2. working to create a relationship that allows for open dialogue; 3. maintaining frequent, positive, two-way communication; and 4. acknowledging parents' choices and goals for their child and responding with sensitivity and respect to their preferences and concerns.

Source: Adapted from NAEYC (2009).

Types of Observations

There are numerous types of observation methods. The most common ones are as follows:

- Reflective journal or diary
- Narrative description
- Time sampling
- Event sampling
- Frequency count
- Duration record
- Checklist
- Rating scale
- Photographs
- Videotaping

The first two observation types listed are more informal, and the last four are more formal. The ones in the middle may be either depending on how they are created and conducted. **Informal observations** are free-flowing and less structured, while **formal observations** are more structured and controlled (Goodwin & Driscoll, 1980, 1982). Whether an observation is formal or informal, it is important to not use the child's full real name. Use only a pseudonym (false name) or just the child's first name. Some observations, such as photographs and videotapes, require parental and child permission.

A **reflective journal or diary** (Billman & Sherman, 2003) selects and describes a particular behavior or emotional expression of the child and then reflects on the meaning or interprets the behavior or expression. This reflection or interpretation is informal and may change after repeated objective observations. The date and time are also noted, along with a name or another identifying reference for the child. The defining elements of this type of observation are the selected behavior or expression and an interpretation of it. (See Figure 6.1 for an example.)

Narrative descriptions are informal observations as well. They differ from reflective observations in that they are more general and basic. They are written descriptions of general behavior (Lay-Dopyera & Dopyera, 1982) rather than observations of a specific behavior. Narrative descriptions can become more formal in nature if they are very detailed and have a strong and strict objective (Bentzen, 2000; Irwin & Bushnell, 1980). However, they keep their general nature (see Figure 6.2).

Time sampling is observation that seeks to quantify the number of times a specific behavior occurs during a specified amount of time (Irwin & Bushnell, 1980; Wortham, 2005). For instance, you can count the number of times a young child says "bye-bye" during 10 intervals of 15 minutes each throughout the day. Time sampling is usually used when the behavior or expression of interest occurs frequently.

Another type of sampling is **event sampling**. Event sampling is used when the focus of the observation occurs less frequently or rarely. Perhaps there is a young child who engages in power struggles with his or her teachers, but not very often. Then you can observe using event sampling, a richly descriptive recording of an infrequent behavior or expression every time the behavior or

Figure 6.1	A Journal Account

A Journal Account

March 16. When I first got there, I gave K. (nine-month-old female) her bottle and she fell asleep between my legs, so I had to be careful and put her in the playpen and still have her sleep. She did open her eyes, but I just rubbed her stomach and she fell back to sleep . . . She hadn't eaten any breakfast and they (the other teachers) thought that she was either cutting some teeth or was sick.

March 23. K. had a fall today on the slide. She climbs up the steps, then sits on the top, but when she slides down, she loses control. She hit her head and got a rug burn. (The other teachers) told me that she's a daredevil. She keeps on climbing up the slide even though she has fallen down a couple of times.

April 1. Today when I got there I set up the water table. They were all so excited. It was amazing to see them get excited about just water. It's not just water to them; it's something new and different. They must all like to take baths. They even screamed when I was pouring the water in. They had a good time splashing in the water. Sometimes they would get carried away and splash each other in the face . . . K. would get so excited that she would scream and, boy, does she have a scream. (The teacher) says that she likes to hear her own voice.

April 20. K. was aggressive today. She hit C. and made her cry . . . Today we played some music while they were playing. It seems to calm them down. Today, though, they were all aggressive. They have a soft, cushiony tunnel that they like to play with. Both E. and K. were trying to get into it at the same time. They were wrestling each other, laughing most of the time; but then the hitting and hair pulling started.

April 27. K. was my buddy today for a while. She wanted me to help her go up and down the slide. I must have done it about five times. She is having problems with her teeth so she wanted (the teacher) to give her bottle today, not me.

May 6. K.'s mom came in worried because she saw blood on K.'s car seat. R. told her she had a paper cut when she came in. (Her mom) took K. with her for an hour before she had class.

May 11. Today was such a nice day out that we decided to take the infants for a walk after we had snack and changed diapers . . . K. fell asleep in the back of the wagon. Her head was leaned way back and everyone would look at her as we were walking through campus. We just told everyone that she had a bad night. Our walk lasted about forty minutes.

May 13. K. is going all day without a bottle now. She will be one on the 24th of May. Her mom told us that she thought it would take her longer to get K. off the bottle. To get her to sleep, we usually just rock her.

Source: Billman and Sherman (2003).

Figure 6.2 | Narrative Description

Observer's Name   <u>Alice Thompson (Teacher)</u>

Child/Children Observed   <u>Melissa L.</u>

Child's/Children's Age(s)   <u>4 years, 3 months</u>   Child's/Children's Sex   <u>Female</u>

Observation Context (home, child care center, preschool, school)   <u>Children's Delight Preschool</u>

Date of Observation <u>January 10, 1999</u>   Time Begun <u>9:20A.M.</u>   Time Ended <u>9:30A.M.</u>

Brief Description of Physical and Social Characteristic of Observation Setting

Children are busily engaged in various free play activities. The overall mood seems upbeat. Of the usual 15 children who are enrolled, only 12 are here today—three are ill, according to the parents' telephone communications with the director this morning. Although the children's moods seem good, they are more quiet than usual—not as much loud talking as sometimes takes place.

Objective Behavioral Descriptions (OBD) and Interpretations: *Narrative Description*

OBD 1: [Time Begun 9:20A.M.   Time Ended 9:22A.M.]
Melissa (M.) arrives about 35 minutes after the other children have arrived and started their activities. She puts her coat in her cubby and then stands in the doorway of the main classroom and looks around; she remains motionless for about ½ minute, moving only her eyes as she glances at other children and their activities.

Interpretation 1:
Melissa seems shy, almost withdrawn. From moment of arrival, she seemed reluctant to enter into things. May be because she didn't want to come in first place; her reluctance was mentioned by her mother several days ago. No specific reason was offered.

OBD 2: [Time Begun 9:22A.M.   Time Ended 9:24A.M.]
M. walks towards reading area on far side of the room from the cubbies. As she walks, she scrapes the toe of her right foot at each step, doing this for about 5 feet. She passes by the puzzle table where 2 children are seated; no communication is exchanged. She walks to a table with some books lying on it. Tina, José and Miguel are seated at the table; Jose and Miguel are sharing a book, Tina (T.) is watching them "read." Melissa says nothing to the three children as she sits down.

Interpretation 2:
Melissa still seems uncertain: even her motor behaviors seems restricted; she walks slowly, shuffling, as though unsure of herself and of her relationship with the other children or her environment. Seems to have trouble deciding what to do. Not at all communicative; makes no overtures to any of the children who were "available" for such.

OBD 3: [Time Begun 9:24A.M.]   Time Ended 9:29A.M.]
José and Miguel don't look up or acknowledge Melissa in any way. Tina says "Hi, Melisa, wanna read a book with me?" M. cocks her head to one side and says, "I don't know how to read." T. replies "We can look at the picture." M. looks over towards the big block area and without looking at T., says, "OK." Tina smiles and goes to a shelf containing a number of books. M. picks up one of the books already on the table and flips through the pages. T. returns with a books and says, "I like this one, let's look at this one." M. merely nods; T. sits down close to M., but M. moves slightly, keeping a distance of about 6–8 inches between her and Tina.

Interpretation 3:
Tina seems outgoing and friendly as Melissa approaches; M. is still uncommunicative; still seems shy and uncertain; speaks softly as though afraid of being heard. Tina persists in spite of M.'s apparent lack of enthusiasm. M. also seems distractable or inattentive. She shies away from T.'s efforts to get close physically. Tina moves at a quick pace—much more energetic than M.

OBD 4: [Time Begun 9:29A.M. Time Ended 9:30A.M.]
José looks up and says, "Hey, you two, wha' cha doin'?" Tina tilts her head upward, thrusts out her chin slightly and says, "Never mind, we're busy." Melissa says nothing, but gets up from the table and walks toward big block area. Miguel still reads.

Interpretation 4:
Tina is much more outgoing and sure of himself than M. T. didn't interact too much w/ José and Miguel; may have felt left out of their activity. T. definitely seemed pleased to see M.; displayed no unfavorable response to M.'s "unsocial" behavior. T.'s response to José was quite assertive, but in a friendly way; almost like she claimed Melissa as her playmate, may be in retaliation for the two boys ignoring her earlier. M. still seems uninterested, even uncertain of what to do.

Source: Bentzen (2000).

expression occurs (Gander & Gardiner, 1981; Wortham, 2005). You may also want to note what happens before and after this behavior or event in order to understand it better, which can help with subsequent assessment, evaluation, communication, and teaching.

A **frequency count** is simple and usually informal. You simply count the number of times a behavior or an expression happens during the observation. This observation method may be used to establish a baseline of a behavior or an expression. A frequency count is often followed or accompanied by a **duration record**, which is the recording of how long a behavior or an expression lasts (Goodwin & Driscoll, 1982).

A **checklist** is always prepared beforehand and linked to a specified context and, therefore, is a formal observation method (Bentzen, 2003; Brandt, 1972). The checklist observation method lists the presence or absence of a characteristic or an action in a given context (Bentzen, 2003; Brandt, 1972). A checklist seems simple, but must be prepared ahead of time (see Figure 6.3).

Figure 6.3	"Concepts About Print" Checklist

COMPETENCIES	FALL	MIDYEAR	SPRING
1. Book Concepts			
1.1 Front cover			
1.2 Back cover			
1.3 Title			
1.4 Title page			
2. Book Handling Skills			
2.1 Holds the book right-side up			
2.2 Turns pages from the front			
3. Directionality			
3.1 Left-to-right page sequence			
3.2 Left-to-right sentence			
3.3 Top-to-bottom			
3.4 Return sweep			
4. Reading Concepts			
4.1 Understands that print carries specific meaning			
4.2 One-to-one correspondence (points to each word)			
5. Letter Concept			
5.1 Points to a letter			
6. Word Concept			
6.1 Points to a word			
7. Precise Literacy Terms			
7.1 Title			
7.2 Author			
7.3 Illustrator			

Sourece: Adapted from Clay, M. M. (1993).

With a **rating scale**, a value or judgment of relative degree is placed on a behavior or an expression. Rating scales usually have at least three levels of value degree but may have as many as seven or more (Bentzen, 2003; Wortham, 2005). The rating scale in Figure 6.4 has three levels of value degree. Rating scales may be used to observe and judge characteristics or actions, as well.

Photographs and videotapes are used in everyday life and, hence, easily defined. However, they have only recently been accepted as valid observational methods. Photographs and videotapes are permanent and vivid records of behavior and expressions. As mentioned above, permission should be obtained from the parents and perhaps the children themselves. Photographs and videotapes can capture examples of focus behavior and/or expressions, and then the photograph or videotape can be interpreted or explained with another more traditional method.

Figure 6.4	"Concepts About Print" Rating Scale

Code: 1 = No Evidence 2 = Developing 3 = Mastered

COMPETENCIES	1	2	3
1. Book Concepts			
1.1 Front cover			
1.2 Back cover			
1.3 Title			
1.4 Title page			
2. Book Handling Skills			
2.1 Holds the book right-side up			
2.2 Turns pages from the front			
3. Directionality			
3.1 Left-to-right page sequence			
3.2 Left-to-right sentence			
3.3 Top-to-bottom			
3.4 Return sweep			
4. Reading Concepts			
4.1 Understands that print carries specific meaning			
4.2 One-to-one correspondence (points to each word)			
5. Letter Concept			
5.1 Points to a letter			
6. Word Concept			
6.1 Points to a word			
7. Precise Literacy Terms			
7.1 Title			
7.2 Author			
7.3 Illustrator			

Sourece: Adapted from Clay, M. M. (1993).

Choosing which observation method to use is a very important decision for you as a teacher to make. The observation method you use may highlight or bring to life a certain behavior or expression that might not be noticed at all with another type of observation. And, most naturally, what you observe will be an influence on your teaching style, methods, and philosophy.

Observation, assessment, and evaluation are aids in instructional planning and practice.

How Observations Influence Teaching

As a teacher you can utilize observations to uncover patterns of behavior and expression in children. You may then interpret these patterns and compare them with appropriate norms and expectations of development (Wortham, 2005). It is very important to be as sensitive and objective as possible when observing. It is also important to be sensitive when interpreting the observations and to realize that interpretations may change after successive objective observations or further reflection. As a trained teacher, you can rely on your education and experience with children to help you interpret the observation. After observing, interpreting, and reflecting, take this information and use it to enhance the development of the child or children. Observations allow you to know where children are positioned along the developmental continuum and where they need to go next to further their development. Then you as a teacher provide the appropriate experiences to assist the children with growing, learning, and developing (Dodge, Heroman, Charles, & Maiorca, 2004). You create, arrange, or plan for experiences and lesson plans that help further the children's development.

HOW DO TEACHERS ASSESS AND EVALUATE YOUNG CHILDREN?

Observation, interpretation, and reflection occur over and over again at various time points during the teaching of young children. At one point, the interpretative step becomes more of an assessment or evaluation as a value or judgment comes into play. Some teachers of young children are uncomfortable with assessment and evaluation and wish they were not necessary. This is because young children grow and change constantly at varied rates. However, if done objectively, sensitively, and professionally with an awareness of the teacher's own filter, assessment and evaluation can aid young children as they grow, develop, and learn.

In all actuality, you as a teacher are already "assessing" young children when you observe them because we all have an observation filter that we use to "make sense of" or value/judge children's behaviors and expressions. But more formal assessment furthers the observation and assessment process because with assessment some criteria or standards are used to judge children's behavior, some decisions are made, and some actions are taken. An evaluation is a more involved assessment with more than one piece of evidence. Evaluation criteria or standards are more inflexible; the evidence is stronger and more numerous, and the value judgment is more consequential and final. Evaluation also examines the educational program in which the young children are learning. The differences between observation, assessment, and evaluation are differences of degree. With observation, you as the teacher try to be objective, but acknowledge you have your own filter. Assessment provides criteria or standards upon which you as the teacher judge children's behavior and expressions. Decisions and actions also come into the picture with assessment. Evaluation is assessment taken to another degree where the value judgment is more inflexible, consequential, and final. Evaluations are concrete, far-reaching, and definitive. Evaluations also judge the young children's educational program.

Types of Assessments and Evaluations

When trying to decide how to assess and evaluate children, there are many types of assessments and evaluations from which to choose, including criterion-referenced and norm-referenced assessments. **Criterion-referenced assessments** are based on some outside objective criteria or standards and compare young children with those criteria or standards. Teachers usually create these criteria based on some information or skill or ability they think the children they are teaching should have mastered. Examples might include a spelling test in first grade or an assessment of gross motor skills or language ability in preschool. An assessment is **norm-referenced** if it compares young children with other typically developing children who are the same age and at the same developmental level. Most norm-referenced assessments are also standardized. **Standardized assessments and tests** have standard and averaged, norm-referenced scores that are derived by giving the assessment or test to a large number of young children who are representative of all young children in the nation.

There are also alternative and performance assessment methods. With **alternative assessments**, students actually create a response or an answer instead of choosing a premade answer or response from a list. Open-ended questions, interviews, and portfolios are examples of alternative assessments. For example, you as a teacher may want to gain an understanding of how well children process emotions. You can observe them on the playground and in the classroom as they process their emotions, or you can give them an interview about processing emotions. You can also create an "emotional processing" portfolio. Introduced in Chapter 4, a portfolio is an example of a student's work, which can include standardized test scores, interview transcripts, pictures, and videos.

With **performance assessment** the children are required to emit some type of "real-world" behavior. Perhaps you will have them write and recite a poem or story, or demonstrate a science experiment. Grading of performance assessments by its nature is a bit subjective and complicated. It is akin to judging a figure skating contest. Figure skating judges make very fine-tuned subjective judgments based on their knowledge, personal tastes, and experiences. However, by creating the judgment criteria beforehand and allowing for flexibility, performance assessment can give the teacher and children a more "real" understanding of the children's abilities.

In terms of evaluation, there are formative and summative evaluations. **Formative evaluations** allow for change in the educational program or more learning and growing by the children evaluated. Midterm grades in elementary school can be seen as formative. **Summative evaluations** are final, with major decisions and actions following. Examples of summative evaluation are final, end-of-the-year grades and state criterion-referenced standards tests upon which grade promotion and funding decisions are sometimes made in high-stakes environments. Evaluations can also be standardized, just as assessments are standardized. Standardized evaluations make use of standardized measurement instruments. However, the capacity for change and flexibility exists no

Promoting Optimal Development

The New TeamS Assessment Model

A current trend in assessment is a team of professionals conducting the assessment with input from family members. In 1996, the federal government sponsored such a model of assessment, TeamS, that was to link assessment with intervention (instruction in an educational setting). This new TeamS model also helped to answer questions that teachers and parents had about particular cases of child learning or development that were complicated (Westby, Dominguez, & Oetter, 1996). This new TeamS model is for children from birth to age 6 years and requires attention to the neurological (relating to the brain and nervous system) underpinnings of performance, assessments carried out in natural/realistic environments, consideration of the whole child, and a team of professionals who share ideas, write collaboratively, and provide services. The team of professionals includes psychologists and medical doctors. There is an observational framework that guides the team (see Figure 6.5).

Using this type of framework and approach can aid in uncovering the supportive factors and risks that impact a child's development. This type of approach and model can assist you as a teacher as you strive to utilize observations, assessments, and evaluations to promote optimal development in the children you teach.

Figure 6.5	The Child Quality of Life Membership: Personal Sense of Competence

DEVELOPMENTAL
- Physical
- Emotional
- Intellectual
- Spiritual

ENVIRONMENTAL INFLUENCES
- Home
- Child Care
- School
- Community Activities

FOUNDATIONS FOR PROCESSING INFORMATION
- Sensory Registration, Processing, Integration
- Orientation, Discrimination
- Movement
- Self-Regulation

GIVENS
- Predispositions
- Basic Biological Drives

LEARNING BY DOING
- Exploration
- Physical Interaction
- Social Interaction
- Communication

COMFORT/SAFETY CYCLE
- Comfort/Safety
- Confidence
- Risk Taking
- Competence

Source: Adapted from Westby (1996).

matter what type of assessment or evaluation is utilized. As a teacher of young children, you may find it helpful to think of every evaluation as formative and to allow for change as you and the child grow and learn after it is administered.

Young children are assessed and evaluated in many domains of their development, and some assessments and evaluations cover multiple domains. Young children are assessed and evaluated in the physical, cognitive, linguistic, social/emotional, mathematical, health/wellness, and other domains. Some assessments and evaluations cover multiple domains (see Table 6.2).

The assessments in Table 6.2 cover multiple domains and have more than a single score. Some of the domains covered are socioemotional development, self-help skills, and even academic areas such as spelling and mathematics. Some assessments exist, however, that only cover one domain or academic area (see Table 6.3).

A variety of evidence and tools can be used to observe, assess, and evaluate. In addition to taking notes, teachers can collect pictures, writing samples, and video footage with consent.

The previous set of assessments and tests (Table 6.3) measure a single domain/area of child development. Most often these single tests measure an entity called **intelligence**. Intelligence is one's ability to reason and solve problems cognitively. Any subscales in the previous set of assessments are a limited number of items that measure the same ability or skill or domain in relation to an assessment of some larger or overarching domain.

The assessments and evaluations above are some of the most common ones used that are seen as valid for middle-class European Americans (Whites). However, their validity for ethnic minorities has been questioned for many decades (Boone & Adesso, 1974; McCullough, 1992), even though ethnic minorities are becoming more familiar with and scoring better on these tests in general (Butler-Omololu, Doster, & Lahey, 1983). Nevertheless, other tests and testing systems have been created to be more culture-specific or culture-fair. Even the NAEYC (2009b) recognizes the importance of this concern as it continues into this decade.

Some Assessments and Evaluations for Ethnic Minorities

The second edition of the Kaufman Assessment Battery for Children (KABC; Kaufman & Kaufman, 2008) is known to be culture-fair. The KABC can be utilized with children aged 3 to 8 years and beyond. This test was normed with children from various ethnic groups, and only slight differences in scores were found between them. This may be because verbal responses and cultural content are minimized with this test and because there are two models of interpretation that can be used. The first model of interpretation includes culturally sensitive scoring of verbal responses, and the second model excludes verbal ability altogether. This is a test of cognitive ability or intelligence with five scales: simultaneous intelligence, sequential intelligence, planning skill, learning skill, and knowledge.

There is also the Learning Potential Assessment Device (LPAD) that was developed by Feuerstein (1980) in Jerusalem. The LPAD is another viable assessment tool for minorities. A dynamic assessment that highlights a young child's learning potential, it is considered dynamic because of its flexibility in scoring. It also points out possible intervention methods that may be necessary. For instance, if a child has multiple or severe developmental delays, then intervention may be necessary.

| Table 6.2 | Common Assessments and Evaluations With Multiple Domains |

NAME	COVERAGE	ADMINISTRATION
Denver II (Frankenburg & Dodd, 1990)	Screening test that covers self-help skills, social development, and language development, as well as fine and gross motor skills	Administered to children from infancy to 6 years and has the reputation of being easy to use and quick
DIAL III (Diagnostic Indicators for the Assessment of Learning) (Mardell-Czudnowski & Goldenberg, 1998)	Assesses motor, cognitive, and language areas	Easy and quick to administer and is usually used to screen young children aged 2 to 6 years
Ages and Stages Questionnaire (ASQ) (Bricker & Squires, 1999)	Assesses language, fine and gross motor skills, and social/emotional development	Administered by parents or caregivers and is fast to complete—mostly used to uncover delays in development that children aged 4 months to 5 years may have
Brigance Diagnostic Inventory of Early Development–Revised (Brigance, 1991)	Assesses self-help skills, fine and gross motor skills, language skills, and cognitive skills	Teachers can administer the Brigance to children from birth to 7 years of age with some training, or a psychologist or counselor can administer the Brigance
McCarthy Scales of Children's Abilities (McCarthy, 1983)	Assesses cognitive, verbal, and quantitative reasoning ability; perceptual/performance problem-solving ability; memory; and motor development	Utilized with children aged 30 months to 8 years of age—aids in the identification of children with slight disabilities
HighScope Child Observation Record (COR) (HighScope, 2003)	Assessments of seven developmental domains (initiative, creativity, social skills, language skills, mathematics, musical aptitude, and movement)	Viewed as an alternative assessment method—assesses children 30 months to 6 years of age and requires you as a teacher to take extensive notes
Battelle Developmental Inventory (BDI-2) (Newborg, 2003)	Covers five areas of child development (social/emotional domain, adaptive/self-care domain, motor domain, communication, and cognition)	Administered by a team of professionals to children from birth to age 8 years
Peabody Individual Achievement Test–Revised (PAIT-R) (Markwardt, 2008)	Assesses academic achievement in six content areas (general information, reading recognition, reading comprehension, mathematics, spelling, and written expression)	Normative scores for this assessment were recently updated for children in kindergarten through third grade and beyond

The SOMPA is a testing system that is fully named the System of Multicultural Pluralistic Assessment. It is normed separately for Black, White, and Hispanic children aged 5 to 11 years. What is unique about this assessment is that it includes a parent interview. This system of standardized tests must be interpreted by trained professionals. It measures a young child's ability in cognition, sensorimotor skills, and adaptive behavior. It has been shown to be helpful in placing young children in special education and gifted education classes (Talley, 1979).

The last test to be discussed is the Black Intelligence Test of Cultural Homogeneity (Williams, 1972). This is a culture-specific, vocabulary-type intelligence test. Black children usually score higher on it than White children or children from other ethnic/racial groups, because it is based on their

Table 6.3   Common Assessments of Single Domains

NAME	COVERAGE	ADMINISTRATION
Wechsler Preschool and Primary Scale of Intelligence (WPPSI) (Wechsler, 2002)	Verbal IQ, a performance IQ, and the full-scale IQ	Professional counselor or psychologist must administer and interpret this test; administered to children aged 30 months to 7 years and 3 months
Wechsler Intelligence Scale for Children, Fourth Edition (WISC–IV) (Wechsler, 2003)	Test has four composite indices and a full-scale IQ score—four composite indices are verbal comprehension, perceptual reasoning, processing speed, and working memory	Used with children aged 6 years to 8 years and beyond by a trained professional
Stanford-Binet Intelligence Scales for Early Childhood (Roid, 2003)	Assesses five domains of cognitive intelligence—fluid reasoning (flexible problem solving), knowledge, quantitative reasoning, visual-spatial processing, and working memory (only computes a single IQ score)	Administered by a trained professional to children aged 24 months to 7 years and 3 months
Peabody Picture Vocabulary Test (PPVT–4) (Dunn & Dunn, 2004)	Focuses on vocabulary	Quick to administer and can identify certain developmental delays and disabilities—used with young children aged 30 months to 8 years and beyond

Source: Hudson, R. F., Lane, H. B., & Pullen, P. C. (2005). Reading fluency assessment and instruction: What, why, and how? *Reading Teacher, 58*(8), 706. Published with permission by Wiley.

culture and linguistic style. This test was developed to ameliorate environmental differences and test bias against Black children on other intelligence tests (Boone & Adesso, 1974). Since it is a culture-specific test, it is not recommended for children of other cultures.

The tests and assessments mentioned above are some of the most common that are marketed and utilized with young children today. There exist other assessments and evaluations and tests that are still being developed and researched or are used mostly in research settings. These newly created and developing assessments measure various areas of child development, academic achievement, and intelligence as well. Some of these are mentioned briefly in the next section.

Current Research Assessments and Evaluations

Researchers who work with young children assess children's development much like teachers of young children do. These researchers have utilized some assessment methods and instruments that teachers may not consider using. However, well-informed teachers may want to use them to supplement assessments they may already be using. These assessments measure development in areas such as social skills/friendships, cognitive development, competence and social acceptance, movement, literacy, and mathematics. Since they are newer and under development, the criteria for and evidence of these assessments are different than those for some of the more traditional assessments.

In the area of social development, teachers and researchers often use peer assessment in research settings with preschool and early elementary children (Yugar & Shapiro, 1996, 2001). These ratings are used to assess social skills and friendships. In general, these assessments ask peers to nominate, rate, and answer questions about networking concerning other young children/peers in

Professionalism & Policy

Curriculum-Based Assessments

Should the use of curriculum-based assessments be strongly advocated as a recommended practice in early childhood and early elementary settings? Assessment researchers Neisworth and Bagnato (2000) define curriculum-based assessments as "a form of criterion-referenced measurement wherein curricular objectives act as the criteria for identification of instructional targets and for the assessment of status and progress" (p. 20).

Curriculum-based assessments are often nonstandardized, but many more standardized and commercial ones are becoming available (Pretti-Frontczak, Kowalski, & Brown, 2002). These types of assessments often are child-centered and activity-centered, which means they focus on the child and the actual curricular activities the child completes as part of the learning experience. They allow for teaching that is individualized and based upon children's strengths, interests, and emerging skills (Bredekamp & Copple, 1997). However, these types of assessments are not used as often as is optimal (Pretti-Frontczak et al., 2002) because they are usually not standardized, and that makes comparison of children harder. However, some still advocate that these types of assessments should be developed more by researchers and teachers in the early childhood field and that their use should be more strongly encouraged by policy advocates.

The social skill level of young children can be seen through naturalistic observation.

their classes. These types of assessments do not always match with teacher or parent ratings of young children's social skills or friendships. These ratings can, however, be stable and reliable when quality of the relationship is taken into account. Therefore, peer assessments can be useful to teachers in that they give a more multidimensional picture of social development in young children.

Naturalistic observation is one of the best methods for measuring social skills (Merrell, 2001), and occurs when young children are observed without manipulation in their naturally occurring daily routine. The PLAY naturalistic observation system measures social (and cognitive) competence in preschool children (Farmer-Dougan & Kaszuba, 1999). It is shown to be both **reliable** and **valid**. It is reliable because the assessments that different teachers and researchers give are in agreement. It is valid because it correlates well with other standard measures such as the Battelle Developmental Inventory (BDI) (Harrington, 1985). The BDI has been a long-standing and recognized assessment. Since the PLAY assessment is based on naturalistic observation, it promotes an ease of translating the findings into learning and educational activities and strategies for young children.

It should be noted that the PLAY observational assessment also measures general cognitive competence (Farmer-Dougan & Kaszuba, 1999). Utilizing the observational assessment in this manner is also reliable and valid. This represents another possible assessment you can use to measure cognition in the young children you teach to get a broader picture of their abilities.

BEST

Practices Naturalistic Observation When Assessing Social Skills

Naturalistic observation is one of the best methods for measuring social skills. Naturalistic types of observation are especially needed for later stages of screening and identification (Merrell, 2001). In other words, screening young children and identifying the children's educational needs after the preschool years and during the early elementary school years is critical. We have presented a specific method that is reliable and valid for measuring social competence in children. However, there are some potential issues with observational assessments that can be overcome with sensitive and objective observation. Some of these issues and possible solutions are listed in Table 6.4.

Table 6.4	Some Potential Threats to the Validity of Behavioral Observations, and Possible Solutions to These Threats	

PROBLEM	POTENTIAL CONSEQUENCES	POSSIBLE SOLUTION
Poorly defined observational domains	Observational recording system is either too cumbersome or too vague.	Carefully define and select behaviors to be observed based on assessment problem and intervention goals.
Unreliability of observers	Observers drift from original definitions; interrater reliability decreases.	Provide high quality initial training; conduct periodic reliability checks and retraining.
Lack of social comparison data	Interpretations of behavior are not based on a normative perspective; deviancy may be under- or overestimated.	Include typical or randomly selected participants in the same setting for behavioral comparison.
Observer reactivity	Participant behavior is influenced by the presence of the observer.	Select and participate in observational settings in a discrete, unobtrusive manner.
Situational specificity of behavior	Interpretations of observational data may not represent the larger picture.	Conduct observations in multiple settings; do not overgeneralize from limited data.
Inappropriate recording techniques	Behaviors are not adequately depicted; inappropriate conclusions are reached.	Select recording systems to carefully match the behavioral domain.
Biased expectations of the observer	Borderline behaviors may be systematically coded in a biased manner.	Resist pressure to confirm expectations of persons with vested interest; remain scrupulously objective in coding behavior.

Source: Adapted from Merrel, K. W. (2001). *Assessment of children's social skills: Recent developments, best practices, and new directions.* Pg. 8. Copyright © 1999 by Lawrence Erlbaum Associates, Inc. Reprinted with permission of the publisher.

There exists another measure of competence and social acceptance of young children in the research literature, namely the Pictorial Scale of Perceived Competence and Social Acceptance for Young Children (PSPCSAYC) (Harter & Pike, 1984). This scale is from the child's point of view and is designated for children aged 4 to 7 years. This scale utilizes a series of pictures and questions and purports to "interview" the children. It is generally well accepted in the literature, but not for assessing low-income, urban children (Fantuzzo, McDermott, Manz, Hampton, & Burdick, 1996), for whom the scores of this assessment are not reliable and valid.

There also exists an assessment titled the Movement General Outcome Measurement for infants and toddlers from birth to age 3 years (Greenwood, Luze, Cline, Kuntz, & Leitschuh, 2002). This measure, used mostly by researchers, is important because it relates to physical, social/emotional, and cognitive development. It only takes 6 minutes to administer and measures movement skills and growth in correspondence with age. Teachers of young children could use this measure to supplement other assessments of infants and toddlers because it is reliable and valid (Greenwood et al., 2002).

Other research assessments are available. For instance, researchers have developed a rubric as a performance-based assessment of student writing in early elementary grades (second and beyond) (Novak, Herman, & Gearhart, 1996). **Rubrics** are scaled assessments that judge whether students can perform a certain task. This rubric is somewhat reliable and valid but still needs some development. However, the rubric is highly usable by teachers of young children. As the rubric is used more and developed further, it may be suitable for widespread, standardized assessment.

In addition, reading fluency has been shown to be an important literacy skill (Hudson, Lane, & Pullen, 2005). The main reason reading fluency is important is its relationship to reading comprehension. However, it is not usually contained in traditional standardized tests and assessments of young children. Table 6.5 shows five assessments that are recognized in the research literature on reading fluency. Some are standardized, and some are more observational in nature.

Measuring number sense in young children aids teachers in assessing early mathematical understanding (Clarke & Shinn, 2004). There exist four experimental research measures that are currently reliable and valid. These four measures are also sensitive enough to identify children who may be at risk in the area of later mathematics achievement. These four experimental measures are simple and are usually included in the general mathematics curriculum in first grade. The measures are oral counting, number identifying, quantity discriminating, and missing number naming. These task measures are easily defined with the exception of quantity discriminating. The quantity discriminating measure task consists of the first graders deciding which number is bigger based on visually shown representations of numbers—for instance, asking a child what number is bigger: a visually represented display of 3 or a visually represented display of 10.

The research and current methods of assessment presented here are not meant to be exhaustive. There are many more assessments in the research and experimental literature that teachers of young children may want to explore to gain a fuller, richer picture of the development, skills, and abilities of the children in their classrooms. The methods mentioned here just reveal the possibilities for other reliable and valid assessment options that exist for the teachers of young children.

How to Use Effective Assessment to Improve Teaching

Much is said currently about intentional teaching (Epstein, 2009; Jeske, 2010; NAEYC, 2009b). Mentioned in the first section of this textbook (see Chapter 1), intentional teaching is helping children learn through both child-centered and adult-centered interactions. The NAEYC (2009b) states that intentional teachers purposefully and thoughtfully choose when to be child-centered or adult-centered. In fact, intentional teachers are purposeful and thoughtful in all decisions (Epstein, 2009; Jeske, 2010; NAEYC, 2009b). In relation to assessment, intentional teachers use formative

Table 6.5

Table 6.5   Reading Fluency Assessments

ASSESSMENT	PUBLISHER	DESCRIPTION
AIMSweb Standard Reading Assessment Passages (RAPS)	Edformation	AIMSweb RAPS provide teachers with passages for quick but accurate formative assessment of students' oral reading fluency. These assessments are a curriculum-based measurement (CBM) system that is intended to assist teachers in making instructional decisions and monitoring student progress. RAPS have been field-tested and validated. The AIMS web system includes a web-based software management system for data collection and reporting.
Dynamic Indicators of Basic Early Literacy Skills (DIBELS)	University of Oregon and Sopris West	DIBELS contains a subtest of Oral Reading Fluency and Retail Fluency for students in the first through third grades. The Oral Reading Fluency is standardized and individually administrated. Students read a passage aloud for one minute. The number of correct words per minute. Students read a passage aloud for one minute to provide the oral reading fluency rate. The Retail Fluency is a measure of comprehension that accompanies the Oral Reading Fluency assessment.
Gray Oral Reading Test, Fourth Edition (GOR–4)	PRO-ED	The GORT–4 is a norm-referenced measure of oral reading performance. Skills assessed include rate, accuracy, fluency (rate and accuracy combined), comprehension, and overall reading ability (rate, accuracy, and comprehension combined)
National Assessment of Educational Progress (NAEP) Fluency Scale	National Center for Education Statistics (NCES)	The NAEP Fluency Scale provides a descriptive guide for oral reading performance based on the student's "naturalness" of reading. The student's performance is rated on a 4-point scale, with emphasis placed on phrasing of words, adherence of syntax, and expressiveness. Accuracy and rate are measured and determined by calculating the correct words read per minute.
Reading Fluency Monitor by Read Naturally	Read Naturally	The Reading Fluency Monitor is an assessment instrument that allows teachers to monitor students' progress. Fall, winter, and spring administrations are recommended. Grade-level passages are available for Grades 1–8, as well as a software program for reporting and record keeping.

Source: Hudson, R. F., Lane, H. B., & Pullen, P. C. (2005). Reading fluency assessment and instruction: What, why, and how? *Reading Teacher*, 58(8), Pg. 706. Published with permission by Wiley.

assessment and other informal assessments to guide their teaching of young children. The results of these formative and informal assessments allow the teachers to know where the children may have misunderstood or where the children have some delays. Then the teachers can make informed, intentional lesson plans to enhance the learning of the children they are teaching.

Additionally, Epstein (2009) suggests that certain skills are better taught as child-centered and certain skills are better taught as adult-centered. For instance, with language development, conversational skills are learned better if children guide their own learning. However, vocabulary is learned better with adults guiding the children's learning (Epstein, 2009). A professional teacher will assess these skills and then implement lessons and activities appropriately to teach these skills. The assessment allows the teacher to know where the child is developmentally and which method to take in teaching the skill, whether child-centered or adult-centered.

Using assessment intentionally to subsequently teach a young child is also supported by the NAEYC (2009b). The NAEYC supports teachers purposefully adapting and planning curriculum based on careful observation and documentation as a manner of improving teaching. Indeed, assessment is seen as an integral part of intentional and effective teaching by many in the field of early childhood education.

WHAT ARE SOME ASSESSMENT AND EVALUATION CONCERNS?

Throughout this chapter, the authors have relayed to the reader the importance of observing and assessing as objectively and sensitively as possible. It is important to acknowledge that we all have an observational filter that influences our judgments and assessments of young children. Our filters are a major concern related to all categories of observation and assessment that are mentioned and discussed in this section of the chapter. The concerns to be discussed are psychometrics (statistics), communicating with parents, accountability, test bias, age at assessment, and environmental assessment. All of these concerns are critical considerations when making and utilizing observation and assessment techniques with young children.

Psychometrics

Statistical concerns about observation, assessment, and evaluation have been mentioned throughout this chapter. Concerns such as reliability and validity have been mentioned and defined briefly in relation to naturalistic observation. Those issues are mentioned again and expanded upon here.

Reliability concerns the issue of whether or not a measure computes the same score again and again. For example, if a young child completes a rating scale on Tuesday at 9 a.m., will the score be statistically the same when the child takes the same test on Friday at 1 p.m.? There is also the issue of **inter-rater reliability**, which refers to whether or not different people utilizing a certain measure get the same score. Inter-rater reliability is really important when using teacher-devised tests or more performance-based tests, such as judgments of oral presentations, reflective journal writing, or portfolios. These types of tests (evaluation methods) are not standardized or normed on large populations of young children. Performance-based tests, in particular, are based considerably on the judgments or values of individual scorers/graders. Therefore, establishing inter-rater reliability is quite necessary. Rubrics help with inter-rater reliability of qualitative or performance-based assessments. Rubrics are scoring/grading frameworks that relay criteria and standards for scoring or grading work and behavior.

Validity is another psychometric issue/concern when conducting observations, assessments, and evaluations. Validity is a determination of whether or not a test measures the entity it purports to measure. In other words, does an assessment of socioemotional development measure that dimension, or does it measure some other dimension such as cognitive development or science knowledge? There are varying types of validity, just as there are varying types of reliability such as general reliability and inter-rater reliability. There is **face validity**, which determines whether or not an assessment looks like it measures what it purports to measure. There is also **content validity**, which establishes whether or not the material on the assessment covers and includes the appropriate information for the domain or developmental area it purports to cover. **Construct validity** is another type of validity that concerns whether or not the items or questions on different sections of an assessment stay together statistically. For instance, an assessment of mathematical and scientific knowledge should have two statistical constructs. The mathematical items should stay together statistically, and the science items should stay together statistically. The items should correlate. The last type of validity to be discussed is **concurrent validity**. This type of validity concerns whether or not two assessments of the same content correlate with each other and is important when creating a new measure or assessment. It is important to gain concurrent validity with an already established measure or assessment.

As with reliability, validity is a special concern with qualitative or performance-type assessments. Face validity and content validity are easier to establish than construct or concurrent validity with performance-based assessment. This is because with performance-based assessment, young children are actually acting and behaving in direct relation to the content. For instance, assessing a young child's athletic ability by how well the child performs has face and content validity. It is important to note that standardized assessments may sometimes have a considerable amount of construct and concurrent validity, but less face or content validity. This is because with standardized assessments, children are usually sitting and writing down answers. In this instance, assessing a young child's athletic ability with a paper-and-pencil test has great construct and concurrent validity, but less face or content validity.

It is very important that the observations, assessments, and evaluations that you as a teacher utilize be both reliable and valid. These measures have a great impact on the young children you teach. They also impact how you communicate with and relate to parents, as well as the accountability standards on which you may be judged.

Communicating With Parents and Family

At some point, you as a teacher will find it necessary to talk with parents or other family members about the growth and development of the young children that you teach. Perhaps a child is developing typically, or maybe a child is below or above the average/norm expectations. Whatever you are communicating to the parents, it is important that you know very well both the child and the assessments used; that you collect a variety of assessments, which are qualitative/nonstandardized and quantitative/standardized over time; and that you be sensitive and respectful in your communications. One way of aiding in this communication process is to videotape children's behavior and development. Be sure to get the parents' permission and to conduct the videotaping objectively, sensitively, and respectfully (Hundt, 2002). An example of this is sharing videotapes of children's behavior with parents.

A video of a child's behavior can capture the child's ability and developmental level (Hundt, 2002). It is also useful for capturing social/emotional expressions and interactions. Videos take place in a given context that is real, play-based, and performance-like. Usually, videos of this type are not conducted in a controlled laboratory. Moreover, videos can aid in your communication with parents during parent-teacher conferences and increase parent communication in general (Hundt, 2002). The videos can directly illustrate points about children's behavior or development.

Here are some tips, from Hundt (2002) and the authors of this textbook, to help you as a teacher when you share videos with parents and family members as a communication tool:

- Establish that the video is one piece of evidence in the child's portfolio.
- Communicate sensitively with parents the objectives of the videotaping.
- Give the parents a context when sharing the video.
- Realize that videotaping is time-consuming.
- Allow parents to videotape their child at home and share these recordings with you.
- Allow parents to communicate their perspectives and viewpoints to you.

Communicating with parents and other family members about young children's development and assessment results takes sensitivity, patience, and understanding. You as a professional teacher have to consider culture, language, special needs, your own filter, and other concerns. It is important to respect the needs, fears, and positions of the children's family members.

There are a number of other ways to improve communication with parents such as newsletters, photographs, the judicious use of e-mail, parent boards and councils, and parent surveys. All of these methods can, in some ways, be used to communicate assessment and evaluation information. You as a teacher may also be prepared with suggestions for activities and strategies for the parents and family members to interact with the child at home. It is important to remember that communication is a two-way street. It is also important to remember to be objective, sensitive, and respectful. Realize, too, that parents and families have their own set of experiences, expectations, philosophies, and standards just as you as the teacher do. For example, you may think that celebrating a child's birthday with cupcakes is a good thing. The families of the children you teach may not agree with celebrating birthdays at all, or they may want healthier food served at the celebration. Observing and assessing young children from these families during a birthday celebration at the school may not be optimal.

With sensitivity and planning, sharing with a family about a child's development can be a positive experience.

Accountability and High-Stakes Testing

Not only do you as the teacher have to communicate with parents; you must also communicate the results of your assessments and evaluations to other stakeholders and interested parties, such as politicians, school board members, and taxpayers. You will be held accountable for the progress, learning, and development demonstrated by the children you teach. There are standards that you as a teacher and the children you teach have to meet. Most states have or are in the process of developing early learning foundations for infants, toddlers, and preschoolers. Most states have standards for the early elementary grades up to third grade and beyond.

This level of responsibility may seem to be a lot of pressure to put on you as a teacher and the children you teach. However, there are positives to assessment and accountability. When assessment is done correctly, it can be an aid in improving instructional practices and strategies. Assessment and accountability can be utilized to make sure that all children are treated fairly despite their race, ethnicity, socioeconomic status, or special need. Assessment and accountability can illustrate the wonderful tremendous work that you as a teacher of young children have accomplished. The opening vignette illustrates just such an example of how assessment can aid teaching.

In order to ensure that observations, assessments, and evaluations are used appropriately, you as a teacher of young children must become knowledgeable about the assessments you utilize. You must learn how to communicate the results of assessments to all stakeholders. Most important, you must conduct your assessments objectively and sensitively. Remember that the future of the children you teach, the families you serve, and your own career path depend on the results of your teaching as assessed by observations, assessments, and evaluations.

Test Bias

Observations, assessments, and evaluations can be biased whether they are standardized or not. Even qualitative and performance-based assessments can be biased because we observe from our filter of experience, culture, and philosophy. The cultural bias of standardized tests is well

Consider This   Assessing the Development of Infants

Melinda, a concerned, loving grandparent, has a grandson who was born prematurely. At birth, he had a low weight, could not eat without assistance, and could not regulate his body temperature. When it was recommended that her infant grandson be assessed, Melinda thought that prospect was ridiculous. She wondered what a premature infant could demonstrate. But now she sees that the professional making the recommendation wanted to help her grandson reach his full potential. The professional wanted her grandson to "be all that he can be." Testing is part of that process, and after the assessment Melinda and her daughter knew what to do to help further his development.

How do you as an early childhood professional feel about assessing infants? Why do you think some family members and early childhood professionals do not agree with assessing young infants?

documented (Santos, 2004). It is hard to make a test that is culture-free (Wortham, 2005), but some tests are more culture-fair. These tests have been mentioned previously in this chapter.

There are several things that teachers can do to minimize the effects that test bias has on students' performance records. Allowing multiple assessments of various types to go into a child's portfolio will help ameliorate test bias. Allowing parents to advocate for their child and have some input into the testing process will also help ameliorate test bias. The authors suggest that there are two important considerations to take into account when assessing young children: (1) Try to be as objective and sensitive as possible, and (2) try to treat each assessment as a formative one (not a summative one) that informs as to how to help a young child grow and develop.

Age at Assessment

At what age should we begin assessing young children? That is another question of concern with observations, assessments, and evaluations. There exist assessments of children as infants, and some of these assessments are mentioned in this text. As mentioned before, California is in the process of creating early learning foundations for infants. Assessment of early elementary-aged children is quite routine in most states, counties, and school districts. The key thing to remember is that in the early years, development sometimes occurs slowly and sometimes occurs rapidly and in spurts; additionally, there is a lot of individual variation in the developmental rates of young children (NAEYC, 2009b). Utilize assessments that are as developmentally appropriate as possible. Also, remember that development is quite fluid and variable in young children.

The Environment

The last concern to be addressed is the environment. Just as a child's age should be considered when conducting observation, assessment, and evaluation and using its results, the environment should also be considered. The child may behave differently in separate environments, such as home and school or home and educational center. The child may behave differently depending on the people in his or her environment at that time. Therefore, it is important to consider the child's environment. Thelma Harms, a well-known and celebrated early childhood professional, and her colleagues have developed some standardized observation assessments that measure the child's care and educational environment. These assessments/scales measure infant and toddler environments, early childhood environments, school-age environments (mostly for after-school care environments), and family child care environments. These assessments also gather information about special needs and diversity. There are also two standardized assessments by Bradley and Caldwell (1977, 1979) that measure the home environment: one for infants and toddlers, and another for early childhood/preschool-aged children. Recent research shows that these assessments can also be used to measure the environment of family child care homes (Bradley, Caldwell, & Corwyn, 2003). Conducting these assessments can aid in understanding and communicating with parents and families. For example, scores on environmental assessments might uncover that a young child acts differently at school than at home. With this information, the child's family and teacher can cooperate to aid the child by making the two environments more similar and suitable for promoting optimal development. Using all of these environmental instruments to assess the environment at home and at school can give you as a teacher important insight into why a young child in your care may be developing or behaving in a certain manner.

Summary

Professional and knowledgeable teachers can learn so much just by observing the children they are teaching. They can come to understand where the children are in each developmental domain. They can also understand what skills they have taught well and what skills still need more practice. Acute observation is important because in today's educational environment both formative assessment and summative assessment are unavoidable. All quality assessments are based on good observations.

Professional assessment may be detailed, but if carried out meticulously and carefully, it can help you as a teacher to complete your duties. Assessment can help you to further the development of the children you teach. It can also help you to gain support and validation for your efforts. The key to assessment is carrying it out sensitively and objectively and using the right type of assessment for your purpose. With patience and some work, assessment can actually become a friend to the professional early childhood educator.

Key Terms

Alternative assessments 149	Face validity 158	Observation 142
Assessment 142	Formal observations 143	Performance assessment 149
Checklist 146	Formative evaluations 149	Rating scale 147
Concurrent validity 159	Frequency count 146	Reflective journal or diary 143
Construct validity 158	Informal observations 143	Reliable 154
Content validity 158	Intelligence 151	Rubrics 156
Criterion-referenced	Inter-rater reliability 158	Standardized assessments and tests 149
assessments 149	Narrative Descriptions 144	Summative evaluations 149
Duration record 146	Naturalistic observation 154	Time sampling 144
Evaluation 142	Norm-referenced 149	Valid 154
Event sampling 144	Objective 142	Validity 158

Reflection, Application, and Analysis Questions

1. Name and describe three positives to assessment in terms of how it can aid you as a teacher when working with young children and their families.

2. Early childhood educators will use formative assessment the most, but can you think of a situation when it would

be wise to use summative assessment? Name and describe the situation, and then delineate three reasons why this choice would be made.

3. Name and describe three positives about normative standardized assessments.

4. Create a rubric that you as a teacher could use to assess a child's performance in language production.

5. Should ethnic minorities be assessed with the typical and usual assessments, or should there be alternative assessments for them? Please state your beliefs, and then support your beliefs with three fully described reasons.

Extension Activities

1. Go to a place that has lots of children such as a mall, a playground, a park, or a zoo. Pick a place where you can see plenty of children. Then try to observe one or two children intently and take notes. Try applying what you have learned from this textbook so far to what you see the children doing. Record the terms and concepts from this textbook in your journal, by describing them in action from the children's behavior. Watch the children for an hour or two, and apply all of the terms that you see emerge from the children's actions.

2. Interview a preschool or early elementary school teacher in your local neighborhood by asking five basic questions. Ask this teacher how he or she assesses the children he or she teaches. Then ask the teacher how he or she uses those assessments and what are the results of those assessments. Then ask the teacher how the school, school district, and public use those assessments and how that impacts his or her classroom and the children he or she teaches. The teacher's answers to these five questions will be illuminating to you as you learn more about early childhood education.

Additional Readings

Assessing young children is an important task. A teacher has to be prepared and objective. These additional readings can assist teachers as they carry out this duty.

Billman, J., & Sherman, J. (2003). *Observation and participation in early childhood settings.* **New York: Merrill.**
This book gives general information about different types of assessment and observation methods. It also teaches how to interact with children. Activities are included in each chapter.

Witte, R. H. (2012). *Classroom assessment for teachers.* **New York: McGraw-Hill.**
This book provides up-to-date information about classroom assessment. It is based on the inquiry-oriented approach and

demonstrates the relationship between assessment and teaching. It also discusses contemporary issues in assessment.

Wortham, S. C. (2012). *Tests and measurements in early childhood education* **(6th ed.). New York: Merrill.**
The sixth edition of this book provides general information about assessment in young children. It also discusses how to assess, and presents principles for identifying quality assessments in, young children.

On the Web

American Institutes for Research - *http://www.learningpt.org/*
This website created and monitored by the American Institutes for Research contains evidence-based information about the process of assessing and assessments, and is good for teachers and parents.

Council of Chief State School Officers - *www.ccsso.org*
The Council of Chief State School Officers website explains who the organization is and what it does. Information about state and some federal assessment systems is available.

National Association of School Psychologists - *www.nasponline.org*
This is the official website of the National Association of School Psychologists, which publishes a number of assessments used in schools around the country. This site is also good for teachers and parents.

Student Study Site

Visit **www.sagepub.com/gordonbiddle** to access several study tools including eFlashcards, web quizzes, links to SAGE journal articles, web resources, video resources, lesson plan templates, and more.

Lesson Plan:

"Do I Know Who I Am?"

Subject:

General realization you are separate from others and are your own person.

Focus:

Recognizing oneself in the mirror.

Overview:

Around 15 to 21 months of age, children begin to recognize themselves in the mirror. This new awareness comes about because of cognitive advances. This new awareness also marks basic observation and evaluative skills.

Purpose:

To help infants/toddlers become aware of themselves in the mirror. This represents cognitive and evaluative advances in addition to social and emotional advances.

Objectives:

1. Assist with obtaining self-recognition.

2. Assist with obtaining general self-awareness.

3. Advance cognitive development and, in turn, social and emotional development.

4. Advance basic observation and evaluative skills.

Resource Materials:

- Several mirrors.
- Red lipstick.
- A visually interesting hat.

Activities and Procedures:

1. Stand the mirrors on the floor at the child's eye level in several strategic places.

2. When the child notices a mirror, put some lipstick on the child's nose.

3. See if the child touches his or her nose or the nose in the mirror.

4. Let the child explore and experience the situation, giving the child time to notice the lipstick on the mirror image.

5. Verbally ask the child questions such as "Who is that?" and "Where is that red nose?"

6. If the child still doesn't seem to notice anything, repeat the same steps with the visually interesting hat.

Tying It All Together:

This is a fun and interesting activity for both the child and the teacher. With infants/toddlers who don't react to their mirror image, you may want to repeat the activity after a few weeks. Eventually, the child's development combined with the repeated experience will facilitate skill development. Although elements of emotional and social development are present in this activity, basic observation and evaluation skills are also present. Remember that all the domains of children's development are interrelated, especially at this young age.

Visit **www.sagepub.com/gordonbiddle** to access templates of these lesson plans.

Lesson Plan:
"Did I Count That Right?"

Early Childhood
(3 to 5 yrs)

Subject:
Basic counting ability and evaluation.

Focus:
Checking to see if you have counted the objects correctly.

Overview:
With the emergence of one-to-one correspondence, young children can count small numbers of objects accurately.

Purpose:
To help young children remember to check the accuracy of their counting by simply counting the objects again.

Objectives:
1. To learn, practice, and reinforce basic counting skills.
2. To learn to be careful when counting and to check one's accuracy.
3. To develop basic observation and evaluation skills by simply checking counting accuracy.

Resource Materials:
- A set of three to five manipulatives such as LEGO bricks, checkers, or dominoes.

Activities and Procedures:
1. Place the set of manipulatives in front of the preschooler.
2. Ask the child how many there are.
3. If the child dos not automatically count them by pointing to each one, ask the child to count them.
4. If the child still does not count them by pointing to each one, ask the child to count and point to each one while counting.
5. Then ask the child if the number is correct.
6. Then ask the child to recount them being sure to point to each one while counting.
7. Then ask the child if he or she is sure the number is correct.

Tying It All Together:
Most preschoolers can count at least three objects, and some can count five or more. The skill to emphasize in this lesson is checking to see if the counting is accurate. This is a basic observation, assessment, and evaluation skill that preschoolers can develop.

Visit **www.sagepub.com/gordonbiddle** to access templates of these lesson plans.

Lesson Plan:

Peer Assessment of Spelling Quizzes

Subject:

Spelling, language arts.

Focus:

Obtaining an understanding of assessment processes through peer assessment.

Overview:

Being able to observe, assess, and evaluate is a good skill set to develop. In the right classroom environment with positive and supportive relationships among peers, children can begin to develop these skills in the context of language arts.

Purpose:

To help children develop observation, assessment, and evaluation skills.

Objectives:

1. To help young children create a positive and supportive environment among peers.

2. To develop observation, assessment, and evaluation skills.

3. To increase spelling accuracy.

Resource Materials:

- A spelling list from the current unit of study.
- Written and verbal models of the current word list spelled accurately.
- A positive and supportive classroom environment.

Activities and Procedures:

1. Complete the spelling test as normal, but change the assessment process.

2. Have the children grade each other's spelling tests.

3. The children must be prepared to know that this type of assessment is coming.

4. The children must be given a rubric or some guidelines for assessing the spelling test.

5. Be sure the children understand the rubric or guidelines before grading each other.

6. Check the accuracy of the children's assessment before recording the final grades.

Tying It All Together:

Peer assessment is a wonderful experience for students if completed in a positive and supportive classroom. This experience will no doubt develop the students' observation, assessment, and evaluation skills. However, this experience will enhance their social and emotional development as well.

Visit **www.sagepub.com/gordonbiddle** to access templates of these lesson plans.

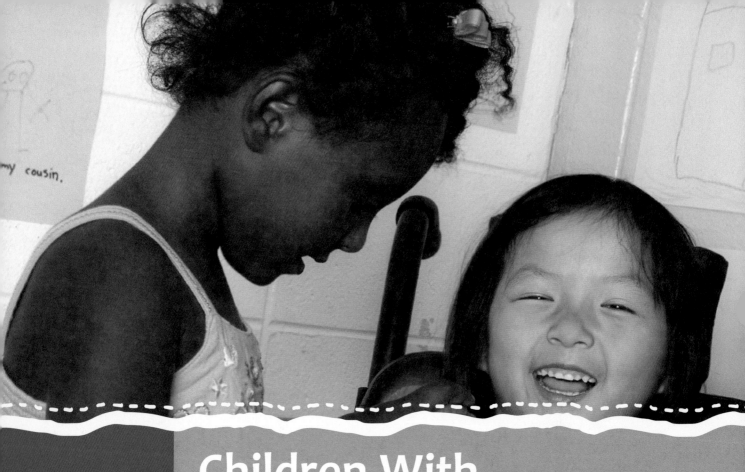

CHAPTER 7

Children With Exceptional Needs In Early Childhood Education

This chapter will help you answer these important questions:

- How has the field of special education evolved?
- What is the spectrum of IDEA disability categories?
- What is the role of the early education professional in the special education cycle?
- What types of special education services are available to children with special needs?
- How has assistive technology improved access and removed barriers for children with special needs?
- How does inclusion of children with special needs in early childhood education settings promote learning?
- How do schools respond to the needs of children who are gifted and talented?
- What are best practices for communicating with parents and families of children with exceptional needs?

Vignette: Educational Accommodations

Margarita is a kindergarten teacher who works for a school district that supports the inclusion of students with exceptional needs in regular education classrooms. She is both excited and nervous to start the new school year. She has prepared the classroom environment to provide a wide range of learning experiences for her students. Margarita has taught children with various learning needs during her career, but this time she will support a child diagnosed as being on the autism spectrum. Tommy has expressive and language delays and will require augmentative communication adaptations throughout the school day. Margarita has received educational training and participated in the development of an individual education program (IEP) for Tommy. During the school year she will collaborate with the special education teacher, the speech and language pathologist, the occupational therapist, and an instructional assistant. Margarita will provide Tommy the educational accommodations he requires.

Margarita wants to create a learning environment that promotes inclusiveness and acceptance of all children with diverse cultural, linguistic, and special needs backgrounds. She will prepare her students to meet the required standards while supporting Tommy's unique academic needs. She is aware that there will be challenges ahead; nevertheless, she also believes that a relationship of collaboration and problem solving with the special education team will make the experience rewarding for all of the children.

The full **inclusion** in early childhood education settings of children with special needs and children who are typically developing has evolved into one of the most important aspects of effective programming for young children. Full inclusion implies that children with special needs will receive all instruction in a regular classroom with supports and aids. Needless to say, however, adherence to recent legislation—the **Individuals with Disabilities Education Act (IDEA)**, which requires that all general education systems provide comprehensive and individualized services to all children with special needs—has been wrought with challenges and some hesitation on behalf of early childhood educators. This is perhaps due to the very complex nature of the process of inclusion in early childhood education programs, which requires early childhood teachers' knowledge and understanding of atypical development, the use of screening and assessment tools, and various

Key Elements
for Becoming a Professional

NAEYC DEVELOPMENTALLY APPROPRIATE PRINCIPLE 3

Development and learning proceed at varying rates from child to child, as well as at uneven rates across different areas of a child's individual functioning.

Interpretation

All children, including those with special needs, will demonstrate a wide range of physical, cognitive, communication, and social/emotional skills. This variation is normal, but the early child professional needs to have knowledge of typical child development to determine if a child will require special education intervention.

NAEYC DEVELOPMENTALLY APPROPRIATE PRINCIPLE 5

Early experiences have profound effects, both cumulative and delayed, on a child's development and learning; optimal periods exist for certain types of development and learning to occur.

Interpretation

There are many factors, both biological and environmental, that can disrupt development. During sensitive periods, a child must receive stimulation to develop normally. Early intervention can have a positive influence on infants, toddlers, and preschoolers, particularly those with special needs.

NAEYC STANDARD 1: PROMOTING CHILD DEVELOPMENT AND LEARNING

a. Knowing and understanding young children's characteristics and needs

b. Knowing and understanding the multiple influences on development and learning

c. Using developmental knowledge to create healthy, respectful, supportive, and challenging learning environments

NAEYC STANDARD 4: TEACHING AND LEARNING

a. Building close relationships with children and families

b. Using developmentally effective teaching and learning strategies

c. Having sound knowledge of academic disciplines and content areas

d. Combining all of these to give children experiences that promote development and learning

assistive technologies. **Assistive technologies** include devices and services for students with special needs that allow them to participate and be successful in school (National Association for the Education of Young Children [NAEYC], 2012).

Over the past few years, the role of regular education teachers has increased significantly as they seek to implement, monitor, and adjust specific intervention strategies to enhance all children's optimum success in inclusive early childhood education settings. Hence, the knowledge, skills, and attitudes of early childhood educators are tantamount to ensuring effective practice for children with special needs.

Children with exceptional needs include children with special needs and those with gifts and talents. Children with special needs require special education services to meet their potential. While children who are gifted and talented are not eligible for special education services, they do require a differentiated curriculum or accelerated instruction. Some children can simultaneously have both a disability and a gift or talent. In our opening vignette we learned about Tommy, a child who has autism. Autism is a spectrum disorder, which means that children can have symptoms that fall on a continuum of severity. **Autism spectrum disorders** are pervasive developmental disorders that can be characterized by (1) impairments in reciprocal interactions, (2) impairments in verbal and nonverbal communication skills, (3) repetitive behavior, (4) intellectual delays, and (5) fine and gross motor delays.

As a professional in early childhood education, you will have many opportunities to teach children with exceptional needs in your classroom. It is important to consider that children with exceptional needs in the regular classroom form a community of learners where every child has unique strengths and challenges.

HOW HAS THE FIELD OF SPECIAL EDUCATION EVOLVED?

In our opening vignette we met Margarita, a kindergarten teacher, who will welcome Tommy as part of an inclusive regular education program. Today, a child diagnosed as being on the autism spectrum can be successfully integrated into a regular classroom with appropriate support. The Education for All Handicapped Children (EAHC) Act of 1975, now known as the Individuals with Disabilities Education Act (IDEA), was the first federal law to ensure that students like Tommy, who qualify for special education services, receive a **free and appropriate public education (FAPE)**. Prior to the act, many states had laws excluding students who were deaf, blind, emotionally disturbed, or mentally retarded from public schools (Bursztyn, 2007; U.S. Department of Education, 2005). FAPE is defined as special education and related services designed to meet the unique needs of the child, provided at no cost to the parents. A brief history of special education is necessary as it will provide some context for working with parents and advocacy groups committed to the full inclusion of children with special needs, like Tommy, in regular education classrooms. Table 7.1 provides a summary of historical events in the field of special education along with educational implications for students with special needs.

Table 7.1 will be useful as you learn about special education and related services for children with special needs. Basic knowledge of federal laws and procedures will empower you as a professional in early childhood education. This knowledge will also help you advocate for students with special needs.

From Segregation to Inclusion

During the 19th century, early attempts to educate children with special needs took place in private or state institutions for the mentally retarded, blind, or deaf. The 1950s led to the development of self-contained classrooms within public schools. For example, children with mental retardation, hearing and visual impairments, emotional disturbance, and physical disabilities were placed in classrooms segregated from their peers without disabilities (Winzer, 1993). Some local school districts opened special schools for children with special needs, further isolating them. Children with special needs eventually gained equal access to public education following federal legislation and landmark court cases as noted in Table 7.1.

The integration of children with special needs in public schools prevents isolation and offers broader opportunities for bonding and friendships.

Education for All Handicapped Children Act

In 1975, the Education for All Handicapped Children (EAHC) Act (Public Law 94-142, Part B) mandated states to provide a free and appropriate public education (FAPE) to all students with special needs ages 5 to 18 years in the **least restrictive environment (LRE)**. The concept of LRE emphasized the importance of providing children with special needs instruction in the regular classroom, to the maximum extent possible. According to Burns (2007), the least restrictive environment is defined as the "regular classroom, but 'environment' also includes the physical environment, the curriculum, other students in the classroom, and the classroom teacher" (pp. 37–38). Although not mentioned in the law, **mainstreaming** gained support and is based on the idea that children with special needs can participate in the regular classroom during specific times to the extent that it meets their individual needs. Students must demonstrate that they can learn the same material at the same rate as their peers who exhibit typical development.

The EAHC Act required that regular education teachers learn about the assessment techniques used to identify children for special education and about the interventions to serve them. The law mandated that parents be part of **multidisciplinary teams** where professionals from various disciplines came together to identify and place students in special education programs. Moreover, legislation required an **individual education program (IEP)**, or a written plan to help meet the special learning and social needs of each child.

By 1986, amendments to the EAHC Act led to the passage of Public Law 99-457 (Part C), which established a federal preschool program, extending special education services to children ages 3 to 5 years. The government also established an early intervention program for infants and toddlers with developmental delays or disabilities from birth to 2 years of age. States were required to develop an **individual family service plan (IFSP)** for all infants and toddlers with special needs. The IFSP is similar to the IEP, but it prioritizes developmental outcomes and the needs of the family. You will learn more about the content of IEPs and IFSPs later in this chapter.

Individuals with Disabilities Education Act

In 1990, the Individuals with Disabilities Education Act (IDEA) replaced the EAHC Act. IDEA added two new disability categories: autism and traumatic brain disorder. IDEA required that all early childhood programs be prepared to provide services to children with special needs. This included

YEAR	HISTORICAL EVENT	EDUCATIONAL IMPLICATIONS
1965	Elementary and Secondary Education Act (Public Law 89-10) and the ESEA Amendments (Public Law 89-313)	Schools can apply for grants to help educate children with special needs. However, schools are not mandated to educate students with special needs. The Office of Special Education is created.
1970	Diana v. California State Board of Education	Plaintiffs filed on behalf of Diana, a Spanish-speaking student, alleging that the Monterey County school system had misdiagnosed her as mentally retarded on the basis of an intelligence test administered in English. Court ruled Spanish-speaking children had to be retested in their native language.
1971	Pennsylvania Association for Retarded Children (PARC) v. Commonwealth of Pennsylvania	Supreme Court ruled that children with mental retardation could not be denied equal access to public education by the state. Children with special needs were entitled to receive a free and appropriate public education similar to that afforded to students without disabilities.
1972	Mills v. Board of Education of the District of Columbia	The court ruled that a school district was responsible for providing free public education services to children with exceptional needs or paying for placement in private schools. The expense of educating a child with special needs was not justification for children to remain out of school.
1973	Section 504 of the Rehabilitation Act	This law passed to protect individuals with a physical and mental impairment that substantially limits one or more of their daily living skills, including learning, from discrimination.
1975	Education for All Handicapped Children Act (EAHCA) (Public Law 94-142)	This law mandates all school districts to educate students with special needs between ages 3 and 5 years. Prior to this law most children with special needs were excluded from the educational system or placed in private institutions.
1979	Larry P. v. Riles	This California court case spoke to the overrepresentation of Black students in educable mentally retarded (EMR) classrooms based on the use of an intelligence test. California schools were banned from using intelligence tests on the basis that they were culturally biased against Black children. This law only applied to California.
1986	The EAHCA is amended with the addition of Public Law 99-457 (Part C).	Establishes a federal preschool program extending special education services to children ages 3 to 5 years. An early intervention program is also established for infants and toddlers with developmental delays or disabilities from birth to 2 years of age.
1989	Daniel R. R. v. State Board of Education	The court ruled that inclusion in a regular prekindergarten was inappropriate for Daniel, a child with mental retardation. Daniel required constant attention from the teacher and the aide, received little educational benefit, and was disrupting the class. Daniel was removed from the regular education classroom and placed in a special day class.
1990	The EAHCA is amended and now called the Individuals with Disabilities Education Act (IDEA) (Public Law 101-476).	Addition of autism and traumatic brain injury as disability categories. Extends special education services to include social work and assistive technology. Requires schools to provide bilingual special education programs for students with special needs.

1990	Americans with Disabilities Act (ADA) (Public Law 101-476)	Protects equal opportunity to accommodations. ADA adopts the Section 504 regulations as part of the ADA statute. This has significant implications for teachers and schools because it requires that modifications and accommodations be made for students in the regular classroom. Section 504 plans become common in schools and benefit some students who do not qualify for special education, such as children with attention deficit disorder or attention deficit/hyperactivity disorder.
1997	Individuals with Disabilities Education Act (Public Law 105-17)	Regular education teachers are now required to attend IEP meetings. There is an increased focus on giving students with special needs access to the regular curriculum. The amendment calls for students with disabilities to take part in state- and districtwide assessments. States are allowed to extend the use of the disability category of developmental delay for students through the age of 9 years.
2001	No Child Left Behind (NCLB) Act	School-age students with special needs are expected to achieve the same learning outcomes as their peers who are typically developing but with adaptations and accommodations to the curriculum. NCLB requires that 95% of students with special needs be included in state accountability systems. Law does not apply to preschool children with special needs.
2004	Individuals with Disabilities Improvement Act is reauthorized (Public Law 108-446). It is still referred to as IDEA.	There is increased accountability at the state and local levels, as more data on outcomes are required. A response-to-intervention (RTI) model is introduced to address academic problems in a timely manner and reduce the number of students disproportionately represented in special education. Early intervention service funds allow students to receive intervention without having to qualify for special education.

designing facilities and outdoor play structures to accommodate children with disabilities. IDEA provisions also mandated programs to provide assistive technology to increase student participation and access to the curriculum. The various levels of assistive technology will be covered later in the chapter.

Individuals with Disabilities Education Improvement Act

The Individuals with Disabilities Education Improvement Act of 2004 was a reauthorization of IDEA. Let's summarize Parts B and C of IDEA. Part B establishes funds to ensure that children and students age 3 through 21 years (some states extend services until the age of 22) receive a free and appropriate public education, or FAPE. Part C provides funds to state education agencies to develop and implement a statewide, comprehensive, coordinated, multidisciplinary, interagency system that provides early intervention services for infants and toddlers with disabilities and families under the age of 2 years (U.S. Department of Education, 2005). Services are also extended to infants and toddlers who are "at risk" of experiencing substantial developmental delay if these services are not provided. IDEA 2004 was aligned with the No Child Left Behind Act of 2001.

No Child Left Behind Act

The passage of the No Child Left Behind (NCLB) Act of 2001 brought significant educational reform to all students. NCLB legislation requires states to develop curriculum standards for K–12 students. Students with exceptional needs are expected to achieve the same learning outcomes as their peers who are typically developing but with adaptations and accommodations to the curriculum. NCLB requires that 95% of students with special needs be included in state accountability systems. For

more information about NCLB, refer to Chapter 16. Let's turn now to how children are classified into categories of disability.

WHAT IS THE SPECTRUM OF IDEA CHILDHOOD DISABILITY CATEGORIES?

IDEA's disability categories guide how states define disabilities and develop eligibility criteria. States also monitor disproportionate representation of students from culturally and linguistically diverse backgrounds being served in special education programs.

Children with special needs received the right to a free and appropriate public education (FAPE) in 1975.

Disability Categories

IDEA defines 13 disability categories that can have an adverse educational impact for children with special needs. Table 7.2 lists the disability categories and the number of children ages 3 through 8 years who qualified under each category in 2010.

Table 7.2 shows that the highest number of children between the ages of 3 and 4 years qualified for special services due to a developmental delay. IDEA allows state and local districts to use the term *developmental delay* for children up to the age of 9 years experiencing delays in physical development, cognitive development, communication development, social/emotional development, or adaptive development. It should be noted that while IDEA provides definitions for disability categories, each state can define disability and determine who is eligible. Often, the IFSP or IEP team will decide a child exhibits "developmental delay" to avoid classification of students at an early age. Table 7.2 indicates that by age 5 years, the number of children diagnosed with a developmental delay declined sharply while the number of children with a specific learning disability consistently showed a yearly increase. The number of children diagnosed with intellectual disabilities increased significantly between the ages of 3 and 8 years. Other categories that showed a large increase were other health impairment and traumatic brain injury.

Also noteworthy is that the number of children labeled as autistic increased across all age levels since 2005 (U.S. Department of Education, 2010). For instance, there was an average 60% increase among children ages 3 to 8 years. It is paramount that regular education teachers be prepared to plan instruction for and assess children who fall along the autism spectrum. Recall from our vignette that Margarita has received educational training and participated in the development of an IEP for Tommy. Educating children with autism requires knowledge of developmental milestones and systematic interventions. For example, children with autism demonstrate delays in social development and will require a social skills program to learn appropriate behaviors necessary for participation in social situations. Teachers can use play within the curriculum to teach important social skills (Jamison, Forston, & Stanton-Chapman, 2012).

Disproportionate Representation in Special Education

The disproportionate representation of students from culturally and linguistically diverse backgrounds in special education is reflected across all states and is a serious concern. Black, Latino, and Native American students, as well as English language learners (ELL), have historically been

Table 7.2
Children and Students Served Under IDEA, Part B, in the United States and Outlying Areas, by Age and Disability Category, 2010

DISABILITY CATEGORY	3-YEAR-OLDS	4-YEAR-OLDS	5-YEAR-OLDS	6-YEAR-OLDS	7-YEAR-OLDS	8-YEAR-OLDS
Specific learning disabilities	1,326	2,120	6,449	20,845	53,530	104,860
Speech/language impairments	66,804	112,909	159,637	202,810	199,450	177,513
Intellectual disability	2,284	3,039	6,705	15,398	16,539	21,674
Emotional disturbance	277	641	2,240	6,167	11,218	16,326
Multiple disabilities	1,809	2,173	5,480	6,295	7,088	8,271
Hearing impairments	2,532	3,006	3,611	4,255	4,731	5,099
Orthopedic impairments	2,035	2,426	3,022	3,675	4,191	4,125
Other health impairments	3,892	5,264	10,855	20,039	30,882	41,485
Visual impairments	927	1,124	1,396	1,660	1,922	2,075
Autism	10,515	15,379	23,357	30,585	34,667	34,307
Deaf/blindness	62	77	91	83	84	99
Traumatic brain injury	256	350	476	647	876	1,149
Developmental delay	85,234	112,916	74,033	45,737	35,135	23,679
All Disabilities	177,953	261,460	295,832	354,625	399,520	439,479

Source: U.S. Department of Education. (2010). *Report of children and students served under IDEA, Part B, in the U.S. and outlying areas, by age and disability category.* Data file, Office of Special Education Programs, Data Analysis System. Retrieved from http://www.ideadata.org/populationdata.asp

disproportionately represented in special education classes (Artiles, Rueda, Salazar, & Higareda, 2002; Blanchett, 2010; Dunn, 1968; Losen & Orfield, 2002). African American boys are significantly overrepresented in the disability categories of intellectual disability and specific learning disability (Council for Exceptional Children, 2002). Similarly, Artiles et al. (2002) reported an overrepresentation of English language learners in the intellectual disability and speech and language impairment disability categories. Moreover, they found that English language learners receiving instruction in English immersion programs over bilingual programs were almost 3 times more likely than other children to participate in a special education program. Overall, children with special needs from culturally and linguistically diverse backgrounds often receive inadequate special education services, they have limited access to a high-quality curriculum and high-quality instruction, and they are often isolated from their peers who are nondisabled (Losen & Orfield, 2002). In fact, these students are underrepresented in less restrictive educational environments, despite the social consensus that inclusion benefits all students (Skiba, Poloni-Staudinger, Gallini, Simmons, & Feggins-Azziz, 2006).

WHAT IS THE ROLE OF THE REGULAR EDUCATION TEACHER IN THE SPECIAL EDUCATION CYCLE?

The role of the regular education teacher in the special education process is essential. Teachers often begin the referral process and take a central role in supporting students who are struggling in the classroom. Recent legislation has increased the responsibilities of regular education teachers at all levels of the special education cycle, as illustrated in Figure 7.1.

Professionalism & Policy

Special Education Racial Disparity

All teachers need to be prepared to work with children with special needs. The problem of disproportionate representation in special education impacts teachers of both special education and regular education. In 2004, IDEA included regulatory requirements addressing disproportionality and overidentification. States must have policies, practices, and procedures in place to prevent the disproportionate representation of students in special education; for example, they must report special education placement based on race and ethnicity.

It is important to consider that most children do not enter school diagnosed with a disability. Teachers of regular education refer students for evaluation, and these students will likely qualify for special education. Along with school-level policies and practices, teacher perceptions and decisions impact the observed racial disparity within special education (Losen & Orfield, 2000). As a professional in early childhood education, it is important to be aware of your own biases and assumptions regarding students from culturally and linguistically diverse backgrounds as you will play a critical role in the special education cycle.

Child Find

Child Find is a mandate of IDEA that requires states to identify, locate, evaluate, and track students with special needs from birth through age 21 years. Moreover, states are required to implement a multidisciplinary system of early intervention services for infants and toddlers with special needs. Early childhood teachers who suspect that a student has a disability and is in need of special education services need to refer the child for evaluation within a reasonable time.

Referral

Teachers are required to assess children's development prior to kindergarten to document progress and to determine if there are developmental delays in cognitive, social, emotional, language, or physical development. As an early childhood professional working with infants, toddlers, and preschool children, it is essential that you have a foundation in learning theories and developmental stages as young children develop at different rates. This knowledge base can help you make a determination if a referral for diagnostic testing is required.

Your responsibility as a K–3 teacher is to begin a referral to the **student study team** when a student is experiencing academic or behavior difficulties. The student study team evaluates the student's performance, makes recommendations, and develops a plan to ensure student success. The student study team includes the parent, the teacher, and a special education representative. As the referring teacher, you will provide background information regarding the child's academic progress or behavioral challenges as well as interventions that you have tried in your classroom. Under IDEA, some important questions need to be addressed before a student can meet eligibility criteria: Did the student participate in a reading program that emphasizes the essential components of reading instruction? These include phonemic awareness, phonics, fluency, vocabulary, and comprehension. Does the child have health, vision, or hearing problems? Is the student limited in English proficiency?

The team may suggest further modifications to be implemented and documented before an evaluation is started. When the parent makes a formal request for an evaluation, this supersedes the student study team process and begins timelines set by states. Most states require an assessment be completed within 60 to 65 days of obtaining parental consent. Some parents may

Figure 7.1 **The Special Education Cycle**

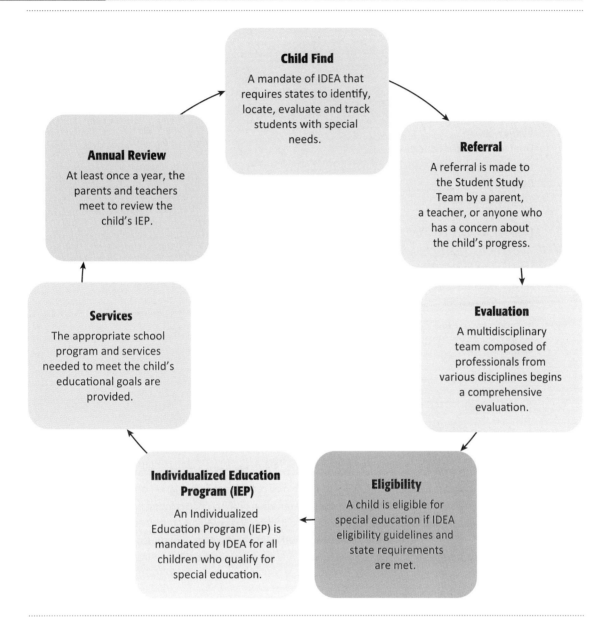

work with an advocate organization to ensure they understand disability rights and special education regulations. Figure 7.2 shows a request for assessment letter for parents adapted from an advocacy organization.

Evaluation

Once a child is referred for special education, a multidisciplinary team composed of professionals from various disciplines begins a comprehensive evaluation to determine if the student meets state eligibility criteria for special education. Based on the referring problem, the team may consist of a school psychologist, a speech and language therapist, a physical therapist, an occupational therapist, a behavior interventionist, and/or a special education teacher. As a classroom teacher, you will need to

| Figure 7.2 | Sample Parent Letter/Request for Assessment |

Terry Smith
Address
City, State Zip Code
Telephone Number
Date

Stanley Becker
Director of Special Education
Local Unified School District
Address
City, State Zip Code

Dear Mr. Becker,

I am writing to refer my son, Alex, for assessment to determine if he is eligible for special education services and support. He is not progressing in school. He is 7 years old and attends Valley Elementary School.

I request that the Sunshine Elementary School District conduct a comprehensive assessment that includes:

1. A psychological evaluation to determine his learning potential.

2. An occupational therapy assessment.

3. A speech and language evaluation.

I also request that my son be evaluated under Section 504 of the Rehabilitation Act of 1973 for the presence of any educational service needed, which may require accommodation or program modification not available under special education or if my child is found not eligible for special education. I also request that the Section 504 coordinator be present at the initial IEP meeting to discuss the results of these evaluations and plan for Alex's continued education. Please ensure that I get copies of the assessment reports one week before the IEP meeting.

Sincerely,

Terry Smith

Source: Adapted from Community Alliance for Special Education & Disability Rights California. (2011).

provide classroom work samples, informal assessment results, and observational notes (Burns, 2007). A student will be administered a variety of standardized tests to determine if a disability is present.

Eligibility

A student is eligible for special education if IDEA eligibility guidelines and state requirements are met. Eligibility criteria will vary by state, so become familiar with your state's requirements. Schools have traditionally relied upon a **significant discrepancy formula** that requires that the student have a significant discrepancy between intellectual ability and academic achievement. For example, a student may have high average ability but be performing well below average in an academic subject area. Under IDEA 2004, school districts can apply to use an innovative approach known as **response to intervention (RTI)**. The National Center on Response to Intervention (n.d.) provides a definition:

> Response to intervention integrates assessment and intervention within a multi-level prevention system to maximize student achievement and reduce behavior problems. With RTI, schools identify students at risk for poor learning outcomes, monitor student progress, provide evidence-based interventions and adjust the intensity and nature of those interventions depending on a student's responsiveness, and identify students with learning disabilities.

RTI emphasizes that schools administer **universal screenings** to all children that include low-cost quick testing during the academic year in order to assess the effectiveness of the curriculum and instruction, as well as to address academic problems in a timely manner. Additionally, RTI expands the identification procedure to include statewide achievement group-administered tests to determine special education eligibility. Schools have to show evidence of equitable access to high-quality standards-aligned instruction and intervention.

Students Who Are Not Eligible

Students who are not eligible for special education may qualify for modifications or accommodations through Section 504. Section 504 of the Rehabilitation Act of 1973 passed to protect individuals with disabilities from discrimination. Individuals with a physical and mental impairment that substantially limits one or more of their daily living skills, including learning, are entitled to protection under the law. The Americans with Disabilities Act (ADA) adopted the Section 504 regulations as part of the ADA statute. Today, Section 504 has significant implications for teachers because it requires that modifications and accommodations be made for students to help them succeed in the regular classroom. Students with an "other health impairment" such as AIDS or attention deficit disorder (ADD) can have a Section 504 plan. For example, some accommodations may include changes to the classroom environment and preferential seating, adaptive aides or technology, small group instruction, extra time to complete assignments or homework, parent/teacher conferences, and support with organization and planning. The role of the Section 504 coordinator is to provide assistance in developing a plan for students who require accommodations. As a professional, you should be familiar with various modifications and accommodations to help children succeed in the classroom.

Individual Education Program

As you may recall, an individual education program (IEP) is mandated by IDEA for students between the ages of 3 and 21 years who qualify for special education. The IEP is a written document that includes (1) disability eligibility, (2) present levels of educational performance, (3) goals and objectives that correspond to the unique needs of the student, and (4) accommodation and adaptations used in the classroom and statewide testing (Rinaldi & Samson, 2008). IEP annual goals have to enable the child to access and participate in the regular education curriculum. IEPs that are culturally and linguistically relevant should describe the extent to which English language learners will participate in bilingual education or an English as a second language (ESL) program.

IDEA requires that the IEP meeting include members from both special education and regular education programs. Regular education teachers who are working directly with the student are mandated to attend. Refer to Figure 7.3 for an overview of the IEP team.

Figure 7.3   IEP Team Members

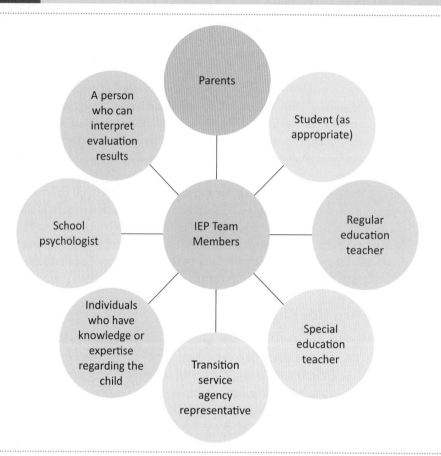

Source: Adapted from www.ed.gov

As an early education professional, you will need to understand the IEP process and the content of the IEP to be an active participant in the development of the plan (Kamens, 2004). According to Weishaar (2001), participation in the IEP process allows the regular education teacher to gain knowledge about the student and learn what needs to be accomplished in the classroom, make suggestions about the supplemental aids and services needed to accommodate the student, and assist in creating and implementing behavioral interventions. The parents should also be actively engaged as equal partners in the IEP process. A third member of the IEP team is a local education agency representative who has knowledge of necessary resources to ensure that the IEP is implemented. For instance, a Section 504 coordinator should be available when a student does not meet eligibility criteria for special education but does meet eligibility criteria for a disability category. The fourth member should be the special education teacher. The final member may be the student when appropriate.

Writing an IEP requires that the members of the IEP team set realistic and achievable goals (Edelen-Smith, 1995; Kamens, 2004). The IEP needs to include goals that are connected with grade-level standards. Davis Holbrook (2007) presents a seven-step process to use in developing a standards-based IEP:

1. Consider the grade-level content standards for the grade in which the student is enrolled or would be enrolled based on age.

2. Examine the classroom and student data to determine where the student is functioning in relation to the grade-level standards.

3. Develop the present level of academic achievement and functional performance.

4. Develop measurable annual goals aligned with grade-level academic content standards.

5. Assess and report the student's progress throughout the year.

6. Identify specially designed instruction including accommodations and/or modification needed to access and progress in the general education curriculum.

7. Determine the most appropriate assessment options.

It is not a good idea to have the IEP written before the meeting. The IEP should be developed during the meeting so that all members can participate in developing the plan. IEP members can contribute present levels of performance, determine eligibility, recommend services, and discuss accommodations (Burns, 2007). If a student is found eligible for special education and the parents agree to services, the IEP is implemented immediately. The IEP is then reviewed annually.

The majority of infants and toddlers with disabilities receive early intervention services within the home setting.

Individual Family Service Plan

As noted earlier, under Part C of IDEA an individual family service plan (IFSP) is written for infants and toddlers under the age of 3 years who qualify as having a disability or are considered "at risk" of experiencing a substantial developmental delay without these services. IDEA requires that the multidisciplinary team be composed of the parent and two or more individuals from separate disciplines, one of whom has to be the service coordinator who facilitates the coordination of services for each service plan. However, multiple agencies may be involved with a family. An IFSP must be completed 45 days after the parent makes a referral. An essential component of an IFSP is a statement of the child's present levels of development across all developmental domains (i.e., physical development [including vision, hearing, and health status], cognitive development, communication development, social or emotional development, and adaptive development). The Office of Special Education and Rehabilitative Services (OSERS) offers a sample IFSP that you will find useful (http://www2.ed.gov/policy/speced/reg/idea/part-c/model-form-ifsp.pdf).

The IFSP differs from an IEP in several ways (Bruder, 2000):

- It revolves around the family, as it is the family that is the constant in a child's life.
- It includes outcomes targeted for the family, as opposed to focusing only on the eligible child.
- It includes the notion of natural environments, which encompass home or community settings such as parks, child care, and gym classes. This focus creates opportunities for learning interventions in everyday routines and activities, rather than only in format-driven, contrived environments.
- It includes activities undertaken with multiple agencies beyond the scope of Part C. These are included to integrate all services into one plan.
- It names a service coordinator to help the family during the development, implementation, and evaluation of the IFSP.

An annual review is completed for every student who qualifies for special education. The IFSP meeting is held annually, but a review is needed every 6 months (without the need for a meeting). Members of the IEP team reconvene to determine if the student has met the goals and objectives written on the educational plan annually. The student may be evaluated to determine if special education services are still required.

WHAT TYPES OF SPECIAL EDUCATION SERVICES ARE AVAILABLE TO CHILDREN WITH SPECIAL NEEDS?

In this section we will review the special education services available to children with special needs. We begin with early intervention services for infants and toddlers.

Early Intervention Services for Infants and Toddlers

The IFSP indicates who will provide the services to the child and where they will be provided. For instance, the IFSP may indicate that a toddler will receive physical therapy twice a week. IDEA encourages teachers to provide early intervention services within the home environment. The IFSP team determines services based on the needs of the family to promote optimal development of the infant or toddler. Recent revisions to Part C of IDEA include the use of scientifically based research when providing early intervention services; that a service provider is no longer required to speak exclusively in the native language of the child at all times; that flexibility is built into the IFSP to allow parents to choose the continuation of early intervention services after a child turns 3 years old and is ready to begin kindergarten; and an educational component that promotes school readiness, preliteracy, language, and numeracy skills. An infant or a toddler who meets eligibility criteria is entitled to any of the early intervention services listed below (IDEA, 2004):

- Family training, counseling, and home visits
- Special instruction
- Speech-language pathology and audiology services, and sign language and cued language services
- Occupational therapy
- Physical therapy
- Psychological services
- Medical services only for diagnostic or evaluation purposes
- Early identification, screening, and assessment services
- Health services necessary to enable the infant or toddler to benefit from other early intervention services
- Social work services
- Vision services
- Assistive technology devices and assistive technology services
- Transportation and related costs that are necessary to enable an infant or a toddler and the infant's or toddler's family to receive another service described above

Special Education Programs and Services for School-Age Children

School-age children qualify for special services for various reasons. The level and intensity of services depend on the goals and objectives written in the IEP. School-age children can be served in a regular education class or in a self-contained class.

Resource Specialist Program

The resource specialist program (RSP) or special education teacher provides instructional support services to students diagnosed with a specific learning disability. Generally, all schools house an RSP on site. Resource specialist teachers work with students individually or in small groups in a regular classroom or RSP classroom. For example, a resource specialist teacher may help a student who struggles to learn to read by emphasizing phonological processing or the ability to process the sounds in language. Students who have a specific learning disability in the area of reading are often referred to as dyslexic. Students with **dyslexia** have a problem processing language in the area of phonology (Shaywitz, 2008).

As noted in our vignette, the special education teacher will assist Margarita in carrying out educational accommodations for Tommy. Because Tommy will be required to participate during circle

With curriculum modifications a child with autism can learn how to participate during circle time.

time, both teachers, along with the instruction assistant, will work collaboratively to support Tommy. Children with autism often have difficulty during circle time because it requires "social proximity, participation with peers in a group activity, receptive language skills, understanding abstract language (e.g. calendar, weather), and sustained attention" (Barton, Reichow, Wolery, & Chen, 2011, p. 4). However, circle time will provide a structured opportunity for Tommy to use language and learn social skills. With the support of the instructional assistant, Tommy can carry out a specific role or tasks during circle time to increase his participation.

Special Day Class

A special day class is an intensive educational program for students with special needs. IDEA indicates that placement of an exceptional student in a separate classroom is only done when "the nature or severity of the disability is such that education in regular classes with the use of supplementary aids and services cannot be achieved satisfactorily" (IDEA, 2004). Students in special day classes are typically mainstreamed for a part of the school day. For instance, a student with spina bifida who has a history of hydrocephalus may require intensive support in a special day class due to medical needs. Although there is individual variation, some children with spina bifida may experience problems with reading, math, attention, and language. Successful mainstreaming needs to take into account the child's physical disability. For instance, structural changes to a school playground can make the setting accessible for children with spina bifida, allowing them the opportunity to socially interact with their peers who are typically developing (Farrell, 2009).

Separate School Facility

Students with severe disabilities require special education services in a separate school facility. When a school district does not have the staff or adequate resources to meet the student's individual needs, placement in a private or public facility will take place. For example, a student with a severe physical disability, learning difficulties, or behavioral problems may receive intensive special services in a separate school facility.

Consider This Full Inclusion

Robert has worked in a special education school where he has taught students with severe emotional, developmental, and physical disabilities for 20 years. He believes that due to budget cuts school officials have opted to educate more students with special needs in regular classrooms because it is twice as costly to educate a student in a private school for students with special needs. The move has been praised by special education advocates and parents. However, Robert argues that the trend toward inclusion is not optimal for all students with special needs. He fears that many of his students are being set up for failure in regular classrooms.

What do you think are the benefits of educating a student with special needs in a regular education program?

HOW HAS ASSISTIVE TECHNOLOGY IMPROVED ACCESS AND REMOVED BARRIERS FOR CHILDREN WITH EXCEPTIONAL NEEDS?

Children with special needs are participating in larger numbers in various educational programs with the assistance of technology. Assistive technology supports function in the areas of mobility, self-care, communication, learning, and social participation.

Assistive Technology Act

The Assistive Technology Act of 2004 provides federal funds for states to develop training and to increase their capacity to provide assistive technology devices and services. The act defines an assistive technology device as "any item, piece of equipment, or product system whether acquired commercially off the shelf, modified, or customized, that is used to increase, maintain, or improve functional capabilities of a child with a disability" (U.S. Department of Education, 2006). An exception to the term is a surgically implanted device. Assistive technology benefits children with a wide variety of disabilities, encompassing both cognitive and physical impairments, to participate fully in school-related activities (Foster, 2007). According to the NAEYC (2012), "When used thoughtfully, these technologies can empower young children, increasing their independence and supporting their inclusion in classes with their peers. With adaptive material, young children with disabilities can be included in activities in which they once would have been unable to participate" (p. 9). Examples of both high-tech and low-tech assistive technology devices are presented below (IDEA, 2004):

- Pencil grips
- Calculators
- Braille readers
- Adaptive spoons
- Power and manual wheelchairs
- Augmentative communication devices (speech-generating devices), voice amplifiers, and speech recognition devices
- Other orthotics and prosthetics, such as hearing aids and electric larynxes
- Accessibility adaptations, such as ramps, stair glides, lifts, and grab bars
- Equipment and technology for school, such as enlarged computer keyboards, text-to-speech software, voice recognition software, and adaptive sports equipment

A variety of assistive technology services are available to support children with special needs. An assistive technology service is "any service that directly assists a child with a disability in the selection, acquisition, or use of an assistive technology device" (IDEA, 2004). The following is a summary of assistive technology services available (IDEA, 2004):

- The evaluation of the needs of such a child, including a functional evaluation of the child in the child's customary environment
- Purchasing, leasing, or otherwise providing for the acquisition of assistive technology devices by such a child
- Selecting, designing, fitting, customizing, adapting, applying, maintaining, repairing, or replacing assistive technology devices, such as those associated with existing education and rehabilitation plans and programs
- Training or technical assistance for such a child or, where appropriate, the family of such a child
- Training or technical assistance for professionals (including individuals providing education and rehabilitation services), employers, or other individuals who provide services to, employ, or are otherwise substantially involved in the major life functions of such a child

Augmentative and alternative communication (AAC) systems are designed to facilitate or compensate, temporarily or permanently, for severe speech or language impairments of students who have difficulty communicating verbally or in writing. An example of an AAC system is aided language stimulation. It is "used with a facilitator who highlights symbols on the user's communication display as he or she interacts and communicates verbally with the user" (Beck, 2002, p. 44). Children who experience speaking as a challenging task can use an electronic speech machine, or they can learn to type into a communication device that can speak for them.

Assistive technology is changing constantly due to innovations in the field. The early childhood education teacher can add assistive technology devices as part of the tools available to improve children's ability to express needs, wants, and thoughts.

Early Literacy Development Through Assistive Technology

Assistive technology can be used to promote early literacy among preschool children with special needs. Beck (2002) studied how the use of assistive technology promoted early literacy skills among exceptional children in a preschool classroom. Children used various types of assistive technology in the classroom:

- Picture communication symbols (key vocabulary related to the book or theme of the week)
- Adapted books, used at circle time and placed in the reading corner
- A BIGmack—a single message communication device, programmed to repeat a story's line
- A computer with IntelliKeys, IntelliPics, and Overlay Maker, an alternative keyboard and software

The special education teacher posted a picture communication symbol schedule on the board, with a picture symbol and an associated word. This activity exposed students to print and stimulated vocabulary development. Students were able to receptively and expressively identify the words. Picture communication symbols were also used by the teacher and speech language pathologist to create storyboards based on books used at circle time and placed in the reading corner. Further, children learned their names by first pairing them with a symbol.

The teacher used BIGmack to facilitate active student participation during shared reading. The teacher programmed a message from a book being read during "language" circle that the student activated with a switch.

The software programs IntelliPics and Overlay Maker allowed the teacher to create computer-based books. Each page contained a symbol, sound, and movement that corresponded to the book. These books became learning centers, allowing children to work independently on the computer.

While some students used the low-tech adaptations created with picture communication symbols to read books, others preferred to use high-tech computer programs. Using IntelliPics, the teacher prepared an electronic book of *Brown Bear, Brown Bear, What Do You See?* to allow students the opportunity to read an entire book independently. This was accomplished by the student activating a switch that prompted the program to turn a page on the screen, speak the text, and produce a story illustration.

Assistive technologies provide young children with disabilities the opportunity to actively participate in the classroom setting to promote the development of emergent literacy. The resources listed in Table 7.3 may be useful for you as you prepare to support children with special needs in your classroom.

Under Section 504 of the Rehabilitation Act, schools are required to provide auxiliary aids to exceptional children with hearing, vision, or speech impairments to ensure effective communication. Additionally, schools must include provision of supplementary aids and services determined appropriate and necessary by the student's IEP team. It is important to note that there are many barriers to successful implementation of assistive technology. These barriers include "staff training and attitudes, assessment, planning and funding issues, equipment issues, and time constraints" (Foster, 2007, p. 79). Despite these initial barriers, you should strive to incorporate these devices as they promote higher levels of student participation and independence. It is essential that you request training on the use of assistive technology devices.

Table 7.3   Assistive Technology Resources for Children With Special Needs

ASSISTIVE TECHNOLOGY RESOURCES	
BIGmack	www.ablenetinc.com
Boardmaker	www.mayer-johnson.com
IntelliTools (IntelliPics, IntelliTalk, and Overlay Maker)	www.intellitools.com
SOFTWARE RESOURCES	
Kid Pix Deluxe	Broderbund Software
Chicka Chicka Boom Boom	Davidson & Associates Inc.
The Cat in the Hat	Broderbund Software
The Backyard	Broderbund Software
Preschool JumpStart	Knowledge Adventure Inc.
Bailey's Book House	Edmark

HOW DOES INCLUSION OF CHILDREN WITH SPECIAL NEEDS IN EARLY CHILDHOOD EDUCATION SETTINGS PROMOTE LEARNING?

Children with special needs are participating in general education in higher numbers. As a society, we are moving toward inclusion of children with special needs as part of the regular curriculum. This implies that schools have to adapt their curriculum for wider participation of children with special needs. Prior to IDEA, students with special needs were considered the primary responsibility of special education teachers and were educated in separate classrooms. Today, the IEP team is required to discuss the opportunities children with special needs will have to participate in the regular classroom. The IEP team makes the determination if inclusion will benefit the child. While inclusion does not necessarily mean that the regular classroom is the best learning environment for the child, the trend toward inclusion is growing.

Children with special needs require many opportunities to develop academic and social skills in an inclusive classroom with peers who are typically developing.

Inclusive Preschool Programs

Returning to our vignette, we learned about Margarita and her excitement and nervousness about teaching Tommy in her kindergarten classroom. Because Margarita has participated in the development of the IEP, she has knowledge of Tommy's strengths and areas of need. Tommy has extensive language and communication delays, but with assistive technology and augmentative devices he will be able to participate in the regular education classroom. The goals listed in his IEP include (1) purposeful communication, (2) social skills development, (3) play, and (4) academic skills training. Tommy will receive support from special education personnel including the special education teacher, the instructional aide, the speech and language therapist, and the occupational therapist. The special education teacher will collaborate with Margarita to implement evidence-based intervention strategies such as curriculum modifications, embedded learning opportunities, and peer mediation (DeVore, Miolo, & Hader, 2011). The instructional assistant will support the development of social and behavioral skills during circle time. The speech and language pathologist will work on social pragmatics to help Tommy learn social interaction skills. The occupational therapist will assist Tommy with independent living skills at home.

Inclusive education promotes classrooms as learning communities where each member is valued and respected. According to Sappon-Shevin (2007), "Within inclusive settings, students are not only exposed to a wide array of people and their differences, but also learn how to talk about these differences, to ask thoughtful questions, to connect" (p. 18). She goes on to share that "children who grow up in inclusive settings grow up to be comfortable and knowledgeable about many differences" (Sappon-Shevin, 2007, p. 19). Teachers working in inclusive classrooms should set high expectations for all students, taking into account developmentally appropriate practices and individual differences.

Challenges to Inclusion and Mainstreaming

Some of the challenges posed to the concept of inclusive education include lack of time, training, or resources; effect on other children; and cost. An additional concern is that a student with a disability

Students with autism spectrum disorder in an inclusive classroom can develop social communication by using concrete visual scripts.

will demonstrate unsuccessful classroom performance even with accommodations, as noted in *Daniel R. R. v. State Board of Education* in 1989. IDEA does not require that all students with disabilities participate in a regular education classroom. However, students in all disability categories can participate in the regular education classroom. According to Burns (2007),

> The key to 100% inclusion is the designation of consultant teacher services whereby a certified special education teacher provides direct and indirect services in the regular classroom. Direct services include direct teaching by the special education teacher to both disabled and nondisabled children. Indirect services include planning, curriculum modification, accommodations, aide supervision and all other activities that will support success by a child with a disability in the regular classroom. (p. 46)

As illustrated in the opening vignette, Margarita will receive support from the special education teacher, the speech and language therapist, and the occupational therapist. This will help ensure that Tommy has a positive experience in an inclusive classroom.

HOW DO SCHOOLS RESPOND TO THE NEEDS OF CHILDREN WHO ARE GIFTED AND TALENTED?

While students with disabilities receive provisions under IDEA, these do not apply to children who are **gifted and talented**. The Jacob K. Javits Gifted and Talented Students Education Act of 1988, reauthorized under the No Child Left Behind Act of 2001, defines students who are gifted and talented as those who "give evidence of high performance capabilities in areas such as intellectual, creative, artistic, or leadership capacity or in specific academic fields, and who require services or activities not ordinarily provided by the school in order to fully develop such capabilities." In 2008, the National Association for Gifted Children redefined giftedness:

> Gifted individuals are those who demonstrate outstanding levels of aptitude (defined as an exceptional ability to reason and learn) or competence (documented performance or achievement in top 10% or rarer) in one or more domains. Domains include any structured area of activity with its own symbol system (e.g., mathematics, music, language) and/or set of sensorimotor skills (e.g., painting, dance, sports).

Some students who are gifted and talented also have a disability and are defined as **twice exceptional learners**. A student may have not only a gift, talent, or high ability but also a disability that impacts the student's ability to achieve based on his or her potential (Kalbfleisch & Iguchi, 2008). For instance, a student may be gifted in math but have a special learning disability in the area of writing.

The Practice of **Research** and **Theory**
Autism Spectrum Disorders

Hart and Whalon (2011) present evidence-based intervention strategies to assist children with autism spectrum disorders (ASD) to develop functional communication skills in both academic and social settings. Teachers have to make social communication a critical instructional goal. The authors suggest that teachers need to develop familiarity with a variety of evidence-based practices that have been demonstrated to reliably and meaningfully improve outcomes for students. These strategies include flexible grouping (a form of peer-mediated instruction), concrete supports (i.e., visuals), self-management, and video modeling.

- Flexible grouping strategies have allowed students with ASD to develop increased social communication. These strategies include cooperative learning and classwide peer tutoring.

- Concrete supports, such as visuals and scripts, help the student with ASD to effectively participate in flexible grouping strategies. Scripts can be visual and/or written prompts used by the student to facilitate participation in an interaction.

- Self-management is a strategy that reduces student dependence in independent or group activities. A teacher can develop a self-monitoring checklist that explicitly depicts the steps needed to complete an activity.

- Video modeling is a strategy that teaches a student how to use social communication in order to initiate interactions with others. The strategy limits the amount of social information by targeting a behavior in isolation. Each behavior is practiced in the natural classroom setting, such as during cooperative learning groups, to promote generalization.

Each school district will determine how a student will be identified, what teacher qualifications will be, and the types of programs offered (Gallagher, 2002). The underrepresentation of ethnically diverse gifted students in gifted and talented programs is a severe problem (Gentry, Hu, & Thomas, 2008). According to the National Research Center on the Gifted and Talented (NRC/GT) (http://www.gifted.uconn.edu/nrcgt .html), the traditional identification criteria, such as the use of intelligence tests, have resulted in the underrepresentation of students with various backgrounds, including African Americans and Latinos, as well as students with special needs and students from low-income backgrounds. Howard Gardner proposed the theory of multiple intelligences and argues that there is no single intelligence (refer to Figure 7.4). According to Gardner (2008), instead of settling for an intelligence test score, we should ask students to carry out a task to determine if they have mastered the task.

Gifted and talented children can have musical aptitude.

Figure 7.4   Theory of Multiple Intelligences

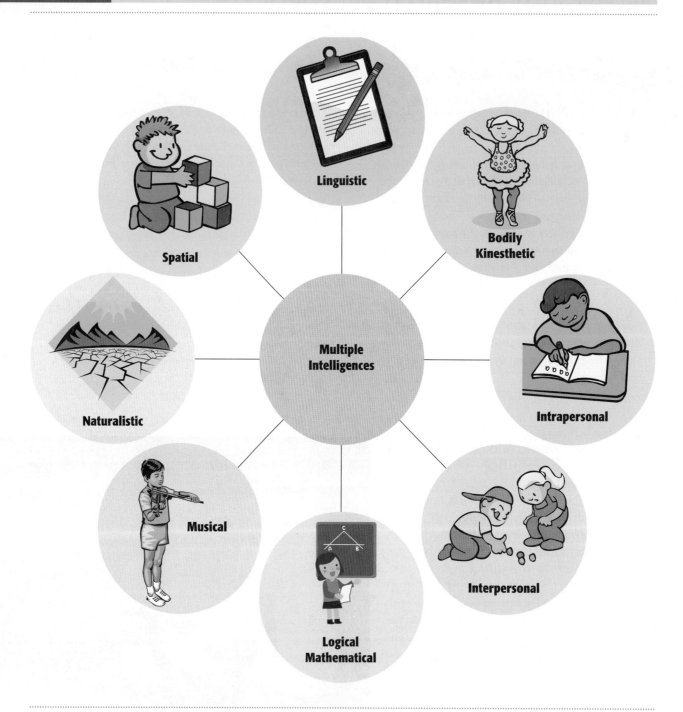

Programs for Students Who Are Gifted and Talented

School districts may develop programs for students who are gifted and talented that range from special day classes to services delivered in the regular classroom. Components of a gifted and talented education (GATE) program can include acceleration and enrichment.

Acceleration and Enrichment

Two approaches for educating students who are gifted and talented are **acceleration** and **enrichment**. Acceleration can involve a student moving rapidly through a curriculum, skipping a grade, or starting school at an earlier age. Enrichment involves providing a student with supplementary materials or learning opportunities commensurate with his or her ability level. Examples of differentiated curriculum or instruction include an advanced mathematics program, an advanced creative arts curriculum, and special computer lessons. In the case of preschool children, instruction may include an advanced early literacy curriculum.

Children who show a keen ability to build with Lego bricks have advanced creativity and problem-solving skills.

WHAT ARE BEST PRACTICES FOR COMMUNICATING WITH FAMILIES OF CHILDREN WITH EXCEPTIONAL NEEDS?

The early childhood education professional recognizes the importance of family involvement to increase children's development and learning. Effective communication with families also can strengthen early childhood education programs.

Communicating With Parents of Children Who Are Gifted and Talented

Parental involvement and family engagement are key features of successful gifted and talented programs, particularly for students who are culturally, linguistically, and ethnically diverse (Briggs, Reis, & Sullivan, 2008). Parent outreach efforts are essential since parents observe their children outside of the classroom and can provide critical information about any gifts or talents a child has. The National Association for Gifted Children (www.nagc.org) is a valuable resource for parents of children who are gifted and talented.

Communicating With Parents of Children With Special Needs

As an early childhood educator, you need to learn how to communicate effectively with families of children with special needs. IDEA requires that parents be actively involved in their child's education. You have an important responsibility to provide resources and guidance, and to serve as an advocate for families. Moreover, it is essential that you develop strategies to promote involvement of all families. Over the last 40 years, research has demonstrated that family involvement is critical to children's development, school readiness, academic achievement, improved behavior and social skills, and high school graduation (Westmoreland, Rosenberg, Lopez, & Weiss, 2009; Weiss & Stephen, 2009). While this is important for all children, it is

Preschool children can develop writing concepts when exposed to an advanced early literacy curriculum.

Audio Books	http://www.bookshare.com
Boardmaker	www.mayer-johnson.com
Intellitools (Intellipics, Intellitalk, and Overlay Marker)	www.intellitools.com
Portable Word Processors	http://www.neo-direct.com
Electronic Math Work Sheets	http://www.mathtalk.com/

SOFTWARE RESOURCES

Learning for Children	ATKidSystems
Cosmos Learning Systems	ATKidSystems
Math and Music	Rock N Go
CompuThera	Equidel
Special Needs Software	Laureate Learning System
Videos for Modeling Social Skills	Model Me Kids
Kid Pix Deluxe	Broderbund Software
Preschool Jumpstart	Knowledge Adventure, Inc.
Bailey's Book House	Edmark
Text to Speech	Kurzweil 1000
Picture This (Graphics)	Silver Lining Multimedia, Inc.

particularly crucial for economically disadvantaged and immigrant children. Weiss and Stephen (2009) contend that "proposed solutions to reformulating NCLB, as well as current thinking about education reform broadly, emphasize that the solution includes opening the school doors to welcome the broader family and community partnerships" (p. 3).

Families of children with special needs face many challenges, one of which is learning how to communicate with education professionals. It is imperative that teachers maintain regular communication with parents to build positive relationships. The following are special education professional practice standards applicable to all professionals working with families of children with special needs (Council for Exceptional Children, 2009):

1. Develop effective communication with parents, avoid technical terminology, use the primary language of the home, and use other modes of communication when appropriate.

2. Seek and use parents' knowledge and expertise in planning, conducting, and evaluating special education and related services for persons with exceptionalities.

A "precocious reader" is defined as a child who is able to read fluently and with understanding at a very young age without receiving direct instruction in reading (Stainthrop & Hughes, 2004). Children with precocious reading ability can be encouraged to apply this ability to develop early writing concepts through the instructional strategy of interactive journals. Preschool children who participated in this teacher-directed writing strategy were able to advance to the alphabetic writing level in the writing process (Valero, 2002). Interactive journals provide a meaningful and authentic approach to teaching children about the writing process. This instructional strategy is taught within the context of an optimal learning environment (Ruiz, Figueroa, & Garcia, 1996).

THE PROCESS

1. The teacher asks the student to draw a picture of his or her choice in the journal. (The student can draw and/or make a writing attempt.)

2. Upon completion of the journal entry, the student shares it with the teacher, who facilitates a meaningful communicative exchange. (This interaction is a critical component of interactive journals.)

3. The teacher then writes a question in the student's journal based on the content of the entry.

4. The student is encouraged to provide a written response while the teacher scaffolds (i.e., the teacher elongates a word by emphasizing each sound).

5. The student is asked to read his or her written response.

---

3. Maintain communications between parents and professionals with appropriate respect for privacy and confidentiality.

4. Extend opportunities for parent education utilizing accurate information and professional methods.

5. Inform parents of the educational rights of their children and of any proposed or actual practices that violate these rights.

6. Recognize and respect cultural diversities that exist in some families with persons with exceptionalities.

7. Recognize that the relationship of home and community environmental conditions affects the behavior and outlook of the exceptional person.

Helping Families Access Needed Resources

One of the most important ways to support parents of children with exceptional needs is to provide them with resources to help them navigate the special education or gifted education process. In the case of children with special needs, you may start by providing parents with a glossary of terms related to children with disabilities and information on national service organizations and technology centers (Kroth & Edge, 2007). In addition, you can arrange for parent workshops on computer technology to present state-of-the-art computer programs available to promote communication and early literacy. Kroth and Edge (2007) have developed a handout that you can provide to parents who have recently learned that their child has a disability (refer to Figure 7.5).

Dealing With Your Feelings About Your Child With Special Needs

Many parents have written or talked about the feelings they have after learning that their child has a disability or special needs. The shock may set in at birth or upon diagnosis during childhood. These feelings are normal and should not cause you to feel guilty. Feelings that parents of a child with special needs have include the following:

Denial

- You may understand what someone has told you about your child but cannot accept it as truth.
- You may say, "I just don't believe that my child is handicapped," or ask, "What did I do to make this happen to my child?"

Guilt

- You might say, "It's my fault this happened."

Anger

- When doctors, nurses, family members, school staff, or friends do not understand your feelings, you may feel angry and frustrated and lash out.
- You may ask, "Why did this happen to me?"

Resentment

- You may feel burdened by the added responsibilities that come with a child with special needs.
- Seeing parents with a child who is nondisabled may be upsetting to you.

Fear

- You may be afraid about what will happen to your child and how the disability will affect his or her life.
- You may worry about how you are going to deal with the responsibilities of having a child with special needs.
- You may feel alone and that no one understands your situation.
- You may be afraid to leave your child with someone else, even if only for a few hours.

Grief

- You may feel a great sadness about having a child with disabilities.
- You may cry or feel like crying often.
- You may say, "This is not the child I expected or 'wanted.'"
- You may feel tired and worn out. Every day may seem like a lifetime.

Acceptance

- All children, with and without disabilities, give pleasure as well as pain to their parents.
- Accepting and coping with a child's disability is an ongoing process.

When you have come to accept your child's disability, you may experience feelings of

- Hope
- Joy in small successes
- Pride
- Satisfaction

Source: Kroth, R. L., & Edge, D. (2007). *Communicating with parents and families of exceptional children.* Denver, CO: Love Publishing.

Summary

Special education is a dynamic and evolving field that has experienced many changes since the hallmark federal legislation, the Education for All Handicapped Children (EAHC) Act of 1975, now known as the Individuals with Disabilities Education Act (IDEA). IDEA mandates that children with exceptional needs have access to a free and appropriate public education in the least restrictive environment. States are required to provide early intervention services to infants and toddlers through an individual family service plan (IFSP). An individual education program (IEP) is required for students ages 3 to 21. IDEA mandates how states and public agencies provide early intervention, special education, and related services to students with exceptional needs. The alignment of IDEA and the No Child Left Behind (NCLB) Act of 2001 expanded the role of the regular education teacher and produced many changes for students with special needs. Federal legislation required that all students have access to the general education curriculum and be part of state accountability systems. Whereas children with special needs were once excluded from public schools, today children from all disability categories can have the opportunity to receive instruction in the regular education classroom, to the maximum extent possible. More preschool children are participating in inclusive settings than ever before. To ensure the success of exceptional children in inclusive programs and classrooms, a collaborative relationship between the regular education teacher and special education personnel is essential.

As an early childhood professional, you will teach students with various disabilities, gifts, and talents. A student with exceptional needs can have a disability or may be gifted and talented. Twice exceptional learners include students who are gifted and talented and have a disability. While IDEA does not apply to students who are gifted and talented, state education agencies do develop innovative programs to provide enrichment and acceleration. A persistent challenge for gifted education in the United States is the underrepresentation of students who are ethnically diverse in gifted and talented programs. Many studies in the field of special education have also focused attention on the disproportionate representation of African American, Latino, and Native American students in special education. You have learned in this chapter about the important role you will have in the special education cycle. As a professional, you will need to advocate for children with exceptional needs and their families. This includes removing barriers to increase learning and to increase participation.

Key Terms

Acceleration   191

Assistive technology   170

Augmentative and alternative communication (AAC) systems   185

Autism spectrum disorders   170

Child Find   176

Children with exceptional needs   170

Dyslexia   183

Enrichment   191

Free and appropriate public education (FAPE)   170

Gifted and talented   188

Inclusion   169

Individual education program (IEP)   171

Individual family service plan (IFSP)   171

Individuals with Disabilities Education Act (IDEA)   169

Least restrictive environment (LRE)   171

Mainstreaming   171

Multidisciplinary team   171

Response to intervention (RTI)   179

Significant discrepancy formula   179

Student study team   176

Twice exceptional learners   188

Universal screening   179

Reflection, Application, and Analysis Questions

1. Assess how federal legislation has impacted the education of children with special needs.

2. Illustrate the special education cycle. What is the role of the regular education teacher?

3. Compare and contrast the components of an IEP and an IFSP.

4. What types of assistive technology devices are used to improve the educational opportunities of students with special needs?

5. Why is it important for classroom teachers to be familiar with enrichment activities for students who are gifted and talented?

Extension Activities

1. Interview one or two teachers who have a student with special needs. Ask the teachers to share what modifications and accommodations they make to help the student participate and learn in the classroom.

2. Research evidence-based interventions for children who fall on the autism spectrum and write in your journal about how these interventions promote learning and social skills.

3. Investigate what enrichment programs are available in a local school district for students who are gifted and talented.

Additional Readings

The field of early childhood education has been driven by educational research that supports the role of the teacher as a professional. The readings below will augment the knowledge base you will develop as an early childhood education professional.

Farrell, M. (2008). *Educating special children: An introduction to provision for pupils with disabilities and disorders*. New York: Routledge.
This book is a great resource for early childhood students and educators as it provides a fundamental understanding of the provisions for children with special needs.

Gottlieb, M. (2006). *Assessing English language learners: Bridges from language proficiency to academic achievement*. Thousand Oaks, CA: Corwin Press.
This book is a good resource for teachers working with English language learners. It provides strategies for appropriate assessment that can be used to plan instruction. Various examples of evaluation instruments are included.

Grant, K. B., & Ray, J. R. (2010). *Home, school, and community collaboration: Culturally responsive family involvement*. Thousand Oaks, CA: Sage.
This book provides more detailed information on your role as a teacher in promoting family involvement. Included is information about how to work effectively with families of exceptional children.

Villa, R. A., & Thousand, J. S. (Eds.). (2005). *Creating an inclusive school* (2nd ed.). Alexandria, VA: Association for Supervision and Curriculum Development.
This book begins with a historical perspective on inclusive education and the rationale for creating and maintaining inclusive schools. It also includes promising practices that foster inclusive education.

On the Web

American Academy of Special Education Professionals - *http://aasep.org/*
This link takes you to the American Academy of Special Education Professionals (AASEP). AASEP builds community among special education professionals. If you are interested in a professional board certification in special education, visit this website.

Autism Speaks - *http://www.autismspeaks.org*
The website for Autism Speaks offers information about autism, research, family services, and advocacy.

Children and Adults with Attention Deficit/Hyperactivity Disorder - *http://www.chadd.org/*
This nonprofit website is from the Children and Adults with Attention Deficit/Hyperactivity Disorder (CHADD), a membership organization that provides education, advocacy, and support to parents and their children with ADHD.

Council for Exceptional Children - *http://www.cec.sped.org*
The Council for Exceptional Children website seeks to improve the educational success of children and youth with disabilities and/or gifts and talents. It is a valuable resource for educators working with exceptional children and for parents.

National Center on Response to Intervention - *http://www.rti4success.org/*
This link takes you to the National Center on Response to Intervention. The mission of the center is to provide technical assistance to states and districts and to build state capacity to support schools in their implementation of proven methods. The response-to-intervention (RTI) model integrates instruction and assessments. RTI can serve as a prevention model, allowing schools to follow students who are not progressing in general education.

Student Study Site

Visit **www.sagepub.com/gordonbiddle** to access several study tools including eFlashcards, web quizzes, links to SAGE journal articles, web resources, video resources, lesson plan templates, and more.

Lesson Plan:

Things We Eat

Subject:

Vocabulary development.

Focus:

Use of functional words.

Overview:

Infants and toddlers with special needs should have the opportunity to hear language within meaningful contexts to increase their vocabulary.

Purpose:

To help infants and toddlers learn new words needed to communicate with caretakers and get their needs met.

Objectives:

1. Learn functional words.
2. Say single vocabulary words.
3. Advance language development and, in turn, emotional and social development.
4. Assist with verbal expression.

Resource Materials:

- Infant/toddler picture book about food (e.g., *Scratch and Sniff: Food*).
- Small photo book in which to place pictures of the child's favorite foods.
- Small pieces of food appropriate to the child's level.

Activities and Procedures:

1. Sit with the child on your lap or in close proximity and let the child explore the book.

2. Read the book to the child and emphasize the words of the food items.

3. Use plastic food as props for toddlers.

4. During mealtimes, present some of the food items (if appropriate) from the book.

5. Ask the child to point to the correct food item you have verbally expressed and offer some to eat.

6. On subsequent days, ask the child to say the word of the food item (provide the word, if necessary).

Tying It All Together:

Have the parents participate in the lesson by creating a small photo book with their child's favorite foods. Encourage the parents to review the vocabulary words at home. Children with special needs will benefit from many opportunities to learn new vocabulary words within meaningful contexts.

Visit **www.sagepub.com/gordonbiddle** to access templates of these lesson plans.

All About Books

Subject:

Early literacy skills.

Focus:

Concepts about print (directionality, the message is in the print, one-to-one correspondence, return sweep, front and back part of a book, how to turn the pages, etc.).

Overview:

Preschool children need extensive opportunities to interact with text. Shared reading is an instructional strategy that early childhood education teachers can use to promote early literacy and language development.

Purpose:

To help young children with special needs develop important concepts about print.

Objectives:

1. To learn concepts about print.

2. To develop prediction skills (i.e., what the story will be about, what will happen next).

3. To increase enjoyment of books.

Resource Materials:

- Big shared reading books with simple, patterned, and predictable text that students can learn through repeated readings.
- Mini shared reading books based on the big books/poems/song charts.
- Paper.
- Nontoxic crayons.
- Popsicle sticks to make pointers.
- Brown paper bag to make puppets.

Activities and procedures:

1. Decide ahead of time what concept about print you will emphasize each day.

2. During circle time, draw students' attention to the cover page of the big book. Read the title, and introduce the illustrator and the author. Ask students to look at the illustration and predict what the story will be about. Facilitate participation by accessing students' background knowledge. Once students have shared their predictions, lead to a brief discussion about the story line, drawing on their prior knowledge and personal experiences in order to connect them to the story.

3. Do a picture walk with the students explicitly through the text, page by page, eliciting information from them about what they see and what they think is happening.

4. Read the book and demonstrate book handling skills.

5. During reading center, provide each child with a mini book so that the students have the opportu- nity to practice book handling skills. Have them chorally read the book.

Extension Activities:

- Make variations of the class books to read in the reading center.
- Make take-home books to reread to family members.
- Make pointers by gluing miniature book characters onto them to use while reading to practice the concept of directionality.
- Have students color drawings of the book characters and glue them onto paper bags to make puppets used for role-play during the story.

Tying It All Together:

Concepts about print are important precursors to reading. Children between the ages of 3 and 5 years learn that print, not pictures, carries the message. Children also learn literacy terms such as *letter, word,* and *capital.* Children with special needs can learn these skills through repeated demonstrations and hands-on activities.

Visit **www.sagepub.com/gordonbiddle** to access templates of these lesson plans.

ABC Name Chart

Subject:

Language arts/reading.

Focus:

Learning letter names and sounds using personal names.

Overview:

By using an ABC Name Chart, children with special needs will be exposed to letter names and sounds within a meaningful context. Learning the names of the members of the classroom promotes social interactions.

Purpose:

To help children with special needs develop letter recognition, letter identification, and letter-sound correspondence.

Objectives:

1. Develop letter recognition.

2. Develop letter identification.

3. Develop letter-sound correspondence.

4. Learn personal names of classmates and teachers.

Resource Materials:

- ABC Name Chart (an oversized laminated chart with each letter of the alphabet delineated within a box).
- Laminated 3 × 5 pictures of each child and adult in the classroom with the person's name written on the bottom.
- Velcro (used to attach pictures to the chart).

Activities and procedures:

The following activities are done throughout the school year for no more than 8 to 10 minutes a day.

1. During circle time, each child has the opportunity to place his or her picture on the chart. (Teacher shows picture: "Mary, come and place your picture on the first letter of your name. Your letter is *M*. Put your picture next to your letter. Class, can you say *Mary*? What is her letter?") Repeat during the week to promote letter recognition.

2. During circle time, the teacher selects one child at a time to place a classmate's picture next to his or her letter. (Teacher shows picture: "Who can tell me what letter Daniel's name begins with? Put Daniel's picture next to his letter.") Repeat during the week to promote letter identification.

3. During circle time, the teacher selects one child at a time to place a classmate's picture next to his or her letter. (Teacher shows picture: "Who can tell me what sound Kenny's name begins with? Put Kenny's picture next to his letter.") Repeat during the week to promote letter-sound correspondence.

Tying It All Together:

During free-choice time, students can demonstrate what they have learned when they choose their ABC Name Chart as an activity. If all of the letters on the chart are not represented with a classroom member, use pictures of family members and familiar staff in the school.

Visit **www.sagepub.com/gordonbiddle** to access templates of these lesson plans.

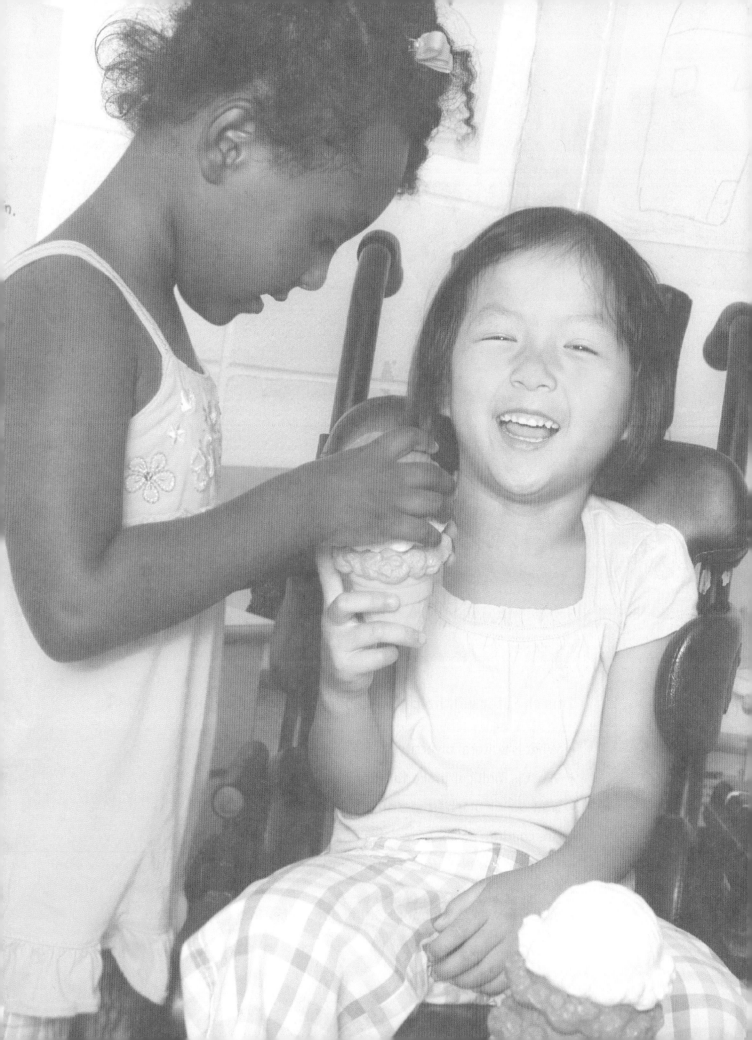

Diversity in Early Childhood Education

This chapter will help you answer these important questions:

- What is cultural diversity?

- What is multicultural education?

- How do we teach from a multicultural perspective?

- Are children aware of racial differences?

- How can multicultural programs involve family members and the wider community?

- What do we know about cultural differences in the special education system?

Vignette: Brown Like Me

At a low-performing, high-poverty public school, Maya is the only African American child in a kindergarten classroom. Twelve children are Spanish-speaking; 10 of the children's parents are from Mexico, and 3 are from other countries in Central America. The remaining children are Asian American (from the Philippines, Vietnam, and Laos). Most of the children are second-language learners, and all receive free or subsidized lunch.

Recently, the teacher asked the children to make an art project that consisted of drawing, cutting, and pasting a puppet. The teacher gave brief verbal directions. The children were also shown a teacher-made sample, and there was a chart posted above the art supplies with written directions. The teacher provided boxes and baskets with colored paper, fabric scraps, yarn, and buttons for students to use in their project.

The teacher was helping the children staple the completed puppets. Maya handed the teacher her puppet and said, "Look, she's brown like me."

"Yes, she has a beautiful brown skin like you," the teacher said with a smile. Maya had also created braids identifying her hair. The teacher said, "Look at these beautiful braids and at those dark black eyes! This is very nice, Maya!" While this interaction between the teacher and Maya was going on, the other children gathered to admire Maya's artwork.

Maya, a kindergartner, is comfortable presenting that she and her puppet have a different skin color and hair type. She expresses her ethnic identity and awareness of skin color through her behavior, language expression, and social and cognitive ability. While doing the project, Maya decided how she was going to individualize the puppet to make it an affirmation of herself. Thinking analytically about her ethnic identity, using her fine motor skills, and having the determination to accomplish her project are examples of cognitive achievements. Her enthusiasm to convey her thoughts to the teacher through language is evidence of strong social and communication skills. This example shows that opportunities arise for educators to expand and promote multiculturalism in the classroom. The teacher took Maya's self-awareness and the children's interest in examining skin and hair differences as an opportunity to discuss ethnic identity and diversity and decided to read a book about cultural differences at the end of the day.

Key Elements
for Becoming a Professional

NAEYC DEVELOPMENTALLY APPROPRIATE PRINCIPLE 8

Development and learning occur in and are influenced by multiple social and cultural contexts.

Interpretation

Teachers need to understand the influence of sociocultural contexts and family circumstances on learning, recognize children's developing competencies, and be familiar with the variety of ways that children may demonstrate their developmental achievements.

NAEYC STANDARD 2: BUILDING FAMILY AND COMMUNITY RELATIONSHIPS

a. Knowing about and understanding diverse family and community characteristics

b. Supporting and engaging families and communities through respectful, reciprocal relationships

c. Involving families and communities in their children's development and learning

Many of today's preschools and elementary schools are faced with cultural, ethnic, special needs, gender, religious, and socioeconomic diversity, which calls for multicultural education programs that reflect an understanding of and respect for young children's differences. The multicultural education movement has particular relevance for the new century because teachers and schools will always be encountering culturally diverse students due to the continuing influx of people into the United States. This education movement is equally relevant because of the recent perspective, shared by many, that diversity enriches, rather than weakens, a nation. This chapter examines the fundamentals and principles of culture, ethnicity, and multicultural education. It also considers the importance of involving families and the community in the classroom.

Children feel comfortable and express an understanding of racial identity as early as 3 years of age.

Teaching in today's classroom, with its diverse population of students, is different from teaching 50 years ago. Demographic changes in the classroom serve teachers with complicated challenges and demands. According to Lieberman (1992), this change in our society is exerting potentially profound effects on teaching and learning: "Teaching is affected not only by what the teacher does, but by the context within which teaching takes place: the kinds of students, the content of the curriculum, and political and social forces within as well as surrounding the school" (p. 6). When teaching, we have to create the appropriate curriculum content for each specific group of students and their families. The preschool and elementary curriculum has to be infused with diverse materials and activities, and it must include people such as teachers, parents, and educators who can provide opportunities for children to come in contact with meaningful diversity issues. Several researchers have presented analysis of the changing context of education (Darling-Hammond & Snyder, 1992; Lieberman, 1992; Little, 1992), and these analyses suggest that the traditional acceptance of school success for some and failure for others is changing. Simply stated, "There is a growing consensus that the United States cannot maintain its democratic foundations or its standard of living unless all students are much better educated" (Darling-Hammond & Snyder, 1992, p. 13). The schools' new mission—to "ensure high levels of student learning for all"—means that schools must succeed in reaching diverse learner populations (Darling-Hammond & Snyder, 1992, p. 11). If children fail, not only the children are considered at fault, but the school and the teachers are also to blame. Merely delivering instruction, whatever the outcome, is no longer enough.

Classroom practices are changing from teacher-directed instruction toward student-centered learning. Student-centered learning includes things that are seen in the classroom, such as creating an environment that actively engages students in learning, building upon student strengths and abilities, involving students in higher-level thinking and problem solving, and making learning more individualized within a group setting. What we are seeing outside the classroom are things that influence student learning, the school environment, parental involvement in the education of children, and teacher involvement in school governance.

The role of the teacher is also one that is changing in many ways. Teaching responsibilities are more complex; teachers, for example, are becoming accountable for their teaching and their students' learning, for making school-level decisions, for taking the lead in program development, and ultimately for encountering and handling pressures from outside the school.

Because classroom and teaching practices are changing, a multicultural education becomes a fundamental and vital part of children's educational development.

WHAT IS CULTURAL DIVERSITY?

The diverse new population includes students who come from a variety of cultures. To be more effective in this multicultural environment, teachers must understand the impact and interactions of culture within the classroom. Let's begin by defining culture. To define the term *culture* can be problematic since anthropologists and sociologists have defined culture in a variety of ways over the years. Prior to the late 1950s, culture was typically defined in terms of patterns of behavior and customs. As part of a more recent movement, Spradley and McCurdy (1975) define culture as "the acquired knowledge that people use to interpret experience and to generate social behavior" (p. 5). They also claim that cultural understanding "is like a recipe for producing behavior and artifacts" (Spradley & McCurdy, 1975, p. 5). Another definition of culture comes from LeVine (1984), who defines culture as "a shared organization of ideas that includes the intellectual, moral, and aesthetic standards prevalent in a community and the meanings of communicative actions" (p. 67). Combining these definitions, **culture** is therefore the pattern of knowledge, skills, behaviors, attitudes, beliefs, and material artifacts produced by a human society and transmitted from one generation to the next. Furthermore, culture is the whole of humanity's intellectual, social, technological, political, economic, moral, religious, and aesthetic accomplishments (Pai, Adler, & Shadiow, 2006). Therefore, the culture to which we belong becomes the origin of our identity. Culture provides individuals with a sense of power and confidence. It provides the psychological and moral values of what is acceptable and not acceptable, which, in essence, allows us to develop a purpose for our life.

Because members of a specific culture allocate meaning, value, and significance to things, events, and behavior, culture should be seen as a constellation of behaviors created by humans. These units of behavior are the creations of human beings' exclusive ability to "originate, determine, and bestow meaning upon things and events in the external world and [their] ability to comprehend such meanings" (White & Dillingham, 1973, p. 1). For example, an ordinary cow in American culture is valued for its milk and meat, but the same cow in Hinduism becomes sacred because it is a symbol of God's generosity to humankind. It follows, then, that the meaning and significance of objects, events, and behavioral patterns should be understood and appreciated within a specific cultural context (Pai et al., 2006).

Understanding our own culture and other cultures can help us to clarify why we behave in certain ways, how we perceive reality, what we believe to be true, what we build and create, and what we accept as good (Bennet, 2007). It is especially important to understand the tenets of culture in a complex society such as the one in the United States where people of diverse national origins live and a variety of cultures coexist along with the predominant Anglo Western European culture.

WHAT IS MULTICULTURAL EDUCATION?

Like culture, **multicultural education** has many definitions. Some definitions, for example, speak to the perspectives of specific disciplines, such as education, anthropology, sociology, and psychology. Other definitions address the views of professional organizations that are concerned with school curriculum and teacher practices. Bennet (1995), for instance, defines multicultural education as an approach to teaching and learning that is based upon democratic values and beliefs, and that seeks to foster **cultural pluralism** within culturally diverse societies. Cultural pluralism is an ideology characterized by mutual appreciation and respect between two or more ethnic groups. In a culturally pluralistic society, members of a diverse group are allowed to maintain many of their cultural practices as long as they conform to those practices deemed necessary for the survival of the society as a whole. Therefore, "cultural pluralism is an ideal state of societal conditions characterized by equity and mutual respect among existing cultural groups" (Bennet, 1995).

Teaching in a multicultural setting involves promoting a positive attitude toward differences and focusing less on stereotypical attitudes or differences that may seem strange. Gay (1979) has illustrated basic multicultural strategies that are appropriate to include in an elementary school. Different instructional approaches are shown in Table 8.1, which includes the emphasis of each approach and the features that create a culturally pluralistic curriculum. In a preschool setting, for example, the use of toys, games, or books is an excellent way to introduce young children to global education (Swiniarski, 1991). When children play with diverse sets of materials, they notice the similarities and differences between people. Additionally, reading a book that depicts children with special needs can captivate children's interest. Some toys that are common worldwide include the following:

- Dolls
- Toy animals
- Musical instruments
- Puzzles
- Construction toys
- Cars, trucks, and planes
- Puppets

Books to consider:

- Books that represent children in your classroom
- Books that introduce new information and ideas to children
- Books that introduce children to a variety of topics and cultural artifacts
- Books that introduce children to different customs and traditions

HOW DO WE TEACH FROM A MULTICULTURAL PERSPECTIVE?

In order to teach effectively in a multicultural setting, we as educators have to self-evaluate by considering how diversity is present in our own lives and how it affects our behaviors in the classroom. If we are to teach our best in a multicultural environment, it is extremely important to become aware of how we develop these internal thinking processes. A process of self-reflection is needed to evaluate the way we think about cultural differences. If you grew up in an open-minded environment where cultural differences were accepted and valued, the outcome of your behavior toward others is likely a positive one. Even though many people accept and value differences and diversity, others do not. Unfortunately, adults continue to pass on to children their misconceptions or unconscious thoughts about people who are different from themselves. Bringing these unconscious thoughts to a conscious level can help us to identify how our biases may influence our perceptions of others. Such an evaluation of how we think is often the beginning of opening up to differences.

Teachers Developing a Cultural Awareness

Because our culture helps us decide how we think, feel, and behave, it becomes the lens through which we evaluate other ethnic groups. As humans, we may view other cultures as unequal or inferior because of their differences; this common perspective is known as **ethnocentrism**. This ethnocentrism, where one's own culture is viewed as the natural way of being, obviously prevents us from understanding other cultures. Through the process of reflection and self-evaluation, we can overcome ethnocentrism and learn about, respect, and function comfortably with other cultures.

Table 8.1   Strategies for Incorporating Multicultural Content Into the Early Childhood Curriculum

APPROACH	EMPHASIS	BASIC FEATURES
Integrative multicultural basic skills	Social skills, intellectual skills, literacy skills, functional survival skills	Use cultural perspectives, content, material, and experiences to teach basic educational skills
Modified basic skills	Fundamental skills, social action skills, decision-making skills, ethnic literacy	Use ethnic materials to teach basic skills, enhance student ethnic identity, and expand awareness of multiethnic perspectives; address ethnic/racial and gender stereotypes
Conceptual approach	Concepts from multiple disciplines (e.g., social science, such as power identity, ethnicity, culture survival, communication, change, racism, socialization, and acculturation)	Analyze concepts within an interdisciplinary framework using comparative and multiethnic perspectives
Thematic approach	Themes characterizing the human condition, social realities, and cultural experiences of ethnic groups in the United States (e.g., ethnic identity, the role of ethnic groups in society, struggles against injustice, and the quest for freedom)	Focus on themes rather than ethnic groups and treat themes from interdisciplinary perspectives; examine inter- and intragroup diversity
Cultural components	Culture and traditions of ethnic groups, including perceptions, behavior and communication patterns, socialization processes, value systems, and interpersonal interaction styles	Emphasize identification of cultural features for specific groups; rely on ethnic source materials (e.g., literature, histories, folklore, customs, traditions, and religious heritage)
Branching designs	Idea, issue, concept, or problem extended from one discipline to another (e.g., analysis of protest as manifested in civic, literary, and artistic areas)	Organize the curriculum to allow for more integrated, in-depth, and cohesive treatment of content

Source: Hernandez, H., *Multicultural education: A teacher's guide to linking context, process, and content*, 2nd edition, © 2001. Adapted by permission of Pearson Education, Inc., Upper Saddle River, NJ.

Through repeated exposure from parents, teachers, neighbors, television, and other media that reinforce approval of people different from themselves, children start to internalize these values.

One goal of multicultural education is to develop a cultural awareness of the skills, attitudes, and knowledge that are essential for living and functioning in both an ethnic culture and the universal American culture (Banks, 1987, pp. 35–36). One way for us to develop such a cultural awareness is to see how someone from another culture perceives or misperceives us. For example, the views of international students and visitors in the United States can trigger deeper insights into our own culture.

Another way to develop cultural awareness is to become attentive to and critically examine how personal thinking patterns influence your classroom decisions:

1. When making decisions regarding your capabilities to teach and your students' abilities to learn, acknowledge how you are dependent on your internal and external judgments, as well as how you are influenced by the judgments of others. Examine your patterns of thinking and make changes when necessary. For example, being aware of your own unintentional stereotypical comments may demonstrate your need to further your own education about certain diversity issues.

2. Become aware of how you respond to differences in students' appearances, values, and behaviors. Becoming aware will help uncover issues that may reflect bias or negativity toward others. Evaluate differences in factors such as ethnicity, language, gender, socioeconomic status, and sexual orientation, and deem them just as important as factors that teachers normally consider when planning instructional events, such as age, grade level, social skills, and academic ability.

Effective teachers generally form their teaching perspectives by drawing on the cultural practices of the learners. To learn about these cultural practices, a teacher can use adults within a specific cultural community as a primary source of information. Teachers can also learn from the learners' own backgrounds, including their cultural experiences and perceptions, by asking questions of parents or previous teachers. Information from these two sources is simple to gather and important to include in the curriculum. Effective teachers understand how to draw relevant information, such as cultural practices, from the social and cultural context of the classroom and then use what they learn to enhance their teaching. By doing this they develop a teacher perspective that is, in effect, multicultural. The next section will further discuss how you can become an effective teacher when you implement a multicultural approach to teaching.

A teacher giving a lesson to a diverse group of students during reading time.

Preparing Teachers for Multicultural Programs

Teachers play a vital role in shaping children's cultural perceptions. If teachers display that they value cultural and ethnic diversity, children will imitate this behavior. Therefore, modeling acceptable behavior toward people who dress, speak, or look unlike you will be important for shaping the actions of the children in the classroom. Teachers should be vigilant about not tolerating culturally insensitive behavior, such as children teasing and ridiculing other children because of their differences.

A multicultural curriculum should emphasize and represent the beliefs, art, folklore, history, and science of many different cultures. Recognizing children's beliefs, traditions, and uniqueness, for example, gives both the child and the parents the respect and value they deserve. The holiday traditions that different people value become an important opportunity for children to learn about diversity. However, educators should be aware that not every holiday, such as Christmas, is celebrated by every child's family, and such holidays should therefore not be used as a theme in the classroom. The National Association for the Education of Young Children (1996a) provides these suggestions:

- Parents and teachers need to ask why children should learn about a particular holiday and whether it is developmentally appropriate.
- Celebrations should be connected to specific children and families within the group.
- Children should be encouraged to share their feelings and information about the celebrations they have.
- Every ethnic group represented within the classroom should be honored through celebration of a holiday or cultural tradition.
- Activities should demonstrate respect for the customs of different cultures.
- Parents and teachers need to work together in planning these special events.

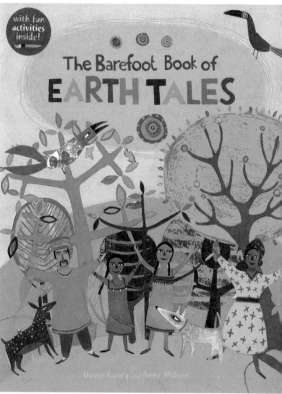

It is important that multicultural books be made available in the classroom and used during lessons and story time.

Adding different themes or holidays into the curriculum is not an easy thing to do. Teachers are required to investigate the children's cultural beliefs, talk to parents, and research information or topics they are not familiar with. The next section mentions several approaches that a teacher should consider when incorporating multicultural themes into the curriculum.

Integrating Multicultural Education Into the Curriculum

The multicultural curriculum should be infused with activities, materials, and people. Derman-Sparks, Ramsey, and Edwards (2011) recommend the antibias curriculum. The philosophy of the antibias curriculum is to raise awareness by allowing people to analyze things from different perspectives: "Differences are good; oppressive ideas and behaviors are not" (Derman-Sparks, 1989, p. 53). The antibias curriculum "sets up a creative tension between respecting differences and not accepting unfair beliefs and acts" (Derman-Sparks, 1989, p. 53). Implementing this curricular approach requires careful planning, self-assessment, and communication with other educators, teachers, and parents. Although this curriculum requires dedication and commitment, it gives children and adults many rewards.

To become an effective teacher and ensure success in the classroom using this antibias curriculum, teachers should take a five-step approach (Derman-Sparks, 1989):

Step 1. *Make a personal commitment.* To make this curriculum a reality, teachers must spend considerable time and energy. Diversity issues must be a high priority.

Step 2. *Organize a support group.* Gathering perspectives and feedback from peers is essential for rethinking the teaching of diversity.

Step 3. *Do consciousness-raising (self-awareness) activities.* Self-awareness was described earlier in this chapter. Essentially, teachers need to become aware of their own feelings toward cultural, racial, and ability differences.

Step 4. *Make a plan for implementing the curriculum.* Through an evaluation of the physical environment, a critique of current activities, and observations of children, teachers can make plans for implementing antibias activities.

Step 5. *Move slowly and carefully.* Integrating diversity issues into the curriculum is hard work and requires careful planning. Moving more slowly helps ensure success.

Another researcher who has developed a multicultural content approach, James Banks, has identified four basic approaches to multicultural education. He argues that "it is unrealistic to expect a teacher to move directly from a highly mainstream-centric curriculum to one that focuses on decision making and social action" (Banks, 1997, p. 242). Thus his approaches provide various levels of multicultural awareness. His approaches are commonly used in multicultural classrooms nationwide.

According to Banks (1997), here are the four approaches teachers should use as they develop a multicultural curriculum:

The Contribution Approach—curriculum includes content about holidays and celebrations of various ethnic groups, especially at the early childhood and elementary level. Thus, children learn about Black History Month, Cinco de Mayo, and Asian Pacific American Heritage Week.

The Ethnic Additive Approach—content about minorities is added to the curriculum without substantially changing its goals or structure.

The Transformation Approach—changes the basic assumptions of the curriculum "and enables students to view concepts, issues, themes, and problems from different perspectives and points of view" (Banks, 1997, p. 31). Curriculum is aimed at helping learners understand events and society from the perspectives of various groups, rather than simply from the dominant culture.

Decision Making and Social Action Approach—suggests that once learners have studied an issue and have drawn their own conclusions, they should be able to take personal, social, or civic action.

The contribution and additive approaches present content about minorities, women, and other underrepresented groups from the perspective of the dominant culture rather than those of the groups being studied. The contribution approach does not change the actual curriculum. The selected individuals being studied are those whose ideas have contributed to the larger society. The additive approach, similar to the contribution approach, adds some multicultural content into the curriculum without changing the traditional structure of the core curriculum. This approach demands less time and effort from a teacher and therefore is the one many teachers prefer.

The transformation approach includes examinations of issues, events, and problems from the point of view of the groups most affected (such as minorities, women, or other underrepresented groups). Gay and Banks (cited in Banks, 1997), for example, would argue that teaching the American Revolution would require treatment of political, military, socioeconomic, philosophical, and geographical aspects that involve various groups such as Europeans, American Indians, African Americans, and others.

Finally, the social action approach utilizes the transformation approach and then broadens its scope by having students use what they learn to effect social change. This approach focuses on decision-making skills, reflection, and political and social efficacy. Teachers encourage students to engage in activities that would help improve their schools, their neighborhoods, their communities, and society overall. Teachers play a vital role in this approach. "Teachers are agents of social change who promote democratic values and the empowerment of students" (Banks, 1997, p. 240).

There are various ways to integrate multicultural education into any curriculum. Teachers must find an approach or a method with which they and their school are comfortable and one that is effective for their students.

ARE CHILDREN AWARE OF RACIAL DIFFERENCES?

Teaching from a multicultural perspective includes examining and being aware of differences and at some point will likely involve the impact of race. Before we answer whether children are aware of racial differences, we must first define race and ethnicity in order to better understand how these terms relate to children's awareness of diversity.

The term **race** was developed by anthropologists more than a century ago to describe the physical and biological characteristics of different people throughout the world. It is a social-historical concept that is greatly dependent on a society's perception that physical and biological differences exist and that these differences are important. Establishing the racial categories of individuals often proves to be difficult because of the wide variety of traits and characteristics people share. For example, we all have different skin color, hair color, and texture, and there may be some commonality and variations among some groups, but there is only one human race. Some researchers suggest that race, as conceptualized in the United States, is equivalent to the term **caste,** a group in society based on hereditary status, wealth, profession, or race, in other countries (Gollnick & Chinn, 2006). This comparison seems appropriate when you consider that the term *race* and the act of racial identification have both been used by policy makers and society to classify groups of people as inferior or superior to other racial groups, which has resulted in discrimination and inequality against people of color.

The term **ethnicity** examines people's national origin, religion, or race, and any combination thereof. Characteristics associated with ethnicity include a sense of identity and a group image derived from contemporary cultural patterns, shared political and economic interests, and involuntary membership (Manning & Baruth, 2000). Ethnicity can also include belonging to a community of people within a larger society that is set apart from the larger group due to cultural characteristics such as language, religion, or tradition. The main reason why individuals would identify with a particular ethnic group is due to being set apart because of their physical or cultural attributes or both.

Young children often discuss racial and ethnic differences and issues of diversity with more ease and "matter-of-factness" than do older children or adults. Because of young children's curiosity, awareness, and comfort level, researchers and educators have suggested that multicultural education begin during infancy (Swick, Boutte, & Van Scoy, 1994). From birth to 8 years of age, children develop perceptions and attitudes toward people who differ from themselves in terms of socioeconomic status; gender; physical, mental, and social capabilities; and religion. Children develop these perceptions and attitudes through the process of socialization; that is, if a child grows up in a segregated White environment, the social interactions that this child has will influence his or her attitude. Developing attitudes toward others based on difference is an indicator that children notice racial and ethnic differences (see Table 8.2).

Because children's ethnic, racial, and cultural attitudes are more strongly influenced during the early childhood years than at any other point in their lives (Neugebauer, 1992), this is a great time to help them to be culturally sensitive. Kevin Swick (1991), a researcher who studies multicultural family involvement, presents three reasons for taking a multicultural approach to teaching early in a child's life: (a) The early childhood years are the most influential period for shaping children's cultural understanding, attitudes about culture, and perspectives of different cultures; (b) parents are the most powerful models, guides, and designers of children's social and cultural experiences; and (c) teachers' use of parent and family involvement strategies is highly influential in promoting multicultural learning. Since children are in an impressionable period, the early childhood years are the best time to foster culturally sensitive children.

Research About Children's Racial Awareness

The classic "Doll Study," conducted by Kenneth Clark and Mamie Clark (1939), tested young children's racial awareness, preferences, and self-identification. The researchers showed young African American children a Black doll and a White doll and asked the children which doll

> (a) you like to play with or the doll you like best, (b) is the nice doll, (c) looks bad, (d) is a nice color, (e) looks like a White child, (f) looks like a colored child, (g) looks like a Black child, and (h) looks like you. (Clark & Clark, 1939, p. 595)

Table 8.2 Children's Stages of Racial Awareness

Infants: Children at this age are developing a sense of self-awareness.

- They distinguish familiar people and explore faces to differentiate who they are.
- They develop a sense of fear of strangers.
- They develop a sense of trust for the people around them.
- They experience and show fear and anger.

Toddlers: Children at this age are discovering a sense of self as an individual.

- They start experiencing embarrassment.
- They expresses their sensitive emotions and are able to notice the feelings of other people.
- They start understanding the behaviors of others.
- They begin asking "What's that?"

Age 2: Children at this age are naming people with the words me, mine, and you.

- They begin to develop their independence and having a sense of control.
- They identify the physical characteristics of the self and classify others by their gender.
- They begin learning the names of the primary colors.
- Are able to differentiate the Black and White colors.

Age 3 to 4: Children at this age have improved at seeing differences among people.

- They are able to recognize and match people according to their physical characteristics; however, they are unable to understand that people's skin color and gender persist for life.
- They are vulnerable in believing stereotypes.
- They create wrong associations and often overgeneralize.
- They start asking the "why" questions.

Age 5 to 6: Children at this age comprehend cultural uniqueness and enjoy exploring cultural heritage of classmates.

- They are able to identify stereotypes.
- They delve into what is real and pretend, fair and unfair.
- They begin to think with a rigid mentality and behavior.
- They demonstrate aggression when presented with insults and name-calling.

Age 7 to 8: Children at this age begin to have a sense of gender and racial constancy.

- They become familiar with membership in a group; and become members of groups to distinguish themselves from others.
- They become aware of racism against their own group.
- They begin asking "What are you?"
- They expect correct information from others.
- They are developing a sense of personal strength.

Age 9 to 12: Children at this age are becoming conscious of and attentive to world events.

- They are aware of their ancestry, history, and geography.
- They comprehend what it feels like to have shame and pride.
- They are able understand the self in another's shoes.
- They are conscious of the cultural and political values around them.
- They have a clear understanding of racism.
- They are able to compare and contrast minority and majority perspective.
- They are able to use their abilities to take social action.

Source: Adapted from Derman-Sparks, L. (1989).

The results from this study revealed that young Black children raised in the 1930s preferred White dolls. Over the years, replications of this study using a variety of methods and settings have revealed that White children identified with their skin tone more often than Black children (Goodman, 1964). Black children, on the other hand, rejected their own ethnic group and had greater preferences for White skin tone (Clark & Clark, 1947; Greenwald & Oppenheim, 1968; Lewis & Biber, 1951; Morland, 1962, 1966). A more recent study by Jordan and Hernandez-Reif (2009) revealed a different finding that related to children having more options when asked to pick a best friend. These options were cartoon characters who had greater skin tone variations (dark brown, medium brown, light brown, and white cartoon characters), unlike the original study by Clark and Clark (1939) where children had to choose between Black dolls and White dolls.

Clark and Clark's (1939, 1947) research findings and interpretation of the Black children who preferred the White dolls rather than the dolls that matched their own identity have remained controversial and up for debate among many. Some early researchers interpreted this behavior to mean that Black children had low self-esteem. Other explanations are that the Black children were simply trying to please the White researchers or that the children had picked up societal messages that being White is better (York, 2003).

The results of these studies suggest that children as young as toddlers develop preferences associated with skin color. As young as 3 or 4 years of age, White children being part of a dominant culture start to form negative attitudes about people who are different from them, and this is due to a lack of awareness or experience with people of color. This is also the age where preschoolers are in what is known as the question-asking stage, referring to being curious and wanting to know about the world around them. Children of color, on the other hand, do not seem to develop negative attitudes toward White people. Frances Aboud (1988) explains that children of color are better at classifying faces by color and that they are very aware of their and other people's skin color. At the age of 5 years, all children start identifying correctly their own ethnicity. This is the age where they begin to differentiate between the real and the pretend, and they may start choosing friends of their same sex and ethnic group. By the age of 7 years, children realize that their skin color will remain constant. They start understanding that they are members of a family and are part of a culture, religion, classroom, state, and country. It is very important to understand that young children learn about race, ethnicity, and culture as a part of trying to make sense of the world around them. Therefore, adults should help children develop an awareness of differences and explain their interest in knowing about other people.

Classroom activities such as this first-grade self-portrait project that focuses on skin color, hair color, and features can help children understand and appreciate differences.

Children's Formation of Ethnic Identity

Children develop their ethnic identity primarily from their family's ethnic cultural heritage. They become aware of their own characteristics, those of their families, and other people's physical and cultural characteristics early in their development. From birth through adolescence, children are socialized by their parents, peers, and community, which helps them form and develop their ethnic identity. According to Spencer (1985), the process by which young children present their ethnic identity and include it in their personal and group identity varies through their development. Though they share similarities, the three concepts of ethnicity, ethnic group, and ethnic identity are different, as illustrated in Table 8.3. Gradually, young children start to figure out how they are the same as or different from other people. One could therefore argue that ethnic identity is a developmental process that goes through continuous changes.

Because ethnicity is a major component of culture, knowledge of culture is essential to understanding ethnic identity. In turn, culture plays a major role in the development of ethnic identity; therefore, ethnic identity is usually considered within a cultural context (Hernandez-Sheets, 2005). For example, White U.S. citizens whose heritage comprises multiple European origins might assume that a mixture of ethnic groups makes their ethnic heritage nonexistent. It becomes nonexistent

| Table 8.3 | Ethnicity, Ethnic Group, and Ethnic Identity Distinctions |

ETHNICITY	ETHNIC GROUP	ETHNIC IDENTITY
Ethnicity is part of people's personal and cultural history. This category includes all of the cultural, psychological, and social phenomena associated with a particular group. It focuses on the ways social and cultural practices intersect during interactions among diverse groups.	An ethnic group is a distinctive social group in a larger society whose members set themselves apart or who are set apart by others due to distinctive cultural patterns, beliefs, histories, values, attitudes, languages, national origins, and physical traits.	Ethnic identity is a personal process, influenced by membership in an ethnic group. It forms within the child and develops throughout the life span. Ethnic identity has individual and group components, is not necessarily limited to one group, and can be internally driven, externally imposed, or both.

Source: Sheets, R. H. *Diversity pedagogy: Examining the role of culture in the teaching-learning process*, 1st edition, © 2005. Adapted by permission of Pearson Education, Inc. Upper Saddle River, NJ.

because they don't share cultural practices with a specific ethnic group. On the other hand, White U.S. citizens whose heritage originated from a single European group or region (e.g., Italy) have a cultural heritage that allows them to assume their ethnicity as Italian American.

Researchers studying ethnic identity report that ethnic identity begins at birth, at the earliest interactions between the child, his or her family, and the community (Spencer, 1985). When young children start self-labeling, it is because they have had direct contact with their immediate surroundings (e.g., family, society, or physical environment) such that they have learned the language, values, and beliefs of a specific group; share the skin color of a group; have membership in a particular group; and have perceived some sort of difference from others. This in turn shapes their ethnic individuality and membership in that ethnic group. This personal (ethnic identity) and social group (ethnic group) identity (a) promotes cognitive growth and social skills valued in the children's homes and communities, and (b) determines how children view themselves. Culture plays a major role in shaping ethnic identity because children are socialized by their parents, society, and peers and thereby learn how their ethnic heritage takes part in their lives.

The Process of Socialization

Through the process of socialization, children learn the values, behaviors, and social patterns of their ethnic group before they gain the ability to self-label. Hernandez-Sheets (1998), for example, argued that 5-year-old African American, Mexican American, Laotian American, and African American and White biracial children were able to precisely classify themselves within their ethnic group. In order to prove differences from others, these children readily used specific physical markers (eye shape, skin tone, and hair texture) and cultural elements (native language, food preferences, and ways of eating) as indicators. Hernandez-Sheets (1998b) also found that children used what they perceived to be socially accepted reasons to classify others. They would say a peer is "Laos" because "my daddy said so" or someone is "Mexican" because "he was born in the hospital" (Hernandez-Sheets, 2005, p. 57).

Young children are socialized to use a variety of physical traits that consist of color terms such as *Black, White,* and *Brown* and other ethnic descriptions such as *Chinese, Mexican,* and *Japanese* in order to describe themselves and others. In one study, children aged 3 to 5 years from a variety of racial groups categorized people ethnically as Chinese or Japanese on the basis of eye shape and skin color (Ramsey, 1986). In a kindergarten classroom, 5-year-old Samantha, upon noticing Gabriel's eye shape, explained that Gabriel (a native Spanish speaker) should speak "Mexican" because when he was asked, "What are you?" he responded, "I'm Mexican, don't you know? I speak Spanish"

(Hernandez-Sheets, 2005). It is clear by this example that both Samantha and Gabriel were socialized to use ethnic terms to describe the self.

Children Learning Culture

The early socialization that children receive from their families impacts children's values, beliefs, and other behaviors. The ways parents or caretakers hold, bathe, dress, feed, and talk to a baby are early examples of the process of learning the family's culture. Through the process of socialization, parents, extended family, neighbors, and society teach children which behaviors are desirable and undesirable in order for them to function successfully in society. Parents, caregivers, and teachers teach children certain ways of dealing with situations, and when confronted with a new situation, children will use those particular ways of doing things in order to figure out how to solve the new problem. As children interact with others in their society, this process of learning cultural practices continues throughout life.

HOW CAN MULTICULTURAL PROGRAMS INVOLVE FAMILY MEMBERS AND THE WIDER COMMUNITY?

In order for a program to successfully involve families as part of the children's education, educators must know the community to which the families belong and understand the cultures of those families. Understanding the culture, language, and ethnic background of the children, their families, and the community will help you get parents involved in their children's education.

It is very important to work with parents and gain their assistance with the planning and implementation of a diverse curriculum. Collaborating with parents in an effort to find resources and activities that encourage pride in students' diversity can be a positive step for many teachers.

Consider This Physical Differences

As a kindergarten teacher, Yolanda gets to introduce and talk about differences between the self and others. Yolanda has a very culturally and ethnically diverse classroom—Maria is Mexican American, Tanika is African America, and Bobby is Korean American. A very memorable experience occurred when these three children were involved in a small group math lesson with the assistant teacher. Bobby, excited and engaged, kept blurting out the answers. Maria, upset at Bobby because he was not taking turns, said loudly, "Stop it! It's my turn! Anyway, your eyes are squished!" Bobby, surprised at the outburst and perceiving that "squished" was an insult, yelled back. "No, they're not!" "Yes, they are!" "No, they're not!" The bickering went back and forth.

Finally, Bobby looked at Yolanda and asked poignantly, "Are my eyes squished?" Yolanda waited a moment, and then responded, "Yes, they're oval. They're a soft brown color and actually quite beautiful," she said. Yolanda then grabbed a mirror and asked Bobby to look in it. The other children, watching what Yolanda was doing, grabbed small handheld mirrors from the basket in the housekeeping area and returned to the rug.

Maria looked at her eyes closely and then stared at Bobby's eyes. She said, "We both have brown eyes." Tanika, searching her eyes, commented, "Mine are mostly round, but they're pretty, too. Right?" Throughout the rest of the day, most of the children in the class freely examined and discussed the differences and sameness of their eyes.

If a young child approaches you and asks why your skin color is light or dark, how would you react to that question? And what would you say?

BEST ~~~~~~~~~~~~~~~~~~~~~~~~~~~~~~~~

Practices The Influence of Family in Socializing Children

Families pass their culture on to their children by socializing their children to become members and participate in a particular culture. Although a family may live in the United States, it may function within a subculture based on its ethnicity, socioeconomic class, religion, or sexual orientation. Parents, being the primary caretakers, are the primary socializing agents. Parents socialize children to encourage the development of those qualities and attributes required for their expected adult roles in their particular subculture or society. To illustrate this, Barry, Child, and Bacon's (1957) study assessed 104 societies to find out whether the child-rearing practices of parents in industrialized societies, such as the United States, differed from those of parents in

agricultural societies, such as India. They found that parents in industrialized societies socialized children for achievement and independence, whereas parents in agricultural societies socialized children for obedience and responsibility. Another study compared European American and Japanese mother-infant interaction and found that European American mothers interacted more vocally with their infants, whereas the Japanese mothers exhibited more body contact with their infants and, in so doing, soothed them into quiescence. The European American infants tended to be more vocal, active, and explorative of their environment than the Japanese infants, who tended to be more passive *(Caudill, 1988).*

Many parents may not get involved in their children's education because they are not directly made to feel welcome either by the teacher or by the school. And this may be in part because most schools reflect the dominant culture and language rather than the family's own. Therefore, school personnel will need to reach out to the parents, rather than simply wait for them to show up at a meeting. Parents and teachers must become partners in the teaching process in order to have the true collaboration that is required in multicultural education. To establish such partnerships, teachers need to listen to parents and participate in the community in order to develop a range of teaching strategies that are congruent with the home cultures of their students. At home parents can participate in this partnership by supporting their children's learning but may need concrete suggestions from the teacher. Often parents will only seek this information from teachers who they believe care about their children. Based on his study, Bronfenbrenner (1974), a big proponent of parental involvement, articulated the following regarding parent-teacher partnerships:

> The evidence indicates that the family is the most effective and economical system for fostering and sustaining the development of the child. The evidence indicates further that the involvement of the child's family as active participant is critical to the success of any intervention program. Without such family involvement, any effects of intervention, at least in the cognitive sphere, are likely to be ephemeral, to appear to erode rapidly once the program ends. In contrast, the involvement of the parents as partners in the enterprise provides an on-going system which can reinforce the effects of the program while it is in operation, and help to sustain them after the program ends. (p. 55)

In addition to parents, the community can be a great resource in a multicultural classroom. Educators can learn much about cultures in the community through participation in cross-cultural activities and by inviting community members into the school. Community speakers and helpers should represent the diversity of the community. Teachers should select speakers in different roles and from different age-groups to present relevant information for the students. If you as an educator encounter a problem with certain community members regarding objectionable content and activities presented in a specific curriculum, you should not be discouraged from teaching about different cultures or special needs. Instead, you should investigate that community's sentiments before introducing new material. Educate parents on issues or topics that may be controversial. Explaining to parents the importance of the topic for their children's education and the ways it can contribute to their children's knowledge will make parents feel included in decisions about their children's learning.

Program Models for Involving Parents and the Community in Multicultural Education

Over the past several decades, researchers have created a variety of program models and services with the intent to involve parents, particularly African American parents, in early childhood programs. Among these precursors to multicultural education as we know it today were an "infant stimulation through family life education" program in Schenectady, New York (Ligon, Barber, & Williams, 1971) and Ira Gordon's (1971) well-known home visitation programs in Florida that utilized a teacher's aide. Another program, the Carnegie Infant Education Project (Lambie, Bond, & Weikart, 1974), constructed curriculum to increase a mother's awareness of her infant's growth and her ability to enhance this growth. Each of these early programs promoted parents' involvement in their children's learning and enhanced the parents' own growth and development as adults.

Other programs involved home visits and entering the homes of children and their families. Susan Grey (1971) and colleagues developed a home visitation technique for preschool mothers at the George Peabody College Demonstration and Research Center for Early Education (DARCEE). Levenstein's (1970) Verbal Interaction Project was based on the belief that parents could be taught to stimulate their children's intellectual development. Many early programs of parent involvement relied exclusively on parent group meetings, such as that conducted by Karnes, Hodgins, Teska, and Kirk (1969). Sometime around the 1970s, the Home Start program employed home visitors whose qualifications were friendly attitudes, suitable cultural and language backgrounds, and successful experience as parents, rather than academic credentials. The Home Start program and other parental involvement programs of that period emphasized the importance of cultural and language awareness (Midco, 1972).

During the 1970s, attempts to involve parents were measured by changes in parenting skills, parents' self-esteem, building trust among parents and educators, and parents' acceptance of the value of education for their children. The research findings often showed that many conditions, such as working multiple jobs or single parenting, were caused by poverty, minority status, or personal stress, and these conditions were a barrier to parents becoming involved in their children's education. Parents found the effort involved in participating in parent education programs was just another impediment or life stressor. However, parents knew all too well then, as they do now, that such programs made a difference to their own personal growth and their children's education.

Boutte (1999) provides some of the important findings from these earlier programs, which, in fact, have long-lasting implications for today's educators:

- All parents need to fully understand and appreciate the significance of their behavior in shaping children's lives; for example, the attention parents pay to a child's expressions of pleasure and parents' listening skills and demonstrations of interest greatly impact the child.

- Parent involvement should be sought cross-culturally. Certainly, parental involvement is not just a problem for the poor or people of color. Parenting skills are needed at all levels of society; people from all cultures can use more skills in this area.

- Teaching parents effective parenting skills by modeling and demonstrating works better than simply talking.

- Parents need to be involved early on in the school life of their children if they are to become active participants in school activities later.

- No single approach to parent involvement matches every parent's ability to participate.

- School personnel must make a wide variety of outreach efforts in order to meet the developmental and educational needs of children and parents.

- Parent involvement efforts may require a lot of patience, and the results may not be immediately apparent.

- Regardless of the level of involvement in their children's learning experiences, parents can benefit from knowledge about the ways children develop emotionally, socially, physically, and cognitively and how this information relates to their growing child's personality and ability to succeed in school.

- Parents must feel rewarded for being involved in their children's educational progress.

- Observation skills are very important for parents to acquire; becoming informal child-watchers is crucial in order to understand the relationship between a child's developmental stage and the child's ability to learn new skills.

- Parents need to know how to take advantage of the many opportunities for children to learn routines and activities in the home environment that can create learning, problem solving, and positive socialization experiences.

- Parental involvement does not result in cognitive gains alone. Emotional goals may be more lasting and more significant. Social development outcomes are also a very important aspect of parent involvement.

- The interactions of teachers with parents strongly affect children's learning.

Building collaboration between parents, families, and schools requires that schools and teachers be familiar with the cultures of the children and their families. Clearly, this is a gigantic task but an important one. Effective teachers are knowledgeable about their students' cultures, recognize their students' strengths and weaknesses, and have a positive attitude toward differences.

WHAT DO WE KNOW ABOUT CULTURAL DIFFERENCES IN THE SPECIAL EDUCATION SYSTEM?

Multicultural education doesn't only include appreciation of cultural diversity; it also provides equality for all individuals, including children with special needs. Providing these children the opportunity to interact in regular classrooms—to be mainstreamed—can be an advantage for both children with special needs and their peers. Such advantages for special needs children include the opportunity to experience regular education, develop friendships with peers who are typically developing, and receive realistic life experiences that prepare them to live in the community (Wolery & Wilbers, 1994). Children without disabilities can also benefit from interacting with children who have special needs because they can develop an accurate view about disabilities, can form positive attitudes about people who are different, and can have the opportunity to view children who have succeeded despite many challenges.

Early childhood special education (ECSE) is a federal and state government-funded program that provides services for children under 9 years of age and their families when a child has a disability or developmental delay. It provides infants, toddlers, and their families with early intervention to address the special needs that these young children may have. This program is part of the Individuals with Disabilities Education Act (IDEA), a federal law that guides special education. As you may remember from Chapter 7, if a child has been identified as having special needs, the child will receive an individualized education plan (IEP) or individual family service plan (IFSP). Guidelines for the development and implementation of the IEP and/or the IFSP are specified by IDEA.

Early Intervention

ECSE offers three types of early intervention programs to infants and toddlers. The first is for children with developmental delays. The law requires that these delays be "measured by appropriate diagnostic instruments and procedures" and asserts that they may be present in one or more of the five developmental domains: physical, cognitive, socioemotional, language, and adaptive (IDEA, 1991). The second type of program is for children who "have a diagnosed physical or mental condition which has a high probability of resulting in developmental delay" (IDEA, 1991). Most states list Down syndrome, fragile X syndrome, and similar chromosomal disorders; sensory disorders such as deafness or blindness; and neuromuscular disorders, such as cerebral palsy, as conditions that can result in developmental delays. The last program type allows the

An aide helps a student with special needs complete an assignment.

state to serve infants and toddlers without developmental delays or diagnosed conditions who are at risk as defined by the state. Each individual state has the authority to set its own definition of such terms as *developmental delay, diagnosed conditions,* and *at risk*, which provides flexibility in deciding which children will be served by these special programs. At first, many states communicated an interest in serving at-risk populations, and in 1989, more than 39 states included provisions for serving at-risk infants and toddlers. Three years later that number dropped to 13 states, and in 2000, only 9 states were serving at-risk infants and toddlers (U.S. Department of Education, 2000, p. A-293).

Preschool Special Education

Children between the ages of 3 and 5 years are eligible nationally for preschool special education services if they have one of 10 recognized disabilities: "mental retardation, hearing impairments including deafness, speech or language impairments, visual impairments including blindness, serious emotional disturbance, orthopedic impairments, autism, traumatic brain injury, other health impairments, and specific learning disabilities" (IDEA, 1991). Mainstream and special education preschool programs will usually serve children until they enter elementary school or until they reach 6 years of age.

Developing an inclusive environment to serve these preschoolers with special needs consists of four guidelines that teachers can use to design the physical space (Wolery & Wilbers, 1994):

1. When needed, help children learn to play with toys and materials. Some young children with disabilities may benefit from initial adult assistance in playing with typical early childhood materials. With sensitive guidance, these children, like children without disabilities, can greatly benefit from these play experiences.

2. Select toys and materials that appeal to students. Through careful observation, teachers can learn which play materials students with special needs enjoy. These favorites should be provided on a regular basis to encourage creative play experiences.

3. Provide play materials that engage children in playing, interacting, and learning. When possible, toys and materials for children with disabilities should be selected to promote the type of learning identified in their IEPs.

4. Adapt toys and materials where needed. Some toys and materials cannot be manipulated because of physical limitations. Adaptations such as battery-powered toys that can be manipulated with switches and wheelchair-accessible sand play areas outdoors help ensure that all children benefit from quality play experiences.

Early Primary Special Education

The number of children in special education in the public schools has increased dramatically since the 1980s, with the majority of all children in such programs categorized as having a learning disability (e.g., attention deficit disorder [ADD] and attention deficit/hyperactivity disorder [ADHD]). See Table 8.4 for a description of other learning disabilities (Bennet, 2007). The second most common disability, and the one impacting English language learners (ELL), is language disorder. A language disorder can be defined as a child or an adult having trouble understanding other people **receptive language** or having trouble sharing his or her thoughts, ideas, and feelings completely **expressive language**. The possibility of ELL students being labeled with a language disorder is based on the referral of a teacher due to low academic performance. That is, the child is not learning English in the expected time frame and is not performing academically at the same level as his or her monolingual peers.

Schools and teachers that are in a multicultural setting need to create a learning environment that is supportive of all children's cognitive, socioemotional, physical, and ethnic differences, thus being responsive to their needs as individuals (Osher, Woodruff, & Sims, 2005).

Table 8.4	Characteristics of Children With Learning Disabilities

CHARACTERISTIC	DESCRIPTION
Poor academic achievement	Children with learning disabilities (LD) often have difficulty in one or several subject areas. Their performance is often uneven; for example, they may excel in math but struggle with writing.
Perceptual-motor difficulties	Children with LD often have trouble interpreting sensory stimuli and distinguishing left from right. They may exhibit a lack of motor coordination.
Speech and language delays	Children with LD often show delays in language, including slow speech and poor word retrieval.
Faulty memory and logic	Children with LD often have trouble remembering or thinking through problems in school.
Hyperactivity/attention deficits	Some children with LD show extreme degrees of activity in school. They may have great difficulty attending to classroom tasks.

Source: Modified from Trawick-Smith, 2006.

Promoting Optimal Development

Supporting Multicultural Education

What can parents and teachers do to promote multicultural education?

- *Recognize* that because we live in a racist and biased society, we must actively foster children's antibias development. We need to be cognizant that we all are constantly and repeatedly exposed to messages that subtly reinforce biases.

- *Create* an environment at home or at school that gives messages that deliberately contrast with the prevailing biased messages of the wider society.

- *Provide* books, dolls, toys, wall decorations (paintings, drawings, photographs), TV programs, and recordings that reflect diverse images that children are not likely to see elsewhere. These materials should reflect diversity in

  o Gender roles (including men and women in nontraditional roles)

  o Racial and cultural backgrounds (e.g., people of color in leadership positions)

  o Capabilities (people with disabilities doing activities familiar to children)

  o Family lifestyles (varieties of family composition and activities)

- *Show* that you value diversity in the friends you choose and in the people and companies you choose for various services (e.g., doctor, dentist, car mechanic, teachers, stores).

- *Make it a firm rule* that a person's identity is never an acceptable reason for teasing or rejecting him or her.

- *Initiate* activities and discussions with the goals of building positive self-identity and teaching the value of differences among people.

- *Talk* positively about each child's physical characteristics and cultural heritage. Tell stories about people from your ethnic group of whom you are especially proud.

- *Help* children learn the differences between feelings of superiority and feelings of self-esteem or pride in their heritage.

- *Provide opportunities* for children to interact with other children who are racially or culturally different from themselves and with people who have various disabilities.

- *Respectfully listen* to and answer children's questions about themselves and others. Do not ignore questions, change the subject, sidestep, or admonish the child for asking a question.

- *Teach* children how to challenge biases about who they are. By the time they are 4 years old, they become aware of biases directed against aspects of their identity. Teach them to recognize stereotypes and caricatures of different groups. Young children can become adept at spotting "unfair" images of themselves and others if they are helped to think critically about what they see in books, TV, movies, and comics.

- *Use accurate and fair images* in contrast to stereotypic ones, and encourage children to talk about the differences in these images. For example, at Thanksgiving time, greeting cards that show animals dressed up as "Indians" with buckskins and feather headdresses abound. This can be contrasted with real images of Native Americans.

- *Let children know* that unjust things can be changed. Encourage children to challenge bias and give them skills appropriate to their age level.

Source: Derman-Sparks, Gutierrez, & Phillips (1989).

Summary

Cultural diversity and multicultural education are important in our lives. This chapter examined the purpose of teaching in a multicultural classroom as well as the approaches to teaching in a multicultural program. As educators, we have to self-evaluate by considering how diversity is present in our lives, how it functions in our students' lives, and how it affects our behaviors. Through the process of self-evaluation and reflection, we can reduce or overcome ethnocentrism. Children at a young age are socialized to learn the values, behaviors, and social patterns of their ethnic group. Young children will learn different beliefs and behaviors depending on the availability of role models or the influence of socialization agents. When thinking about diversity and multiculturalism, we must think of gender, ethnicity, religion, socioeconomic status, and exceptionality differences, such as having a physical and/or a learning disability. There are many advantages to mainstreaming children with special needs in regular education classrooms. Such advantages include building friendships with children who are typically developing, and obtaining realistic life experiences.

Key Terms

Caste   213

Cultural pluralism   207

Culture   207

Early childhood special education (ECSE)   220

Ethnicity   213

Ethnocentrism   208

Expressive language   222

Multicultural education   207

Race   213

Receptive language   222

Reflection, Application, and Analysis Questions

1. Reflect on your upbringing. What culturally diverse experiences did you encounter as a young child, in middle childhood, and/or as an adolescent?

2. Define ethnocentrism, and explain how to reduce ethnocentric beliefs.

3. Identify three things that a multicultural curriculum should emphasize and represent.

4. Explain Banks's (1997) four approaches to developing a multicultural curriculum.

Extension Activities

1. Interview a teacher or an administrator at a preschool or an elementary school to determine the type and level of parent involvement at that school. List all parent activities that the school offers (parent-teacher association, open houses, home visits, etc.).

2. Acquire community resources (posters, postcards, and cultural artifacts, such as clothing, jewelry, and pictures) so that students can make connections between school, home, and community. What kind of lessons will your students be gaining by acquiring a connection between home and school?

3. Encourage students to become aware of and appreciate their own physical traits and to respect the differences of others. Provide young children with handheld mirrors for them to view their faces and other parts of their body. What kind of lessons could be learned in the classroom by giving children handheld mirrors?

Additional Readings

The following list of readings will be useful for those who are interested in keeping up with the most current developments.

Alba, R. D. (1990). *Ethnic identity: The transformation of White America.* **New Haven, CT: Yale University Press.**
Richard D. Alba's work examines the changing role of ethnicity in the lives of Americans from a broad range of European backgrounds. Using data from in-depth interviews with more than 500 people, he shows that while the ethnic origins of White Americans have less and less import in such measurable areas as educational and occupational achievement and marriage, they are still salient in more subjective ways.

Gonzalez-Mena, J. (1992). Taking a culturally sensitive approach in infant-toddler programs. *Young Children,* **47(2), 4–9.**
This article discusses ways for caregivers to improve sensitivity toward cultural and individual differences and increase communication across cultural barriers. It describes four possible outcomes of conflict that arise because of cultural differences among families and caregivers.

Van Ausdale, D., & Feagin, J. R. (2001). *The first "R": How children learn race and racism.* **New York: Rowman & Littlefield.**
Using ethnographic data from a study of children in a racially and ethnically diverse preschool in an urban area, this book examines how young children learn about race and racism. The authors' numerous vignettes reveal a world of unexpected sophistication and complexity in these 3- to 5-year-olds.

York, S. (2003). *Roots and wings: Affirming culture in early childhood programs.* **St. Paul, MN: Redleaf Press.**
This book explores how multicultural and antibias issues affect the classroom, what multicultural education is, and what culturally responsive care and education looks like on a day-to-day basis. It offers concrete ideas and activities to early childhood teachers, program directors, teacher trainers, and parents to help implement culturally relevant and antibias education in the classroom.

On the Web

Council for Exceptional Children - *http://www.cec.sped.org/*
The Council for Exceptional Children (CEC) is the largest international professional organization dedicated to improving the educational success of individuals with disabilities and/or gifts and talents. The CEC advocates for appropriate governmental policies, sets professional standards, provides professional development, advocates for individuals with exceptionalities, and helps professionals obtain conditions and resources necessary for effective professional practice.

Family Diversity Projects - *http://www.familydiv.org/index.php*
Family Diversity Projects is a nonprofit organization located in Amherst, MA. It has created six award-winning traveling rental photo-text exhibits that tour communities nationally and internationally. The exhibits are perfect for diversity events in schools, colleges, community centers, conferences, libraries, hospitals, mental health centers, and museums.

National Association for Multicultural Education - *http://www.nameorg.org/*
The National Association for Multicultural Education (NAME) is a nonprofit organization that advances and advocates for equity and social justice through multicultural education. NAME today is an active, growing organization, with members from throughout the United States and several other countries. Educators from preschool through higher education and representatives from businesses and communities compose NAME's membership. Members in many local communities and states have formed NAME chapters that serve the same networking, support, and outreach functions on the local level, similar to the national network.

Student Study Site

Visit **www.sagepub.com/gordonbiddle** to access several study tools including eFlashcards, web quizzes, links to SAGE journal articles, web resources, video resources, lesson plan templates, and more.

Lesson Plan:

I Am Unique

Subject:
Multicultural education.

Focus:
Learning to describe the self.

Overview:
Children will learn to appreciate themselves and others.

Purpose:
To identify how similar and different we all are.

Resource Materials:
- Children's fingers.
- Optional: pictures. (You can take the children's pictures with a digital camera and decorate your bulletin board.)

Activities and Procedures:
This is a finger play to do with children during circle time. Children will point first to themselves, then to a part of the body that describes the self:

1. My head is different from your head. My head has long black hair that is straight. (Describe the uniqueness of your hair color, length, texture, etc.; point to yourself, then to your head.)

2. I am different from my eyes to my nose; my eyes are black, blue, or green. (Describe the color of your eyes and wiggle your nose as you point to it; point to yourself, then to your eyes and nose.)

3. I come from a place that is far and wide. (Point to yourself, then spread your arms wide open.)

4. A place where we all smile instead of cry. (Act like you are tracing your lips into a smile, and bring your hands down your eyes as if you were crying.)

5. I am very different as you can see. (Point to yourself, then to a friend.)

6. But I still have a lot of love in me! (Point to yourself, then place a hand over your heart and hug yourself.)

Tying It All Together:
Encourage families to get involved in sharing their unique stories and experiences. These experiences can be used to help the children in the classroom begin to understand other cultures. This knowledge of the cultures of their classmates helps students learn to respect diverse cultures.

Visit **www.sagepub.com/gordonbiddle** to access templates of these lesson plans.

Developing a Multicultural Book

Subject:

Multicultural education.

Focus:

Learn about different beliefs, customs, and traditions.

Overview:

After the children have finished their multicultural books, ask them to read the pictures or stories to the class.

Purpose:

To learn about and appreciate different cultures and traditions.

Objectives:

- Increase understanding of cultural diversity.
- Have an understanding of different attire and artifacts that are used in different cultures.
- Learn about one's own and other cultures and traditions.

Resource Materials:

- Construction paper or cardboard.
- Old magazines.
- Glue.
- Ribbon.

Activities and procedures:

1. Teachers ask children to cut out various pictures from magazines (old *National Geographic* ones are great).

2. Make a book by using construction paper or cardboard.

3. Children glue pictures of different ethnic groups, attire, and artifacts onto the pages, punch holes, and add ribbon to make the book.

4. Have children dictate their thoughts about the pictures (the different people, clothing, and artifacts) to you.

5. Write their responses down on the relevant page.

Tying It All Together:

Encourage families to get involved in sharing their unique stories and experiences. These experiences can be used to help the children in the classroom begin to understand other cultures. This knowledge of the cultures of their classmates helps students learn to respect diverse cultures.

Visit **www.sagepub.com/gordonbiddle** to access templates of these lesson plans.

Lesson Plan:
Dream Catcher

Source: Adapted from http://www.kinderart.com/camp/rainbowdreamcatcher.shtml and http://www.kinderart.com/multic/

Subject:

Native American history.

Focus:

Understanding the meaning of the dream catcher.

Overview:

Have some students share their dream catcher and explain the things they added to represent themselves.

Purpose:

To familiarize students with Native American arts and crafts through legends, and to reveal the origin of the popular decorative art called a dream catcher.

Objective:

To learn about Native American folk tales, legends, and stories.

Resource Materials:

- Paper twist ribbon (sold in a roll—one roll is enough for 12 hoops of 6 inches each).
- Yarn or string in any color.
- A variety of beads and feathers in assorted colors.

Activities and Procedures:

Begin by showing the class examples of dream catchers. You might tell them the story of the Lakota spirit of wisdom named Iktomi who disguised himself as a spider to visit the Lakotas' leader. Iktomi took the leader's willow hoop and told him about the importance of the cycle of life. Iktomi spun a web in the leader's hoop and told him that the "dream catcher" would catch the leader's good dreams and let the bad ones fall through the web's center. This would help the leader and his people realize their dreams and ideas. To read the story of the Iktomi dream catcher, visit http://www.dreamcatchers.org/dcat16T.html.

1. Precut the hoops from the paper ribbon and tape the open end to create a circle.

2. Have students tie an anchor knot with the yarn/string from one side of the hoop to the other in order to create a line across the hoop's center.

3. Have students continue to create their dream catcher's "web" by stretching the yarn/string across the hoop's center in different directions. (Note: If they want to include beads in the web, they must string them before they tie off the yarn/string onto the edge of the hoop.)

4. Tie two or three pieces of yarn/string on the bottom of the dream catcher hoop to suspend beads and feathers, and include a small loop of yarn/string at the hoop's top to hang your dream catcher.

5. Make sure all knots are nice and tight to keep the dream catcher's web intact.

Tying It All Together:

Discuss with the children of the importance of various beliefs, customs, and traditions of the Native American culture.

Visit **www.sagepub.com/gordonbiddle** to access templates of these lesson plans.

Guidance in Early Childhood Education

This chapter will help you answer these important questions:

- What are the theoretical foundations of guidance?

- How does a teacher guide behavior?

- What individual needs of children should be considered?

- What is the family's role in guidance?

- What types of classroom environments facilitate guidance and positive behavior?

Vignette: Snack Attack

It is not uncommon for early childhood teachers to have problems with children who want to eat their snack before it is time, especially if the snack is something yummy such as Goldfish crackers or Cheerios. Let's go back in time and see how Liz's teachers guided her behavior at each level in order to keep her from eating snack too early.

Liz loves Goldfish crackers and Cheerios. This has been true ever since she was a toddler. If those were the snacks being placed on the table, Liz would notice them immediately through her sense of smell. As a toddler, Liz would always want to eat the Goldfish crackers right away. Her teachers would guide her behavior by distracting her and redirecting her energy. They would turn Liz away from the tables with snack on them, place her somewhere far from these tables, give Liz her favorite toy, and encourage her to play.

Later in her preschool years, Liz still loved the same crackers and cereal. Because she was older, she needed a discipline strategy that was a little more involved. This time the teachers talked to Liz and explained to her about nutrition and schedules. They also let her know that in a few minutes it would be snack time if she could just wait patiently. They encouraged Liz to go play with some other toys and games. They promised to call her name as soon as snack was ready, and these good early childhood education teachers kept their promise.

In early elementary school, Liz's love of these snack treats soared. When Goldfish or Cheerios were served, she would beg the teacher for some early snacks before all the other children. Guiding Liz's behavior at this age was more complex and took more than one strategy. This time the teachers gave Liz a contingency, telling her that if she waited she could have snack first. The teacher also praised her every 15 minutes during snack preparation whenever she was happily involved in another activity and not circling around the snack preparation table.

G uiding a young child's behavior is one of the most important duties of an early childhood professional. Through guidance from early childhood teachers and other adults in their lives, children—even children with special needs (Jolivette, Gallagher, Morrier, & Lambert, 2008)—learn how to interact socially, regulate their emotions, and regulate their behavior (Gartrell, 2005). Guidance techniques are best learned and practiced before a teacher even steps into a classroom with young children, through role-play in preservice

Key Elements
for Becoming
a Professional

classes. With reflection and evaluation, guidance techniques will evolve as the early childhood teacher learns and becomes more professional (McFarland, Saunders, & Allen, 2009).

Learning how to discipline or guide young children is an area of knowledge that assists teachers as they prepare to teach young children. **Guidance**, or discipline, of young children is an art, and it requires special skills. Best if accomplished in a firm, yet gentle and sincere, manner, guidance involves teaching a young child to distinguish between appropriate and inappropriate behavior. This chapter focuses on guidance and offers some methods for guiding behavior. The chapter begins with the theoretical underpinnings of guidance. Next come strategies and methods of guidance divided into three sections. The first section contains general guidance methods that the teacher can use, such as the following:

- Natural and logical consequences—helping children through and letting them experience the ordinary result of their actions.
- Evoking new behaviors—behaving and interacting with children in such a manner that they react in a positive way.
- Environmental manipulations—setting up and arranging the environment in such a way as to avoid negative behaviors.
- Fostering prosocial behavior—using strategies that bring about behavior from children that considers the thoughts, feelings, and needs of others.

The next two guidance methods focus on how the day flows. These two methods are as follows:

- Scheduling and routines—prearranging the day to keep the children interested and avoid conflict.
- Transitions—making changes and passages during the day as smooth and seamless as possible.

The third section of guidance strategies lists and describes various other specific guidance strategies such as these:

- Problem ownership and problem solving—helping children see the problem as a result of their actions and helping them take the necessary steps to solve it.
- Active listening—really listening to children and reflecting back through talk what they are feeling, thinking, and saying.
- "I" messages—helping children see that you view their behavior as wrong and that their behavior makes you uncomfortable.
- Attention—giving attention and praise to good, positive behavior.
- Redirection—providing alternative materials and activities for children to engage in.
- Discussion—helping children talk out the problem among themselves to arrive at a solution.
- Time-out and time-in—stopping children from participating in an activity until their behavior improves, and keeping children close to you and giving suggestions and models of appropriate behavior.

Also covered in this chapter are children's individual needs, which parents and teachers should consider when applying guidance methods, and the family's role in guidance. The individual needs are as follows:

- Health: Is the child ill, and is it affecting his or her behavior?
- Temperament: What is the child's temperament, and what are some ways of interacting fruitfully with the different temperaments?

- Peers: What are the child's peers teaching and demonstrating?
- Attachment disorders: Does the child have an insecure attachment to a primary caregiver that is influencing his or her behavior?
- Special needs: Does the child have a diagnosed or undiagnosed special need that is influencing his or her behavior?

As stated previously, this chapter concludes with the family's role in guidance. A discussion about how to build a partnership with parents is followed by what can be considered the family's unique role in guidance.

WHAT ARE THE THEORETICAL FOUNDATIONS OF GUIDANCE?

This section of the book discusses knowledge and procedures that can help prepare you for teaching young children. This specific chapter focuses on guidance. Having knowledge and strategies for guiding or disciplining young children is quite important for early childhood educators. As with most areas in early childhood education, there are theories that underlie the reasoning, knowledge base, and methods. Specific theories of guidance exist as well. Three of these theories—social constructivism, social learning theory, and learning theory—were briefly covered in Chapter 4. These theories will be elaborated and extended in this chapter, along with other theories that will be new to the reader.

As with many areas of early childhood education, guidance has underlying theoretical strands. In other words, there are theoretical bases for the guidance methods utilized by early childhood teachers and suggested for use by the families of young children. Traditional theories such as social constructivism, learning theory, and social learning theory add to the theoretical foundation of guidance methods. Other theories have been developed and named after specific people, such as Dreikurs's and Gordon's theories of guidance. These five theories are the main ones that underlie the guidance methods of early childhood education. Let us begin with the traditional theories of social constructivism and learning.

At times in this textbook, when discussing theories, we have a central scenario. Here is a scenario that offers a real-life, specific illustration of how each theory views and interprets the scenario. The following scenario, which is typical on first-grade playgrounds, will be interpreted by each of the five guidance theories.

The female children on the playground are all playing hopscotch, which just happens to be by the basketball court. The two basketball teams of mostly male children keep throwing the ball out of bounds or running out of bounds and interrupting the hopscotch game. Pretty soon a yelling and pushing match ensues that is mostly along gender lines, as some children at this age believe the opposite gender has "cooties."

Different theoretical lenses will yield various approaches for guiding the behavior of young children and responding to behavior on the playground.

Social Constructivism

Social constructivism is one of the major theories of early childhood education (Vygotsky, 1962, 1978). In social constructivism, the approach to guidance is based on the belief that children create their own reality and that subsequent behavior is based on experience interacting with people and objects in their world. Social constructivist terms such as *zone of proximal development, scaffolding, private speech,* and *self-regulation* apply most directly to guidance. As you may recall from Chapter 2, the zone of proximal development (ZPD) is the difference between what children can accomplish alone and what children can accomplish with a more knowledgeable and skilled person helping them. Scaffolding, as described in Chapter 4, is gradually helping children arrive at a new point of knowledge or skill by giving them hints and suggestions, but not doing the work for them. **Private speech** occurs when children uses their words to guide their thoughts, behaviors, and emotions.

Simply put, teachers and parents help children monitor their own behavior through scaffolding children's behavior in their ZPD. In the beginning, teachers and parents help children understand what behavior is appropriate and the reasoning behind appropriate behavior. Then parents and teachers help children internalize these behaviors and the accompanying reasoning. Soon the chil-

dren will guide their own appropriate behavior through private speech. For instance, in our hopscotch and basketball scenario, the children are acting as they are because of the messages and tools the people and the culture around them have given them. The culture told or showed them that yelling and shouting are the ways to solve problems. It is the job of the teachers on the playground to give the children new knowledge and show them strategies to scaffold their learning about how to solve their problem. The playground teachers will have to show, tell, and scaffold the children's learning a number of times before the children internalize the new behavior, knowledge, and problem-solving strategies. **Self-regulation** is a state of being for the child—a skill or an ability that teachers and parents try to foster within the child. Children who are self-regulated can control their own behavior and emotions and exhibit them in a socially acceptable manner. Ultimately, this, a self-regulated child, is the goal of a professional teacher's guidance. Early childhood teachers strive with their guidance methods to foster self-regulation in the children they teach. These children will be able to guide and control their own behavior and emotions.

Learning Theory

Learning theory, also referred to as behaviorism, is a basic and widely known child development theory (Skinner, 1953; Watson, 1913). This theory is closely related to guidance principles for young children. Operant learning and positive reinforcement are concepts from learning theory that can be applied to the guidance of young children. **Operant learning** is the process of gaining new knowledge or developing through rewards from other people in the environment. Positive reinforcement, closely related to operant learning, is the actual act of rewarding a young child when the child exhibits behavior. Hopefully, it is the behavior that is appropriate and favored. As you can see, these two concepts are closely related. One term/concept is from the perspective of the child and relates to the whole process. This term is *operant learning*. The other term, *positive reinforcement*, introduced in Chapter 4, is more specific and relates to the actions of other adults or children who are guiding a certain young child's behavior. One cannot say enough about the importance of positive reinforcement. It has a great impact on the children's emotions, motivation, and behavior. Positive reinforcement is a better choice than punishment when selecting guidance techniques.

A child is learning operantly when, for example, a boy realizes that hitting his sister makes her cry and then allows him to take the toy that he wants from her. Although teachers and parents of young children may not want children to learn this particular behavior, this process is a clear

Technology can be rewarding for children, but should parents use it as a positive reinforcement or take away access as punishment?

demonstration of operant learning that happens often. Keeping with this same scenario, the young boy's sister has reinforced his behavior. On a positive note, a teacher or parent can positively reinforce the young boy by rewarding him with his favorite toy when he gives his sister's original toy back to her.

In terms of our playground scenario, the teachers can reward the children who are behaving appropriately and not yelling and shoving. The other children, seeing that this is the appropriate behavior and the way to get rewards, will soon modify their behavior in order to receive rewards from the playground teacher as well.

Social Learning Theory

Social learning theory is another major theory of child development (Bandura, 1977, 1986, 1992). The social learning concepts of observational learning

Children learn a great deal from observing the behavior of the adults in their lives.

and modeling relate to the process of guiding young children. **Observational learning** is learning that happens when watching another child or adult get rewarded for some behavior. Once a young child watches another person get rewarded for his or her behavior, the child is likely to display that behavior, too. The child or adult who initially exhibits the rewarded behavior is **modeling**. It may be quite simple to see how these concepts can be utilized to guide the behavior of young children, but perhaps an illustration is in order. For instance, let's say Suzy sees Jane share her apple slices with a friend. Her teacher then gives Jane a hug and tells her that she is such a good sharer and the teacher is proud of her. Little Suzy observes this interchange and then shares her apple slices with a friend. The teacher then gives Suzy a hug and calls her a good sharer. Suzy's behavior was influenced by observational learning. Jane modeled the appropriate behavior for Suzy. In the scenario that began this section of the chapter, the playground teachers can again reward children who are acting appropriately. The difference with social learning theorists (as opposed to learning theorists or social constructivists) is that they focus on the modeling of the appropriate behavior and give a name to the learning that takes place within the children who are misbehaving. This type of learning is observational learning, which takes some thought. Suzy does not just react without any thought. She thinks about the appropriate behavior she observes being modeled.

Dreikurs's Guidance Methods

Rudolf Dreikurs based his theory of guidance on the work of psychiatrist Alfred Adler (Dreikurs & Cassel, 1972; Dreikurs & Soltz, 1964). Adler's basic tenet that all humans have goals that underlie their behavior is a framing principle of Dreikurs's theory and guidance methods. Dreikurs believed that inappropriate behavior has an underlying goal or goals. These goals and accompanying behaviors are initiated and activated when a young child experiences discouragement. Dreikurs believed there to be four underlying goals to misbehavior that go in a steplike sequence. The goals (steps) are attention, power, revenge, and inadequacy.

Attention

It is good to give attention to a child who exhibits appropriate behavior. However, it is best to ignore the bids for attention of a child who is exhibiting inappropriate behavior. This will probably make the child increase the bad behavior in amplitude and frequency.

Power

The child will also advance to the next step or goal, which is power. If the child does indeed engage you in a power struggle, it is best that you as a teacher or parent not participate in the power struggle. Not participating may neutralize the behavior or escalate it. However, young children need to learn that there are acceptable and unacceptable methods for asserting power.

Revenge

If the behavior escalates, this means the child is still feeling discouraged. He or she will now try to get revenge. The child will try to hurt another person. This may be a person more or less powerful than the child. The child will probably try to get revenge on the person who ignored his or her initial bid for attention, but not always. The child is actually seeking revenge because he or she is in pain and feels discouraged, and it is important to remember this. At this point, a teacher or parent should try to encourage the child and help him or her feel accepted.

Inadequacy

If the child continues to feel discouraged, he or she will progress to the fourth goal, inadequacy. This goal does not seem to make sense intuitively. At this point, the child is really discouraged and might feel helpless. It is advisable at this time for teachers or parents to give the child encouragement, praise, and support.

Encouragement and Praise

According to Dreikurs (Dreikurs & Cassel, 1972; Dreikurs & Soltz, 1964), encouragement and praise are very specific actions to take. By **encouraging** children, you accept them as they are and increase

their self-esteem and confidence. Encouragement focuses on abilities and accomplishments that contribute in some way to the whole group. An example encouraging statement is "Thank you for picking up your blocks. The classroom is organized better, and now everyone can have a snack."

Praise relates to an adult's (i.e., a teacher or parent's) approval of a child. Praise also focuses on children's action, but the message of adult approval is huge. An example praise statement is "Thank you for picking up your blocks. You are such a good helper, and I am so proud of you." Encouragement and praise support the child in a different way.

Natural and Logical Consequences

Dreikurs (Dreikurs & Cassel, 1972; Dreikurs & Soltz, 1964) introduced the natural and logical type of guidance. When using this type of guidance, you

Natural and logical consequences help young children understand the outcomes of their behavior.

allow children to experience the **natural consequences** of their actions, what would occur naturally. Your guidance leads to the **logical consequence** of the children's actions, what would logically be thought of as a consequence. The philosophy behind this guidance method is that children can control their behavior and the consequence they receive. This approach applies to both punishment and positive reinforcement. More discussion and examples follow in the section "How Does a Teacher or Parent Guide Behavior?"

Gordon's Guidance Methods

Gordon (1974, 1976) based his suggested guidance methods on humanistic theory. His methods are suggested for use by parents and teachers, and include problem solving and ownership, active listening, and "I" messages. These guidance techniques are staples in every early childhood educator's repertoire.

Problem Solving

Problem solving is the act of helping children think about and solve their own guidance issue. You begin by acknowledging a child's feelings. Then you state that the behavior is not acceptable. Then you guide the child to a more acceptable alternative through a few questions. For instance, you can say, "I know you are angry right now because Todd took the toy boat. However, it is not OK to bite Todd. What can you do instead? What words can you use to express yourself? Do you see any other toys in the room that interest you?"

Problem Ownership

Problem ownership helps with solving the problem. It is important to communicate whether the problem is located with the child, with the teacher, or with the relationship between the child and the teacher. If the problem is located with the child, you may use either problem solving or active listening to get to a resolution. When the problem is located with the child, usually he or she is trying to send you a message.

Active Listening

Problem solving was described in a preceding paragraph. **Active listening** is the process of reflecting back to children in words what they are trying to communicate. You repeat or rephrase what they are saying in a way that helps them clarify what they are feeling and thinking. This type of reflecting or active listening helps children solve their guidance issue. An example of active listening is "You seem sad. It also seems that you want to be happy again. What can we do to help you be happy again?"

"I" Messages

If the problem is located with the teacher, Gordon (1974, 1976) suggests using **"I" messages**. With "I" messages, you own the problem and express to the child how you feel, why you feel that way, and why you would like the child to change a particular behavior. An example of an "I" message is "I see you are playing with the dishes. It makes me uncomfortable when you throw them, because the dishes might break or some of your friends might get hurt." More examples and discussions of guidance follow in subsequent sections of this chapter.

HOW DOES A TEACHER OR PARENT GUIDE BEHAVIOR?

A teacher may use any of the guidance methods defined and described in this text. However, a few techniques are used regularly and routinely by numerous early childhood teachers of children from birth to 8 years old. The guidance techniques mentioned in this section are having appropriate expectations, limits and choices, natural and logical consequences, evoking new behaviors, environmental manipulations, and fostering prosocial behaviors. **Guidance techniques** are styles of interacting with children that discipline them and show them positive and socially appropriate

General and specific methods of guidance can help early childhood teachers prevent and remedy negative behavior, such as throwing objects.

behaviors. **Evoking behaviors** is the process of interacting with children in such a manner that positive and socially appropriate behaviors are emitted. **Environmental manipulations** are actions that arrange or prepare the physical environment of the classroom in order to elicit positive and socially appropriate behaviors from young children. **Prosocial behaviors** are behaviors that benefit someone else; in addition, the child who emits these behaviors has little expectation of gaining any benefit for him- or herself.

Expectations, Limits, and Choices

When a teacher or parent is implementing guidance, having the appropriate expectations makes all the difference. It is not realistic to expect a 6-month-old to feed him- or herself, and a child should not be punished if unable to perform this action. Having the appropriate expectations in the beginning starts guidance efforts off on the right path. This general rule of having the correct expectations applies to preschoolers and kindergarteners as well.

Another general overall strategy that goes along with having appropriate expectations is establishing limits and choices (Flicker & Hoffman, 2002). Simple, logical limits with two choices are the best ways to obtain appropriate behavior from children. A few simple, logical limits that children understand help them behave appropriately. After setting the limits, the next step is to communicate the limits to the children (Flicker & Hoffman, 2002). Convey the classroom limits to the children verbally, in written form, and in pictorial form. Repeat these limits and refer to them as often as needed. To illustrate, perhaps a rule in your first-grade classroom is that students must ask for permission to sharpen their pencils. What if the students' kindergarten teacher let them sharpen pencils at will? This might cause the students to have trouble remembering and following the rule. Instead

Promoting Optimal Development

Behavior Expectations

What are appropriate behavior expectations for preschoolers and kindergarteners, and how do they vary?

According to NAEYC Standard 1c, teachers should use developmental knowledge to create learning environments. This mandate applies to discipline standards as well. According to some well-known theories in early childhood education (cognitive development and psychosocial theories, for example), the transition from preschool to kindergarten coincides with some developmental changes. For instance, the transition from preoperational thinking to concrete operational thinking happens at this time. Young children go from symbolic thinking to concrete thinking. Also to be noted in the socioemotional realm is the transition from autonomy to industry.

Young children go from wanting to do things themselves to comparing themselves to others. This translates into different behavioral expressions and subsequently the necessitation for different behavioral expectations. Theoretically, it is easier for a kindergartner to share. These children are also more independently capable and are beginning to compare abilities. Therefore, the discipline strategies utilized with preschoolers will be different from those used with kindergartners, but emotional well-being must still be facilitated. To give a practical example, a preschooler who takes a toy from another child is probably acting out of egocentrism and the belief that the toy is his or hers. That same behavior in a kindergartner probably is based in aggression or intent to harm. Regardless, the discipline of each child should be warm and consistent.

of getting upset and frustrated as a teacher, just verbally stating this rule in the beginning and having written and pictorial reminders posted around the classroom will help students remember this new rule. Soon the first graders will be asking permission before going to sharpen their pencils.

Natural and Logical Consequences

Introduced earlier in this chapter, natural and logical consequences as guidance techniques let children experience the consequences or outcomes of their actions and behaviors. This may seem simple, but many parents and teachers try to "rescue" children from the consequences of their negative behavior and not give them any consequences. For example, let's say that Felicia eats some cookies before dinner even though she was explicitly told not to do so. The logical consequence of this action is that Felicia will not be allowed any dessert after dinner. Another example is that Steve keeps hitting his little brother and taking away a treasured toy. His parents or a teacher can step in and give him two choices. Either Steve can stop hitting his younger brother and share the toy, or Steve can have the toy taken away for a period of time until he learns the appropriate way to share the toy with his little brother. These two choices represent logical outcomes of Steve's actions. A natural outcome of his actions would be his brother not wanting to play with him anymore.

Evoking Behaviors

Besides letting young children experience natural and logical consequences, teachers can work to evoke positive and appropriate behaviors in children. This is a general strategy that is most helpful with infants and toddlers but may be used with older children as well. Caregivers and parents can evoke behaviors from young children by using a cluster of strategies. First, the environment can be arranged in such a way as to invite appropriate behaviors. Some examples of this are having several of the same toys to lessen the number of quarrels, blocking access to dangerous or forbidden areas, and allowing enough room for play. Second, attention can be given to appropriate behavior. When a child behaves appropriately, the teacher or parent can give the child lots of attention. Receiving this type and amount of attention increases the odds that this type of behavior will be repeated. Scaffolding, mentioned earlier in the chapter, is a third strategy. Teachers can work to build appropriate behavior in children by aiding them and giving them structure with scaffolding. Modeling is a fourth strategy that was also mentioned earlier. Adults can model the appropriate behavior and/or reward other children who model the appropriate behavior. This works to increase the odds of other children repeating this behavior. Fifth, a young child's behavior can be shaped through positive reinforcement. By reinforcing appropriate behavior or actions that approximate appropriate behavior, adults can actually shape a child's behavior. The reinforcement increases the likelihood that the appropriate behavior will be repeated. Positive reinforcement, mentioned earlier, and shaping are learning theory concepts. Evoking appropriate behavior is a general guidance strategy that can be enacted with a number of specific guidance techniques.

Environmental Manipulations

As briefly mentioned above, teachers and parents can set up or change the environment in order to guide young children's behavior. This general strategy, environmental manipulations, can be quite effective at alleviating some inappropriate behaviors. For instance, separating the block area from the large muscle/gross motor area with a physical barrier can alleviate inappropriate behavior such as knocking over block towers or tripping other children with train tracks. The physical environment should be arranged thoughtfully and critically. Teachers have to give attention to how the room is arranged, even in early elementary classrooms. How are the children sitting? Are they in rows or clustered groups? Where are the learning materials placed? Do they promote self-help and follow the flow of the day? Giving some time and thought to the arrangement of the physical environment is a good guidance strategy.

Fostering Prosocial Behavior

Prosocial behaviors are behaviors or actions that are good for another person but do not necessarily benefit the person who emits the actions. When fostering prosocial behavior, it is good to examine one's own guidance methods as they are quite important for helping children develop appropriate social skills (Lawhon & Lawhon, 2000). In fact, it is quite important for teachers to evaluate and reflect on their own behavior when guiding the behavior of young children (McFarland et al., 2009). This is because young children model what adults do. The methods and techniques for fostering prosocial behavior will be discussed in depth in Chapter 11. Here we will briefly mention some of them, as they are good general methods for guiding behavior of all young children (Elksnin & Elksnin, 2000): taking advantage of "teachable moments" that occur naturally, modeling prosocial behavior, role-playing in the natural setting, encouraging self-talk, discussing prosocial behavior and the outcomes and emotions associated with it, and encouraging deliberate practice of prosocial behavior. As always, focus on what prosocial behavior is valued by the setting or culture that you and the children are in at the time.

BEST

Practices Guiding the Behavior of Toddlers, Especially When They Bite

Toddlerhood is a special time in development. It seems as though toddlers have behaviors and actions that are anything but prosocial. How can a teacher or parent foster positive behavior in a toddler, especially when biting occurs? Here we will relay a general framework for guiding the behavior of toddlers and some specific actions to take when a toddler bites. In general, adults who work with toddlers may take these four steps to work with toddlers: (1) support their development, (2) plan the environment, (3) adjust guidance methods for the toddler's developmental level, and (4) adjust play activities for the toddler's developmental level (Abraham, 2002). You can support toddlers' development by building their trust, communicating with them, getting down on their level, using music as a tool to communicate with them, staying close to them, and being careful not to overstimulate them. As with children of any age, preparing the environment is important. With toddlers, be sure to have a safe, clean environment that is baby-proofed. Have sturdy, durable climbing toys; have ample space for playing; mark play spaces with rugs, tape, or physical barriers; and arrange the room so that toddlers are always in view, even if you are changing another child's diaper. In order to modify guidance techniques for toddlers, it is important to understand and respect the toddler's developmental level. You may also want

to use techniques such as redirection, discussion (in words the toddlers understand), and modeling very often. Be sure to be consistent, stay close, and smile a lot! You also need to understand toddlers' developmental level to adjust their play activities. Have duplicates of a variety of toys and educational materials for activities to keep their attention, and help with sharing. Use music, allow for exploration, develop their imaginations, and respect their attention span, which can lengthen a bit with the right materials and activities.

But what about when a toddler bites? What should you do then? Be as quick to act as possible. Get down on the child's level and say something such as "No biting. We do not hurt our friends. That is not nice." Your voice tone should be calm, but firm. Give attention to the child who was bitten and have the biter apologize (in words he or she can verbalize). Also give the biter some simple verbal phrases and words to use if he or she faces the same circumstances again. Often toddlers bite when they cannot express themselves verbally. Try to discern the circumstances that came before and accompanied the biting. Watch for those circumstances again in the future, and try to prevent them. If the biting continues, parents and behavior specialists may need to be consulted.

WHAT ROLES DO SCHEDULES AND ROUTINES PLAY IN GUIDANCE?

Schedules and routines are very important when it comes to guiding young children. The development of very young children, such as infants and toddlers, thrives in the presence of schedules and routines. Schedules and routines help young children trust the environment and adults around them. For older children, the predictability of schedules and routines helps them feel comfortable and have some sense of "control" in their day. Schedules and routines are even important in early elementary grades (see Figure 9.1).

Schedules that are well planned and well thought out help with guidance of children. There should be a balance of high- and low-energy activities. This helps keep the children's attention, keep them active, and foster better behavior. The predictability of a schedule helps children know what to expect, which helps them behave better. An important part of scheduling is well-planned and smooth transitions.

Within every schedule comes time to transition from one activity to another. In general, it is good to schedule these so that children's time is not wasted and children do not have to wait. Help them transition from one activity to another with music, familiar activities, or familiar sayings as cues or signals. For instance, the song "It's Howdy Doody Time" could signal cleanup and preparation for recess.

Two of the more important transitions are drop-off and pickup times. At drop-off it is important to welcome each child and family and communicate with the adults. Some children may need more support than others when separating from their parents. These children may need a comfort object from home or some concentrated and warm attention from a teacher. At pickup time, you as the teacher can share positive and important information about each child's day with the parent or family member who comes to pick up the child. It is important to prepare children for the arrival of an adult to take them home. This can be done with verbal statements, music, or some other cue.

Figure 9.1   Daily Schedule Example

SCHEDULE

Free Time Art Activity
Cleanup
Calendar Circle and Singing
Small Group Learning Centers
Wash Hands/Snack Time
Outside Time
Cleanup Outside
Sharing and Story Time
Dismissal

WHAT ARE SOME SPECIFIC TECHNIQUES FOR GUIDING BEHAVIOR?

Besides the more general methods mentioned above, there are some specific guidance techniques and strategies that teachers and parents can utilize on a day-to-day and moment-by-moment basis. These techniques and strategies are just as important as the general methods mentioned in this chapter, and include

- Attention
- Redirection

Figure 9.2 **Benefits of Choice-Making Opportunities**

Choices in daily routines produce positive behavior and developmental outcomes.
1. Independence
2. Self-monitoring of appropriate behaviors
3. Improved sense of control over the environment
4. Active participation in the environment
5. Improved performance
6. Increased sense of well-being
7. Connections between natural consequences and responsibility
8. Decrease in inappropriate behavior

Source: Exceptionality by Lawrence Erlbaum Associates Inc. Reproduced with permission of Lawrence Erlbaum Associates Inc. in the format republish in a book/textbook via Copyright Clearance Center.

- Ignoring
- Problem solving and problem ownership
- Active listening
- "I" messages
- Discussion and verbalization of emotions
- Time-out and time-in

The first three strategies work especially well with very young children, such as infants and toddlers, but can be used with older children as well. The other strategies work well with older toddlers, preschoolers, and early elementary children.

Attention

Giving attention to any human being helps foster trust and signals to that person that you value him or her. This is especially true with young children. Giving positive attention to appropriate behavior goes a long way to ensure that the person who demonstrated the behavior will repeat and value it. But remember that giving attention to negative behavior may also increase the frequency of that behavior. On the other hand, smiling and giving positive attention to positive behavior goes a long way with young children.

Redirection

When the children are young and the misbehavior is minor and easy to correct, it may be wise to just redirect the child. **Redirection** is giving the child an alternative activity or toy and thereby deflecting the child's attention from inappropriate behavior. This can be as simple as turning a young child away from a hot stove and rolling him or her a ball. Another example is distracting a child from knocking over a block tower by anticipating the action and asking the child to ride a bike before it happens.

Ignoring

Just as giving attention to a behavior reinforces it, ignoring a behavior helps it decrease. **Ignoring** a behavior means not giving any attention or reinforcement to that behavior so that it will stop. This type of guidance works best when the behavior of focus is not dangerous in any way. Tantrums and attention-seeking behaviors that are inappropriate, but not unsafe, illustrate behaviors that can be ignored. When ignoring a child's behavior, suggest some alternative behaviors that would receive your positive attention or a reward of some kind. This teaches the child how to obtain positive rewards and positive attention with appropriate behavior. For example, if little Johnny always has tantrums at cleanup time, you can tell him that if he cleans up, you will help him, and then he can go outside (or participate in some other rewarding activity). Simply say this so he can hear you, and then ignore the tantrum. Go about the business of helping other children clean up the room. Soon little Johnny will get the message, stop the tantrums, and help clean the room. Once he does, give him plenty of positive attention and help.

Gordon's Theoretical Concepts Revisited

Problem ownership, active listening, and "I" messages were mentioned earlier in this chapter. They are reiterated here because they work well as general and specific techniques. To summarize, these three methods work together to help children solve their own problems through owning and discussing them. If a child is trying to give you a message, listen to and reflect on it. Then help the child solve the problem. If the problem is yours, as a teacher or parent, give an "I" message. Tell the child how you feel about his or her behavior and why it is wrong. Then guide the child to a solution or more appropriate behavior. The following examples from early elementary classrooms illustrate these concepts. Let's imagine that Suzi has trouble being still in class and always taps her pencil on the desk and hums. Help Suzi first own the problem, then solve it. Tell her that she is stopping the rest of the class from learning and that she must find alternative activities and times for releasing her energy. Then ask her how she can release her energy in a more appropriate fashion. Or, alternatively, you may listen to and reflect on Suzi's message and help her solve her problem. Tell her that you understand she has lots of energy to release, but it is not the appropriate time. Ask her to tell you how and when it is more appropriate to release her energy. The third strategy, "I" messages, can be accomplished by telling Suzi that you cannot teach the other students well when she taps and hums and that she is frustrating you. Ask her to tell you what she can do to release her energy in a more appropriate time, place, and manner.

Discussion

In general, discussion of behavior and emotions is a good guidance technique. **Discussion** consists of helping children talk about their behaviors or emotions, why they are inappropriate, and what can be substituted that is more appropriate. This type of strategy works well with older children. However, simple discussions can work with older toddlers as well. In the examples from the preceding section, Gordon's (1974, 1976) theoretical concepts were used to discuss Suzi's inappropriate behavior. However, discussion can be utilized as a technique without following Gordon's concepts. For example, let's say Ted is angry because he keeps losing one-on-one basketball games with Fred. Ted then kicks the basketball off of the court. First have Ted retrieve the ball. Then discuss with him what his feelings are and why he's feeling them. Then ask him what are some more appropriate actions for expressing those feelings and what he can do to win a basketball game (or some other game) in the future. Discussion is a technique that works well with older children and helps them learn more appropriate behavior.

Time-Out and Time-In

Time-out is a discipline strategy that parents and teachers use often. **Time-out** involves sending children away from a situation that may be inappropriately rewarding or overstimulating them. Time-outs usually happen if the inappropriate behavior is repeated continually, and are sometimes seen as an alternative to physical punishment. The child goes to a corner, seat, or space set aside for time-out periods. Usually, the time-out lasts one minute for every year in the child's age. Time-out does not teach children the appropriate behavior in which they should engage. Therefore, it should be used in conjunction with discussion or attention for appropriate behaviors.

Time-in, a newly emerging technique of guidance, involves children in appropriate activities and fulfills their needs. It works well with toddlers, preschoolers, and young elementary children. When instances of discipline are necessary, the teacher responds by keeping the child close, giving suggestions for appropriate behavior, modeling appropriate behavior, and giving huge amounts of praise and attention when the appropriate behavior is emitted by the child (D. Wessels, personal communication, September 2006). This is sometimes referred to as the "Velcro approach." This helps the child learn the appropriate behavior and allows the teacher to take advantage of "teachable moments."

WHAT INDIVIDUAL NEEDS OF CHILDREN SHOULD BE CONSIDERED?

This section of this chapter examines individual factors that may come into play when applying appropriate discipline strategies to young children's behavior. These individual factors include health, temperament, peers, attachment disorders, and special needs. For the purposes of this section, **health** can be considered basic physical and biological well-being. **Temperament** is the biologically based foundation of personality. **Peers** are friends who are at or near the same age or developmental level. **Attachment disorders** are personality disorders that stem from an insecure attachment. Special needs are disabilities that range in atypicality from learning disability to mental illness (see Chapter 7 for more on children with exceptional needs). These factors can influence a child's behavior, and teachers and parents must consider them when applying discipline techniques.

Health

For some children with medical conditions, the use of guidance techniques should be carefully adjusted. Children with asthma usually also have allergies (Delaney, 1971). This is because they can have asthma attacks that last from 15 minutes to several hours; therefore, cooperation is needed between the medical community, the parents, and the teachers (Delaney, 1971). When young children feel unwell, they may not behave properly. The possibility of a health problem should be taken under consideration when young children misbehave.

Temperament

There are three major categories of temperament: easy, slow-to-warm, and difficult (Thomas & Chess, 1969). The slow-to-warm and difficult temperaments may benefit from adapted guidance techniques. For instance, putting a positive slant on a difficult child's self-assertion is the mark of a sensitive teacher (Thomas & Chess, 1969). For example, the sensitive teacher would describe

Using this type of paddle device is not necessary in order to properly guide children's behavior. It is usually not allowed in public schools, but may be in some private schools.

Professionalism & Policy

Advocating for Children and Against Physical Punishment

In an effort to improve on discipline strategies, physical punishment has long been thought of as inappropriate for young children. However, some parents still use it and justify it with religious reasons or by saying that it didn't harm them when their parents used it. As professionals in early childhood education, it is up to us to educate our students' families about the use of physical punishment. The use of physical punishment by itself does not teach young children what behavior is appropriate, and it models the use of aggression to solve problems. If physical punishment is used, it should be as gentle as possible and not escalate to abuse. Also, it should be accompanied by a more positive discipline technique such as redirection, discussion, or problem ownership.

What are some ways that early childhood professionals can advocate against the use of physical punishment? They can advocate for laws forbidding physical punishment in early childhood classrooms. They can give workshops to parents about successful alternatives to physical punishment. These workshops should contain real-life scenarios, problem solving, and actual role-playing in order for the parents to learn optimally. Additionally, giving these workshops in faith-based or community-based settings can help. The workshops can teach preservice early childhood educators and parents alternative methods of discipline. Videos and role-plays can accompany these classes as well.

The best way early childhood professionals can advocate against physical punishment is by not using it themselves. They can model appropriate discipline for other adults. At least, if parents or other adults insist on using physical punishment, early childhood professionals can give them the main reasons for not using physical punishment (i.e., it does not teach and models aggression). They can also tell these adults how to use physical punishment more appropriately, intermeshed with other more positive and appropriate discipline techniques.

this child as strong-willed. To be effective, teachers can also utilize respect, objectivity, environmental structure, and limit setting (Soderman, 1985). These are the types of discipline technique adaptations an early education teacher can make in response to the individual factor of temperament. It is also important for mothers of fearful/anxious children to use gentle discipline and de-emphasize power assertion (Kochanska, 1995). The dynamics of this may be the same for teachers as well.

Peers

The way young children interact with their peers may impact their acceptance by their peers, but teachers pay a role in this process as well (Hazen, 1982). Teachers can guide young children into play groups, assist with communication skills, and comment positively when the children demonstrate pleasant and correct social behavior. It is important that teachers help children who are rejected and neglected by their peers through the use of guidance techniques. Helping these children to learn communication skills and the other behaviors necessary to make friends is important for setting them on a positive developmental trajectory.

Peers are a big influence on the type of behavior that young children exhibit.

Attachment Disorders

Children who are insecurely attached may develop attachment disorders. This is not good for children, their families, their community, or society in general. The use of gentle discipline techniques by the mother (and perhaps the teacher) influences a child's attachment security and aids in creating a secure attachment. Both of these factors, discipline techniques and attachment security, contribute to whether or not young children show an orientation toward internalization, or internalizing negative feelings. Gentle guidance techniques lead to more compliance with demands and more secure attachment.

Special Needs

Children with disabilities may require an adaptation in guidance techniques. Children with special needs may develop more persistent and consistent behavior problems (Jolivette et al., 2008). Special needs can range from a heart anomaly, to a physical deformity, to dyslexia or disgraphia (writing disability). Behavioral and socioemotional disorders are other forms of special needs (Skinner, Neddenriep, Robinson, Ervin, & Jones, 2002). Having students report incidents of prosocial behavior helps to ameliorate social behavior problems in some classroom situations (Skinner et al., 2002). For example, having students report kind acts, such as sharing, and rewarding those acts are more effective for reducing social behavior problems such as hitting or bullying than focusing on and punishing social behavior problems.

When working with children with special needs, it is important to remember the IDEA laws. These laws and other related laws were discussed in Chapter 7, and suggest implementing guidance practices schoolwide in the preschool and early elementary years (Conroy & Davis, 2000). These laws are collectively called the Individuals with Disabilities Education Improvement Act of 2004. They call for equity, accountability, and excellence in education for children with disabilities (www.ed.gov/IDEA), as described in detail in Chapter 7.

Positive behavior support (PBS) is an especially useful framework when working with children with special needs. However, PBS can be used with children who are typical as well as atypical (Jolivette et al., 2008) (see Figure 9.2). PBS is an early intervention program that teaches young children a variety of appropriate responses to challenging situations. The levels of PBS progress from positive relationships, to classroom-level prevention, to teaching appropriate social

Figure 9.3	Probable Reasons Why Young Children Use Problematic Behavior Instead of Their Language Skills

- The child has a language delay (e.g., expressive and/or receptive), deficit, or disability.
- It is more efficient for the child to use his or her behavior than to verbally or gesturally communicate.
- The child has learned it is more effective or expedient to use his or her problem behavior than other forms of communication.

Source: Jolivette et al., (2008) p. 83.

and emotional behaviors, to intense interventions with a specific child. Intense interventions may include removing a child or having a specialist in the classroom to assist the child.

HOW TO SUPPORT GUIDANCE THROUGH THE USE OF PARENTS AND FAMILIES

Having teachers, parents, and families cooperate with the use of discipline strategies is an ideal situation. However, the culture and beliefs of the parents and families should be respected and considered. If there is a conflict between parental values and early childhood philosophy, just state your views and philosophies in a nonjudgmental fashion and try to be as supportive as possible of the parents' culture and values. Try to focus on the guidance process and not the guidance outcome when cultural values come into conflict (Gonzalez-Mena & Shareef, 2005). For example, focus on the guidance technique used and not the cessation of inappropriate behavior.

Building Partnerships With Parents

The first step in gaining cooperation is building a partnership with the parents and families. It is best to start having frequent, informal, positive contact with parents and other family members as soon as the child enters the early childhood program. This type of contact helps to build a trusting partnership (Gestwicki, 2000). Therefore, from the very beginning of your relationship with the parents and families of the children in the program, try to have frequent and positive contact.

If inappropriate behavior escalates, it may be necessary to work with both the child and the child's family. Perhaps workshops on parenting, discipline, and guidance may help all families with children in your early childhood program. These workshops may be targeted at certain children and families, but it is best to invite all families to the workshops. This prevents the targeted families from feeling embarrassed. Parts III and IV of the textbook have accompanying workshops in the ancillary materials that are appropriate for families. The general outline of these workshops can serve as a guide for you, the early childhood professional. Remember that the reason behind having parent education workshops is to give parents good parenting strategies that are supported by research and theory (Webster-Stratton, 2000).

Consider This Consistent and Effective Guidance

"My mommy lets me throw things," shouted Brian while hurling another plastic block across the play area. Brian's teacher Charlotte knew this wasn't the case, but in order to truly handle Brian's behavioral issues she knew that it would be important to involve Brian's parents. Charlotte recognizes that teachers have to work as a team with parents and family members when it comes to guidance techniques. She believes children need consistency, and family members need to feel respected. However, Charlotte understands that oftentimes differing cultural values come into play, and

it can be difficult to reach common ground. Since Charlotte works with children from diverse cultures, she is very aware of the need to respectfully communicate with the family members of the children she teaches.

Do you believe a child's educational setting and a child's home setting should have consistent discipline? How would you respond if a student in your class claimed your rules did not apply because they did not match the rules at home?

The Family's Unique Role

Every child's family is unique and different. As mentioned above, each family has its own culture, beliefs, and values. In fact, it may be helpful to think about the fact that each family has a "culture" of its own that is only partially related to race, ethnicity, and religion. The behaviors and beliefs of a child's family help to shape the child's behavior and beliefs. Because parents and other family members share similar genes and similar home environments with the children in the program, their behaviors and beliefs impact a child's behaviors and beliefs greatly. This influence may be stronger than any influence an early childhood teacher may have over the child's behaviors and beliefs. Each family is unique, and the family members play a very important role in their child's life, even in terms of guidance and discipline (see Figure 9.4). Therefore, early childhood teachers must think carefully about how to interact with families in regards to guidance techniques.

Intervening when children are young can produce positive results for years to come.

WHAT TYPES OF CLASSROOM ENVIRONMENTS HELP FACILITATE GUIDANCE AND POSITIVE BEHAVIOR?

Early childhood education teachers can create an overall environment in their classrooms that will be conducive to positive behavior from children and to the overall success of the application of guidance techniques. The encouraging classroom, the peaceable classroom, and the responsive classroom are three types of classroom environments that help facilitate guidance. All three of these classroom environments have a different flavor and have arisen from various diverse needs.

Figure 9.4	The Reflective Practitioner

1. Recognizes the ethical nature of working with parents and families.

2. Maintains a clear focus on the goal of enhancing growth and development in both parents and children.

3. Takes responsibility for establishing collaborative relationships with parents and researchers to improve practice.

4. Takes responsibility for continuing to develop technical expertise based on theory, research, and practice.

5. Understands the critical role of artistry/intuition in parent education practice and works to articulate and enhance this artistry.

When you are creating and conducting parent education workshops, it is important to be reflective, especially when the topic is guidance of young children.

Source: Adapted from Group Parent Education. © 2004 SAGE Publications, Inc.

The **encouraging classroom** puts particular emphasis on the daily schedule, room arrangement, and curriculum modification and development (Gartrell, 2001). Another focus of this classroom type is teaching democratic life skills. **Democratic life skills** include expressing emotions in a manner that does not hurt another person and working well in small groups. This classroom type arose as a response to an overuse of time-out. In this classroom, the teachers work as a team to reduce the number of conflicts that may arise from the schedule, classroom layout, and/or curriculum. This classroom type emphasizes caring inside of the physical limits of the classroom. In other words, when inside the walls of this classroom, young children are to be caring toward each other.

The **peaceable classroom** is a model that arose in response to the amount of violence to which children are exposed (Levin, 1994). Teachers in the peaceable classroom try to ameliorate the violence to which children are exposed that negatively impacts the children's development, thoughts, and feelings. The teachers try to help children cope with violence in appropriate and meaningful ways. This classroom type focuses on violence prevention and intervention. The teachers help the children in their classroom to experience safety and trust. The children should feel safe in the classroom environment in terms of their feelings, bodies, ideas, and possessions. The children should also feel that the teacher trusts them enough to work out their own problems when conflicts arise.

The **responsive classroom** focuses on supporting children's socioemotional development, especially in the early elementary years (Horsch, Chen, & Wagner, 2002). It arose out of the fact that having a developmentally appropriate classroom is necessary, but not always sufficient, to alleviate students' behavioral problems, and, in fact, can aggravate behavior problems if proper guidance techniques are not in place. In this classroom type, teachers endeavor to build a responsive classroom by focusing on socioemotional needs and creating caring, respectful schools. The teachers in these classroom types utilize morning meetings, rules with logical consequences, guided discovery, classroom organization, academic choice, and assessment and reporting to parents. By using these tools, the teachers help the children they are teaching to develop cooperation, assertion, responsibility, empathy, and self-control. Academically, the children gain deeper knowledge of the subject matter, reasoned decision making, and motivation for learning.

Even the way in which you arrange and organize your classroom can impact the effectiveness of your guidance techniques.

Summary

Early childhood teachers' guidance methods are quite important. It is good for you to understand the theories of guidance, some proven guidance methods, and some of the choices for organizing your classroom. Remember that when you are guiding young children's behavior you are teaching them appropriate responses to certain situations. A main goal is for children to be able to regulate and control their own emotions and behavior. It is important for you to also communicate with the parents and family members of the students you teach. The parents and family members are your partners in helping guide young children's behavior.

Key Terms

Active listening   237
Attachment disorders   244
Democratic life skills   249

Discussion   243
Encouraging   236
Encouraging classroom   249

Environmental manipulations   238
Evoking behaviors   238
Guidance   232

Reflection, Application, and Analysis Questions

1. Which theoretical lens is the best for deciding how to discipline a toddler? Name and describe the theory and give three reasons why it is the best one.

2. Which theoretical lens is the best for deciding how to discipline a third grader? Name and describe the theory and give three reasons why it is the best one.

3. Are the two theories you named in Questions 1 and 2 the same or different? State five reasons why this may be the case, whether they are the same or different.

4. What is the "logic" behind letting a child experience the natural consequences of his or her actions? Do you agree with it or not? Define or describe the logic, and then describe three reasons why you agree or disagree.

Extension Activities

1. How do you feel personally about physical punishment and young children? We know that as early childhood professionals you do not support and will not engage in physical punishment with the young children you teach. However, what are your personal beliefs? Take a few moments to reflect and/or write in your journal about your personal feelings toward physical punishment and young children.

2. It is important that you communicate and cooperate with the parents and families of the children you teach. Take a few moments to reflect, and then write down two strategies for accomplishing this important aim in your journal.

Additional Readings

Guidance of young children is a controversial topic. There are many views and perspectives based on culture, religion, and experience. As an early childhood professional, try to base your guidance techniques on research, theory, and best practices.

Campbell, D., & Palm, G. F. (2004). *Group parent education: Promoting parent learning and support.* Thousand Oaks, CA: Sage.
This is a very comprehensive book that discusses parent education through group workshops. It covers rationale, frameworks, skills needed, and issues. This book is particularly helpful when designing guidance workshops for parents.

Gartrell, D. (2004). *The power of guidance: Teaching social-emotional skills in the early childhood classroom.* Clifton Park, NY: Thomson Delmar Learning.
This book was noted by the NAEYC as a comprehensive member benefit. It is a collection of writings that help early

childhood educators understand the why of children's behaviors. Strategies for teaching appropriate social responses are also thoroughly discussed.

Gonzalez-Mena, J., & Shareef, I. (2005). Discussing diverse perspectives on guidance. *Young Children, 60*(6), 34–38.
This is a very important article for early childhood educators who are working in a multicultural setting. It is especially important for educators who have not experienced bias or oppression to relate to the guidance practices of parents and families who have experienced bias and oppression. One of

the main points of this article is that discussing diverse guidance perspectives should be a process, with little emphasis on outcome.

Williams, K. C. (2009). *Elementary classroom management: A student centered approach to leading and learning.* **Thousand Oaks, CA: Sage.**

This book is particularly helpful for early elementary school educators. It is useful as young children transition from early childhood to middle childhood. The principles of autonomy, belonging, competency, democracy, and motivation are elaborated and discussed as they pertain to guidance.

On the Web

Guidance Techniques - *https://utextension.tennessee.edu/publications/Documents/sp489-C.pdf*
This is an 8-page publication. It offers guidance suggestions including building confidence, offering choices, and being an example. It also contains some scenarios for role-play and practice.

IDEA '97 - *www.ed.gov/IDEA*
This website contains laws concerning the education of children with special needs. Their rights are also contained in these laws. It is important for early childhood educators to become familiar with these laws.

Suggested Guidance Techniques - *http://extension.oregonstate.edu*
A variety of guidance technique publications are available at this site. Put the words *guidance* and *discipline* in the search box and read some of the articles from your results.

Student Study Site

Visit **www.sagepub.com/gordonbiddle** to access several study tools including eFlashcards, web quizzes, links to SAGE journal articles, web resources, video resources, lesson plan templates, and more.

Lesson Plan:

"I Am Learning Manners"

Subject:

Etiquette/manners.

Focus:

Etiquette while self-feeding with eating utensils.

Overview:

Once a toddler begins to self-feed with eating utensils, much development can happen in more than one developmental area. For instance, physical and motor development, language development, cognitive development, and social emotional development all are enriched during mealtimes. One method teachers can use to assist with this development is to have family-style meals with older toddlers and model appropriate development and mealtime interactions.

Purpose:

To enrich a toddler's development during mealtimes.

Objectives:

- Teach toddlers appropriate manners during mealtimes through modeling.
- Socialize toddlers by modeling appropriate mealtime behaviors.
- Enrich toddlers' meal experience through interaction with other children and adults.

Resource Materials:

- A table appropriately set for eating a meal.
- A booster seat for the toddler.
- Toddler-sized utensils along with child and adult utensils.
- An appetizing meal.
- Pleasant conversation with appropriate manners.

Activities and Procedures:

1. Have all children and at least one adult sit at the table that is set for a meal.

2. Begin passing the food around in child-sized containers for self-serving, remembering that the toddler(s) may need assistance.

3. Begin eating and having pleasant conversation, making sure to follow your etiquette rules and manners.

4. Point out and highlight appropriate manners during the conversation and mealtime.

5. After the meal is complete, have older children clean their spots, putting food in the trash and dishes in the sink or a small plastic washtub.

6. Make sure that everyone washes their hands.

Tying It All Together:

Mealtimes are great for socialization and learning, especially in family-style arrangements. This way the teacher can model appropriate behavior, monitor the children, and assist children when necessary. Pleasant conversation adds to the atmosphere and teaches and socializes children as well. By modeling, monitoring, and assisting, the teacher is actually guiding the children's behavior and helping the children to learn how to guide their own behavior, too.

Visit **www.sagepub.com/gordonbiddle** to access templates of these lesson plans.

"What Do I Do With This Feeling?"

Subject:

Self-regulating and guiding emotions and behavior.

Focus:

Learning to handle and respond to one's own anger.

Overview:

Some of the activities are planned, but at other times take advantage of teachable moments.

Purpose:

To help young children respond appropriately to their own anger.

Objectives:

1. To learn how to express anger appropriately.
2. To learn how to behave appropriately when angry.
3. To learn to self-regulate emotions and behavior.
4. To increase emotional competence.
5. To increase behavioral competence.

Resource Materials:

- *Emily's Tiger,* by Miriam Latimer.
- Paper.
- Nontoxic crayons.
- Nontoxic markers.
- Pencils.

Activities and procedures:

1. Read and discuss the book by Miriam Latimer during circle time.

2. Engage children in a structured or free-play art activity where they draw angry faces and the appropriate behavior to accompany the feeling of anger.

3. Take advantage of teachable moments, when children are angry. Get down at their level and help them express their anger appropriately and understand how they are feeling and why they are angry.

4. When you are angry, turn it into a teachable moment by verbally and appropriately expressing your anger. Focus words on how you are behaving to express anger and model appropriate behavior.

Tying It All Together:

Learning to appropriately express anger can take a lifetime. However, young children can begin to learn by seeing the adults react to anger around them. *Emily's Tiger* is a wonderful story about a little girl who does not know how to respond to her own anger until her grandma models how to handle anger. This book is educational and entertaining. It is a great piece for fostering discussion about self-regulating one's anger.

Visit **www.sagepub.com/gordonbiddle** to access templates of these lesson plans.

Lesson Plan:
Taking Turns

Subject:

General guidance.

Focus:

Learning to take turns.

Overview:

It is important for children to learn to take turns in life to get access to popular and interesting objects and activities. This learning and socialization process can be reinforced at school when children need to take turns on computers or other popular objects in the classroom.

Purpose:

To give children rules and underlying reasons for taking turns.

Objectives:

1. Help children learn the rules surrounding taking turns in your classroom.
2. Help children learn the reasons for taking turns.
3. Help children learn when to take turns.
4. Help children learn why taking turns is valued.

Resource Materials:

- Signs posted around the classroom where it is appropriate to take turns, for instance by the water fountain, by the class pet, by the computers.
- A list of three to five rules that apply to taking turns with these objects.
- A list of three to five reasons why taking turns is valued.

Activities and Procedures:

1. Very early in the academic year, take time to go over rules concerning taking turns, reasons for taking turns, and why taking turns is valued.

2. Also talk about when taking turns is necessary, being sure to point to different objects in the classroom where taking turns is appropriate.

3. Post signs around the classroom where appropriate.
4. Also post rules, reasons, and values.
5. Remind children of the rules when it becomes necessary.
6. When adults must take turns, verbalize why and how this is done.

Tying It All Together:

Taking turns is an inevitable and necessary part of life. Explaining the rules and why taking turns is valued can help young children comply. Socializing young children to take turns is a benefit to them and society.

Visit **www.sagepub.com/gordonbiddle** to access templates of these lesson plans.

PART IV

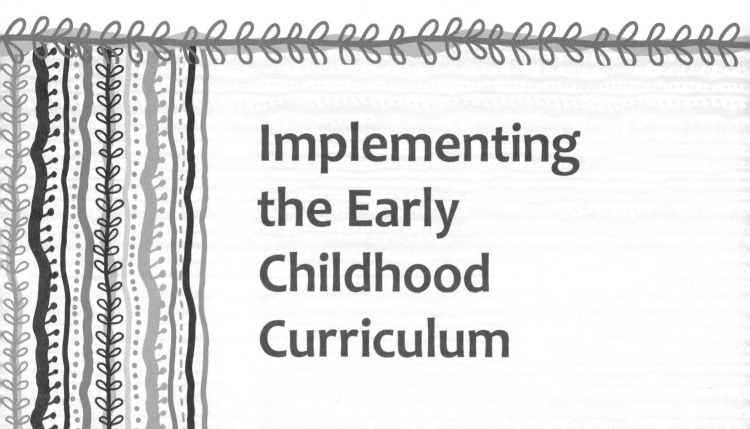

Implementing the Early Childhood Curriculum

CHAPTER 10

Play and the Learning Environment

This chapter will help you answer these important questions:

- Why is the physical environment important for learning and play?

- What are some learning environments?

- What are the developmental characteristics of play?

- How do we distinguish play from other behaviors?

- What are the theories on play?

- How can teachers use play to help children learn and develop?

Vignette: Let's Make Lunch

Gabriela, a 4-year-old preschooler, is sitting in a playhouse by a table with a plastic plate, cup, and utensils. She calls out, "Do you want to eat lunch? Come on, it's lunchtime!" Aviva, also 4, answers, "Wait." She wraps up a doll in a cloth and comes in and sits opposite Gabriela. Aviva says, "I want to help you make a sandwich." Gabriela says, "OK, let's make lunch." In the playhouse, there are plastic slices of bread, ham, tomato, and lettuce. Each child starts preparing her sandwich, and when they finish, the two girls sit and pretend to eat. Aviva then says, "I am thirsty; can I have some orange juice?" Gabriela says, "Yes, let's have some orange juice." Gabriela pretends to pour orange juice into a cup. Aviva then pretends to drink from the cup. Adam, another 4-year-old, approaches and says, "I want to play." Gabriela tells him, "You have to knock on the door to come in." Adam knocks on the imaginary door, and Gabriela asks, "Who is it?" Adam answers, "It's Adam." Gabriela then pretends to unlock and unbolt the door. Gabriela invites Adam in and asks him, "Do you want some orange juice?" They all sit down together and pretend to drink orange juice.

P lay is very significant for a child during the early childhood years. Therefore, knowledge of the development of different types of play gives educators and parents a foundation for proper teaching strategies. Goodman (1994) reported that the preeminent teaching for young children happens at the midpoint of a continuum between play and work. Professional early childhood teachers who are aware of and comprehend developmental theories of play are better prepared to use play as a context for instruction and assessment. They also understand the importance of play in social, emotional, cognitive, physical, and motor domains of development. Therefore, it is extremely important that teachers of young children have a strong academic background in the study of play to best evaluate problems and offer appropriate support to children who have a hard time playing, such as children with physical disabilities.

The vignette presented at the beginning of this chapter is an example of play, and most observers would describe it as cooperative play, when a group of children play and interact socially together. Play is an important element of a child's life. It helps children achieve mastery in certain skills, and they learn to have control over their environment. The environment and play are important elements that support each other. Even though the concept of play seems very simple, in reality the study of play is quite complex, as you will learn in reading this chapter. This chapter first discusses the definition of the physical environment and play, the defining characteristics of play, and the leading theorists. It goes on to examine the importance of play and the significance of play in children's development.

WHY IS THE PHYSICAL ENVIRONMENT IMPORTANT FOR LEARNING AND PLAY?

A well-arranged environment should enhance children's development through learning and play. It facilitates classroom management and supports the implementation of curricular goals and objectives (Catron & Allen, 2007). The way the **physical environment** is designed and configured influences how children feel, act, and behave. The physical environment allows growth and development through activities and materials in defined play areas. Room arrangement for play activity plays an important role in students' social and language interactions. Poorly designed classrooms can cause disruptions and negative social interactions among students and/or between students and the teacher. For example, having the reading and writing center next to the music area would cause disruptions among children who are trying to concentrate on the skill of writing. Students can become frustrated when they do not have an organized environment to call their own (Clayton & Forton, 2001).

The physical environment is a direct image of the teacher's planning and the student's learning. It is where both teachers and students will spend most of their time and a place they can call their own and relate to. It should be well organized, comfortable, and personable and offer a variety of manipulates for cognitive, social, emotional, and physical development (Catron & Allen, 2007).

Definition of the Environment

To understand play, we first must understand the importance of the environment in the eyes of children and adults. Some people may see the environment as insignificant, but for teachers, parents, and educators it is something that needs to be considered a high priority. **Environment** is defined as the physical environment, its surroundings, and a specific setting (Vickerius & Sandberg, 2006).

The physical environment will vary depending on the age and number of children in the classroom, as well as the goals of programs and specific activities in the classroom. The infant classroom, for example, will designate the eating, sleeping, diapering, and play areas as primary for activities. However, the most important space in which activities will be performed is the play area. The play area of infants needs to be configured so that they can grasp and reach age-appropriate toys or pull themselves up when practicing standing or walking (Vance & Boals, 1989). Infants will need to be down on the floor exploring their environments with toys to look at, listening to things around them, feeling, chewing, pushing, pulling, stacking, rolling, turning, squeezing, and shaking (Vance & Boals, 1989). To maximize infant supervision, it is best to have all the activities in one room. This includes the sleeping area. Some researchers have recommended a separate room for sleeping (Willis & Ricciuti, 1974); others, however, have found that sleep patterns are not adversely affected by having a sleeping area in the same room as a play area (Twardosz, Cataldo, & Risley, 1974). Having a cozy, warm, and homelike environment in the classroom provides infants with a healthy social/emotional environment.

The physical environment for a toddler classroom has eating, napping, diapering, toileting, and playing areas. Play continues to be very important, and learning centers become more obvious for this age-group. Areas are subdivided into dramatic, block, art, library, manipulative, and science learning centers. Toddlers need spaces that allow them to experiment, explore, and discover things around their environment. They are constantly moving or on the go and need many opportunities to practice newly emerging skills (Vartuli, 1987).

The preschool classroom will have similar physical space needs to the toddler classroom. The only difference is the diapering area, no longer needed in the preschool classroom. Therefore, eating, napping, toileting, and play areas continue to be essential. Learning centers are emphasized in the preschool classroom; such centers include block, art, library, pretend or dress-up, science, and music, just to name a few.

WHAT ARE SOME LEARNING ENVIRONMENTS?

Decisions about how the classroom or physical environment is arranged will depend on the philosophy and goals of the teacher. Depending on the teacher's objectives, the room arrangements and placement of instructional materials will differ; however, certain essential features will need to be in every classroom (Hand & Nourot, 1999). For example, one teacher's belief is that children become more literate through participating in a broad range of activities that include read-aloud and group reading. Given this belief, the teachers will make sure that their classrooms have a comfortable library area, that the children can access many literacy materials without asking for them, and that they have table space for reading and writing silently.

Learning Centers

Learning centers, also known as learning areas, are a system that is used to arrange a classroom or organize materials in a classroom. The term *learning center* has been judged by many because it has a connotation that learning takes place only in these specific centers (Brewer, 2004). The essential discussion underpinning this topic is that learning occurs every day and everywhere, whether it is inside or outside the classroom. Therefore, for purposes of clarifying the term, a learning center is defined in this text as a specific location where instructional materials are placed and organized in a classroom.

Some of the learning areas that are most common and that you will see in the early childhood classroom are art, library/listening/writing activities, blocks, dramatic play, science/discovery activities, and manipulative/mathematics/games. Keep in mind that these areas will need to consider the children's ages, interests, and abilities, and thus will need to change accordingly.

Materials and Equipment for Early Childhood Classrooms

Play materials in the classroom are extremely important for multiple developmental perspectives such as cognitive, social/emotional, physical, and language. Teachers need to be cognizant of the age-appropriate play material/equipment and furniture for the classroom. Table 10.1 includes some common learning centers and materials that preschool and primary-grade teachers have found to be beneficial.

Preparing the Physical Space for Play

In structuring the physical environment for play, consider these questions: How is the space arranged, both indoors and outdoors? Are there clearly marked areas in which children may find the housekeeping, reading, and block materials? Is there enough space between the areas to walk around? All of these features of a classroom will foster children's freedom to choose their own activities, which in turn develops the complexity of their play as well as encourages ongoing play.

In addition to the arrangement of the classroom, size is important. Research on children's play environments indicates that between 30 and 50 square feet of usable space per child represents an ideal size for indoor environments. Spaces with less than 25 square feet per child generally lead to increases in aggression and unfocused behavior for children (Smith & Connolly, 1980). For teachers,

Table 10.1   Materials and Equipment for the Early Childhood Classroom

DRAMATIC PLAY

- Child-sized kitchen equipment (with pots and pans)
- Dishes and silverware
- Tables and chairs
- Telephones
- Child-sized ironing board and iron
- Child-sized cleaning equipment (brooms, mops, dustpan, etc.)
- Assorted dolls
- Doll clothes
- Doll bed, carriage
- Dollhouse, furniture
- Assorted tubs, buckets, dishpans
- Assorted dress-up clothing and costumes

BLOCKS

- Blocks
- Block accessories (people, cars, safety signs, etc.)
- Small blocks (sets of cubes, small colored blocks)
- Sturdy wooden vehicles (cars, trucks, boats, planes, tractors, fire engines, buses, helicopters)

ART

- Adjustable easels
- Brushes (half-inch to 1-inch widths)
- Liquid tempera paint (in a variety of colors)
- Painting smocks
- Crayons
- Colored chalk
- Clay
- Scissors
- Glue
- Paper (construction paper in a variety of colors, tissue paper, newsprints, white drawing paper)
- Drying rack for paintings
- Miscellaneous supplies (fabric scraps, rickrack, yarn, ribbon, glitter, buttons, natural materials)

LIBRARY/LISTENING/WRITING

- Computer and printer
- Typewriter
- Paper (various colors, sizes, shapes) and writing instruments (pencils, markers)
- Tape recorder, tapes, books with tapes
- Record player
- Flannel board with stand and flannel pieces
- Books (professional and published by classroom authors)
- Magazines

MANIPULATIVE/GAMES

- Hand puppets
- Puzzles
- Games (board games)
- Beads and strings
- Sewing cards
- Manipulative materials (ranging from stacking rings to very complex materials)
- Tinkertoys
- LEGO bricks, Bristle Blocks

SCIENCE/DISCOVERY

- Aquarium
- Terrarium
- Magnets of various kinds
- Magnifying glasses
- Prism
- Metric measuring equipment, test tubes, slides, petri dishes
- Pattern blocks
- Pegs and pegboards
- Scales
- Rhythm instruments
- Sandbox
- Water table with top
- Workbench with equipment

PHYSICAL EDUCATION

- Balance beam
- Tumbling mat
- Rocking boat
- Steps
- Walking boards
- Jungle gym
- Fabric tunnel
- Sawhorses
- Climbing ladder, climbing rope
- Balls of various sizes
- Ropes, hula hoops
- Bowling set
- Outdoor equipment (gardening tools)

Source: Adapted from Brewer, J. (2004).

crowded physical spaces promote more directive teaching and limit opportunities for social interaction among children. In thinking about room arrangements, you may want to consider both the spaces arranged for children's play and the surrounding space, which is the area needed for people to move about. Space generally shapes the flow of play and communication in the classroom or outdoors (Kritchevsky, Prescott, & Walling, 1977; Loughling & Suina, 1982).

Setting Up the Classroom

Research has indicated that the way the classroom is arranged and the way it looks are significant because they influence children's and adults' behavior. Therefore, when setting up the classroom, teachers should consider the following suggestions:

1. Centers should have multiple uses, not just serve one specific center topic.

2. Have as much natural light in the classroom as possible. Natural light reduces energy use but, most important, enhances task performance and improves the appearance of an area.

3. Keep noisy and quiet areas separate. Noisy areas such as dramatic play and music should be located at one end of the room, opposite to the quiet area. This will allow each area to have its activities in a comfortable location.

Figure 10.1 illustrates how an indoor classroom is arranged, and Figure 10.2 shows the arrangement of an outdoor classroom.

A Safe Environment

A safe environment encourages exploration and play behaviors in young children. Therefore, a safe environment is very important for teachers of young children and child care centers. When parents bring their children to a child care center, they expect them to be safe. They assume the playground, equipment, toys, and other materials will be safe for children to use and that teachers will carefully supervise their activities (Wellhousen, 2002). These expectations require teachers to be well informed and knowledgeable about how to create and maintain environments that ensure children's health and safety.

To avoid injuries and age confrontations, infants and toddlers are expected to have a separate play area from the preschool children. A large, open space, free from obstacles, for the play area is encouraged for very young children. This type of area helps infants and toddlers move about and explore their environment without any hesitation.

Fire Safety. Fire regulations require that fire extinguishers, as well as smoke and carbon monoxide detectors, be present and in working condition in all classrooms. Fire exits, fire alarms, and fire escapes should be labeled clearly, and staff should be familiar with the location of building exits and emergency procedures. In order for children to be familiar with fire drill routines, teachers should be trained and conduct regular fire drills. This would allow children not to be frightened if a real emergency did occur.

Sanitation and Bathroom Facilities. Classroom toys and other equipment are required to be sanitized on a daily basis, as this will reduce germs from spreading around. All child care centers are required to have adequate washing sinks, toilets, soap dispensers, and a towel rack. Having the right size fixtures allows children to care for their own needs. The bathroom facilities need to be accessible to both indoor and outdoor play areas. Health regulations require one toilet and sink for every 10 to 12 children in a child care facility.

Lighting, Ventilation, and Temperature. Adequate lighting is of the essence in a classroom. Of course, the most desirable light is natural light coming from windows and/or glass doors; however, if this is not available, a no-glare light would do just fine. Windows and glass doors that are reachable to young children should be made of safety glass or plastic to avoid serious injuries to children if a window or door is broken. Doors and windows should be covered with blinds or shades to control the light and should also have locks. All rooms should have appropriate air ventilation and heating for a comfortable classroom environment.

Figure 10.1   Indoor Settings: Preschool and Kindergarten

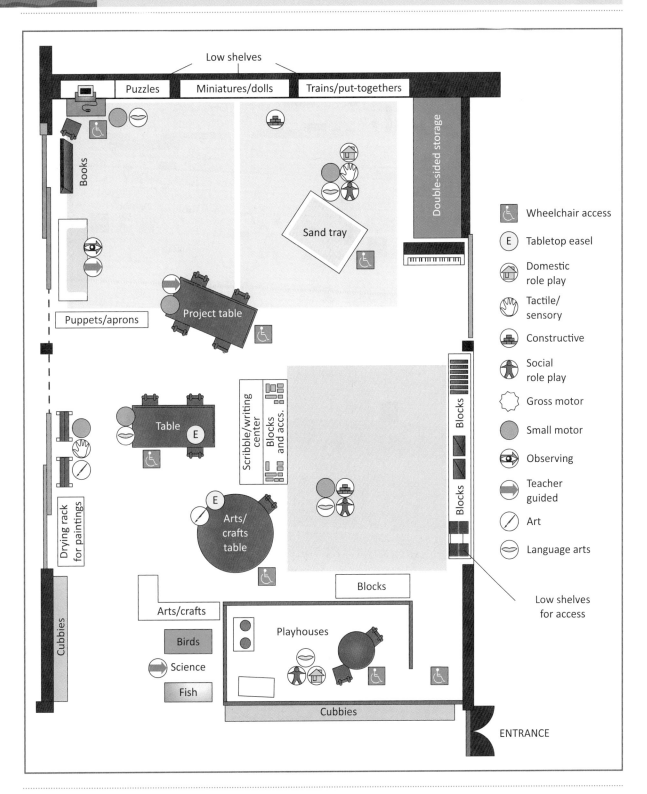

Source: Van Hoorn, Nourot, Scales, and Alward (2005). *Play at the Center of the Curriculum*, 5th Edition, © 2011. Adapted by permission of Pearson Education, Inc., Upper Saddle River, NJ.

Figure 10.2   Outdoor Settings: Preschool and Primary Grades

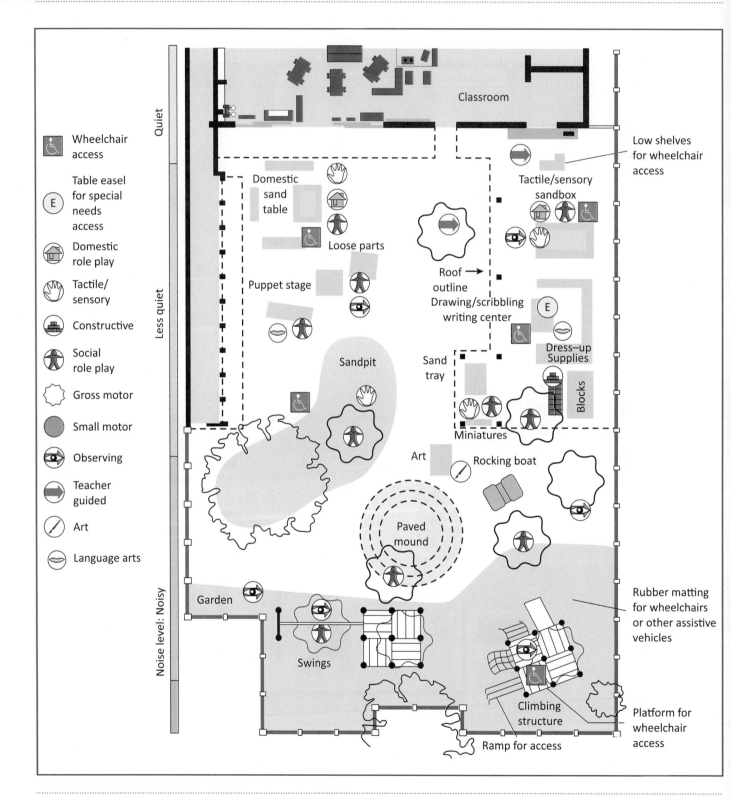

Source: Van Hoorn, Nourot, Scales, and Alward (2005). *Play at the Center of the Curriculum*, 5th Edition, © 2011. Adapted by permission of Pearson Education, Inc., Upper Saddle River, NJ.

The Practice of **Research** and **Theory**
The Importance of Physical Education in Preschool

When children are engaged in play in any type of environment (either indoor or outdoor), they are naturally involved with some physical movement. Researchers on physical education and movement emphasize that the preschool years are a fundamental period for the development of motor skills (Wellhousen, 2002). In 1992, the Council on Physical Education for Children published an article that emphasizes the appropriate physical movements for preschoolers enrolled in child care centers. This article also presents five premises for understanding preschoolers' physical education:

1. When it comes to motor development, 3-, 4-, and 5-year-old children are different from elementary-age children. Young children are perfecting their fine and gross motor skills at ages 3 to 5, unlike the elementary-age children who have accomplished their motor skills.

2. Young children learn through interaction with their environment. Children learn best when they are socially interacting with other people and with objects in their environment.

3. Teachers of young children serve as guides or facilitators. Teachers are in a classroom not just to tell children what to do but to guide and assist them through the learning process.

4. Young children learn and develop in an integrated fashion. Play is the cornerstone for multiple disciplines, such as art, language, and physical education.

5. Planned movement experiences enhance play experiences.

Further, the National Association for Sport and Physical Education (Council on Physical Education for Children, 1992) recommends that preschool programs incorporate physical education into their curriculum. Preschoolers who enjoy and participate in physical activities develop positive attitudes toward health and fitness. Involvement during the preschool years is the first step toward becoming a physically educated person who

- has learned the skills necessary to perform a variety of physical activities,
- participates regularly in physical activity,
- knows the implications of and the benefits from involvement in physical activities, and
- values physical activity and its contributions to a healthy lifestyle (Wellhousen, 2002).

Definition of Play

Play, on the other hand, is difficult to define. Many educators and philosophers have defined the term, each adding some variation to its meaning. The broad category of activities that are covered by the term *play* include a great variety of behaviors, such as swinging, sliding, running, digging in the dirt, building with blocks, dancing to music, making up nonsense rhyming words, dressing up, and pretending. Because of this variety, no one definition of play can adequately describe its many facets.

Some may argue that play does not need to be defined, explained, or studied; most people would recognize play when they see it. Play is often interpreted as the opposite of work, something that is done on the weekends, during vacations, or with children. Understanding the term *play* from an academic point of view is critically important to early childhood educators.

Many researchers have tried to define play, in particular Erik Erikson, Jerome Bruner, and Lev Vygotsky. They have been able to contrast their research studies of play in order to better define it. Erikson (1963), for example, suggested the following definition:

> When man plays he must intermingle with things and people in a similarly uninvolved and light fashion. He must do something which he has chosen to do without being compelled by urgent

Young children learn the most when they are actively interacting with other people and manipulating objects in their environment (Kamii & DeVries, 1978; Piaget, 1952). Experienced early childhood teachers who instantly see these benefits set up indoor play environments to reflect this philosophy. However, setting up an outdoor environment is more challenging; children do not have the opportunity to manipulate outdoor toys or objects as readily, with the exception of sand, water play, and tricycles (Frost, Bowers, & Wortham, 1990). A solution to incorporating outdoor toys is having movable toys, or accessory materials that are manipulated by children. Examples of movable toys include outdoor blocks, boards, crates, sawhorses, and cable spools. Classroom materials that are used indoors such as puzzles, books, and art supplies can also be used outdoors (Frost & Wortham, 1988). All young children will need time and opportunity to become familiar with outdoor toys, materials, and equipment in order to discover the different ways to interact with them. In particular, to teach children with special needs, much repetition is required for them to learn from the materials. Therefore, movable toys, materials, and other equipment should not be changed or removed too often (Klein, Cook, & Richardson-Gibbs, 2001). An example of movable equipment that should not be removed is an obstacle course. Young children should be given the opportunity to interact with this equipment until they have had a chance to master it completely.

interests or impelled by strong passion. He must feel entertained and free of any fear or hope of serious consequences. He is on vacation from social and economic reality—or as is most commonly emphasized: he does not work. (p. 212)

Bruner (1972), a distinguished psychologist, defined play as the following:

Play appears to serve several centrally important functions. First, it is a means of minimizing the consequences of one's actions and of learning, therefore . . . [it is] . . . a less risky situation . . . Second, play provides an excellent opportunity to try combinations of behavior that would, under functional pressure, never be tried. (p. 693)

According to Bruner, play can be seen as the main opportunity for children to take risks without fear of failure. His definition also proposes that creativity and play activities are closely related. That is, if children explore and experiment in their play, the possibilities for creative outcomes are greatly enhanced without the fear of failure. For example, a toddler playing with Play-Doh can creatively explore and experiment freely as there is no right or wrong way to create and mold with this material.

Vygotsky offered additional insight into childhood play. For Vygotsky, imaginative play is the main focus for the general development of the child. He suggested that we must challenge the child to increasingly higher levels of functioning, what he referred to as the zone of proximal development (see also Chapters 2 and 4):

Play creates a zone of proximal development in the child. In play, the child always behaves beyond his average age, above his daily behavior; in play it is as though he were a head taller than himself. As in the focus of a magnifying glass, play contains all developmental tendencies in a condensed form and is itself a major source of development. (Vygotsky, 1978, p. 102)

Early childhood teachers go to great lengths to create play-based learning activities, but it can be difficult to assess if play is freely chosen in these developmentally appropriate preschool classrooms. If a child made a game out of an assigned task, would you consider it work, play, or both? As a teacher giving a lesson in your classroom, you would consider this work. The challenge is to be able to recognize that play provides developmental context and content for early learning, which then raises questions about the exact definition of play (Slentz & Krogh, 2001).

The Benefits of Play in the Environment

Play is a necessary element of healthy development for children of all ages. Play influences all areas of development; it offers children the opportunity to learn about the self, others, and the physical environment (Catron & Allen, 2007). It encourages aspects of social, emotional, cognitive, and physical development that cannot be achieved any other way. Children learn how to interact with peers when engaged in play activities while also building on important schemas about the real world. Although play has been looked at by many as just a time filler for caretakers, much research has been dedicated to the benefits of play that would suggest that play is vital for every child.

Through play, children build important knowledge that encompasses many developmental domains, such as literacy and mathematics. Even in the earliest years, children become familiar with words by playing with books or other materials that have letters on them. Throughout the school years, children are constantly developing their language skills through play, as well as learning important roles that pertain to the real world (Seefeldt, 2001). For example, when children are engaged in playing "house" or "dress up," they are often interacting with one another, which is important for language development while applying and modifying their current knowledge about the real world.

During play, children are also able to begin their gender identity process; they establish relationships with one another, thus creating a sense of intimacy. Also, play is children's means of self-expression, which is important for their emotional development. While engaged in play, children feel safe and are able to express any part of themselves at that moment without worrying about reprisal. Children learn how to express their feelings; they use play to relax tension and anxiety, release aggression, and express conflict. See Table 10.2 for a thorough list of benefits that play offers children.

Children should be engaged in a variety of physical activities that are safe.

WHAT ARE THE DEVELOPMENTAL CHARACTERISTICS OF PLAY?

Piaget's and Vygotsky's contributions to our understanding of the characteristics of play are in the dimensions related to abstract thinking and the creation of rules (Van Hoorn, Nourot, Scales, & Alward, 2007). Piaget (1952) saw play as the construction of knowledge within the individual child by interacting with the object (toy). On the other hand, Vygotsky (1978) perceived play as a social interaction (two children playing together) and believed children learn about the self through their interactions with others. Ultimately, it is through the act of play that children come to see the developing self. Mead (1934), another researcher, found that play is the major vehicle for young children to learn to differentiate their own perspectives from those of others (Catron

Table 10.2	The Multiple Benefits of Play

1. Development of motor skills	7. Vocabulary growth
2. Sharpening of the senses	8. Increased concentration
3. Expression of emotions—empathy	9. Flexibility
4. Sharing, turn taking—harmony	10. Role taking
5. Ordering, sequencing	11. Expansion of imagination and creativity
6. Delay of gratification	

Source: Adapted from Goldstein, J. H. (1994).

& Allen, 2007). When children play "pretend" and undertake other children's roles, they come to view their own behavior from the perspectives of other children. According to Mead, the young child functions in the pretend play, achieving a role transformation from the self to others (Van Hoorn et al., 2007). Similarly, Smilansky (1990) explained this developmental process as the beginning stages of role-play. The child simply becomes or pretends to be a doctor, nurse, chef, or teacher and then returns to being the self.

Cognitive Development and Play

To show how play functions and develops as a complex, adaptive system as children grow older, it is helpful to review some of the commonly recognized forms and developmental sequences of play. Sara Smilansky (1990) provides a model presenting five basic forms of play:

1. **Functional play** or exploratory play. This type of play is a sensorimotor approach in which a child learns the nature of his or her surroundings. Such examples include dumping, filling, stacking, water play, and outdoor play.

2. **Constructive play** describes children combining pieces or entities, such as with blocks. The purpose of this type of play is to make something and/or work out a problem.

3. **Dramatic play** entails pretending. The child pretends to be someone else, for example the teacher or a fireman. This type of play does not require any social interaction with other children. See the example provided below.

Ricky is 4 years old and is playing with a fire truck in front of his house. He is pretending to drive a fire truck. As he drives his truck, he sounds the sirens, screaming, "Whee-ooh! Whee-ooh!" He is speeding to get to the fire. As he arrives at the fire, he connects the fire hose to the fire hydrant and holds the hose toward the fire. He then raises the tall ladder all the way up to the top floor of the building. He holds the hose and shoots at the flames. He makes a sound of relief, saying the fire is gone and the building is saved.

4. **Sociodramatic play** is a form of dramatic play with more than one player socially interacting around a theme and a time trajectory over which the play continues and evolves. Children enact real-life types of play activities.

Jeffrey and Brian are 7 years old and are playing together at a park. The two boys are imitating army men and are pretending the play structure is their ship. Brian exclaims, "Take the wheel—I see land!" Once they decide they have landed, they proceed to crawl on the wood ships, dragging their stomachs to a nearby tube. Both boys struggle in the new shelter and take their shoes off. After whispering for some time about the enemy, they continue to throw their shoes and make explosion noises. Following the shoe explosions, both boys take off in opposite directions screaming and looking for cover.

These boys are engaged in sociodramatic play. They have taken an object (their shoes) and turned it into something completely different, drawn from their imaginations. Also, they are not just children anymore; they have taken on the role of people in the army. Not only are they army men, but they are busy running from pretend people. In addition, they have taken a typical play structure and turned it into a ship.

5. **Games with rules** encompass cooperative play, often with winners and losers. These games are distinguished by child-controlled rules and thus are different from the competitive games usually called "sports." Children begin the games with rules stage at about age 6.

Games with rules become more evident as children move from early into middle childhood. This type of play behavior suggests that children are understanding the social rules of our culture.

Social Development and Play

A number of researchers have suggested different types of models to describe children's social play. Mildred Parten (1933) presented a model of socialization skills in play that is considered one of the best in the field. Parten states that children engage in solitary play until about 2 1/2 years of age. Children move from solitary play into parallel play, associative play, and then cooperative play.

1. **Solitary play**—Children play alone, usually with toys that are different from those of the children playing nearby. Children at this stage make no attempt to get close to or interact with others. Clearly, the level of social interaction at this point is very low. It is important, however, to realize that despite its lack of social value, solitary play should be encouraged as a part of a young child's activities. Much of an elementary child's day, for example, is spent doing independent seatwork. Children who have learned to be comfortable in solitary play are more likely to succeed in working independently.

While playing with blocks, the infant is learning by using the sense of touch.

2. **Parallel play**—Children from 2 1/2 to 3 1/2 years old continue to play independently, but now they are among their peers and use toys that are similar to those of the children around them. Just as parallel lines run side by side, children in this play stage play beside, but not with, others. There is an awareness of the children nearby but little interaction, as in the following example of parallel play:

Sarah and Madison are both 26 months old and are playing in the sandbox. Both girls are digging holes and filling up buckets with sand. Although they are both engaged in the activity, they do not speak to one another or interfere with each other's area. After some time of playing in the sand, their only interaction with each other is when Madison takes Sarah's bucket and a conflict arises. When the bucket is returned, the two girls go back to playing in the sand, keeping to themselves for the remainder of the time.

3. **Associative play**—As children mature, they begin to engage in associative play, which begins at about 3 1/2 years old. In this type of play, children truly play with others. Children loan and borrow play materials among one another. Parten (1933) suggests that at this point, the associations are more important than the play activity itself. Children begin to form small playgroups and spend considerable time moving from one activity to the next, with playmates remaining together. The following is an example of associative play:

Jessica is almost 4 years old and has a younger brother who is 16 months. She carefully watches over him and is often instructing him in what he can and cannot do. When he wanders off, she is quick to stop him from going anywhere, even when it is unnecessary to do so. He usually consumes most of her time; however, today her friend Kelly comes to the park. Within moments of the two girls spotting one another, Jessica loses all interest in her brother and replaces it with interest in Kelly. Jessica is following Kelly all over the play structure, and the girls become nearly inseparable during their playtime. When the girls decide to go down the slide, Kelly instructs Jessica to go down the other slide (which is parallel to her slide) so they can go down at the same time. Then the two girls choose the swings for some entertainment, but quickly change their minds when they see that only one is available and they wanted to swing together. At the end of the play day, Jessica's brother attempts to come on the play structure, and Jessica instructs him to go away and tells him, "There are no babies allowed here." When Kelly states, "It's OK—he can play with us," Jessica yells for her brother to come back.

As children pretend to be a doctor and a patient, they learn the rules and roles of those positions.

These girls demonstrate associative play. They are discussing what they are going to do and disregard plans that do not allow the two of them to be together. Also, they decide together who can be a part of their play and who cannot; when Kelly gives her approval of the new child in their play, Jessica is quick to agree.

4. **Cooperative play**—This final type of social play begins to take place at about 4 1/2 years of age. Parten (1933) describes this as the highest level of social play; it is characterized by children playing in groups as they did in associative play, but now the children demonstrate division of labor, whether working on a group project or cooperating to attain a common goal.

Cooperative play is a more sophisticated type of play because it requires the process of negotiation among two or more children. An example of this negotiation process is when three children are pretending to work in a hospital setting. One child pretends to be the doctor, the second a nurse, and the third the patient. First, they negotiate by alternating their roles in the play, then they make suggestions about the plot, and one suggests they pretend that the patient has a cut and is bleeding and needs stitches and a bandage.

Emotional Development and Play

Play is an excellent vehicle for helping children with their emotional development (Johnson, Christie, & Yawkey, 1999). Children can master emotional issues such as anxiety, frustration, normal developmental conflicts, traumatic situations, unfamiliar concepts, and overwhelming experiences in their play. That is, play helps children find new ways of dealing with their emotions and their reality. As children play, they explore the properties of things and extract information about their environments. They imitate, re-create, and rehearse roles that help them understand and solve problems related to everyday living. They form relationships, share, cooperate, master their feelings, extend the range of their experience, test ideas, and form associations between things, events, and concepts.

Another major emotional benefit of play is that it gives children numerous opportunities to feel good about themselves. Because there is no right or wrong way to play, children have multiple experiences in play, which positively influences their concepts of self.

Language Development and Play

The act of play is influential in learning language and communication skills. When children are engaged in play, they use language to interact with their peers; as they interact, they are using different tones and sounds to regulate their speech, and are developing new vocabulary. Several researchers have argued that play and language promote children's development of expressive tones as well as their perception of the rules underlying the use of voice or conversation patterns of language (Bergen, 2002). Children are also able to improve their oral and written language skills. The language used in play, for example, encourages the development of **metalinguistic awareness**—the ability to reflect consciously on the linguistic operations and analytical orientations of language—which generates literacy development. This metalinguistic awareness allows children to think about the words they will be using in their conversations. Children experiment with words and manipulate their use, meaning, and grammar. Through words, children experiment with rhythm, sound, and form (Johnson, 1928). Garney (1990) proposed that *every* characteristic of language can be better understood through play.

Physical Development and Play

A major characteristic of play is being active through dancing, jumping, throwing, running, and generally moving around. And children often strengthen their **gross motor development** through the use of their large muscles in these activities (Gallahue, 1982). Other types of play activities, such as cutting, eating, writing, buttoning, painting, and dressing, provide for their **fine motor development**, or refinement of the skills that require the use of smaller muscles. Through play, children are naturally able to use and learn to refine their gross and fine motor skills and coordination. As children get older, they use their muscles in continually more complex ways, integrating large and fine muscle movements with visual perception (Henniger, 2008).

Creativity and Play

Through creativity, children use their imagination to invent or produce something new. The early years are very important for the development of creativity; young children have many opportunities to express and develop their creative talents. For example, during free play, young children experiment with things and ideas and create new combinations that they have never experienced before. Wasserman (1992) states it this way: "The creation of new ideas does not come from minds trained to follow doggedly what is already known; the creation comes from tinkering and playing around, from which new forms emerge" (p. 134). Children develop their creativity in play situations that require them to use their imagination (Singer, 1973). Therefore, play materials are supposed to help elicit new ideas for children. Fostering creativity in children helps them promote healthy development and happy dispositions.

Developmental Benefits and Play

In addition to its developmental benefits, play provides a joyful experience for children, and it opens up the world to a child. No matter how eager we may be as early childhood educators to provide purposeful play opportunities for children that will enhance development and lead to learning, we must never forget that one of the greatest gifts of childhood is the ability to pursue seemingly insignificant interests and to explore tiny details to one's heart's content. Play is a marvelous, renewable resource in the life of a child. Play can follow any path the child desires and will end when the child decides to move on to something else or when the demands of living in the world intrude on the child's own agenda.

Play is practical, authentic, and an often suggested educational endeavor for young children who are gaining much of their knowledge about the world through their senses. Young children are very much dependent on sensory learning and physical contact with their environment (Catron & Allen, 2007). When play is sense based, it encourages children's active involvement and is relevant and meaningful to them since they find it easier to attend and remain interested. When children are active in their play, learning becomes much easier.

These young children are playing with shapes and organizing and sorting them.

Consider This The Importance of *Play*

Susan is a grandmother who raised her three kids in the mid-1960s. When she was raising her kids, she did not know much about the importance of play and the benefits that play has for children. The research was not as evident, and parents did not know that play forms the foundation for cognitive, creativity, and language development. Susan thought that when her children were playing, they were just having fun and entertaining themselves. She never thought that their play promoted their intellectual and social development. She is glad to see and read the extensive research people have done in the area of play. Her grown-up daughter has benefitted from reading the research on play because she has exposed her kids, Susan's grandchildren, to quality books and exploratory toys that engage and challenge the mind.

How would you respond if a parent asked why the children in your care were allowed to spend so much time playing or told you that play has no contributions to learning in a child's development?

HOW DO WE DISTINGUISH PLAY FROM OTHER BEHAVIORS?

Agreement about definitions allows researchers to compare results from study to study and to establish consensus on what is being observed. Existing theories tend to agree on certain features that distinguish play from other behaviors (Rubin, Fein, & Vandenberg, 1983). Rubin et al. (1983), for example, have identified five characteristics that have been used to define play. These include (a) active engagement, (b) intrinsic motivation, (c) attention to means rather than ends, (d) nonliteral behavior, and (e) freedom from external rules.

Active Engagement

Children are active agents in their environments. They explore and figure out how to communicate and respond to events and people around them. Through the process of play, children engage in learning about the world by constructing knowledge through interaction with the people and the things around them (Chaille & Silvern, 1996). Children are active agents in their environment, for example, by being exposed to a variety of toys that will challenge their thinking skills and support the process of learning.

Intrinsic Motivation

Intrinsic motivation is the inherent yearning for children to do something tangible because they will learn something new from their experience. Children are motivated to choose new playthings or activities because they offer a new challenge on a familiar experience. For example, LEGO bricks, the popular children's toys, provide the opportunity to apply familiar constructive play skills in an innovative, comprehensive way. Children also use familiar objects or activities to offer a safe outlook on a new and perhaps discrepant experience (Monighan-Nourot, Scales, Van Hoorn, & Almy, 1987). For example, after seeing her mom prepare her lunch, Gabriela was seen playing in the playhouse, preparing herself a meal. Gabriela was performing a familiar activity based on her prior observation and experience.

Attention to Means Rather Than Ends

While in play, children are less worried about a particular goal than they are about various methods of reaching it. Because the children themselves are establishing their own goals, the goals may change as play progresses. Once a child learns how to solve a puzzle, she or he might stack the pieces in new arrangements or use them in a completely different activity.

Nonliteral Behavior

Nonliteral behavior, which begins as early as the first year of life, is the distinctive feature of symbolic play (Fein, 1975). Children transform objects and situations to fit their play theme, such as pretending their fingers (their thumb and pinky) are a telephone. This concept of make-believe is thought to be a key factor in the hypothetical or "as if" types of reasoning called for in scientific problem solving (Fink, 1976). Make-believe may also play a part in the use of abstract symbols (Fein, 1981; McCune, 1985, 1986; McCune-Nicolich, 1981).

Existence of Implicit Rules

Although there are no externally enforced rules in the types of play preschool children engage in, play often has **implicit rules**, maintaining the fantasy and reality distinction. An illustration is a group of children playing "doctor." The behaviors of a girl playing the role of the doctor and a boy playing the patient with a scraped knee reveal the two children's understanding of the rules pertaining to the roles of doctor and patient, as well as the children's understanding of their relationship (Monighan-Nourot et al., 1987).

Children are also capable of creating rules when entering a play situation. They develop a plan and presume their roles. This process of following rules and taking a role is an intrinsically motivated experience for children. Through this experience, children learn to understand their own roles and the rules that define them. Most important, children learn the roles and rules of others (Fein, 1984; Monighan, 1985). As a teacher, you can observe not only the play, but also the behind-the-scenes negotiations between the children that form the rules of their play. This observation will provide you with information of how children negotiate rules and understand the rules of their play.

WHAT ARE THE THEORIES ON PLAY?

Within the last two decades, researchers have proposed important theories to support the understanding of the behaviors seen in children's play. Mellon (1994) described two types of theories: classical (pre-1920) and contemporary.

Classical Theories

Before the 1920s, classical theories of play emerged from philosophical thinking on the nature of childhood and the perceived value of playful activities. These theories highlighted the biological and innate aspects of play, using both physiological and evolutionary explanations instead of focusing on the children's variations of activities. Classical theories attempt

A preschooler is actively engaged in riding a tricycle.

to explain the reason that play exists and its meaning. Gillmore (1971), a researcher on play, summarizes the classical theories of play—surplus energy, relaxation, recapitulation, and pre-exercise—as follows:

Surplus Energy Theory. Friedrich Schiller (1878/2003), a German poet, suggested the surplus energy theory. This theory proposes that play is a method of removing from any living being the excess energy that is available after meeting the basic survival needs. He further explained that play is an activity that individuals use to replenish the energy lost. The idea with surplus energy theory is that play is the opposite of work; that is, when you are at play you are engaged in a recreational activity, and when you are at work you are engaged in some sort of labor, something that you may not enjoy.

Relaxation Theory. The relaxation theory (Patrick, 1916) proposes that, through play, individuals restore the energy that they exhausted during their work. Hence, after working for a period of time, individuals need to play to relax and to generate sufficient reserve energy for work.

Recapitulation. G. Stanley Hall (1906), an American psychologist, found and established his recapitulation theory from Charles Darwin's theory of evolution. Recapitulation can best be seen as the psychological evolution and relaxation theory as the physiological evolution. In the recapitulation process, children repeat the human race's stages of development in their play. Play is an inherent manner of discontinuing primitive skills and drives that individuals have inherited from the time civilization began. When individuals use play to migrate through these primitive stages, they become prepared for the endeavors of adult life.

Pre-exercise. Karl Groos (1901), a zoologist, studied play behavior first in animals and later in humans. He recognized many of children's play behaviors in adult games, customs, and competitions. Groos, through his research created a system that grouped the different types of play, such as games with rules, rough-and-tumble play, and dramatic play. Play, according to Groos, encourages children to emulate behaviors that are similar to adult roles, which in turn they will assume in the future. For instance, children enact parental roles in dramatic play (e.g., a child pretending to drive a car to go to work). The pre-exercise theory suggests that play is a natural way of preparing children for the endeavors of adult life because their play experiences are similar to those they will encounter as they get older.

These four classical theories are believed to be inadequate today because they are derived from philosophical principles rather than empirical research studies (Ellis, 1973). In addition, the classical theorists did not address the theoretical facts to inform their ideas. However, the classical theories are the foundations for the contemporary theories of play, which are discussed next.

Contemporary Theories

Contemporary theories of play give emphasis to the psychological value and significance of a child's social, cognitive and emotional development. In other words, they address the importance of higher levels of thinking and symbolic thought. Unlike classical theories, contemporary theories are supported by empirical research. Contemporary theories consist of psychoanalytic, arousal modulation, metacommunicative, and cognitive theories (Mellou, 1994).

Psychoanalytic

Sigmund Freud (1923/1973) hypothesized that play performed a special function in children's emotional development. Play achieves a therapeutic effect; it enables children to relieve themselves of negative emotions and replace them with more positive ones. This therapeutic effect facilitates children's ability to play freely so that they can disengage themselves from any negative feelings brought on by traumatic experiences or personal confrontations. Play activities and explorations help the children to better understand distressing events and to search for alternative meanings that embrace pleasurable feelings and forgo unpleasant ones (Wehman & Abramson, 1976).

Arousal Modulation

This theory describes how play lets individual children find sources of stimulation to capture certain information to learn about the world around them. Berlyne (1969), a researcher in this area, speculated that there is a need in children's central nervous system to keep arousal at an optimum level. Too much stimulation (e.g., seeing a strange object) increases arousal to distressingly high levels, steering children to participate in activities that reduce stimulation (e.g., looking at an already familiar object). Lack of stimulation reduces arousal to lower levels, creating monotony and boredom. The child then strives to seek more stimulation, which Berlyne (1969) calls "diverse exploration" (p. 797).

Metacommunicative

Children's play is found when children interact among each other to create a make-believe behavior (Bateson, 1955; Frost, 2010). When playing make-believe, children are imitating real-life behaviors. Consequently, children learn about (a) the make-believe play with objects, often forcing reality to conform to their own point of view, and (b) the real life play behavior, which is a transition between pretend play and nonplayful play activities. Play is the **metacommunicative** (connecting the thought processes of two people and using language to describe events) perspective of what people consider their cultural and personal reality, meaning that play and pretend are important for children's intellectual growth.

Cognitive

Piaget (1952) and Vygotsky (1967) are the principal originators of cognitive development theory. The theory is about the construction of thought processes and intelligence. In other words, as humans we are able to acquire knowledge, to reason, and to make decisions. Piaget states that children acquire knowledge though the dual processes of assimilation and accommodation (see Chapter 4). In assimilation, children learn new material from the outside world and fit it into their existing knowledge. For accommodation, children adjust their knowledge to the new information being presented. For example, children will adjust the newly incorporated knowledge, compare it, and notice that it does not match with the information that they already know. Usually, assimilation and accommodation will occur at the same time, creating a state of balance or equilibrium. Both assimilation and accommodation are to maintain a balance between the structure of the mind and the environment. We tend to balance assimilation and accommodation to create a stable understanding of the world around us. For play, assimilation takes dominance over accommodation; that is, children assimilate new intellectual materials or ideas (Fein & Schwartz, 1982; Frost, 2010) instead of accommodating to the realities that they have seen and heard about.

Piaget's (1952) cognitive theory consists of three stages of play:

1. Functional play, also known as sensorimotor

2. Symbolic play

3. Games with rules

Children progress through these stages in a conforming sequence. As children advance through the stages, they acquire new skills and move from one level of mastery to another An infant playing with a rattle (functional play) will learn eye-hand coordination, and will improve this skill to the point of moving to the next level of mastery (symbolic play).

Vygotsky (1967) believed that conflict and problem solving are the essential characteristics of development. His primary focus of research was the belief that individuals need social interactions in order for learning to take place. His theory includes three important social-cognitive processes:

1. The zone of proximal development (see Chapters 2 and 4) is the difference between what a student can accomplish with help, under the guidance of or in collaboration with the teacher, a peer, or a parent, and what he or she can do alone without help.

2. Movement from interpersonal to intrapersonal knowledge involves moving from understanding concepts developed between two or more people interacting to how these concepts get internalized through the use of internalized speech.

3. Transition from implicit rules to explicit rules is moving from a behavior that is based on events remembered by the children to actually taking a role in the play behavior and playing fairly.

According to Vygotsky (1962) and other researchers who have studied cognitive development, a variety of intellectual skills are enhanced during symbolic or dramatic play. Make-believe helps children understand the objects they depict in their dramatic play. Objects used in symbolic play represent ideas and situations. Vygotsky (1967, 1978) noted that these objects support children's development of thought.

HOW CAN TEACHERS USE PLAY TO HELP CHILDREN LEARN AND DEVELOP?

Teachers can help children learn through the process of play by planning and organizing learning areas. It has been documented that learning areas assist children in the development of socioemotional, cognitive, and physical growth (Shipley, 2007). Learning areas provide children with the opportunity to explore and experience feelings and cognitive tasks while using motor skills that are crucial later in life (Shipley, 2007). See Table 10.3 for the kinds of practices teachers can be involved in; for example, if the teacher is doing a unit project on the ocean, having sand and water play is a great way for children to become familiar with aspects of the ocean. When planning the creation of centers, teachers should consider the following:

1. Determine developmental goals and objectives.

2. Know principles of learning and children's learning styles.

3. Design and set up learning centers.

4. Evaluate the learning environment.

Adapting Play to Individual Learners

As we have seen, play fosters children's development; this idea is no different for children with disabilities. More children with disabilities will have access to the mainstream classroom due to

Providing a variety of toys and opportunities for children to play with them will assist with their creativity.

Table 10.3   Procedures to Follow as an Early Childhood Teacher

1. Children should be free to choose their own play experiences.

2. The environment should offer play alternatives that are meaningful and accessible to children.

3. Play experiences should be based on objectives derived from observations of children in order to facilitate developmental progress from their present level to a higher level of development.

4. Teachers should plan a range of play experiences from the simple to the complex and begin with very concrete learning challenges in which the concepts or skills to be mastered are clear and observable to the learner.

5. A balance of structured and open-ended activities should be provided.

6. A balance of individual and group activities to allow for children's unique learning styles should be provided.

7. Equipment, materials, and supplies should be placed in well-defined learning centers that ensure children's receipt of messages from their environment about what they should be doing and learning in each learning center.

Source: Adapted from Shipley, D. (2007).

mandated inclusion policies and the implementation of less restrictive environments, so chances are that teachers will have a child in their classroom with special needs (see Chapter 7). When children with disabilities enter the classroom, the teacher should be aware that these children might require more time, instruction, or help to be included in the classroom. It is important and helpful for the teacher to be well informed about the specific disability of a child and how to adapt play appropriately.

Children who have difficulty with learning, memory, or problem solving can gain a great deal through the practice of play. For example, if a teacher facilitates the right opportunities, these children can benefit from such activities as classifying, identifying, sorting, matching, problem solving, seriation, number concepts, and spatial concepts (Wasserman, 2000). Similarly, children with communication problems can become more skilled at using signs in their play, and they improve their ability to communicate in increasingly complex ways. Play enhances the developmental process by providing situations to practice symbols that result in language. For example, symbolic play (e.g., playing to be "Mommy" by making lunch) is important for later development because it is an indicator of the development of representational thought, which helps stimulate children's language comprehension skills.

The idea that "children learn through play" has directed early childhood teachers for decades. This simple phrase provides the rationale for several models of early childhood programs and different theoretical approaches. It has also become a way of explaining almost anything that a professional early childhood teacher does to keep children occupied in the classroom. The emphasis on learning through play will continue. The fact that children are active learners who construct their own knowledge and understanding of the world through play experiences has become a cornerstone of professional early childhood educators. As a professional educator, you must be increasingly ready to give children more of the responsibility for their own learning.

Professionalism & Policy

Technology in the Classroom

Since the 1970s, technology has become a major part of today's culture and has found itself in almost every classroom. Technology brings many benefits to child development. While children pretend to talk on old cell phones, they are becoming familiar with how the phone works. Computer games are not only fun for young children; they also provide important eye-hand coordination and an early introduction to the keyboard (which is necessary for later years in school and work). Games can also enhance cognitive development. Television programs such as *Dora the Explorer* and *Go, Diego, Go!* interact with viewers, asking them questions and introducing Spanish during the show.

Summary

Defining the term *play* has been a challenge for many researchers and educators. Most theories suggest that play behavior is voluntary, enjoyable, and pleasurable to children. Having an understanding of these theories is important because it provides guidelines to researchers and educators to help promote educational play in young children. The classical theories of play are derived from philosophical principles rather than empirical research studies (Ellis, 1973); they also lack the current theoretical knowledge of energy, instinct, evolution, and development. Therefore, these theories are believed to be inadequate by today's standards. The contemporary theories, on the other hand, explore and explain different aspects of child development in order to understand how kids grow, behave, and think.

Some of the benefits of play, including social, emotional, cognitive, and physical development, cannot be achieved any other way. Children learn how to interact with peers when engaged in play activities while also building on important schemas about the real world. Play is an enjoyable experience for all children. Children of all ages will spend many hours participating in play activities because play supports their understanding of their social environment and facilitates their efforts to build a realistic sense of self (Spodek & Saracho, 1994). Play has a great value in that it assists children in exploring and understanding various roles and social interaction techniques.

Key Terms

Associative play   270

Constructive play   268

Cooperative play   270

Dramatic play   268

Environment   258

Fine motor development   271

Functional play   268

Games with rules   269

Gross motor development   271

Implicit rules   274

Metacommunicative   276

Metalinguistic awareness   271

Parallel play   269

Physical environment   258

Play   265

Sociodramatic play   268

Solitary play   269

Reflection, Application, and Analysis Questions

1. Describe and provide two examples of Vygotsky's idea of the zone of proximal development as it relates to play.

2. Provide examples of the relationship between language development and symbolic play.

3. What theoretical view of play do you consider the most important for a child's development?

4. Reflect on and discuss with a classmate some of the play development issues that teachers must keep in mind when planning the environment to promote the play of children with a physical disability.

Extension Activities

1. Interview an adult who attended kindergarten prior to 1960. Observe a kindergarten and compare the two types of play experiences.

2. Observe and record young children during play. Categorize the play activities using theories of play discussed in this chapter (e.g., surplus energy, relaxation, pre-exercise, and recapitulation theory).

Additional Readings

The following list of readings will be useful for those who are interested in keeping up with the most current developments.

Broadhead, P., Howard, J., & Wood, E. (2010). *Play and learning in the early years.* Thousand Oaks, CA: Sage.
This text examines current theoretical perspectives on play. Examples of recent and innovative play research are presented from a range of disciplinary and methodological perspectives. With contributions from leading play scholars, it brings together theory, research, policy, and practice in relation to play and learning in early childhood settings.

Casey, T. (2010). *Inclusive play: Practical strategies for children from birth to eight* (2nd ed.). Thousand Oaks, CA: Sage.
This is a practical and child-focused book that gives you the tools you need to make sure all the children in your classroom are included and involved in play opportunities.

Inside the second edition, updated content includes a new chapter on risk and challenge in play, new case studies, international perspectives, full coverage of the birth to 8-year age range, and consideration of inclusive play from a children's rights perspective.

Goncu, A., & Gaskins, S. (2007). *Play and development: Evolutionary, sociocultural, and functional perspectives.* Mahwah, NJ: Erlbaum.
The editors of this textbook explore assumptions about play and its status as a unique and universal activity in humans. Topics covered in this text include evolutionary foundations and functions of play, children's play as cultural interpretation, and the use of imagination in children's play.

On the Web

Circle Time - *http://www.badghill.pair.com/circtime/subpgs/toylinks.htm*
This website provides information about toy safety, as well as annotated links to toy stores and manufacturers. It also offers practical information for parents on the best books for kids.

Games Kids Play - *http://www.gameskidsplay.net*
This website provides a description of children's games, game rules, the appropriateness of each game for children, and game safety. It also contains all-time favorite rhymes.

KidSource Online - *http://www.kidsource.com*
This is an informative website for parents and children. Elementary-grade children can get assistance with their homework with the useful link to Homework Helpers. Parents can read articles on education, health, and safety.

A Parent's Guide to Nature Play: How to Give Your Children More Outdoor Play . . . and Why You Should! - *http://www.greenheartsinc.org/uploads/A_Parents__Guide_to_Nature_Play.pdf*
This guide provides parents with information on outdoor play. It gives you a perspective on how childhood has changed from 30 years ago and how you can incorporate outdoor activities in a child's life.

Play, Creativity, and Lifelong Learning: Why Play Matters for Both Kids and Adults - *http://www.helpguide.org/life/creative_play_fun_games.htm*
This is an article from HelpGuide.org, a nonprofit source for parents and educators. This article presents important information that was introduced in this chapter about play and its benefits for both children and adults.

Student Study Site

Visit **www.sagepub.com/gordonbiddle** to access several study tools including eFlashcards, web quizzes, links to SAGE journal articles, web resources, video resources, lesson plan templates, and more.

Sensory Exploration

Subject:

Learning through the senses.

Focus:

Use language to describe, explain, and elaborate on children's discoveries.

Overview:

Children will be exploring through the use of their senses.

Purpose:

According to Piaget, children learn through exploration of their environment during the first two years of life. Providing children with opportunities that allow them to exercise their senses is important for young developing minds.

Objective:

To promote language development, thinking, and problem solving. Children will

- Be able to use their senses to learn about their environment.
- Develop a sense of confidence.
- Have the opportunity to socially interact with other children and adults.

Resources and Materials:

None.

Activities and Procedures:

Allow infants and toddlers to explore each of the materials that will engage their various senses. Teachers or other adults can play with children to facilitate their learning.

- Sense of Touch: *Touch a Box*
  - Set out one large box, big enough for a child to crawl into.
  - Line the walls of the box with different textured paper or material. The child will have fun exploring this sensory cave.
- Sense of Hearing: *Sound of Bottles*
  - Collect some small plastic bottles and fill them with items that make a different sound (e.g., salt, beans, paper clips, rice).
  - Let the children shake the bottles to listen to the sounds.
  - Caution: Be sure to supervise this game and that the children do not attempt to open the bottles.

- Sense of Smell: *Smelly Cups*
  - Set out two or three paper cups.
  - Place a cotton ball in each cup, upon which you have placed a scent (e.g., coffee, lemon extract, floral perfume).
  - Have the children tell you what each cup smells like. If they do not know the name of the smell, they can tell you if they like the smell or not.
- Sense of Vision: *Color Areas*
  - Set out a red piece of paper.
  - Ask the children to look around the room for small objects that are the same color as the red paper, and have them place the objects on the paper.
  - Continue with other colors, if interest lasts.

- Sense of Taste: *The Taste Test*
  - Set out two mini snacks. Have the children try both of them and tell you which one they like best.

- Variation: Set out two snacks, one salty and one sweet. Have the children tell you which snack is salty.

Tying It All Together:

Providing activities that require the use of their senses is important for developing children. The senses are used to receive information about the world around us and to find out what is being communicated to us from our environment. By doing this activity, children are processing the information they receive and are gaining knowledge.

Visit **www.sagepub.com/gordonbiddle** to access templates of these lesson plans.

Representational Objects

Subject:

Cognitive and physical development.

Focus:

Promoting critical thinking with an emphasis on fine and gross motor skills.

Overview:

This activity will encourage children to remember prior knowledge and stimulate their curiosity.

Purpose:

Representational toys look like real objects in our society and environment. Many representational toys allow children to project their emotions, process feelings, and develop certain skills.

Objectives:

Encourage children to

- Make logical distinctions.
- Be able to identify, compare, and contrast objects.

Resources and Materials:

- Puzzles for fine motor skills.
- Blocks for sensorimotor skills in young children and dramatic play in older children.

Activities and Procedures:

Allow preschoolers to explore with the puzzles and blocks that will engage their fine motor skills.

- Teachers/adults can play with children to facilitate their learning.
- Preschoolers need to master their fine motor skills, and puzzles will aid in developing fine motor coordination. Have preschoolers explore using the blocks. You will observe the process of stacking and knocking over blocks, and you may allow the child to do this multiple times. For older preschoolers, observe the process of building something using the block or using the blocks as props (e.g., telephones).

Tying It All Together:

Ask the children if they were able to put the puzzle together. What was challenging about putting the puzzle together? Playing with different types of toys provides children with opportunities to combine spoken language with imagination, to imitate, and to pretend to be someone or something else. It stimulates all areas of children's growth and can in turn affect their success in school.

Visit **www.sagepub.com/gordonbiddle** to access templates of these lesson plans.

Lesson Plan:

The Animal World

Source: http://school.discoveryeducation.com/lessonplans/programs/animalColorsShapes

Subject

Science

Focus:

To learn and discover about the differences in the animal kingdom (classification, physical characteristics, and life cycle).

Grade:

Kindergarten to third grade (5- to 8-year-olds).

Objectives and Purpose:

- Understand that animals come in different colors and shapes.
- Describe the purpose of color in the animal world.
- Use different colors and shapes to create pictures of animals.

Resources and Materials:

- Crayons.
- White construction paper (1 sheet per student).
- Print images of different animals.
- Different-colored construction paper cut into different-sized triangles, circles, squares, and rhomboids.
- Glue.

Activities and Procedures:

- After reading a book about animals, ask students to share examples of shapes they have seen. What body part of most animals is circular? What animals have triangles?
- Talk about the children's favorite animals. What colors can be found on them? Discuss some of the purposes of color in the animal world. Why are the feathers on most male birds brightly colored, while female birds have gray or brown feathers? How do some animals use color to stay hidden?
- Share print images of animals. Talk about the different colors and shapes of these animals. Tell students that they are going to create pictures of animals with different shapes. They will also draw a picture of the animal's habitat.
- Demonstrate using a print image as an example. Talk about the animal. In what kind of environment would you expect to find this animal? Have students describe where this animal might live. Does it live in a desert or a forest?

- Next, talk about the different shapes students might see on the animal. What shape are its ears? What shape is its body?
- Use different-sized construction paper shapes to create the animal. Arrange the shapes on the background habitat, being sure to tell students that you will not use glue until it looks the way you want it to. Finally, glue the shapes on the background habitat. Demonstrate using crayons to make additional lines that should appear (such as whiskers) on the animal.
- Making sure that students understand what they are supposed to do, give them print images of animals, and tell them to choose one to copy for their picture. Have them first draw the background habitat and then use the paper shapes to make their animal. Check student work before allowing them to glue their animal shapes to the background.

- Once students have finished their pictures, ask volunteers to share them. Talk about the shapes they used. Discuss the colors of the animals. Ask about the animals' habitats. Does the color of blend into its habitat? Display th in the classroom.

Tying It All Together:

This activity promotes creativity, vocabulary growth, and understanding of story sequencing. Not only is this activity cognitively stimulating; it also encourages language development. It allows children to interact with others socially while having fun in the process of learning about animals in their environment. The important thing is for children to use their imagination and have fun drawing and playing with toy animals.

Visit **www.sagepub.com/gordonbiddle** to access templates of these lesson plans.

Emotional and Social Development

This chapter will help you answer these important questions:

- What are the major theoretical perspectives on emotional and social development?

- What are emotions, and what is emotional competence?

- What is social competence?

- What is attachment, and why is it important?

- What are other important issues in emotional and social development?

Vignette: Big Girl

Here's a story of 24-month-old Christina. She and her 6-year-old sister are the lovely daughters of a single father. Her father has an authoritative parenting style, so he lets Christina explore her environment within limits while he shows her plenty of love and support. He also aids Christina with transitions and stays close when she interacts with her peers, as she has a slow-to-warm-up temperament.

Christina's father is interested in potty training her in a few months, so now he is gathering as much information as he can. He is reading books, doing Internet searches, and talking to other parents. He also asks the experts, his daughter's pediatrician and child care teacher. He gets lots of helpful advice, but he trusts his daughter's child care teacher the most.

She advises him not to rush Christina or overly stress her. She suggests that Christina will demonstrate signs when she is ready for "big girl" underwear by pulling on her diaper when it is soiled and by showing an awareness of the process. The child care teacher also suggests that Christina's father point out to Christina how her sister and other slightly older children use the bathroom. The teacher also cautions that even when Christina is potty trained, she may still have an occasional accident. But, because Christina has a slow-to-warm-up temperament, the child care teacher really emphasizes that Christina's father wait for Christina to give him signs that she is ready for potty training since this is a maturational process.

The emotional and social domain of development is linked to other developmental domains and is quite important itself. In some ways, as a professional teacher, you must instruct children as to what emotional and social responses are appropriate for their culture and society. You must also assist parents with ideas and strategies for promoting optimal emotional and social development in their children. Parents may be curious about why young children act a certain way, and as a professional teacher you can explain the importance of emotional and social concepts when facilitating young children's development. This domain is important and can be facilitated by the adults in a child's life much like the domains of physical or language development.

As can be seen in the chapter opening vignette, young children's emotional and social development depends on their maturation and readiness, as well as the environment around them. This means that children need to be developmentally ready to reach emotional and social milestones, and children's environment needs to simultaneously foster the development of these milestones in order for the children to reach

Key Elements
for Becoming
a Professional

NAEYC DEVELOPMENTALLY APPROPRIATE PRINCIPLE 7

Children develop best when they have secure, consistent relationships with responsive adults and opportunities for positive relationships with peers.

Interpretation

This principle applies to many areas of development and many teaching strategies for teachers of young children. However, the influence and profound relevance for emotional and social development are evident. The adults and peers in a young child's life can significantly impact the child's emotional and social development.

NAEYC STANDARD 1: PROMOTING CHILD DEVELOPMENT AND LEARNING

a. Knowing and understanding young children's characteristics and needs

b. Knowing and understanding the multiple influences on early learning and development

c. Using developmental knowledge to create healthy, respectful, supportive, and challenging learning environments

them. More specifically, according to the vignette, Christina will show signs of emotional and social readiness to potty train, encouraging her father to facilitate the process. She also has a slow-to-warm-up temperament, which means she takes her time to adjust to transitions, new situations, and new people. Her father aids her in this process with his authoritative parenting, which is good for Christina's overall development and assists her temperamental pattern. As you will see in the balance of this chapter, Christina's environment and her maturational readiness have given her a good start in the domain of emotional and social development. As you continue to read, this will become more clear and defined.

In this chapter, we continue our exploration of the development of young children by examining another foundational aspect of development: emotional and social development. We'll begin with a brief look at how the major theoretical perspectives—behaviorism, constructivism, social constructivism, and psychosocialism—explain emotional and social development. Then we'll discuss the most important topics in emotional and social development, including

- Development of emotions—children's expression and experience of feelings
- Development of social competence—children's ability to have positive, productive relationships with others
- Development of attachment—children's bonds with their caregivers

We'll conclude the chapter with a review of other relevant issues in emotional and social development, including

- Prosocial behavior—children's ability to develop helping behaviors, such as sharing
- Gender roles—children's views of themselves and others as girls and boys, including their beliefs about gender-appropriate objects and activities
- Diversity—differences among children in demographic characteristics such as culture, ethnicity, language, and religion
- Working with children who have special needs—how to keep children's special needs from hampering their development
- Resilience—children's ability to overcome obstacles and fulfill their potential
- Bullying—how bullying in the early years can impact a child's development

Throughout the chapter, we'll see how emotional and social development are interrelated. Thus, whether you're considering how to meet standards, write lesson plans, or carry out any other aspect of good teaching, you should remember not to focus just on areas such as cognition and language, but to teach to the whole child.

WHAT ARE THE MAJOR THEORETICAL PERSPECTIVES ON EMOTIONAL AND SOCIAL DEVELOPMENT?

In Chapter 4, we reviewed various theoretical perspectives on child development as a whole. In this section of the book, we briefly discuss how four of these perspectives—behaviorism, constructivism, social constructivism, and psychosocialism—shed light on the specific areas of children's emotional and social development. To understand these theoretical perspectives, consider the following example and how each might view it.

Lakshmi is a 5-year-old girl who attends a preschool program. Melissa, her best friend in the program, is very good at soccer—when the class plays soccer, everyone wants to play on the same team as Melissa. Yesterday when Lakshmi's mother picked her up at the preschool, Lakshmi insisted on going to the playground to practice soccer so she could become as good as Melissa.

In this example, behaviorists such as John B. Watson and B. F. Skinner wouldn't focus on Lakshmi's desire to play soccer like Melissa. Behaviorism, defined in Chapter 4, focuses on observable behavior and how the observable stimuli in our environment shape our behavior through such mechanisms as conditioning and reinforcement. Behaviorists would try to determine which environmental stimuli caused Lakshmi's behavior—for example, by seeing whether Lakshmi had previously been rewarded for becoming good at sports or for duplicating a friend's accomplishments.

In contrast, constructivists such as Jean Piaget believe that as young children experience the world, they actively try to make sense of it (see Chapter 2). They experiment with physical objects, think about real events, and *construct* their own ideas about what the world is like and how it works. They then use these constructions to organize their behavior, including their emotional and social interactions. So how might a constructivist interpret Lakshmi's desire to become good at soccer? A constructivist would say that after experimenting with soccer, Lakshmi has decided that it is desirable and emotionally satisfying to play that sport. Since making a decision that seems sensible, she consciously decides to prioritize soccer in her life. She has constructed her own ideas about what soccer is and what soccer can add to her life.

From the theoretical perspective of Lev Vygotsky, who originated the idea of social constructivism (see Chapter 4), this theory focuses on the role of culture in giving young children the tools to construct knowledge. Through language and the other socially transmitted tools that culture provides, children actively progress to higher levels of mental functioning through apprenticeships. That is, young children interact with people from their culture who are more knowledgeable and skilled and in the process learn what is valued and believed in their culture. This knowledge is then translated into behavior, including emotional and social interactions. From this theoretical perspective, we can say that Lakshmi has noticed that her culture values playing sports such as soccer. She has adopted this viewpoint and learned valuable cultural lessons and skills from playing soccer like her friend.

The psychosocial approach of Erik Erikson (see Chapter 4) relates directly to emotional and social development. From the psychosocial perspective, young children go through a series of crises in their social world that they can resolve adaptively or not so adaptively—that is, young children have to actively come to terms with the social realities of their life in order to develop normally. Resolving crises helps young children develop emotional and social traits such as trust, autonomy, initiative, and industry. This theoretical perspective says that Lakshmi is trying to feel industrious and compare favorably with her friend.

Lakshmi's desire to be a better soccer player can be interpreted in numerous ways depending on which theoretical lens is used to describe it.

WHAT ARE EMOTIONS, AND WHAT IS EMOTIONAL COMPETENCE?

Every young child has **emotions**—feelings that influence the child's thoughts and behaviors. Emotions typically develop in a regular fashion and are crucial in enabling children to relate to others and in shaping their behavior in terms of social and cultural norms. Because emotions are so fundamental to social interactions, teachers of young children need to understand children's emotions, how emotions develop, which emotions children exhibit, and how children learn to express emotions. Without such understanding, teachers won't be able to help children develop their emotions and express them in healthy, productive ways. In this section of the chapter, you will observe how language development and emotional development are related. As we mentioned earlier, social and emotional development are related to other areas of a child's development. For instance, language relates to emotional development because communication is important to social interaction and emotional expression (Bloom, 1993).

The Development of Emotions

Young children's emotions are often categorized into primary emotions and secondary emotions, based on development. Anger, sadness, joy, surprise, and fear (Izard et al., 1995) are called **primary emotions** because they are the first emotions to appear, around the age of 2 months, and have biological roots (Izard, 1993). However, it seems that some experience with the world is necessary to fully express those primary emotions, which are not present at birth (Lewis, Alessandri, & Sullivan, 1990; Sullivan, Lewis, & Alessandri, 1992). Around 2 months, babies begin to express joy (a positive primary emotion) with a social smile—that is, a smile in direct response to another person's smile (Malatesta & Haviland, 1982). The negative primary emotions—anger, sadness, and fear—generally begin to emerge around the age of 6 months (Izard et al., 1995). During this time, it is important for parents and other adults to help infants learn to name their emotions (Adams, 2011). This is so infants can learn to express their emotions in a socially appropriate manner.

Two aspects of the primary emotion fear—stranger anxiety and separation anxiety—play an interesting role in the life of young children because they signal a cognitive advance as well as a social advance. **Stranger anxiety** is the uncomfortable, anxious feeling a child experiences when a stranger approaches. **Separation anxiety** is the uncomfortable, anxious feeling a child experiences when a primary caregiver leaves. Stranger anxiety usually appears around the age of 6 months, peaks around 8 months, and then declines gradually (Schaffer & Emerson, 1964; Sroufe, 1977; Witherington, Campos, & Herenstein, 2001). Separation anxiety tends to appear around 6 months also, but peaks around 14 months and then declines gradually for most infants and toddlers (Honig, 2005; Kagan, Kearsley, & Zelaxo, 1978; Weinraub & Lewis, 1977). Both anxieties are of particular interest to teaching professionals who encounter them. Children who exhibit one of these anxieties demonstrate that they are able to differentiate among the people in their environment and realize which caregivers can fulfill their needs. As an early childhood educator, be prepared for children at this age to cry and fuss when a parent leaves them. These children will also cry, fuss, and cling to a well-known caregiver when a stranger approaches. Being patient and comforting during these times will aid the children until they naturally develop beyond this stage. As the children move through stages and their expression of primary emotions changes, they also begin to demonstrate secondary emotions.

During the second year of life, children first express the **secondary emotions**—embarrassment, shame, guilt, envy, and pride (Lewis, 1998). Embarrassment tends to appear earliest, with the others following. Typically, children are able to express all of the secondary emotions by age 3 or 4 years (Lewis, Alessandri, & Sullivan, 1992; Lewis & Ramsay, 2002; Stipek, Recchia, & McClintic, 1992). These feelings are called secondary because they appear later in early childhood, and to develop the secondary emotions young children need to at least recognize themselves as distinct individuals, separate from other people. In addition, development of some secondary emotions requires that children understand the rules and standards of their culture, society, or social group (Lewis, 1998). For example, 12-month-olds who wet their diapers will feel no embarrassment, but a 3-year-old who has a potty accident will. The 3-year-old realizes that wetting one's underwear is not culturally acceptable. Adult reactions to children, not just socialization, are an important influence on the development of the secondary emotions (Alessandri & Lewis, 1996). To illustrate, parents or other caregivers who put lots of blame on their children for mistakes and errors or place severe limits on their children's behavior may cause an excessive amount of guilt, negatively affecting the development of emotions.

The Expression of Emotions and the Development of Emotional Competence

Children generally express their emotions early in some basic form, such as smiling, laughing, or crying. As children grow older, gain experience, and expand their social and cognitive abilities, the range of situations in which they are able to express emotions increases. This demonstrates the relationship of cognition to social and emotional development. From this reality, one can see how cognition is related to emotional expression because as cognition becomes more complex, so does

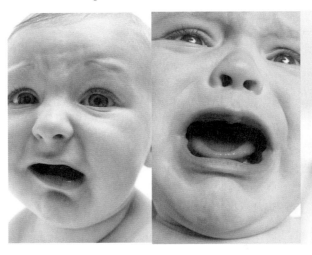

Even in their earliest months, young babies' faces can communicate volumes about their emotions.

social interaction. Advances in cognition help with self-knowledge and understanding our own and others' thoughts and feelings (Harter, 1986; Moses, Coon, & Wusinich, 2000; Wellman, Phillips, & Rodriguez, 2000). For example, toddlers at the beginning of Piaget's preoperational stage (see Chapter 2) may have difficulty expressing their emotions with words and may bite (refer to the *Best Practices* box in Chapter 9 [p. 240] for more on children who bite). But, preschoolers may learn to use their words to express their emotions. Cognitively, the preschoolers are approaching concrete operations and are gaining more logic in their thought.

With these cognitive gains come other maturational developments such as **social referencing**— the ability to understand the emotional expressions of other people, especially primary caregivers, and to respond accordingly—which begins to develop at a very early age. Three-month-olds can realize when their mother is happy, sad, or angry and will usually react appropriately (Haviland & Lelwica, 1987; Montague & Walker-Andrews, 2001), and this ability is usually quite well developed by the age of 7 or 8 months (Soken & Pick, 1999). Young children use social referencing to understand situations and to know which emotions are appropriate to express in which situations (Soken & Pick, 1999).

Children also develop greater ability to regulate their emotions appropriately—to experience and express different degrees of joy, fear, embarrassment, and so on, depending on the situation. For instance, children may experience mild to moderate joy when a caregiver gives them a hug. This joy is probably increased if a child is fed by a caregiver after a period of hunger. Therefore, children come to understand and regulate emotions as they mature, develop, and gain experience. The combination of these abilities—to understand their own and other people's emotions and to appropriately regulate the expression of their own emotions—is referred to as **emotional competence**. The achievement of emotional competence assists with positive future development.

Supporting the Development of Emotional Competence

You, as the teacher, can use the following strategies to help young children learn to express their emotions appropriately and productively:

- Model appropriate emotional expression yourself.
- Become more self-aware about your own emotions and how to handle them—by keeping a journal in which you record your emotions and reflect on how you expressed them.

Young children learn very quickly how to respond to their primary caregiver's emotions.

- Teach young children how to delay gratification and control their impulses.
- Help young children understand their emotions and the emotions of others by encouraging them to use their words—to talk about their emotions.
- Take advantage of teachable moments (defined in the following section) to help young children understand their emotions and the emotions of others.

To elaborate on the strategies above, there are a number of instances throughout a typical day when you can model appropriate emotional expression for young children. For example, whenever you are angry, you can verbally express your anger in a calm manner by simply stating you are angry and how to solve the problem while having a calm expression on your face. Anger can easily lead to harmful behavior and is an emotion that children need guidance to handle appropriately. You as the teacher can appropriately model emotions such as joy or pride in a personal success. Self-reflection, such as keeping a journal, is also good practice. Remember, young children look to the adults in their lives to guide them.

Teaching young children how to delay gratification and control their impulses may not be as easy as appropriately modeling emotions. However, it is important for emotional competence. Giving children verbal strategies such as counting to 10 before acting or telling themselves out loud "I can do it in 5 minutes" helps them delay gratification and control impulses. They can also sit on their hands or close their eyes. Explicitly showing young children these strategies and guiding them in the usage of the strategies can enhance their emotional competence.

Another way to enhance emotional competence, especially the aspect of learning to understand their own and others' feelings, is to teach young children to express their emotions with words. If children hurt others, you can help them understand a hurt child's feelings by relaying to them with words the feelings of the hurt child and encouraging them to use their words to apologize. To teach children to understand their own emotions, sadness for example, directly say to them, "You are sad about what happened." In these examples, labeling, defining, and describing emotions for young children help to enhance children's emotional competence.

The timing for using the above strategies is very important. If you can use one of the strategies during a teachable moment, it can be more effective. **Teachable moments** are times when an event or a behavior occurs naturally during the day and then you as a professional teacher take that moment to teach a related concept or further the children's development in a related domain. You can make use of teachable moments to support the development of emotional competence: read books about emotions and emotional expression that relate to emotions expressed during the day; address sadness, anger, and hurt as soon as they occur; point out these emotions in adults; and talk about them with the children.

WHAT IS SOCIAL COMPETENCE?

Social competence means being able to maintain good social relationships with other people while also being able to achieve one's goals in and through those relationships (Rubin, Bukowski, & Parker, 1998). Like emotional competence, social competence is an important skill for young children to develop. Further, there is an important relationship between emotional competence and social competence: Young children who are emotionally competent are likely to be socially competent too. Research demonstrates the importance of the relationship between emotionally competent

Early childhood teachers are instrumental in helping young children understand their emotions and the emotions of their peers.

coping strategies and temperament for developing prosocial behavior (Blair, Denham, & Kochanoff, 2004). Therefore, understanding how children develop and express social competence is just as important for teachers of young children as understanding emotional development and expression.

Influences on Social Competence

Important influences on the social competence of children include parents, peers, culture, and teachers— which is no surprise, given the large effects of these forces in all aspects of children's lives. In this section, we'll discuss how parents, peers, and culture affect children's development of these skills. Then we'll discuss how teachers can influence and support the social competence of the children in their classes.

Parents

Mothers are an important influence on their children's social competence (Garner & Estep, 2001; Rubin, Cheah, & Fox, 2001; Zhou et al., 2002), and this influence, which is clearly evident during the preschool and early elementary school years, can be both positive and negative. Additionally, fathers are important, even during infancy and the toddler years, and can parent better if given information on emotional and social development (Zero to Three, 2010). With mothers, research indicates that preschool-age children whose mothers direct more than the normal amount of anger at them have reduced emotional competence (Garner & Estep, 2001). This lack of emotional competence is related to reduced social competence. Laboratory research also indicates that mothers who are overly **solicitous** or overly controlling and interfering when it comes to behavior of their preschool-age children don't seem to guide their children's behavior appropriately during teaching tasks, and their children seem to be shier and less socially competent than normal (Rubin et al., 2001).

Mothers can positively influence their child's social competence, for example, during playdates for preschool-age children. They can monitor their children indirectly rather than directly (Ladd & Golter, 1988). Direct monitoring is becoming involved in the children's play and solving problems and managing conflicts for them. Indirect monitoring is keeping a watchful eye on the children while they are interacting with their peers and only intervening when the need arises. With indirect monitoring, parents guide children in solving their own problems and managing their own conflicts.

There are other ways that parents influence the social and emotional development of their children. Research with mothers of children in early elementary grades indicates that mothers who are warm and who express positive emotions have a positive influence on their children's social competence. However, it is hard to be sure about this conclusion because there is also an effect in the reverse direction—that is, children's display of social competence (e.g., by showing empathy toward other children) leads mothers to display positive emotions (Zhou et al., 2002). This picture is even more complicated by the fact that permissive parenting (described below), which includes expression of warmth, does not lead to social competence. This is because permissive parents usually do not give their children any limits. So the behavior of warm, positive parenting by itself is not enough to produce social competence. Warm, positive parenting with reasonable limits reflects a parenting style that supports the social competence of young children.

Attachment (a special bond defined later in this chapter) to the mother also influences a child's social competence, as does the mother's parenting style. Children who are securely attached to their mother tend to view other people more positively and do more exploration, exhibiting social competence. Viewing people positively creates an overall general atmosphere that is conducive to good relationships, which leads to social competence (Bowlby, 1988). Besides influencing a child's attachment, style of parenting can influence the child's social competence as well.

Parenting style is a concept aimed at describing how parents treat their children across two broad dimensions: responsiveness and demandingness. Responsiveness (also referred to as parental warmth or supportiveness) is how sensitive, supportive, and acquiescent parents are to children's needs and demands. Demandingness (also referred to as behavioral control) refers to how much parents insist that their children obey family rules and act in mature ways, how strictly parents supervise and discipline their children, and how willing parents are to confront children who disobey. The four generally recognized parenting styles can be described as follows (Baumrind, 1967, 1971; Maccoby & Martin, 1983):

- **Authoritative parenting style**—parents are warm and nurturing; they set and enforce clear, reasonable rules and limits; they use supportive disciplinary methods rather than punishment.
- **Authoritarian parenting style**—parents are not very warm or nurturing; they have many rules and set strict limits; they expect their children to obey orders without explanation.
- **Permissive parenting style**—parents are very warm and nurturing, but have few rules and set few limits; they are lenient and avoid confronting their children.
- **Uninvolved parenting style**—parents tend not to parent much at all; they show little warmth and have few rules or limits.

Table 11.1   **How Different Parenting Styles Lead to Various Outcomes for Children**

PARENTING STYLE	MIDDLE CHILDHOOD	ADOLESCENCE
Authoritative	High cognitive and social competence	High self-esteem, excellent social skills, strong prosocial concern, high academic achievement
Authoritarian	Average cognitive and social competence	Average academic and social skills
Permissive	low cognitive and social competence	Poor self-control and academic performance; drug use
Uninvolved/Neglectful/Indifferent	Low cognitive and social competence (aggressive and disruptive)	Poor self-control and academic performance; hostility, rebelliousness, drug abuse

The **authoritative** parenting style is related to a number of good outcomes in children's emotional and social development, including better-than-average levels of social competence (Hart, Newell, & Olsen, 2003). Remember Christina in our beginning scenario? Her father's authoritative parenting style will be quite useful as he helps her potty train because he will implement a combination of warmth and structure. Table 11.1 shows more outcomes of different parenting styles. In contrast, the other three parenting styles are not as successful in promoting children's social competence in the culture of the United States (Hart et al., 2003). Parenting styles are illustrated further in Figure 11.1.

Parenting styles vary among different social ethnic groups in the United States; there are some exceptions to the authoritative parenting style being the most successful at promoting social competence. For instance, urban African American mothers are generally controlling and strict disciplinarians (authoritarian style). However, this type of parenting protects their children from crime and antisocial peers and may be quite adaptive (Mason, Cauce, Gonzales, & Hiraga, 1996; Ogbu, 1994). In general, African American parents also use oral stories and proverbs to teach their children limits and demonstrate love (Hale, 1991). This "softens" their authoritarian style. Mexican American parents who speak Spanish and have recently immigrated may also have a more controlling style, but this is also adaptive in that it helps their children adjust to a new and confusing culture (Hill, Bush, & Roosa, 2003).

At this point, you might be wondering why the discussion of parents' influence on their children's social competence has mainly focused on mothers. It's true that fathers influence their children's social competence too. One study shows that authoritative parenting is favorable in both mothers and fathers, especially when addressing the complexity of a young child's play behavior (Clawson & Robila, 2001). Another study shows that a father's thoughts about his child's play and the strategies he uses to involve himself in his child's play influences his child's social competence (McDowell, Parke, & Spitzer, 2002). Additionally, studies show that fathers' interaction in parent-child play predicted higher social competence in their children than mother-child play (Pettit, Brown, Mize, & Lindsey, 1998). Moreover, the advice a father gives to his child about social interactions and behavior is linked more strongly to social competence than advice from mothers. Indeed, fathers play an important role in helping their children obtain and maintain social competence.

| **Figure 11.1** | **The Two Dimensions of Parenting and the Four Parenting Styles** |

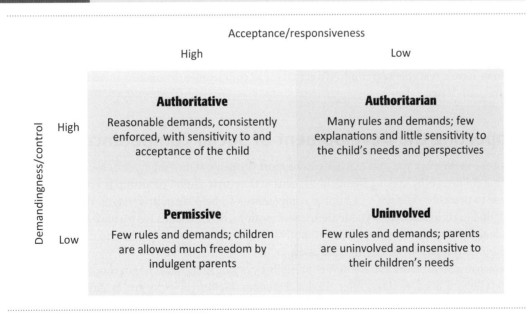

Source: Adapted from Smith, M. (2001).

Peers

Children enjoy learning from older or more knowledgeable peers (Azmitia, 1992; Brown, 1997; Johnson & Johnson, 1989; Lynch & Simpson, 2010). Not only do children learn academically from peers; they also learn socially. Indeed, peers are wonderful at teaching children skills that promote social competence, such as sharing and resolving conflicts (Caplan, Vespo, Pedersen, & Hay, 1991; Lynch & Simpson, 2010). Children learn how to share toys by interacting with each other or watching other peers share toys successfully. Interactions among children of different ages, where the older children have higher status, can help both the older and the younger children increase social skills. The older children gain in leadership ability, compassion, and assertiveness (Whiting & Edwards, 1988), while the younger children learn how to defer gracefully and how to seek assistance (Rubin et al., 1998). Interactions among children who are the same age (within a year) and of equal status can also promote social competence, in that children learn such skills as negotiation, cooperation, and compromise. Additionally, whether in mixed-age or same-age groups, interacting with peers who are also friends helps to increase social competence, because friendship is a context that promotes learning about the important foundations of social relationships, such as loyalty, intimacy, and mutual affection that make relationships more satisfying and fulfilling. Young children who have loyalty, intimacy, and mutual affection in their relationships are seen as more socially competent.

The parenting style that is used has a big influence on a young child's social competence.

Culture

Cultures differ in what they value. At the broadest level, we can divide cultures into two different types: collectivist and individualistic. **Collectivist cultures** emphasize the values of harmony, respect for authority, and group welfare, whereas **individualistic cultures** emphasize the values of self-expression and individual achievement (Cole, Bruschi, & Tamang, 2002). But within these two types of cultures, there are also other differences. Cultural values that get expressed are important because these values influence children's behavior and development.

Children behave in ways that reflect the values of their culture. In classrooms where most children are from the majority culture, children from other cultures with different values may behave in ways that don't seem socially competent to the majority-culture children. Such perceptions can, of course, have a real effect on children's actual social competence, by making them uncomfortable, shy, and withdrawn.

Supporting the Development of Social Competence

One of the main ways you as a teacher can support the general development of social competence in young children is by making friendship a focus of the curriculum. Friendship is a context that you can use to promote children's emotional competence—to help them understand the emotions of others and to recognize and regulate their own emotions. Since friends have a stake in each other's good feelings, friendship gives children motivation for mastering the ability to develop socially acceptable strategies for achieving their goals.

You can also promote social interaction skills by organizing children into cooperative learning groups (Bergin, Ford, & Hess, 1993; Taylor, Peterson, McMurray-Schwarz, & Guillou, 2002), by making sure that interactive toys, such as balls and blocks, are available (Taylor et al., 2002), and by helping children work toward reciprocity in their relationships—for example, by encouraging them to share. And of course you should model appropriate social behavior while also acknowledging

Promoting Optimal Development

Diversity and Social Competence

Children entering kindergarten are expected to have achieved a certain level of social competence: They must be able to get along with the other children in their class, be accepted by them, and be able to make friends. Given the significant and growing diversity in many U.S. kindergarten classes, it is important/relevant/necessary to ask which diversity-related factors might affect children's ability to display this necessary level of social competence.

The first factor involves the differences between the individualistic culture of the United States and the collectivist cultures of many other countries. In U.S. classrooms, collectivist cultures are often represented by children from Asian countries. Because Asian cultures tend to emphasize the group over the individual, Asian children often learn to avoid expressing themselves forcefully, and they put their individual goals aside in favor of helping the group achieve its goals. For this reason, Asian children often seem shy to mainstream U.S. children. Their appearance of shyness may be reinforced by their desire for group harmony and their respect for authority. This shyness is often seen as a lack of social competence by socializing agents in the United States.

Another diversity-related factor that impacts social competence is socioeconomic status (SES). Children from some low-SES homes, especially boys, often seem more aggressive than middle- or high-SES children (Loeber & Stouthamer-Loeber, 1998; Tolan, Gorman-Smith, & Henry, 2003). A probable reason for this is that low-SES parents often lead stressful lives, are not able to monitor their children enough, and, perhaps, use more aggressive disciplinary methods with their children,

which can have the effect of teaching their children that aggression is the solution to conflict (Kilgore, Snyder, & Lentz, 2000; Laird, Pettit, Bates, & Dodge, 2003). But whatever the causes of higher-than-average levels of aggressive behavior in low-SES children, one effect is reduced social competence—that is, more conflict with other children, fewer friendships with a narrower range of other children, and lower achievement of social goals.

Interestingly, the negative effects of cultural differences and of differences in socioeconomic status seem to be less severe for girls than for boys. Girls are usually more socially competent than boys, probably because girls tend to be more emotionally competent than boys—they understand their own and others' emotions better than boys do, and they are better than boys at regulating their own emotions. In addition, girls are less inclined than boys to use violence (physical aggression) to resolve conflicts. It is striking that these differences between girls and boys hold true for both African American and European children and for children from both low-SES and middle-SES homes, as you can see in Table 11.2 (Smith, 2001).

This information is very important for teachers of young children. Early childhood professionals need to know how to promote social and emotional competence in children from all cultures, especially if the classroom is diverse and especially when children's culture is different from their own. It is important also to help children learn socially appropriate responses to children whose culture may differ from their own. Having knowledge and reflecting on personal beliefs can assist teachers of young children as they help their students develop optimally in the area of emotional and social development.

and rewarding children who behave in socially appropriate ways (Taylor et al., 2002). Research indicates that children's development of social competence is best promoted by these kinds of holistic and comprehensive teacher interventions, especially in the early elementary school years (Aber, Brown, & Jones, 2003). Additionally, current research demonstrates that in the early elementary school years helping young children adopt a social development goal (prosocial goal) increases feelings of belongingness and lessens loneliness. Social development goals or prosocial goals are related to enriched academic achievement (Mouratidis & Sideridis, 2009). This is because prosocial goals, wanting to help others, increase feelings of connectedness.

Next, we'll discuss a more specific strategy you can use to promote children's social competence—sociodramatic play; and we'll follow this with discussion of a common obstacle to the development of social competence—aggression.

Table 11.2	The Relationship Between Emotional and Social Variables and Peer Social Acceptance for African American Preschoolers

VARIABLE	PEER PERCEPTION
Emotional Competence	
Emotion Knowledge	⬆
Violent	⬆
Behavior Regulation	
Delay of Gratification	⬆
Social Competence	
Aggression	⬇
Social Problems	⬇

Source: Adapted from Smith, M. (2001).

Sociodramatic Play

In **sociodramatic play** children take on roles and use objects as they act out dramatic scenarios. For example, children might play "house"—a girl takes on the role of "Mommy" and a boy the role of "Daddy" while another girl plays "Baby," and they all act out getting up in the morning and having breakfast. There are several reasons why this type of play leads to enhanced social competence for the children (Farver, Kim, & Lee-Shin, 2000; Rubin et al., 1998). It lets preschool-age children try on socially valued roles (Goencue, Mistry, & Mosier, 2000).

- Children learn to agree on shared meanings—for instance, that Matthew is "Daddy" and that a classroom desk is their kitchen table.
- Children learn to compromise and negotiate as they deal with issues such as two girls who both want to be "Mommy."
- Children learn to express negative emotions and deal supportively with the negative emotions of others, which leads to emotional competence.
- Children learn to trust their playmates and form close emotional bonds with them.
- Children gain communication skills and develop their capacity for caring.

Most young children engage in sociodramatic play, but teachers can encourage this, help all children participate, and make the play richer and more effective. For instance, teachers can encourage children to let shy or unpopular children join in the sociodramatic play. They can also rotate the materials in this play area and provide realistic props from at least three different sociodramatic themes. Having more themes in play makes it a richer experience. Being sure to include "male" props is also an important element of enriching young children's dramatic play, allowing a wider range of social roles to be explored by children of both genders.

Aggressiveness and Social Competence

At every age, teachers are likely to treat young children differently based on how aggressive or sociable they seem, which can impact children's social competence. For example, if a child is perceived as shy, or not very sociable, teachers are more likely to initiate contact with that child. In contrast, children who frequently initiate contact with teachers are perceived as aggressive, while those least involved in contact with the teacher are perceived as more sociable and as having fewer behavior problems (Coplan

& Prakash, 2003). These teacher perceptions, in turn, influence how children view and interact with each other. For instance, a teacher may become impatient with a child who solicits his or her attention constantly. The other children may notice this irritation and start to ignore or bully the child. This is not a situation that promotes social competence in any of the children. This situation could also occur if a teacher reacts similarly to other aggressive acts such as hitting, biting, or taking another's toys. **Aggression** is behaving in a manner that hurts another person. Learning how to control and appropriately express aggression is important for obtaining social competence.

Research shows that teachers whose training enables them to respond appropriately to aggressive behaviors can increase their students' social competence (Aber et al., 2003). With training, you can help aggressive children develop better strategies for getting along with others, which leads to fewer and less severe conduct problems, lower levels of depression, and fewer and less violent aggressive fantasies. And these findings hold for children of diverse backgrounds, including European, African American, and Latino children. A teacher's style of interaction, knowledge about aggressiveness in children, and perceptions of children's behavior can have a dramatic, positive impact on children's social competence and interactions with peers. The teacher's training would provide research-based strategies with examples and include role-playing and simulations.

Bullying is a relatively new concept in awareness for early childhood professionals and a special concern. Later on in this chapter this concept is explored further by reviewing and examining the work of Crick, Casas, and Ku (1999). Bullying also relates to aggression in the classroom. Indeed, as young children develop, many concepts and contexts are interrelated.

WHAT IS ATTACHMENT, AND WHY IS IT IMPORTANT?

Attachment refers to the type of emotional bond that young children have with their primary caregivers. Early attachment relationships are the foundation for all other intimate relationships that a person develops throughout life (see Figure 11.2). Researchers have defined four different types of attachment, or the ways babies organize their behavior in response to their primary caregivers. One type is secure attachment, and the others are three different types of insecure attachment. The behavioral descriptions that follow represent what might happen with these four forms of attachment. Children's behavior is not always predictable and has to be observed for a long period of time in order to present a pattern (Honig, 2002). Let's look at some attachment types to see if they remind you of any young children you know:

- Babies with **secure attachment** feel safe, secure, and free from stress when close to their primary caregivers. They explore their environment freely, using their primary caregivers as a secure base. Typically, their primary caregivers are sensitive, responsive, and reliable. These babies usually smile when their caregivers approach and will explore their environment while a caregiver is near. These caregivers come to understand what the various cries of their infants mean. They feed their children when the children are hungry and change the children's diapers when they are dirty. This type of attachment produces the best developmental outcomes. As a teacher, you can assist young children in developing secure attachments.
- Babies with **insecure-avoidant attachment** are less compliant with their primary caregivers than are securely attached babies and may also show anger and lack of trust. Their primary caregivers tend to be emotionally unexpressive, rigid, compulsive, and resentful of their predicament (being with a child). These babies show a lot of anger when a caregiver leaves. They do not comply with caregiver requests or suggestions. These caregivers do not respond appropriately to their children's attempts to communicate. Their limits and guidance of the children may go from one extreme to another.
- Babies with **insecure-ambivalent attachment** want comfort from their primary caregivers but cannot seem to accept it. Their primary caregivers are inconsistent in their caregiving

BEST

Practices Bullying and Relational Aggression— What an Expert Has to Say

Christina Short (personal communication, January 11, 2006), a child development expert, has worked in the field for 15 years and has a master's degree. Her master's thesis (Short, 2007) investigates relational aggression, a form of bullying. Bullying is defined as aggressive behavior aimed at hurting, intimidating, or controlling others through physical, verbal, or emotional abuse, real or threatened.

The reasons for bullying differ depending on the age and experience of the children involved. According to Short, the likely explanation for why preschoolers bully is that they are trying to get their needs met or they are attempting to gain control of a situation. Preschoolers who have been victims of bullying by a sibling or an older peer may think that bullying works and then try it in the preschool classroom. With older children, the explanations for bullying are much more varied. Short points to research that shows older children may bully for one or more of the following reasons: They think aggression and impulsiveness pays, they enjoy the submission of others, they think bullying seems like fun, they have low levels of empathy, they have generalized hostility toward others, they may have seen aggressive models, they are bored with school, or they believe bullying will help them achieve some goal (Rigby, 2001).

Another form of bullying that teachers should be aware of is called relational aggression, which often occurs in the context of a peer clique, a tightly knit group of children who exclude other children from the group. Relational aggression–type bullying takes place when this exclusion involves hurtful behavior, usually talk, aimed at letting excluded children know that they aren't wanted. Short

finds that relational aggression happens more with girls than with boys, because the types of social relationships found in cliques are particularly important to girls, especially around third grade. Relational aggression that continues over a number of years can have powerful negative effects on the excluded child, including suicide and violent outbursts.

Short has devised the following three-step process as an approach to handling bullying in the preschool classroom:

1. Use reflective listening and talk about feelings. For example, say something like "Your words aren't kind. You sound angry."

2. Use perspective taking through conversation. That is, talk to aggressive children and help them see how the victim of the bullying feels. Say something like "Sam is crying. Can you see that? Why do you think Sam is crying? How do you think Sam feels?"

3. Use problem solving through conversation. That is, help aggressive children see that they can solve a problem by talking to an injured child after damage. For instance, say something like "How can we make Sam happy again? Sam is our friend, and we want him to be happy again. What can we do to make Sam happy again? Maybe we can apologize to Sam for calling him a 'dodo bird.'"

In early elementary classrooms, says Short, you have three main goals related to handling and eliminating bullying: You want to build trust and community in the classroom; you want to give children opportunities to be open and honest, both in real situations and in sociodramatic play; and you want children to learn how to advocate against bullying.

practices—sometimes they are responsive to their baby's needs and sometimes not. These babies might smile when a caregiver picks them up, but then start crying. These caregivers respond to their baby's cries sometimes, and at other times they do not respond. Sometimes these caregivers feed their babies when they are hungry, and sometimes they do not.

- Babies with **insecure-disoriented-disorganized attachment** behave in contradictory ways, without any apparent goal. Usually, they have experienced abuse, trauma, or significant loss, and often their primary caregivers have too. These caregivers may physically or emotionally abuse their children or neglect them. Sometimes these caregivers are just too overwhelmed to respond appropriately. Babies with this type of attachment might smile at their parents yet seem fearful. These parents may not feed their children for a long period of time, or may abuse them in some manner.

These descriptions imply that the characteristics of a child's primary caregiver are the most important influence on the type of attachment the child develops (see Table 11.3). For most infants, the primary caregiver is the mother, and research has shown that the main determinant of attachment security is maternal sensitivity (National Institute of Child Health and Human Development [NICHD], 2001). That is, the more the mother is sensitive to the child's needs and is reliable in meeting those needs, the more likely the child will display secure attachment. Conversely, the more the mother is insensitive to the child's needs or inconsistent in meeting them, the more insecure the child's attachment will be.

Early childhood professionals know that these considerations apply to them too. That is, they too need to be sensitive and responsive to the needs of children in their care, in order to help those children develop secure attachment. However, the more hours a young child spends in care away from the mother, the more important is maternal sensitivity in fostering secure attachment. Indeed, when measuring attachment, mothers play a central role.

Assessment of Attachment: The "Strange Situation"

The usual way of assessing attachment is by a procedure called the **strange situation**. The procedure takes about 20 minutes and works as follows:

1. A child 12–18 months old and the child's primary caregiver (usually, a parent) go into a room containin to toys and other objects that children this age like to explore.

Figure 11.2	Features of Infants of Different Species

Source: Adapted from Shaffer, D. R. (2005).

CHARACTERISTIC	DESCRIPTION
Sensitivity	Responding promptly and appropriately to the infant's signals
Positive attitude	Expressing positive affect and affection for the infant
Synchrony	Structuring smooth, reciprocal interactions with the infant
Mutuality	Structuring interactions in which mother and infant attend to the same thing
Support	Attending closely to and providing emotional support for the infant's activities
Stimulation	Frequently directing actions toward the infant

Source: Shaffer (2005).

Note: These six aspects of caregiving are moderately correlated with each other.

2. The parent sits quietly while the child explores.

3. A stranger enters the room and talks with the parent; then the stranger approaches the child, and the parent leaves inconspicuously.

4. While the parent is absent, the stranger gears his or her behavior to that of the child.

5. The parent comes back and greets and comforts the child; the stranger leaves inconspicuously. Then the parent leaves again.

6. The child is alone.

7. The stranger reenters and again gears his or her behavior to that of the child.

8. The parent comes back again and greets and picks up the child; the stranger leaves inconspicuously.

The child's behavior when the parent comes and goes is the basis for classifying the child into one of the attachment categories, as shown previously on pages 300 and 301.

Attachment and Temperament

Temperament and attachment are different, but they interact and influence each other. Because of temperament's influence on attachment, it is important to understand the different temperament characteristics of children. Temperament, introduced in Chapter 9, is the foundation of personality, the usual or average emotional and behavioral response a child gives to various situations. Temperament has a biological basis (from genetic roots) that results in certain characteristically typical response styles and behavioral patterns (Teglasi, 1995; Thomas & Chess, 1977). Thomas and Chess (1977) uncovered three basic temperament styles: easy, difficult, and slow-to-warm-up. Children with **easy temperaments** are flexible and predictable, and generally display a positive mood. Children with **difficult temperaments** have lots of energy and intensity, irregular moods that are usually negative, and a hard time adjusting to making transitions, new people, or new situations. Children with the **slow-to-warm-up temperament** are generally thought of as shy. They have difficulty adjusting to transitions and new people and situations, too. However, their reactions are not as intense as those of the child with a difficult temperament. It is important to remember that these patterns have a biological basis and that children with all temperament types can develop successfully with guidance from the adults around them.

One example of a slow-to-warm-up temperament is Christina in our opening scenario. To facilitate her development and maintain a secure attachment, this temperament suggests that her father should ease her into this new transition from diapers to "big girl" underwear. As he potty trains her, he might want to help her transition by gradually introducing the new ideas and behaviors associated with potty training and preparing his reactions or response since he will likely encounter repeated attempts at training his daughter. Patience and gentle interactions aid in guiding the behavior of children with Christina's temperament toward positive development and help them continue a positive attachment to their caregivers.

Children with any temperament type—easy, slow-to-warm-up, or difficult—can be securely attached. The key with attachment is for the child's caregiver to be responsive and consistent. A caregiver who responds to a child's needs in a stable manner will facilitate a secure attachment with all temperament types, including a difficult child.

As mentioned above, temperament is related to and can influence attachment. Accordingly, we can say temperament and other biological traits influence social and emotional development as well as emotional expression and social interaction (Rothbart & Bates, 1998). Just imagine parenting a child who has difficulty with transitions versus parenting a child who is flexible, predictable, and generally positive. What would your social interactions be like in both instances? What type of emotions would everyone involved express more often? Children with different temperamental characteristics produce different social interactions and evoke varied emotional responses from their caregivers. This in turn impacts how securely children attach to their caregivers, whether the caregiver is a parent or a teacher.

Other Factors That Influence Attachment

What can influence children's type of attachment besides maternal sensitivity and the other characteristics of primary caregivers discussed above? Research indicates that the following factors can be associated with insecure attachment:

- Biological vulnerability—such as a temperamental proneness to distress
- Limited exploratory competence—not feeling secure in exploring the world
- Adoption—separating and transitioning from biological parents to adoptive parents
- Child abuse—severe and of various kinds

Stability of Attachment

What is the likelihood that a child's attachment type will change over time? Research in the United States indicates that children's attachment categorization seems to be relatively stable from infancy through the preschool years (Main & Cassidy, 1988; NICHD, 2001), and research in Germany indicates similar findings (Wartner, Grossman, Fremmer-Bombik, & Suess, 1994). Considering both countries together, attachment stability from infancy through the preschool years ranged from 76% to 86%—that is, three quarters or more of children don't change their attachment type over that period of their lives. However, when we consider a longer period, infancy through adolescence, the results are less certain, due to such factors as differences in measuring attachment and such negative life events as parental drug use or divorce. While some research has found that attachment stability over that time period is as high as 77% (Hamilton, 2000), other research has found significantly less stability (Lewis, Feiring, & Rosenthal, 2000). Most researchers on this topic seem to agree, though, that negative life events such as divorce and parental drug use are related to changes in attachment type between infancy and adolescence and can have the effect of turning securely attached infants into insecurely attached adolescents (Hamilton, 2000; Lewis et al., 2000). Therefore, caregivers and teachers of young children should try to be as consistent in their behavior and as sensitive to their children's needs as possible.

Supporting Secure Attachment

Because young children are likely to attach to their teacher as well as to their parents, teachers should be aware that they play a role in supporting secure attachment. The amount of influence a teacher has on attachment depends on the child's age and the amount of time spent with the child. Before 30 months of age, it seems that young children can have a stable, secure attachment to a teacher only if they have that teacher for an extended time. After 30 months of age, however, young children seem able to develop a stable, secure attachment to a teacher regardless of whether the teacher is familiar or not (Howes & Hamilton, 1992).

Like parents, teachers help promote secure attachment by being sensitive and positively responsive to the young children in their care and by providing them with support and stimulation. Research has shown that smiling at young children and reading to them helps parents promote secure attachment (De Wolff & Van Ijzendoorn, 1997; Koren-Karie, Oppenheim, Doley, Sher, & Etzion-Carasso, 2002), and these types of interactions may be helpful for teachers too.

Professionalism & Policy

Parenting Classes?

In early childhood education classes, a frequent topic of discussion is whether parents could improve their parenting skills by taking a class. People preparing to adopt a child from the foster care system have to take parenting classes, but should naturally expectant parents also have to take classes? The issue of attachment makes this question even more important. Early secure attachment is invaluable as a foundation for future intimate relationships, so why not require all parents to develop the skills they need to help their children become securely attached? Even if we agree that states or federal agencies should require parents to learn parenting skills, we then have to ask, "Which parenting skills should be learned?" The skills parents use vary not just across the diversity of ethnic, cultural, and socioeconomic groups but also across particular individual parents, yet the majority of children are securely attached. Perhaps the question should be "How do we improve the parenting skills of parents with insecurely attached children?" But this raises the same question of which skills to teach, as well as the question of how to identify the insecurely attached children.

WHAT ARE OTHER IMPORTANT ISSUES IN EMOTIONAL AND SOCIAL DEVELOPMENT?

In this section, we'll discuss other topics related to children's emotional and social development. These include the development of prosocial behavior (introduced in Chapter 9), the development of gender role concepts, diversity-related issues, concerns related to children with special needs, the concept of resilience, and bullying. As the heading above indicates, these are equally important issues in children's development.

Prosocial Behavior

People engage in prosocial behavior when they help or assist others, without any other apparent benefit to themselves. Young children may first behave prosocially by sharing a toy or by patting a friend on the back when the friend is hurt. Prosocial behaviors such as sharing and showing empathy are important indicators of emotional and social competence. In contrast, a lack of prosocial behavior in young children is associated with mental health problems that tend to worsen as time passes (Strain & Odom, 1986). Some young children show such behavior more than others, but as a teacher it is important to foster prosocial behavior because it leads to positive developmental outcomes.

Fortunately, there are ways parents and teachers can help young children develop prosocial behavior. The most obvious but also the most powerful of these methods is for parents and teachers to model prosocial behavior for young children (Bandura, 1989; Eisenberg & Fabes, 1998). For example, teachers can hand a Kleenex to a child who sneezes or has a runny nose. Usually young children who see this will imitate the teachers' behavior. Adults can also praise children's prosocial behavior to make them feel good about it and to reinforce it. Research indicates that, to be most effective, such praise should be given only intermittently and only after little time has elapsed following the behavior. This will help young children generalize their prosocial behavior and apply it to new situations (Elksnin & Elksnin, 2000).

Other effective techniques for fostering prosocial behavior in young children include the following (Elksnin & Elksnin, 2000):

- Role-play prosocial behavior in its natural setting. For instance, help children get up and check on their physical and emotional state during outside or recess time as it occurs.

- Focus on prosocial behavior that is valued by the setting or culture. For instance, if the culture or setting values sharing, then focus on sharing behavior in the young children for whom you care.

- Teach young children to engage in self-talk about prosocial behavior and self-reinforcement for prosocial behavior. You can give them words for why sharing is important and how it benefits the sharer, for example.

- Teach prosocial behavior naturally or incidentally—that is, teach it during teachable moments. This basically suggests that you teach sharing, helping, and other prosocial behaviors as they happen in life. When a child shares an object, you can praise the child for doing it right there in front of all the children immediately when it occurs.

- Discuss the outcomes of a child's prosocial behavior (or lack of it) with that child. Talk to the child about the outcome and results of sharing. Tell the child how both parties are satisfied and conflict is avoided by sharing or taking turns with a prized toy.

One child hands another a tissue, demonstrating that even young children can exhibit prosocial behavior after it is taught or modeled.

- Help children become more aware of the emotions associated with prosocial behavior (or the lack of it). Talk to the children about how sharing makes them feel and also about how it makes other children involved feel.

- Deliberately encourage young children to practice prosocial behavior. Give children a chance to role-play giving a tissue or helping someone who has fallen. Make suggestions to children to carry out these types of behaviors, or praise and reward these behaviors as they occur naturally.

Gender Role Concepts

Gender roles refer to the different ways that males and females are expected to think, feel, and behave. The specific differences in these expectations vary depending on culture, ethnicity, religion, *and* socioeconomic status of particular groups of people. And these expectations are different for people of different ages—little girls aren't expected to act like adolescent girls, and neither young children nor adolescents are expected to act like adults.

Adults begin to teach boys and girls their appropriate gender role from birth. In the United States, babies born in hospitals, for example, often are given hats and blankets of the gender-appropriate color—blue for boys, pink for girls. Even before birth, parents who know the baby's gender may paint and decorate the baby's room with colors and objects that, to them, are "right" for a baby boy or girl. So from the earliest age, children begin the process of **gender typing**—learning that they are either a boy or a girl and interpreting how a boy or a girl should behave in their society. The exact methods of gender socialization vary by nation and culture, although by around the age of 3 years, most children understand that they are a boy or a girl (Thompson, 1975). However, it isn't until the age of 5 to 7 years that most children realize that their gender is a fixed characteristic, permanent and unchangeable.

At the age of 3 years, when children realize what their gender is, they also begin to acquire **gender role stereotypes** (Kuhn, Nash, & Brucken, 1978)—beliefs about the types of toys, behaviors, and activities appropriate for each gender. For example, children at this age believe that girls like to play with dolls while boys like to play with trucks, or that girls play house while boys climb trees. These kinds of stereotypes seem to multiply in the early elementary school years and

In the United States, children are socialized into their gender role very early in life.

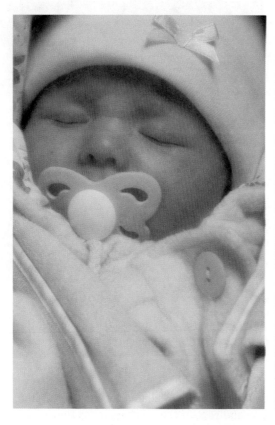
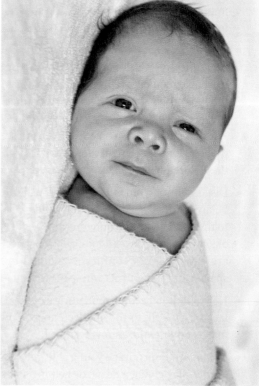

solidify by age 8 (Serbin, Powlishta, & Gulko, 1993; Welch-Ross & Schmidt, 1996; Williams & Best, 1990), as children draw more distinctions concerning which behaviors are appropriate for which gender.

Teachers can play a role in giving young children alternatives to the gender roles and gender stereotypes to which children cling. Alternatives can be offered by modeling nonsexist roles, by providing gender-neutral toys (especially for toddlers), by providing books and other materials that demonstrate males and females in nontraditional roles, and by direct and explicit discussion of stereotyping. All of these strategies can be used when a teacher is attempting to dispel strict gender roles and stereotypes (Click & Parker, 2009; McDaniel & Davis, 1999; Nodelman, 1999; Sheldon, 1990). Some examples include the following: Male teachers can be nonsexist role models in the early childhood classroom; gender-neutral toys for toddlers include stacking rings and shape sorters; other neutral toys are those with colors of yellow and green rather than pink and blue; female firefighters and male nurses in books, pictures, and other materials serve to reduce gender stereotypes; and discussion of stereotypes with children who are 3 to 8 years of age helps dispel myths about gender-appropriate activities, possessions, and behavior. As young children are developing their gender role concepts, teachers can certainly play the role of offering alternative views rather than reinforcing restrictive stereotypes.

Children do not always display behavior that is consistent with the gender stereotypes.

Diversity

Families in the United States aren't all the same—they are diverse in culture, ethnicity, language, religion, socioeconomic status, and many other characteristics (see Chapter 8). Regardless of such diversity, however, parents love their children and provide them with the kind of support they need for healthy emotional and social development (Schmitz, 2005). However, as we saw in our discussion of diversity as it relates to the development of social competence, children from different families, brought up by parents with different varied beliefs, values, and parenting styles, may think, feel, and behave very differently in the classroom. And children's behavior can result in nonmajority children being treated very differently. The reasons behind these variations in treatment can fluctuate widely—from a simple lack of understanding of the meaning of a child's behavior to wholesale approval or disapproval of a child based simply on the group to which the child belongs. Whatever the reasons, when variations in treatment take a negative form, the child's emotional and social development, and the child, are harmed.

Early childhood teachers have a responsibility to do all they can to prevent this from happening and to make sure that they promote the emotional and social development of every child in the class. What should you be aware of, and what should you do to achieve these goals? First, you should try to become aware of your own beliefs about people from different groups. This will help you avoid automatically applying those beliefs to the children in your class, so you can view each child as the unique individual he or she is. You also need to become aware of the different kinds of threats faced by children considered nonmajority, or "different."

Consider, for example, preschool children who speak their home language—a non-English, "foreign" language—in class. Research indicates that families with mothers who show pride in their culture through use of their native language provide stimulating home environments that enhance children's emotional and social development (Schmitz, 2005). If these children are isolated or made fun of in class because they use a non-English language, the good done through the use of that language at home will be undone by the treatment they receive at school. In this case, to promote these children's positive development, the teacher needs to show them and the other children in the class that the use of their home language is accepted and valued. To do this, the teacher might try a "game" activity, asking the children to provide the words in their language for objects in the classroom. The other children could join in and promote the emotional and social development of all the children in the class.

Another threat to the positive development of nonmajority children is posed by teachers who expect that these children will not perform as well as children from the majority culture. Low teacher expectations can lower children's academic self-concept, or sense of how good they are at acquiring knowledge and mastering skills, which in turn can lead them to fulfill a teacher's low expectations (Kuklinski & Weinstein, 2001). You as a teacher of young children should be careful not to place this burden on nonmajority children and should train yourself by being very conscious and deliberate to have and show high expectations for all students, regardless of their background. This is especially important in the early years, when differences in the way teachers treat children can have severely negative effects (Kuklinski & Weinstein, 2000, 2001).

Finally, we all know that some people in the mainstream, majority culture harbor many **negative stereotypes** about minority groups—beliefs that all members of a particular group share one or more negative characteristics. As we acquire our culture, we all learn these stereotypes and, over the course of our lives, have to learn how to overcome them so that we can see each person as an individual apart from his or her group memberships. Teachers need to understand that minority children learn these stereotypes too, which exposes them to **stereotype threat**—the fear that, no matter what they do, they will be judged to have the stereotyped negative attributes of their group (Steele, 1997). The stress of dealing with this fear can cause children as young as 6 years of age to perform poorly in school (McKown & Weinstein, 2003). Teachers of young children should make a special effort to be sensitive to children affected by negative stereotypes and to ameliorate the impact of these stereotypes in their classroom. Teachers may be able to accomplish this by simply verbalizing their belief in a student's abilities. Clearly the answer to diversity-related issues is not to ignore differences and assume everyone is the same but rather to acknowledge and discuss the remarkable uniqueness of each individual and thus promote positive emotional and social growth for all children.

Children With Special Needs

Children with special needs include those with a wide range of disorders and disabilities, as well as those who are gifted in various ways (see Chapter 7). In some cases, children with special needs can be identified as early as infancy. In general, the earlier a special need is identified and appropriately responded to, the better it is for the child's emotional and social development (Roth-Hanania, Busch-Rossnagel, & Higgins-D'Alessandro, 2000; Squires, 2000). Teachers, clinicians, and other interventionists play an important role in working with young children with special needs (Squires, 2000; Williams, 2001), and for the optimal development of the children, parents and other family members should be included as well (Prizant, Wetherby, Rubin, & Laurent, 2003).

The most important thing for a teacher to realize about young children with special needs is that they are children. Just like other children, they need to develop emotional and social competence, make friends, play with other children, and become an integral part of classroom activities. The following general suggestions for working with children with special needs (Williams, 2001) can also be specifically applied to promoting their emotional and social development:

- Use positive reinforcement to shape children's behavior. For example, you can reinforce young children's sharing behavior by praising them after they let another child play with their toy.
- Use individualized assignments that appeal to children's special interests, broaden their horizons, or accommodate their special limitations.
- Break down assignments into small units, and give frequent feedback.
- Time children's work sessions, and perhaps lessen their workload. For instance, a heavy workload can cause stress, which may cause a socially or emotionally vulnerable child to behave inappropriately. Lessening the workload or dividing the work into timed units may lessen the stress and improve the child's behavior or social interactions.
- Be firm but realistic about your expectations for the quality of children's work. For example, a child with special needs might not draw a picture of a friend as well as another child might, but if the child does his or her best, you can praise the effort just as you would praise the effort of any other child.

As we mentioned above, families should be involved in the education and treatment of children with special needs. This involvement, though, will only fully support the child's emotional and social development if the families are supported too, by being provided with information about their children's needs and about the strategies they can use to help their children. Families may also need support in dealing with the stress of having a child with special needs, in setting priorities, and with having realistic expectations and goals for their child and for their everyday family life (Prizant et al., 2003). As a teacher interested in promoting emotional and social well-being, you may be able to provide some of this information and support, but you should also be aware of and able to recommend services that families can turn to for help.

Resilience

In relation to emotional and social development, **resilience** can be briefly defined as children's ability to overcome obstacles and fulfill their potential. A more comprehensive definition is as follows: "Resilience is being able to thrive, mature, and increase competence in the face of adverse (biological or environmental) circumstances. In order to do this a person must draw upon all of their environmental, biological, and psychological resources" (Gordon, 1993, p. 5).

Consider This Responding to Children With Special Needs

Judy was a little uncertain about how the children would react to her newest student Bob because Bob is in a wheelchair and 3-year-olds are naturally curious. Before his first day of class, Judy brought in a wheelchair from the local hospital. The children took turns sitting in the wheelchair and pushing each other around. Judy communicated to the children that they should be sensitive and respectful to Bob. But most important, once Bob arrived, she let the students see her be sensitive and respectful too. They quickly saw that she treated him just like she treated them. After 6 months, Bob fit right into the class. He felt comfortable, and the other children were comfortable with him.

Think back to your younger years and the first time you met a child with special needs. Do you remember your reaction? How did the reaction of the adults around you impact your own reaction as a child? How will you react as a teacher of young children when a child with special needs enters your classroom?

The adversities that young children have to overcome to fulfill their emotional and social potential include internal factors such as physical handicaps and learning disabilities, as well as external factors such as child abuse and poverty. By overcoming such factors, a child is resilient, a term that in the field of early childhood education means that a child must meet certain criteria. The generally accepted criteria for considering young children resilient is that they demonstrate competence in two or more areas despite facing two or more adversities. The areas of competence are academic competence, developmental competence, social competence, and behavioral competence (Glantz & Johnson, 1999; Gordon Rouse, 1998, 2001). While academic competence is demonstrated by achieving good grades, and developmental competence is demonstrated by reaching appropriate developmental milestones, the focus here is on resilience defined by social competence and behavioral competence. Social competence has been defined as being able to maintain good social relationships while also being able to achieve one's goals. **Behavioral competence** is demonstrated by exhibiting socially acceptable behaviors. The relationship between these two concepts is clear and does exist, but a child can be socially competent without being behaviorally competent.

When we look at resilient children who have overcome adversities to demonstrate behavioral and social competence, we can usually identify one or more important protective factors that help them in their struggle. **Protective factors** are categorized into three groups: individual characteristics, the family environment, and the environment and institutions outside the family (Werner & Johnson, 1999; Werner & Smith, 2001). It is important to note that all children need environmental supports in order to display resilience (Glantz & Johnson, 1999); protective individual factors alone aren't enough. This fact is illustrated by Figure 11.3.

Protective individual characteristics include the right kind of temperament, high physical energy, good problem-solving ability, and good communication skills, but other familial and outside factors help children obtain and maintain resilience. Having these skills helps young children obtain and maintain social competence in the most stressful and challenging circumstances. Being able to solve problems and communicate well will help children obtain a wanted goal, such as a toy or a good grade, in a socially acceptable manner without resorting to aggression.

Relational aggression isn't good for the social and emotional development of young children.

The most helpful protective factor in the family environment is for the child to have at least one adult in the family who is stable, caring, and trusting and who also promotes the child's autonomy and initiative. Outside the family, protective factors include religious and educational institutions that support the family, enhance the child's self-esteem, and convey positive values (Werner & Johnson, 1999). These protective factors can provide an avenue for children in adverse situations to continue to develop emotional and social competence. Teachers are a vital part of the child's supportive environment (Gordon Rouse, 1998, 2001).

Bullying

In a landmark 1999 study, Nicki Crick and colleagues demonstrated that bullying exists even during the preschool years. **Bullying** is intentionally causing physical or emotional and social harm to one's peers. Bullying, sometimes referred to as peer victimization, comes in two basic forms: physical aggression and relational aggression (Crick et al., 1999). **Physical aggression** is intentionally

Figure 11.3   Factors Related to Resiliece

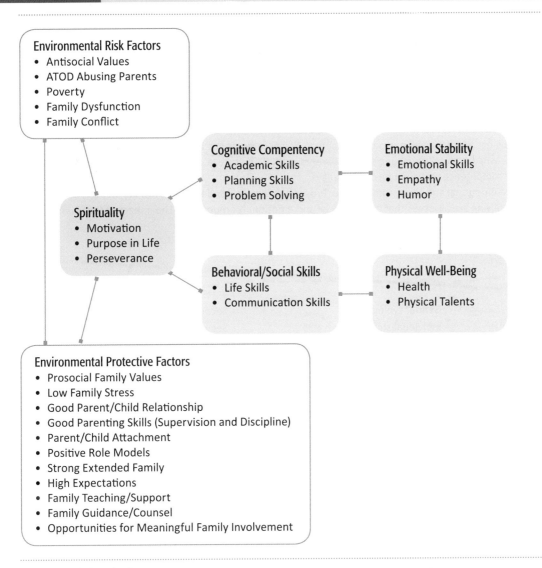

Source: Glantz and Johnson (1999).

harming someone physically by hitting, biting, kicking, or committing some other physical act. **Relational aggression** is intentionally harming someone emotionally or socially by harming the person's reputation, calling the person names, or hurting the person's feelings. Boys are more likely to be victims of physical aggression, and girls are more likely to be victims of relational aggression (Crick et al., 1999). However, victims of both kinds of aggression are likely to have emotional and social issues with their growth and development.

The seeds of bullying may be planted in preschool, but they grow in early elementary and beyond. Current research demonstrates the importance of cross-racial/ethnic friendships for increasing peer support and lessening bullying, both physical and relational (Kawabata & Crick, 2011). Research also shows that the developmental trajectory may be different for males and females, but that negative one-on-one peer relations are the key (Murray-Close & Crick, 2006). This research suggests that teachers of young children pay close attention to negative one-on-one relationships and increasing the number of high-quality peer friendships. It also suggests using the relationships, both positive and negative, that occur in real life to foster social skills and competence (Murray-Close & Crick, 2006).

Summary

There are four major theoretical perspectives that relate to emotional and social development, namely behaviorism, constructivism, social constructivism, and psychosocialism. Each perspective views and explains children's behavior from a different lens, and emphasizes the importance of attachment.

Attachment is an emotional bond that young children have with their primary caregivers. Early attachment relationships are the foundation for all the other intimate relationships that the person develops throughout life. It is best for young children to be securely attached.

Emotions are feelings that influence a child's thoughts and behaviors. Emotional competence is the ability to regulate the expression of emotions and understand one's own emotions, as well as the emotions of others. Helping young children label their emotions increases their emotional competence, as does giving them strategies for coping with negative emotions.

Young children are social beings and want to be socially competent. Social competence is the ability to maintain good relationships with other people while accomplishing one's goals. Parents, a child's culture, a child's peers, and a child's teacher all influence the amount of social competence that a young child displays.

Other vital issues influence emotional and social competence. Prosocial behavior, gender roles, diversity, being a child with special needs, resilience, and bullying are all issues that impact social and emotional competence. The impact of these issues can be strong and follow young children throughout their developmental trajectory.

Key Terms

Aggression   299

Attachment   299

Authoritarian parenting style   294

Authoritative   295

Authoritative parenting style   294

Behavioral competence   310

Bullying   310

Collectivist cultures   296

Difficult temperament   302

Easy temperament   302

Emotional competence   291

Emotions   289

Gender roles   306

Gender role stereotypes   306

Gender typing   306

Individualistic cultures   296

Insecure-ambivalent attachment   299

Insecure-avoidant attachment   299

Insecure-disoriented-disorganized attachment   300

Negative stereotypes   308

Parenting style   294

Permissive parenting style   294

Physical aggression   310

Primary emotions   290

Protective factors   310

Relational aggression   311

Resilience   309

Secondary emotions   290

Secure attachment   299

Separation anxiety   290

Slow-to-warm-up temperament   302

Social competence   292

Social referencing   291

Sociodramatic play   298

Solicitous   293

Stereotype threat   308

Strange situation   301

Stranger anxiety   290

Teachable moments   292

Uninvolved parenting style   294

Reflection, Application, and Analysis Questions

1. Which theoretical lens gives the clearest framework for social and emotional development? Name and describe the theoretical framework and give three reasons why you feel it is the best lens.

2. Which of attachment's influences is the most important? Name and describe the most important influence, in your opinion, and give three reasons why it is the most important.

3. How can parents foster secure attachment, even if their child is in child care? Name and describe three strategies parents can use to foster secure attachment in their child. At least two of these should specifically relate to children in child care.

4. Is there such a thing as an invulnerable child (one who is always resilient)? State whether or not invulnerable children exist, and then give three reasons why they exist or do not exist.

Extension Activities

1. Observe an ordinary parent interacting with his or her children in an everyday setting such as the mall, a grocery store, a restaurant, or a park. Write down notes in a journal of the exact words and behaviors in an objective fashion.

Then try to interpret the character and nature of the interaction, assessing the amount of warmth, limits set, and discipline techniques. Then try to discern the type of parenting style being displayed.

2. Although attachment can only truly be measured at specific ages with specific measures such as the strange situation, try to assess who is the main attachment figure in your life right now. Ask yourself who is your main emotional and social support, and with whom you share victories and disappointments first or most frequently. This person is probably your main attachment figure. Depending on who you are and where you are in your development, this could be a parent, a grandparent, or another relative. It could also be a friend or a significant other.

Additional Readings

Fostering emotional and social development is just as important as fostering cognitive development. Some early childhood educators would say that the emotional and social domain is even more important than the cognitive domain. As a teacher of young children, you must give attention to both areas.

Howes, C., & Ritchie, S. (2002). *A matter of trust: Connecting teachers and learners in the early childhood classroom.* **New York: Teachers College Press.**
This text presents an application of attachment theory to teacher-child relationships. It also suggests strategies for facilitating positive student behavior and positive, warm classroom environments. Some of the pedagogical features are stories and narrative examples.

Hyson, M. (2003). *The emotional development of young children: Building an emotion-centered curriculum* **(2nd ed.). New York: Teachers College Press.**
This text is in its second edition. It highlights the research on emotional development that has occurred over the last two decades. The author links emotional competence to educationally significant early childhood outcomes, such as school readiness. She also lays out plans for developing an emotion-centered curriculum.

Kostelnik, M., Whiren, A., Stein, L., & Gregory, K. (2006). *Guiding young children's social development: Theory to practice.* **New York: Delmar.**
This book offers a framework based on theory and research. This framework of social development relays practical strategies for developing a child's self-esteem or social competence. Suggestions for infusing these ideas into learning environments are also relayed.

On the Web

Center on the Social and Emotional Foundations for Early Learning - *http://csefel.vanderbilt.edu*
This site is funded by the federal government's Department of Health and Human Services. One of its main goals is promoting the social and emotional development of children in order to deter and ameliorate challenging behaviors. The site also has culturally sensitive information about training, technical assistance, and evidence-based practices.

National Center for Early Development and Learning - *www.pbrooks.com/store/ncedl.htm*
This website is backed by the latest research and the federal government's Institute for Education Sciences. It contains information about social and emotional development in terms of the latest research findings, news reports, and products. It is backed by the University of North Carolina with the University of Virginia and the University of California, Los Angeles.

National Institute of Child Health and Human Development: Child Development and Behavior Branch - www.nichd.nih.gov/CRMC/cdb/p_cog.htm
This website is part of the federal government's National Institutes of Health. It shares information about funded projects on social development, affective development, child maltreatment, and violence. The funded projects focus on typical development and children who develop in high-risk settings.

Student Study Site

Visit **www.sagepub.com/gordonbiddle** to access several study tools including eFlashcards, web quizzes, links to SAGE journal articles, web resources, video resources, lesson plan templates, and more.

Subject:

Self-awareness and recognition.

Focus:

Recognizing oneself in a mirror.

Overview:

Around 15 to 21 months of age, children begin to recognize themselves in the mirror. This is a special time of development and discovery, and the experience can be enriched in specific ways.

Purpose:

To help infants/toddlers become aware of themselves in the mirror. This is an important milestone related to the expression of emotions and general self-awareness.

Objectives:

- Assist with obtaining self-recognition.
- Assist with obtaining general self-awareness.
- Advance cognitive development and, in turn, emotional and social development.
- Assist with obtaining emotional expression.

Resource Materials:

- Several mirrors.
- Red lipstick.
- A visually interesting hat.

Activities and Procedures:

1. Stand the mirrors on the floor at the child's eye level in strategic places.

2. When the child notices a mirror, put some lipstick on the child's nose.

3. See if the child touches his or her own nose or the nose in the mirror.

4. Let the child explore and experience the situation, giving the child time to notice the lipstick on the mirror image.

5. If the child still doesn't seem to notice anything, repeat the same steps with the visually interesting hat.

Tying It All Together:

This is a fun and interesting activity for both the child and the teacher. You might want to get the parents involved by suggesting ways they could do the activity at home. With infants/toddlers who don't react to their mirror image, you may want to repeat the activity after a few weeks. Eventually, the child's development combined with the repeated experience will allow the child to recognize that it is him- or herself in the mirror.

Visit **www.sagepub.com/gordonbiddle** to access templates of these lesson plans.

"I'm Not Happy!"

Subject:

Emotional competence.

Focus:

Expressing emotions verbally.

Overview:

Some of the activities are planned, but at other times take advantage of teachable moments.

Purpose:

To help young children verbally express positive and negative emotions.

Objectives:

- Learn how to express positive and negative emotions verbally.
- Enrich emotional communication skills.
- Increase emotional competence.
- Increase social competence.

Resource Materials:

- *Alexander and the Terrible, Horrible, No Good, Very Bad Day,* by Judith Viorst.
- Pictures of adults and children of different genders, races, and ethnic groups expressing various emotions.
- Paper.
- Nontoxic crayons.
- Nontoxic markers.
- Pencils.

Activities and procedures:

1. During circle time, do either of these activities:
   A. Read and discuss the book by Judith Viorst, OR

   B. Look at and discuss the emotions expressed in the pictures, and ask children to talk about those emotions.

2. Engage the children in a structured or free-play art activity where they draw faces to correspond with various emotions and then label the emotions verbally and graphically, with pictures.

3. Take advantage of teachable moments when children are having trouble expressing their emotions. Get down on their level and help them understand how they are feeling at that moment; get them to talk about and express their feelings in their own words.

Tying It All Together:

The verbal expression of emotions is an important skill, especially for young boys. The emotional and social development of girls, too, will be helped tremendously by verbally expressing their emotions.

Visit **www.sagepub.com/gordonbiddle** to access templates of these lesson plans.

Lesson Plan:
"Mommy and Daddy Love Me!"

Subject:

Emotional understanding and emotional competence.

Focus:

Gaining a concrete understanding of love.

Overview:

Emotions are complex and hard to understand. This combination of planned activities will help young children understand emotions better and will benefit their overall development.

Purpose:

To help children gain a concrete understanding of love.

Objectives:

- Help young children understand and express love better.
- Increase young children's emotional competence.
- Increase young children's social competence.

Resource Materials:

- *Love You Forever,* by Robert Munsch.
- Pictures of children and adults of different genders, races, and ethnic groups hugging, holding hands, and smiling at each other.

Activities and Procedures:

1. During language or English class, read and discuss the book by Robert Munsch.

2. During social studies class, look at and discuss the pictures.

Tying It All Together:

Love is an abstract concept. Elementary children may not be able to understand it fully because, according to Piaget, at this age they are only able to reason about concrete things. Showing children love in books and pictures can make this abstraction more concrete and help them understand it better.

Visit **www.sagepub.com/gordonbiddle** to access templates of these lesson plans.

CHAPTER 12

Language and Literacy Development

This chapter will help you answer these important questions:

- What are the language rules?
- What are the theories of language development?
- How do children acquire a second language?
- How do children develop literacy?
- What are the methods for teaching reading?

Vignette: Story Time

In Ms. Sherri's kindergarten class, the children were having story time. Ms. Sherri had just finished reading The Magic School Bus Blows Its Top: A Book About Volcanoes, *and she had just started asking them questions about the story. She asked the class, "Who can tell me what the first page tells you?" Amanda, Jenny, and Alex all raised their hands eagerly to answer. "Amanda," said Ms. Sherri, and Amanda described the characters and what they were doing. Alex jumped in and added that there was a volcano, and it was erupting. Ms. Sherri went on to ask another question as she turned the page: "Tell me what is happening at this point in the story." Josh raised his hand and said that lava and smoke were coming out of the volcano. Samantha yelled out, "That is an active volcano!" Jeremia, who had been listening this whole time and hadn't raised his hand, suddenly asked, "Why do volcanoes erupt?"*

The kindergartners in Ms. Sherri's classroom are a perfect example of young children's competence in language. The vignette presents a setting where children benefited from listening to the story, listening to the responses and expertise of others, receiving feedback from the teacher and other children, and problem solving. We also see from the vignette that the teacher was assessing the children for new vocabulary learned from the story and comprehension.

Language development is a major accomplishment during the preschool and kindergarten years, unless there are developmental delays that impede children from developing normal language acquisition. **Verbal language** development is the foundation for later literacy development (reading and writing). In this chapter, we provide a general introduction to the study of language development and consider five major questions that will help you understand how children acquire their first and second languages. We also explore the importance of literacy development, emergent literacy, and different techniques for teaching young children reading. In addition, we will focus on the ways teachers can support young children's language and literacy development.

As human beings, we use language to communicate—to express our thoughts and feelings with one another. The most common tool to express this communication is verbal and written language. Language, introduced in Chapter 5, is a powerful tool that allows children, at a very young age, to learn to express their needs, emotions, and desires and give and receive information. In short, it allows them to better understand the world in which we live.

As a natural process of human development, children learn such skills as listening and speaking without any formal instruction. Children learn these language skills by socially interacting with others in a language environment. Robinson, Ross, and Neal (2000) have reported that children as young as 4 or 5 years can understand and use the **basic grammar** (rules that govern the structure of phrases and clauses) of their native tongue, for example "I have" versus "She has." In addition, studies have revealed that children learn the five general language rules before entering school: phonology (sound system), morphology (rules regarding words), semantics (meaning of words), syntax (grammatical structure), and pragmatics (appropriate usage) (Robinson et al., 2000). We will discuss these five language rules in the section to follow.

WHAT ARE THE LANGUAGE RULES?

Infants have the ability to produce a broad array of sounds. The sounds infants make, during what is called the **babbling stage**, develop into the sounds heard in adult language. The sounds infants hear in the adult language are the sounds they put together to make sense of their world; some examples of words infants put together based on what they hear are *mama* and *mo* (more). These are indicators of the beginning of a child's mastery of the phonetic rules of language.

Phonology

We begin to see language growth in the toddler years. Toddlers will move from one spoken word to more decisive speech that will expand their vocabulary and express their wants and personal needs. They also become aware that everything in their environment has a name and are exploring, repeating, and learning new words (Machado, 2012). The toddler years are when children learn the **phonology** of their native language—the study of sounds concerned with the rules governing the structure, distribution, and sequencing of speech sounds. As one researcher said, "The young language learner must classify sounds into recognizable types of groups while he or she is possibly experiencing the speech of a variety of people in a variety of settings" (Geller, 1985, p. 36). A challenging task that toddlers must accomplish is using spoken language in a continuous flow of word sounds, such as completing the five-word sentence "I am going to school." A **phoneme** is the smallest unit of sound that distinguishes one word from another, and toddlers learn to differentiate each word meaning. For example, in *read* and *bead*, the phonemes /r/ and /b/ serve to distinguish the difference in these two words. English has 50 phonemes, and all 50 sounds are achieved by most children around the age of 7 or 8 years (Machado, 2012).

Morphology

Morphology is the study of the structure and content of words. Morphologists examine the patterns of word formation and create rules that model the language one speaks. The root words are considered the smallest grammatical units, called morphemes. Children learn new words and word forms when they start to understand that combinations of sounds have structure and meaning. For example, they can correctly make words past tense such as *went* for *go* and plural such as *dogs* for *dog*. Children are able to understand the rules

Cooing, babbling, and crying are babies' first sounds.

of morphemes before they enter school. They are not thinking of the rules of words as adults do. However, they demonstrate their awareness of the rules when they **overgeneralize** and say "wen-ted" instead of "went." Overgeneralization is when we draw conclusions that are very general and without facts. Children are capable of learning the rules for changing words early in their development. Researchers argue, however, that some words are not learned until 6 to 10 years of age (Akhtar & Tomasello, 1997; Wood, 1976).

Semantics

Semantics is the study governing the meaning of words and word combinations. When children learn and store the sounds and patterns of a new word, they are learning to express the meaning depending on the situation in which the words are used. When the young child hears the sound and the meaning of a word, he or she is taking in the meaning. The meaning of the words, however, are learned when the child is active, or involved in the process of the experience. For example, a young child may not understand the meaning of the word *rain* because he or she has not physically experienced the rain. This concept and intellectual building that the child is experiencing is a result of language development and trying to make sense of the surrounding world. Both Vygotskian (1962) conceptual knowledge and Piagetian (1955) stages of intellectual development address the stages of children's thinking as it relates to language development.

Children at the sensorimotor stage use single words as if they were entire sentences, developing a sentence dictionary with "meanings tied to functions that words perform" (Wood, 1976, p. 150). Consider Carlos, a 20-month-old who is looking for his father. Carlos first runs around the house, saying "Daddy?" meaning, "Where is Daddy?" Then he looks in the bedroom and shakes his head from side to side, saying "Daddy," meaning "Daddy's not in the bedroom." Then, he goes to the kitchen and, with his hands on his hips, yells "Daddy!" meaning "Daddy, come here!"

While at the preoperational stage (refer back to Chapter 2) of language acquisition, children use separate words from a sentence and attach a meaning to the word that infers concrete actions. Children become aware that words have more than one meaning and are able to understand this concretely but not abstractly. For example, ask a child to define a vehicle. Children at this stage are able to define it, saying something like "A vehicle has wheels, you drive it, and it takes you places." But when it comes to abstract thinking, a vehicle is much more complex to define; for example, a vehicle can be defined as having four wheels, an engine, and a steering wheel; an object that moves on rails such as a streetcar; or the part of a balloon for carrying people.

At the concrete operational stage (refer back to Chapter 2), children's understanding of the meaning of words increases, and they develop word dictionaries—unabridged. A child at this stage understands the function of a vehicle and may define it as a source of transportation such as a car, a motorcycle, a bicycle, a wagon, a train, a ship, or an aircraft.

Syntax

Syntax refers to word order or grammar that prescribes how words are combined to create sentences. As children's language develops, they learn that word order is important in producing meaning and in understanding other people's messages. The rules of grammar are said to be "in the heads" of native speakers, a "mental grammar," allowing children to create and understand grammar with extraordinary ease and speed (Jacobs, 1995, p. 4). Carlos, for example, brought his shoes when told to "go get your shoes." He was able to understand the action verb *get* without any formal teaching. With Carlos's grammatical knowledge, he is now able to produce and understand a wide range of new words. Brain development researchers believe that there is a "critical time period" for acquiring syntactic understandings, and consider this period to be around 5 or 6 years of age (Nash, 1997, p. 54).

Pragmatics

Pragmatics is a set of rules concerned with the way language is used within different social contexts. Heath (1983), Labov (1970), Tizard and Hughes (1984), and Vygotsky (1962) pointed out that children learn from the conversations they have with others from the community in which they live. Different social and cultural practices will be taught to children based on the specific rules of conversation of their home, social, or cultural customs. For example, the U.S. public school system uses the syntactic rules of Standard English and the politeness rules of a middle-class society. Other types of syntactic rules pertain to telephone conversations, classrooms, doctor-patient relationships, jokes, and rituals (Otto, 2009). Children, early on, begin to learn that there are "polite and proper" ways to say things depending on where they are. For example, a 5-year-old boy may use the polite convention of saying "please" whenever he is at school but not at home, where it may not be used as much. When school language practices are too different from a child's at-home language, teachers must respect that child's language and teach the child new sets of rules for different social contexts.

Language learning is an ongoing process. The verbal and rule development of the phonology, morphology, semantics, syntax, and pragmatics are learned early as children socially interact with adults in their environment. As children progress in school, new learning will be built upon the basic language structures that children learn in their own social and cultural community of speakers. Figure 12.1 provides you with the pragmatics of language development that children go through.

| Figure 12.1 | Pragmatics of Language Development |

Functionalist Model

Morphology

Semantics

Phonology

Syntax

Pragmatics

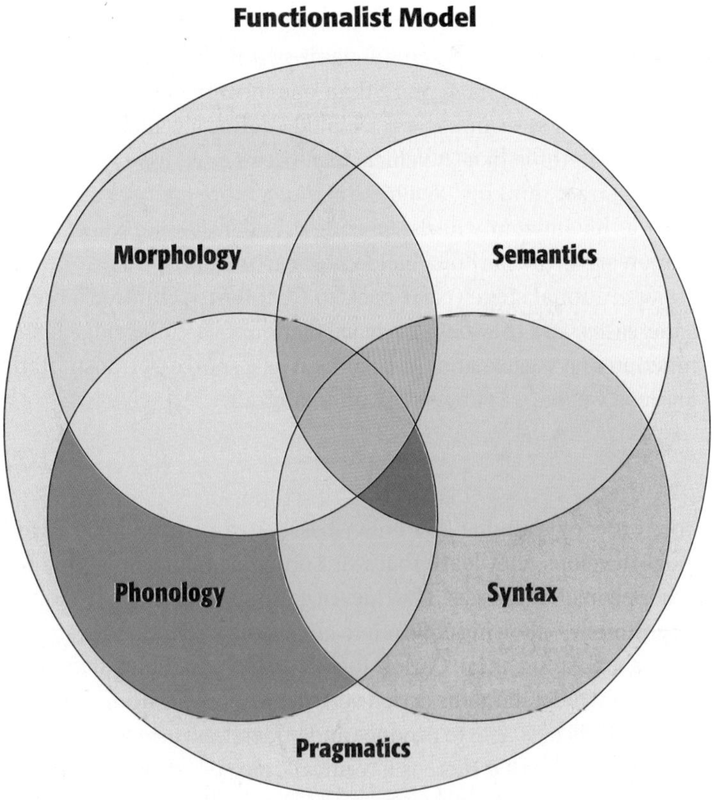

Consider This Phonological Awareness and Rhyming

Veronica is an experienced kindergarten teacher. Throughout her years teaching, she has seen an increase in children whose home language is other than English. When she is in the classroom teaching a new vocabulary word, she tends to say the sounds of the words very slowly to emphasize the smallest unit of sounds in each word (phoneme). She also changes the sound values by overstressing her mouth movement or by clapping or holding up a finger for each new sound. Most kindergarten programs today include phonological awareness in their curriculum. Rhyming and counting syllables are phonological awareness exercises used in the classroom.

Why do you think rhyming might be an important exercise for literacy development? Can you think of other exercises you might use in your classroom to promote phonological awareness?

WHAT ARE THE THEORIES OF LANGUAGE DEVELOPMENT?

There has been much research by scholars in the field on the understanding of how we as humans learn language. Scholars from multiple fields of study—human development, linguistics, sociology, psychology, anthropology, speech-language pathology, and zoology—have contributed to our understanding of language development theory.

The Behaviorist Model

Behavioral theorists believe that behaviors are shaped by responses to other behaviors so that behaviors that are reinforced become strengthened and behaviors that are punished become suppressed. Therefore, the environment elicits language, and children "learn language as adults reinforce their verbalizations" (MacWhinney, 1997, p. 278). Through constant reinforcement, children recognize language as a means of gaining control over their environment (MacWhinney, 1997). The child behaves "as though he had learned the rules" as a result of this generalized imitative repertoire (Peterson, 1971, p. 6). Children become more familiar with language as they grow older and learn the more complex structures of language, which are continually reinforced by parents and teachers (Brown, 2006).

The Nativist Model

Three advocates of the nativist model (also known as the innatist model) are Chomsky (1965), Lenneberg (1967), and McNeill (1966), who believe that children are "prewired" for language and that language is a process of normal maturation. Chomsky explains children's ability to produce and understand new and novel sentences as an innate capacity—known as the language acquisition device (LAD)—dedicated to language and not to other forms of learning. According to Chomsky (1965), children do not just repeat expressions they've learned but test the rules they've formulated about their language. Children refine and generate a wide range of expressions from the particular sentences or expressions they hear (Machado, 2012).

Lenneberg (1967) maintains that language development is biologically determined and that its onset is regular and consistent among all children in all cultures. And McNeill (1966) believes children instinctively understand that there are root structures of sentences from which all other sentence types are generated. Through early hypothesizing and trial and error, children formulate the rules for transforming the basic structures of sentences into all sentence types.

The Interactionist Model

The **interactionist** considers certain functions of language to be maturational and genetically determined. In other words, an interaction between the child's innate language abilities and the child's environment facilitates language development and reasoning. The nativist (Lenneberg, 1967) maintained that language development is biologically determined. The interactionist also believes that language development is genetically determined; however, the difference is that language development is dependent on the maturational stages of the child. This interaction enables the child to formulate rules for communicating in that environment. Two proponents of this theory are Vygotsky (1962) and Piaget (1955), who see language and thought as related developments that occur during different stages of development: sensorimotor, preoperational, concrete operational, and formal operational.

Piaget (1955) maintains that language develops along with the child's capacity for logical thought, judgment, and reasoning, and that language reflects these capacities. He notes that children have certain biological capacities for language learning, but as these internal structures grow and develop, children must interact with their environment and absorb these elements into their internal structure before the next stage takes place. Children need a language-rich environment in order to be able to construct the phonetic, morphemic, syntactic, semantic, and pragmatic rules of language. They also need to practice language in a variety of ways, for a variety of purposes.

Social interaction between an infant and other more capable peers (parents, siblings, teachers, etc.) is a critical mechanism for children's language acquisition. Vygotsky (1962) viewed language as a uniquely human ability that exists independent of general cognition, starting at about age 2 years. Prior to this time, general cognition and language are intertwined, but at about age 2, these two processes begin to develop as separate capabilities. According to Vygotsky, children develop **external speech** during the sensorimotor stage. Speech may accompany action, but it is not connected to an understanding of speech as communication. Vygotsky maintains that human consciousness develops through words. During the preoperational stage, this **egocentric speech** becomes inner speech, a sort of unconnected talk that one hears in one's head. At the same time, children become conscious that through speech they can communicate ideas and concepts to others. This awareness becomes apparent in children's language development as they become interested in learning the names of things and constantly ask to be informed.

Vygotsky (1962) emphasizes the importance of adults' role in children's language development. He maintains that children develop their understanding of the rules and function of language from the adults who use that language in a regular and consistent manner. In the beginning, children have some concept of the meanings of adults' language even before they can pronounce the words. These vague concepts come closer to adult meanings in a series of more complex ways (not unlike Piaget's stages) as children interact with the adults. During these stages, adults supply more context to concepts as children build and refine their own meanings. Though the children construct meanings, the adults determine the direction of their thinking process.

Other researchers emphasize how the adult language environment can affect the more complex development of a child's language and thus the child's capacity for thought (Tizard, 1981). Bernstein (1970) and Elardo, Bradley, and Caldwell (1977) have revealed that different parental language styles and interactions result in differing scores on children's intellectual and language tests. Parental styles that include such characteristics as reading to children, mealtime conversations, role-playing in pretend games, expanding children's language, and engaging children in different verbal interchanges are related to children's more extensive use of language and increased problem-solving ability (Honig, 1982).

HOW DO CHILDREN ACQUIRE A SECOND LANGUAGE?

Students whose primary language (L1) is other than English are faced with the challenge of learning a new language (L2) that has different characteristics from their primary language. The phonetic, morphemic, syntactic, semantic, and pragmatic aspects of the two languages may be significantly different. Languages from the same "language family" have similar characteristics and features, whereas languages from different language families will be dissimilar (Crystal, 1987). For example, Spanish and French are considered to be in the Indo-European (Romance) language family and have some similarities such as the use of an alphabetic writing system and similar word stems (Otto, 2009). In contrast, Spanish and Chinese belong to different language families and are distinctly different in not only the writing system used but other aspects of language as well, including four of the five general rules of language—phonetics, morphemics, syntax, semantics, and pragmatics. The similarities or differences between the two languages influence second language acquisition. Children who are attempting to learn a language from a different language family will find it more difficult than if they were attempting to learn another language from the same language family. As the second language is learned, children build on their understanding of language by making connections and comparisons between their first and second languages. A second language that is noticeably different from the first language will require more effort to learn.

Bilingual children acquire their first and second language simultaneously with ease.

Bilingualism

Bilingualism is a term that depicts the process whereby children acquire two languages. If children learn more than two languages, they are considered to be multilingual. When children acquire two or more languages from birth, the process of learning is called "simultaneous," whereas other children acquire additional languages in a "sequential" manner.

De Houwer (1995) argues that children develop a second language similarly to how they learn their first language. With regard to syntax (the rule for the formation of grammatical sentences), Meisel (1993) concludes that "the sequence of grammatical development in each of the bilingual children is the same as in monolingual children's acquisition of the respective language and is guided by the same underlying logic" (p. 371). Bialystok (2001) also agrees; however, he holds some reservation, believing that vocabulary develops separately for each language, and that vocabulary knowledge does not transfer from one language to another. Ultimately, there seems to be substantial agreement that the processes of bilingual language acquisition are similar to those of monolingual language acquisition.

Simultaneous Bilingualism

The child who acquires two or more languages from birth acquires these languages simultaneously, or through **simultaneous language acquisition**. These children usually receive language input in two or more forms from their parents, grandparents, other close relatives, or child care providers. Simultaneous language acquisition occurs before the age of 3 years. This process of acquisition can be characterized as follows (Grosjean, 1982):

- Initial language mixing, followed by a slow separation and increasing awareness of the differences
- Influence of L1 on L2 when the environment favors one
- Avoidance of difficult words and constructions in the weaker language
- Rapid shifts in the dominance of either language with environmental shifts
- Final separation of the phonological and grammatical systems but enduring influence of the dominant system in vocabulary and idioms

Children who are growing up as simultaneous bilingual students can continue developing their knowledge of vocabulary and grammar in English and in their native language only if both languages are exposed. In most cases, however, one language prevails, becoming more dominant than the other.

Sequential Bilingualism

Through **sequential bilingualism**, the child learns two languages in succession before developing proficiency in one of the languages. Children acquire two or more languages because parents prefer to use just one language from birth and wait to introduce an additional language, or because input from one language may not be available directly after birth. For example, the child may start to attend child care with a provider who speaks a different language. This is the case for many immigrant children in the United States. This sequential learning seems easiest for younger children in their accent and grammar, but there is no empirical evidence that younger children are any more successful with vocabulary and syntax.

Most children who are bilingual develop one language, such as Spanish, at home and a second language, such as American English, with peers or in school, usually after age 3 years. Although humans are capable of acquiring a second language at any age, by the late teens it is difficult for a speaker to acquire native speakers' pronunciation in a second language. In part, this difficulty may be that adult speakers use the communication strategies of their primary language to interpret the second language (Tao & Healy, 1996, 2002). Therefore, children seem to have an advantage in second language attainment but not in the rate of learning the second language (e.g., DeKeyser, 2000; Krashen, Long, & Scarcella, 1979; Slavoff & Johnson, 1995).

Code Switching

Bilingual speakers often demonstrate evidence of **code switching**, or shifting from one language to another. Code switching does not reflect language deficiencies as was once believed; rather, it is the result of functional and grammatical principles and is a complex, rule-governed phenomenon. Code switching is systematically influenced by the context and the situation in which the individual lives (Auer, 1984; McClure, 1981; Penalosa, 1981; Poplack, 1981; Sanchez, 1983). Children start by code switching single words, switching from one language to another (Lanza, 1992). Adults, on the other hand, tend to replace whole sentences (Huerta-Macias, 1981). This typically occurs when a concept label is not available in the language being used (e.g., proper noun or new terminology, such as that referring to technology) or if a specific meaning is needed (Baker, 1996; Bhatia & Ritchie, 1996; Cloud, Genesee, & Hamayan, 2000; Lessow-Hurley, 2000).

Code switching for children appears to be a function of the participants in a conversation (McClure, 1981). Three characteristics of the participants in a conversation are essential: perceived language proficiency, language preference, and social identity (McClure, 1981). Children under age

5 years use proficiency and preference decisions for code switching. Older children make finer distinctions and will consider the individual they are addressing more often before they code switch.

The exact reason why people code switch is unknown. However, the phenomenon is believed to be controlled by social or psychological factors, such as to show ethnic unity (Cloud et al., 2000; Lessow-Hurley, 2000). Huerta-Macias (1981) provides two reasons: (1) It may sustain the retention of the first language while a second is acquired, and (2) once the two languages are acquired, code switching may ensure that both are used.

Bilingualism and Brain Development

Learning a second language may influence in how the brain is organized. Brain organization is contingent on a number of factors, such as the age at second language acquisition, the method of learning, the patterns of usage, and the similarity of characteristics of the languages (De Groot & Van Hell, 2005; Paradis, 2004). Learning a second language may involve right-hemisphere mechanisms not involved in individuals who are monolingual. If a second language is learned before puberty, there may be symmetrical brain representation—a balanced brain image—within the two hemispheres (Paradis, 2004). If the second language is learned after puberty, it may result in more complex brain organization and thus less symmetrical lateralization—less balance in one side of the brain (Paradis, 2004).

Bilingualism and Cognitive Development

Individuals who are bilingual typically attain high levels of language proficiency before the effects of bilingualism are evident in cognitive development, but there is a very strong relationship between bilingualism and cognitive development. It has been reported that individuals who are bilingual are better in classifying objects, creativity, concept formation, memory, metalinguistic awareness, problem solving, role taking, science concepts, social sensitivity, and understanding complex instructions (Eckstein, 1986; Fang, 1985). High-functioning children as young as 5 to 6 years exhibit higher divergent thinking, imagination, grammatical awareness, perceptual organization, and reading achievement (Ricciardelli, 1992).

HOW DO CHILDREN DEVELOP LITERACY?

Young children and adults have the capacity to speak, listen, read, write, and think, and these are all the elements of literacy (see Chapter 5). Unlike speaking and listening, which are natural processes; reading and writing are skills that have to be taught.

Language as the Foundation for Literacy Development

Young children's oral or expressive language develops in stages, beginning with cooing around 6 to 8 weeks of age. At around 4 to 6 months, most infants will begin to babble. Later on, their babbling reflects or echoes the intonation and expressive **prosody**, or rhythm of spoken language, such as the intonation of speech, of their home language (echolalic babbling; see Chapter 5). At around 1 year of age, most infants will use single words and/or develop two- to three-word utterances, a process known as telegraphic speech (see also Chapter 5). In order to create developmentally appropriate learning activities for both infants and toddlers, the early childhood teacher needs to be aware of each child's level of oral language.

The development of spoken language competencies is a major accomplishment during the preschool years. All children will become relatively fluent in their primary language during the first

4 years unless there are developmental delays, cognitive impairments, or physical speech impediments. The ability to use language to communicate affects children's learning and their daily social interactions. Understanding spoken language gives children the foundation for later development of reading and writing skills, and "what children bring to the printed page and to the task of writing is knowledge of spoken language" (Moats, 2000, p. 16).

Language development and literacy awareness begin right after birth. During the first 5 years of life, the child's brain is developing very rapidly, and acquiring verbal language skills becomes very important. This is why exposure to a rich literacy environment, one that is full of books and oral and written language, is crucial.

Teachers should encourage parents to develop a routine of reading to children every day.

Children first construct concepts about books and how print works; and then begin to attend to aspects of the print that surrounds them. This is followed by growth of phonemic awareness and acquisition of phoneme-grapheme (alphabet) knowledge. As children construct knowledge about print and the relationship between print and speech, they also are building oral language skills that support their progress as they encounter the demands of first grade and begin to move into conventional forms of reading and writing. (Dickinson, Wolf, & Stotsky, 1993, p. 376)

Children who are learning how to read and write learn quickly that books convey meaning through print. They first visualize the pictures, connect the pictures with their own experiences, and then monitor them—asking themselves if the pictures and experiences make sense. Second, they see print (a word or sentence) and realize that it represents a spoken message. In addition, young children come to an understanding that each word is composed of letters and that these letters appear in a certain order.

The 8-month-old who cuddles up on his or her father's lap to look at a picture book is developing early literacy understanding. The 18-month-old scribbling on a piece of paper is preparing for writing in later childhood. Through these and other early learning experiences, very young children slowly gain knowledge of literacy concepts such as beginning at the front of the book and moving sequentially to the back, reading each line of print from left to right, and being aware that print has meaning (Bobys, 2000).

Emergent Literacy

The belief that learning to read and write has much in common with spoken language development is called **emergent literacy** (Sulzby & Teale, 1991). Emergent literacy has also been referred to as early literacy development. This approach endorses the belief that children begin learning about reading and writing as early as infancy. With appropriate materials and supportive adults, young children construct knowledge about print and gradually become more literate (Yaden, Towe, & MacGillivray, 2000). Adults can help young children grow into readers and writers if they engross children in a print-rich environment and provide guidance during their developmental process.

Emergent literacy behavior is the foundation for children's spoken language and their knowledge of written language. As a teacher, you can observe preschoolers engaged in emergent literacy behavior when they participate in literacy-related events with others as well as when they interact with reading and writing on their own. When they are engaged in these behaviors, such as participating in book sharing, interpreting environmental print, and attempting to write, and when they read what they write, they are using their spoken language competencies.

The Four Components of the Language Arts Curriculum

Children entering kindergarten begin an educational system that is totally different from their preschool setting. One of the most dramatic differences presented in kindergarten is the curriculum. The language arts curriculum, for example, focuses on the following four components: listening, speaking, reading, and writing.

Listening

Children will develop the ability to listen so they can make meaning of their environment. The National Council of Teachers of English (NCTE) has identified four types of listening: marginal, appreciative, attentive, and analytical (NCTE, 1954). Listening can be done as children go about their own tasks while only marginally hearing what is being said or what is happening. One can listen for entertainment or pleasure and develop an appreciation for language and environmental sounds. Early in life, children discover that they must listen carefully and attentively in order to gain information. Last, children will listen to speech to understand and analyze how what is happening or spoken will affect their own situation. They will be able to vary their listening strategies appropriately. Seating children in a circle is a good activity for listening. Circle time allows children to look at the person speaking and hear what others are saying.

Speaking

Children will develop the ability to speak clearly, correctly, and distinctly so they can be understood at school, at home, and in the larger community. Children require life experiences to help them make their needs and wants known, to give directions to others, to influence others, and to speak so as to interpret a story, a poem, and characters in a play.

Children need to learn that the manner in which they speak depends on the situation. Informal speech is appropriate with friends and family, but more precise speech is appropriate at school. Children recognize that very clear and often formal speech is required in school when the teacher employs this language in giving directions for a school report.

Reading

Children will develop the ability to read a variety of increasingly difficult material in order to gain and interpret information, follow directions, locate materials, and derive pleasure and enjoyment.

Young children first learn to gain information and interpret signs from the environment. It may be that children first notice changes in the faces of their caregivers and interpret their moods, or they may notice clouds in the sky and know they may need a raincoat. Children also learn that pictures give meaning and that they can gain information and pleasure from them.

Children progress to understanding that what seem like scribbles have meaning. They will begin to understand that the person reading is gaining meaning from those scribbles and that the sound of the words ends when the print ends. In a print-rich environment, children learn to recognize letters and words and eventually become aware of the relationships of sounds to letters and words. Finally, they learn a system for figuring out the unknown parts of a passage and discover that they are reading, and they learn to read different types of texts and establish different reasons for reading.

Writing

Children will develop the ability to write in an increasingly complex and precise manner in order to show appreciation, share information, request things, and give pleasure and amusement.

In early school and home environments, children need experiences making marks on paper and pretending to write. As these scribbles become more like letters and the nonsense letters come closer to phonetic spellings, children discover that these marks have meaning. Children's first discovery of connecting words and concepts is often their own name, and they become fascinated with the results.

From these beginnings children learn the often difficult, but exciting, task of putting their words and thoughts on paper. They eventually learn that there are different purposes for writing and that the style of writing changes with the purpose.

Creating a Rich Literacy Environment

Early childhood and elementary school teachers should provide children with meaningful written materials that will lead to literacy development. The most obvious literacy learning materials are books. Starting in the infant and toddler programs, teachers should provide children with access to a wide variety of books and should read to individual or small groups of children (Kupetz & Green, 1997). Key elements of creating a print-rich environment include the following (Christie, Enz, & Vukelich, 2003, as cited in Henninger, 2005):

- *A variety of materials for reading.* In addition to books, classrooms should have many types of print that serve real-life functions (labels on food items, restaurant menus, road signs, etc.).

- *Diverse writing materials.* A well-equipped writing center should be the focus of these activities, with materials available throughout the classroom that encourage children (or adults) to record important written communications (title of artwork, description of a block structure, stories to accompany flannel board figures, etc.).

Promoting Optimal Development

Key Emergent Literacy Behaviors During Picture-Book Sharing With Adults

Books intended to tell young children a story contain limited print and more pictures. The purpose of a picture book is to communicate to young children the importance of reading. The following are examples of adult and child behavior during picture book reading:

- Shared gaze, looking at illustrations to which the parent is pointing

- Facial expressions indicating comprehension or prediction of book content

- Attempts to turn pages and assist in holding the book

- Demonstration of memory for story content by verbal and nonverbal behaviors (gestures, verbalization, or sounds) in predicting upcoming events portrayed in the picture/storybook

- Use of gestures or questionlike verbalizations to elicit responses from parent

- Participation in labeling objects or actions pictured, or in asking for the parent to provide the label, indicating listening vocabulary and expressive vocabulary

Source: Adapted from Otto, B. (2006). Language development in early childhood. Upper Saddle River, NJ: Pearson Prentice Hall.

- *Display of children's written products.* Teachers help children see the importance of writing by displaying their stories, books, and letters to friends and families.

- *Integrated print materials.* Written materials should be connected with ongoing activities in the classroom. Gardening activities outdoors could be connected to teacher-recorded stories of children's gardening experiences, labeling of plant rows, recordings of plant growth, and books in the library center about aspects of gardening.

- *Literacy as part of routines.* Literacy activities can be highlighted during the routines of the school day. Attendance charts, hot and cold lunch counts, daily schedule, the Pledge of Allegiance, and a weather chart can be used for meaningful reading and writing experiences.

In addition to infants and preschoolers, kindergartners and elementary school-age children need a print-rich setting. Teachers should select books that are functional and provide educational messages. Children's work should be posted on bulletin boards, on blackboards, and in play areas, along with their own messages, labels, lists, and beginning writings. Writing and art centers should contain a variety of papers, pencils, crayons, paintbrushes, and magic markers. And children should be given time and opportunity to discover what makes reading and writing work for them.

A developmentally appropriate classroom provides a safe and secure environment for all children. In addition to providing supportive opportunities for physical growth, cognitive development, and emotional well-being, this environment needs to provide opportunities to develop language competencies. A literacy-rich environment will have these five characteristics:

1. A special area of the room for book sharing
2. A variety of language- and literacy-related activities embedded throughout each day
3. Opportunities for interaction and conversation
4. Opportunities for conceptual development through exploration and interaction
5. Developmentally based learning materials

Exploring Art Through Literacy

Much of what we do with books is focused on reading and comprehension. Oftentimes we forget that these books contain art, another mode of communication and learning about our environment, society, and cultures. The art and illustrations presented in picture books are the beginning of young children's use of visual symbols that contribute to their later abilities to communicate through reading and writing (Edwards & Willis, 2000). In today's technological world, young children are exposed to the use of different visual media—television, computers, and videos—and should be encouraged to make graphic representations of their favorite character on paper. Teachers should also encourage young children to analyze and critique what they see in those visual images. Children who have artistic talent may better be able to reveal their reading comprehension in their artistic strengths than if they are limited to a more traditional form of representing literacy, such as writing.

Encourage children to express their understanding of stories through artwork.

Learning Materials and Activities

A language- and literacy-rich classroom will have materials that have been chosen to fit the developmental needs of the children in the classroom. For example, in an infant and toddler classroom, the books need to be very sturdy and heavy-duty, such as cardboard, or be laminated because young children are just learning how to manipulate objects and often will mouth or chew on an object as they explore its features. The books should have pictures and big print since the children will be viewing and not reading at this age. When older toddlers begin to show interest in drawing and writing, they will need to have materials that fit their developmental needs. For example, toddlers will need large and thick pieces of paper—for fine motor skills, which refer to the control of arm and hand movements, particularly in the wrist, small joints, and muscles of the fingers (Biel & Peske, 2005)—for their endeavors in early writing since they are in the process of developing small-muscle coordination. Other materials such as water markers, which are washable and non-toxic, and chalk should be available to children for practicing their writing and scribbling.

In order to keep children interested and motivated in language and literacy, the reading materials should be engaging and stimulating so that the children's curiosity is invigorated. In addition to a wide variety of appropriate books, stuffed animals and puppets that resemble storybook characters will add interest to picture-book sharing and will encourage children to participate verbally (Soundy, 1997). Figure 12.2 provides a list of literacy skills that children should have based on their age and grade.

A well-balanced preschool curriculum provides learning opportunities that enhance acquisition of phonetic, morphemic, syntactic, semantic, and pragmatic language knowledge. After teachers have established the individual needs of their children in the classroom, a more exclusive curriculum and language goals should be developed for those children. Ultimately, the curriculum and lesson plans should have clear, rational, and purposeful activities. Many sources of curriculum ideas and activities describe how to conduct specific activities but do not indicate why these activities should be used. As a result, teachers may implement activities without a full awareness of the potential of curriculum and language goals to foster language development. When teachers have a strong educational rationale for each learning activity, implementation of each activity is more focused, and assessment of the learning outcome is more direct. When activities are implemented without a clear rationale or objective, the focus may simply be on keeping the children busy.

Preschool learning activities and their potential for fostering language development are described in four categories of activities: exploratory, computer-based, teacher-guided, and routine.

Infants are learning how to manipulate objects and will learn first about books through touching and chewing.

- *Exploratory activities.* Exploratory activities encourage independence and curiosity. Many preschool programs have learning centers that promote unstructured and open-ended activities. Teachers plan these learning centers but allow children to decide how they will interact with the materials provided. Exploratory centers may focus on activities such as block play, drama (office, dress-up, kitchen), reading, listening, writing, and art. Another venue for unstructured activity is the outdoors where teachers continue encouraging language development. In all areas, it is important to remember that the exploratory nature of the activity requires that the children have an opportunity to interact independently with the materials with only a minimum of adult guidance or intervention. Many activities have general purposes and goals such as improving children's physical development, social interaction and collaboration, conceptual development, and problem-solving skills (Bredekamp & Copple, 1997; Lindberg & Swedlow, 1980). Obviously, language development should be part of these goals, specifically since we know that social interactions and collaboration with other children, such as when they manipulate and talk about things they have created together, will promote language development. Language goals should be emphasized that assist children in using language to solve problems, inquiring about their creative endeavors, and describing their play activity or project.

- *Computer-based media.* Computers are growing in popularity in preschool classrooms. The Internet and other software programs are having a positive impact on children's reading skills. A study done by the Pew Research Center in 1998 reported that adults with Internet access spend less time viewing the news and more time reading it on the Internet. Even though this study does not apply to children, it does suggest that online activities require both reading and writing skills and that children tend to embrace the behaviors of their parents. Computers have helped the youngest children to become writers. When used for writing and reading—through games, art, music, or other software—computers seem to stimulate children to talk more, plan more, think more, and write and read more (Mambretti, 1999; Smith, 1988). The concern has been not whether computers should be in the classroom but how they should be used (Mambretti, 1999; Smith, 1988).

- *Teacher-guided activities.* Both large and small group activities are designed and directed by the teacher, and group size is an important factor to consider when deciding which type will be appropriate. It is easier for teachers to plan for an entire class group, but small groups are more suitable for young children because they provide greater intimacy, opportunity for conversation, and feedback.

The lengths and frequency of whole-class activities should be limited with very young children due to the wide range of attention spans among this age-group. These children will vary in their listening comprehension skills, and some may not be able to attend to speech that is directed to the whole group. Teachers should encourage children to participate in large group activities, but participation should be voluntary, and children should not be disciplined for choosing not to join in with the large group.

Figure 12.2	Literacy Skills According to Young Children's Developmental Stages

During the kindergarten year, children will be able to achieve the following:

- Recognize the letters of the alphabet.
- Recognize and associate roughly 20 letters and their sounds.
- Begin to have an understanding of phonemic awareness (each word has its own sound).
- Begin reading and writing simple consonant-vowel-consonant words.
- Be able to recognize a few simple sight words.

During the first-grade year, children will be able to achieve the following:

- Have an understanding of short and long vowels.
- Be able to combine the "b" and "r" and "t" and "h" sounds, to make the "br" and "th" blends.
- Be able to read simple words, sentences, and stories.
- Have an understanding of the word endings *-ed* and *-ing*.
- Be able to read simple sight words, for example *is, was, have,* and *are.*

During the second-grade year, children will be able to achieve the following:

- Be able to combine vowels, making the sounds "ea" and "ai."
- Be able to spell complex words.
- Be able to combine two words to make a whole, for example *cow* plus *boy* to make the word *cowboy.*
- Increase their vocabulary and word recognition.

Source: Adapted from Parlapiano (2006).

- *Routines.* Routine activities happen on a normal basis and serve the institution's needs, such as taking attendance or taking care of children's physical needs—snack time, dressing to go outside, paying attention, listening to instructions, or changing diapers. Routines often go unnoticed because they are not credited with any opportunity for important learning. However, routine activities provide opportunities for acquiring important language knowledge, such as conversational skills (during snack or lunch time) and listening skills (when children listen to each other speak). Establishing specific language goals for daily routine activities can help encourage development of conversational skills (pragmatic knowledge) as well as enhance the other four forms of language knowledge: phonetic, morphemic, syntactic, and semantic.

Planning for Language and Literacy Teaching

Teachers provide a rich environment for high-quality interactions with the child that encourage articulation, receptive language, expressive language, and written language. Teachers should give clear directions, have children ask questions, and provide them with an age-appropriate answer. For example, repeat a phrase from a child's last sentence that asks the child to try again: "You want what?" Or cast the question back to the child by changing the phrase: "Where did you put it?"

Try to understand what the child means, regardless of the actual language used. What is the purpose and intent beyond the words the child may have used? This is very important for children who are English language learners and toddlers.

Have children state their thoughts out loud. For example, "Tell me what you think is going to happen if I let go of the ball."

Storybook reading has been shown to be crucial for emergent literacy and language acquisition. Researchers feel that storybook reading "bridges the development of oral language skills and the emergence of print literacy" (Rice, 1995, p. 8). It has been reported that children who have had familiarity with early story sharing also have "greater success in learning to read and write" (Slaughter, 1993, p. 4). Research has highlighted the following benefits to children from storybook sharing (Morrow, 1989):

- Increased interest in reading
- Increased familiarity with written language
- Increased vocabulary development
- Awareness of story structure

Language-related goals for storybook activities include increasing children's listening comprehension and vocabulary, helping children become aware of the relation between speech and print, and encouraging children to learn how to sequence events and to recall sequences of events.

Children's Books

Every classroom should have a book collection that invites children into its library center. Book covers should be at the children's eye level. The International Reading Association (1998) suggests that a classroom library for elementary children should have at least five books for every child. Some of these books can remain in the center throughout the year, but rotating the books by removing or storing some from time to time and supplying different books will make the area more interesting. The school should develop guidelines that outline the rules and responsibilities of book handling. These rules should be designed to encourage children to return books to shelves, turn pages carefully, and respect quietness in the area.

Many types of children's books are available. Other varieties of novelty books are also available: bath-time floating books, bedtime books that are soft, pocket-sized books, jumbo board and easel books, lift-the-flap books, movielike flipbooks, glow-in-the-dark books, potty training books, and sing-a-story books. Additional types of books appropriate for the young child are described by Kupetz and Green (1997):

- *Rhythmical language books.* Books with rhymes and lullabies (e.g., Mother Goose) are some of the first to interest very young children.

- *Point-and-say books.* Containing pictures or photographs of familiar animals, toys, family members, and the like, these books allow the adult to point to the pictures and say their names. Eventually, children can do the pointing and become more involved in the reading.

- *Touch-and-smell books.* Children are presented with different textures to touch and/or a variety of smells to get them actively involved in exploring these books.

- *Board books.* These durable books are made of boardlike materials that withstand the banging and chewing of young children.

- *Early picture storybooks.* Many children are ready for books with simple story lines and clear illustrations that help tell the story.

Older children may require different types of books, and Neuman and Roskos (1993) suggest the following categories of books for preschool and primary school-age children:

- *Action books.* These books contain mostly pictures and have pop-ups, pull tabs, and other movable parts to encourage a child's active participation.

- *Informational books.* Books that share specific content on topics of interest to young children through words and pictures fit this category. Stories about how milk is produced (Carrick, 1985) or the life of a squirrel (Lane, 1981) are examples.

- *Picture books.* Books of this type contain mostly pictures and have limited print. Young children can learn many of the conventions of reading books (e.g., reading each page from left to right and top to bottom) while enjoying the pictures.

- *Predictable books.* These books have repetitive patterns that make it easy for children to predict what comes next. Many of the Dr. Seuss books fit this category.

- *Storybooks.* Although they contain pictures on most pages, these books provide children with an interesting story line to follow.

- *Wordless books.* Children can use the pictures in these books to tell their own stories.

- *Beginning chapter books.* These books are more like those for adults. They have limited pictures, have complex plots, and are organized into chapters. Parents or teachers often read these books to primary school-age children.

Books should be accessible and at eye level to all children.

Parental Involvement

Parents can be instrumental in fostering literacy development in their children. The home setting plays a critical role in providing literacy-related experiences for young children. The context and quality of children's interactions with adults are associated with children's early literacy transactions. Home environments where young children have shown evidence of emergent literacy can be characterized by the following nine features:

- Parents value literacy.
- Parents use reading and writing in their daily activities.
- Parents engage children in frequent book sharing.
- Parents encourage children's early literacy explorations.
- Parents respond positively to children's questions.
- Parents value children's early attempts to draw and write.
- Parents engage children in frequent conversations.
- Parents are sensitive to their children's developmental level and prior experiences.
- Parents use scaffolding and mediation.

Machado (2012) notes that literacy development at home and school is affected by three factors: (1) setting, (2) modeling, and (3) planned and unplanned events. The setting is the home or school where books, toys, materials, supplies, and space to read are made available. Family economics is a big factor because it may determine the opportunities and materials that are available to the child at home. However, parents' creativity and resourcefulness may overcome the lack of financial resources. Parents can promote literacy by devoting their time, attention, and sensitivity rather than money (Mavrogenes, 1990).

Modeling positive attitudes toward reading and writing can be done by parents, older children, and adults. Reading newspapers, magazines, or books is a positive modeling technique. Finally, planning a trip to the library or museum or playgroup activities that involve reading and writing can make literacy development fun and entertaining. Other interesting and unplanned places for literacy development include grocery stores, post offices, and banks. Ask the children to draw what they observe at various places and to talk about these places and their experiences.

WHAT ARE THE METHODS FOR TEACHING READING?

There is a continuing controversy and debate over what approach to use for teaching reading. Some researchers support one method over the others. In order to thoroughly explore what approach is best, we must compare the three methods.

Whole-Language Approach

The **whole-language approach** is a philosophical view of how children learn both oral and written language. Learning to read and write, as well as learning to speak, is achieved by observing the process used by those who have acquired the skills, by experimenting, and, finally, by figuring out the cues in order to extract meaning and to communicate. This approach emphasizes the interrelatedness of the language arts skills—listening, speaking, writing, and reading—and the interrelatedness of learning to read in all curriculum areas.

Goodman, Smith, Meredith, and Goodman (1987) point out that reading is a constructive process and that children first get meaning from symbols in context by using inferring, predicting,

Many public and private schools throughout the country have instituted family literacy programs. These programs allow children to bring books home in order to engage parents in assisting their children with reading. A book bag literacy program designed by preschool and elementary teachers of students from families with low socioeconomic status has used Title I funds (the Elementary and Secondary Education Act [ESEA] provides financial support to states and school districts to meet the educational needs of at-risk students) and money donated by the National Parent Teacher Association to buy bags and books for the parents (Barbour, 1998/1999). The bags are lent to families and checked in and out by the teachers. Parents first receive a letter explaining the program; then the parents, children, and teacher promise to fulfill the expectations. The expectations consist of parents reading to the children on a daily basis, children caring for the bags, and teachers managing the program.

Source: Barbour (1998/1999) in Robinson, Ross, & Neal (2000, p. 72).

Recommendations from teachers based on the outcomes of the program are as follows:

- Take a lot of time to prepare and organize.
- Make sure the items in the bag are replaceable.
- Encourage parents' participation and assistance in making activities.
- Arrange for reliable parents to handle check-in/checkout procedures.
- Include ideas for extension activities (conversation starters, places to visit, words to finger-plays and songs).
- Keep track of the bag's contents.
- Allow children to check out a new bag only after all items in a previous bag are returned.
- Be flexible in the length of loan time, depending on children's interest.
- Keep costs low, by minimizing the use of consumables.

confirming, and correcting strategies. Linguistic principles are learned not as isolated units but simultaneously as children use these strategies to understand and construct the meaning of any given text.

Whole-Word Approach

The **whole-word approach** is a reading method that teaches children to "sight read" words; that is, they become able to pronounce a whole word as a single unit (Mayer, 2003). Whole-word instruction involves associating word names with printed words. By repeated exposure to words, especially in meaningful contexts, it is expected that children will learn to read the words without any conscious attention to single units. Therefore, whole-word recognition, or the development of a whole-word vocabulary, is a goal of whole-word instruction. The idea behind this approach is that children can learn to recognize words through repeated exposure. Children are taught to read whole words and then parts of the words, whereas phonics teaches children to read parts of the word, then the whole word.

Phonics Approach

The **phonics approach** to teaching reading stresses the sounds of letters and words. The proponents of phonics instruction argue that letter-sound correspondence enables children to make automatic connections between words and sounds and to sound out words and read them on their own. Reading using the phonics method emphasizes the understanding that sounds and letters have a relationship. Children are able to combine sounds into words, for instance, sounding out each letter of the word *cat*. Following this example, the child learns that the letter *C* has the sound of "c" as in *cow*. Then the child learns how to blend letter sounds together to make words like *cat*.

Ultimately, researchers have reported that none of these approaches is right for every child in every situation, and teachers are encouraged to try employing more than one approach. Recognizing that individual children differ in ability, interest, and learning styles is crucial to determine the type of reading method to be taught. A study conducted by researchers at New York University in 2007 revealed that all three methods work together, and the three reading approaches do not conflict but, rather, work together to determine the speed of reading.

Summary

Growth in language ability is at its fastest rate of development during the preschool years. During this period, young children accomplish difficult language tasks. They learn their native language sounds (phonetics) and successfully produce an increasing number of sounds. Language, like cognitive, social/emotional, and physical abilities, emerges in a progressive manner, in stages that are interconnected. Understanding these growth systems promotes appropriate teaching practices and behaviors.

Preschool teachers can then influence children's emergent literacy behavior through fostering the awareness of sounds in language and language-rich activities. As children are being exposed to various reading, writing, listening, and speaking experiences, they will more often come into contact with new vocabulary words.

Both parents and teachers should continue supporting and encouraging children who are bilingual with the development of their native language competencies and oral development in their second language.

Creating a book bag literacy program or lending libraries in the classroom can foster home school literacy connections and help parents understand the importance of reading at home.

Key Terms

Babbling stage   320

Basic grammar   320

Behavioral theorists   323

Bilingualism   325

Code switching   326

Egocentric speech   324

Emergent literacy   328

External speech   324

Interactionists   324

Language acquisition device (LAD)   323

Morphology   320

Nativist model   323

Overgeneralize   321

Phoneme   320

Phonics approach   337

Phonology   320

Pragmatics   322

Prosody   327

Semantics   321

Sequential bilingualism   326

Simultaneous language acquisition   325

Social interaction   324

Syntax   321

Verbal language   319

Whole-language approach   336

Whole-word approach   337

Reflection, Application, and Analysis Questions

1. Provide one example of each language rule (phonology, morphology, semantics, and syntax).

2. We learned in this chapter that bilingual children acquire their second language very similarly to how they learn their first language. Explain why.

3. How do children learn to read?

4. Find a recently published article on whole-language and phonics instruction, and write the pros and cons of each method.

Extension Activities

1. Observe a teacher interacting with a preschool child. Examine the type of speech the teacher uses and how the child interacts with him or her.

2. Learning to read and write is facilitated by social interactions. Based on your own experience, how can you support this?

Additional Readings

The following list of readings will be useful for those who are interested in keeping up with the most current developments.

Bowerman, M., & Levinson, S. C. (Eds.). (2001). *Language acquisition and conceptual development.* **Cambridge, MA: Cambridge University Press.**

This text examines the relationship between child language acquisition and cognitive development. This book brings two vital strands of investigation into close dialogue, suggesting a synthesis in which the process of language acquisition may interact with early cognitive development. It provides empirical contributions based on a variety of languages, populations, and ages, and its theoretical discussions cut across the disciplines of psychology, linguistics, and anthropology.

Dumas, L. S. (1999). Learning a second language: Exposing your child to a new world of words boosts her brainpower, vocabulary and self-esteem. *Child, 72*(74), 76–77.

This article presents brain research that indicates that learning a second language is a powerful experience that helps the brain of young children develop.

Pence, K. L., & Justice, L. M. (2008). *Language development from theory to practice.* **Upper Saddle River, NJ: Pearson Education.**

Each chapter of this text bridges language development theory and practice by providing students with a theoretical and scientific foundation to the study of language development. The authors emphasize the relevance of the material to students' current and future experience in clinical, educational, and research settings.

Whitehead, M. R. (2007). *Developing language and literacy with young children* **(3rd ed.). Thousand Oaks, CA: Sage.**

This textbook gives parents, teachers, and other professionals a confident understanding of communication and language development for children from birth to age 8 years. This book examines the range of elements that are typical of communication and language activities: thinking, feeling, imagining, talking, listening, drawing, writing, and reading.

On the Web

National Center for Family Literacy - *http://www.famlit.org/*
This website from the National Center for Family Literacy (NCFL) provides information to families by educating and improving family literacy programs. The organization's emphasis is on family literacy because families are the force of their children's education. The NCFL works with community partners to develop model programs and innovative laboratories.

Bank Street College of Education: Early Literacy Guide - *http://www.bankstreet.edu/literacyguide/early.html*
This website provides background information on literacy and early reading, sample lesson plans, activities, and information on other literacy and reading resources. It also includes information on English language learners.

Everything ESL.net - *http://www.everythingesl.net*
This website provides practical links to help educators understand the needs and challenges of English language learners. It also provides lesson plans, teaching tips, and the stages of second language acquisition.

Student Study Site

Visit **www.sagepub.com/gordonbiddle** to access several study tools including eFlashcards, web quizzes, links to SAGE journal articles, web resources, video resources, lesson plan templates, and more.

Lesson Plan:

Goodnight Moon

Subject:

Language, vocabulary, and rhyming development.

Focus and Overview:

This is a bedtime story. It describes the process of a child saying goodnight to everything around him or her.

Purpose:

A highly acclaimed bedtime story introduces rhyming to young children. This classic story is about a bunny describing his bedtime rituals of saying goodnight to several things in his bedroom.

Objectives:

- Awareness of receptive and expressive knowledge.
- Observing and exploring written language.
- Observing the environment.
- Awareness of day and night times.

Resources and Materials:

Goodnight Moon by Margaret Wise Brown.

Activities and Procedures:

1. Read the story to the infant/toddler, emphasizing and enunciating the sound of each word.

2. After reading each page, ask questions about the story and assess the child's comprehension (e.g., Where is the red balloon? What do you see in this picture? Who are you going to say goodnight to?).

3. If the infant/toddler babbles, respond to the babbling. Responding to or imitating the intonation and rhythm of adult conversation reinforces language development.

4. Hold a conversation about the things observed in the book and then ask about the familiar things or objects the child sees in his or her room. Holding a conversation between infants/toddlers and adults adds new words and provides more structure, form, and content to the child's language repertoire.

Tying It All Together:

This lesson plan promotes new vocabulary growth, visual discrimination, and understanding of story sequencing. Not only is this activity cognitively stimulating; it also encourages language development. It allows children to interact with others socially while having fun in the process of learning about things in their environment.

Visit **www.sagepub.com/gordonbiddle** to access templates of these lesson plans.

Learning the Alphabet

Subject:

Literacy and alphabet development.

Focus and Overview:

Select any alphabet book available in your class (e.g., *ABC* by Dr. Seuss).

Purpose:

Introduce the letters, capital and lowercase, and key words beginning with specific letters.

Objectives:

Introduce the letters of the alphabet, letter recognition, and letter sounds.

Resources and Materials:

- Manuscript paper.
- Pencil.

Activities and Procedures:

1. Introduce the alphabet book (show the pictures), read the book, and discuss the various letters and their sounds.

2. Assign each student a letter. If your class is large, you may place students into groups of three and assign them the same letter.

3. Have students write their name and their assigned letter on the manuscript paper.

4. Ask the students to think of other words that start with the same letter. You might need to assist them in writing those words (e.g., A = *Apple, Alligator, Astronaut*). Have them practice sounding out the first sound of the letter.

5. Integrate each letter of the alphabet with other subjects, including art, math, music, science, and outside activities.

6. Give each student an opportunity to show his or her letter and tell about other words that start with the same letter. Display all the letters alphabetically around the class.

Tying It All Together:

This lesson plan encourages children to listen carefully to each letter sound. Children can practice saying the sounds of the letters of the alphabet. They can also discriminate the sounds by listening to the phonemes of each word (e.g., *cat* and /c/ vs. *bat* and /b/).

Visit **www.sagepub.com/gordonbiddle** to access templates of these lesson plans.

Lesson Plan:

Blending and Decoding Words

Subject:

Phonemic awareness.

Focus and Overview:

Learning about blending words. Having kids blend sounds to make words is an essential step in learning to read. This lesson provides children with sounding out consonant-vowel-consonant (CVC) words.

Purpose:

Introduce children to consonant and short vowel sounds and to blend these sounds together to make words.

Objectives:

Children will be able to recognize rhymes, decode printed words, and understand that words are made up of sequences of individual sounds.

Resources and Materials:

1. A selection of second- and third-grade-level reading books.

2. Index cards.

3. Paper and pencil.

Activities and Procedures:

1. Introduce the lesson by having children select a book, based on their reading level and interest. Review the components of blending sounds, CVC, and the high-frequency words.

2. Ask them to make flash cards (from the index cards) of the high-frequency words that are presented in their reading book.

3. Have students identify and blend the compound words (words that you can combine: *base* and *ball* = *baseball*). Have them write those compound words on a piece of paper.

4. Have students identify challenging words and say the word in pieces (CVC). Have them write down the challenging word and break it down.

Tying It All Together:

As you introduce the lesson, you will need to model how to blend words, write the CVC words, and present the high-frequency words. You will need to enunciate and stretch challenging words by saying them slowly.

Visit **www.sagepub.com/gordonbiddle** to access templates of these lesson plans.

CHAPTER 13

Mathematics, Science, and Technology

This chapter will help you answer these important questions:

- How does mathematics, science, and technology understanding enhance development?

- What are some appropriate skills for children to have during the early childhood years?

- What are some appropriate knowledge areas for children during the early childhood years?

- What are some common core standards in these subject areas?

- What are appropriate knowledge and attitudes in these subject areas for early childhood teachers?

- How does a teacher plan for mathematics, science, and technology teaching?
- How does a teacher utilize computers and other technologies appropriately and effectively?
- How does a teacher educate parents about the importance of this area and assist them with teaching their children at home?
- What are some cultural and socioeconomic differences of knowledge and skills in young children?

Vignette: Ethan the Engineer?

Kohji is a 30-year-old computer engineer with a 24-month-old son named Ethan. Kohji is very determined that his son will become an engineer and asks his child's teacher what can be done at 24 months to help his child love mathematics and science and want to become an engineer and follow in his dad's footsteps. The teacher enthusiastically tells Kohji that at 24 months children have a rudimentary understanding of number sense and classification and that this can be fostered with activities involving manipulatives. The teacher also suggests that Kohji share his joy of mathematics and science with his son, by letting him see Kohji interacting happily with manipulatives, numbers, calculators, and the like. However, she also suggests that Ethan will demonstrate his own love for these areas and others naturally as he grows and that Kohji should not push Ethan "too hard."

Kohji goes home and ponders how to demonstrate number sense and classification with manipulatives and make it fun. He buys books that classify objects by function, color, and size. He reads those books to his son Ethan. He also buys three boxes of crayons to see if Ethan can tell which three crayons are green, blue, brown, purple, and other colors. He makes small piles of crayons and large piles of crayons and labels them. Then he asks his son Ethan to point to the small pile and the large pile. He also begins putting Ethan on his lap when he creates and works with spreadsheets or calculates bills.

Ethan seems to thoroughly enjoy interacting with mathematics and science concepts with his father. He loves listening to the sound of his father's voice, sitting on his father's lap, and seeing his father smile. That love and enjoyment transfers to the concepts of number sense and classification, making Kohji's goal reachable. If this love of mathematical and scientific concepts is nurtured continually, Ethan just might become an engineer!

C hildren are excited to learn most concepts during the early years if taught concretely and with enthusiasm. This love of learning extends to mathematical, scientific, and technology concepts, as long as that material is presented in the same manner. However, when a young child's teacher emphasizes memorization, it can lead to having a bad attitude concerning these concepts and subject areas. Professional early childhood teachers focus on letting the young child play, explore, or question. Early childhood education teachers, from infant teachers to third-grade teachers, can instill a yearning for mathematical, scientific, and technology concepts if they act as professionals. This may require early childhood teachers to overcome their own phobias and/or negative attitudes toward these concepts. It may also require teachers to improve their mathematical, scientific, and technology knowledge and skills. However, as the field of early childhood education professionalizes, teachers' professionalism has to increase, too. Hopefully, this chapter leaves you excited about mathematics, science, and technology.

The opening vignette demonstrates just how early children have rudimentary understanding of mathematical and scientific concepts. It also shows that understanding can be nurtured and fostered. What can also be gleaned from the vignette is the relationship between this domain and the social/emotional and language domains. Mathematical, scientific, and technological reasoning are impacted by and, in turn, impact social/emotional and linguistic interactions, knowledge, and skills. Therefore, these domains are best taught in an integrated fashion. Mathematics, science, and technology are related to other developmental areas and contribute to the development of the whole child.

Professional early childhood educators will address and include mathematics, science, and technology in the early childhood education experiences they create for their young students. They will be aware that young children are quite capable, and that their job is to maximize all of the children's capabilities. However, maximizing children's capabilities is currently not always accomplished (National Research Council, 2001a, 2001b), especially in the area of mathematics, science, and technology concepts. A professional also must have the right attitude toward and understanding of these concepts. This reality is becoming more and more apparent (Saracho & Spodek, 2009) and is recognized by the National Association for the Education of Young Children (NAEYC). Early childhood teachers need knowledge, understanding, and the right attitudes in regard to these subject areas in order to maximize young students' learning. Therefore, a chapter on mathematics, science, and technology is included in this textbook, because these subjects are related to and enhance all areas of development.

HOW MATH, SCIENCE, AND TECHNOLOGY UNDERSTANDING ENHANCES DEVELOPMENT

Constructivism, being active in creating people's understanding of the world around them, is the main theory that gives foundational support to math and science understanding. This theory, constructivism, is created like most theories by scientific reasoning (see Chapter 4). The scientific process consists of the steps used by scientists to create and further knowledge and is also mentioned in Chapter 3. Constructivism and the scientific process, especially constructivism, are the basis of most learning during early childhood and are particularly important for math, science, and technology.

The main champions of constructivism are Piaget (1950) and Vygotsky (1978), with Vygotsky (1978) emphasizing the social aspects of constructivism. Piaget (1950) believed that children construct their knowledge of the world through their actions and their senses. In other words, what children do to objects and people in their world and what information they take in through their senses creates their knowledge and understanding of the world. Vygotsky (1978) added the social aspect of constructivism to his theory. He believed that knowledge is constructed by groups and cultures collectively. Therefore, one child's knowledge of the world is influenced by the group or culture to which the child belongs and in which he or she interacts. Each group or culture has its own tools, artifacts, values, and reasoning process. Children from each group or culture value and reason as their group or culture does. Children from one group or culture see the world differently than children from another group or culture. With this reality, more objectivity is needed when making theories and creating facts.

The scientific process came into being as a matter of adding more objectivity to theoretical, intellectual, and philosophical pursuits. The steps of the process allow theorists to be more certain about the facts they create and obtain. The main steps of the scientific process are to first complete an informal observation, then formulate a question (hypothesis) or problem that flows from the initial observation, then gather data formally, next analyze the data, and last formulate facts and share the facts with others. Other slight variations to the scientific process exist. For instance, not all variations begin with informal observations, and some variations place data collection before hypothesis generation. Moreover, other versions of the scientific process conclude with revising the initial observation or theory. Nevertheless, this scientific process is followed in general by professional teachers in the field of early childhood education as they generate theoretical facts. Early childhood teachers go through this process daily as they observe and teach young students.

Wolfinger (1994) also believes that there is a certain approach that professionals take when employing the scientific method. This approach includes having objectivity, a willingness to suspend judgment, skepticism, respect for the environment, and a positive approach to failure. Early childhood education teachers can impart this information and professional approach to the young elementary school children they teach during lessons and activities on the scientific method.

Coming to understand the world, constructivism, and generating theoretical facts appropriately, or the scientific process, is what undergirds mathematical and scientific reasoning. However, these two concepts (constructivisim and the scientific process) truly support all learning and reasoning. Therefore, mathematical and scientific reasoning underlie all of early development. For instance, in the scenario above as Ethan learns about math, science, and technology from his father, he also enhances his language and social/emotional development. Ethan is learning the definition and use of terms. Ethan is also learning how to interact with others. Development in the domain of mathematics and science is integrated with development in other early childhood domains. As children learn number sense, they learn when they are full (which relates to a certain amount) or when someone has more or less of a substance. As children learn to classify, they learn which objects are toys and which are not. The skill of classification also teaches them which utensil goes in the bathroom (toothbrush) and which in the kitchen (fork or spoon). Truly, mathematics, science, and technology concepts are integrated with and enhance all early childhood development.

Given that young children have an ability to comprehend mathematical, scientific, and technological concepts and that this understanding enhances development, what skills are appropriate for them to learn and at what age? What does an average 18-month-old or 3-year-old know about science, math, and technology? Is it really appropriate for Ethan in our vignette to have number sense and classification skills?

First, it is important to remember that early exposure to technology and media, if not done in a developmentally appropriate manner, may not be helpful for skill development (American Academy of Pediatrics, 2009). Even educational videos and TV programs do not seem to enhance skill development if exposure happens before age 2 years (American Academy of Pediatrics, 2009). Indeed, once young children begin watching television, videos, and other media, teachers and parents should monitor and limit their viewing. Some fast-paced cartoons are actually harmful for developing cognitive skills (American Academy of Pediatrics, 2011). Moreover, television and media exposure should be limited to only two hours a day (American Academy of Pediatrics, 2010). Instead, children should be entertaining themselves the majority of the time with creative and social pursuits that do not involve media and television. Most important, when considering mathematics, science, and technology, teachers and parents need to know when to expect certain skills to develop and how to foster those skills.

WHAT ARE SOME APPROPRIATE SKILLS?

Some researchers have found very basic understanding of **number sense** as early as 5 months old (Starkey & Cooper, 1980; Starkey, Spelke, & Gelman, 1990). Number sense is a basic understanding of number or quantity. This basic understanding is communicated with basic language in a consistent fashion around 18 to 24 months of age, making this skill easier to see, assess, and foster (Baroody, 2004; Fuson, 1988; Gelman & Gallistel, 1978). Therefore, Ethan's teacher is correct in his advice, and Ethan's father, Kohji, is appropriate in fostering Ethan's number sense.

Classification is grouping objects and people based on characteristics (see Chapter 4). This begins to emerge as young as 3 months (Barrera & Maurer, 1981; Legerstee, 1997). Therefore, Kohji may cultivate and enhance this ever-important skill in his son Ethan with the manipulatives and other concrete objects. As with other skills and abilities that infants acquire, the classification skill becomes more accurate and complex as children develop. As young children age, they learn to classify by more complex and abstract properties, such as materials or color shades (National Council of Teachers of Mathematics [NCTM], 2000). Classification is an important skill because it not only underlies mathematics and science, but is related to other important domains in a young child's life. Take, for instance, language and social development; learning grammar is aided by classification as is learning to behave appropriately in the social realm. The integrated nature of the classification skill is illustrated by Figure 13.1.

Seriation is putting items in order by weight, amount, size, or other related characteristic and going from smallest amount to largest amount or vice versa. Seriation is a type of patterning that appears in basic form early but really develops during the preschool and early elementary years (Flavell, 1963; Klein & Starkey, 2004; Starkey, Klein, & Wakeley, 2004). It is important for early childhood educators to create seriated patterns for young children as examples and then give the young children opportunities to seriate some objects by themselves. Repeated exposure, experience, and practice seem to be the key for this skill.

Patterning is broader than seriation and means putting objects, people, or sensations in some sort of repeated order. Even sounds and movements can be put into a pattern. Patterning starts before age 2 years, but can be seen more readily during the preschool years, ages 3 to 5, and keeps on developing in complexity, detail, and accuracy as young children develop (Flavell, 1963; Klein & Starkey, 2004; Starkey et al., 2004). Patterns are ever present in the lives of young children. Although this skill is important for mathematics and science understanding, it is also integrated into other domains and areas of a child's life, such as physical/motor development with dancing and other movement. Patterns and mathematics and art are related. The same basic patterns that underlie mathematics also underlie visual and performing arts. Early childhood teachers can foster patterning skills with music. For instance, they can clap a rhythmic pattern and have the young students repeat the same pattern.

Figure 13.1	The Integrated Nature of Classification

SUBJECT MATTER	SCIENCE	MATHEMATICS	MUSIC/ MOVEMENT	LANGUAGE ARTS	SOCIAL STUDIES	ART
Activities	• Sorting objects • Categorizing objects	• Sorting objects	• Classifying instruments • Identifying movements	• Explaining • Reading	• Collecting props	• Selecting and organizing • Drawing

Source: Adapted from Charlesworth, R. & Lind, K.K. (2003).

Number concepts are properties and functions of numbers. In general, there are two number concepts, counting and more complex arithmetic, that categorize skills in young children. Counting ability appears around age 2½ or 3 years. This ability is usually enhanced by teachers and parents alike through practice with books, songs such as "Three Little Ducks," and everyday routines such as setting the table for dinner or folding laundry. It is very important when learning to count that children develop **one-to-one correspondence**. One-to-one correspondence is the awareness and knowledge that each individual number in a counting sequence refers to one object.

Arithmetic usually happens in the early elementary school years, but may occur earlier. **Arithmetic** is understanding how numbers function. In other words, arithmetic is addition, subtraction, multiplication, and division. Number

Numerical patterns can be found in artistic expression.

concepts are quite abstract, and young children learn best with the use of contextualized learning and concrete objects. Going back to our vignette, Kohji has the right idea with books, crayons, and real-world spreadsheets. These same concrete objects can be used in the early childhood classroom.

Measurement is calculating the quantity or amount of something. Young children can measure length, height, weight, volume, mass, or area. Obviously, measurement ability is better as children develop more. At approximately 3 years of age, children can make general comparisons by saying that something is bigger or heavier, and so on. They can also order three objects by size (Clements, 2004a). By age 5 years, children understand that measurement involves the reoccurrence of equal-size units (Clements, 2004a). Early elementary-age children can understand standardized measurement units such as inches, feet, ounces, and pounds. Children can understand and enjoy measurement if taught with activities that are concrete and relate to their lives. Counting teaspoons of chocolate syrup while putting them into a glass of milk or counting how many feet deep is the swimming pool is the type of activity that makes measurement enjoyable and fun. The swimming pool can be visited as a class field trip, or this activity can be substituted with measuring each child's height or arm length.

Geometry is the study of the properties and relationships of two- and three-dimensional shapes. This definition may make it seem that geometry is too advanced for young children. However, the children can learn the basics of geometry at young ages, as their world is filled with interesting shapes. Once children begin to recognize shapes, around age 3 years or younger, they have rudimentary geometrical knowledge. Around the age of 5 or 6 years, children can use shapes to create other objects and combine shapes to make other shapes or objects (Clements, 2004a). Preschool-age children can also rotate shapes in space or recognize shapes that have been rotated (Clements, 2004a). Early elementary students can understand three-dimensional shapes, and they also understand that shapes come in a number of varieties (see Figure 13.2). Additionally, early elementary students can understand more complex relationships among shapes. For instance, early elementary students can understand how triangles can fit inside other shapes such as squares, rectangles, or octagons. Teaching these concepts with manipulatives such as blocks really helps young children grasp geometric concepts and reasoning. Teachers can foster these skills and concepts with simple shape puzzles or more complex puzzles where one shape goes into another shape.

Figure 13.2   **Triangles of Different Sizes**

In learning about the relationships of shapes, children need a basic understanding of space (NCTM, 2000; Smith, 2001). Coming to understand space means understanding distance, location, direction, and orientation (Clements, 1999). Understanding these concepts comes with maturation and experience. Therefore, it is important to give children experience with geometric concepts, shapes, and space concepts. Experience with actual physical movement in space is also important to learning these concepts, which is another reason why mathematics and science concepts are important and an example of how these concepts enhance a young child's development. Experience with spatial language is also important. It helps children if teachers and parents use words such as *up, under,* and *around.* Using these types of space words, in context with concrete examples, helps children understand geometric concepts.

Language and Concept Formation

Calendar time presents an opportunity for learning mathematics through everyday occurrences.

Language is important for communicating an understanding of concepts, including mathematics and science concepts. Therefore, it is important when teaching mathematics and science concepts to young children to use the proper language. An example of this is found in the previous geometry section. However, teaching and giving children the appropriate language is important for teachers and parents to do for all mathematics and science concepts. For number sense, counting in the correct sequence or pattern is important. With classification, teachers and parents can introduce color names and words such as *hard* and *soft.* In general, terms such as *cylinder, long, round,* and *far* can be spoken and repeated in the context of real-world experiences in order to teach young children the language of mathematics and science.

We have addressed some skills that young children can develop in the early years, but what about mathematical and scientific knowledge? What domains can children learn about in the early years? Of course, there are arithmetic, algebra, and geometry. Do other domains that children can learn about exist? The correct answer may not be obvious, but yes, children can learn about other domains such as physical science, space science, and environmental science. Physical health and nutrition are also domains about which young children can learn. The health and nutrition domain will be explored extensively in Chapter 14 but will also be mentioned briefly in this chapter.

WHAT ARE SOME APPROPRIATE KNOWLEDGE AREAS?

Fractions

Young children have an intuitive sense of parts and wholes and really come to understand fractions around second and third grade. **Fractions** are the numeric representations of part and whole relationships, especially equal parts. At first, children can be exposed to whole numbers, and then they can group pieces of the whole numbers into patterns. This happens around age 3 years (Payne, Towsley, & Huinker, 1990). Eventually, with enough practice, young children come to understand fractions such as one half, one third, and one fourth. Again, this skill comes to young children in second and third grade, and early childhood teachers cannot "push" the skill on young children any earlier (NCTM, 2000). As children become more familiar with fractions, they begin using vocabulary associated with fractions with more accuracy. Words such as *more, less,* and *same* and later *half, third,* and *fourth* become part of a young child's vocabulary.

Fractions relate to many situations in daily living, even lunch, in the early childhood classroom. Creative early childhood teachers find ways to introduce math concepts throughout the day.

In order to teach young children about fractions, early childhood teachers can have fun and use their imaginations. For instance, children can make patterns with colored marbles or cardboard circles. An example is a pattern of three blue marbles and two red marbles. In this example, three fifths of the marbles are blue, and two fifths of the marbles are red. In fact, mathematical art is a field of mathematics (Kenney & Bezuszka, 2007). In mathematical art, teachers are encouraged to have their students create art with number patterns. This type of fun activity strengthens knowledge about number patterns and geometry. The patterns can be created by hand or with technology aids (Kenney & Bezuszka, 2007). Advanced patterns can be used with older children, but simple patterns can be used with early elementary and preschool children.

Additionally, mathematics can be made fun and meaningful by using language and music. Mathematical language associated with fractions can be introduced with books and manipulative activities. Music, movement, and art can also be incorporated into mathematical and science lessons that focus on fractions. For instance, students can learn simple music rhythms by clapping their hands. They can clap to half notes and quarter notes and focus on the fractional relationship between those two types of notes.

Promoting Optimal Development

Characteristics of an Effective Science Program

Young children are capable of learning science if it is taught concretely with enthusiasm. Even in early childhood, children are capable of grasping these concepts, and in order to assist them in developing optimally, there are some ideas and procedures to keep in mind when presenting science to young children. Think back to or reread NAEYC Developmentally Appropriate Principle 5 at the beginning of this chapter. It states that early experiences are profound and that there are optimal times for the development of certain concepts Therefore, professional early childhood teachers

- build on children's prior experiences, backgrounds, and early theories (children have their own basic theories of these subject matter areas);

- draw on children's curiosity, while encouraging them to pursue their own questions and develop their own ideas;

- engage children in in-depth exploration of a topic over time in a carefully prepared environment;

- encourage children to reflect on, represent, and document their experiences, and to share and discuss their ideas with others;

- embed science in children's work and play;

- integrate science with other domains; and

- provide access to science experiences for all children.

Source: National Academy of Sciences and Karen Worth (2009).

Data Collection

Data collection is a fundamental step in the scientific method where young children systematically record their numeric or verbal observations. Around 3½ to 4 years of age, children can begin systematic data collection (Clements, 2004b). They can classify, work with patterns, and measure (Clements, 2004b; Klein & Starkey, 2004). They can also detect the characteristics of objects (Clements, 2004b). Repeated exposure to these types of experiences in a fun manner with manipulatives and other concrete objects, while recording the data, helps young children improve in this important area of knowledge. For instance, children can measure and record the length of each person's hair. They can also record the frequency with which each child sharpens a pencil or raises his or her hand. These experiences that are relevant and related to everyday life help make math and science fun.

Life Science

Life science is the study of living beings and their environments and life cycles. Basic life science concepts can be mastered by young children in the early elementary grades. To begin, children need to understand the difference between living and nonliving things. For instance, plants and kitty cats are alive, but robots and cars are not. Children need repeated exposure and comparisons to nonliving and living things to understand their characteristics and needs. Young children can also understand that living things have different structures and functions. Additionally, they come to understand in early elementary grades that living things have different journeys and, therefore, come to live, reproduce, and die at different rates and under different circumstances. The National Science Education Standards (National Research Council, 1996) can be a guide to teachers of young children about when to introduce such concepts.

Physical Science

In the early elementary years, the basic physical sciences are physics and chemistry. **Physics** is the study of matter and energy and comes to mind frequently when thinking of physical sciences. **Chemistry**, the science of substances and their combinations, is also a basic physical science that can be taught in early elementary grades. In the early years, teachers of young elementary children can focus on energy and the characteristics and movement of objects and substances (National Research Council, 1996). Again, it is helpful to make the learning of physical science fun and to integrate it with other subject areas such as language, art, and music. Activities that involve bubbles, wind, water, and cooking can focus on physics and chemistry. For instance, students can record how fast liquid water travels and compare it with how fast frozen water (ice) travels.

Earth and Space Science

Children in early elementary grades are capable of learning about the earth and space. This science is the study of earth and space substances and properties. In the early elementary grades, students may learn about various substances concerning space and science. These substances include water, soil, rocks, and minerals. As with all scientific inquiries, children begin with early steps of the scientific method: observe, describe, and record. Helping children see and understand the natural changes that occur with earth and space substances is the basis of this science, and this learning can happen in early elementary grades. Next children can begin grouping these substances based on certain properties. As always, it is important to integrate these concepts into other curricular areas and make the learning applicable to life and fun (National Research Council, 1996).

Earth and space science are fascinating areas of study for young children and are made concrete by studying the Earth's solar system.

Environmental Science

In the early years, **environmental science** focuses on making children aware of their world, introducing basic concepts, and teaching young children about actions to take to protect the environment. The 1996 National Science Education Standards separate environmental science from other earth and space sciences. In environmental science, children learn about how population, resources, science and technology, and environmental changes impact their own life. More practical examples of earth science topics are water, garbage, and plants. Teaching children how the elements of these topics influence human beings and how human beings influence them in return is early elementary environmental science.

Health and Nutrition

Health and nutrition are two of the main foci of Chapter 14 but are mentioned briefly here as well. Health and nutrition are actually scientific topics (National Science Education Standards, 1996). Since they impact our everyday lives so fundamentally, we do not think of them in that way. Teachers can help young children understand the basics of nutrition, hygiene habits, and exercise. These teachers can also help young children develop appropriate habits. Again, these science lessons can be integrated with the rest of the curriculum and made to be fun. For instance, students can bring in vegetables from home and make a salad. Then the teacher can read a book about how vegetables grow, and children can write about which vegetable is their favorite.

The beginning sections of this chapter focus on mathematics and science concepts. The next section of the chapter focuses on issues surrounding the teaching of mathematics, science, and technology in the early years. These issues include common core standards, teacher attitudes, planning for teaching, relating to and teaching ethnic minority and other populations, and educating and assisting parents. A professional early childhood education teacher will address these issues with seriousness and enthusiasm. Let us explore these issues now, beginning with common core standards.

WHAT ARE COMMON CORE STANDARDS?

Common core standards have been developed for kindergarten through third grade and beyond in the area of mathematics (National Governors Association Center for Best Practices & Council of Chief State School Officers, 2010). Frameworks for common core standards have been developed for science and technology education for the same age-groups. The standards are being promoted by the National Academy of Sciences and other national professional organizations. These standards and frameworks state what skills and knowledge children should have in kindergarten to third grade and beyond. It is important for teachers of young children to be familiar with these standards.

In kindergarten mathematics, some of the skills students are expected to master include comparing numbers and analyzing shapes. Students are also expected to be able to classify objects and compare measurable characteristics of objects. In first grade, some of the skills students should acquire include telling and writing time, as well as adding and subtracting within the number 20. By the end of second grade, students should understand place value, understand the equal groups of objects that are the basis of multiplying, and work with money. There are other skills, of course, that students acquire in second grade. By the end of third grade, students should multiply and divide within the number 100, understand fractions, and solve problems with four steps, among other skills.

Along with the skills mastered at each grade level come standards for mathematical practice. These practice standards are also important for teachers of young children. The practice standards guide teachers in creating lesson plans and actually teaching the appropriate and standard skills, behaviors, and attitudes to young children. These eight practice standards provide teachers with goals, and are as follows:

1. Make sense of problems and persevere in solving them.

2. Reason abstractly and quantitatively.

3. Construct viable arguments and critique the reasoning of others.

4. Model with mathematics.

5. Use appropriate tools strategically.

6. Attend to precision.

7. Look for and make use of structure.

8. Look for and express regularity in repeated reasoning.

Although common core standards do not exist in the areas of science and technology, a framework for kindergarten to third grade and beyond does exist. This framework, which will be developed into common core standards in the future, has the following three dimensions:

1. Scientific and engineering practices.

2. Crosscutting concepts.

3. Disciplinary core ideas in science.

The subelements of these dimensions include developing and using models, patterns, and heredity (National Academy of Sciences, 2011, 2012).

Since common core standards already exist or are being developed, the teachers of young children must teach these concepts. Having the appropriate knowledge helps, but teachers need the right attitudes when teaching mathematics, science, and technology. The next section of this chapter addresses teacher attitudes toward these subjects.

WHAT ARE APPROPRIATE KNOWLEDGE AND ATTITUDES FOR EARLY CHILDHOOD TEACHERS?

More often than not, early childhood educators do not have knowledge of or attitudes toward mathematics and science that facilitate teaching these concepts effectively (Copley, 2004; Philippou & Christou, 1998). This knowledge and these attitudinal deficits are similar for inservice and preservice teachers alike (Zacharos, Koliopoulos, Dokimaki, & Kassoumi, 2007). This reality leads to ineffective teaching of these concepts in the early years (Thompson, 1984; Zacharos et al., 2007). Additionally, the teachers' attitudes toward mathematics and science may impact their students' attitudes (Zacharos et al., 2007). Some teachers do not think that teaching mathematics and science is even appropriate during the early years (Zacharos et al., 2007). These attitudes and beliefs are extremely hard to change (Pajares, 1992). However, Zacharos and others (2007) have these suggestions for changing these maladaptive attitudes: (a) help early childhood educators see the theories and the relationship between those theories and teaching approaches; (b) focus on the social aspects of creating scientific knowledge; (c) link professional knowledge and skills of mathematics and science with cultural elements of education; (d) teach early childhood educators about mathematics and science in an interactive cooperative manner; and (e) acknowledge that real-life experiences teaching these concepts will help early childhood educators solidify their knowledge and come to understand the interrelatedness of these concepts to other early childhood domains.

Burns (1992) really emphasizes that teachers and students need to know why they are using the rules and procedures of mathematics. Teaching mathematical reasoning or the "why" of mathematics is hard to accomplish and assess. However, knowing how to reason in mathematics helps you know how to apply the knowledge gained in one task to another task. This transfer of training is particularly important. Early childhood teachers of mathematics and science need to have reasoning skills and abilities so that they may impart these skills and abilities to the young children that they teach. And, sometimes, these same teachers may need to explain the reasoning to the parents of the children they teach.

HOW TO UTILIZE COMPUTERS AND OTHER TECHNOLOGIES APPROPRIATELY AND EFFECTIVELY

The appropriate use of computers and other technologies in early childhood education is a topic that garners much discussion. However, the NAEYC accepts technology use if done in a developmentally appropriate fashion, and the use of computers and other technologies is obtaining more mainstream acceptance among educators of young children (Moomaw & Davis, 2010; NAEYC, 2009b). Some of the keys to successful use of and teaching about and with technology are integrating the skills and concepts into other content and developmental areas and allowing children to utilize as many senses as possible to explore. Other important keys are considering the early childhood teacher's beliefs, attitudes, and practices; considering the interactive nature of the technology; and evaluating and using technology guided by research-based recommendations (Hillman & Marshall, 2009; Ihmeidah, 2010; Moomaw & Davis, 2010; Zucker, Moody, & McKenna, 2009).

Teachers' attitudes, beliefs, and practices may be the most important factors that influence young children's experiences with technology. These attitudes, beliefs, and practices are formed before and during teacher training and can last a long time without any change despite professional development opportunities (Henning, Peterson, & King, 2011; Liu, 2011; O'Brien, 2010). Even when teachers believe that mathematics, science, technology, and their requisite standards are viable, the degree to which the teachers implement the standards and teach these subjects varies widely by teacher and by grade level (Klieger & Yakobovitch, 2011).

Technology can be used successfully with young children from 3 to 8 years of age. Technology can even be used as a teaching aid with children who have special needs. A variety of technologies can be used, from computers, to tablets, to e-books, to assistive technologies. Tablets have successfully been

Consider This Teaching How and Why in Math

"Three plus three is six!" "Four plus four is eight!" chanted the children in Mrs. Simpson's class. Out of the corner of her eye she spotted Teddy's hand waving back and forth. "Yes, Teddy?" she asked. "Why is three plus three six? I think three plus three is eight!" Teddy responded. This caught Mrs. Simpson off guard. The question rang again in her head: "Why does three plus three equal six?" Quickly she crossed the room and grabbed her box of colored

marbles. Soon she began sorting and counting all of the marbles—first finding three green marbles, then adding three additional green marbles, and finally counting with Teddy and the class, "One, two, three, four, five, six!"

In your early mathematics courses, were you taught the "how" and "why" of mathematical formulas? If a student asked you how to multiply, how would you explain?

BEST

Practices Roles of an Effective Teacher

Effective early childhood teachers must not only have the right attitude; they must behave in a certain manner and play a certain role. When it comes to mathematics and science, this role is quite important.

Effective teachers

- create a physical, social, and emotional environment that supports inquiry;

- observe children and act on those observations;
- acknowledge children's work;
- extend children's experiences, which are based on their work;
- lead activities with children that extend their thinking; and
- deepen children's understanding through discussion, questions, representation, and documentation.

Source: National Academy of Sciences and Karen Worth (2009).

used to teach young children aged 3 to 6 years some technical drawing skills. The tablets increased children's interest in drawing, and their engagement with the technology increased with the age of the children (Couse & Chen, 2010). Research and experience indicate that technology can aid in enthusiasm for learning, particularly in mathematics and science curricula (Thomas, Barab, & Tuzun, 2009). Additionally, the use of technology can actually improve the learning of concepts and skills if done appropriately and with enhancing teaching strategies such as scaffolding (see Chapters 4 and 9), giving specific feedback, and collaborative learning (Roschelle et al., 2009). This early foundation also aids in the learning of more complex concepts and skills in the later elementary school years when children learn subjects such as astronomy and general critical thinking (Suh, 2010; Sun, Lin, & Yu, 2008).

Young children with special needs can utilize and benefit from technology in their classroom as well. Technology can help children who are deaf learn sign language (Snoddon, 2010). In addition, research demonstrates that technology can help young children with special needs spend more time on task, submit more assignments, and work more independently, without asking the teacher as many questions (Poel, 2010). This is because the technology helps the children to be more independent learners. Moreover, technology can be used successfully to assist and aid children with special needs such as muscular dystrophy (Heller, Mezei, & Avant, 2009). Assistive technology is discussed in depth in Chapter 7 of this textbook.

HOW TO MAKE CONNECTIONS BY EDUCATING AND ASSISTING PARENTS

Parents are a child's first and primary teachers for most of the early years. It is important for early childhood educators to make connections and partnerships with the parents in teaching young children. This is especially true for mathematics, science, and technology concepts and skills.

Just as some early childhood educators have had negative and ineffective prior experiences with mathematics and science, some parents have had those same experiences. So what can an early childhood educator do? The authors of this textbook make the following suggestions: (a) Increase your own knowledge of this area and reflect on your own attitude; (b) help the parents of your children do the

When it comes to learning in mathematics and science, parents are truly role models for their children and partners with their children's teachers.

same; (c) help parents see how mathematics, science, and technology concepts are related to other early childhood domains and subject areas; (d) help parents see how their children have the basic skills necessary to understand these concepts at young ages; (e) help parents see how mathematics, science, and technology concepts relate to everyday life; (f) emphasize to the parents the importance of their role as teachers and role models; and (g) emphasize to the parents the importance of their role as organizers, monitors, and assistors with home learning experiences and homework from you, the teacher. Parents truly are their child's first teachers.

Returning to our opening vignette, Kohji is already excited about teaching his child math and science concepts. However, not all parents have this enthusiasm, and their role in assisting in their child's learning is crucial. In this case, the teacher's knowledge, attitude, and behavior are crucial. Early childhood teachers must professionally relay to parents their important role in assisting and monitoring their children's learning. This can be done through communicating with the parents formally, as in newsletters, or informally, as during pickup time. Kohji is on his way, but he may lose his enthusiasm if he finds opposition from other parents or Ethan's teachers. Both teachers and parents play separate, but significant, roles in children's learning.

HOW TO ADDRESS CULTURAL AND SOCIOECONOMIC DIFFERENCES IN MATHEMATICAL AND SCIENTIFIC KNOWLEDGE AND SKILLS

For two decades or more, mathematics and science educators have been interested in the different skills and abilities of different cultures and socioeconomic groups (Saxe, 1981, 1991; Ma, 2003a, 2003b). Investigations of this phenomenon have discovered that processes of symbol organization vary across cultural and socioeconomic groups. For instance, not all numeric systems are based on sets of 10 as in the United States (Saxe, 1981). These researchers have also come to realize, through the theorizing of Vygotsky (see Chapter 4) and subsequent research, that mathematical and scientific understandings are socially organized and socially constructed (Saxe, 1981, 1991). However, some universals do still exist such as the importance of Piaget's concepts (see Chapter 4) and the fact that all children seem to have a notation system for numbers before they can conserve numbers (Saxe, 1981, 1991). Social organization and construction, though, lead to achievement gaps in these subject areas, especially in math. For instance, research shows that 5-year-olds from China score higher on tests of early numeracy than 5-year-olds from Finland and England. Moreover, the 5-year-olds from Finland score slightly higher than those from England (Aunio, Aubrey, Godfrey, Pan, & Liu, 2008). Kindergarten children in the United States also show differences (Coley, 2002). Socioeconomic status is the biggest discriminate when considering mathematics skills and knowledge, with students from higher-income families in the United States scoring better than students from lower-income families. Ethnic differences in mathematics skills and knowledge are very slight, with Asian Americans and European Americans scoring higher than African Americans and Hispanic Americans. These slight differences are mostly due to the higher numbers of African Americans and Hispanic Americans living in poverty (Coley, 2002).

However, early childhood teachers can ameliorate these differences with good instruction. It is important to note that interventions and teaching strategies exist that can virtually equalize the knowledge and skills of the various cultural and socioeconomic groups. So, what does this mean for the early childhood education teacher? The authors of this text have the following comments and suggestions. First, remember how important the early years are for laying a foundation for learning and enjoying mathematics and science for a lifetime. Second, remember it is important to assess where the student is at the beginning, to find the student's baseline, and to improve on the student's knowledge and skills. Third, remember to connect the student's in-class learning to learning in the real world. Fourth, remember that not all students in your class have the same culture or the same previous experience with mathematics and science. Fifth, remember to involve the student's parents and other family members in the learning of mathematics and science, when appropriate, in a respectful manner. All adults in the child's life work on the same team.

HOW TO PLAN FOR TEACHING MATHEMATICS, SCIENCE, AND TECHNOLOGY EDUCATION

The early childhood educator plans for teaching these concepts by understanding them and having the appropriate outlook (Burns, 1992; National Research Council, 2001a, 2001b). It is important to know the range of when certain abilities come into existence. Then the lessons should include the appropriate tools, such as concrete objects or assistive technologies. Next, the teaching should be presented with enthusiasm and accuracy. This is much the same as planning for teaching in all early childhood areas.

NAEYC Recommendations When Planning for Mathematics in the Early Childhood Curriculum

The NAEYC has some strong suggestions for developmentally appropriate planning in early childhood classrooms for mathematics. These include recognizing that children enjoy making sense of their experiences with mathematics, building on children's intuitive thoughts, and supplying accurate mathematical knowledge, formulas, and language. The NAEYC also suggests promoting reasoning and problem solving in spontaneous "teachable moments" (see Chapter 11) and in planned activities. They also suggest it is most optimal that topics be taught in the order suggested by research and that all major content areas be addressed (NAEYC, 2009).

NAEYC and Planning for Science in the Early Childhood Curriculum

The NAEYC has basically one guiding principle for planning science curricular experiences for young children. This principle has a few segments. NAEYC suggests that early childhood teachers when planning lessons for science recognize young children's curiosity, focus on science in everyday life, and give children fun experiences that teach key concepts and skills in the realm of science.

NAEYC and Planning for Technology in the Early Childhood Curriculum

The NAEYC has three main axioms when it comes to planning for technology use in early childhood programs. First, the organization says to thoughtfully use technology as a tool to aid children and allow them to learn at their own pace. Second, it says to place technology in the room in order to enhance interaction, talking, cooperating, and helping. Allow children to explore what is possible. Third, the organization says to have enough equipment for deep engagement by both boys and girls (NAEYC, 2009b).

Researchers and practitioners both have been concerned for decades about what software is developmentally appropriate for young children (Shade, 1994). As mentioned previously, it can be harmful, and exposure to it for young children should be limited and monitored. However, how does a teacher or parent know what software is developmentally appropriate? A software evaluation form does exist, and it contains the following criteria:

1. Is it age appropriate?
2. Does the child have control?
3. Are instructions clear?
4. Does complexity increase?
5. Can the child do it independently?
6. Does the process engage children?
7. Does the software model the real world?
8. Are the technical features appropriate?
9. Are there object transformations?
10. Can children test alternative choices?
11. Is diversity represented?

Haugland (2012) has created criteria for assessing software and websites, too. Her criteria are similar, but she also includes nonviolence as a criterion. With checklists and rating scales such as these, parents and teachers have to use their own judgment and be vigilant.

The NAEYC and Fred Rogers Center released a position statement on technology and interactive media in January 2012. It contains a general position, 16 principles, and six recommendations. In the statement, both organizations acknowledge that technology and interactive media (software and websites) can be used intentionally and developmentally appropriately to promote learning and development in young children. The keys really are being intentional and developmentally appropriate. The recommendations include providing balance and leadership when working with interactive technology and media. Indeed, all teachers and parents of young children should provide balance and leadership when it comes to the learning and development and education of the young children they impact.

Summary

Mathematics, science, and technology are important domains of early childhood education that are related to other areas of development, such as language and the arts. It is important for early childhood educators to nurture mathematics, science, and technology learning with enthusiasm. Current research shows that young children have a rudimentary grasp of mathematics, science, and technology concepts and are quite capable of learning more as they grow and develop.

Some of the same theoretical underpinnings of mathematics and science, such as constructivism and the scientific method, underlie other developmental areas such as language and social relationships. Therefore, it is best to teach mathematics, science, and technology in an integrated fashion and to relate the teaching of the concepts to real-life experiences. Some of the skills children learn come early, such as classification. Other skills come later, such as geometry and fractions. When teaching young children these concepts, it is important to use proper terms and language.

There are other concerns to consider when teaching mathematics and science to young children. For instance, how does one plan, and what is developmentally appropriate? These are questions a professional early childhood educator will ask. Professional early childhood educators will have the appropriate knowledge, skills, and attitudes themselves. They will understand the "why" and know how to reason with and apply these concepts to new situations. Professional early childhood educators will impart the joy and value of mathematics and science to the parents of the children they teach in a respectful manner. They will also know how to teach these concepts to children from various cultural and socioeconomic backgrounds. Above all, they will be enthusiastic and professional while teaching these concepts to young children.

Key Terms

Arithmetic 349

Chemistry 353

Constructivism 346

Data collection 352

Environmental science 353

Fractions 351

Geometry 349

Life science 352

Measurement 349

Number concepts 349

Number sense 348

One-to-one correspondence 349

Patterning 348

Physics 353

Seriation 348

Reflection, Application, and Analysis Questions

1. Name and describe three important lessons about teaching mathematics and science that can be learned from ethnic minority cultures or cultures in other countries.

2. What is the difference between optimizing a young child's learning in mathematics, science, and technology and "pushing" a young child? How will children act if they are learning optimally, and how will they act if being pushed? What are the results of optimal learning, and what are the results of pushing? Name and describe at least four differences.

3. Be honest about your own knowledge, attitude, and behavior when it comes to mathematics, science, and technology. Name and describe three or more strengths or positives you have in this domain and three or more challenges. Come up with strategies for ameliorating the challenges.

Extension Activities

1. Interview both a preschool teacher and an elementary school teacher about their mathematics, science, and technology attitudes. Compare their attitudes to examine similarities and differences.

2. What are your own beliefs about exposing young children to technology? Take some time to reflect, and then write in your journal what you think is the appropriate age to begin exposure and appropriate amount of daily exposure. Then support your beliefs with evidence.

Additional Readings

Teaching young children math, science, and technology in a developmentally appropriate manner is an exciting challenge. Early childhood educators must prepare for and approach these lessons and teachings with professionalism, creativity, and enthusiasm. To do this, early childhood educators may need to enlist parents, increase their own knowledge base, and increase their own self-efficacy in this domain.

James, A. (2006). *Preschool success: Everything you need to know to help your child learn.* Indianapolis, IN: Jossey-Bass.
The main audience for this book is parents of preschoolers. However, the information is good for early childhood educators, too. It contains many specifics about the mathematics and science skills and concepts that preschoolers are able to comprehend.

Lalley, J. P., & Miller, R. H. (2006). Effects of pre-teaching and re-teaching on math achievement and academic self-concept of students with low math achievement. *Education, 126*(4), 747–755.
This study demonstrates that preteaching and reteaching have a positive impact on both math achievement and academic self-concept. Students' understanding of math concepts, problems, and computation is increased with both methods. Preteaching really has a significant impact on academic self-concept.

Prairie, A. P. (2005). *Inquiry into math, science, and technology for teaching young children.* Clifton Park, NY: Thompson Delmar Learning.
This book targets teachers of young children from infancy to early elementary. It discusses inquiry as a scientific process and how to integrate it into the teaching of mathematics, science, and technology. It also relays ideas about how to integrate mathematics, science, and technology into other areas of the early childhood curriculum.

On the Web

HighScope - *www.highscope.org*
HighScope is an early childhood education organization, and this is its official website. This organization stresses a three-step process of research, application, and validation and offers professional development and information that is valuable for teachers, administrators, parents, researchers, and policy makers. Mathematics, science, and technology are some of the domains covered in the information that is shared and produced by this organization.

National Council of Teachers of Mathematics - *www.nctm.org*
This is the official website of professionals who teach mathematics. It communicates the collective and public voice of these professionals and advocates for and supports quality learning of mathematics for all students.

National Science Teachers Association - *www.nsta.org*
This is the official website for science teachers and all others committed to science education. It advocates for and supports "excellence and innovation in science teaching and learning for all." Some of the guiding principles for the represented organization are to champion science literacy, value scientific excellence, and enhance teaching and learning through research.

Student Study Site

Visit **www.sagepub.com/gordonbiddle** to access several study tools including eFlashcards, web quizzes, links to SAGE journal articles, web resources, video resources, lesson plan templates, and more.

"I Can Group Objects!"

Subject:

Basic mathematics and science.

Focus:

Classification.

Overview:

This skill is present in rudimentary form at 3 months and evolves and becomes more complex throughout early childhood. Enthusiastic environmental facilitation of this skill gives young children the chance to practice.

Purpose:

To allow infants to discover their ability in this domain and give them practice with this domain in a concrete, realistic, and relevant fashion.

Objective:

- To uncover infants' ability to classify objects.
- To tie this ability to real-life situations.
- To give an infant practice at classifying objects.

Resources and Materials:

- White plastic spoons and white toothbrushes.
- An enthusiastic and supportive caregiver.

Activities and Procedures:

1. Begin doing this with a 9- to 10-month-old infant who has the motor skills and life experience to assist the activity.

2. Have the infant sit up on his or her own or prop the infant up in a caregiver's lap.

3. Place a single pile of 3 spoons and 3 toothbrushes in front of the infant.

4. Allow the infant to just play with the objects naturally, by putting them in his or her mouth, holding them, and placing them down. Watch how the infant begins to naturally put them in groups by function.

5. If this does not happen naturally, give the infant verbal prompts. Say, "What do you do with these?" "Where do you find these?" and "When do you use these?" (Although infants this age can't produce very many words, they have receptive language and can understand these simple questions.)

6. Repeated exposure may be needed for some infants.

7. Maturation and experience and deliberate connection to real life may also be needed for some infants, who will come to classify these objects after a few more months of learning and growing.

Tying It All Together:

Remember that infants begin classifying objects early. They may also be able to classify more objects than they can communicate to adults. If the infant is unable to classify the objects at first, keep trying. You may need to do this activity a number of times and allow the infant to grow and experience some more before he or she is able to demonstrate this skill. You may also have to deliberately tie this lesson to real-life experience in order for the infant to understand. Remember not to give up or get frustrated. Continue to present the spoons and toothbrushes to the infant with support and enthusiasm.

Visit **www.sagepub.com/gordonbiddle** to access templates of these lesson plans.

Lesson Plan:

"I Can Recycle!"

Subject:

Environmental science.

Focus:

Basic recycling.

Overview:

Children aged 3 to 5 years can learn the basics of recycling and its value to them and others.

Purpose:

To give young children an early introduction to recycling and its importance to them, other humans, and the earth.

Objectives:

- To teach preschoolers the basics of recycling.
- To teach preschoolers the importance of recycling.
- To facilitate positive lifelong habits in preschoolers.
- To help preserve the earth.

Resources and Materials:

- Simple rules about what materials are recyclable in your area.
- Real-life concrete examples of those materials.
- Real-life concrete examples of containers that receive those materials.

Activities and Procedures:

1. Begin a conversation about waste, materials, and recycling. Ask children what they do with certain materials at home and at school.

2. Specifically, begin talking about recycling. Explain that certain materials are used again so they don't go in the regular garbage. Ask children about their experience with recycling.

3. Tell children about the rules for recycling in your area at school. Depending on the age makeup of the group, you may want to write down a few of the rules and read them to the children or have the children read them.

4. Bring out your real-life examples of recycling materials and receptacles. Describe the materials one at a time and place them in the proper receptacle. Then have children follow your example.

Tying It All Together:

Very young children can learn to recycle. It is a good, positive habit that can start early and continue throughout childhood and adulthood. This science lesson is very relevant to a child's life and quite important, too.

Visit **www.sagepub.com/gordonbiddle** to access templates of these lesson plans.

Lesson Plan:

All Forms of Water

Subject:

Physical science.

Focus:

Transformation of matter.

Overview:

Water comes in a few forms; it can be liquid, solid, or steam. This lesson helps children see the various properties of water in all of its forms. This lesson illustrates how the same matter can take different forms.

Purpose:

To introduce basic transformational concepts of the physical sciences.

Objectives:

- To gain knowledge about basic transformational concepts.
- To gain experience with these concepts using the concrete example of water.
- To discuss how these concepts relate to other domains of development and academics.

Resources and Materials:

- Ice cubes.
- A cup of water.
- A boiling container of water that is letting off steam.
- A microwave or hot plate to boil the container of water.
- Safety equipment.

Activities and Procedures:

1. Begin the discussion by asking the children to define and describe water.

2. As they are talking, frame the discussion to talk about how water changes and the different forms it has.

3. Ask them what kind of science is demonstrated as water changes form.

4. Then bring out your resource materials. Let the children see and experience the materials, while being safe.

5. Then ask them to describe water again, focusing on the properties of each form that water takes.

Tying It All Together:

Physical science is very abstract and can be a challenge even for adults. However, water is around in everyday life. This lesson makes the principles of matter transformation very concrete and comprehensible for the children.

Visit **www.sagepub.com/gordonbiddle** to access templates of these lesson plans.

CHAPTER 14

Movement, Health, and the Physical Curriculum

This chapter will help you answer these important questions:

- What are the theoretical underpinnings of physical development?
- What are the components of physical development?
- What are the various types of movement?
- How do you integrate physical and motor development into the curriculum?
- What are some guidelines concerning movement?

Vignette: Big Sister Sally

Sally is in kindergarten and is taking gymnastics. She is learning how to walk on the balance beam. Her teacher has her start by walking on a ribbon taped to the gymnastics mat. Then her teacher holds her hand as she walks on a balance beam only a foot off the floor. Next, her teacher will have her walk on this low balance beam by herself with her arms out horizontal to the ground.

Sally really likes walking on the balance beam with her teacher and wants to teach her 18-month-old sister, Megan. Sally tapes a ribbon to her bedroom floor and has Megan walk in a straight line on the ribbon. Megan really likes her big sister and wants to please her; however, Megan cannot walk straight on the ribbon. Sally tries to help Megan by holding her hand, but Megan still cannot walk straight on the ribbon. At 18 months, Megan is still not neurologically and physically mature enough to walk a straight line on the floor.

Sally is frustrated until her mom tells her that, even with her help, her sister is too little to walk a straight line. Sally's mom suggests that she help her sister walk backward or up stairs, which are more developmentally appropriate milestones for Megan. Sally gives this a try and finds that she can help her little sister walk backward and up stairs. Soon Megan can walk backward all by herself, but she still needs a little help up stairs.

I t may seem that children's physical development occurs automatically without much assistance or "teaching" by the early childhood teacher. However, professional early childhood teachers include health, nutrition, movement, games, and other exercises in their curriculum. In order for children to reach their optimum level of physical development, planning and thought concerning health, physical development, and motor skills must go into lesson planning. Taking professional responsibility in this area of development means understanding theory, being knowledgeable about ages and stages, understanding nutrition, and being aware of safety. After reading this chapter, you should understand the importance of physical development and how to facilitate it.

Chapter 14 ends the section of the textbook that emphasizes theory, different developmental areas, and developmentally appropriate lesson plans. Specifically, Chapter 14 addresses physical developmental components and their variations by age, gender, and culture, and touches on

Key Elements
for Becoming a Professional

NAEYC DEVELOPMENTALLY APPROPRIATE PRINCIPLE 1

All domains of development and learning—physical, social and emotional, and cognitive—are important, and they are closely interrelated. Children's development and learning in one domain influence and are influenced by what takes place in other domains.

Interpretation

Children are thinking, moving, feeling, and interacting human beings. To teach them well involves considering and fostering their development and learning in all domains.

NAEYC STANDARD 1: PROMOTING CHILD DEVELOPMENT AND LEARNING

c. Create great environments where all children thrive. Early childhood professionals use their understanding of children and children's developmental influences to create great environments where all children can develop optimally.

special needs. Chapter 14 also relays guidelines and important issues to consider when integrating physical development into the curriculum. These issues are space, safety, health education, nutrition, obesity, and relating to parents and families.

WHAT ARE THE THEORETICAL UNDERPINNINGS OF PHYSICAL DEVELOPMENT?

Basically one major theory and two principles are utilized heavily in understanding physical development: the maturational theory and the cephalocaudal and proximodistal principles. Maturational theory examines the engine or "how" physical development occurs, as well as the limits of physical development. The two principles of development address the direction in which physical development occurs, or the "where."

Maturational theory relays how neurological development and timing basically set the course for physical development (Shonkoff & Phillips, 2000). For instance, a child does not have the motor control to grasp with the hand until his or her hand is neurologically mature enough. Neither can he or she crawl or walk until neurologically and physically mature enough. Of course, other developmental facets besides maturation come into play. Neurological maturation creates a timeline and some limits in terms of development, but nutrition, experience, and practice also influence the rate of development. Children need good nutrition in order to grow on schedule neurologically and physically. They also need experience and practice in order to be able to grasp with their hands, crawl, or walk.

The two principles of development describe the general direction in which physical development occurs. The **cephalocaudal principle** states that development generally progresses from head to tail (foot). This is why young babies usually have heads that are larger than the rest of their bodies. The **proximodistal principle** states that development progresses from inside the body to the outer extremities. This explains why babies can control their back and/or torso before their fingers or toes (see Figure 14.1).

| Figure 14.1 | **The Progression of Human Growth** |

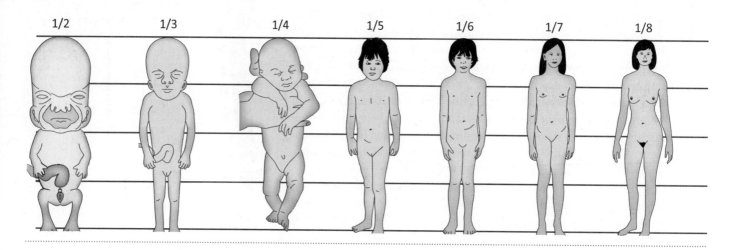

Source: Adapted from Papillia, Olds, and Feldman R.D. (2007).

WHAT ARE THE COMPONENTS OF PHYSICAL DEVELOPMENT?

There are three major components of physical development: sensoriperceptual development, physical growth, and motor skill development. Each component is associated with average milestones and age ranges derived from theory and research. However, the timing of when children achieve these milestones varies according to gender, culture, and whatever special needs a child may have.

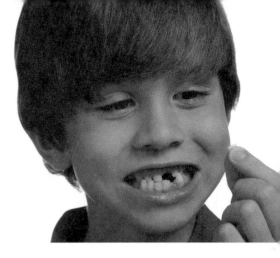

Losing teeth is a typical physical developmental milestone of young children.

Sensoriperceptual Development

Sensory capabilities are present before birth and continue developing after birth. Touch, smell, taste, hearing, and sight all develop quite rapidly in the early months. The five senses are integrated by cross-modal perception (see Chapter 5). As senses develop, a baby can begin to coordinate sight and hearing or smell and taste. For instance, remember the last time you had pizza? Didn't the smell of the pizza make your taste buds tingle, allowing you to "taste" the pizza before actually putting it in your mouth? This is a direct experience of cross-modal perception, the integration of the senses.

As young children age, their senses mature, and they make meaning of and come to understand sensory information better. This is **sensoriperceptual development**. Young children use sensory information to guide their physical and motor movements. As the teacher, you can awaken a child's senses in your lesson planning by taking multimodality into account (Allen & Marotz, 2003). **Multimodality** indicates that sensory information comes through more than one sensory venue at a time. For instance, if you take young children on a hayride, they can see, feel, and smell the hay. If they crumple it, they can hear it. Some young children may even be tempted to put it in their mouth and taste it. All of the children's senses are involved in learning about the hay at various ages.

There are a few early sensoriperceptual capabilities that develop, such as binocular vision, eye-hand coordination, depth perception, and haptic perception. **Binocular vision** is the ability to focus using both eyes, and this develops around 4 or 5 months of age (Bushnell & Boudreau, 1993). **Eye-hand coordination** is the ability to coordinate hand movements with visual cues. Surprisingly, this ability also develops early in life, around 4 months of age. **Depth perception** is a skill that develops in conjunction with motor skills and involves realizing that surfaces are not always flat; surfaces may have two or three dimensions. This begins developing around the age of 3 months but is not fully developed until much later when babies begin to crawl (Bushnell & Boudreau, 1993). **Haptic perception** is learning about objects through touch. Once babies start handling objects, they learn about size, texture, and other characteristics of objects. The development and proper functioning of sensoriperceptual abilities are quite important. These physical abilities relate to cognitive and social emotional functioning as well. This is because the sensoriperceptual abilities create mental images (schemes, as described in Chapter 4) that serve as a foundation for movement, solving problems, and forming relationships (Bagdi, Vacca, & Waninger, 2007).

Sensory information comes in through the various senses at different ages.

Physical Growth and Motor Skills

Physical growth happens quickly in the early years, especially during the first year (Kuczmarski et al., 2000). The average baby is usually 7 or 8 pounds at birth. Then the baby doubles his or her weight in 6 months and triples his or her birth weight in 1 year. At 1 year old, rapid growth slows to a gain of about 5 pounds a year. Length at birth is approximately 20 inches. At 1 year of age, height is approximately 30 inches, and, at 2 years, it is close to 35 inches. Thirty-eight inches is the typical height at 3 years of age. From age 3 to 6 years, children typically gain 2 to 3 inches and 4 to 6 pounds annually. These growth patterns continue into the early elementary years, too.

A number of physical and motor milestones occur during the early childhood years. Some of the basic ones were mentioned in Chapter 5. Here, the authors will discuss other, more complex and specialized milestones, such as discovering handedness, buttoning, jumping, hopping, and balancing. These usually occur during the preschool and early elementary years.

Physical and motor milestones can be roughly divided into two categories, fine motor and gross motor (see Chapter 5). Fine motor skills involve the small muscles of the hands and fingers, while gross motor skills involve large muscles of the arms, legs, and torso. These fine and gross motor skills develop rapidly, especially during the preschool years.

The skill of balancing develops as young children grow.

In terms of fine motor skills, **handedness** or hand preference usually develops around age 3 years. Some children never develop a preference for either hand. Around age 3 years or before, children become better with dressing skills such as buttoning, zipping, snapping, and tying. Four-year-olds can handle the basics of dressing and grooming, and 8-years-olds have mastered these skills (Allen & Marotz, 2003; Keogh & Sugden, 1985).

Large muscles and gross motor skills also develop complexity during the preschool and early childhood years. Walking becomes more balanced and graceful. Children can finally walk up and down stairs by themselves around the age of 4 years (Allen & Marotz, 2003; Gallahue & Ozmun, 1998; Keogh & Sugden, 1985). Little Megan in our earlier scenario has a few years ahead of her before she can accomplish this feat. Around the latter part of the second year, young children can technically run with moments when both feet are in the air (see Chapter 5). Around age 4, there is marked improvement in running and, by age 8, speed, control, and synchrony of running have improved (Allen & Marotz, 2003; Gallahue & Ozmun, 1998; Keogh & Sugden, 1985).

Even more complicated movements are jumping and hopping. **Jumping** is being up in the air with both feet above the ground, and this skill develops before hopping. **Hopping** is being up in the air with one foot in the air. In other words, the feet are separated, and one foot is a little higher than the other. In the latter part of the second year, children begin jumping from a step and master this skill around age 3. They also begin jumping straight up starting from the floor at age 3, and at 4 years of age, they can jump over objects (Allen & Marotz, 2003; Gallahue & Ozmun, 1998; Keogh & Sugden, 1985). Hopping begins during the latter part of the third year.

Balancing means keeping straight and level while performing simple and complex gross motor skills and is important for self-confidence and movement coordination (Keogh & Sugden, 1985). Remember young Sally and her sister, Megan, in our opening scenario? It is not until age 3 that children can balance standing on one foot for 5 seconds. At 2 years of age or just before, young children can balance while walking a straight line on the floor, just like Megan in our beginning scenario will be able to do in a few months. Children can also walk backward with balance at around 2 years old. Then, at 3, they can balance on one foot. By age 8 or before, children can walk heel-to-toe forward and backward on a balance beam (Keogh & Sugden, 1985).

The basic facts about physical growth and skill development are fascinating, but the variances associated with age, gender, various types of movement, and the issues concerning movement discussed in the rest of this chapter are even more exciting and interesting. For example, what can boys do physically with ease that challenges girls and vice versa? The answer to this question, and more, is covered in the rest of the chapter, so you as a future teacher should keep reading.

Differences in Physical and Motor Development

Some age differences were relayed above, and more are included here. Generally, young children get taller and weigh more with age. Their motor skills become more refined and more complex and more graceful. However, there are differences in how boys and girls develop. In terms of gender, male babies are more likely to die within the first year. If they do not die and are healthy, they are usually taller and heavier than female babies (Cratty, 1986). There are also a few slight differences in motor skills between male and female babies (Cratty, 1986). At 6 years of age, girls have more accurate motor movements, while boys have more forceful and complex actions. At 8 years of age or slightly older, boys can throw a small ball 70 feet, while girls can only throw it 40 feet. On the other hand, girls run slightly faster than boys, at an average speed of 17 feet per second, while boys run an average speed of 16.5 feet per second (Cratty, 1986).

Additional cultural and socioeconomic differences impact physical and motor development, and they begin with mortality during the first year. Just like male babies, ethnic minority babies in the United States, such as African American and Native American babies, are more likely to die within the first year of life. The reasons for this vary, from access to health care, to the mother's behavior during pregnancy and after birth, to birthweight (American Public Health Association, 2004; Kochanek & Smith, 2004). If they survive, African and African American babies tend to sit, walk, and run sooner than babies from other ethnic groups. On the other hand, Asian babies seem to pace slower than other ethnic groups with those motor skills (Gardiner & Kosmitzki, 2005). Unfortunately, ethnic minority children in the United States are also more likely to be impoverished, and poverty in the younger years is associated with health and physical problems such as anemia, asthma, and poor nutrition (National Center for Health Statistics [NCHS], 2004). Ethnic minority children in Black and Hispanic groups also tend to be immunized at a lower rate than White children (Chu, Barker, & Smith, 2004). These cultural and socioeconomic problems impact physical and motor development.

Children with a variety of special needs may also have delayed physical and motor development (Deiner, 2004). Obviously, children with physical disabilities will need support and adaptations when developing physical and motor skills, sometimes including the use of assistive technologies. A wheelchair is an example of an assistive technology device. What may not be as obvious is that children with socioemotional and cognitive special needs may also

Flexibility and resilience characterize physical development and physical skills.

need support and adaptation. For instance, a child may be depressed or have dyslexia. These young children with socioemotional or cognitive special needs can also be delayed in their physical and motor development. (More information about this area is contained in Chapters 7 and 8.)

WHAT ARE THE VARIOUS TYPES OF MOVEMENT?

Children from birth to age 8 years engage in various movement activities, from the basic sensorimotor skills such as tracking objects with eye movements to complex skills such as dancing and organized sports. As children engage in these activities, which range from vigorous and physical to quiet fine motor activities, they are afforded practice in their physical and motor skills. We will begin by discussing sensory activities, then move to fine motor movements, and end with gross motor movements.

With sensory activities and movements, children can engage in sensing objects and materials. They can touch sandpaper, smell bananas or vanilla, taste apples, listen to bells, and see complex drawings or three-dimensional objects. These types of activities, which can be introduced to children (even infants) daily, allow them to use their cross-modal perception abilities to match smells and tastes or sounds and sights. Children can also classify objects by categories and put objects in order according to size. And they can play in sand and water. All of these activities and movements are very common activities for young children.

Fine motor activities include handling manipulatives, drawing, and utilizing eye-hand coordination skills. **Manipulatives** include puzzles and games with small pieces, such as LEGO bricks, bingo tokens, and dominoes. In the beginning, when the children are young, the puzzles should have knobs and large pieces; however, by age 8 years, a young child can put together a 50-piece puzzle with medium-sized pieces. Children can also draw and paint with large crayons or paintbrushes and then move on to smaller artistic utensils. For eye-hand coordination, children can string beads and use lacing cards and peg boards with colors and shapes.

BEST
Practices   Facilitating Movement During the Kindergarten Year

Movement is important in all early childhood years from infancy to third grade. However, lately there has been an emphasis on developing skills through instruction and not just allowing free play, especially in kindergarten (Manross, 1994, 2000). According to the National Association for the Education of Young Children (2009b), children in kindergarten need two 30-minute sessions of moderate to vigorous physical activity each day. Ideally, the sessions involve play and the intentional learning of specific skills. Additionally, both fine and gross motor movement should be addressed inside the kindergarten classroom as well as outside. Moreover, children should have the right equipment (plastic stairs and/or a rocking horse inside and a teeter-totter and/or hopscotch game pattern outside) and time to practice their skills. Professional kindergarten teachers have the right knowledge and skills and attitude. They play an important role in the quality of movement experiences that their kindergarten children have. These teachers should promote and encourage the requisite attitudes and habits for joyful, lifelong involvement in movement activities.

Eye-hand coordination can be facilitated with gross motor movement, too. For example, children can learn and practice how to throw and catch. First, young children can practice the movements alone and isolated. Then, throwing and catching can be combined in noncompetitive games, then competitive games, and finally organized sports. Young children also participate in other gross motor activities in outdoor play such as running and climbing. Inside, they can climb structures, play with blocks, and have organized physical fitness activities. The number of sports available for young children to play has increased over time to include golf, tennis, soccer, tag football, T-ball, softball, gymnastics, martial arts, and different types of dancing. The following section provides more information about movement.

HOW DO YOU INTEGRATE MOTOR AND PHYSICAL DEVELOPMENT?

How will you as a teacher facilitate motor and physical development? What are some standards, guidelines, and tips you can use? Of what issues do you need to be aware? Read on to find out.

Current Standards and Guidelines for Movement and Physical Activity

Did you know that guidelines exist for physical activity at every age of childhood, even infancy and toddlerhood? The National Association for Sport and Physical Education (NASPE) has produced five guidelines for infant physical activity (see Table 14.1) and five guidelines for toddler and preschooler physical activity (see Table 14.2). Infant guidelines encourage daily physical exploration of the infant's environment, safe settings without restricted movement, daily promotion of movement

Table 14.1	Five Guidelines for Infant Physical Activity

GUIDELINES FOR INFANTS	
Guideline 1	Infants should interact with caregivers in daily physical activities that are dedicated to exploring movement and the environment.
Guideline 2	Caregivers should place infants in settings that encourage and stimulate movement experiences and active play for short periods of time several times a day.
Guideline 3	Infants' physical activity should promote skill development in movement.
Guideline 4	Infants should be placed in an environment that meets or exceeds recommended safety standards for performing large-muscle activities.
Guideline 5	Those in charge of infants' well-being are responsible for understanding the importance of physical activity and should promote movement skills by providing opportunities for structured and unstructured physical activity.

Source: Reprinted from *Active Start: A Statement of Physical Activity Guidelines for Children From Birth to Age 5*, with permission from the National Association for Sport and Physical Education (NASPE), 1900 Association Drive, Reston, VA 20191, www.NASPEinfo.org

Table 14.2   **Five Guidelines for Toddler and Preschooler Physical Activity**

GUIDELINES FOR TODDLERS	
Guideline 1	Toddlers should engage in a total of at least 30 minutes of structured physical activity each day.
Guideline 2	Toddlers should engage in at least 60 minutes—and up to several hours—per day of unstructured physical activity and should not be sedentary for more than 60 minutes at a time, except when sleeping.
Guideline 3	Toddlers should be given ample opportunities to develop movement skills that will serve as the building blocks for future motor skillfulness and physical activity.
Guideline 4	Toddlers should have access to indoor and outdoor areas that meet or exceed recommended safety standards for performing large-muscle activities.
Guideline 5	Those in charge of toddlers' well-being are responsible for understanding the importance of physical activity and promoting movement skills by providing opportunities for structured and unstructured physical activity and movement experiences.
GUIDELINES FOR PRESCHOOLERS	
Guideline 1	Preschoolers should accumulate at least 60 minutes of structured physical activity each day.
Guideline 2	Preschoolers should engage in at least 60 minutes—and up to several hours—of unstructured physical activity each day, and should not be sedentary for more than 60 minutes at a time, except when sleeping.
Guideline 3	Preschoolers should be encouraged to develop competence in fundamental motor skills that will serve as the building blocks for future motor skillfulness and physical activity.
Guideline 4	Preschoolers should have access to indoor and outdoor areas that meet or exceed recommended safety standards for performing large-muscle activities.
Guideline 5	Caregivers and parents in charge of preschoolers' health and well-being are responsible for understanding the importance of physical activity and for promoting movement skills by providing opportunities for structured and unstructured physical activity.

Source: Reprinted from *Active Start: A Statement of Physical Activity Guidelines for Children From Birth to Age 5*, with permission from the National Association for Sport and Physical Education (NASPE), 1900 Association Drive, Reston, VA 20191, www.NASPEinfo.org

skills (evoking the skills), and furthering young children's movement skills (getting motor skills to develop to the next level). Toddler and preschooler guidelines cover similar territory but contain more specific language and time periods, structured and unstructured play, indoor and outdoor safety, and designated periods of time.

Consider This Physical Education

Melinda, a new early childhood education teacher, took her children out to the playground for some physical education (PE). She started dividing the students into teams when Juan protested, "We don't want José on our team—he is too slow!" Melinda did not know how to respond and continued dividing students into teams. Juan strategized with his fellow teammates: "OK, we'll make José go last." Later that afternoon, Melinda decided to consult with Sara, a master teacher who had many years of experience. "The key to successful PE is maximum participation, with all kids participating at all times," declared Sara. "There should be no waiting and no limitations. Physical education in the early elementary years should be noncompetitive and allow for skill development, social interaction, and creativity." Sara suggested that in the early years a game such as tag that involves the whole class is great for building awareness and skills. This is how PE was before it became rule-based and competitive. "We're returning to that old model once again," Sara noted.

Reflect back on your early days of physical education. Did teachers emphasize maximum participation or competition? Did teachers emphasize strict adherence to rules or creativity? As a teacher, how would you respond if your students wanted to keep score or exclude other students?

There are also guidelines for the early elementary years. In 2009, NASPE called for a comprehensive school physical activity program. The guidelines for the comprehensive program are detailed, specific, and divided into the following categories:

- Quality physical education.
- School-based physical education opportunities.
- School employee wellness and involvement.
- Family and community involvement.

In some ways, the new guidelines are reminiscent of earlier years.

Space

Adequate space is important for optimal facilitation of physical growth and motor skill development. Young children need space indoors and outdoors. In fact, a child's awareness of general space and personal space is one of the basics of physical education in the early years (NASPE, 2004, 2009). The space for physical activity should also be prepared properly. For infants, the keys to physical development and growth are safety and few restrictions (NASPE, 2004). Unstructured and structured spaces are key for preschoolers and toddlers. The unstructured space should invite young children to play with a few carefully placed objects such as scarves and tumbling mats. The structured space should be prepared for teacher-facilitated, planned activities such as body puzzles or tag (NASPE, 2004). Appropriately prepared space is also important during early elementary years. Structured and unstructured spaces prepared both outdoors and indoors are quite important for physical growth and motor skill development (NASPE, 2009). These various types of spaces help a child learn and practice.

Safety

Space for young children's physical development should be safe, especially for young infants, but indeed for young children of all ages. NASPE (2004, 2009) offers safety guidelines for children

Simple and noncompetitive games such as tag can enhance physical development.

Safe spaces are important for infants and toddlers, even if the play space is outside.

of all ages. Young children should be safe indoors and outdoors in terms of equipment and adult supervision. Remember our scenario at the beginning of this chapter? The gymnastics teacher started Sally with a line of ribbon on the floor, a deliberate step to keep her safe while learning. Safety is important for all teachers to remember, and safety information should be shared with parents and other family members. Most states and counties have safety guidelines that teachers must follow closely, but it is a general suggestion to have a certified professional inspect any young children's playground (Wallach, 1999). Additionally, two well-known observation instruments, HOME (Home Observation and Measurement of the Environment) (Bradley, Caldwell, & Corwyn, 2003) and ECERS (Early Childhood Environmental Rating Scales) (Harms, Clifford, & Cryer, 2005), have safety items or subscales that can be used to assess a child's environment. HOME is for home environments, and ECERS is for preschool environments. For elementary school, there is also SACERS (School-Age Care Environmental Rating Scale). The importance of safety cannot be overstressed, because accidents are the leading cause of death in the early childhood and early elementary years (NCHS, 2004).

Arranging the Environment for Physical Activity

Adequate space and safety are important concerns when arranging the environment for physical activity. There are other concerns, too, such as size of space and flow of activities. Space can be used either inside or outside as long as the space is large enough and safe. There are also certain concerns for children with special needs in order that they may be included in the physical activities (Rouse, 2009). For preschool and early elementary children, space can be arranged for specific games and activities. For instance, the environment can be set up for games such as "Four Corners" and "Grand Prix" (see Figures 14.2 and 14.3). These are specific, fun activities that allow for the practice of skills, such as balance, eye-hand coordination, and speed. The environment can also be divided into stations that assist all children, including those with disabilities, in learning movement fundamentals (Rouse, 2009). Each station can allow for the exploration and practice of different skills, such as spatial awareness.

Health and Health Education

Ensuring adequate space and safety are not enough to promote and facilitate optimal physical and motor development in young children. Children's overall general health must also be considered, and information about health must be communicated to their primary caregivers. In order for young children to develop optimally physically and motorically, their general overall health is quite important. Space and safety are not adequate for optimal physical growth or motoric development; health is an additional element to consider when promoting and/or facilitating physical development. Health information should also be shared with parents, during day-to-day interactions, parent-teacher conferences, newsletters, and workshops.

Teaching young children about healthy habits and the importance of being healthy and making healthy choices must be integrated into your lesson plans. The importance of mental health for young children of all ages, even infants, should not be forgotten.

General health, physical health, and mental health are all important. These concepts and ideas should be taught to young children deliberately, and you should build partnerships with health providers in the community, such as physicians, nurses, dentists, therapists, psychiatrists, pharmacists, and dieticians. These partnerships are positive relationships in which the health providers give services and information and accept referrals. Communicating with these professionals and parents is very important, especially when considering immunizations, dental care, exposure to lead and other environmental hazards, and physical fitness. The involvement of the entire community is particularly important in keeping young children healthy who are most at risk, such as those in poverty (Proctor & Dalaker, 2003).

Immunizations and Vaccines

Immunizations and vaccines help prevent childhood diseases such as measles, whooping cough, and polio. Immunizations begin in infancy and continue into adulthood. A good number of early childhood education institutions require that the recommended immunizations be obtained in order for children to enroll and attend on a regular basis. Because of immunization, incidences of the targeted childhood diseases fell more than 95% from 1993 to 2000 (American Academy of Pediatrics Committee on Infectious Diseases, 2000). However, as mentioned above, ethnic minorities are less likely to be immunized than White children (Chu et al., 2004), and some parents choose not to immunize their children because of the unproven relationship of immunization to autism (Mitka, 2004; Parker, Schwartz, Todd, & Pickering, 2004). As a teacher, it is important that you work with the children under your care, their parents, and the community's health care professionals to do what is best for each child.

Dental Care

Dental care and tooth decay also concern young children from infancy and beyond. Sweet beverages such as 100% juice can cause tooth decay (Marshall et al., 2003) in children as young as 1 year of age and should be consumed in small amounts. It is also important for young children to be given fluoride and receive dental care on a regular basis. This may begin with children as young as 1 year old but should not start later than their third year. Professional early childhood teachers use this

Figure 14.2   **Four Corners**

Source: Adapted from Landy and Burridge (2000).

information to teach their students, inform the parents, and secure needed services from dental professionals in the community.

Environmental Hazards

Exposure to lead and other environmental hazards such as smoke is related to cognitive, behavioral, and neurological deficits (American Academy of Pediatrics Committee on Environmental Health,

Figure 14.3   **Grand Prix**

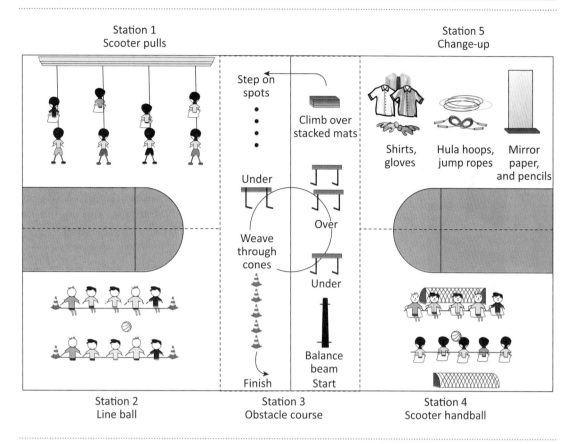

Source: Adapted from Rouse (2009).

1998; Canfield et al., 2003; Tesman & Hills, 1994). Once a child is exposed to lead, the damage may be irreversible (Bellinger, 2004). Therefore, it is very important to be aware of lead levels in paint, toys, clothing, candy, food, and water. Most important, high-risk children (those in houses with lead-based paint) should have the lead levels in their blood checked. It is important for you as a teacher to prevent and help parents to prevent children's exposure to lead, by educating the parents about possible lead in paint, toys, clothing, candy, food, and water. The elimination of exposure to other environmental hazards such as smoke and pollution is also suggested. Such toxins are related to a number of childhood illnesses, such as asthma, and can also cause death (DiFranza, Aligne, & Weitzman, 2004).

Physical Fitness

Physical fitness is a special concern in modern U.S. society during the early childhood and elementary years. However, the concern may begin as early as infancy and the toddler years. As the physical education guidelines mentioned earlier in the chapter established, children should be allowed space, time, opportunity, and incentive to be physically active. Lack of physical fitness along with improper nutrition is related to childhood obesity and diseases related to being overweight (American Academy of Pediatrics

Committee on Nutrition, 2003; Chen et al., 2004). Physical activity and fitness education are important to include in the daily lives of young children. As a teacher, you should work with the children in your care, their parents, and their family members to impress upon them the positive impact physical activity has on physical growth, motor skills, general and mental health, and overall well-being.

Nutrition

The U.S. Department of Agriculture (USDA) along with the U.S. Department of Health and Human Services (USDHHS) updates nutrition guidelines periodically. In September 2005, along with new guidelines for people age 2 years and up, they created a new food guide pyramid that includes physical activity and fitness. These new guidelines give science-based information, recommend relative amounts of food groups, and emphasize choice. The deliberate addition of physical activity and the separation of vegetables and fruits are also important.

As you can see in Figure 14.4, it is a colorful pyramid with steps on the left side and colored triangles of various sizes inside. The size of the inner triangles is relative to the amount of that food group to be eaten. Separately, the food groups are grains, vegetables, fruits, milk and milk products, meat and beans, and oils. Figure 14.4 is the kids' version with a young girl running up the steps on the left side and explanations of the pyramid's various components.

The food dietary guidelines changed in 1995. The new guidelines gave science-based information, recommended relative amounts of food groups, and emphasized choice. The deliberate addition of physical activity and the separation of vegetables and fruits were also important. In 2011, nutrition guidelines changed once more (www.choosemyplate.gov). The visual is now a plate with triangular portions of fruits, vegetables, grains, and proteins, with a cup of dairy nearby. The related educational materials for teachers suggest ways to make fruits and vegetables more palatable, to decrease the intake of sweets, and to model positive and healthy eating habits for young children (see Figure 14.5).

Obviously, nutrition is important for physical growth and motoric skill development in young children. For instance, children who are malnourished will not be as tall as their genetic potential dictates and may become obese. It is important for you not only to serve nutritious food but to teach young children and their parents about nutrition and to model good nutrition habits, for instance having fresh fruits and vegetables at birthday parties.

The importance of nutrition begins even before pregnancy and continues through the prenatal period. If you have parents who are considering another pregnancy, they may ask questions about nutrition. Other questions that parents may have are whether to breast-feed or use formula and which formula is best. They may want to know how much formula or breast milk to give at certain ages. They may also want to know when to start rice cereal and how much rice cereal to give. You need to be prepared to work with these parents and community health professionals, such as gynecologists, to find appropriate answers.

As the young children in your care grow, you and their parents will need to make decisions about what types of food to feed them, how often to feed them, and how much of each type of food to feed them. Making the right decisions about nutrition and physical activity will help you prevent children from becoming malnourished or overweight. **Malnutrition** can occur when children eat insufficient amounts and/or types of food needed to maintain healthy body

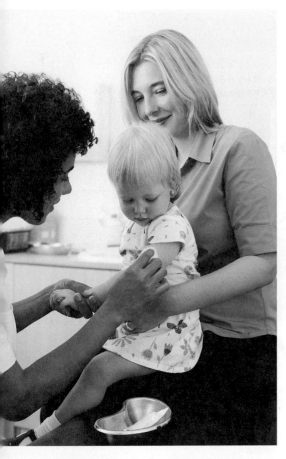

Parents and health care professionals, along with teachers, must work together to protect and promote good health in young children.

Figure 14.4   **Kid Food Guide Pyramid**

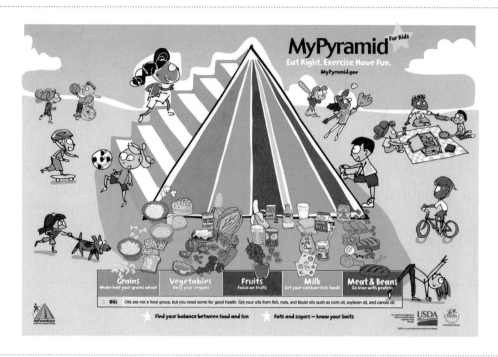

Source: United States Department of Agriculture.

functions. This is often coupled with insufficient interaction and physical activity. **Overweight** children eat too much food or too much of the wrong types of food and do not partake in enough physical activity. In general, children grow rapidly, and their nutrition needs change rapidly until age 3 years, when fewer calories are required in proportion to their weight (American Academy of Pediatrics Committee on Nutrition, 2003). At age 5 or 6 until age 8 and beyond, children need approximately 2,400 calories a day, and approximately one third of their calories should come from fat (USDA & USDHHS, 2000). This should be accompanied by regular physical activity.

Childhood Obesity

Being extremely overweight with excess fatty tissue is called **obesity**. Obesity can become a problem for children around 24 months of age (Hedley et al., 2004; Institute of Medicine, 2004; Ogden, Flegal, Carroll, & Johnson, 2002). Currently, of children age 6 years and over, around 9 million are obese (Institute of Medicine, 2004). Obesity is more of an issue for families of all ethnic groups with low socioeconomic status, or SES (American Academy of Pediatrics Committee on Nutrition, 2003). Some of the reasons for this are poor food quality and lack of exercise or movement. Families with low SES do not have resources for high-quality food and may not have adequate space, equipment, or opportunity for exercise and movement. Additionally, parents in low-SES families may not have education or knowledge about the importance of quality food and exercise. Some cases of obesity have

Good maternal nutrition during pregnancy is extremely important.

Figure 14.5 Adult Food Guidelines

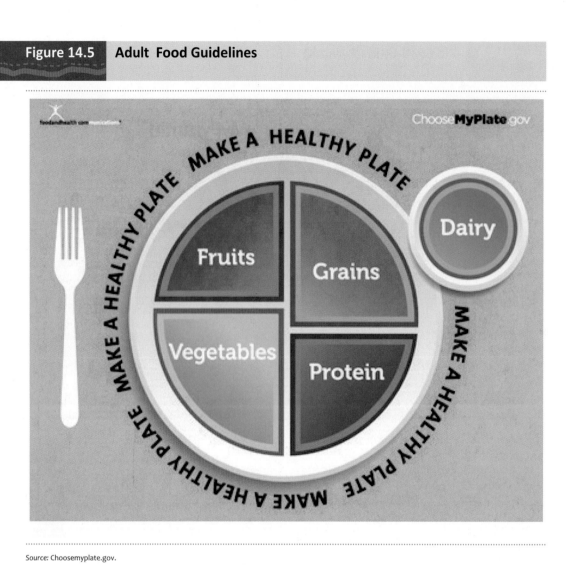

Source: Choosemyplate.gov.

biological causes, but most cases have environmental roots (American Academy of Pediatrics, 2003). However, some of the environmental factors come from parents, especially overweight parents (American Academy of Pediatrics Committee on Nutrition, 2003). Overweight parents create environments that perpetuate bad nutrition and exercise habits. It is important to intervene early in cases of obesity (American Academy of Pediatrics Committee on Nutrition, 2003; Quattrin, Liu, Shaw, Shine, & Chiang, 2005). The keys of intervention are food intake in terms of types of food and amount along with physical activity. You as a teacher can influence the food intake and participation in physical activity of young children directly and indirectly through educating their parents.

Early intervention in cases of obesity is important (American Academy of Pediatrics Committee on Nutrition, 2003; Quattrin et al., 2005) because obesity is related to serious childhood illnesses such as hypertension, which can occur in children as early as age 8 years (Muntner, He, Cutler, Wildman, & Whelton, 2004). Some children may also develop high cholesterol and diabetes from high insulin (American Academy of Pediatrics Committee on Nutrition, 2003; NCHS, 2004), and some obese children may experience depression, exhibit behavior problems, and suffer from low self-esteem (American Academy of Pediatrics Committee on Nutrition, 2003; Datar & Strum, 2004; Mustillo et al., 2003). As a teacher, you can influence the food intake and participation in physical activity of young children directly in your educational setting through modeling and education. You also influence children indirectly through educating their parents. It is very important for you as a professional teacher to teach young children and their parents and families about obesity and how to prevent it. To do so, do not hesitate to form partnerships with other community professionals such as nurses and dieticians.

Communicating With and Involving Parents and Families

We believe that it is just as important to communicate with parents and family members about physical growth and motor skills as it is to talk to them about cognitive and socioemotional development and health and wellness. In addition to teaching young children about these matters in a developmentally appropriate manner, a professional teacher models the behavior and shares information and knowledge with parents and family members. Although family or cultural beliefs and values may come into play, it is important for you as a professional to emphasize what is good for the young children in your care based on sound early childhood principles and research. The knowledge you gain from this text and will gain in future course work is your guide to aiding parents and families as they facilitate their young children's physical growth, motor skills, and general health.

Good communication with parents leads to optimal physical development in young children.

As a professional teacher, you may have to go the extra mile to communicate with parents and family members. This may involve networking with other community professionals in order to provide all of the information needed. You may also have to provide parents with workshops, recipes, newsletter articles, and informal advice concerning physical development and motor skills. You should also be prepared to listen to parents and have them share some of their knowledge and expertise with you. If the early childhood setting where you work has a parent board or council, this group can aid in educating and involving all parents and family members in issues and events concerning physical growth, motor development, and health. It is your duty as an early childhood educator to facilitate optimal development of the whole child, and physical growth, motor skills, and health habits are an important part of that duty.

Being a professional early childhood teacher means integrating physical development and motor skills into your curriculum. You should impress upon family members the importance of enhancing physical development, motor skills, and good health habits. Developmental areas such as perception, health, nutrition, and dental care should not be ignored. In addition to teaching young children about these matters in a developmentally appropriate manner, a professional teacher models the behavior and shares information and knowledge with parents and family members.

Summary

It is important to include aspects of physical development such as health, nutrition, movement, games, and exercise in the early childhood education curriculum. This part of the curriculum deserves as much thought and planning as the other areas of development. It is important to plan for the facilitation of physical and motor development.

Theoretically, physical development is the unfolding and maturation of genes and biology. However, children also need environmental assistance through proper nutrition, experience, and practice in order to develop optimally. All components of physical development, from cross-modal perception to balancing, need genes, biology, and environmental facilitation. The same holds true for all the various types of movement.

One of the key issues in this area of development is integrating it into the early childhood education curriculum. There are professional and national standards as guides and suggestions. These standards apply to such issues as space, safety, health, nutrition, and involving parents and families. Communicating and coordinating with families is quite important for early childhood educators.

Key Terms

Balancing   372
Binocular vision   371
Cephalocaudal principle   370
Depth perception   371
Eye-hand coordination   371
Handedness   372

Haptic perception   371
Hopping   372
Jumping   372
Malnutrition   382
Manipulatives   374
Maturational theory   370

Multimodality   371
Obesity   383
Overweight   383
Proximodistal principle   370
Sensoriperceptual development   371

Reflection, Analysis, and Application Questions

1. What is maturational theory? Define it thoroughly and give three specific examples of the theory in action with young children.

2. Which component of physical development is the most essential? State your choice and then give and defend three reasons why the component is the most important.

3. How would you communicate with a parent that his or her child has a significant gross motor delay? What documentation would you have? In what setting would you communicate this information? What form would the communication take? What follow-up would there be?

4. How would you communicate to a parent the importance of making his or her home safe for physical development? What documentation would you have? In what setting would you communicate this information? What form would the communication take? What follow-up would there be?

5. Let's say you are a preschool teacher with a nutrition unit to plan. You decide to have the preschool children make and eat their lunch for one day in school. What would you have them make? What safety considerations would you have? How would you integrate other parts of the curriculum such as mathematics and social/emotional development?

Extension Activities

1. Contact two local preschools and two local elementary schools, and determine what is on their menus for that month. Then analyze them in terms of nutritional information presented in this chapter. How are local schools doing in your area with regard to nutrition for young children?

2. Reflect on your early school experiences with physical education. Think about how you felt about those experiences. Then write in a journal about your early feelings and how those experiences impact your current physical exercise practices and habits.

Additional Readings

Physical development is an important area of development in young children that early childhood educators must nurture. Development in the physical area impacts all other areas of development. It is also important to share the importance of physical development with parents and other family members.

Flamenbaum, R. K. (Ed.). (2006). *Global dimensions of childhood obesity.* **New York: Nova Science.**
This edited volume contains chapters by world-famous experts on obesity. It examines the latest research and reasons for obesity in children.

Harcourt Health and Fitness. **(2007).**
Published and authored by Harcourt, this program helps students develop a lifetime of healthy attitudes and

behaviors. It has real-world applications and also helps build character. The contribution of physical activity is highlighted.

The Developmental Benefits of Playgrounds. **(2004).**
This is written and published by the Association for Childhood Education International. It puts forth appropriate playground equipment and appropriate uses for the equipment. It also stresses the importance of play and movement. It discusses individual differences in children's abilities in this area.

On the Web

Bright Futures - *www.brightfutures.org*
This website is located at Georgetown University and receives funding from the Maternal and Child Health Bureau. The purpose of the website is to promote health in children. It emphasizes the importance of trust in the health care professionals who take care of children. Some of the materials are available online.

Illinois Early Learning Project - *www.illinoisearlylearning.org*
This is a state-run website that provides information to caregivers involved in the lives of young children. Here the caregivers, whether parents or teachers, can find evidence-based advice. The site also contains information about standards and benchmarks for physical and other areas of development as established by the state.

Scholastic - *www.scholastic.com*
This is a commercial website for a children's publisher that publishes *Early Childhood Today.* It contains a blog titled "Christina's Classroom" that has entries from a real-life kindergarten teacher. Some of her entries concern physical development and physical education.

Student Study Site

Visit **www.sagepub.com/gordonbiddle** to access several study tools including eFlashcards, web quizzes, links to SAGE journal articles, web resources, video resources, lesson plan templates, and more.

Infant/ Toddler
(Birth to 3 yrs)

Lesson Plan:
"I Am on the Move!"

Subject:
Gross motor skills.

Focus:
Beginning to creep or crawl.

Overview:
Infants begin to crawl at anywhere from 6 months to 10 months. This process and phase of development can be aided by environmental facilitation.

Purpose:
To get infants moving. This important physical milestone also aids in cognitive and social development.

Objectives:
- To begin infants' movement.
- To expand infants' exploration space.

Resource Materials:
- A happy and supportive caregiver.
- An interesting and colorful favorite toy.

Activities and Procedures:

1. Place the infant on his or her stomach on a comfortable and safe surface.

2. Move approximately 2 feet away.

3. Smile wide and encourage the infant to come toward you for about 1 minute.

4. Then put the toy down in front of you and encourage the infant to come and get it.

5. Greet all movements toward you or the toy with warm enthusiasm and applause.

Tying It All Together:
Creeping and crawling are very important milestones. They increase the amount of exploring an infant can do. As stated above, they also enhance cognitive and social development because of the increased exploring and interaction with other humans and objects.

Visit **www.sagepub.com/gordonbiddle** to access templates of these lesson plans.

"I Can Brush My Teeth!"

Subject:
Health.

Focus:
Dental hygiene.

Overview:
Teeth brushing is usually taught at home, but can be taught at school as well. Children in all day programs should brush their teeth once while there.

Purpose:
To teach about dental hygiene in general and teeth brushing specifically.

Objectives:
- To gain knowledge about dental hygiene.
- To increase teeth brushing skills.
- To practice teeth brushing skills.

Resource Materials:
- A sink with mirror.
- A cup.
- A toothbrush.
- Toothpaste.

Activities and Procedures:
1. Ask the children who knows how to brush their teeth and have them describe it.

2. Then tell the children verbally how to brush their teeth, making sure to fill in gaps in their knowledge.

3. Demonstrate how you brush your teeth in front of the sink and mirror.

4. Have children brush their teeth in front of the mirror as you watch and assist.

Tying It All Together:
Dental hygiene is sometimes a forgotten art. Teeth brushing is important for physical and socioemotional development. It is good for children to learn how, to practice, and to develop an appreciation for teeth brushing.

Visit **www.sagepub.com/gordonbiddle** to access templates of these lesson plans.

Lesson Plan:
"I Can Cook!"

Subject:

Nutrition.

Focus:

Making nutritious meals.

Overview:

There are many simple nutritious meals that young children can make with the assistance of an adult. For this lesson plan, we will make a simple vegetable salad with cubed chicken. It would be nice if some of the vegetables were grown in a garden that the children tend and cultivate.

Purpose:

To help children understand that nutrition can be fun and tasty.

Objectives:

- To gain nutrition knowledge.
- To obtain skills to create a nutritious meal.
- To satisfy hunger in a nutritious manner.

Resource Materials:

- Lettuce, tomatoes, cucumbers, mushrooms, and other basic salad vegetables prechopped by an adult.
- Chicken breast that has been precubed by an adult.
- Sufficient number of bowls and forks.
- Healthy salad dressings such as oil and vinegar.

Activities and Procedures:

1. Have everyone wash their hands.
2. Then the children can take turns putting the vegetables and chicken in their bowl. You may want them to tear the lettuce leaves some.
3. As the children are preparing their salad, you can talk about from where the food comes, how to carefully and safely chop it, and its nutritional value.
4. Once the salads are prepared, add a teaspoon or two of dressing and enjoy.

Tying It All Together:

Cooking activities are great learning opportunities for young children. In terms of physical development, they teach about nutrition. However, including a garden in the lesson adds science to the equation. If measuring and counting are involved, then mathematics is added. Of course, social development is included with lessons of manners and polite social conversation while eating.

Visit **www.sagepub.com/gordonbiddle** to access templates of these lesson plans.

PART V

Trends and Issues in Early Childhood Education

Considerations for Engaging Parents, Family, and Community

This chapter will help you answer these important questions:

- How has the traditional American family evolved?

- What is the definition of family structure and family function?

- What is effective parental involvement and engagement?

- What is culturally sensitive engagement of families?

- What is the role of family and community in fostering children's development?

Vignette: Community Support and Collaboration

Not too long ago, a young, undocumented mother enrolled her 3-year-old daughter, who was abused by her biological father, in a local Head Start program. For a period of 2 years, this young mother transported her young child to the Head Start program on a bicycle, with periodic transportation assistance provided to her by the Head Start family support services worker assigned to the family. During the family's enrollment period—and with the very able assistance and support from the family support services worker—this mother separated from the child's father, acquired her legal status as an American citizen, obtained appropriate counseling and play therapy referrals to local community resource agencies for herself and her young daughter, and obtained a job working at a local thrift store chain. Over time, this young mother was promoted to the rank of manager at the thrift store, and she and her daughter were eventually relocated to another community by the company. The young child successfully transitioned from the full-day Head Start program to traditional kindergarten, thus beginning her trajectory in formal schooling.

The above vignette conveys the transformative power of effective preschool programs and caring communities and the resilience of disenfranchised families. It is quite apparent that family and community are important in the lives of young children between birth and 8 years of age. As a matter of fact, as you may remember from Chapters 2 and 4, there exists a common phrase that has become a part of Western society's lexicon most recently: "It takes a village to raise a child." Made infinitely popular in the early 1990s by the former first lady and U.S. Secretary of State Hillary Clinton—this famous saying certainly resonates with the beliefs and values of early care and education professionals. This old adage, which has roots in ancient villages on the continent of Africa, places a great deal of value on the role and function of family and community life in the lives of young children. As early childhood professionals, we recognize that the optimum care and education of our nation's youngest children are linked to caring and responsive parents, families, and communities. As you may recall from Chapter 4, ecologist Urie Bronfenbrenner's theory of ecological development clearly conveys the impact that the various layers of the social system have on families. We will revisit Bronfenbrenner's theory at greater length in this chapter.

Would you agree that the traditional American family of the 21st century has undergone significant change over the course of the past 50 years? The family, as we once knew it, has faded in the distance. Social scientists of every ilk consider today's family an ever-changing institution. As we closely examine family demographics such as culture, race, and socioeconomic status, as well as the current sociopolitical landscape, the discussion of family in the context of today's society is a complex and intriguing topic. Our knowledge and understanding of family systems theory and dynamics, family cycles, alternative family structures, parenting styles, the functionality and dysfunctionality of families, parents as educational partners, parents as advocates, coparenting, noncustodial parenting, the impact of community/societal dynamics on the family, and so many other family-related topics too numerous to name can serve us well as we seek to provide enhanced services for young children in our care. These and other topics will be discussed at length in the pages ahead.

HOW HAS THE TRADITIONAL AMERICAN FAMILY EVOLVED?

During the previous century and right up to this present day, the evolution of the traditional family has been shaped by a complex cluster of culture and familial decision making that has morphed the American family into many different configurations, some of which are hardly recognizable to most people. Over the years, American families have been shaped by the consequences of very personal decision making, culture, family history, religious practices and customs, motivational levels of individual family members, and each family member's external or internal locus of control (i.e., how the member views the forces that shape his or her life and the degree to which the individual feels in control of his or her own destiny). Families have also been bombarded by the influence of cultural shifts, economic swings, social-political trends, immigration laws, education policy, laws governing society, calamities and catastrophes of every type, and global as well as international events.

To better understand the dramatic shifts that families have endured over the past several years, it is important to view growing families within the context of environmental systems—the sociocultural contexts of educational settings, communities, and the broader society. As professionals in the field of early childhood education, our knowledge and application of contextualist theories—bioecological, sociocultural, and family systems—as well as our use of helpful strategies for optimizing children's development, are critical and can lead to increased effectiveness in engaging families. Understanding the concepts inherent in Vygotsky's sociocultural theory, Bronfenbrenner's bioecological theory, and family system cycles can shed light on the dynamic nature of the institution of family. The three contextualist theories discussed below convey critical relationships or systems among children, families, and communities that are not only complex but differentiated. As educators, the better we understand these relationships, the more adept we become at using family engagement practices that are supportive, comprehensive, and authentic. Let's take a few moments to explore these contextualist theories.

Bronfenbrenner's Bioecological System of Development

You may recall from Chapter 4 that theorist Urie Bronfenbrenner understood the importance of nurturing adults in the lives of young children. Bronfenbrenner's theory, which was recently renamed *bioecological* systems theory (see Chapter 2), stresses the importance of children's biology as a primary factor in the interplay between children and their environment, and the environment's vital role in advancing children's development. Bronfenbrenner's theory affords us the opportunity to view the impact of environmental influences on children's development from a very comprehensive vantage point. Figure 15.1 illustrates the dynamic nature of the child and family's environment by showing the interconnections among the various bioecological systems discussed in Bronfenbrenner's theory.

Bronfenbrenner believed that educators must become aware of the systems that surround the development of the child and their impact on the child's development. Bronfenbrenner's bioecological

The traditional American family has evolved to include families with varying gender, racial, and generational makeup.

systems theory is likened to the crust or foundation of the earth; it consists of multiple layers. These environmental systems or layers, according to Bronfenbrenner, are always transforming over the course of the child's development, impacting the child's existence and the existence of the adults that compose the child's social system.

Bronfenbrenner's theory consists of three nested systems: (1) microsystems, (2) exosystems, and (3) macrosystems (see also Chapter 4). The microsystem is the innermost level and consists of the child's immediate environment—the child's home, family, peer group, kindergarten classroom, religious institution, or other setting. These contexts compose children's realm of personal experiences. The mesosystem constitutes the interactions or connections between and among the various settings at this and other levels, as well as the interactions between and among the various elements or settings belonging to the three systems (i.e., a troubled 6-year-old girl might be required by the school psychologist to participate in a program aimed at curtailing aggression in young children). The exosystem consists of events that have the potential to influence the child's development but only indirectly. For instance, a recently divorced single mother may become angry and punitive toward her 5-year-old daughter, which can ultimately impact the child's adjustment behavior. The macrosystem represents the culture and the subcultures in which the child lives and includes the ideals, values, and traditions that are often a part of a particular region's identity. Thus, a child growing up in some urban American cities today might experience the brunt of lawlessness and unprecedented violence due to the paucity of public funding (some cities have recently filed for bankruptcy) and the dearth of law enforcement personnel, resources for vulnerable families, and intervention services for at-risk populations. Finally, Bronfenbrenner recognized that family interrelationships are often modified with the passage of time, and that societal and sociohistorical trends can also impact family life. The chronosystem, according to Bronfenbrenner's theory, recognizes the timing of these adjustments and the relative age and station of the child during these

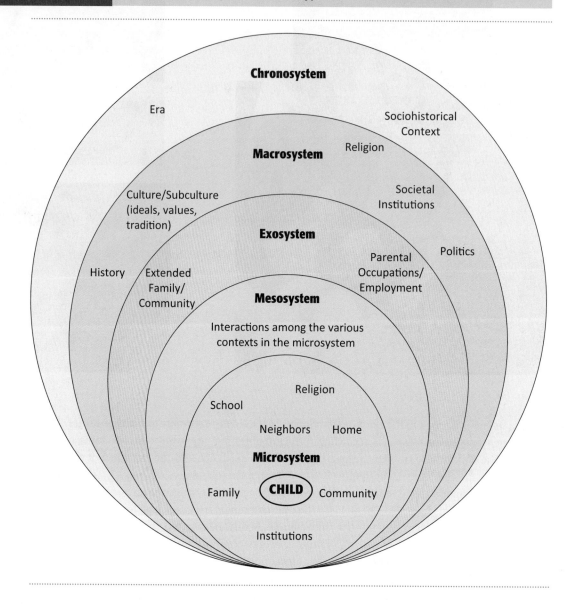

periods, including the impact of these changes on the developing child (Bronfenbrenner, 2005). For instance, as mentioned earlier, during the 1980s and early 1990s, many children in Harlem, New York, were forced to live with their grandparents, other relatives, and other designated legal guardians due to the AIDS epidemic, which left many of them orphans.

According to Bronfenbrenner, many environmental influences can impact the development of the child; however, simply being aware of them is not sufficient. Early childhood professionals can join forces with legislators to craft policies and social agendas that support the development and protection of young children and the ability for growing families to thrive in today's society.

Vygotsky's Sociocultural Theory

As discussed in Chapter 4, Vygotsky's theory of sociocultural development underscores the influence of the critical nature of children's social world on their ongoing development. Much of the recent research in the area of child development explores the cultural contexts of children's lives and is beginning to shed some light on whether children everywhere follow the same developmental pathways or whether developmental pathways are limited to certain environmental situations (Goodnow, 2010). According to Vygotsky, we gain knowledge only through the repeated interactions with others who are a part of our social space; and, for young children, much of their learning is the result of regular interactions with more expert or capable others (i.e., older children, adults, knowledgeable family members) in their world. Children's learning takes place in the zone of proximal development (see Chapter 2), that place where children are beginning to acquire certain skills and concepts but cannot master them without help from a more capable other. Children rely heavily on adult assistance and support to tackle new developmental challenges. Vygotsky also believed that language or the communication between children and more capable others is the primary medium that helps children master culturally meaningful tasks and responsibilities. Knowing this, teachers of young children must support children's development of their "mother tongue"—the language of their home.

This photo depicts a child learning in the zone of proximal development.

The values, beliefs, customs, and practices of sociocultural groups are transferred to young children who are in a unique position to acquire the "thinking patterns" and "doing behaviors" specific to a particular cultural group. Hence, children, in various cultural groups, develop very unique developmental strengths and capabilities. Often in the early childhood classroom, there is diversity (the subject of Chapter 8) among children with regard to the food they eat, their specific ways of eating, the holidays they celebrate, and so on. Among diverse groups, there are also specific beliefs about family, gender roles, the role of fathers in the lives of young children, and the family's role in the child's educational process. The family's behavior patterns are rooted in these beliefs. Educators must therefore abandon their assumptions or preconceived notions about families and refrain from judgments of value regarding families' beliefs and practices. They must find creative ways of both recognizing and validating all families' values, traditions, ways of behaving, and unique approaches to life.

Inasmuch as children learn in the contexts of family and relationships, sometimes their unique contextual experiences cause them to display certain social behaviors in educational or preschool settings that are unacceptable (e.g., aggressive, biting, or hitting behavior). Recognizing that much of young children's behavior is the result of family expectations, reinforcement and punishment of children's behaviors should move teachers to effectively engage the family in the proactive process of addressing the behavior and the use of positive guidance techniques. In this instance, it is not enough for the teacher to simply work with the child independently in establishing ground rules; rather, the teacher is expected to enlist the family's support in helping the child learn prosocial behaviors. In the field of early childhood education, our work with youngsters is a family affair.

Family Systems Theory

In family systems theory, when something happens to one family member, the event or episode is viewed as impacting everyone else in the family. This is because family members are interconnected or function as a system or group (Olson & Defrain, 1994). The following three models of family systems theory explain the interactive nature of family systems as a key determinant of children's growth and development.

Developmental Contextualism Model

In family systems theory, the family is viewed as a dynamic context wherein children are both changed and change agents. Additionally, as in Bronfenbrenner's bioecological model, the child-family dynamic is reciprocally linked to other contexts such as school or community. According to Lerner (1989), development in these contexts is both bidirectional and dynamic, and it must include aspects of biology, psychology, sociology, and history in order for researchers to better understand disparities in human development. In the **developmental contextualism** model, a focus on biology and context—or the dynamic interplay between nature and nurture—is central to our understanding of family functioning and the development of individual family members. The fact that families can acquire the necessary resources to impact their *own* development is a comforting thought, which can greatly influence teachers' work with families. It, therefore, fuels the need for early childhood educators to work closely with families *and* the community, and to consider the many levels of influence on the development of children and their families. So, for example, a family service worker at a local Head Start program might assist a young family with a child who is at risk for obesity and diabetes with accessing a clinic to ensure that the child is placed on a steady regimen

Figure 15.2	The Circumplex Model of Family Systems

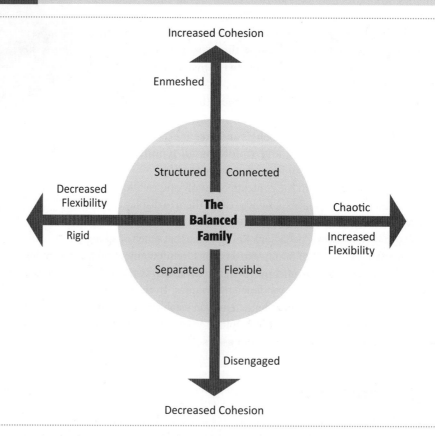

Source: Adapted from Couchenour and Chrisman (2011, p. 14).

of diet and exercise. This simple step might significantly enhance the self-efficacy of both the child and the family, and the child's subsequent schooling success as well.

Circumplex Model

In the circumplex family systems model, Olson and Fuller (2003) demonstrate the interconnectedness or degree of cohesion (togetherness) among members (see Figure 15.2). **Cohesion** refers to the feelings members have toward each other, the kinds of activities in which they engage, and the amount of time members spend with each other. According to the research of Olson and Gorall (2003), the degree of cohesion among family members can be placed on a continuum that includes the following benchmarks: disengaged/disconnected, somewhat connected, connected, very connected, and enmeshed/overly connected. Balanced families are somewhat connected, connected, or very connected, and dysfunctionality occurs at either extreme (disengaged or enmeshed) (Olson & Gorall, 2003).

Families can also be defined in terms of their flexibility. **Flexibility** refers to the ability of family members to be flexible in their roles and the amount of power ascribed to these roles. The flexible continuum includes rigid/inflexible, somewhat flexible, flexible, very flexible, and chaotic/overly flexible. As with the cohesion continuum described above, the middle levels of flexibility are considered to be characteristic of a balanced family, and the two extreme levels of flexibility are unique to unbalanced families (Olson & Gorall, 2003).

Communication among family members is also a critical factor when defining family, and it is the basis of familial relationships. Family communication is the mechanism through which families can appropriately create and maintain cohesion and flexibility over time. This includes the family's ability to listen, speak, clarify, demonstrate respectfulness, and show concern, as well as each family member's capacity and willingness to self-disclose. Parents whose style of child rearing is authoritative in nature (see Chapter 11) maintain effective communication with their young children, offering them appropriate explanations when disciplining or setting limits for them.

Family systems theory underscores the ability of families to change over time, and understanding this can inform our work with families. Families with young children are more closely knit (have greater cohesion) than families with older children because of the need for teenagers to exercise their independence. When children are young, families tend to do everything together. Similarly, families with older adolescents have been found to demonstrate more flexibility than they did just before their first child was born; families with young children have tight routines and schedules that often limit flexibility.

Family Life Cycle

The last family systems theory to be discussed is the family life cycle, which is also linked to Bronfenbrenner's earlier work. Carter and McGoldrick (1999) expanded Bronfenbrenner's bioecological theory to include horizontal or developmental stressors (marriage, transition to parenthood, illness, etc.) and vertical stressors (poverty, oppression, addition, family myths/secrets, loss of leisure time, etc.). In the **family life cycle model**, theorists Carter and McGoldrick postulate that families are composed of people who have a shared history and a shared future that encompasses an entire

Today's families have hectic schedules that often require them to maintain strict routines and schedules.

emotional system of several generations. Furthermore, the relationships among family members undergo various transitions over the course of the family's life cycle (Carter & McGoldrick, 1999). In the family life cycle model, relationships among family members take precedent over family function, and relationships across the generations determine how successfully families move from one cycle to another. What is important for early childhood educators to remember about this particular family system is that young children are always growing and developing in the context of the family life cycle. Carter and McGoldrick's theory includes six phases that family members undergo: (1) single young adults leaving home, (2) marriage: the new couple, (3) families with young children, (4) families with adolescents, (5) launching children, and (6) families in later life. According to Carter and McGoldrick, Stage 3 is often the "pressure cooker" of the family cycle. During this phase, parents are earnestly trying to care for their young children, cultivate their marriages and relationships, and balance household, job demands, and child care simultaneously. Early childhood educators and administrators must be sensitive to the stressors confronting growing families during this period. They can do this by ensuring

The Practice of **Research** and **Theory**

Shared and Nonshared Environments

What makes you so very different in lifestyle, temperament, and social competency when compared with your younger or older sibling? Why might each child growing up in the same household react to and recount family experiences in such markedly different ways? How can two siblings raised by the same parents in the same home end up on two opposite ends of the "life productivity" continuum? For example, one sibling turns out to be a Rhodes Scholar teaching at an Ivy League school and a prolific writer, and the other sibling is sentenced to life in prison for committing a murder. There has been a good amount of research on siblings' development and the impact of shared and nonshared environments. It is false to assume that children raised together share the same home environment. Research has found that children are less impacted by shared environments (such as siblings growing up in the same home and having the same parents) than they are by nonshared environments, such as individual experiences, peers, teachers, and communities. Some social scientists suggest that the impact of the nonshared experience is so significant that parenting has little to no impact on children (Harris, 1998, 2002; McLeod, Wood, & Weisz, 2007). But recent studies refute this assertion and reaffirm the influence of parents in the lives of children (Baumrind, 2005; Chan & Koo, 2010). The degree to which family stressors like the loss of employment, acute or chronic illness of a family member, relocating to a new home/community, or divorce can adversely impact children's development depends on a number of different factors (Berger, 2011). The child's genetic composition, level of resiliency, age, temperament, gender, "goodness of fit" with the parent, and other factors matter greatly. Likewise, some influences—school, neighborhood, extracurricular, and after-school activities—are not shared because family socioeconomic status and neighborhood contexts change (Simpkins, Fredricks, Davis-Kean, & Eccles, 2006).

Maternal attitudes toward children and differential treatment of children can render very different child-rearing experiences and opportunities for siblings. A study of identical twins reared by their biological parents found that nonshared aspects of the siblings' upbringing are significant in the lives of children, but parental influence matters as well. Mothers who were more negative toward one of their twins resulted in that twin engaging in more antisocial and problematic behavior, like fighting, stealing, and hurting others, than the co-twin. Therefore, even among identical twins, each child's experience as a family member is quite unique and can affect development over time (Caspi et al., 2004). And just as parents can provide varying experiences for their biological children, teachers' interactions with children can result in a very different (unique) experience for each child in their preschool classroom.

that children are afforded quality care, arranging parent meetings and scheduling events conducive to parents' schedules, and being flexible around program policies and procedures (arrival and pickup times), when feasible. The family life cycle is replete with transitions at every phase (see Figure 15.3).

Diverse Family Structures

In 2010, the Pew Research Center in Washington, D.C., launched a special investigation of the changing demographics of U.S. families. The institute utilized data from a half-century of census reports and a small nationwide survey of 2,691 people to help shed light on the ever-changing family structures in the United States since 1960. The center claims that, as a research entity, it does not promote any particular ideology, and the sole intent of the report is to explain familial changes occurring in the United States. Although 2,691 people was a rather small sample size and not large enough to be generalizable to the U.S. population, the report did reveal some interesting and continuing developments in the U.S. family structure within the last half of the 20th century.

Reviewed in the Pew analyses were individuals from different demographic subgroups including those defined by marital and family circumstance, class, age, race, gender, and religion. The report asked the following questions: "Is marriage becoming obsolete? Why have marriage rates dropped more for some groups than others? To what extent does the growing marriage gap align with a growing economic gap? How much have gender roles within marriage changed? How does it define family?" (Pew Research Center for the People and the Press, 2010). The Pew researchers found that while marriage is more common for college-educated adults and less common for people of poverty, marriage is still declining among both groups. Also in 1960, 68% of people in their 20s were married, yet in 2008, only 26% of these individuals were married. The report also found that cohabitation

Figure 15.3	The Family Life Cycle

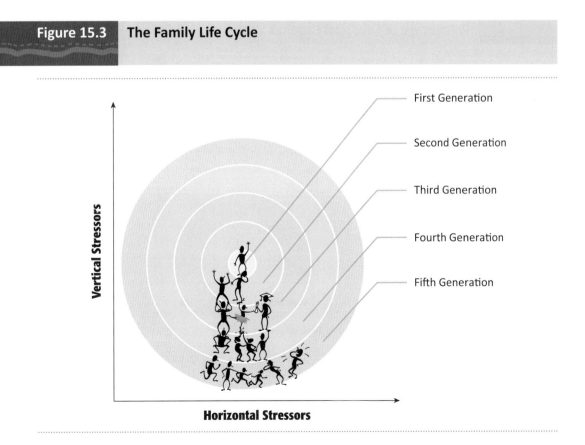

without marriage has doubled since 1990. Interestingly, though, the survey results found that "the family" remains resilient, although marriage is on a steady decline. Perhaps it is more accurate to state that reproduction abounds in light of declining marriages; the report indicated that births to unmarried women moved from 5% in 1960 to 41% in 2008. With regard to race, of the number of Black women giving birth in 2008, an unprecedented 72% were unmarried. This compares with 53% of unmarried Hispanic women and 29% of White unmarried women giving birth during the same period (Pew Research Center, 2010). It is clear from Figure 15.4 that the United States exceeds several industrialized nations in divorce rates.

Although marriage is waning in the United States, still about 54% of all 6- to 11-year-olds live in two-parent homes, usually with their biological parents. This arrangement constitutes the nuclear family (coined after the tightly connected particles of the nuclear atom), considered the most traditional family structure—though some parents in today's nuclear family may not be legally married. Table 15.1 includes the variety of family structures that exist today.

Gay and Lesbian Parenting—Same-Sex Couples

Today, there exist disparate views among early childhood professionals and educators in general concerning young children who are raised by same-sex parents. This type of family structure is more common in today's world than ever before, especially when we consider the composition of the family 50 years ago. Individuals' varying perspectives are shaped by their religious beliefs, prejudices, biased thinking and practices, upbringing, beliefs, customs and practices of family members, and their race of ancestors, political landscape, sexual orientation or identity, and many other factors

Figure 15.4 | **Divorce Rates Among Industrialized Countries and the Percentage of Divorced Families With Young Children**

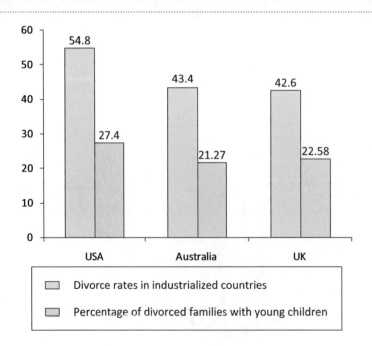

Source: Adapted from http://www.abs.gov.au/AUSSTATS/abs@.nsf/Lookup/4102.0Main+Features30March+Quarter+2012; http://www.darndivorce.com/divorce-rates-around-the-world/; http://nitawriter.wordpress.com/2007/04/04/divorce-rates-of-the-world/; and http://www.oecd.org/els/familiesandchildren/45583012.pdf

Table 15.1   Descriptions of Today's Family Structures

- Adoptive parents: These parents assume legal custody or guardianship of related or unrelated children for an indefinite period.

- Foster parents: These parents assume legal guardianship or custody of related or unrelated children for extended or brief periods of time.

- Grandparents alone: These grandparents assume responsibility for children in the absence of their biological parents—who may be dead, incarcerated, addicted to drugs, or mentally or physically sick.

- Same-sex parents: Less than 1% of two-parent families are headed by a same-sex couple (gay or lesbian), whose legal status (married, step-adoptive) varies.

- Stepparent family: People typically remarry, and when children from a former relationship come to reside with the biological parent and the stepparent, they are a part of a stepparent family. If the stepfamily includes children born from two or more previous families or relationships, this structure is referred to as a **blended family.**

- Single mother, never married: One-parent families are increasing but, on the average, have fewer children than two-parent families. About a third of all American children live in single- or one-parent families. About 40% of all U.S. children are born to unmarried mothers. But many of these mothers marry by the time children attend school.

- Single mother divorced, separated, or widowed: About half of all marriages in the United States end in divorce.

- Single father: About 1 in 5 divorced, separated, or widowed dads has custody of his children and raises them without a wife.

- Grandparent alone: At times, a single grandparent, typically female, assumes sole responsibility for a child.

- Extended family: When children live with a grandparent or other biological family members as well as with one or both parents, they belong to an extended family. The authors are convinced that there are significant anecdotal data that point to an increase in the number of extended family arrangements during the first decade of the 21st century due to the great recession (Berger, 2011; Children, Youth, and Families Education and Research Network, n.d.). Many families who lost their homes doubled up (moved in) with relatives, many of whom were grandparents, uncles, and aunts living under the same roof.

can greatly influence an individual's level of responsiveness and effectiveness when working with same-sex families. Years ago, parents who divorced a heterosexual partner lost custody of their children because of the then commonly held belief that homosexuals were not suitable parents. Today, while there still exist a few U.S. states that ban gay and lesbian couples from adopting children, some U.S. jurisdictions hold that sexual orientation in itself is irrelevant to custody of children. Research substantiates the claims of many who believe that children raised by same-sex couples fare as well as or better than, in some cases, youngsters raised in two-parent households (Bos, van Balen, & van den Bloom, 2007; Tasker, 2005).

Gay and lesbian couples have been found to be just as committed to parenting children as their heterosexual counterparts and, in some cases, even more committed to the rearing of children (Bos et al., 2007; Tasker, 2005). When it comes to raising children, family functionality; the degree of openness, honesty, and encouragement displayed by adults; parents' level of education and earning

potential; and so on are what matters in the scheme of things, not the sexual orientation of two adults living under one roof. Furthermore, young children raised by gay and lesbian parents do not differ from their peers who are raised by heterosexual parents on a number of different measures such as mental health, peer relations, and gender role identity—and the vast majority of these youngsters develop a heterosexual orientation. While society's attitude toward gay and lesbian parenting steadily improves, gay and lesbian parents do fear that their children will be ostracized because of their parents' sexual orientation. Hence, the main distinction between children of gay and lesbian couples and children of heterosexual couples is that, at times, these children are plagued by issues related to living in an unsupportive society (Berk, 2012).

Gay couples are just as committed to their children as heterosexual couples, and like their peers, many children of gay couples undergo typical developmental phases that lead to well-adjusted adult lives.

Grandparents as Caregivers

One popular family structure that has emerged in most recent years is grandparents as caregivers. The vast majority of grandparent couples or single grandparents spend an inordinate amount of time with their grandchildren during special holidays or on the weekends. As a matter of fact, today, more children than ever permanently reside with their grandparents. Nearly 2.4 million U.S. children live with their grandparents and apart from their biological parents in a so-called "skipped-generation family" arrangement (U.S. Census Bureau, 2010; Berger, 2011, p. 275). Not only are grandparents legal guardians, but great-grandparents are also included in this number. Grandparents are getting younger, and people, invariably, are living much longer—perhaps a result of improved medical advances and an increased life span among aging adults. Grandparent caregiving typically involves women rather than men (grandfathers often participate as well), usually includes two or more children, extends across all ethnic groups (although this practice has been found to be less prevalent among Caucasian families), and is the result of parental substance abuse, illness, child neglect and maltreatment, adolescent parenthood, or any other circumstance that places children at risk (Fuller-Thomson & Minkler, 2005, 2007; Minkler & Fuller-Thomson, 2005). As a result of the AIDS epidemic in the United States during the 1980s and 1990s, many grandparents and great-grandparents became surrogate parents for their biological grandchildren whose parents died from the insidious disease. Thus, grandparents often assume the parenting role under tremendous duress (harshness) and must contend with the task of advancing children's development, which has already been compromised by unfavorable child-rearing circumstances. At times, biological children interfere and tend to violate child visitation rights and child custody. And while many of these skipped-generation families are afforded some financial support, funds are inadequate to meet the material and physical needs of youngsters; some grandparents have fixed incomes and are barely scraping by. These circumstances can often take a toll on the health of older adults, resulting in caregivers who are significantly stressed and emotionally overrun. There is a tremendous need for federal and state entitlement programs and city municipalities to provide grandparents with the necessary materials, resources, referrals, and interventions to be effective guardians of their grandchildren. As grandparents increasingly become the significant caregivers in children's lives, it is necessary that teachers of young children become more adept at working with a range of families. Recommended child-rearing techniques that appear effective with young growing families may be found to be ineffective with older caregivers who may be less flexible

Consider This Father and Daddy

John and Thomas moved into a new neighborhood and signed their infant son up for day care at the local child care center. The young boy, exhibiting typical development, was curious and eager to meet new people. He affectionately referred to one parent as "Father" and the other as "Daddy," and both would switch between dropping off and picking up their son from day care. Life was good for this family, but there were some challenges too. As John and Thomas's son grew older, children began to ask the boy questions about his two dads, and some parents raised questions about John and Thomas's

participation as classroom helpers. However, the teachers' treatment of families was undifferentiated. By treating John and Thomas the same as all of the other parents, their son's first day care teacher helped set the tone for this family's acceptance in the community and their son's success at school.

What are your thoughts regarding same-sex parents raising children participating in your preschool program? How would you respond to students' questions about a child with two dads?

and/or willing to try new ways of interacting with their grandchildren. Furthermore, connecting grandparents with social service agencies that provide respite for guardians may greatly mitigate grandparents' feelings of despair and may facilitate their ability to work conjointly with teachers in promoting children's development.

But, for the most part, grandparents can be very acceptable and appropriate caregivers. They provide emotional stability, warmth, and nurturance for children, and they are often wholly committed to children's growth and well-being. The deep and long-lasting relationships that are forged between children and their grandparents last a lifetime and can mitigate more pronounced and prolonged problems with adjustment and development (Poehlmann, 2003). For many grandparents, the opportunity to raise their grandchild affords them yet another chance at child rearing and an opportunity to invest in a life that they hope will yield large dividends—grandchildren who are successful, independent, and contributing members of society.

WHAT IS THE DEFINITION OF FAMILY STRUCTURE AND FAMILY FUNCTION?

What family structures are more conducive to effective family functioning? In other words, what structures produce positive family-child outcomes? The term family function refers to how a family provides for its members; it is the way in which a family works together to meet members' individual needs. Family structure, on the other hand, is defined as the legal and genetic relationships that bind people together, which include nuclear and extended family members, stepfamily members, and others (Berger, 2011). Family function and family structure are interrelated. According to Berger (2011), family function is far more important than family structure at every developmental phase. Infants need responsive caregiving; children in early childhood need guidance, social interactions that propel their development, and a sense of industry; children in middle childhood need stability and a sense of routine; teenagers need autonomy, encouragement, and effective relationships with adults to help them make good choices; young adults need peace and privacy; and older adults need respect and appreciation. Personal assets such as level of education, maturity, and earning potential facilitate the level of functionality of the family. Coparents, living under one roof, support and encourage one another, and both become wealthier and healthier than they would have if they were single and living on their own. Likewise, shared parenting decreases

the likelihood of child abuse, maltreatment, and neglect and affords children certain assurances such as assistance with homework and school projects, cultivating peer relationships, material resources, and basic security (Berger, 2011).

Dual-Earner Families

In dual-earner families, the father's willingness to assist with child care is tantamount. The male's involvement in child care has increased tremendously over the course of the past 30 years. But fathers' increased engagement in child-rearing chores has resulted in an increased incidence of work-life family conflicts (Galinsky, Aumann, & Bond, 2009). The male's assistance in carrying the load can go a long way in a relationship. Not only does the male's willingness to carry the load reduce maternal stress, but his increased interactions with children as a result of increased engagement in child rearing positively impact children's cognition. Paternal involvement is linked to increased cognitive involvement in children, more mature social behavior, flexibility at viewing gender roles, and enhanced mental health in adulthood (Coltrane, 1996; Pleck & Masciadrelli, 2004). Research has found that happier fathers tend to be more involved fathers. But the causal relationship between parental engagement and happiness can be unclear. Do happy fathers tend to be more engaged with their children, or does becoming engaged with their children make fathers happier? What do you think?

Grandparents are reliable and effective guardians for their grandchildren. For many children from low socioeconomic backgrounds, grandparents provide the much needed stability in children's lives.

Maternal Employment

According to the U.S. Census Bureau (2011), single and married women have joined the labor market in record numbers, and the proportions are nearly equal among the two groups. For very young children, the impact of maternal employment on children's development is contingent upon quality and responsive caregiving and the quality of the parent-child relationship. Oftentimes, mothers as well as fathers in dual-earner families struggle with feelings of guilt when they are forced to place their very young children in group care for extended hours, sometimes 8 to 10 hours a day. Parents can be made to feel at ease, and children's development is enhanced, when early care and education programs include adequate care and attention to children, provide quality learning experiences that promote children's development in all domains (cognitive, physical, socioemotional), pay attention to the health and safety of youngsters, and demonstrate professional caregiving—the program ensures continuity of care for children and minimal turnover of staff as well as employs staff who have relevant training and advanced degrees.

For some mothers, especially single moms, the demands at work can inflict undue stress and pressure, placing children at risk for ineffective parenting. Research has found that mothers working long hours and those subjected to a negative work environment displayed reduced parent sensitivity and engaged in fewer adult-child joint activities, which resulted in children with deficit cognitive abilities that persisted throughout adulthood (Brooks-Gunn, Han, & Waldfogel, 2002; Bumpus, Crouter, & McHale, 2006; Strazdins, Clements, Korda, Broom, & D'Souza, 2006). When long hours and negative work milieus are juxtaposed with low-socioeconomic-status wage-earner mothers, the results are even worse. These mothers are likely to develop maternal depression, and children are often subjected to harsh and inconsistent discipline (Raver, 2003). Working parents need support from their places of work and their communities to assist them in raising their children. Part-time work and flexible work schedules, sufficient paid leave and family health insurance policies, and equal pay and employment opportunities for mothers can help boost their morale and socioeconomic status.

Divorce and Its Impact on Young Children

Researchers have found a link between low socioeconomic status and development. Underemployment, unemployment, low wages, blighted living conditions, substandard housing, and limited or unsuccessful schooling experiences can produce significant stress in the home. And when stress is persistent, adults typically become tense and hostile toward their partners and children (Conger et al., 2002; Parke, Coltrane, Fabricius, Powers, & Adams, 2004; Parke, Simpkins, et al., 2004). These conditions impede the growth of both children and parents. Hence, there are two essential factors that adversely impact family function in every possible structure: low income and significant family conflict. The persistence of these two factors can lead to divorce.

It is quite sobering to know that about 45% of all marriages today will end in divorce. It is equally disturbing to know that of these 45% of marriages, about half involve children. At any given time, one quarter of American children reside in a single-parent household. Although most of the children of divorced parents live with their mothers, the number of fathers as custodial parents continues to rise steadily (Federal Interagency Forum on Child and Family Statistics, 2008). Children spend a significant amount of their early childhood years in a single-parent home. Sometimes parents remarry, and children are once again required to make adjustments in their living arrangements and status, family roles, and responsibilities. About two thirds of divorced parents marry again, and about half of the children in these situations soon undergo yet another major change, the breakup and divorce of their parent's second marriage.

Divorce can have a pernicious effect on young children.

Children's ability to fare under these difficult circumstances depends on several different factors: the custodial parent's psychological well-being and maturity, the child's temperament and personality, the social supports that are available to the family, and the social networks within the surrounding community (Hetherington, 2003).

Since divorce is so prevalent in our society, some legal researchers have sought to reduce the stigma of divorce by referring to postdivorce family relationships as "binuclear families" (Karpf & Shatz, 2005). People are therefore discouraged from using language like "broken home." These researchers promote cooperative parent alliances and encourage a renegotiation of rules and boundaries to shape new **coparenting relationships**. Among the issues that are explored within the new coparenting relationships, consider these questions:

- How much time does each parent plan to spend with children following a divorce?
- Is each parent motivated to become a collaborative coparent, or is a "parallel parenting" arrangement preferred?
- How will coparents divide child care responsibilities?
- Do the coparents expect the same rules to apply in each household (discipline, chores, allowances, bedtimes, curfews)?

- How will coparents negotiate important decisions, and are unilateral decisions permissible?
- How will information about children's physical states, daily routines, weekly schedules, and school issues be exchanged between the coparents?

Since most divorces occur during the early childhood years, it is absolutely important that early childhood professionals assist families in ensuring that divorces are significantly less impactful on children. This can be facilitated if divorced families uphold certain basic rights of children, as outlined in Table 15.2.

Reconstructing Fathers

In 1999, Silverstein and Auerbach began to dismantle or deconstruct the notion that young children thrive best when they are raised by both biological parents working in collaboration as opposed to single mothers. These authors adopted a neoconservative view of parenting, which rejects the notion that the criteria for parenting must include parents who are mature, married, and self-supporting; who are not handicapped by substance abuse or by disabling mental illness or defect; and who have no prior convictions for crimes (Lykken, 2000). This is in keeping with Westman's (1994) proposal that called for the need to bestow "parental licensure" on "would-be parents" and constituted an ultra-conservative view of parenting. According to Silverstein and Auerbach, single women who decide to have a child on their own are off the hook; for instance, they need not convince a family court judge of their fitness and/or ability to provide the child with some suitable paternal surrogate. But the argument regarding the need for children to be raised by both biological parents can be supported by some alarming statistics. Since 1960, the United States has experienced an increase in crime, violence, and antisocial behavior and related social pathology. And there is a striking relationship between fatherless child rearing and social pathology. More than two thirds of school dropouts, delinquents, children who are abused or murdered, and juvenile murderers are from homes where the father is absent (Lykken, 2000). In 1994, a study regarding the truancy behavior of elementary school youngsters found that 70% of these children were being reared by a single mother (Foster, 1994). While it is important to indicate that antisocial behavior, increased incarceration rates, truancy, increased numbers of high school dropouts, and fatherless child rearing bear no direct causal connection, one would have to conclude that a father's presence in the home

Table 15.2	Seven Basic Rights of Children During Parental Divorce

CHILDREN HAVE THE RIGHT TO
1. understand that the decision to divorce was not their fault but their parents' decision;
2. not be asked to serve as a spy or mediator, and never be interrogated about a parent's private life;
3. maintain independent relationships with each parent, and respect differences in parenting styles in each parent's home;
4. be free from witnessing parental conflict and from having to side with one parent;
5. have regular access and consistent time with each parent;
6. be free from hearing disparaging comments made by one parent about the other; and
7. maintain relationships with extended family members on both sides of the family.

Source: Adapted from Karpf and Shatz (2005).

and engagement with his children matter greatly. A study by Harper and Mclanahan (1998) found that although increased crime rates among Black boys in inner cities could be attributed to factors such as extreme poverty conditions, living in "bad" neighborhoods, and being born to teenage mothers, the major contributing factor to the boys' incarceration by age 30 years was family structure.

It is important to note that a young person living under certain negative conditions may be motivated to become successful—to turn the tide, so to speak. There is supporting evidence that arduous family circumstances motivate success in education and aid psychological maturation, and some children coming from disadvantaged backgrounds can attain high achievement (Cho & Campbell, 2011). High achievement does not automatically mean a child is functioning well, or that all needs are being met in this child's life. Even resilient children need support and care during situational struggles.

Research supports the fact that fathers can be a critical factor in the child's overall growth and development.

However, we should never assume that most children will somehow rise to the occasion. There is one important fact to remember: Resilient children are more the exception than the rule. It is now time for early childhood professionals to reconstruct fatherhood because father involvement levels the playing field and makes the impossible possible in the lives of children.

Father/Male Involvement

Some of you might have heard of the saying or perhaps recall the popular TV show *Father Knows Best*. This 1960s comedy, which was enjoyed by hundreds of thousands of TV viewers, conveyed the very conservative notion that not only was the "father" the head of the family, but the father knew best when it came to matters regarding the growth and overall well-being of his children. In this sitcom, the father was often portrayed as overly engaged in the lives of his children, and he was always the one who made the major decisions related to the family. Looking back, this depiction of fathers was somewhat faulty and laced with chauvinism (unreasonable devotion to the opposite sex, especially males), but it was in lockstep with the tenor of the times.

However, not too long after the portrayal of fathers in this light, the family as an institution entered into what many refer to as a major state of flux. Hence, as already indicated, a very different picture of the family structure and function began to emerge. Due to such factors as lack of education, lack of commitment, and high divorce rates, over the years, fathers have been virtually absent from their homes and disengaged in development of their children. For the very first time, researchers began to make the connections between absent fathers or the lack of "father figures" in the lives of children and the subsequent negative impact on children's educational, social, and emotional development. Fathers who remain involved and who use good child-rearing techniques contribute greatly to the well-being of children of both genders, with boys showing special benefits.

Thus, children in general fare better when there is involvement and participation of a male or father figure. The engagement of fathers in the rearing of children is so critical that it has been written into public law. Not only does the well-known, government-run Head Start program require parent involvement on all levels, including classroom interaction with children and participation

In the 1960s and 1970s, the traditional role of fathers was quite pervasive.

in program policy making and decision making, but it should be noted that the term *parent involvement* is mentioned in the federal legislation promulgated during George W. Bush's presidency (2001–2009) known as No Child Left Behind more than 300 times (Martinez & Perez, 2008). More specifically, with regard to male interaction with children and along with the acknowledgment that men and women are inherently different, the nature, strength, and uniqueness of males have some very powerful influences on developing children. "A study of low-income Early Head Start fathers found a link between fathers and play with their 2-year-olds, which resulted in better language and cognitive skills in the children a year later, even when controlling for mothers' behavior" (Hall, 2008, p. 6). In addition, it has been discovered that the strength of interactivity of the father tends to encourage curiosity and helps children control their emotions and enjoy surprises (Hall, 2008).

There are a number of ways fathers or **surrogate fathers** (serving as a deputy or substitute, in place of the biological father) can become engaged in their children's lives. Male participation in the PTA (Parent Teacher Association) is one of the most effective ways that fathers can become engaged in children's educational processes. Participating in such an organization not only affects the life of one's own child or children; it can also help other children who may not be as fortunate to have a male role model in their lives. Sharing in the activities and responsibilities of the PTA affords fathers an opportunity to stay abreast of the school programs and policies, to participate in educational workshops, and to engage in decision-making processes (school policies and practices) impacting children.

More and more in our educational settings, we see fathers assume nontraditional roles of engagement and involvement—roles typically reserved for mothers. Today, fathers are breaking the mold when it comes to what constitutes typical male involvement and engagement. In July 2007, the PTA elected the first national male president-elect in its 111-year-long history (Martinez & Perez, 2008, p. 19). Men, therefore, are beginning to make great strides in these types of organizations by assuming major leadership roles. The contributions of male involvement in the education of their children cannot be minimized.

Overall, males' involvement has a powerful impact on the lives of children, and it has been well established that their involvement is just as important, if not more important, than that of their female counterparts. The involvement of supportive fathers or males results in a world of good for a young child and can often be one of the greatest gifts ever offered to a child. But whether fathers, mothers, or both; extended family members; grandparents; legal guardians; a good neighbor; or other adults are engaged in the lives of children, the most important fact remains: that adult involvement at any level can make a difference in subsequent outcomes for children.

Characteristics of Competent Families

Now that we have an increased understanding of some possible causes of family dysfunction and "family trouble," it is a good idea to review the characteristics of the competent or functional family, as shown in Table 15.3.

Table 15.3	Characteristics of Competent Families

A belief and sense of commitment toward promoting the wellness of individual family members as well as of the family unit

Appreciation for the small and large things that individual family members do well and encouragement to do better

The ability to communicate with one another in a way that emphasizes positive interactions

Concentrated effort to spend time and do things together, no matter how formal or informal the activity or event

A sense of purpose that permeates the reasons and basis for "going on" in both bad and good times

A varied repertoire of coping strategies, and the ability to see crises and problems as an opportunity to learn and to grow

A clear set of family rules, values, and beliefs that establish expectations about acceptable and desirable behavior

A balance between the use of internal and external family resources for coping and adapting to life events and planning for the future

Source: Adapted from Lewis, J. M., Beavers, W. R., Gossett, J. T., & Phillips, V. A. (1976).

WHAT IS EFFECTIVE PARENTAL INVOLVEMENT AND ENGAGEMENT?

Parent involvement is not a new concept. Parents' involvement and engagement in their children's educational experiences have roots in the very early stages of early childhood education in the United States. As a matter of fact, the presence of parental engagement in early childhood education settings dates back to the early 1930s and 1940s. Mothers, in particular, assume the roles of **paraprofessionals** and volunteers in the classroom. "Such a close involvement in their children's classroom lives offered opportunities for mothers to enrich the lives of their children and themselves" (Gestwicki, 1992).

While the term *parent involvement* may seem self-explanatory to many, there is a need to fully explicate its meaning. What constitutes parent involvement? **Parent involvement** is

> an all-inclusive term used to describe all genres of parent-program interaction such as policy making, parent education, fundraising, volunteering time, and even parents' simple exchange of information of various sorts with staff. Under the general goal of continuity of care, the desired end result of parent involvement is enhanced parenting and improved care and education for children. The parent-involvement continuum runs from an expectation of parent control to complete subservience of parents to professionals in the field of early care and education. Parents may be cast in a variety of roles from experts (on their own children) to students, thus placing them in positions ranging from servants to **savants** [learned, eminent scholars]. (Pettygrove & Greenman, 1984, p. 89)

Parent involvement, therefore, runs the gamut from low-level involvement such as participation in newsletters to high-level involvement consisting of interacting with children in the classroom. Of course, it is always better for parents to assume a level of involvement that will produce the greatest benefits for all parties involved—child, teacher, and parent.

Professionalism & Policy

Poverty in the United States

The infomercials on TV depicting poor children from around the world may cause viewers to believe that poverty and blighted living conditions only exist in remote countries on the continents of Asia, Africa, and South America. But these kinds of living conditions are just as apparent in the United States as in many underdeveloped nations. The stark reality of children living in dire straits and abysmal poverty in the United States, a country whose leaders often boast of its status as one of the richest global economies in the world, is both disheartening and sobering. The great recession, from which many people are still reeling, has had a devastating impact on our country's most vulnerable populations—poor families. The term *poor families* refers to individuals with incomes below the federal poverty level (FPL), as defined by the U.S. Census. In 2010, the average FPL for a family of four was $22,314. How can today's family of four get by on a meager household income of just $22,000 a year? Today, in New York City, one of the largest cities in the country, there is a high prevalence of concentrated poverty (the number of people living in extreme poverty neighborhoods). According to data collected from the U.S. Census Bureau, since 2008, the number of people living below the FPL in New York City grew exponentially—by more than 120,000—to more than 1.6 million in 2010. Additionally, in 2010, 1 in 3 of New York City's children lived in poverty, up from 1 in 4 two years previous. Throughout the city, 298,000 poor people live in extreme poverty neighborhoods (where the poverty rate exceeds 40%). In New York City, more than 200,000 children—or 1 in 10—reside in neighborhoods where more than 40% of the residents live below the federal poverty level. Overall, 1 in every 10 children in New York City lives in a neighborhood where the poverty level exceeds 40%. While citywide, concentrated poverty has declined in the past decade, the reality is that a large number of New Yorkers still live in extreme poverty (Citizens Committee for Children, 2012). It is also important to note that for many of these families, the burdens of personal poverty are exacerbated by living in overwhelmingly poor neighborhoods. In neighborhoods with high concentrated poverty, individuals confront many obstacles such as a dearth of employment and educational opportunities, high crime rates, poor housing conditions, scarce communal resources, and significant obstacles to prosperity. In many of these neighborhoods, even banks are hard to find. It is also important to note that, as is the case across many U.S. communities, extreme poverty neighborhoods are often predominantly Black and Latino. Our country's public policies or lack thereof seem to disregard the plight of "poor" families. President Barack Obama has often used the words "ladders of opportunity to lift [poor] people into the middle class" as a metaphor to convey the sense of urgency and our nation's moral imperative to care for all of its citizens. He contends that as a nation, we can no longer afford to prevent progress by raising the ladder on the poor—which was the same ladder that many others used to get where they are today. The stalemate that exists among congressional members regarding the continued funding of entitlement programs for "poor families" at appropriate levels is concerning to many. Popular entitlement programs like Medicaid, food stamps, and Temporary Assistance for Needy Families (TANF), which came into existence with the dismantling of welfare, are essential programs that can make a real difference in the lives of young children and their families. As a country, we must recognize that the continued well-being of those families who are faring well is contingent upon the overall stability and progress of all U.S. families. Early childhood educators must be vigilant in their efforts to connect families to available resources in their communities. And the better these connections, the more we increase the likelihood that young children and their families will not only survive but thrive.

According to Bredekamp and Copple (1997), programs successfully engage parents when they

- develop program goals in collaboration with families;
- develop reciprocal and collaborative relationships with families;
- involve parents' participation in program decision making;
- assess and plan for individual children;
- demonstrate teacher sensitivity to and respect for families' preferences and concern;
- create a mechanism for teachers and parents to frequently share knowledge about children's growth and learning; and
- facilitate family linkages with service providers and conduct interdisciplinary case conferencing with families for the purposes of sharing pertinent developmental information about children and facilitating transitions.

Early childhood programs and schools that successfully engage families are family centered in their approach. This means that teachers extend the boundaries of their work with young children to include the family, and extend their social contexts as a basis for supporting children's growth. These teaching staffs appear to be well equipped in the areas of understanding relationship development, developing shared goals for the child, working with children in family contexts, coherent and integrative work with families, and the ability to work in high-stress situations (Powell, 2003).

Effective family engagement occurs when conferences with families are well planned and executed.

It is a given that parental involvement in the educational experience of children is not only crucial but instrumental in serving both the child and the school system. "The truth is that there is a direct link between parent involvement and student achievement. Decades of research show that students succeed when a parent is involved in their child's education, regardless of race, religion, or socioeconomic status" (Martinez & Perez, 2008, p. 18). When people become parents, active participation in their child's education is really not a choice, but rather one of their major responsibilities.

There are several ways to facilitate parents' involvement in their children's education. Parents can participate in educational workshops that may include topics related to child development or creating a supportive learning environment at home. Other types of parent involvement may include taking part in organizations such as the PTA, staying in close communication with the child's teachers by attending parent-teacher conferences (see Table 15.4), working closely with children to acquire or facilitate the learning of new concepts and skills by utilizing curriculum-related suggestions and materials at home, and engaging in meaningful volunteer assignments in the classroom. Regardless of the type of involvement, parental participation is irreplaceable; there is no effective substitute. The key to children's overall success in their school trajectory is parents' and teachers' capacity to build strong partnerships and cooperative relationships with one another. Research has found that involved parents transcend socioeconomic status. Children whose parents are engaged in their educational process are more likely than those whose parents are disconnected to be promoted, attend school regularly, be more adept in social skills, adjust well to school, and benefit from long-term positive consequences such as completing high school and seeking postsecondary education. In short, the more involved parents are in their youngsters' educational experiences, the more likely

Table 15.4	Tips for Effective Conferences With Families

BEFORE THE CONFERENCE:

- Notify the family and coordinate a mutually convenient time and place. Make certain to convey the purpose of the meeting to the family. Ask the family members about their preferred language. (It might be necessary to secure a translator.)

- Prepare for the conference. Review the child's folder, gather examples of the child's work, and prepare materials.

- Plan an agenda jointly with the family, if appropriate.

- Arrange the environment. Make certain to ensure comfortable seating and a good vantage point for the family to review the child's work, and avoid authoritarian posturing by not sitting behind your desk.

DURING THE CONFERENCE:

- Remember to welcome and establish rapport with the family.

- Restate the purpose of the conference, any time limitation, and options for follow-up.

- Encourage the family and accentuate the positive.

- Provide the family with an opportunity to ask questions and share.

- Listen, pause intermittently, exercise appropriate nonverbal and verbal communication techniques, ask clarifying questions, and take notes.

- Develop a collaborative action plan, if necessary, and follow up.

- Summarize and remember to end the conference on a positive note.

it is that children will perform better (Henrich & Blackman-Jones, 2006). Other benefits resulting from parent involvement may include children possessing higher aspirations for themselves, scoring higher on achievement and standardized tests, and having a more positive outlook and attitudes toward math and science.

The benefits of parents working closely with teachers are tremendous and infinitely long lasting. Moreover, this involvement can indeed make a difference in the academic success of children. These benefits are indispensable. Everyone can agree that all children deserve an opportunity to obtain the aforementioned benefits or advantages. When parental engagement is efficacious and mutually beneficial, a win-win situation exists. Considering the myriad of problems that plague our schools today, and the types of challenges that our children often face, optimal parental involvement is an absolute imperative. If the U.S. system of public education, or any system of education for that matter, is to survive and ameliorate over time, then parents of all backgrounds, ethnicities, and socioeconomic backgrounds must become infinitely passionate with regard to their involvement in the education of their children.

Home Visiting

Probably one of the most effective ways to connect with families is through the incorporation of home visiting as a part of the overall program strategy or as the sole technique or strategy to engage families in the education of their children. Home visiting as an effective strategy or service delivery system has its roots in the mid-19th-century United States, and the technique is still in existence today. Home visiting programs like Head Start/Early Head Start, Parents as Teachers, and Home Instruction for Parents of Preschool Youngsters (HIPPY) include a rather elaborate approach to home visiting, which entails a point of entry; the utilization of techniques that create bonds between staff and families; developmentally appropriate child development and literacy activities that build children's enthusiasm for learning, in which parents can easily engage their children, and that quickly demonstrate noticeable effects in children's cognitive abilities; observation and feedback of children's progress and the quality of the parent-child interaction; the exchange of community resource and referral information, and upcoming events; discussion about familial goals and aspirations; modeling of appropriate adult-child interactions; expectations for the subsequent visit; and a point of exit. Finally, home visiting as a strategy is often used by many schools to prove teachers' and schools' interests in families and to help teachers better understand children by viewing children in the contexts of their home and family relationships. Teachers who visit the homes of their children, once or twice a year, build stronger rapport with parents and their children. It has also been found that home visiting as a strategy improves attendance and achievement.

Stages of Parenthood

Our effective work with families as partners in children's educational process, growth, and development can be enhanced by our understanding of parent stage theory. Parents, like children, undergo stages in their development. Parents' emergence through the various stages of parenthood is impacted by children's growth. Therefore, it is conceivable that parents can exist in more than one stage simultaneously, depending upon the different ages of their children. According to Ellen Galinsky (1987), there are six stages of parenthood:

- *Image-making stage:* This stage occurs during pregnancy. Parents form and re-form images of what is to come, for both birth and parenthood. Parents during this stage of growth brace for the inevitable change in themselves and in other adult relationships.

- *Nurturing stage:* This stage begins at birth and extends throughout the first 2 years of life—about the time the child becomes a defiant toddler and is now able to say "No!" This is the time parents contrast their images of the birth of their child with their current reality. Their conceptions of themselves as parents become blurred and are subject to change. They begin to ask themselves questions like "How much time do I give to this child, and how much time do I reserve for me?"

- *Authority stage:* This stage occurs during the child's second to fifth year. During this stage parents ponder the kind of authority figure they will be in the life of the child.

- *Interpretive stage:* This stage begins when the child begins preschool and ends when he or she approaches adolescence. The child's entry into kindergarten or first grade causes parents to review their images and to ask themselves questions related to how realistic and practical they have been. The main task during this phase of parental growth is interpreting. Parents are concerned about how they are being interpreted by their children and how they are interpreting and developing their children's self-concepts. Parents become concerned about their children's profound questions and the kinds of knowledge, skills, and values to promote.

- *Interdependent stage:* This stage of parent development spans the teenage years. The issue that parents struggle with in the authority stage rises to new prominence—often requiring a new solution. Parents begin to form a new relationship with their almost adult children.

- *Departure stage:* This is the time that children leave home and parents evaluate their images of their children's departures by assessing when and how far away their children will go. Parents evaluate whether or not they have successfully achieved the parent–grown child relationship they imagined, and they take stock of their overall success and failures (Galinsky, 1987).

Table 15.5   Considerations for Working With Culturally and Linguistically Diverse Families, and Characteristics of Culturally Responsive Individuals

CONSIDERATIONS WHEN WORKING WITH CULTURALLY AND LINGUISTICALLY DIVERSE FAMILIES

Communicate an attitude of unconditional acceptance and positive regard.

Learn and use children's/families' names (including the proper pronunciation).

Learn and share information (general and specific) about families with appropriate staff, without violating children's/families' right to confidentiality.

Emphasize the similarities more than the differences.

Encourage cultural knowledge sharing.

Be aware of your own attitudes, stereotypes, and expectations.

Allow families to share their knowledge—use families as resources to provide pertinent information about their respective culture.

Communicate that cultural awareness is bilateral.

Invite role models of cultural groups to participate in educational events.

Ensure feelings of belonging.

Assign buddies to each new family and coach the buddies.

Learn the phonemic differences between the families' languages and English.

Recognize and support different learning styles and intelligences.

Use learning materials and props that are authentic and familiar to families.

Celebrate and acknowledge diversity and avoid stereotypical thinking.

Be aware of words, images, and situations that suggest that all or most members of a racial or ethnic group are the same.

Use language and demonstrate behavior that is nonbiased and inclusive.

Avoid the use of qualifiers, which reinforce racial and ethnic stereotypes (i.e., "Geraldo speaks well for a child whose second language is English").

Identify race and ethnic origin only when relevant.

Be aware of language that, to some people, has questionable racial or ethnic connotations.

QUALITIES OF A CULTURALLY RESPONSIVE INDIVIDUAL

Possesses a deep sense of respect for others.

Is aware of his or her own culture.

Has the ability to maintain cultural integrity.

Is knowledgeable of other cultures in the United States.

Seeks and obtains accurate information about families and their cultures.

Avoids making assumptions and generalizations.

Believes that other perspectives are equally valid.

Critiques and analyzes existing knowledge base and practices.

Takes others' perspectives.

Is open, willing, and able to adapt and try new behaviors.

Has good problem-solving skills.

Tolerates ambiguity, conflict, and change.

ideal exists in too few cases. Intimate knowledge of parenting, parenthood, family characteristics, culture, customs, and practices can assist us in our efforts to effectively engage families.

WHAT IS THE ROLE OF THE COMMUNITY IN FOSTERING CHILDREN'S DEVELOPMENT?

You have heard the popular adage "It takes a village to raise a child." And whether you have arrived at this understanding from your direct or indirect experiences with young children is not important. What is important is that you fully recognize that the rearing and teaching of your children is a major task that requires everybody's input. Fostering the effective engagement of the community in the lives of families and young children is a monumental charge but well worth it.

Fostering Community Engagement

Programs like Head Start and Early Head Start that provide comprehensive services for children and families are deliberate about the active engagement of community supports to address the prevalent need of families. It is impossible to have a holistic approach toward engaging families without buy-in, ownership, and support from community agencies. The needs of growing families are often significant, and the limited resources of programs are inadequate to meet the expressed needs of families. It is important to utilize, to the fullest extent possible, the available community resources in order to ensure that families' basic needs are being met. When families' most pressing needs like housing, clothing, and food are met, they are usually less preoccupied and more responsive in the educational process of their children. Linking families to essential community services and resources can have a transformative impact on families as clearly conveyed in this chapter's opening vignette. Below are a few suggestions that can help early childhood educators in their efforts to successfully leverage community resources.

- Know the particular needs of your families and those conditions or circumstances that adversely affect family function and progress.
- Become intimately knowledgeable about the available resources and services that exist in the community.
- Collaborate with families in order to successfully garner support from service agencies and local businesses.
- Maintain an active resource and referral handbook and make certain that it is available in parents' preferred languages.
- Recruit volunteers from local agencies to visit the school to speak with families about available services.

Early childhood education programs can actively engage the community in a number of different ways, such as (1) planning cultural events, carnivals, family nights, and potlucks for families and community members to attend; (2) displaying children's art/written work in local community agencies, organizations, and businesses; (3) working with sororities, fraternities, and local charities who are interested in adopting a family; (4) hosting support groups for parents of children with varying ages and work in conjunction with other entities; (5) encouraging community seniors to visit schools and creating intergenerational programs; and (6) enlisting community members to assist in the classroom as volunteers. When seeking to engage the community at large, it is important that early childhood educators remember that one key element of the relationship between schools and the community must be reciprocity. Both programs and communities have much to offer, and the level of engagement among these two entities is what leads to thriving communities.

Summary

In early childhood education contexts and in elementary schools across the United States, building partnerships with parents and communities is inextricably linked to favorable outcomes for children and families. Effective partnerships with families entail many essential components and considerations. Both political and social forces have resulted in increased connections among parents, schools, and communities. Educators now recognize the benefits of mutual cooperation with families, which can be significant when efforts to engage families in school and community are sincere, informed, and culturally, linguistically, and developmentally appropriate—and when program protocols, policies, and processes are based on best practices. Effective programs recognize the changing nature of families and stay abreast of family trends and adaptations. As families continue to change, it behooves early childhood education professionals to regularly adapt and adopt effective program strategies to engage families.

Key Terms

Chauvinism   409

Cohesion   399

Communication   399

Coparenting relationships   407

Developmental contextualism   398

Family function   405

Family life cycle model   405

Family structure   405

Father Knows Best   409

Flexibility   399

Locus of control   394

Neoconservative   408

Paraprofessional   411

Parent involvement   411

Savants   411

Surrogate fathers   410

Reflection, Analysis, and Application Questions

1. Why is fathers' engagement with their children important to the development of young children? Substantiate your response.

2. In what ways have the traditional family evolved over the course of the past 50 years?

3. As an early childhood professional, how would you facilitate and support the involvement of families and communities?

4. Provide five essential reasons why it is important to engage families in the growth and education of their children.

Extension Activities

1. Take a few moments to reflect about your experiences growing up in your family. What were those experiences like for you? What major theories were at work in your family during that period? Write down your reflective thoughts about your child-rearing experiences.

2. Visit a few of your preschoolers' homes and write down your observations of familial interactions. Of course, be sure to obtain the parents' permission first. In a journal, detail the series of exchanges and interactions, both verbal and behavioral, between you and other members residing in your current household. In light of the many theories presented in this chapter, compare and contrast families, including your own. In your discussion of the families, be sure to maintain anonymity.

Additional Readings

The recommended texts below will provide wide-ranging information relative to today's contemporary family and the most effective strategies for engaging growing families. The texts also include a discussion of such disparate issues as familial drug use and exposure, community and domestic violence, parental discord, and societal toxicity—critical topics of which all early childhood professionals will need to be aware.

Allen, J. (2007). *Creating welcoming schools: A practical guide to home school partnerships with diverse families.* New York: Teachers College Press.

This book provides detailed accounts of schools and diverse families forging partnerships across this country.

Azzi-Lessing, L. (2011). Home visitation programs: Critical issues and future directions. *Early Childhood Research Quarterly, 26,* 387–398.

This article provides a discussion of several aspects of home-visitation programs that warrant further development and evaluation, including the powerful role of context in determining program outcomes, as well as the impact of other factors.

Couchenour, D., & Chrisman, K. (2011). *Families, schools and communities: Together for young children* (4th ed.). Belmont, CA: Wadsworth, Cengage Learning.

This article provides a very comprehensive overview of today's families as well as techniques and strategies for working with families.

Durand, T. (2010). Celebrating diversity in early care and education settings: Moving beyond the margins. *Early Child Development and Care, 180*(7), 835–848.

This article explores issues related to cultural diversity and the need for multicultural sensitivity in early childhood settings.

Klass, C. S. (2003). *The home visitor's guidebook: Promoting optimal parent & child development* (2nd ed.). Baltimore: Paul H. Brookes.

This text provides a detailed overview of the various aspects of children's milieus and practical applications for promoting optimal child growth.

Olson, G., & Fuller, M. L. (2003). *Home-school relations: Working successfully with parents and families* (2nd ed.). Boston: Allyn & Bacon.

This text provides a thoughtful guide to more productive relationships between parents and teachers, homes and schools.

Olson, D. H., & Defrain, J. (1994). *Marriage and the family: Diversity and strengths.* Mountain View, CA: Mayfield.

This article investigates the myriad of strengths and the degree of pluralism in today's marriages and families.

On the Web

Early Childhood Educators' and Family Web Corner - *http://users.sgi.net/~cokids/*
This website provides links to teacher pages, family pages, articles, and staff development resources.

Family Involvement Network of Education (FINE) - *http://www.gse.harvard.edu/hfrp/projects/fine.html*
Under the guidance of the Harvard Family Project, FINE develops human capital for effective family school relationships. Through the provision of rich and diverse offerings of research materials and tools, FINE equips teachers to partner and informs families of leading-edge approaches.

National Coalition for Parent Involvement in Education (NCPIE) - *http://www.ncpie.org/*
NCPIE is committed to developing family-school partnerships throughout America. Its mission is involving parents and families in their children's lives and fostering relationships among home, school, and the community.

National Parent Teacher Association (PTA) - *http://www.pta.org*
The National PTA promotes partnerships that will increase parent involvement and participation in the social, emotional, and academic development of children; it also provides voluntary national standards for parent-family involvement programs.

Student Study Site

Visit **www.sagepub.com/gordonbiddle** to access several study tools including eFlashcards, web quizzes, links to SAGE journal articles, web resources, video resources, lesson plan templates, and more.

CHAPTER 16

Early Childhood Education Policies

This chapter will help you answer these important questions:

- How are education policies enacted?

- What are some hallmark federal early childhood education policies?

- How did the No Child Left Behind Act transform early childhood education?

- What are some model state policies for early childhood education?

- What are some recent and pending federal policies in early childhood education?

- What are some policies that address the family?

Vignette: Policy Preparedness

Lorena, a college senior, knows that her work as an early childhood professional in Arizona will involve supporting English language learners. An initiative passed in 2003 replaced bilingual programs, where children receive some instruction in their primary language, with structured English immersion, which emphasizes learning English for school-age children. Lorena is fluent in Spanish and English; she wonders what impact this will have on her early literacy preschool curriculum. Will she be able to implement best practices for English language learners? For instance, will she be able to provide Spanish instruction in content areas while she supports children's development of English skills? If she decides to pursue her teaching credential, how will state and federal education policies impact her role as a professional? As a teacher, Lorena will be called upon to make many decisions about developmentally appropriate practice in her classroom within the context of federal education policies. At the same time, Lorena will need to become familiar with Arizona state policies that may vary from other state policies.

In this chapter, you will be introduced to various education policies that impact both the field of early childhood education and families with young children. Traditional hallmark policies enacted since the 1960s such as the Elementary and Secondary Education Act, recent policies such as the No Child Left Behind (NCLB) Act of 2001, and pending legislation to reform NCLB will continue to have a major impact on all aspects of early childhood education programs to varying degrees. The policies that have a definitive impact on the field include federal policies as well as model state policies, such as universal preschool and program standards. Understanding the impact of these polices is very important for the beginning early childhood professional. An introduction to the policy-making process will be helpful as you proceed though this chapter. Let's begin with a look at how policies become enacted and some of the goals that drive policy making.

HOW ARE EDUCATION POLICIES ENACTED?

The federal government has enacted many education policies that have shaped the field of early childhood education. Similarly, state departments of education incorporate policies for statewide reform. **Policy making** refers to the act of creating laws that specify the goals of a government. It is important for you to have a foundation in both state and federal policies, as they will impact your role as a teacher. Figure 16.1 is an illustration of the policy-making process.

Figure 16.1 **The Policy-Making Process**

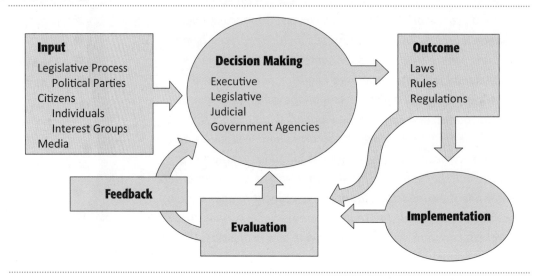

Source: Center for Civic Education. (n.d.).

The policy-making process begins at the input level where an idea, a concept, or a problem becomes identified and individuals address problem-solving solutions. For instance, the idea that all 4-year-old children should have access to a free preschool education is one that many educators, parents, politicians, policy makers, and media have addressed. At the decision-making level, policy makers are informed by both private and public sources. Policy makers may commission a task force composed of researchers and practitioners in a specific field to propose recommendations. For instance, the Task Force on Universal Preschool Education (Maryland State Department of Education, 2007) has informed the state of Maryland of the importance of access to preschool for all children regardless of income level. Similarly, the National Task Force on Early Childhood Education for Hispanics (Working Group on ELL Policy, 2010) has developed policy recommendations for English language learners (ELLs). At the outcome level, policies are written and eventually become laws, rules, and regulations.

Federal policies are adopted by a **state education agency (SEA)** and implemented by a **local education agency (LEA)**. A state education agency, or state department of education, is a state-level government responsible for providing information, resources, and technical assistance to school districts and their residents. A local education agency is a public school district that operates multiple schools. Factors that may impede successful implementation of new policies include cutbacks in federal and state funding, an economic recession, and a shortage of qualified early childhood teachers. Following implementation, policies are evaluated periodically and come up for reauthorization, modification, or elimination. The hallmark education policy, the Elementary and Secondary Education Act (ESEA) of 1965, has undergone various reauthorizations over the years that have led to new program development and modification of existing act provisions. For example, Congress is currently working on reform of the controversial No Child Left Behind Act of 2001, which we will discuss later. Next, let's look at education policy goals that influence reform at the federal, state, and local levels.

Education Policy Goals

Policy making is influenced by the social, cultural, economic, political, and historical contexts of the time. Some of the prevailing factors that influence the goals of federal education policy include educational

The Early Childhood Professional and Education Policies

It is important that teachers be familiar with education policies so that they can interpret the laws and be able to advocate for students and families. Teachers should be able to make decisions about whether laws have been interpreted correctly starting at the state level and ending at the school level. Ultimately, how education laws take shape will depend greatly on the classroom teacher. Involvement with professional local, state, and national organizations keeps teachers informed about laws written for education reform. Teachers can become involved in policy development beginning at the school level and then at the district level. Teacher leaders can provide state policy leaders with their perspective as classroom teachers in how policy impacts children's learning and development. For instance, many states have adopted the Common Core State Standards (CCSS), which provide guidelines on what students should learn at each grade level. The passage of the No Child Left Behind (NCLB) Act of 2001 requires that all students, including students with special needs and English language learners, meet the same rigorous standards. The National Education Association (NEA) is composed of professionals in education and is committed to advancing the cause of teachers. Many teachers have shared their stories about the challenges of implementing NCLB law on the NEA's website (www.nea.org). These teachers' voices play a critical role in how laws are modified and reauthorized.

inequity, poverty, risk, juvenile delinquency, welfare, the working poor, and maternal employment (Kagan & Reid, 2008). Recent legislation goals for education reform include the establishment of high-quality preschools, school readiness, accountability, teacher quality, learning standards, and English language proficiency. What follows is an overview of hallmark federal education policies.

WHAT ARE SOME HALLMARK EARLY CHILDHOOD EDUCATION POLICIES?

As an early childhood professional, you need to have a clear understanding of policy making to influence policy decisions at the local, state, or federal level (International Reading Association [IRA], 2010). Knowledge about education policies will allow you to advocate for the children and families you serve. Your decision making must adhere to children's learning and developmental outcomes (National Association for the Education of Young Children [NAEYC], 2009). Moreover, you must be informed by current knowledge, you must maintain challenging and achievable goals, and your teaching must be intentional.

Elementary and Secondary Education Act

The Elementary and Secondary Education Act (ESEA), passed by Congress in 1965, has been the most widespread federal legislation impacting education. ESEA was part of the "War on Poverty" and the civil rights movement during President Lyndon B. Johnson's administration. A widespread effort was made to address education inequality. The broad education problems of children living in poverty were at the center of education reform (U.S. Department of Health, Education, and Welfare Office of Education, 1969). Education reform was deemed necessary to close the **academic achievement gap**, or the difference in performance on standardized tests between children living in poverty and children from middle-class backgrounds. Similarly, as addressed in Chapter 7, legislation for children with special needs eventually led to the creation of special education programs.

ESEA gave the federal government a significant role in public education. The federal government made an important investment in education, directing funds to research, supplemental services, school libraries, and state departments of education. ESEA addressed the educational and social needs of children beginning in infancy through secondary school. It expanded services to children with disabilities, children with limited English proficiency, and children from migrant and Indian families. ESEA created programs such as Title I, Head Start, and special education, which are discussed next.

Title I

Title I, Education for the Disadvantaged, was one of the most significant provisions of ESEA. It provided federal funding to both public and nonpublic schools. At the public level, state education agencies expanded and improved educational programs for low-income children. The state education agencies then allocated these funds to local education agencies that, in turn, determined which public schools were in need. Schools with high concentrations of educationally disadvantaged children that composed at least 40% of the student population received federal grants. Funds were allocated for professional development, parental involvement, instructional materials, and resources to support educational programs. As a way of helping struggling students, Title I began as a **pullout program** where an instructional assistant worked with students outside of the regular classroom. Eventually, Title I was rewritten to place a larger emphasis on whole-school programs dedicated to improve the overall quality of instruction within regular classrooms.

Head Start

Head Start was an early intervention compensatory program developed to provide economically disadvantaged preschool children and families with comprehensive child development services. As noted in Chapter 3, the Head Start program offered early childhood education, health services, nutrition, social services, and parental involvement. Over time, ESEA increased Head Start student enrollment by requiring that 10% of students be children with disabilities. The Early Childhood Education and Development Act of 1989 expanded Head Start programs to include child care services. The passing of a Head Start reauthorization in 1994 led to the establishment of Early Head Start, extending services to low-income pregnant women, infants, and toddlers. Despite support for Head Start, program funding has not been sufficient to offer services to all children who qualify (Kagan & Reid, 2008). We will learn more about the Head Start program later in this chapter.

Even Start parents receive training on how to be the primary teachers for their child.

Even Start

The Even Start program of 1988 became the first family-centered program established to promote adult literacy and child education outcomes. Even Start allotted funding for the most disadvantaged families in the United States, living well below the poverty level. It targeted parents with low literacy and limited English proficiency, and their children from birth to 7 years of age. Funding grants through the William F. Goodling Even Start Family Literacy Program were intended to break the cycle of poverty and low literacy. Even Start was based on an integrative model that emphasized early childhood education, adult literacy, parenting education, and interactive parent and child literacy activities. To meet federal requirements, Even Start teachers provide families with tools and resources, often through the program model Parents as Teachers (www.parentsasteachers.org). The Parents as Teachers National Center provides resources that include federal and tribal home visiting programs, as well as Promoting Responsible Fatherhood.

Education for All Handicapped Children Act

When ESEA passed in 1965, it did not mandate that schools provide children with special needs with access to a free public education. In fact, many children with special needs did not attend school (Bursztyn, 2007). When Congress passed the Education for All Handicapped Children Act in 1975, it brought awareness to the educational and social needs of children with special needs. The act stipulated that public schools provide students with a free and appropriate education in the least restrictive environment, giving them the opportunity to interact with children in public schools or in the regular classroom. In 1986, amendments to the act were addressed by the Education of the Handicapped Act. The federal preschool program extended services to children 3 to 5 years old while an early intervention program focused on children from birth to age 2 years. In 1990, the act was amended and renamed the Individuals with Disabilities Education Act (IDEA). For a more comprehensive overview of programs serving children with special needs, refer to Chapter 7.

Bilingual Education Act

When Congress passed the Bilingual Education Act of 1968, Title VII, it prompted the development of **bilingual education programs** for school-age ELL students. Bilingual programs vary widely today, but they were originally designed to offer educational programming in the native language while students acquired English language proficiency. At the time, California and Texas were already providing educational programs for ELL students, but the Bilingual Education Act was the first federal policy to provide school districts with federal funding to develop innovative programs for these students. Research funds were appropriated to study ELL students. Schools could provide support to children in their native language until they transitioned into **English immersion** classrooms where they received all instruction in English (Hakuta, 2011). As you read further in this chapter, you will learn how some states across the country have responded to the needs of ELL students. Bilingual education is controversial and has been impacted by social and political issues. As noted in our opening vignette, Lorena will be teaching Spanish-speaking students in a state that has eliminated bilingual education as a program model for school-age children. It is critical that early childhood education teachers be aware of state policies impacting their role as teachers.

Migrant Education

In 1966, an amendment to ESEA, Title I, established the Office of Migrant Education as a separate program that included Migrant Head Start and Migrant Education Even Start. The migrant education program was designed to address the unique educational needs of children of workers in the agriculture and fishing industries. The migrant lifestyle caused disruptions in children's schooling and contributed to educational underachievement. For this reason, migrant children qualified for programs that focused on supplemental and supportive services to remove barriers and promote continuity of education.

Indian Education Act

In 1972, the Indian Education Act focused national attention on the unique educational needs of American Indian and Alaskan children and adults. An amendment to the act in 1974 added a teacher training program and a fellowship program. This was followed by an authorization for gifted and talented education in 1988. A comprehensive focus on both academic and culturally related academic needs was at the center of the 1994 reauthorization of the Indian Education Act (U.S. Department of Education, 2012).

Improving America's Schools Act

An important reauthorization of ESEA was the Improving America's Schools Act (IASA) of 1994, enacted by the Clinton administration. The administration promptly passed the family leave legislation and increased Head Start funding (Kamerman & Kahn, 2001). It also continued funding for Even Start family literacy programs, migrant education programs, and Indian education. While a move toward comprehensive health insurance failed, the Clinton administration made improvements in child health insurance by passing the State Children's Health Insurance Program (SCHIP) law in 1997. ESEA reauthorization also increased funding for Title VII, bilingual education. The Title I program, renamed Helping Disadvantaged Children Meet High Standards, included a provision for accountability results for Title I students. The Goals 2000: Educate America Act of 1994 called for states to develop content standards and challenging state student performance standards. IASA encouraged regular testing of students in reading and math. IASA reflected the future role the federal government would play in prioritizing accountability and the standards-based reform movements of today.

Mobility, poor school attendance, and poverty can negatively impact the educational achievement of migrant children.

The United States has made a significant investment in the education of young children since the Elementary and Secondary Education Act of 1965. Between 1965 and 2001, ESEA programs increased from 6 to 55, and the federal government spent over $140 billion (U.S. Department of Education, 2002). One of the goals of ESEA was to narrow the achievement gap between low-performing and high-performing children through educational equity. This goal was still evident when the Bush administration enacted the No Child Left Behind Act of 2001. As we will see next, NCLB has increased the role of the federal government in stipulating what schools should teach and how student achievement is measured. This has had a transformative effect on the field of early childhood education.

HOW DID THE NO CHILD LEFT BEHIND ACT TRANSFORM EARLY CHILDHOOD EDUCATION?

The implementation of the No Child Left Behind Act of 2001 has posed many challenges for teachers. These challenges include planning for the progress of students with a broad range of instructional needs, implementing nationwide standards, an overemphasis on high-stakes testing, and loss of federal funding for schools that do not meet federal requirements. Let's look more closely at this controversial education policy.

No Child Left Behind Act

NCLB reauthorized the Elementary and Secondary Education Act and held four reform principles: accountability for results, emphasis on scientifically based research, parental choice, and expansion of local control and flexibility. What follows are major provisions of NCLB (U.S. Department of Education, 2001):

- Administer annual, state-standards assessments in reading and math for Grades 3 to 8 and once during high school..
- Be accountable for results.
- Create flexibility at the state and local levels.
- Expand options for parents of children from disadvantaged backgrounds.
- Provide supplemental education services for children in low-performing schools.
- Strengthen teacher quality.
- Offer parents report cards on their public schools.
- Promote English proficiency.
- Require all students in every school to be performing at proficient levels by 2014.
- Integrate scientifically based reading research to ensure all children learn to read.

NCLB targeted accountability and standards-based reform. States were mandated to develop academic standards in reading and math and to align student assessments with these standards. Annual testing, using standardized assessments, was required for 95% of students in Grades 3 to 8 and once in high school. Academic achievement results were to be reported based on disaggregated student subgroups as follows:

- Race
- Ethnicity
- Gender
- English language proficiency
- Migrant status
- Disability status
- Low-income status

Moreover, each state needed to report progress objectives based on the above subgroups. The federal government enforced accountability by establishing **adequate yearly progress (AYP)** reports for every school and district, based on achievement results. States reported student levels of achievement as basic, proficient, or advanced. State education agencies developed timelines for AYP. Local education agencies had flexibility in determining how resources and interventions were directed. After two consecutive years of failing to meet AYP, schools were identified as "schools in need of improvement" and were subject to interventions or restructuring by the state education agency. A system of school improvement interventions implemented for Title I schools was reported, as part of statewide accountability systems. These supplemental services could include tutoring, after-school programs, and summer school programs. States and school districts had to distribute annual report cards to parents, who could also request information regarding teacher qualifications. When a school was labeled as failing, parents could transfer their child to a better-performing public or charter school.

Under NCLB guidelines, **scientifically based research** became the standard and foundation of academic instruction. For the first time, the federal government mandated that state departments of education implement scientifically based reading programs under the Reading First initiative to ensure students reached reading proficiency by the third grade. Let's review scientifically based reading instruction.

Scientifically Based Reading Instruction

NCLB established initiatives to improve reading achievement and to close the achievement gap. These initiatives have brought more attention to the field of early childhood education.

Reading First Initiative

Under NCLB, the Reading First initiative awarded grants to states, which, in turn, awarded grants to schools that documented how they would use scientifically based reading programs to get all students to read by the end of third grade. The National Reading Panel report (National Institute of Child Health and Human Development [NICHD], 2000) presented a critical review of the scientifically based research conducted on reading development and instruction. Based on the findings of this report, the Reading First initiative established that schools adopt evidence-based methods of reading instruction. The report highlighted five essential components of effective reading instruction: phonemic awareness, phonics, fluency, vocabulary, and comprehension.

Competency in these five components requires systematic and explicit instruction (Learning Point Associates, 2004). For instance, phonemic awareness and phonics skills, such as letter sounds and letter names, are taught explicitly and systematically in a hierarchical structure. This approach to reading instruction requires that teachers adopt changes in their delivery models. Reading First funding was distributed to states only when they adopted this prescribed approach to reading instruction. The federal government then monitored state programs to ensure they maintained program integrity.

Educators have expressed concerns over reading approaches that emphasize teaching discrete skills over reading comprehension at the lower primary grades. The National Reading Panel report (NICHD, 2000) informs educators that a preschool and elementary curriculum needs to include a balanced approach for teaching reading. A well-designed reading program promotes learning discrete skills within a meaningful context where reading comprehension is part of the program. This is especially important for English language learners. The National Literacy Panel on Language Minority Children and Youth report (August & Shanahan, 2006) found that although English language learners benefited from direct instruction in decoding, word recognition, and spelling, they did not experience gains in reading comprehension and writing. The report states:

> Instructional approaches found to be successful with native English speakers do not have as positive a learning impact on language-minority students. It is not enough to simply teach language-minority students reading skills alone. Extensive oral English language development must be incorporated into successful literacy instruction. The most promising instructional practices for language-minority students bear out this point: Literacy programs that provide instructional support of oral language development in English, aligned with high-quality instruction are the most successful. (August & Shanahan, 2006, p. 4)

As an early childhood teacher, you will need to take into account the relevant research on the educational needs of a diverse student population. The current knowledge base in early literacy acquisition and reading instruction brings increased attention to the need to prepare preschool children to enter school ready to meet the demands of a standards-driven curriculum. This is a realization that Lorena from our opening vignette confronts as a future preschool teacher.

NCLB encourages preschool programs to also incorporate scientifically based research to promote early literacy skills. Although NCLB legislation has not placed explicit demands on early childhood preschool educators, it has directed policy efforts to emphasize early literacy instruction, accountability systems through early learning guidelines, high-quality preschool programs, and teacher qualifications (Kagan & Reid, 2008).

Good Start, Grow Smart Early Learning Initiative

The Good Start, Grow Smart early learning initiative of 2002, part of NCLB, had the goal to prepare preschool children to enter kindergarten with the skills necessary to be "ready to learn." The initiative was designed to strengthen Head Start, provide support to states and local communities in improving early learning, and inform educators and parents with information on early learning (U.S. Department of Health and Human Services, 2006). Currently, the federal government awards grants to local programs that demonstrate they can provide children with a high-quality environment that incorporates scientifically based research. The three key areas of the initiative are early learning guidelines, professional development plans, and program coordination.

The first key area, early learning guidelines, encourages states to develop guidelines of content standards for children ages 3 to 5 years in the areas of early literacy, language, prereading, and mathematics. These guidelines/standards should be aligned with state K–12 standards. These guidelines are voluntary, but the majority of states have already developed them. The second key area, professional development plans, recommends that states provide professional development to support implementation of early learning guidelines. The third key area, program coordination, suggests that states coordinate services across early childhood programs to ensure more students are provided with high-quality early care and education programs.

High-Quality Programs

Research indicates that participation in high-quality programs correlates with positive student outcomes. Unfortunately, many children in child care attend programs that have little or no quality assurance (Barnett, 2008). The ratio of children to teachers is important to ensure quality during preschool. A high-quality preschool program includes an emphasis on cognitive, language, social, and emotional development, as well as self-regulation. Programs require small class sizes with qualified teachers who are given adequate pay (Barnett, 2008). Quality implies one teacher and an aide for no more than 20 students. In addition, parent partnerships are an important component of these programs.

Currently, many states are in the process of developing a system of quality assurance for all early childhood programs in which the early childhood professional works. For instance, by 2013, Colorado will augment its Quality Rating and Improvement System (QRIS) to make it "inclusive, accessible, available to all child care providers, embedded in licensing, and reflective of evidence based practices for successful outcomes for all children" (Colorado Department of Human Services, 2011). California is developing an Early Learning Quality Improvement System that contains high-quality care features that will align a funding model with a quality rating system (California Department of Education, 2012).

Common Core State Standards Initiative

The Common Core State Standards (Council of Chief State School Officers & National Governors Association, 2010) for K–12 English language arts and mathematics were developed to provide a consistent framework of what students are expected to learn. A framework for K–12 science education from the National Research Council (2011) will serve as the new K–12 science education standards. The English language arts and mathematics standards provide benchmarks for all students, regardless of where they live. These Common Core State Standards build upon the state standards and have already been developed by states across the country. The Common Core State Standards meet the following criteria:

- Fewer, clearer, and consistent
- Aligned with college and work expectations

- Include rigorous content and application of knowledge through higher-order skills
- Build upon strengths and lessons derived from current state standards
- Informed by the standards of other top-performing countries, so that all students are prepared to succeed in our global economy and society
- Based on evidence and research

While the Common Core State Standards focus on learning expectations for all students, they do not stipulate what the process will be in meeting the standards. Teachers will need resources, tools, and time to implement the standards. Additionally, instructional materials and assessment will need to be aligned to the standards. Moreover, educators need to review federal and state policies to ensure alignment between the Common Core State Standards and student achievement.

Early Learning Standards

The Good Start, Grow Smart initiative (U.S. Department of Education, 2002) does not mandate, but highly encourages, states to develop early learning guidelines in the areas of early literacy, language, prereading, and mathematics. State programs have the option of using guidelines or standards already developed. The Florida Department of Education (2011) has developed the Early Learning and Developmental Standards for Four-Year-Olds. They include comprehensive standards for physical development; approaches to learning; social and emotional development; language, communication, and emergent literacy; and cognitive development and general knowledge. The learning and development standards are a valuable tool for early childhood educators who seek to develop a high-quality learning environment.

Currently, there are no national learning standards for infants and toddlers. The Zero to Three National Center for Infants, Toddlers, and Families (2008) has developed the Early Learning Guidelines for Infants and Toddlers to offer guidance for states in the process of developing early learning guidelines. Some states, such as Massachusetts and California, have developed infant/toddler learning standards. The California Infant/Toddler Learning and Development Foundations (California Department of Education, 2009) present competencies most infants and toddlers who are typically developing acquire in the domains of social/emotional, language, cognitive, and perceptual and motor development. The California Department of Education has aligned the learning and development foundations with a curriculum framework and an assessment tool. Table 16.1 provides an example of cognitive foundations for early development of mathematical and scientific thinking, part of the Infant/Toddler Learning and Development Foundations.

The influence of NCLB legislation is also apparent in Head Start preschool programs. The Head Start Reauthorization Act of 2007 highlights program performance standards and guidelines, enhanced program quality, research, professional development, and increased teacher qualifications.

Head Start Program

Despite changing political and fiscal climates, Head Start continues to evolve and has been reauthorized several times. Head Start has enrolled more than 27 million children since it was created in 1965. Head Start is administered through the U.S. Department of Health and Human Services and bypasses oversight from state departments of education.

During the 2008–2009 Head Start program year (U.S. Department of Health and Human Services Office of Head Start, 2010), Head Start reported the following statistics:

- 11.5% of children served were children with disabilities.
- 44,109 children participated in the home-based program.
- 77% of Head Start teachers had an associate's degree in early childhood education.

Table 16.1	Summary of California Infant/Toddler Foundations

SOCIAL/EMOTIONAL DEVELOPMENT

- Interactions With Adults: The developing ability to respond to and engage with adults
- Relationships With Adults: The development of close relationships with certain adults who provide consistent nurturance
- Interactions With Peers: The developing ability to respond to and engage with other children
- Relationships With Peers: The development of relationships with certain peers through interactions over time
- Identity of Self in Relation to Others: The developing concept that the child is an individual operating within social relationships
- Recognition of Ability: The developing understanding that the child can take action to influence the environment
- Expression of Emotion: The developing ability to express a variety of feelings through facial expressions, movements, gestures, sounds, or words
- Empathy: The developing ability to share in the emotional experiences of others
- Emotion Regulation: The developing ability to manage emotional responses with assistance from others and independently
- Impulse Control: The developing capacity to wait for needs to be met, to inhibit potentially hurtful behavior, and to act according to social expectations, including safety rules
- Social Understanding: The developing understanding of the responses, communication, emotional expressions, and actions of other people

LANGUAGE DEVELOPMENT

- Receptive Language: The developing ability to understand words and increasingly complex utterances
- Expressive Language: The developing ability to produce the sounds of language and use vocabulary and increasingly complex utterances
- Communication Skills and Knowledge: The developing ability to communicate nonverbally and verbally
- Interest in Print: The developing interest in engaging with print in books and in the environment

COGNITIVE DEVELOPMENT

- Cause and Effect: The developing understanding that one event brings about another
- Spatial Relationships: The developing understanding of how things move and fit in space
- Problem Solving: The developing ability to engage in a purposeful effort to reach a goal or figure out how something works
- Imitation: The developing ability to mirror, repeat, and practice the actions of others, either immediately or later
- Memory: The developing ability to store and later retrieve information about past experiences
- Number Sense: The developing understanding of number and quantity
- Classification: The developing ability to group, sort, categorize, connect, and have expectations of objects and people according to their attributes
- Symbolic Play: The developing ability to use actions, objects, or ideas to represent other actions, objects, or ideas
- Attention Maintenance: The developing ability to attend to people and things while interacting with others and exploring the environment and play materials
- Understanding of Personal Care Routines: The developing ability to understand and participate in personal care routines

PERCEPTUAL AND MOTOR DEVELOPMENT

- Perceptual Development: The developing ability to become aware of the social and physical environment through the senses
- Gross Motor: The developing ability to move the large muscles
- Fine Motor: The developing ability to move the small muscles

- 26% of program staff members were parents of current or former Head Start children.
- 94% of Head Start children had health insurance.
- More than 228,000 Head Start fathers participated in program activities.

In 2002, as a response to the Good Start, Grow Smart initiative, Head Start began annual testing of all children in early literacy and math with the National Reporting System (NRS) (U.S. Department of Health and Human Services Head Start Bureau, 2003) to document evidence of program effectiveness. Sharp criticism of the reliability of standardized instruments for young children led to the decision to suspend use of results to determine program funding. Continued NRS data collection today is used to measure student outcomes and to plan training programs for all Head Start programs.

Teacher Qualifications

The Head Start Reauthorization Act of 2007 (U.S. Department of Health and Human Services, 2008) contains new requirements for staff qualification and professional development. By September 2013, half of all Head Start teachers nationwide in center-based programs will require a baccalaureate or advanced degree in early childhood education, or a baccalaureate or advanced degree and course equivalent to a major relating to early childhood education, with experience teaching preschool-age children.

For many preschool teachers a degree in early childhood education or a related field will be required to meet federal or state requirements.

Administrators seeking to retain highly qualified early childhood educators need to provide valued workplace supports like health insurance, disability insurance, and a pension plan (Holochwost, DeMott, Buell, Yannetta, & Amsden, 2009). The probability of teacher retention increases after the teacher has remained in one program for 5 years (Holochwost et al., 2009).

English Language Learners

Under NCLB, the Bilingual Education Act, Title VII, was reauthorized as Language Instruction for Limited English Proficient and Immigrant Students, Title III. NCLB required that all English language learners be assessed annually to track English language proficiency in listening, speaking, reading, and writing. States also had to align the content standards with English language proficiency assessments. The following are some of the purposes behind Title III:

- To help ensure that children with limited English proficiency, including immigrant children and youth, attain English proficiency, develop high levels of academic attainment in English, and meet the same challenging state academic content and student academic achievement standards that all children are expected to meet.

- To develop high-quality language instruction educational programs designed to assist state educational agencies, local educational agencies, and schools in teaching children with limited English proficiency, including immigrant children and youth, to enter all-English instruction settings.

- To provide state and local education agencies with the flexibility to implement language instruction education programs, based on scientifically based research on teaching children with limited English proficiency, that the agencies believe to be the most effective for teaching English.

Similar to Erik Erikson's theory of psychosocial development discussed in Chapter 4, growth for parents undergoing these various stages can occur at any time—whenever the parent resolves the clash between an earlier image and reality. Whether a parent assumes responsibility for a baby, faces anger within, or figures out the best way to explain the world to a budding 5-year-old, parents do, in fact, change. Recognizing that parenthood is itself a transformative process and that parents change in relation to growing children makes our work with parents intriguing and full of possibilities.

Related to our understanding of the stages of parenthood is the recognition that parents possess various styles of parenting. Parenting styles (see Chapter 11), which range from authoritative to disengaged (Baumrind, 1967, 1971), can greatly impact family function and the overall growth of children. Our understanding of parenting styles can also influence our work with families and the types of parenting educational experiences we offer families. As humans, we tend to parent the way in which we were parented, and we tend to teach the way in which we were taught. Parenting styles easily become a part of our repertoire of behaviors; most of our parenting behaviors are executed quite subconsciously. How many times has your response or reaction to children mimicked your parents' antics or ways of interacting with children? While it is often difficult to change parenting style, it is possible to increase parents' awareness of the child-rearing technique or parenting style (authoritative) that has been touted as the most successful in yielding the best results. Authoritative parents tend to raise children who are socially adept, articulate, empathetic, successful, and happy. For many early childhood programs, the provision of parenting education workshops is a major ongoing event.

WHAT IS CULTURALLY SENSITIVE ENGAGEMENT OF FAMILIES?

The United States is the perpetual nation of immigrants. Thus, it goes without saying that many of today's families participating in public early childhood programs and early elementary schools are culturally and linguistically diverse. For many of these parents, English proficiency is limited, and some are unfamiliar with the norms, practices, and social landscape of the United States. While many of these families desire to participate in their children's education, their engagement in their child's educational process is often hampered by language and cultural barriers. In order to effectively engage parents, early childhood professionals must consider all aspects of diverse families' functionality and structure, which should also include a thorough analysis of families' cultural styles of parenting, including parents' perspectives and attitudes about schooling, family aspirations, goals and values, the political landscape, and forms of communication among the targeted groups. Researcher Tina M. Durand (2010) urges early childhood professionals to suspend judgments of the practices of those who are different—at least long enough to gain an informed understanding of behavior patterns that are involved familiar as well as the sometimes surprising ways of other communities. Durand further asserts that early childhood educators be reflective, keep their assumptions in check, increase their understanding of the cultural backgrounds of families, be close observers of families that they serve, celebrate the knowledge about the families that they do possess, and honor the word *time*—knowing that difficult situations will not be resolved overnight (Durand, 2010).

Table 15.5 is a rather exhaustive list of considerations for working with culturally and linguistically diverse families and another list that delineates the characteristics of a culturally responsive individual, adapted from the work of Stacey York (2003).

To reiterate, the United States is becoming increasingly diverse, and the "inevitability of the browning of America" is already apparent. Educators and social service providers who work with families, and particularly vulnerable families, must be well versed in the techniques and strategies that effectively engage ethnic and language minority families. It would also be helpful if teachers and other professionals who work with families are truly reflective of the population served, but this

Consider This Highly Qualified Preschool Teachers

Amanda has taught in a Head Start program for the past 10 years. Five years ago, she became a lead teacher. However, she never obtained a college degree and is now at risk of losing her role as a lead teacher if she does not meet federal requirements. Head Start is requiring that 50% of teachers have a bachelor's degree by 2013. After investigating her options, Amanda has decided to attend a program at a local university that has partnered with Head Start, the county offices of education, and the community college district by creating an early

development, care, and education (EDCE) cohort program that addresses the need for well-qualified teachers in the field of early education. The program is designed for working students, so Amanda will be able to take classes in the evening or on the weekend to accommodate her work schedule.

Do you think that it is important for all preschool teachers to hold a degree in early childhood education or a related field?

In some states, such as Texas and California, Latino children represent 50% of the student population (Gandara, 2010). Children who enter kindergarten unable to speak English demonstrate a large achievement gap compared with children who enter with English proficiency (Gandara, 2010). Latino children are the least likely to have access to preschool, and they demonstrate the lowest levels of academic achievement compared with other non-Latino students. Second language learners have the challenge of learning a new language while mastering academic content (Hakuta, 2011). Research shows that it takes 5 to 7 years to learn a new academic language (Cummins, 1981). Unfortunately, not all teachers may have a clear understanding of the nature of second language acquisition, or they may hold false assumptions and misconceptions about how to support English language learners (Espinosa, 2010; Genesee, 2010; Hakuta, 2011). ELL students who participate in **dual-language programs** where instruction is delivered in two languages (e.g., English and Spanish) become fluent in both their native language and English (Hakuta, 2011; Garcia & Frede, 2010; Goldenberg, 2008). The early

Hmong English language learners participate in a dual-language classroom where the goal is to produce biliterate and bicultural students.

childhood professional needs to have knowledge of first- and second-language acquisition and the role of native language in learning to read and write in a second language (IRA, 2010).

Educators, parents, and policy makers may be apprehensive about teaching children in a language other than English (Genesee, 2010). This was made evident in state initiatives to end bilingual education programs. In 1998, California was the first state to pass an initiative to end bilingual education programs in favor of English immersion models. The states of Arizona and Massachusetts soon followed, declaring English as the official language. By 2005, Arizona required that all K–12 classroom teachers, supervisors, principals, and superintendents receive an endorsement in **structured English immersion (SEI)** (Arizona Department of Education, 2011).

The Practice of **Research** and **Theory**
Saint Paul Public Schools for Language Academy Program

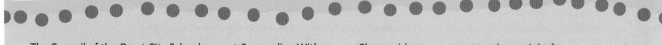

The Council of the Great City Schools report *Succeeding With English Language Learners* (Horwitz et al., 2009) highlighted school district reform efforts impacting English language learners. Saint Paul Public Schools in the state of Minnesota applied research and theory to reform instructional programs for English language learners. In 2005–2006, 42% of the students enrolled were ELL Hmong- and Spanish-speaking students. The district's plan for reform included moving students out of TESOL (Teachers of English to Speakers of Other Languages) centers into mainstream classrooms where they had access to the core curriculum. The key policies and strategies for improving instructions for ELL students included

- Language academies with a collaborative model of instruction
- An emphasis on professional development to support the collaborative structure

- Clear guidance, support, and oversight for implementation
- Employment of school-based accountability to change the culture of schools

The district created Spanish dual-language classrooms and was the first to create a Hmong dual-language classroom in the nation, with the goal of producing biliterate and bicultural students (U.S. Department of Education, 2010). Moreover, the social studies curriculum was embedded with Latino, Hmong, and Somali cultures. Achievement results revealed that Saint Paul Public Schools succeeded in closing the academic achievement gap between ELL students and non-ELL students. Over 50% of ELL students placed within the proficiency level for third grade.

SEI is an intensive English language teaching program for English language learners where instruction is delivered in English. Arizona, California, and Massachusetts use SEI instead of bilingual education programs to meet the legal requirements of state law. In California, for instance, the number of ELL students getting direct support in their native language has dropped sharply (Olsen, 2010).

NCLB legislation does not mandate English immersion programs at the preschool level. However, most states do not implement a systematic approach to English language development and maintenance of the home language (Espinosa, 2010). Let's return to the vignette presented at the beginning of the chapter. Lorena will be working in a preschool program where she will be supporting a large percentage of ELL students from Latino, Spanish-speaking backgrounds. In the United States, over 80% of ELL students come from Spanish-speaking backgrounds (Goldenberg, 2008). Lorena understands the daunting challenge that many of her students will face when they enter kindergarten. Lorena is familiar with state policy in Arizona that requires teachers to teach English in SEI programs where ELL students will need to become English proficient in a year. All materials and instruction will be in English (Arizona Department of Education, 2008). Therefore, one of her goals is to prepare her preschool ELL students to successfully participate in mainstream classroom instruction by using effective strategies for promoting preschool ELL students' language and literacy development (Ford, 2010).

Early childhood professionals need to make many decisions about how to support English language learners in preschool programs. As noted in Chapter 1, your philosophy of teaching will change and develop during your career, especially within the social and historical context of federal and state policies that impact, and will continue to impact, early childhood programs. In the case of

ELL students, your role as an early childhood professional requires that you implement a high-quality early literacy and language program.

WHAT ARE SOME MODEL STATE POLICIES FOR EARLY CHILDHOOD EDUCATION?

States across the country develop innovative policies that can improve current federal policies. It is important that teachers of young children be familiar with both federal and state policies that will impact educational programming and practice.

State-Funded Preschool Programs

State funded preschool programs have grown in most states across the country. The majority of state-funded preschool programs serve students from low-income families and students with disabilities. The field of early childhood education is also impacted by policies developed at the state level. However, these state policies vary across states. Some states, such as Oklahoma, have policies in place to provide voluntary services to all preschool students. In recent years, the state of the economy has brought many challenges to the implementation of early childhood policies. In the 2009–2010 school year, the funding for children in many state preschool programs dropped sharply (Barnett et al., 2010). State cuts to preschool programs have jeopardized quality standards, placing the focus on maintaining program operations versus program quality.

The National Institute for Early Education Research (NIEER) (Barnett et al., 2010) publishes the annual State Preschool Yearbook to provide data on state preschool programs throughout the country. During the 2009–2010 school year, the percentage of 4-year-old children enrolled in state preschools varied widely. The states serving the largest populations of students in state preschool programs were Oklahoma (71%), Florida (68%), West Virginia (55%), Georgia (54%), and Vermont (52%). States that showed a commitment to serving 3-year-old children were Illinois, New Jersey, Vermont, Nebraska, Kentucky, and California. States were also ranked based on 10 quality standards:

English language learners in structured English immersion programs receive direct instruction in English to become English proficient in a year.

1. Comprehensive early learning standards.

2. Teacher has a bachelor's degree.

3. Teacher has specialized training in prekindergarten.

4. Assistant teacher has a Child Development Associate Credential or equivalent.

5. Teacher has at least 15 hours per year in-service training.

6. Class size is 20 or lower.

7. Staff-child ratio is 1:10 or better.

8. Vision, hearing, health, and support services are provided.

9. At least one school meal is included each day.

10. Monitoring of staff and center.

Promoting Optimal Development

Strategies for Promoting Preschool English Language Learners English Language and Literacy Development

Teachers make a difference every day in their classrooms in how they address English language learners' needs. Colorín Colorado is a website that provides research-based information for ELL teachers, as well as information on policies impacting ELL students, and recommendations for instruction and assessment (www.ColorinColorado.org). A recent article found on the website, written by Ford (2010), presents nine strategies for promoting preschool English language learners' language and literacy development:

- Provide explicit, systematic instruction in vocabulary.
- Ensure that ELL students have ample opportunities to talk with both adults and peers, and provide ongoing feedback and encouragement.
- Expose ELL students to rich language print.
- Structure the classroom space and routine to provide scaffolding for ELL students' language learning.

- Encourage continued L1 or native language development.
- Develop early literacy skills (alphabet knowledge, phonological awareness, and print awareness).
- Design instruction that focuses on all of the foundational literacy skills.
- Recognize that many literacy skills can transfer across languages.
- Accelerate English literacy development by helping ELL students make the connection between what they know in their first language and what they need to know in English.

Preschool teachers can promote English language development by incorporating meaningful language and literacy activities in the classroom. While learning English is crucial for ELL students, the development of literacy skills is also important.

States that met all 10 quality standards were Alabama, Alaska, North Carolina, and Rhode Island, plus one Louisiana program. Oklahoma met 9 out of 10 quality standards. The Oklahoma preschool program will be highlighted next because this state has consistently advocated for high-quality preschool programs since 1980.

As noted earlier, Oklahoma's early childhood education program for 4-year-olds ranks first in the nation for access and enrollment. Oklahoma passed an education reform bill in 1990, offering school funding for any district willing to provide preschool to children who qualified for Head Start. By 1998, state funding increased to provide all 4-year-old children with access to free preschool education. Some high-quality program features for 4-year-old preschool children include accessibility to preschool within public schools. Preschool services are free and voluntary. Extra funding is provided to local school districts for children from low-income and non-English-speaking households. Class sizes are 20 students with one teacher for every 10 children. All students receive free vision and hearing screenings. All preschool teachers must hold a bachelor's degree and be certified in early childhood education, as well as participate in continuing professional development. Preschool teachers receive the same salary and benefits as regular public school teachers. Preschool teachers use state-adopted curriculum standards and a school readiness program.

Oklahoma's early childhood program for 4-year-olds established success in the areas of school readiness for receptive vocabulary, math skills, and print awareness (Gormley, 2008; Lamy, Barnett, & Jung, 2005). Receptive vocabulary and print awareness are strong predictors of later success in reading (Snow, Burns, & Griffin, 1998). The Oklahoma early education program demonstrated positive effects similar to those obtained from other high-quality programs across the nation (Lamy et al., 2005). The impact of the program on the school readiness of Latino students is documented by Gormley (2008). In terms of school readiness, Latino children who participated in the program performed one year above Latino children who did not attend. Additionally, children in full-day programs outperformed those in half-day programs. Oklahoma's universal preschool program demonstrates a strong commitment to child-centered policies that promote school readiness for all young children. This innovative program has led the way for other states that have adopted or are in the process of adopting universal preschool programs.

Universal Preschool

Policy makers acknowledge the value of early childhood education and that more attention is being focused on the demand for quality preschool programs for all children despite the economic state of the nation. Many state departments of education have proposed the goal of providing a free public education to all preschool-age children, ending policies that have served only children with low incomes and/or special needs. How states restructure preschool education programs has important educational implications for young children. Universal preschool strives to increase the levels of participation in center-based preschool programs for every 4-year-old child in the country, regardless of parents' income. While the Preschool for All initiative in California failed in 2006, Preschool for All legislation has been passed by Florida, Georgia, Oklahoma, West Virginia, Illinois, and New York to provide universal preschool to all children.

In 2006, Illinois became the first state to offer voluntary universal preschool to all 3- to 5-year-old children. Preschool for All provides high-quality half-day preschool programs. In 2006, Illinois was recognized as a national leader for its commitment to early childhood education by the NIEER (Barnett, Husted, Hawkinson, & Robin, 2006). Both for-profit and nonprofit agencies, as well as faith-based programs, can apply for state grants.

WHAT ARE SOME RECENT AND PENDING FEDERAL POLICIES IN EARLY CHILDHOOD EDUCATION?

The most recent federal policy impacting education today is the American Recovery and Reinvestment Act of 2009. Both the Senate and the House of Representatives are working on the reauthorization of NCLB and ESEA.

American Recovery and Reinvestment Act

In 2009, the American Recovery and Reinvestment Act (ARRA) passed as part of President Barack Obama's response to the economic crisis. A comprehensive list of provisions included health and human services and education. Various early childhood education programs were included in the act, including child care, Head Start and Early Head Start, Title I, school improvement programs, and IDEA. These programs are essential since the number of families living in poverty has increased. Today, children represent 24% of the population but compose 34% of all people living in poverty (National Center for Children in Poverty, 2012). When disaggregated by race/ethnicity, the percentages are staggering. Table 16.2 displays these percentages.

A provision of the ARRA, Race to the Top (2011), is part of the education reform initiative led by the Obama administration's comprehensive learning agenda to increase access to high-quality early childhood education for children from birth to age 5 years. A focus of these efforts is the Race

Table 16.2	Percentage of Children in Low-Income and Poor Families by Race/Ethnicity Living in Poverty in 2010

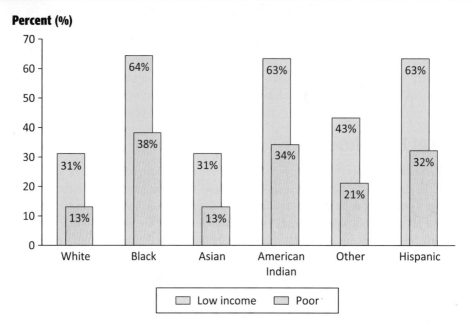

Source: © National Center for Children in Poverty. http://www.nccp.org/publications/pub_1049.html

to the Top Fund awarded to states that can meet benchmarks for reform. According to the U.S. Department of Education, four significant areas of effective education reform strategies involve

- adopting international standards and assessments that prepare students for success in college and the workplace;
- recruiting, developing, rewarding, and retaining effective teachers and principals;
- building data systems that measure student success and inform teachers and principals on how they can improve their practices; and
- turning around our lowest-performing schools.

The Race to the Top–Early Learning Challenge, part of ARRA, is an education reform initiative created to improve child care and strengthen Head Start. The nine states awarded funding are California, Delaware, Maryland, Massachusetts, Minnesota, North Carolina, Ohio, Rhode Island, and Washington. An investment in K–12 education reform was awarded to the states of Arizona, Colorado, Illinois, Kentucky, Louisiana, New Jersey, and Pennsylvania (U.S. Department of Education, 2011).

Early Elementary and Secondary Education Act Reauthorization Pending

ESEA was due for renewal in 2007, but Congress has not passed legislation to reauthorize it. The Obama administration developed the Blueprint for Reform to revamp NCLB in 2010. The U.S. Senate Committee on Health, Education, Labor, and Pensions (HELP) and the Education and Workforce Committee have recently passed bills for ESEA reauthorization as well. Let's review these efforts to amend NCLB.

NCLB and the Blueprint for Reform

The core policies of the Blueprint for Reform to be maintained in the ESEA reauthorization are disaggregation and focus on improving performance for all groups of students, focus on equity, and standards-based reform and accountability. Federal control would be turned over to states to address student achievement, accountability measures, and teacher effectiveness. The Blueprint for Reform brought attention to the overemphasis on tests and the narrowing of the curriculum, as a consequence of NCLB legislation. In Texas, for instance, NCLB and the Texas accountability system "have created formal and informal pressures for bilingual teachers to narrow the curriculum they teach their students, particularly as test time approaches" (Palmer & Snodgrass Rangel, 2011, p. 615).

Another concern with NCLB is that it sets unrealistic goals for student achievement by requiring that children from all subgroups achieve proficient levels in math and English by 2014. In 2010, 38% of the nation's schools had failed to meet AYP. Secretary of Education Arne Duncan informed Congress that 80,000 of the 100,000 schools in the nation would fail to meet federal requirements by 2014 (*New York Times*, 2012). The delay by Congress in reforming NCLB prompted President Obama to grant states waivers around key provisions of NCLB if states showed a commitment to develop education reform closely aligned with the administration's Race to the Top program. Thirty-three states have been approved for waivers (U.S. Department of Education, 2012).

U.S. Senate Committee on Health, Education, Labor, and Pensions

The HELP committee has developed a bipartisan bill for ESEA reauthorization (U.S. Senate Committee on Health Education Labor and Pensions, 2011). In February 2012, Congress voted to pass two pieces of legislation: the Student Success Act and the Encouraging Innovation and Effective Teachers Act. These acts would provide states with the authority to develop innovative programs to meet the needs of students at the local levels (U.S. Department of Education, 2012).

The U.S. House of Representatives' Education and the Workforce Committee

The House of Representatives has passed three authorization bills for ESEA: the Empowering Parents Through Quality Charter Schools Act, the Student Success Act, and the Encouraging Innovation and Effective Teachers Act. The Empowering Parents Through Quality Charter Schools Act would allocate funding for the development of high-performing charter schools. It gives parents more options when their child's school is underperforming. The Student Success Act suggests numerous modifications to NCLB (http://www.edworkforce.house.gov).

The Encouraging Innovation and Effective Teachers Act holds the following education reform items:

- Teacher effectiveness
- School choice
- Increased state and local control of public education reform
- Elimination of ineffective federal programs
- Impact aid support
- Services for homeless students
- Troops to Teachers program

Presently, the Obama administration views the state waivers as preferable to bills produced by either the Senate or the House of Representatives. It is unclear when Congress will reauthorize ESEA. What is clear is that education reform will continue to impact your role as an early childhood provider.

Let's turn to Table 16.3 to get a historical timeline of the federal education policies we have covered to this point.

Table 16.3   Historical Timeline of Federal Education Policies and Events

YEAR	FEDERAL EDUCATION POLICIES AND EVENTS
1965	Elementary and Secondary Education Act (ESEA)
1965	Education for the Disadvantaged, Title I
1965	Project Head Start
1966	Migrant Education Act
1968	Bilingual Education Act
1972	Indian Education Act
1975	Education of All Handicapped Children (EAHC) Act
1988	Even Start
1990	Individuals with Disabilities Education Act (IDEA)
1994	Improving America's Schools Act (IASA)
2001	No Child Left Behind (NCLB) Act
2002	Bilingual Education Act repealed and replaced with NCLB
2004	Individuals with Disabilities Education Improvement Act (IDEA 2004)
2009	American Reinvestment and Recovery Act
2010	Obama administration proposes a Blueprint for Reform of NCLB.
2011	Obama administration approves NCLB flexibility waivers.
2012	U.S. Senate Committee on Health, Education, Labor, and Pensions (HELP) develops bipartisan bill for ESEA reauthorization.
2012	The U.S. House of Representatives Committee on Education and the Workforce passes three bills for ESEA authorization: the Empowering Parents Through Quality Charter Schools Act, the Student Success Act, and the Encouraging Innovation and Effective Teachers Act.

WHAT ARE SOME POLICIES THAT ADDRESS THE FAMILY?

The United States has policies that impact children and their families. Knowledge of these policies is essential to the early childhood professional.

Child Care Policies

The Child Care and Development Fund is a provision of the American Recovery and Reinvestment Act of 2009. It provides federal funds for child care services to low-income parents or parents who receive Temporary Assistance for Needy Families (TANF) to work or to participate in educational or training programs to return to work. Funding is also reserved for children in protective services and for improvements in child care quality and accessibility (U.S. Department of Health and Human

Services, 2012). A move to improve child care quality is significant. While states have invested time and money to develop standards for preschool programs, the same is not evident for state-licensed child care programs. Children in licensed child care programs do not receive the same level of high-quality care and learning opportunities as children in state-funded preschool programs (National Association of Child Care Resource and Referral Service Agencies, 2009). This is disconcerting since the majority of preschool-age children are in state-licensed child care programs. Effective implementation of the recently amended Child Care and Development Fund will help ensure young children in state-licensed child care centers receive access to quality care.

The federal Child Care Subsidy Program established in 2001 assists low-income federal employees with pay for child care. The demand for child care is high—more than 11 million children under the age of 5 years are in child care. Child care is essential since working parents help the economy grow.

While states have developed standards for state preschool programs, the same is not true for state-licensed child care centers.

Health and Well-Being Policies

There are broad support systems in place to help children and families at both the state and federal levels. The Family and Medical Leave Act signed into law in 1993 provides 12 weeks of job-protected unpaid leave for parents to care for a family member. Uninsured children have benefited from federal health care programs such as Medicaid and SCHIP. Children have access to immunizations and regular health care visits. Under the American Recovery and Reinvestment Act, extensive funds were appropriated for improving and preserving health care.

In 2010, the Obama administration reauthorized child nutrition programs through the Healthy, Hunger-Free Kids Act. It increased the number of children who qualify for free meals. Some local education agencies provide up to three meals a day for children from low-income backgrounds.

The Nurse-Family Partnership is a maternal health care, home visiting program for first-time mothers that is devoted to improving outcomes for mothers and families. The program serves mothers with limited economic and educational resources. The program encourages mothers to maintain a healthy pregnancy and provides them with educational resources to improve positive outcomes for children. The Nurse-Family Partnership is an evidence-based public health program that relies on federal and state funding. The program has demonstrated the following outcomes (http:///www.nursefamilypartnership.org):

- Improvements in prenatal health, birth outcomes (including greater intervals between births), child development, school readiness, academic achievement, and maternal employment
- Reductions in child abuse and neglect, early childhood injuries, mental health problems, and crime

Family Literacy Policies

NCLB reauthorized Even Start in 2001, but support for the program has been declining due to poor results on evaluation studies (St. Pierre et al., 2003). Overall, evaluations of this program have been disappointing, prompting policy makers to sharply decrease funding (St. Pierre, Ricciuti, & Rimdzius, 2005). The House Education and the Workforce Committee's Subcommittee on Early Childhood, Elementary, and Secondary Education has proposed repealing the authorizations of Even Start family literacy (National Coalition for Literacy, 2011).

This is disheartening for advocates of Even Start who state that Even Start participants are a very disadvantaged population. Approximately 90% of Even Start families are living at or below the poverty level, and 84% of Even Start adults do not have a high school diploma. Funding for Even Start has decreased 70% since it was enacted. The National Coalition for Literacy (NCL) champions efforts to raise priority for adult education and literacy. NCL has advocated for the Even Start program, raising concerns for the decreased funding allotted to the program (NCL, 2011).

The Head Start program has evolved to include parenting classes that promote self-reliance by addressing illiteracy, substance abuse, and unemployment. The Head Start program promotes adult literacy and vocational education. Similarly, the Workforce Investment Act of 1998 provides access to adult education and literacy.

Education for Homeless Children and Youths

The McKinney-Vento Homeless Assistance Act (1987), Title VII, appropriated funding to states to educate homeless children and youth. The McKinney-Vento Homeless Education Assistance Improvements Act of 2011 required that any state regulations or policies that pose a barrier to enrollment, attendance, or school success, such as compulsory attendance laws, be revised. The Educational Success for Children and Youth Without Homes Act (2009) and the Fostering Success in Education Act (2009) have expanded key provisions of the McKinney-Vento Education for Homeless Children and Youth Program.

While the United States does not have one comprehensive family policy (Kamerman & Kahn, 2001), it does have policies that impact both children and families. As a teacher, it is important to be familiar with policies that impact families, particularly if you are working in a school with a high percentage of children from low-income backgrounds. The Center on the Developing Child at Harvard University (2007) reviewed four decades of program evaluation research that highlights important factors that promote optimal development in the first 5 years. Here are some of the principles that provide a framework for informed policy making:

- Access to medical care for pregnant women and children can help prevent threats to healthy development as well as provide early diagnosis and appropriate management when problems emerge.
- For vulnerable families who are expecting a first child, early intensive support by skilled home visitors can produce significant benefits for both the child and parents.
- For young children from low-income families, participation in very high quality, center-based, early education programs has been demonstrated to enhance child cognitive and social development.
- For young children from families experiencing significant adversity, two-generation programs that simultaneously provide direct support for parents and high-quality, center-based care and education for the children can have positive impacts on both.
- For families living under the poverty level, work-based income supplements for working parents have been demonstrated to boost the achievement of some young children.

This knowledge base will help you as an early childhood education professional engage in informed advocacy for children and the profession. Ultimately, you play an important role in implementing and promoting child and family policies that support children's positive development.

Summary

Legislated public education policies have helped stimulate educational and social reform in the United States. Policies impacting children and families have expanded since the inception of the Elementary and Secondary Education Act of 1965. Children from low-income families and children with special needs have benefited from both federal and state policies. Without these federal policies, many students would not have access to early intervention services, preschool programs, and special education programs. Politicians, educators, and policy makers look to preschool programs, such as Head Start, to provide low-income children with the skills they need to start school prepared to learn and to become productive citizens. The potential impact of early education on social and economic success continues to prompt advocacy for the investment in young children. Universal preschool for all children regardless of income background has achieved notice at both federal and state levels.

NCLB legislation has increased the focus on program standards, extensive personnel training to meet those standards, enhanced program quality and research, improved teacher quality, and increased school accountability. However, many concerns with NCLB have prompted reform movements at both the state and federal levels. Congress has not reauthorized the long overdue Elementary and Secondary Education Act, but the Obama administration has responded by granting states waivers from provisions of NCLB. What is certain is that education reform will bring positive outcomes as well as complex challenges to the field of early childhood education. Early childhood education policies have, and will continue to have, a broad impact on the lives of children and the teachers who prepare them for the future.

Key Terms

Academic achievement gap   425

Adequate yearly progress (AYP)   429

Bilingual education programs   427

Dual-language programs   435

English immersion   427

Local education agency (LEA)   424

Policy making   423

Pullout program   426

Scientifically based research   429

State education agency (SEA)   424

Structured English immersion (SEI)   435

Reflection, Application, and Analysis Questions

1. Reflect on the education policies you have read about in this chapter. Why is it important to have an understanding of how these policies will impact your role as a teacher?

2. Analyze the major provisions of the No Child Left Behind Act. What are the challenges that teachers have had in implementing NCLB?

3. Universal preschool for all 4-year-old children is gaining support across the country. In what ways do children benefit from participation in a quality preschool program?

4. After reading this chapter, what role do you think the federal government should have in providing and setting standards for early childhood education?

Extension Activities

1. Interview a teacher to learn how NCLB has impacted learning and instruction in his or her classroom.

2. Keep a journal for 2 weeks and note the various education topics in the media. Include any magazine or newspaper articles relevant to the themes addressed in this book.

3. Research federal and state policies that impact English language learners in your state. Visit a school and interview an administrator to learn how these policies are being implemented at that school.

Additional Readings

Education policies have important implications for the field of early childhood education and the professional. The following readings inform on the pressing need to use research to help develop policies that promote high-quality programs for young children.

Garcia, E. E., & Frede, E. C. (Eds.) (2010). *Young English language learners: Current research and emerging directions for practice and policy.* New York: Teachers College Press.

This book provides an overview of research, policy, and practices relevant to young English language learners. Some areas of focus include demographics, parental engagement, language development of bilingual children, benefits of preschool education, teacher preparation, and assessment practices.

Kirp, D. L. (2007). *The sandbox investment: The preschool movement and kids-first politics.* Cambridge, MA: Harvard University Press.

The author presents an overview of the impact of policy and research on preschool children in the United States. The need for universal preschool is supported with examples of recent research emphasizing the powerful role of providing high-quality programs in the educational and social outcomes of children.

On the Web

Infant/Toddler Learning and Development Foundations - *www.cde.ca.gov/sp/cd/re/itfoundations.asp*
This link takes you to the California Department of Education to access the state's Infant/Toddler Learning and Development Foundations.

Race to the Top - *http://www2.ed.gov/programs/racetothetop/index.html*
This U.S. Department of Education website provides a description of the Race to the Top Assessment Program and the Early Learning Challenge.

Zero to Three - *http://www.zerotothree.org/*
This is the website for Zero to Three, the National Center for Infants, Toddlers, and Families. It is a national, nonprofit organization dedicated to inform, train, and support professionals, policy makers, and parents.

Student Study Site

Visit **www.sagepub.com/gordonbiddle** to access several study tools including eFlashcards, web quizzes, links to SAGE journal articles, web resources, video resources, lesson plan templates, and more.

Appendix

- -

NAEYC
Code of Ethical Conduct and Statement of Commitment

A position statement of the National Association for the Education of Young Children

Endorsed by the Association for Childhood Education International Adopted by the National Association for Family Child Care

PREAMBLE

NAEYC recognizes that those who work with young children face many daily decisions that have moral and ethical implications. The **NAEYC Code of Ethical Conduct** offers guidelines for responsible behavior and sets forth a common basis for resolving the principal ethical dilemmas encountered in early childhood care and education. The **Statement of Commitment** is not part of the Code but is a personal acknowledgement of an individual's willingness to embrace the distinctive values and moral obligations of the field of early childhood care and education.

The primary focus of the Code is on daily practice with children and their families in programs for children from birth through 8 years of age, such as infant/toddler programs, preschool and prekindergarten programs, child care centers, hospital and child life settings, family child care homes, kindergartens, and primary classrooms. When the issues involve young children, then these provisions also apply to specialists who do not work directly with children, including program administrators, parent educators, early childhood adult educators, and officials with responsibility for program monitoring and licensing. (Note: See also the "Code of Ethical Conduct: Supplement for Early Childhood Adult Educators," online at www.naeyc.org/about/positions/pdf/ethics04.pdf.)

Core values

Standards of ethical behavior in early childhood care and education are based on commitment to the following core values that are deeply rooted in the history of the field of early childhood care and education. We have made a commitment to

- Appreciate childhood as a unique and valuable stage of the human life cycle
- Base our work on knowledge of how children develop and learn
- Appreciate and support the bond between the child and family
- Recognize that children are best understood and supported in the context of family, culture,* community, and society

---

* The term *culture* includes ethnicity, racial identity, economic level, family structure, language, and religious and political beliefs, which profoundly influence each child's development and relationship to the world.

- Respect the dignity, worth, and uniqueness of each individual (child, family member, and colleague)
- Respect diversity in children, families, and colleagues
- Recognize that children and adults achieve their full potential in the context of relationships that are based on trust and respect

Conceptual framework

The Code sets forth a framework of professional responsibilities in four sections. Each section addresses an area of professional relationships: (1) with children, (2) with families, (3) among colleagues, and (4) with the community and society. Each section includes an introduction to the primary responsibilities of the early childhood practitioner in that context. The introduction is followed by a set of ideals (I) that reflect exemplary professional practice and by a set of principles (P) describing practices that are required, prohibited, or permitted.

The **ideals** reflect the aspirations of practitioners. The **principles** guide conduct and assist practitioners in resolving ethical dilemmas.* Both ideals and principles are intended to direct practitioners to those questions which, when responsibly answered, can provide the basis for conscientious decision making. While the Code provides specific direction for addressing some ethical dilemmas, many others will require the practitioner to combine the guidance of the Code with professional judgment.

The ideals and principles in this Code present a shared framework of professional responsibility that affirms our commitment to the core values of our field. The Code publicly acknowledges the responsibilities that we in the field have assumed, and in so doing supports ethical behavior in our work. Practitioners who face situations with ethical dimensions are urged to seek guidance in the applicable parts of this Code and in the spirit that informs the whole.

Often "the right answer"—the best ethical course of action to take—is not obvious. There may be no readily apparent, positive way to handle a situation. When one important value contradicts another, we face an ethical dilemma. When we face a dilemma, it is our professional responsibility to consult the Code and all relevant parties to find the most ethical resolution.

SECTION I

Ethical Responsibilities to Children

Childhood is a unique and valuable stage in the human life cycle. Our paramount responsibility is to provide care and education in settings that are safe, healthy, nurturing, and responsive for each child. We are committed to supporting children's development and learning; respecting individual differences; and helping children learn to live, play, and work cooperatively. We are also committed to promoting children's self-awareness, competence, self-worth, resiliency, and physical well-being.

Ideals

I-1.1—To be familiar with the knowledge base of early childhood care and education and to stay informed through continuing education and training.

I-1.2—To base program practices upon current knowledge and research in the field of early childhood education, child development, and related disciplines, as well as on particular knowledge of each child.

I-1.3—To recognize and respect the unique qualities, abilities, and potential of each child.

I-1.4—To appreciate the vulnerability of children and their dependence on adults.

I-1.5—To create and maintain safe and healthy settings that foster children's social, emotional, cognitive, and physical development and that respect their dignity and their contributions.

---

* There is not necessarily a corresponding principle for each ideal.

I-1.6—To use assessment instruments and strategies that are appropriate for the children to be assessed, that are used only for the purposes for which they were designed, and that have the potential to benefit children.

I-1.7—To use assessment information to understand and support children's development and learning, to support instruction, and to identify children who may need additional services.

I-1.8—To support the right of each child to play and learn in an inclusive environment that meets the needs of children with and without disabilities.

I-1.9—To advocate for and ensure that all children, including those with special needs, have access to the support services needed to be successful.

I-1.10—To ensure that each child's culture, language, ethnicity, and family structure are recognized and valued in the program.

I-1.11—To provide all children with experiences in a language that they know, as well as support children in maintaining the use of their home language and in learning English.

I-1.12—To work with families to provide a safe and smooth transition as children and families move from one program to the next.

Principles

P-1.1—Above all, we shall not harm children. We shall not participate in practices that are emotionally damaging, physically harmful, disrespectful, degrading, dangerous, exploitative, or intimidating to children. *This principle has precedence over all others in this Code.*

P-1.2—We shall care for and educate children in positive emotional and social environments that are cognitively stimulating and that support each child's culture, language, ethnicity, and family structure.

P-1.3—We shall not participate in practices that discriminate against children by denying benefits, giving special advantages, or excluding them from programs or activities on the basis of their sex, race, national origin, religious beliefs, medical condition, disability, or the marital status/ family structure, sexual orientation, or religious beliefs or other affiliations of their families. (Aspects of this principle do not apply in programs that have a lawful mandate to provide services to a particular population of children.)

P-1.4—We shall involve all those with relevant knowledge (including families and staff) in decisions concerning a child, as appropriate, ensuring confidentiality of sensitive information.

P-1.5—We shall use appropriate assessment systems, which include multiple sources of information, to provide information on children's learning and development.

P-1.6—We shall strive to ensure that decisions such as those related to enrollment, retention, or assignment to special education services, will be based on multiple sources of information and will never be based on a single assessment, such as a test score or a single observation.

P-1.7—We shall strive to build individual relationships with each child; make individualized adaptations in teaching strategies, learning environments, and curricula; and consult with the family so that each child benefits from the program. If after such efforts have been exhausted, the current placement does not meet a child's needs, or the child is seriously jeopardizing the ability of other children to benefit from the program, we shall collaborate with the child's family and appropriate specialists to determine the additional services needed and/or the placement option(s) most likely to ensure the child's success. (Aspects of this principle may not apply in programs that have a lawful mandate to provide services to a particular population of children.)

P-1.8—We shall be familiar with the risk factors for and symptoms of child abuse and neglect, including physical, sexual, verbal, and emotional abuse and physical, emotional, educational, and medical neglect. We shall know and follow state laws and community procedures that protect children against abuse and neglect.

P-1.9—When we have reasonable cause to suspect child abuse or neglect, we shall report it to the appropriate community agency and follow up to ensure that appropriate action has been taken. When appropriate, parents or guardians will be informed that the referral will be or has been made.

P-1.10—When another person tells us of his or her suspicion that a child is being abused or neglected, we shall assist that person in taking appropriate action in order to protect the child.

P-1.11—When we become aware of a practice or situation that endangers the health, safety, or well-being of children, we have an ethical responsibility to protect children or inform parents and/or others who can.

SECTION II

Ethical Responsibilities to Families

Families* are of primary importance in children's development. Because the family and the early childhood practitioner have a common interest in the child's well-being, we acknowledge a primary responsibility to bring about communication, cooperation, and collaboration between the home and early childhood program in ways that enhance the child's development.

Ideals

I-2.1—To be familiar with the knowledge base related to working effectively with families and to stay informed through continuing education and training.

I-2.2—To develop relationships of mutual trust and create partnerships with the families we serve.

I-2.3—To welcome all family members and encourage them to participate in the program.

I-2.4—To listen to families, acknowledge and build upon their strengths and competencies, and learn from families as we support them in their task of nurturing children.

I-2.5—To respect the dignity and preferences of each family and to make an effort to learn about its structure, culture, language, customs, and beliefs.

I-2.6—To acknowledge families' childrearing values and their right to make decisions for their children.

I-2.7—To share information about each child's education and development with families and to help them understand and appreciate the current knowledge base of the early childhood profession.

I-2.8—To help family members enhance their understanding of their children and support the continuing development of their skills as parents.

I-2.9—To participate in building support networks for families by providing them with opportunities to interact with program staff, other families, community resources, and professional services.

Principles

P-2.1—We shall not deny family members access to their child's classroom or program setting unless access is denied by court order or other legal restriction.

P-2.2—We shall inform families of program philosophy, policies, curriculum, assessment system, and personnel qualifications, and explain why we teach as we do—which should be in accordance with our ethical responsibilities to children (see Section I).

P-2.3—We shall inform families of and, when appropriate, involve them in policy decisions.

P-2.4—We shall involve the family in significant decisions affecting their child.

---

* The term *family* may include those adults, besides parents, with the responsibility of being involved in educating, nurturing, and advocating for the child.

P-2.5—We shall make every effort to communicate effectively with all families in a language that they understand. We shall use community resources for translation and interpretation when we do not have sufficient resources in our own programs.

P-2.6—As families share information with us about their children and families, we shall consider this information to plan and implement the program.

P-2-7—We shall inform families about the nature and purpose of the program's child assessments and how data about their child will be used.

P-2.8—We shall treat child assessment information confidentially and share this information only when there is a legitimate need for it.

P-2.9—We shall inform the family of injuries and incidents involving their child, of risks such as exposures to communicable diseases that might result in infection, and of occurrences that might result in emotional stress.

P-2.10—Families shall be fully informed of any proposed research projects involving their children and shall have the opportunity to give or withhold consent without penalty. We shall not permit or participate in research that could in any way hinder the education, development, or well-being of children.

P-2.11—We shall not engage in or support exploitation of families. We shall not use our relationship with a family for private advantage or personal gain, or enter into relationships with family members that might impair our effectiveness working with their children.

P-2.12—We shall develop written policies for the protection of confidentiality and the disclosure of children's records. These policy documents shall be made available to all program personnel and families. Disclosure of children's records beyond family members, program personnel, and consultants having an obligation of confidentiality shall require familial consent (except in cases of abuse or neglect).

P-2.13—We shall maintain confidentiality and shall respect the family's right to privacy, refraining from disclosure of confidential information and intrusion into family life. However, when we have reason to believe that a child's welfare is at risk, it is permissible to share confidential information with agencies, as well as with individuals who have legal responsibility for intervening in the child's interest.

P-2.14—In cases where family members are in conflict with one another, we shall work openly, sharing our observations of the child, to help all parties involved make informed decisions. We shall refrain from becoming an advocate for one party.

P-2.15—We shall be familiar with and appropriately refer families to community resources and professional support services. After a referral has been made, we shall follow up to ensure that services have been appropriately provided.

SECTION III

Ethical Responsibilities to Colleagues

In a caring, cooperative workplace, human dignity is respected, professional satisfaction is promoted, and positive relationships are developed and sustained. Based upon our core values, our primary responsibility to colleagues is to establish and maintain settings and relationships that support productive work and meet professional needs. The same ideals that apply to children also apply as we interact with adults in the workplace.

A—Responsibilities to co-workers

Ideals

I-3A.1—To establish and maintain relationships of respect, trust, confidentiality, collaboration, and cooperation with co-workers.

I-3A.2—To share resources with co-workers, collaborating to ensure that the best possible early childhood care and education program is provided.

I-3A.3—To support co-workers in meeting their professional needs and in their professional development.

I-3A.4—To accord co-workers due recognition of professional achievement.

Principles

P-3A.1—We shall recognize the contributions of colleagues to our program and not participate in practices that diminish their reputations or impair their effectiveness in working with children and families.

P-3A.2—When we have concerns about the professional behavior of a co-worker, we shall first let that person know of our concern in a way that shows respect for personal dignity and for the diversity to be found among staff members, and then attempt to resolve the matter collegially and in a confidential manner.

P-3A.3—We shall exercise care in expressing views regarding the personal attributes or professional conduct of co-workers. Statements should be based on firsthand knowledge, not hearsay, and relevant to the interests of children and programs.

P-3A.4—We shall not participate in practices that discriminate against a co-worker because of sex, race, national origin, religious beliefs or other affiliations, age, marital status/family structure, disability, or sexual orientation.

B—Responsibilities to employers

Ideals

I-3B.1—To assist the program in providing the highest quality of service.

I-3B.2—To do nothing that diminishes the reputation of the program in which we work unless it is violating laws and regulations designed to protect children or is violating the provisions of this Code.

Principles

P-3B.1—We shall follow all program policies. When we do not agree with program policies, we shall attempt to effect change through constructive action within the organization.

P-3B.2—We shall speak or act on behalf of an organization only when authorized. We shall take care to acknowledge when we are speaking for the organization and when we are expressing a personal judgment.

P-3B.3—We shall not violate laws or regulations designed to protect children and shall take appropriate action consistent with this Code when aware of such violations.

P-3B.4—If we have concerns about a colleague's behavior, and children's well-being is not at risk, we may address the concern with that individual. If children are at risk or the situation does not improve after it has been brought to the colleague's attention, we shall report the colleague's unethical or incompetent behavior to an appropriate authority.

P-3B.5—When we have a concern about circumstances or conditions that impact the quality of care and education within the program, we shall inform the program's administration or, when necessary, other appropriate authorities.

C—Responsibilities to employees

Ideals

I-3C.1—To promote safe and healthy working conditions and policies that foster mutual respect, cooperation, collaboration, competence, well-being, confidentiality, and self-esteem in staff members.

I-3C.2—To create and maintain a climate of trust and candor that will enable staff to speak and act in the best interests of children, families, and the field of early childhood care and education.

I-3C.3—To strive to secure adequate and equitable compensation (salary and benefits) for those who work with or on behalf of young children.

I-3C.4—To encourage and support continual development of employees in becoming more skilled and knowledgeable practitioners.

Principles

P-3C.1—In decisions concerning children and programs, we shall draw upon the education, training, experience, and expertise of staff members.

P-3C.2—We shall provide staff members with safe and supportive working conditions that honor confidences and permit them to carry out their responsibilities through fair performance evaluation, written grievance procedures, constructive feedback, and opportunities for continuing professional development and advancement.

P-3C.3—We shall develop and maintain comprehensive written personnel policies that define program standards. These policies shall be given to new staff members and shall be available and easily accessible for review by all staff members.

P-3C.4—We shall inform employees whose performance does not meet program expectations of areas of concern and, when possible, assist in improving their performance.

P-3C.5—We shall conduct employee dismissals for just cause, in accordance with all applicable laws and regulations. We shall inform employees who are dismissed of the reasons for their termination. When a dismissal is for cause, justification must be based on evidence of inadequate or inappropriate behavior that is accurately documented, current, and available for the employee to review.

P-3C.6—In making evaluations and recommendations, we shall make judgments based on fact and relevant to the interests of children and programs.

P-3C.7—We shall make hiring, retention, termination, and promotion decisions based solely on a person's competence, record of accomplishment, ability to carry out the responsibilities of the position, and professional preparation specific to the developmental levels of children in his/her care.

P-3C.8—We shall not make hiring, retention, termination, and promotion decisions based on an individual's sex, race, national origin, religious beliefs or other affiliations, age, marital status/family structure, disability, or sexual orientation. We shall be familiar with and observe laws and regulations that pertain to employment discrimination. (Aspects of this principle do not apply to programs that have a lawful mandate to determine eligibility based on one or more of the criteria identified above.)

P-3C.9—We shall maintain confidentiality in dealing with issues related to an employee's job performance and shall respect an employee's right to privacy regarding personal issues.

SECTION IV

Ethical Responsibilities to Community and Society

Early childhood programs operate within the context of their immediate community made up of families and other institutions concerned with children's welfare. Our responsibilities to the community are to provide programs that meet the diverse needs of families, to cooperate with agencies and professions that share the responsibility for children, to assist families in gaining access to those agencies and allied professionals, and to assist in the development of community programs that are needed but not currently available.

As individuals, we acknowledge our responsibility to provide the best possible programs of care and education for children and to conduct ourselves with honesty and integrity. Because of our specialized expertise in early childhood development and education and because the larger society shares responsibility for the welfare and protection of young children, we acknowledge a collective obligation to advocate for the best interests of children within early childhood programs and in the larger community and to serve as a voice for young children everywhere.

The ideals and principles in this section are presented to distinguish between those that pertain to the work of the individual early childhood educator and those that more typically are engaged in collectively on behalf of the best interests of children—with the understanding that individual early childhood educators have a shared responsibility for addressing the ideals and principles that are identified as "collective."

Ideal (Individual)

I-4.1—To provide the community with high-quality early childhood care and education programs and services.

Ideals (Collective)

I-4.2—To promote cooperation among professionals and agencies and interdisciplinary collaboration among professions concerned with addressing issues in the health, education, and well-being of young children, their families, and their early childhood educators.

I-4.3—To work through education, research, and advocacy toward an environmentally safe world in which all children receive health care, food, and shelter; are nurtured; and live free from violence in their home and their communities.

I-4.4—To work through education, research, and advocacy toward a society in which all young children have access to high-quality early care and education programs.

I-4.5—To work to ensure that appropriate assessment systems, which include multiple sources of information, are used for purposes that benefit children.

I-4.6—To promote knowledge and understanding of young children and their needs. To work toward greater societal acknowledgment of children's rights and greater social acceptance of responsibility for the well-being of all children.

I-4.7—To support policies and laws that promote the well-being of children and families, and to work to change those that impair their well-being. To participate in developing policies and laws that are needed, and to cooperate with other individuals and groups in these efforts.

I-4.8—To further the professional development of the field of early childhood care and education and to strengthen its commitment to realizing its core values as reflected in this Code.

Principles (Individual)

P-4.1—We shall communicate openly and truthfully about the nature and extent of services that we provide.

P-4.2—We shall apply for, accept, and work in positions for which we are personally well-suited and professionally qualified. We shall not offer services that we do not have the competence, qualifications, or resources to provide.

P-4.3—We shall carefully check references and shall not hire or recommend for employment any person whose competence, qualifications, or character makes him or her unsuited for the position.

P-4.4—We shall be objective and accurate in reporting the knowledge upon which we base our program practices.

P-4.5—We shall be knowledgeable about the appropriate use of assessment strategies and instruments and interpret results accurately to families.

P-4.6—We shall be familiar with laws and regulations that serve to protect the children in our programs and be vigilant in ensuring that these laws and regulations are followed.

P-4.7—When we become aware of a practice or situation that endangers the health, safety, or well-being of children, we have an ethical responsibility to protect children or inform parents and/or others who can.

P-4.8—We shall not participate in practices that are in violation of laws and regulations that protect the children in our programs.

P-4.9—When we have evidence that an early childhood program is violating laws or regulations protecting children, we shall report the violation to appropriate authorities who can be expected to remedy the situation.

P-4.10—When a program violates or requires its employees to violate this Code, it is permissible, after fair assessment of the evidence, to disclose the identity of that program.

Principles (Collective)

P-4.11—When policies are enacted for purposes that do not benefit children, we have a collective responsibility to work to change these practices.

P-4.12—When we have evidence that an agency that provides services intended to ensure children's well-being is failing to meet its obligations, we acknowledge a collective ethical responsibility to report the problem to appropriate authorities or to the public. We shall be vigilant in our follow-up until the situation is resolved.

P-4.13—When a child protection agency fails to provide adequate protection for abused or neglected children, we acknowledge a collective ethical responsibility to work toward the improvement of these services.

Glossary of Terms Related to Ethics

Code of Ethics. Defines the core values of the field and provides guidance for what professionals should do when they encounter conflicting obligations or responsibilities in their work.

Values. Qualities or principles that individuals believe to be desirable or worthwhile and that they prize for themselves, for others, and for the world in which they live.

Core Values. Commitments held by a profession that are consciously and knowingly embraced by its practitioners because they make a contribution to society. There is a difference between personal values and the core values of a profession.

Morality. Peoples' views of what is good, right, and proper; their beliefs about their obligations; and their ideas about how they should behave.

Ethics. The study of right and wrong, or duty and obligation, that involves critical reflection on morality and the ability to make choices between values and the examination of the moral dimensions of relationships.

Professional Ethics. The moral commitments of a profession that involve moral reflection that extends and enhances the personal morality practitioners bring to their work, that concern actions of right and wrong in the workplace, and that help individuals resolve moral dilemmas they encounter in their work.

Ethical Responsibilities. Behaviors that one must or must not engage in. Ethical responsibilities are clear-cut and are spelled out in the Code of Ethical Conduct (for example, early childhood educators should never share confidential information about a child or family with a person who has no legitimate need for knowing).

Ethical Dilemma. A moral conflict that involves determining appropriate conduct when an individual faces conflicting professional values and responsibilities.

Sources for glossary terms and definitions

Feeney, S., & N. Freeman. 1999. *Ethics and the early childhood educator: Using the NAEYC code.* Washington, DC: NAEYC.

Kidder, R.M. 1995. *How good people make tough choices: Resolving the dilemmas of ethical living.* New York: Fireside.

Kipnis, K. 1987. How to discuss professional ethics. *Young Children* 42 (4): 26–30.

The National Association for the Education of Young Children (NAEYC) is a nonprofit corporation, tax exempt under Section 501(c)(3) of the Internal Revenue Code, dedicated to acting on behalf of the needs and interests of young children. The NAEYC Code of Ethical Conduct (Code) has been developed in furtherance of NAEYC's nonprofit and tax exempt purposes. The information contained in the Code is intended to provide early childhood educators with guidelines for working with children from birth through age 8.

An individual's or program's use, reference to, or review of the Code does not guarantee compliance with NAEYC Early Childhood Program Standards and Accreditation Performance Criteria and program accreditation procedures. It is recommended that the Code be used as guidance in connection with implementation of the NAEYC Program Standards, but such use is not a substitute for diligent review and application of the NAEYC Program Standards.

NAEYC has taken reasonable measures to develop the Code in a fair, reasonable, open, unbiased, and objective manner, based on currently available data. However, further research or developments may change the current state of knowledge. Neither NAEYC nor its officers, directors, members, employees, or agents will be liable for any loss, damage, or claim with respect to any liabilities, including direct, special, indirect, or consequential damages incurred in connection with the Code or reliance on the information presented.

NAEYC Code of Ethical Conduct Revisions Workgroup

Mary Ambery, Ruth Ann Ball, James Clay, Julie Olsen Edwards, Harriet Egertson, Anthony Fair, Stephanie Feeney, Jana Fleming, Nancy Freeman, Marla Israel, Allison McKinnon, Evelyn Wright Moore, Eva Moravcik, Christina Lopez Morgan, Sarah Mulligan, Nila Rinehart, Betty Holston Smith, and Peter Pizzolongo, *NAEYC Staff*

Statement of Commitment*

As an individual who works with young children, I commit myself to furthering the values of early childhood education as they are reflected in the ideals and principles of the NAEYC Code of Ethical Conduct. To the best of my ability I will

- Never harm children.
- Ensure that programs for young children are based on current knowledge and research of child development and early childhood education.
- Respect and support families in their task of nurturing children.
- Respect colleagues in early childhood care and education and support them in maintaining the NAEYC Code of Ethical Conduct.
- Serve as an advocate for children, their families, and their teachers in community and society.
- Stay informed of and maintain high standards of professional conduct.
- Engage in an ongoing process of self-reflection, realizing that personal characteristics, biases, and beliefs have an impact on children and families.
- Be open to new ideas and be willing to learn from the suggestions of others.
- Continue to learn, grow, and contribute as a professional.
- Honor the ideals and principles of the NAEYC Code of Ethical Conduct.

* This Statement of Commitment is not part of the Code but is a personal acknowledgment of the individual's willingness to embrace the distinctive values and moral obligations of the field of early childhood care and education. It is recognition of the moral obligations that lead to an individual becoming part of the profession.

Glossary

Abigail Adams Eliot: An early U.S. 20th-century educator and exponent/founder of the nursery school movement.

Abraham Maslow: Humanist and creator of Maslow's hierarchy of needs.

Academic achievement gap: The difference in academic performance between groups of students. Typically, children living in poverty score lower on standardized tests than their middle-class peers.

Acceleration: An approach to educating students who are gifted and talented that can involve a student moving rapidly through a curriculum, skipping a grade, or starting school at an earlier age.

Accommodation: A term proposed by Jean Piaget that denotes one way that children can adapt new experiences and information. Children modify their mental structures as they compare new information that does not match with the information that they already know.

Accreditation: A process by which an early childhood program voluntarily applies to attain national recognition of its quality.

Active listening: The process of reflecting back to a child in words what he or she is trying to communicate.

Adaptation: The mental process of creating schemes as a result of direct interaction with the environment. This can occur as a result of accommodation or assimilation, and is central to Jean Piaget's theory of cognitive development.

Adequate yearly progress (AYP): The U.S. Department of Education, through the No Child Left Behind Act of 2001, uses this measure to determine how every public school and school district across the country is performing academically based on standardized test results.

Advocates: Supporters of children and families who provide them with assistance and education and speak on their behalf. For example, advocates for special education help families of children with special needs access special education services.

Aggression: Behaving in a manner that hurts another person.

Alternative assessments: Assessments where students actually create a response or an answer instead of choosing a premade answer or response from a list. Open-ended questions, interviews, and portfolios are examples of alternative assessments.

Anthroposophy: A form of spiritual philosophy traced to Rudolf Steiner that promotes the development of spirituality in the person. It is applied in Waldorf schools.

Apprenticeship learning: The process of learning a particular skill or craft under the guidance or supervision of a more expert or learned other.

Aristotle: A philosopher and pupil of Plato who is known for his writings on logic, metaphysics, ethics, and politics.

Arithmetic: Understanding how numbers function. In other words, arithmetic is addition, subtraction, multiplication, and division.

Arousal state: The place or state of being for infants, which includes being asleep or awake. There are six basic states of arousal that an infant experiences during a typical day.

Assessment: Observation that is more systematic and structured and checks to see if goals and objectives are being met. Assessment places a value judgment on the behavior being observed.

Assimilation: A term proposed by Jean Piaget that denotes one way that children can adapt to new experiences and information. Children add new information to their existing knowledge base, sometimes reinterpreting it to fit with their previous knowledge.

Assistive technology: Technology used by individuals with disabilities that allows them to participate in education and facilitates activities of daily living.

Associative play: Beginning at about $3 \frac{1}{2}$ years old, children truly play with others. They loan and borrow play materials among one another, begin to form small playgroups, and spend considerable time moving from one activity to the next, with playmates remaining together. At this point, the associations are more important than the play activity itself.

Attachment: Refers to the type of emotional bond that young children have with their primary caregivers.

Attachment disorders: Personality disorders that stem from an insecure attachment.

Augmentative and alternative communication (AAC) systems: Systems designed to facilitate or compensate for, temporarily or permanently, severe speech or language impairments of students who have difficulty communicating verbally or in writing.

Authoritarian parenting style: Parents are not very warm or nurturing; they have many rules and set strict limits; they expect their children to obey orders without explanation.

Authoritative: Child-rearing practices characterized by high acceptance and involvement, communication, adaptive control techniques, and appropriate autonomy granting and touted as the most successful approach.

Authoritative parenting style: Parents are warm and nurturing; set and enforce clear, reasonable rules and limits; and use supportive disciplinary methods rather than punishment.

Autism spectrum disorders: *Autism spectrum disorder* and *autism* are general terms used to describe pervasive developmental disorders of the brain. These disorders present in varying degrees and are characterized by difficulties in verbal and nonverbal communication, social interactions, and stereotyped behaviors.

Autonomy versus shame and doubt: In Erik Erikson's theory, the psychosocial conflict in toddlerhood that is favorably resolved when parents afford children a certain amount of independence over their actions and bodies.

Aversive stimulation: An aversive stimulus is something that is unpleasant or a form of punishment designed to change behavior.

Babbling stage: During this stage infants have the ability to produce a broad array of sounds.

Balancing: Keeping straight and level while performing simple and complex gross motor skills.

Bank Street School for Children: A school, founded by Lucy Sprague Mitchell in 1916, that educated the whole child, emphasizing how children learn and interact with their environment.

Basic grammar: Rules that govern the structure of phrases and clauses.

Behavioral competence: Demonstrated by exhibiting socially acceptable behaviors in most situations.

Behavioral theorists: Individuals who ascribe to the theory of behaviorism. Behaviorists study behavior that is observable and believe that behaviors are shaped by responses to other behaviors so that behaviors that are reinforced become strengthened and behaviors that are punished become suppressed.

Behaviorism: The study of observable behavior.

Benjamin Bloom: Educator whose efforts helped to broaden educational goals and teacher objectives, developer of a taxonomy of educational skills, a set of educational skills ranging in increasing complexity.

Bilingual education programs: Programs that provide varying instructional approaches for students labeled as English language learners where some academic content is taught in the native language as well as in English. Some programs emphasize proficiency in both languages.

Bilingualism: A term that depicts the process whereby children acquire two languages.

Binocular vision: The ability to focus using both eyes, which develops around 4 or 5 months of age.

Bioecological systems theory: Urie Bronfenbrenner, a theorist who developed the ecological systems approach, renamed his theory to ensure that the name appropriately reflected the interaction between biological processes and their milieu.

Bullying: Intentionally causing physical or emotional and social harm to one's peers.

Burnout: "Physical, emotional, and attitudinal exhaustion" (Hendrickson, 1979).

Caste: A system of social stratification based on hereditary status, wealth, profession, or race.

Cephalocaudal principle: States that development generally progresses from head to tail (foot).

Chauvinism: Militant, unreasoning, and boastful devotion to one's country, race, or sex—especially with contempt for other countries, other races, and the opposite sex.

Checklist: An observation method that lists the presence or absence of a characteristic or an action in a given context.

Chemistry: The science of substances and their combinations.

Child Find: A federal mandate of the Individuals with Disabilities Education Act (IDEA) that requires states to identify, locate, evaluate, and track students with special needs from birth through age 21 years.

Children with exceptional needs: Children with special needs and children with gifts and talents.

Chronosystem: Recognizes the timing of adjustments in familial interrelationships and the relative position of the child during these periods, including the impact of these changes on the developing child.

Classical conditioning: A simple experiment devised by Russian scientist Ivan Pavlov that involves pairing a meaningful stimulus (e.g., food) with a neutral stimulus (e.g., sound of a bell), which had no meaning before conditioning. Also called responsive conditioning.

Classification: Grouping objects and people based on characteristics.

Clinical interview method: Used by theorist Jean Piaget during his countless interviews with scores of children wherein he used a flexible, conversational style of questioning to determine the youngsters' point of view.

Co-constructing knowledge: Based on the philosophy that learning is a socially constructed process. The student acquires knowledge by questioning, identifying, and developing an understanding of the learning event.

Code switching: Involves an individual using more than one language in conversation. It is a complex, rule-governed phenomenon.

Cognitive equilibrium: Mental balance, a process in which theorist Jean Piaget believed that individuals are always engaged to some degree.

Cognitive maps: A type of mental processing by which we can acquire, code, store, recall, and decode information about a specific location, word, idea, or task in our everyday environment.

Cohesion: The act or condition of cohering; tendency to stick together.

Collaborative learning: Group learning in which children impact each other's cognitive structures; they support one another and encourage new ways to think, construct ideas, and reflect on novel material.

Collectivist cultures: Cultures that emphasize the values of harmony, respect for authority, and group welfare.

Communication: The act of transmitting, giving, or exchanging information, signals, or messages such as by talk, gestures, or writing.

Competence: Displaying appropriate abilities and milestones for age and maturity level.

Concrete operational period: In Jean Piaget's cognitive development theory, the third stage of development (6–11 years of age) characterized by increased logical and flexible thought, and the ability to classify objects, seriate, and reverse operations.

Concurrent validity: Type of validity that concerns whether or not two assessments of the same content correlate with each other.

Conservation: The understanding that something remains the same (is conserved) despite alterations in appearance.

Construct validity: Whether or not the items or questions on different sections of an assessment stay together statistically.

Constructive play: Describes children combining pieces or entities, such as with blocks. The purpose of this type of play is to make something and/or work out a problem.

Constructive stage: The final stage of writing, during which children compare and contrast letters and words.

Constructivism: Learning theory based on the work of Jean Piaget, which states that children are active agents who acquire knowledge of the world and their immediate environment through self-reflection and coordination of their personal thoughts.

Constructivist: The notion that individuals are independent and active agents who acquire knowledge and information though self-reflection and coordination of their own thought processes.

Content validity: Establishes whether or not the material on the assessment covers and includes the appropriate information for the domain or developmental area it purports to cover.

Cooperative play: A type of play structure that involves a group of children playing together with the same goal. Children negotiate roles or events such as when children pretend to run a restaurant. Cooperative play constitutes part of the course of the development of play.

Coparenting relationships: Cooperative parenting alliances usually occur between divorced couples, which involve the renegotiation of rules and boundaries relative to child rearing and engagement.

Cortisol: When the brain is stressed, it produces this substance and interferes with brain functioning, growth, and development.

Creeping: Getting around on the hands and knees or the hands and feet (what laypeople call crawling).

Criterion-referenced assessments: Assessments that are based on some outside objective criteria or standards and compare young children with those criteria or standards.

Critical thinking: The process by which individuals evaluate their assertions and claims about an interesting or puzzling phenomenon and provide justifications based on well-documented evidence that has been empirically researched.

Cross-modal perception: The ability to integrate and coordinate information from two or more modalities, or senses, which develops and enriches over time.

Cultural pluralism: An ideology characterized by mutual appreciation and respect between two or more ethnic groups.

Culture: The pattern of knowledge, skills, behaviors, attitudes, beliefs, and material artifacts produced by a human society and transmitted from one generation to the next.

Data collection: A fundamental step in the scientific method where young children systematically record their numeric or verbal observations.

Deferred imitation: The ability to imitate the behaviors of others who are not present.

Democratic life skills: Include expressing emotions in a manner that does not hurt another person and working well in small groups.

Depth perception: A skill that develops in conjunction with motor skills. Depth perception is realizing that surfaces are not always flat; surfaces may have two or three dimensions.

Development: Based in human biology, the process of change and movement in all domains of a child's existence (i.e., cognitive, linguistic, socioemotional, and physical).

Developmental contextualism: The idea that development takes place in and is impacted by environmental contexts.

Developmental stages: A certain sequence of steps most teachers will go through over the first few years of their careers, as described by renowned educator Lilian Katz.

Developmentalists: Individuals who investigate the changes that people undergo in all aspects of their development throughout the life span.

Difficult temperament: Young children who have lots of energy and intensity, have irregular moods that are usually negative, and have a hard time adjusting to making transitions, new people, or new situations.

Direct instruction: An approach to teaching reading that emphasizes systematic and explicit instruction at the lower primary grades. For instance, phonemic awareness and phonics skills, such as letter sounds and letter names, are taught in a hierarchical structure.

Discussion: A guidance technique that consists of helping children talk about their behaviors or emotions, why they are inappropriate, and what behaviors or emotions can be substituted that are more appropriate.

Disequilibrium: A state of imbalance that continuously motivates us to adapt our cognitive structures to restore balance.

Diversity: Refers to differences in students' ethnic, linguistic, and religious backgrounds as well as differences in their experiences, knowledge, and abilities.

DNA: Deoxyribonucleic acid, which is carried in the genes and provides specific instructions to an egg (zygote) to form the body, brain, and specific heritable traits of a growing fetus.

Domain specificity: An element of children's thinking when cognitive levels are not the same in all developmental areas or subject domains. In other words, a child may be at one stage of reasoning in the domain of mathematics and at another stage in the domain of English.

Dramatic play: Entails pretending, in which the child pretends to be someone else, for example the teacher or a fireman. This type of play does not require any social interaction with other children.

Dressing: A self-help skill achieved around 12 months of age. Children start by helping with undressing: Perhaps they remove their socks. Help with dressing starts with pushing their hands and feet through shirts and pants. However, it is not until 3 years old or later that children can completely dress themselves.

Dual-language programs: Programs where instruction is delivered in two languages with the goal of helping children learn a second language.

Duration record: The recording of how long a behavior or an expression lasts.

Dyslexia: Significant problem in learning to read, particularly in decoding and spelling.

Early childhood education (ECE): Refers to the formal education of children from birth through age

8 years. It includes the programs separately referred to as nursery school, child care, day care, preschool, kindergarten, first grade, second grade, and third grade.

Early childhood special education (ECSE): A federal, state-funded program that provides services for children, 8 years old and under, with special needs or developmental delays and their families.

Easy temperament: Young children who are flexible, are predictable, and generally display a positive mood.

Echolalia: When a child makes sounds that approximate words.

Ecology of human behavior: The view that individuals develop within a complex system of relationships impacted by various levels of the immediate environment.

Edward Seguin: A physician and educator who worked with children with developmental disabilities; he is known for implementing sensory training and influencing the work of Maria Montessori.

Egocentric: Self-centered; when children believe everyone sees the world from their point of view.

Egocentric speech: A form of speech that occurs in young children and involves inner speech that does not take another's point of view into consideration.

Elizabeth Palmer Peabody: American educator who launched the first English-language kindergarten in the United States during the 19th century. Elizabeth and her sister, **Mary Tyler Peabody**, were pioneers and primary exponents of the kindergarten movement.

Emergent curriculum: An approach to planning curriculum that builds upon the interests of the children (students) and the teacher.

Emergent literacy: Refers to the reading and writing concepts and behaviors of young children that are the developmental precursors to conventional forms of literacy.

Emotional competence: The ability to understand one's own and other people's emotions and to appropriately regulate the expression of one's own emotions.

Emotions: Feelings that influence a child's thoughts and behaviors.

Encouraging: A guidance technique where educators accept a child as he or she is and increase the child's self-esteem and confidence. Encouragement focuses on abilities and accomplishments that contribute in some way to the whole group.

Encouraging classroom: A classroom that puts particular emphasis on the daily schedule, room arrangement, and curriculum modification and development.

English immersion programs: Programs where all instruction is delivered in English.

Enrichment: An approach to educating children who are gifted and talented that can involve providing students with supplementary materials or learning opportunities commensurate with their ability level.

Environment: The physical surroundings, and a specific setting.

Environmental manipulations: Actions that arrange or prepare the physical environment of the classroom in order to elicit positive and socially appropriate behaviors from young children.

Environmental science: Focuses on making children aware of their world, introducing basic concepts, and teaching young children about actions to take to protect the environment.

Epigenesis: The study of how one's interactions in the environment influence development.

Erasmus: Humanist, scholar, and theologian, a contemporary of Martin Luther.

Erik Erikson: A theorist who contributed significantly to the field of human development. Erikson (1902–1994) viewed the human life span as consisting of various stages, each one involving a psychological crisis or conflict that requires a resolution.

Ethics: Principles that help us make decisions about how to act morally and socially within a specific culture.

Ethnicity: Refers to cultural factors such as national origin, religion, race, or any combination of these.

Ethnocentrism: The tendency to view the standards of one's own ethnic group or culture as superior or natural when compared with another ethnic group or culture.

Evaluation: Judges the worth and value of a behavior, an event, a program, or a teaching strategy based on what is observed.

Event sampling: Used when the focus of the observation occurs less frequently or rarely, a richly descriptive recording of an infrequent behavior or expression every time that the behavior or expression occurs.

Evoking behaviors: The process of interacting with children in such a manner that positive and socially appropriate behaviors are emitted.

Exosystem: In Urie Bronfenbrenner's bioecological systems model, one of three nested levels that comprise local institutions such as the school system, religious organizations, and the workplace.

Expressive language: Being able to communicate with others effectively using language.

External speech: A form of speech that develops before the age of 2 years. External speech is characterized by action, but it is not connected to an understanding of speech as communication.

Extinction or nonreinforcement: Refers to the gradual weakening of a conditioned response that results in the behavior decreasing or stopping. Based on the assumption that responses that are not reinforced are not likely to be repeated.

Eye-hand coordination: The ability to coordinate hand movements with visual cues.

Face validity: Determines whether or not an assessment looks like it measures what it purports to measure.

Family function: A term used to describe how a family provides for its members, or the way in which family members work together to meet each other's individual needs.

Family life cycle model: Emphasizes that families are composed of people across many generations who undergo many transitions as they move along the life cycle and who have a shared history and a shared future that encompasses the entire emotional system.

Family structure: Refers to the legal and genetic relationships that bind people together, which include nuclear, extended, and stepfamily members.

Father Knows Best: A popular television sitcom that aired in the late 1950s and early 1960s.

Fine motor development: Development of skills through the use of small muscles, particularly those in the hands and feet.

Fine motor skills: Skills that involve the small muscles of the hands and fingers.

Flexibility: Family members' adaptability and willingness to switch roles, including their ability to surrender power over time.

Flexibility principle: This happens during the sign and message stage. Children realize letters can be put together in varied arrangements to produce new words, and words can be used to produce sentences.

For-profit: Businesses that produce profit for their owners. In for-profit care centers, after expenses are paid, the remainder is considered profit, and the money goes to the owner.

Formal observations: More structured and controlled observation forms.

Formal operations: In Jean Piaget's theory of cognitive development, the fourth and final stage of development (11 years old to adulthood), characterized by increased systematic logical thought processes and the ability to comprehend and systematically manipulate complex concepts.

Formative evaluations: Allow for change in the educational program or more learning and growing by the children evaluated.

Fractions: The numeric representations of part and whole relationships, especially equal parts.

Free and appropriate public education (FAPE): Special education and related services for children with special needs, provided at no cost to the parents. To the maximum extent appropriate, children with special needs should be educated in the regular classroom with appropriate aids and supports.

Frequency count: A simple and usually informal observation type. An observer simply counts the number of times a behavior or an expression happens during the observation. This observation method may be used to establish a baseline of a behavior or an expression.

Friedrich Froebel: A German educator and originator of the kindergarten educational system.

Froebel's gifts: A series of 10 gifts and associated occupations developed by Friedrich Froebel as part of the kindergarten curriculum, which aimed to develop young students' thinking and coordination abilities.

Functional (or exploratory) play: A sensorimotor approach in which a child learns the nature of his or her surroundings. Examples include dumping, filling, stacking, water play, and outdoor play.

Games with rules: Encompass cooperative play, often with winners and losers. These games are distinguished by child-controlled rules and thus are different from the competitive games usually called "sports." Children begin the games with rules stage at about age 6.

Gender roles: The different ways that males and females are expected to think, feel, and behave. The specific differences in these expectations vary depending on culture, ethnicity, religion, *and* socioeconomic status of particular groups of people.

Gender role stereotypes: Beliefs about the types of toys and behaviors and activities appropriate for each gender.

Gender typing: Learning that one is either a boy or a girl and interpreting how a boy or a girl should behave in one's society.

Generative principle: With this awakening children come to understand that there are rules for putting letters and other writing elements together.

Genes: Units of hereditary information that are composed of DNA (deoxyribonucleic acid) and are the very foundation of human development. Genes are passed on to us by our parents, and they impact every aspect of human development. Life begins with genes.

Geometry: The study of the properties and relationships of two- and three-dimensional shapes.

Gestation: Number of weeks after conception.

Gifted and talented: Students who demonstrate evidence of high performance in areas such as intelligence, creativity, music, arts, leadership, and specific academic areas. Schools may provide acceleration or enrichment approaches to educating students who are gifted and talented.

Goal-directed behavior: By the end of the sensorimotor period, when young infants engage in goal-directed behavior, they are more expansive, creative, and intentional—meaning they are deliberate in their coordination of behavioral schemes as a means to an end.

Grasping: This reflex happens when a small object is placed in a baby's hand. The baby reflexively grasps the object very strongly and tightly to hold on to it.

Gross motor development: Development of skills through the use of large muscles in moving the whole body or large parts of the body.

Gross motor skills: Large muscle movements and control.

Guidance: Teaching a young child what behavior is appropriate and what behavior is inappropriate. Guidance is best if accomplished in a firm, yet gentle and sincere, manner.

Guidance techniques: Styles of interacting with children that discipline them and show them positive and socially appropriate behaviors.

Guided participation: A broader concept than scaffolding, guided participation refers to shared experiences between more capable others and less capable others, with little focus on the aspects of communication, thus allowing for variations across situations and cultures.

Handedness: When a child demonstrates a hand preference.

Haptic perception: Learning about objects through touch. Once babies start handling objects, they learn about size, texture, and other characteristics of objects.

Head control: Means an infant is able to keep his or her head steady in an upright position and move it voluntarily.

Head Start: A preschool program developed in 1965 for low-income children and their families. This is a U.S. federally funded program mandated to meet students' social, emotional, health, nutritional, and psychological needs.

Health: Basic physical, psychological, and biological well-being.

Hearing: One of the five senses, which begins even before birth. A 5- or 6-month-old fetus can hear, but not as well as an adult. Not until they are 2 years old can toddlers hear high-frequency sounds similar to an adult.

Hierarchy of human needs: A pyramid scheme conceptualized and devised by Abraham Maslow to convey that some needs take precedent over others, prompted by Maslow's earlier work with primates.

Hopping: Being up in the air with one foot in the air. In other words, the feet are separated, and one foot is a little higher than the other.

"I" messages: A guidance technique where you own the problem and express to the child how you feel, why you feel that way, and why you would like the child to change his or her behavior.

Ignoring: A guidance technique that means not giving any attention or reinforcement to a behavior so that it will stop.

Implicit rules: The play of children often has implicit rules that allow them to distinguish between fantasy and reality. Children's behavior is based on events they remember from real life.

Inclusion: The concept of full inclusion is based on the idea that children with special needs should receive instruction in regular early care and education settings with children who are typically developing to promote social skills and academic preparation.

Indirect instruction: Based on the constructivist approach to learning that emphasizes the student as an active learner. The teacher takes on the role of facilitator, as opposed to instructor, arranging the classroom environment to promote active student participation.

Individual education program (IEP): A written plan to help meet the special learning and social needs of an individual child with special needs.

Individual family service plan (IFSP): A written plan for infants and toddlers under the age of 3 years who qualify as having a disability or are considered "at risk" of experiencing a substantial developmental delay without these services.

Individualistic cultures: Cultures that emphasize the values of self-expression and individual achievement.

Individuals with Disabilities Education Act (IDEA): Legislation that ensures all children with special needs receive comprehensive and individualized services through special education and related services.

Industry versus inferiority: In Erik Erikson's theory, the psychosocial conflict in early to middle childhood that is resolved when teachers and parents provide children with an opportunity to work cooperatively and effectively with one another, thereby bolstering children's sense of competence and self-efficacy.

Informal observations: Free-flowing and less structured observation forms.

Information processing theory: Antithetical to Jean Piaget's theory of cognitive development. Piaget's theory focuses on distinct stages of cognitive development, whereas information processing theory provides a step-by-step description of thought processes occurring at every age.

Initiative versus guilt: In Erik Erikson's theory, the psychosocial conflict in the preschool years that is resolved when parents support children's sense of purpose and refrain from demanding too much self control, which can lead to guilt.

Insecure-ambivalent attachment: When young children want comfort from their primary caregiver but cannot seem to accept it. Their primary caregivers are inconsistent in their caregiving practices—sometimes they are responsive to their baby's needs, and sometimes not.

Insecure-avoidant attachment: When young children are less compliant with their primary caregivers (compared with babies who are securely attached) and may also show anger and lack of trust.

Insecure-disoriented-disorganized attachment: When young children behave in contradictory ways, without any apparent goal. Usually, they have experienced abuse, trauma, or significant loss, and often their primary caregivers have, too.

Instrumental conditioning: Another term for operant conditioning.

Intelligence: One's ability to reason and solve problems cognitively.

Intentional teaching style: A style of teaching that reflects a balanced approach to teaching where the teacher takes an active role in the teaching of young children and allows for child-initiated learning as well.

Interactionists: Individuals who subscribe to interactionist theory. Interactionists consider certain functions of language to be maturational and genetically determined. The interaction between a child's innate language abilities and the child's environment facilitates language development and reasoning.

Interpsychological: In Lev Vygotsky's sociocultural theory, the process by which learning occurs on the "social plane" or between two people.

Inter-rater reliability: Refers to whether or not different people utilizing a certain measure get the same score.

Intersubjectivity: The process by which two persons begin a task with different understandings but eventually arrive at a shared understanding.

Intrapsychological: In Lev Vygotsky's sociocultural theory, the process by which learning is internalized (within the person).

Intrinsic motivation: Refers to motivation that comes from inside an individual as opposed to from external rewards. Activities are typically pursued for their own sake and provide internal satisfaction.

Intrinsically motivated scholarship: Demonstrated by children who are typically very excited about learning.

Irreversibility: The inability of the child to systematically engage in the mental process of going through a series of steps in a problem and then reversing direction, returning to the initial step. Distinguished from *reversibility*.

Jean-Jacques Rousseau: An 18th-century Swiss political writer and philosopher.

Jean Piaget: A Swiss-born psychologist/philosopher, constructivist theorist, and originator of cognitive development theory.

Jerome Bruner: Early U.S.-born psychologist who has made significant contributions to the fields of educational and developmental (cognitive) psychology.

Johann Heinrich Pestalozzi: An 18th-century Swiss educational reformer.

John Amos Comenius: A 17th-century Moravian educational reformer and theologian.

John B. Watson: An American psychologist and a key player in the development of behaviorist theory.

John Dewey: A U.S. philosopher, educator, and exponent of pragmatism.

John Locke: An empirical philosopher who lived during the 17th century.

Jumping: Being up in the air with both feet above the ground.

Kindergarten: Beginning in the late 18th century, a class for young children, typically comprising 5-year-olds, that prepares them for first grade by providing learning activities and experiences (games, exercises, music, simple handicrafts, etc.) aimed at building their skills and development in the four basic domains: social, cognitive, physical, and emotional.

Kurt Lewin: German American psychologist known for his work in the areas of social/applied psychology, group dynamics, and change theory.

Language: Refers to a whole system of communication.

Language acquisition device (LAD): An innate capacity that gives humans the ability to learn, understand, and produce language.

Lateralization: Lateralization means certain parts of the brain control certain bodily actions and thoughts.

Learning: A relatively fixed or lasting change in the way a child behaves or responds to his or her environment due to experience.

Least restrictive environment (LRE): Emphasizes the importance of providing children with special needs instruction in the regular classroom, to the maximum extent possible.

Lev Semyonovich Vygotsky: A Russian developmentalist who was a leader in explicating the interaction between societal culture and education, the originator of sociocultural theory, and a constructivist.

Life science: The study of living beings and their environments and life cycles.

Literacy: In the early childhood years, literacy involves just a basic awareness and understanding of a subject such as language or mathematics.

Local education agency (LEA): A local education agency is a public school district that operates multiple schools.

Locus of control: The external and internal forces that impact one's life.

Logical consequences: Results of inappropriate behavior that an adult believes to be logical and will lessen the likelihood of that behavior being repeated.

Logico-mathematical knowledge: According to Jean Piaget, knowledge that entails the mental construction of relationships between things.

Loris Malaguzzi: An elementary school teacher who dedicated himself to pedagogical activities within the early childhood education system to join parents and further develop the Reggio Emilia program.

Lucy Sprague Mitchell: A reformer of education who believed in democratic conceptions of education, and whose research interests in children and belief that teachers should understand the development of children led her to establish the Bureau of Educational Experiments, which became the Bank Street School in 1916, now known as Bank Street College.

Macrosystem: In Urie Bronfenbrenner's bioecological systems model, the outermost nested level that comprises cultural values, laws, customs, and resources.

Mainstreaming: Based on the idea that children with special needs can participate in the regular classroom for part of the school day to the extent that it meets their individual needs. Students must demonstrate that they can learn the same material at the same rate as their peers who are typically developing.

Make-believe play: The process of acting out common, everyday experiences and imaginary activities.

Malnutrition: Occurs when children eat insufficient amounts and/or types of food needed to maintain healthy body functions. This is often coupled with insufficient interaction and physical activity.

Manipulatives: Small objects that fingers can interact with that include puzzles and games with small pieces, such as LEGO bricks, bingo tokens, and dominoes.

Margaret and Rachel McMillan: Two sisters who created the first "open air" nursery school in England. They were pioneers who believed in the importance of early childhood education. Their philosophy of learning included a focus on teaching early social skills such as interpersonal interactions, peer relationships, and classroom skills.

Margarethe Meyer Schurz: A proponent of Froebelian educational philosophy and one of the first, unofficially, to administer a kindergarten program in the confines of her home during the mid-20th century.

Maria Montessori: An early-20th-century Italian physician, humanitarian, and educator who established the Montessori method of education, which focused on sense training and guidance as a means of encouraging self-regulation. Her philosophy of teaching has inspired many educators who use her method in public and private Montessori schools across the world.

Martin Luther: A theologian who lived from 1483 to 1546; leader of the Protestant Reformation in Germany; translator of the Bible.

Marxism: The system of thought developed by Karl Marx that consists of an organization of production to directly satisfy economic demands and human needs, so that goods and services would be produced directly for use instead of for private profit driven by the accumulation of capital.

Mary Tyler Peabody Mann: An American educator, reformer, and politician during the 19th century. Mary and her sister, **Elizabeth Palmer Peabody**, were pioneers and primary exponents of the kindergarten movement.

Master teacher: An early childhood educator with at least an associate's degree who mentors teachers with less experience.

Maturational theory: Relays how neurological development and timing basically set the course for physical development.

Measurement: Calculating the quantity or amount of something.

Mental structures: In Jean Piaget's theory, a specific psychological structure or scheme—an organized way of making sense of the world, which changes with age.

Mesosystem: The second nested level of Urie Bronfenbrenner's bioecological systems model that consists of connections between microsystems such as home, school, neighborhood, and child care center.

Metacognition: Awareness of mental activities; thinking about thinking.

Metacommunicative: During play it provides the context of reality that connects the thought processes of two people while using language to describe events.

Metalinguistic awareness: The ability to reflect consciously on the linguistic operations and analytical orientations of language.

Metamemory: The ability to think about and control one's own memory.

Microsystem: In ecological systems theory, the innermost or first level of the nested system that comprises the activities and interactional patterns in the child's immediate environment.

Modeling: When a child or an adult initially exhibits some behavior and is rewarded.

Morphology: The study of the structure and content of words.

Multicultural education: Encompasses the disciplines of education, anthropology, sociology, and psychology, and reflects an approach to teaching and learning that promotes educational equity and social justice.

Multidisciplinary team: A team composed of professionals from various disciplines who conduct a comprehensive educational evaluation to determine if a student meets state eligibility criteria for special education.

Multimodality: Indicates that sensory information comes through more than one sensory venue at a time.

Myelin sheaths: Protective covering over the brain's neurons. These sheaths grow rapidly during infancy and toddlerhood.

Narrative descriptions: Informal observations that differ from reflective observations in that they are more general and basic. They are written descriptions of general behavior, rather than observations of a specific behavior.

Nativist model: Nativists believe that children are "prewired" for language and that language is a process of normal maturation. Also known as *innatist model*.

Natural consequences: Natural results of inappropriate behavior that happen and lessen the likelihood that the behavior will be repeated.

Naturalistic observation: A method for measuring social skills that occurs when young children are observed without manipulation in their naturally occurring daily routine.

Need for achievement and prestige: The fourth stage of Abraham Maslow's hierarchy of needs. In our day-to-day life, the need for achievement and prestige is manifested in a number of ways, such as pursuing an academic degree, purchasing a house, or writing a book. This elevated level of human needs in Maslow's scheme represents our desire for self-respect and the respect of others.

Need for belonging and love: Abraham Maslow's third level on the pyramid, which deals with the social needs of people. Both children and adults need to know that they matter and that someone cares.

Need for security and safety: Abraham Maslow's second level on the pyramid. People of all ages need shelter, a sanctuary or home that makes them feel safe.

Need for self-actualization: The very top of Abraham Maslow's hierarchy of human needs. Children and adults who are self-actualized recognize their full potential and are motivated to become the very best that they can be. They have an enhanced sense of self-efficacy and self-worth.

Needs addressing human survival: At the very basest level of Abraham Maslow's pyramid, these needs consist of food, water, and sleep.

Negative reinforcement: A technique based on B. F. Skinner's theory of operant conditioning designed to increase a behavior by stopping or removing a negative outcome or an aversive stimulus. An example of negative reinforcement is when a student completes an assignment to avoid losing recess.

Negative stereotypes: Beliefs, usually about minority groups, that all members of a particular group share one or more negative characteristics.

Neoconservative: An intellectual political movement that evolved in the late 1970s in reaction to liberal and leftist thought, advocating individualism combined with traditional moral standards.

Neurons: The basic brain cells that carry and store information.

Nonprofit: Programs that do not make a profit from their businesses. Nonprofit monies are incorporated back into the program or are returned to the sponsoring agency.

Norm-referenced: An assessment that compares young children with other young children who are typically developing and are the same age and at the same developmental level.

Number concepts: Properties and functions of numbers.

Number sense: A basic understanding of number or quantity.

Obesity: Being extremely overweight with excess fatty tissue.

Object permanence: Occurs when a young child realizes that an object exists even though he or she does not see it.

Objective: A specific and practical aim for an observation.

Observation: Seeing, noting, and recording specific behavioral phenomena.

Observational learning: Learning that happens when watching another child or adult get rewarded for some behavior.

One-to-one correspondence: The awareness and knowledge that each individual number in a counting sequence refers to one object.

Operant conditioning: A process of behavior modification designed to increase or decrease the occurrence of a specific behavior.

Operant learning: The process of gaining new knowledge or developing through rewards from other people in the environment.

Organization: The process of reordering and connecting new schemes to other schemes to create a more elaborate scheme or cognitive system.

Overgeneralize: Drawing conclusions that are very general and are without facts.

Overweight: When children eat too much food or too much of the wrong types of food and do not partake in enough physical activity.

Paideia: A Greek term that means child rearing and education; a system of instruction in Athens in which students were given a well-rounded cultural education that included such subjects as rhetoric, grammar, mathematics, music, philosophy, geography, natural history, and gymnastics.

Parallel play: Children from $2\frac{1}{2}$ to $3\frac{1}{2}$ years old play independently, but now they are among their peers and use toys that are similar to those of the children around them.

Paraprofessional: A person who is trained to perform certain functions as in medicine or teaching, but who is neither licensed nor credentialed to practice as a professional.

Parent involvement: Parent involvement in early childhood education is the parents and other family members becoming involved in their child's learning process through a partnership with their child's teacher.

Parenting style: A concept aimed at describing how parents treat their children across two broad dimensions: responsiveness and demandingness.

Patterning: Broader than seriation, patterning involves putting objects, people, or sensations in some sort of repeated order over and over again.

Patti Smith Hill: A major proponent and leader in the kindergarten movement and supporter of merging kindergarten and primary education in public schools.

Peaceable classroom: A model that arose in response to the amount of violence to which children are exposed. Teachers in the peaceable classroom try to ameliorate the violence to which children are exposed that negatively impacts the children's development, thoughts, and feelings.

Pedagogical techniques: The art and science of teaching, especially instruction in teaching methods or strategies.

Peers: Friends who are at or near the same age or developmental level.

Perception: The use of the senses to perceive objects; the mental processing of sensory data.

Performance assessment: Where children are required to emit some type of "real world" behavior. Perhaps you will have them write and recite a poem or story.

Permissive parenting style: Parents are very warm and nurturing, but have few rules and set few limits; they are lenient and avoid confronting their children.

Philosophy of teaching: The approach to and beliefs about teaching, it reflects the teacher's values, knowledge, education, and experience, and the needs of the students.

Phoneme: The smallest unit in the sound system of a language that distinguishes one word from another. For example, the word *cat* has three phonemes.

Phonemic awareness: An understanding of the structure of reading and writing.

Phonics approach: A philosophical view of how children should learn to read and write. This method of teaching reading emphasizes decoding and spelling.

Phonology: The study of sounds concerned with the rules governing the structure, distribution, and sequencing of speech sounds.

Physical aggression: Intentionally harming someone physically by hitting, biting, kicking, or performing some other physical act.

Physical environment: Refers to the physical aspects or considerations of a classroom.

Physical knowledge: According to Jean Piaget, knowing the physical properties or attributes of an object, such as its number, size, shape, and color.

Physics: The study of matter and energy.

Planes of development: Based on the Montessori philosophy that states that the child moves to adulthood through a series of developmental periods that are related to the child's physical, mental, and social being.

Plasticity: A property of the brain that allows it to adapt and recover very well if injured. In other words, one part of the brain can take over the functions of another if that section of the brain is weakened or damaged in some manner.

Plato: One of the great ancient Greek philosophers.

Play: The opposite of work, an activity enjoyed by children and adults that offers intrinsic motivation. Play is considered important for development and learning during childhood.

Plutarch: A Greek biographer and historian suspected to have been born in about A.D. 46 and died in about 120.

Policy making: The act of creating laws that specify the goals of a government.

Portfolio: An example of several pieces of a student's work, which can include standardized test scores, interview transcripts, writing samples, pictures, and videos.

Positive behavior support (PBS): An early intervention program that teaches young children a variety of appropriate responses to challenging situations.

Positive reinforcement: A technique based on B. F. Skinner's theory of operant conditioning designed to increase positive behavior based on the assumption that behavior that is rewarded is likely to be repeated. Examples include verbal praise, smiling, a pat on the back, and candy.

Positive self-concept: A person with a positive self-concept believes, perceives, and feels important and capable of learning and doing things.

Potty training: A process that can begin when infants are maturationally able to control elimination, somewhere between 15 and 18 months of age.

Pragmatics: A set of rules concerned with the way language is used within different social contexts.

Praise: A guidance technique that relates to an adult's (teacher's or parent's) approval of a child. Praise also focuses on a child's action, but the message of adult approval is huge.

Prehension: When infants obtain adult-type grasping, around 12 months of age, which can be observed in their ability to use their thumb and forefinger to pick up objects.

Preliteracy: The first stage of reading, where children learn the reasons for reading and writing and make their first attempts.

Preoperational: According to Jean Piaget, during this stage, approximately 18 months to 6 years of age, children know their world through concrete symbols (concrete objects). The hallmark ability for entry into this stage is **object permanence.**

Preoperational intelligence: In Jean Piaget's theory of cognitive development, it occurs between the ages of 2 and 6 years and includes symbolic thought (imagination) and language development. Also referred to as the *preoperational stage of development.*

Prereaching: The first stage of acquiring fine motor skills, which occurs when an infant clumsily reaches for or swats at objects in his or her visual field.

Primary emotions: Anger, sadness, joy, surprise, and fear—these are called "primary" because they are the first emotions to appear and have biological roots and begin around the age of 2 months.

Private speech: When children use their words to guide their thoughts, behaviors, and emotions.

Problem solving: The act of helping children think about and solve their own guidance issues.

Progressive movement: This movement was a period of political, societal, economic, and educational change. The movement championed the important role that government must play in education reform efforts and advocated for a child-centered approach, which gives children the autonomy to grow and learn naturally.

Prosocial behaviors: Behaviors that benefit someone else; in addition, the child who emits these behaviors has little expectation of gaining any benefit for him- or herself.

Prosody: The rhythm of spoken language, such as the intonation of speech.

Protective factors: Factors (internal and external) that help resilient people in their struggle.

Proximodistal principle: States that development progresses from inside the body to the outer extremities.

Pruning: The process by which neuron connections (synapses) are erased or eliminated if environmental experiences do not repeatedly and strongly send information along a specific synapse.

Psychosexual development: In Sigmund Freud's psychosexual theory, the changes in growth that emphasize parents' management of children's sexual and aggressive drives, which will lead to healthy personality development during the first few years of life.

Pullout program: Services to identified students are provided outside of the regular classroom.

Punishment: A technique based on B. F. Skinner's theory of operant conditioning designed to reduce negative behavior by applying an aversive stimulus or removing a desirable stimulus. Examples of punishment include spanking a child after he or she runs into a street, or taking away a toy from a child for hitting a classmate.

Qualitative differences: Variations in how children know what they know.

Quantitative differences: Variations in the *amount* or *degree* of knowledge that each child possesses.

Race: The belief in physical and biological characteristics of different ethnic groups throughout the world. Race has been used to justify social inequalities as natural.

Radical behaviorism: B. F. Skinner's theory of operant conditioning.

Rating scale: A value or judgment of relative degree is placed on a behavior or an expression. Rating scales usually have at least three levels of value degree, but may have as many as seven or more.

Receptive language: Being able to listen and understand what is being said or read.

Recurring: The first stage of writing. This is where young children repeat the same strokes.

Redirection: Giving the child an alternative activity or toy and thereby deflecting the child's attention from inappropriate behavior.

Reflective journal or diary: This type of observation selects and describes a particular behavior or emotional expression of the child and then reflects on the meaning or interprets the behavior or expression.

Reflexes: At birth infants exhibit some inborn, genetic movements or reflexes that help infants interact with their world and survive. Reflexes are only elicited by specific environmental stimuli and may be a signal of whether an infant's nervous system is intact and mature.

Reggio Emilia program: Educators working in Reggio Emilia programs subscribe to an educational philosophy that promotes collaboration and critical thinking skills necessary for a democratic society. A key element of the program is cooperation and collaboration between teachers who work in pairs in each classroom.

Reinforcement: According to Skinner, any consequence that follows a behavior and increases the likelihood of the behavior being repeated.

Relational aggression: Intentionally harming someone emotionally or socially by harming the person's reputation, calling the person names, or hurting the person's feelings.

Reliable: When assessments that different teachers and researchers give at different times are in agreement.

Representational thought: The young child's ability to internalize visual experiences and maintain mental imagery of things not present.

Resilience: Children's ability to overcome obstacles and fulfill their potential.

Response to intervention (RTI): A new approach to intervention for and assessment of students struggling academically or socially. RTI is used to determine eligibility for special education services.

Responsive classroom: Focuses on supporting children's socioemotional development, especially in early elementary years. In this classroom type, teachers endeavor to build a responsive classroom by focusing on socioemotional needs and creating caring, respectful schools.

Reward: In operant conditioning, pleasant consequences.

Rolling: Moving from side to side is a motor milestone that exhibits large muscle control. By the age of 6 months, an infant should be able to roll from his back to his stomach and from his stomach to his back.

Rooting: This reflex happens when you touch a newborn's cheek. The baby will turn his or her head that way in search of something to suck.

Rubrics: Scaled assessments that judge whether students can perform a certain task. Rubrics are scoring/grading frameworks that relay criteria and standards for scoring or grading work and behavior.

Rudolf Steiner: Considered the founder of Waldorf education.

Running: When children move their feet and have an obvious point where their whole body is in the air (off the ground), not mature until around the age of 2 years.

Savant: A learned person, eminent scholar.

Scaffolding: Gradually helping a child to arrive at a new point of knowledge or skill by giving him or her hints and suggestions, but not doing the work for the child.

Schemes: In Jean Piaget's theory, a specified psychological structure or mental frame—an organized way of making sense of experience that changes with age. Also referred to as *schemata* (plural).

Scientific process: The steps used by scientists to create and further knowledge.

Scientifically based research: Under the No Child Left Behind Act of 2001, instructional reading programs primarily used in kindergarten through third grade should be based on rigorous scientific research.

Secondary emotions: Expressed during the second year of life—first embarrassment, followed by shame, guilt, envy, and pride. The child realizes the self is distinct from others to experience these emotions.

Secure attachment: When young children feel safe, secure, and free from stress because they are close to their primary caregiver.

Self-awareness: The ability to perceive or understand our own attitudes, beliefs, behavior, motivation, and personality.

Self-feeding: Begins around 7 months of age, when infants can grasp small pieces of food and place them in their mouths. They can also hold a small spoon. This ability improves around 12 months, again at 18 months, and then again at 24 months, when an infant is fairly proficient with a spoon.

Self-help skills: A set of skills that includes dressing and hand washing, increases children's independence, and impacts their resilience or ability to thrive and survive. These are sometimes called adaptive behavior, because they help young children adapt to their environment.

Self-regulation: A state of being for the child; a skill or ability that teachers and parents try to foster within the child. Children who are self-regulated can control their own behavior and emotions and exhibit them in a socially acceptable manner.

Semantics: The study governing the meaning of words and word combinations.

Semi-clinical interview: Piaget's particular technique of questioning children, a type of "peculiar play situation."

Sensorimotor: Jean Piaget's first stage of development, spanning the first 2 years, during which infants and toddlers think with their eyes, hands, ears, and mouth and other sensorimotor equipment.

Sensoriperceptual development: As young children age, their senses mature, and they make meaning of and come to understand sensory information better.

Separation anxiety: The uncomfortable, anxious feeling a young child experiences when a primary caregiver leaves.

Sequential bilingualism: The process of learning two languages in succession before developing proficiency in one of the languages.

Seriation: Putting in order by weight, amount, size, or other related characteristic and going from smallest amount to largest amount or vice versa.

Sigmund Freud: The father of psychosexual development, who posited that children's inner drives, urges, and unconscious wishes are the basis for their thinking and behavior over their extended life.

Sign and message stage: Children realize letters can be put together in varied arrangements to produce new words and words can be used to produce sentences.

Significant discrepancy formula: A formula used by schools to determine if a student meets state eligibility criteria for special education. A student must have a significant discrepancy between intellectual ability and academic achievement.

Simultaneous language acquisition: The process of learning two languages at the same time.

Sitting: A gross motor milestone where, at first, infants lean forward a little. As they gain balance and support, they do not need to lean forward to sit independently.

Slow-to-warm-up temperament: When children are generally thought of as shy. They have difficulty adjusting to transitions and new people and situations, too. However, their reactions are not as intense as the child with a difficult temperament.

Smell: Develops similarly and is closely connected to the sense of taste. The organs that allow a baby to smell are mature before birth, but research has not shown whether an infant can smell before birth. It is true, though, that infants can smell at birth and discriminate odors.

Social competence: Being able to maintain good social relationships with other people while also being able to achieve one's goals in and through those relationships.

Social constructivism: A term derived from sociological theory of knowledge that underscores individuals' learning as the result of their interactions in a group.

Social interaction: A critical mechanism for children's language acquisition that involves the interactions of an infant with parents, siblings, or teachers.

Social or conventional knowledge: Has roots in social conventions created by people. Jean Piaget recognized that social or conventional knowledge is partly derived from individuals' encounters with other people; children require input from others to build their social knowledge.

Social referencing: The ability to understand the emotional expressions of other people, especially primary caregivers, and to respond accordingly.

Sociocultural theory: A theoretical perspective held by Lev Vygotsky that focuses on how culture—the values, beliefs, customs, practices, and skills of a social group—is transmitted to the next generation.

Sociodramatic play: A form of dramatic play with more than one player socially interacting around a theme and a time trajectory over which the play continues and evolves. Children take on roles and use objects as they enact real-life types of play activities.

Solicitous: Overly controlling and interfering when it comes to behavior of preschool-age children, and not seeming to guide children's behavior appropriately during teaching tasks.

Solitary play: Children play alone, usually with toys that are different from those of the children playing nearby. Children at this stage make no attempt to get close to or interact with others, and the level of social interaction is very low.

Speech: Producing word sounds.

Stage theorist: A researcher (e.g., Jean Piaget) who believes that children's cognitive development consists of four distinct stages, with each stage of development to be qualitatively and quantitatively different from the one that preceded it and the one that will follow.

Standardized assessments and tests: These assessments have standard and averaged, norm-referenced scores that are derived by giving the assessment or test to a large number of young children who are representative of all young children in the nation.

State education agency (SEA): A state education agency, or state department of education, is a state-level government responsible for providing information, resources, and technical assistance to school districts and their residents.

Static reasoning: Thinking that nothing ever changes.

Stepping: This is a reflex. Whenever an infant's bare feet touch a flat surface, the infant reflexively takes steps forward in a rhythmic fashion.

Stereotype threat: The fear of ethnic minorities that no matter what they do, they will be judged to have the stereotyped negative attributes of their group.

Storytelling: The ability to tell stories that enriches children's language development.

Strange situation: The procedural way of assessing attachment.

Stranger anxiety: The uncomfortable, anxious feeling a young child experiences when a stranger approaches.

Structured English immersion (SEI): An instructional approach used to teach English to English language learners rapidly with all content taught in English using materials in English.

Student study team: Consists of the parents, the student (when appropriate), the classroom teacher, and special education representatives who study the student's performance, make recommendations, and develop a plan to ensure academic and social success.

Sucking: This reflex occurs in response to something touching an infant's mouth or lips.

Summative evaluations: Final, with major decisions and actions following.

Surrogate fathers: A person who substitutes, replaces, or assumes the role of the father.

Susan Elizabeth Blow: A devotee of Froebelian thought and principles, and one of the first educators in the late 19th century to officially launch kindergarten in a U.S. public school.

Symbolic thought: When the child enriches his play experiences by allowing an object to symbolize something else.

Synapses: Basic neuron connections that form based on information gathered during environmental experiences.

Synaptogenesis: The process by which different brain neurons connect.

Syntax: Refers to word order or grammar that prescribes how words are combined to create sentences.

Tabula rasa: Literally "blank slate," the notion that children come into the world with a mind like empty paper, which needs to be filled with content. Used by educator John Locke.

Taste: This sense is mature at 14 weeks of gestation. At birth, the infant can discriminate between sweet, sour, and bitter tastes. By the age of 2 years, infants have a sense of what should and should not be salted.

Teachable moments: Times when an event or a behavior occurs naturally during the day and then you as a professional teacher take that moment to teach a related concept or further the children's development in a related domain.

Teacher career developmental stages: A sequence of steps over the first few years of the teaching career.

Teacher competencies: The skills and knowledge early childhood teachers need to posses to be able to work effectively with young children.

Telegraphic speech: A form of speech that involves the use of single words or two- to three-word utterances.

Temperament: The biologically based foundation of personality.

Theory: A formulation of apparent relationships or underlying principles of certain observed phenomena, which have been verified to some degree.

Theory theorists: Researchers who purport that humans are naturally driven to devise theories.

Time-in: A newly emerging technique of guidance that involves children in appropriate activities and fulfills their needs. The teacher responds by keeping the child close, giving suggestions for appropriate behavior, modeling appropriate behavior, and giving huge amounts of praise and attention when the appropriate behavior is emitted by the child.

Time-out: Sending the child away from a situation that may be inappropriately rewarding or overstimulating the child.

Time sampling: An observation type that seeks to quantify the number of times a specific behavior occurs during a specified amount of time.

Touch: The sense that develops first, and is sometimes called the mother of all senses. Some embryos can feel beginning at 7 weeks of age; for others the sense of touch appears when the fetus is 14 weeks old.

Transcendentalism: Any various philosophies that propose to discover the nature of reality by investigating the process of thought rather than the objects of experience.

Trust versus mistrust: In Erik Erikson's theory, the psychosocial conflict in the first year of life in which infants learn basic trust if their basic needs (comfort, food, attention, etc.) are met. If their needs are unmet, the psychological conflict is unresolved, and children learn to become distrustful of others.

Turnover rate: Refers to the percentage of teachers who leave the profession or transfer schools. This is a major concern in American public schools, particularly in high-poverty, high-minority, low-performing schools.

Tutorial intervention: The provision of assistance and support provided to assist another in acquiring a skill or concepts.

Twice exceptional learners: A student may have a gift, talent, or high ability combined with a disability that impacts the student's ability to achieve based on his or her potential.

Two-word utterances/telegraphic speech: When a young child produces two-word phrases such as "up mama."

Uninvolved parenting style: Parents tend not to parent much at all; they show little warmth and have few rules or limits.

Universal screening: Schools administer universal screenings to all children that include low-cost, quick testing three times during the academic year to assess the effectiveness of the curriculum and instruction, as well as to address academic problems in a timely manner.

Valid: When an assessment correlates well with other standard measures.

Validity: A determination of whether or not a test measures the entity it purports to measure.

Verbal language: Language that is the foundation for later literacy development (reading and writing).

Vision: This sense appears at birth but is the newborn's least mature sense. After birth, vision milestones include learning to recognize faces and differentiate between one's mother and strangers (soon after birth), discriminating between two of the four primary colors (2 months of age), developing depth perception (by 3 months of age), and improvement of visual acuity (through 4 years of age when adult-like 20/20 vision is attained).

Visually directed reaching: While reaching to grasp an object at this stage, infants use their eyes to examine the target object's position and to guide the movement of their hand in an attempt to grasp the object.

Waldorf education: A system that serves up to 12th-grade students, and functions independently from political and economic restrictions.

Whole-language approach: A philosophical view of how children should learn to read and write. Whole-language proponents advocate for a constructivist approach that emphasizes meaning followed by form (phonics). For instance, children are taught to read and write using whole texts as opposed to decontextualized words.

Whole-word approach: A reading method that teaches children to "sight read" words, that is, to be able to pronounce a whole word as a single unit.

Working model: A frame of reference that infants tend to tap into as they grow, employed whenever an infant comes in contact with people.

Zone of proximal development (ZPD): The difference between what a child can accomplish alone and what a child can accomplish with a more knowledgeable and skilled person's assistance.

References

Aber, J. L., Brown, J. L., & Jones, S. M. (2003). Developmental trajectories toward violence in middle childhood: Course, demographic differences, and response to school-based intervention. *Developmental Psychology, 39,* 324–348.

Aboud, F. (1988). *Children and prejudice.* New York: Basil Blackwell.

Abraham, C. (2002). Terrific toddlers: Tips for supporting development. *Texas Child Care, 26*(1), 2–9.

Adams, E. J. (2011). Teaching children to name their feelings. *Young Children, 66*(3), 66–67.

Akhtar, N., & Tomasello, M. (1997). Young children's production with word order and verb morphology. *Developmental Psychology, 33*(6), 952–965.

Alessandri, S. M., & Lewis, M. (1996). Differences in pride and shame in maltreated and nonmaltreated toddlers. *Child Development, 67,* 1857–1869.

Allen, K. E., & Marotz, L. R. (2003). *Developmental profiles: Birth to twelve* (4th ed.). Clifton Park, NY: Thomson Delmar Learning.

American Academy of Pediatrics. (2011). *Some children's TV shows are bad for their brains.* Retrieved from www.aap.org

American Academy of Pediatrics. (2009, online periodical). *Television and videos for children under 2 may not influence skill development.* Retrieved from www.aap.org

American Academy of Pediatrics. (2010, online periodical). *AAP updates guidance to help families make positive media choices.* Retrieved from www.aap.org

American Academy of Pediatrics Committee on Environmental Health. (1998). Screening for elevated blood lead levels. *Pediatrics, 101,* 1072–1078.

American Academy of Pediatrics Committee on Infectious Diseases. (2000). Recommended childhood immunization schedule: United States, January–December, 2000. *Pediatrics, 105,* 148.

American Academy of Pediatrics Committee on Nutrition. (1992). Statement on cholesterol. *Pediatrics, 105*(4), 888–895.

American Academy of Pediatrics Committee on Nutrition. (2003). Prevention of pediatric overweight and obesity. *Pediatrics, 112,* 424–430.

American Psychiatric Association. (2000). *Practice guidelines for the treatment of patients with eating disorders* (2nd ed.). Washington, DC: Author.

American Public Health Association. (2004). *Disparities in infant mortality* [Fact sheet]. Retrieved fromhttp://www.medscape.com/viewarticle/472721

Americans with Disabilities Act of 1990, 42 U.S.C.A. § 12101 *et seq.* (West 1993).

Anderson, A. H., Clark, A., & Mullin, J. (1994). Interactive communication between children: Learning how to make language work. *Journal of Child Language, 21,* 439–463.

Appling, R. N., & Jones, N. L. (2005). *Individuals with Disabilities Education Act (IDEA): Analysis of changes made by P.L. 108-446.* Retrieved from http://www.cec.sped.org/Content/NavigationMenu/PolicyAdvocacy/IDEAResources/CRSAnalysis

Antler, J. (1987). *The educated woman and professionalization: the struggle for a new feminine identity, 1890–1920.* New York, NY: Garland Publishing.

Aries, P. (1962). *Centuries of childhood: A social history of family life* (R. Baldick, Trans.). New York: Vintage Books.

Arizona Department of Education. (2008). *Structured English immersion models of English language learners task force.* Retrieved from http://www.azed.gov/english-language-learners/sei/

Arizona Department of Education. (2011). *Structured English immersion, K–12 endorsements.* Retrieved from http://www.azed.gov/educator-certification/files/2011/09/sei-endorsement.pdf

Artiles, A., Rueda, R., Salazar, J. J., & Higareda, I. (2002). English-language learner representation in special education in California urban school districts. In D. J. Losen & G. Orfield (Eds.), *Racial inequality in special education* (pp. 117–136). Cambridge, MA: Harvard Education Press.

Asher, S., Erdley, C., & Gabriel, S. (1994). Peer relations. In M. Rutter & D. Hay (Eds.), *Development through the lifespan: A handbook for clinicians* (pp. 456–488). Oxford, England: Blackwell.

Auer, J. C. P. (1984). *Bilingual conversation.* Amsterdam: Benjamins.

August, D., & Shanahan, T. (Eds.). (2006). *Developing literacy in second language learners: Report of the National Literacy Panel on Language Minority Children and Youth.* Mahwah, NJ: Erlbaum.

Aunio, P., Aubrey, C., Godfrey, R., Pan, Y., & Liu, Y. (2008). Children's early numeracy in England, Finland, and People's Republic of China. *International Journal of Early Years Education, 16*(3), 203–221.

Azmitia, M. (1992). Expertise, private speech, and the development of self-regulation. In R. M. Diaz & L. E. Berk (Eds.), *Private speech: From social interaction to self-regulation.* Hillsdale, NJ: Erlbaum.

Bakhurst, D. & Shanker, S. G., (2001). *Jerome Bruner: Language, Culture and Self.* Thousand Oaks, CA: SAGE.

Bagdi, A., Vacca, J., & Waninger, K. N. (2007). The importance of sensory functioning: Guidelines for infant and toddler caregivers. *Dimensions of Early Childhood, 35*(2), 13–22.

Bahrick, L., & Lickliter, R. (2000). Intersensory redundancy guides attentional selectivity and perceptual learning in infancy. *Developmental Psychology, 36,* 190–201.

Baker, C. (1996). *Foundations of bilingual education and bilingualism* (2nd ed.). Philadelphia: Multilingual Matters Ltd.

Baldwin Dancy, R. (2000). *You are your child's first teacher.* New York: Random House.

Bandura, A. (1977). *Social learning theory.* Englewood Cliffs, NJ: Prentice-Hall.

Bandura, A. (1986). *Social foundation of thought and action: A social cognitive theory.* Englewood Cliffs, NJ: Prentice-Hall.

Bandura, A. (1989). Social cognitive theory. In R. Vasta (Ed.), *Annals of child development* (Vol. 6, pp. 1–60). Greenwich, CT: JAI Press.

Bandura, A. (1992). Perceived self-efficacy in cognitive development and functioning. *Educational Psychologist, 28,* 117–148.

Banks, J. A. (1987). *Teaching strategies for ethnic studies.* Boston: Allyn & Bacon.

Banks, J. A. (1997). *Teaching strategies for ethnic studies* (6th ed.). Boston: Allyn & Bacon.

Banks, M., & Shannon, E. (1993). Spatial and chromatic visual efficiency in human neonates. In C. Granrud (Ed.), *Visual perception and cognition in infancy* (pp. 1–46). Hillsdale, NJ: Erlbaum.

Barbour, A. C. (1998/1999). Home literacy bags promote family involvement. *Childhood Education, 75*(2), 71–75.

Barnett, W. S. (1996). Lives in the balance: Age-27 benefit-cost analysis of the High/Scope Perry Preschool program. *Monographs of the HighScope Educational Research Foundation* (No. 11). Ypsilanti, MI: High Scope Press.

Barnett, W. S. (2008). *Preschool education and its lasting effects: Research and policy implications.* Boulder, CO: Education and Public Interest Center & Education Policy Research Unite. Retrieved from http://epicpolicy.org/publication/preschool

Barnett, W. S., Epstein, D. J., Carolan, M. E., Fitzgerald, J., Ackerman, D., & Friedman, A. H. (2010). *The state of preschool 2010: State preschool yearbook.* New Brunswick: Rutgers, The State University of New Jersey, National Institute of Early Education Research.

Barnett, W. S., Husted, J. T., Hawkinson, L. E., & Robin, K. B. (2006). *The state of preschool 2006: State preschool yearbook.* New Brunswick: Rutgers, The State University of New Jersey, National Institute of Early Education Research.

Baroody, A. J. (2004). The developmental bases for early childhood number and operation standards. In D. H. Clements, J. Sarama, & A. M. DiBiase (Eds.), *Engaging young children in mathematics: Standards for early childhood mathematics education* (pp. 173–220). Mahwah, NJ: Erlbaum.

Barrera, M. E., & Maurer, D. (1981). Discrimination of strangers by the three-month-old. *Child Development, 52*(2), 558–563.

Barry, H., Child, I. L., & Bacon, M. K. (1957). Relation of child training to subsistence economy. *American Anthropologist, 61,* 51–63.

Barton, E. E., Reichow, B., Wolery, M., & Chen, C. (2011). We can all participate! Adapting circle time for children with autism. *Young Exceptional Children, 14*(2), 1–21. doi:10.1177/1096250610393681

Bastick, T. (1999, April). *A three factor model to resolve the controversies of why trainees are motivated to choose the teaching profession.* Paper presented at the Biennial Cross Campus Conference in Education, St. Augustine, Trinidad.

Bateson, G. (1955). A theory of play and fantasy. *Psychological Abstracts Research Report, 2,* 39–51.

Baumrind, D. (1967). Child care practices anteceding three patterns of preschool behavior. *Genetic Psychology Monographs, 75,* 43–88.

Baumrind, D. (1971). Current patterns of parental authority. *Developmental Psychology Monographs, 4*(1, Part 2).

Baumrind, D. (2005). Patterns of parental authority and adolescent autonomy. *New Directions for Child and Adolescent Development, 108,* 61–69.

Beck, J. (2002). Emerging literacy through assistive technology. *Teaching Exceptional Children, 35*(2), 44–48.

Behne, T., Carpenter, M., Call, J., & Tomasello, M. (2005). Unwilling versus unable: Infants' understanding of intentional action. *Developmental Psychology, 41,* 328–337.

Bellinger, D. (2004). Lead. *Pediatrics, 113,* 1019–1022.

Bennet, C. (1995). *Comprehensive multicultural education: Theory and practice.* Boston: Pearson Education.

Bennet, C. (2007). *Comprehensive multicultural education: Theory and practice.* Boston: Pearson Education.

Bentzen, W. R. (2000). *Seeing young children: A guide to observing and recording behavior* (6th ed.). Toronto, Ontario: Thomson Delmar Learning.

Bentzen, W. R. (2003). *Seeing young children: A guide to observing and recording behavior* (7th ed.). Toronto, Ontario: Thomson Delmar Learning.

Berg, W., Adkinson, C., & Strock, B. (1973). Duration and frequency of periods of alertness in neonates. *Developmental Psychology, 15,* 760–769.

Bergen, D. (2002). The role of pretend play in children's cognitive development. *Early Childhood Research and Practice, 4*(1), 2–15.

Berger, K. S. (2011). *The developing person through the life span* (8th ed.). New York: Worth.

Bergin, D. A., Ford, M. E., & Hess, R. D. (1993). Patterns of motivation and social behavior associated with microcomputer use of young children. *Journal of Educational Psychology, 85,* 437–445.

Berk, L. (2012). *Infants, children and adolescents* (7th ed.). Boston: Allyn & Bacon.

Berk, L. E., & Winsler, A. (1995). *Scaffolding children's learning: Vygotsky and early childhood education.* Washington, DC: National Association for the Education of Young Children.

Berlyne, D. E. (1969). Laughter, humor, and play. In G. Lindzey & E. Aronson (Eds.), *Handbook of social psychology* (Vol. 3, pp. 795–852). Reading, MA: Addison-Wesley.

Bernstein, B. (1970). A sociolinguistic approach to socialization with some reference to educability. In F. Williams (Ed.), *Language and poverty: Perspectives on a theme* (pp. 25–62). Chicago: Markham.

Bertenthal, B., & Campos, J. (1990). A systems approach to the development of self-produced locomotion during infancy. In R. Emde & R. Harmon (Eds.), *Continuities and discontinuities of development* (pp. 195–207). New York: Plenum.

Bertenthal, B., Campos, J., & Bennett, K. (1984). Self-produced locomotion: An organizer of social, cognitive, and emotional development in infancy. In C. Rovee-Collier & L. P. Lipsitt (Eds.), *Advances in infancy research* (Vol. 11, pp. 143–191).

Bhatia, T., & Ritchie, W. (1996). Bilingual language mixing, universal grammar, and second language acquisition. In W. Ritchie & T. Bhatia (Eds.), *Handbook of second language acquisition* (pp. 627–688). San Diego, CA: Academic Press.

Bialystok, E. (2001). *Bilingualism in development: Language, literacy, and cognition*. Cambridge, UK: Cambridge University Press.

Biel, L., & Peske, N. (2005). *Raising a sensory smart child: The definitive handbook for helping your child with sensory integration issues*. New York: Penguin.

Billman, J., & Sherman, J. (2003). *Observation and participation in early childhood settings: A practicum guide*. Boston: Allyn & Bacon.

Bjorklund, D. (2005). *Children's thinking*. Belmont, CA: Wadsworth/Thomson Learning.

Blair, K. A., Denham, S. A., & Kochanoff, A. (2004). Playing it cool: Temperament, emotion regulation, and social behavior in preschoolers. *Journal of School Psychology, 42*(6), 419–443.

Blanchett, W. J. (2010). Telling it like it is: The role of race, class, and culture in the perpetuation of learning disability as a privileged category for the White middle class. *Disability Studies Quarterly, 40*(2). Retrieved from http://dsq-sds.org/article/view/1233

Bloom, L. (1993). *The transition from infancy to language: Acquiring the power of expression*. New York: Cambridge University Press.

Bobys, A. (2000). What does emerging literacy look like? *Young Children, 55*(4), 16–22.

Boone, J. A., & Adesso, V. J. (1974). Racial differences on a Black intelligence test. *Journal of Negro Education, 43*(4), 429–436.

Bornstein, M. H., Arterberry, M. E., & Mash, C. (2005). Perceptual development. In M. H. Bornstein & M. Lamb (Eds.), *Developmental science: An advanced textbook* (5th ed., pp. 283–325). Mahwah, NJ: Erlbaum.

Bos, H. M. W., van Balen, F., & van den Bloom, D. C. (2007). Child adjustment and parenting in planned lesbian-parent families. *American Journal of Orthopsychiatry, 77,* 38–48.

Bossey, J. (1980). Development of olfactory and related structures in staged embryos. *Anatomy of Embryology, 161,* 225–236.

Boutte, G. (1999). *Multicultural education: Raising consciousness*. Belmont, CA: Wadsworth.

Bower, T. (1999). New research demolishes link between MMR vaccine and autism. *British Medical Journal, 318,* 1643–1649.

Bowlby, J. (1969). *Attachment and loss: Attachment* (Vol. 1). New York: Basic Books.

Bowlby, J. (1982). *Attachment and loss: Attachment* (2nd ed., Vol. 1). New York: Basic Books. (Original work published 1969)

Bowlby, J. (1988). *A secure base: Clinical applications of attachment theory*. London: Routledge.

Bradley, R. H., & Caldwell, B. M. (1977). Home observation for measurement of the environment: A validation study of screening efficiency. *American Journal of Mental Deficiency, 81*(5), 417–420.

Bradley, R. H., & Caldwell, B. M. (1979). Home observation for measurement of the environment: A revision of the preschool scale. *American Journal of Mental Deficiency, 84*(3), 235–244.

Bradley, R. H., Caldwell, B. M., & Corwyn, R. F. (2003). The child care HOME inventories: Assessing the quality of family childcare homes. *Early Childhood Research Quarterly, 18*(3), 294–309.

Brandt, R. M. (1972). *Studying behavior in natural settings*. New York: Holt, Rinehart, Winston.

Braun S. and Edwards, E. (1972). *History and theory of early education*. Belmont, CA: Wadsworth Publishing Co., Inc.

Bredekamp, S. (2004). Standards for preschool and kindergarten mathematics education. In D. H. Clements, J. Sarama, & A. M. DiBiase (Eds.), *Engaging young children in mathematics: Findings of the 2000 National Conference on Standards for Preschool and Kindergarten Mathematics Education* (pp. 77–82). Mahwah, NJ: Lawrence Erlbaum Associates.

Bredekamp, S., & Copple, C. (1997). *Developmentally appropriate practice in early childhood programs* (Rev. ed.). Washington, DC: National Association for the Education of Young Children.

Bretherton, I., & Munholland, K. A. (1999). Internal working models in attachment relationships: A construct revisited. In J. Cassidy & P. R. Shaver (Eds.), *Handbook of attachment* (pp. 89–111). New York: Guilford.

Brewer, J. (2004). *Introduction to early childhood education: Preschool though primary grades*. Boston: Pearson Education.

Bricker, D., & Squires, J. (1999). *Ages and states questionnaires: A parent-completed, child monitoring system*. Townson, MD: Paul H. Brookes.

Brigance, A. H. (1991). *Brigance diagnostic inventory of early development*. North Billerica, MA: Curriculum Associates.

Briggs, C. J., Reis, S. M., & Sullivan, E. E. (2008). A national view of promising programs and practices for culturally, linguistically, and ethnically gifted and talented students.

Gifted Child Quarterly, 52(2), 130–145. doi:1001177/0016986208316037

Bronfenbrenner, U. (1971). Who cares for America's children? *Young Children, 26,* 157–163.

Bronfenbrenner, U. (1974). *Is early intervention effective? A report on longitudinal evaluations of preschool programs.* Washington, DC: Office of Child Development, U.S. Department of Health Education and Welfare.

Bronfenbrenner, U. (2005). *Making human beings human.* Thousand Oaks, CA: Sage.

Bronfenbrenner, U., & Morris, P. A. (1998). The ecology of developmental processes. In R. M. Lerner (Ed.), *Handbook of child psychology: Theoretical models of human development* (5th ed., Vol. 1, pp. 535–584). New York: Wiley.

Brooks-Gunn, J., Han, W.-J., & Waldfogel, J. (2002). Maternal employment and the child cognitive outcomes in the first three years of life: The NICHD study of early child care. *Child Development, 73,* 1052–1072.

Broude, G. (1995). *Growing up: A cross-cultural encyclopedia.* Santa Barbara, CA: ABC-CLIO.

Brown, A. L. (1997). Transforming schools into communities of thinking and learning about serious matters. *American Psychologist, 52,* 300–313.

Brown, H. D. (2006). Principles of language learning and teaching. New York: Pearson.

Brown, R. (1973). *A first language: The early stages.* Cambridge, MA: Harvard University Press.

Brown, W. (2000). The myth of the first three years. *Early Childhood Research Quarterly, 15*(2), 269–273.

Bruder, M. B. (2000). *The individual family service plan.* Arlington, VA: ERIC Clearinghouse on Disabilities and Gifted Education.

Bruner, J. (1960). *The process of education.* Cambridge, MA: Harvard University Press.

Bruner, J. (1983). *Child's talk: learning to use language.* New York: Norton.

Bruner, J. (1972). The nature and uses of immaturity. *American Psychologist, 27,* 687–708.

Bumpus, M. F., Crouter, A. C., & McHale, S. M. (2006). Linkages between negative work-to-family spillover and mothers' and fathers' knowledge of their young adolescents' daily lives. *Journal of Early Adolescence, 26,* 36–59.

Burns, E. (2007). *The essential special education guide for the regular education teacher.* Springfield, IL: Charles C. Thomas.

Burns, M. (1992). *About teaching mathematics: A K–8 resource.* White Plains, NY: Cuisenaire.

Bursztyn, A. M. (Ed.). (2007). *The Praeger handbook of special education.* Westport, CT: Greenwood Publishing Group.

Bushnell, E. (1985). The decline of visually-guided reaching in infancy. *Infant Behavior and Development, 8,* 139–155.

Bushnell, E. W., & Boudreau, J. P. (1993). Motor development and the mind: The potential role of motor abilities as a determinant of aspects of perceptual development. *Child Development, 64,* 1005–1021.

Bushnell, I., & Sai, F. (1987). *Neonatal recognition of mother's face.* University of Glasgow Report 87/1.

Butler-Omololu, C., Doster, J. A., & Lahey, B. (1983). Peer mediated social skills training with an isolated pre-school child. *Corrective and Social Psychology, 29*(1), 14–16.

California Department of Education. (2009). *Infant/toddler learning and development foundations.* Sacramento, CA: Author. Retrieved from http://www.cde.ca.gov

California Department of Education. (2012). *Early learning quality system.* Sacramento, CA: Author. Retrieved from http://www.cde.ca.gov

Call, J. D. (1984). Child abuse and neglect in infancy: Sources of hostility within the parent-infant dyad and disorders of attachment in infancy. *Child Abuse & Neglect, 8,* 185–202.

Camara, K. A., & Resnick, G. (1988). Interparental conflict and cooperation: Factors moderating children's post divorce adjustment. In E. M. Hetherington & J. Aratesh (Eds.), *Impact of divorce, single parenting, and step-parenting on children* (pp. 169–195). Hillsdale, NJ: Erlbaum.

Canfield, R. L., Henderson, C. R., Cory-Slechta, D. A., Cox, C., Jusko, T. A., & Lanphear, B. P. (2003). Intellectual impairment in children with blood lead concentrations below 10 g per deciliter. *New England Journal of Medicine, 348,* 1517–1526.

Caplan, M., Vespo, J., Pedersen, J., & Hay, D. F. (1991). Conflict and its resolution in small groups of one- and two-year-olds. *Child Development, 62,* 1513–1524.

Caples, S. E. (1996). Some guidelines for preschool design. *Young Children, 51,* 14–21.

Carrick, D. (1985). *Milk.* New York: Greenwillow.

Carter, B., & McGoldrick, M. (Eds.). (1999). *The expanded family life cycle: Individual, family, and social perspectives* (3rd ed.). Boston: Allyn and Bacon.

Case, R. (1985). *Intellectual development: Birth to adulthood.* New York: Academic Press.

Caspi, A., Moffitt, T. E., Morgan, J., Rutter, M., Taylor, A., Kim-Cohen, J., & Polo-Thomas, M. (2004). Maternal expressed emotion predicts children's antisocial behavior problems: Using monozygotic-twin differences to identify environmental effects on behavioral development. *Developmental Psychology, 40,* 149–161.

Cassiday, J., & Berlin, L. J. (1994). The insecure/ambivalent pattern of attachment: Theory and research. *Child Development, 65,* 971–991.

Catron, C. E., & Allen, J. (2007). *Early childhood curriculum.* New York: Macmillan.

Caudill, W. (1988). Tiny dramas: Vocal communication between mother and infant in Japanese and American families. In G. Handel (Ed.), *Childhood socialization.* New York: Aldine de Gruyter.

Center for the Study of Child Care Employment & Institute for Research on Labor and Employment. (2007). *Early childhood educator competencies: A literature review of current best practices, and an online survey process to gather input on next steps for California.* Retrieved from http://www.childcareplanning.org/ECE_educator_competencies_full.pdf

Center on the Developing Child at Harvard University. (2007). *A science-based framework for early childhood policy: Using evidence to improve outcomes in learning, behavior, and health for vulnerable children.* Cambridge, MA: Author.

Chaille, C., & Silvern, S. (1996). Understanding through play. *Childhood Education, 72*(5), 274–277.

Chan, T. W., & Koo, A. (2010). *Parenting style and youth outcomes in the UK.* Retrieved from http://esr.oxfordjournals.org/content/early/2010/03/05/esr.jcq013.abstract

Chang, H., Muckelroy, A., & Pulido-Tobiassen, D. (1996). *Looking in, looking out: Redefining child care and early education in a diverse society.* San Francisco: California Tomorrow.

Chang, H., & Sakai, L. (1993). *Affirming children's roots: Cultural and linguistic diversity in early care and education.* San Francisco: California Tomorrow.

Chatting-McNichols, J. (1992). *Montessori programs in public schools.* ERIC Digest, EDO-PS-92-7. Urbana, IL: ERIC Clearinghouse on Elementary and Early Childhood Education.

Chen, C., Greenberger, E., Lester, J., Dong, Q., & Guo, M. (1998). A cross-cultural study of family and peer correlates of adolescents misconduct. *Developmental Psychology, 34,* 770–781.

Chen, W., Li, S., Cook, N. R., Rosner, B. A., Srinivasan, S. R., Boerwinkle, E., & Berenson, G. S. (2004). An autosomal genome scan for loci influencing longitudinal burden of body mass index from childhood to young adulthood in white sibships: The Bogalusa Heart Study. *International Journal of Obesity, 28,* 462–469.

Children's Defense Fund. (2011). *The state of America's children.* Retrieved from http://www.childrensdefense.org/child-research-data-publications/state-of-americas-children-2011/

Children, Youth, and Families Education and Research Network. (n.d.). *Practical research-based information from the nation's leading universities.* Retrieved from http://www.cyfernet.org/

Cho, S., & Campbell, J. R. (2011). Differential influences of family processes for scientifically talented individuals' academic achievement along developmental stages. *The Roeper Institute, 33,* 33–45.

Chomsky, N. (1965). *Aspects of the theory of syntax.* Cambridge, MA: MIT Press.

Chomsky, N. (1968). *Thought and language.* New York: Harcourt, Brace, Jovanovich.

Chrisman, K., & Couchenor, D. (2002). *Healthy sexuality development: A guide for early childhood educators and families.* Washington, DC: National Association for the Education of Young Children.

Christie, J., Enz, B., & Vukelich, C. (2003). *Teaching language and literacy: Preschool through the elementary grades* (2nd ed.). New York: Longman.

Chu, S. Y., Barker, L. E., & Smith, P. J. (2004). Racial/ethnic disparities in preschool immunizations: United States, 1996–2001. *American Journal of Public Health, 94,* 973–977.

Citizens Committee for Children. (2012, April). *Concentrated poverty in New York City: An analysis of the changing geographic patterns of poverty.* Retrieved from http://resourcelibrary.gcyf.org/node/4014

Clark, K. B., & Clark, M. P. (1939). The development of consciousness of self and the emergence of racial identification in Negro preschool children. *Journal of Social Psychology, 10,* 591–599.

Clark, K. B., & Clark, M. P. (1947). Racial identification and preference in Negro children. In T. M. Newcomb & E. L. Hartley (Eds.), *Readings in social psychology* (1st ed.). New York: Holt, Rinehart & Winston.

Clarke, B., & Shinn, M. R. (2004). A preliminary investigation into the identification and development of early mathematics curriculum-based measurement. *School Psychology Review, 33*(2), 234–288.

Clawson, M. A., & Robila, M. (2001). Relations between parenting style and children's play behavior. *Journal of Early Education and Family Review, 8*(3), 13–19.

Clay, M. M. (1993). *An observation survey of early literacy achievement.* Portsmouth, NH: Heinemann.

Clayton, M., & Forton, M. B. (2001). *Classroom spaces that work.* Greenfield, MA: Northeast Foundation for Children.

Clements, D. H. (1999). Geometric and spatial thinking in young children. In J. V. Copely (Ed.), *Mathematics in the early years* (pp. 66–79). Reston, VA: National Council of Teachers of Mathematics.

Clements, D. H. (2004a). Geometric and spatial thinking in early childhood education. In D. H. Clements, J. Sarama, & A. M. DiBiase (Eds.), *Engaging young children in mathematics: Standards for early childhood mathematics education* (pp. 267–298). Mahwah, NJ: Erlbaum.

Clements, D. H. (2004b). Major themes and recommendations. In D. H. Clements, J. Sarama, & A. M. DiBiase (Eds.), *Engaging young children in mathematics: Standards for early childhood mathematics education* (pp. 7–75). Mahwah, NJ: Erlbaum.

Click, P., & Parker J. (2009). *Caring for school aged children* (5th ed.). Clifton Park, NY: Cengage Learning.

Cloud, N., Genesee, F., & Hamayan, E. (2000). *Dual language instruction: A handbook for enriched education.* Boston: Heinle & Heinle.

Cohen, A. J. (1996). A brief history of federal financing for child care in the United States. *The Future of Children, 6*(2), 26–40.

Cohen, D. H. & Rudolph, M. (1977). *Kindergarten and early schooling.* Englewood Cliffs, NJ: Prentice Hall.

Cohen, N. E. (1996). *Reinventing early care and education: A vision for a quality system.* San Francisco: Jossey-Bass.

Cole, P. M., Bruschi, C. J., & Tamang, B. L. (2002). Cultural differences in children's emotional reactions to difficult situations. *Child Development, 73,* 983–996.

Coley, R. J. (2002). *An uneven start: Indicators of inequality in school readiness* [Policy information report]. Princeton, NJ: Educational Testing Service Policy Information Center.

Colorado Department of Human Services. (2011). *Quality rating and improvement system: The next generation.* Denver, CO: Author. Retrieved from http://colorado.gov

Coltrane, S. (1996). *Family man.* New York: Oxford University Press.

Community Alliance for Special Education & Disability Rights California. (2011). *Special education rights and responsibilities* (10th ed.). San Francisco: Author. Retrieved from http://www.disabilityrightsca.org/pubs/504001.pdf

Conger, R., Wallace, L., Sun, Y., Simons, L., McLoyd, V., & Brody, G. (2002). Economic pressure in African American families: A replication and extension of the family stress model. *Developmental Psychology, 38,* 179–193.

Connecticut Department of Public Health. (2011, November 16). *Program descriptions.* Retrieved from http://www.ct.gov/dph/cwp/view.asp?a=3141&q=387170&dphNav=|&dphNav_GID=1823

Conroy, M. A., & Davis, C. A. (2000). Early elementary-aged children with challenging behaviors: Legal and educational issues related to IDEA and assessment. *Preventing School Failure, 44*(4), 163–168.

Conway, J. (1997). *Education technology's effect on models of instruction.* Retrieved from http://copland.udel.edu/~jconway/EDST666.htm#cogapp

Coplan, R. J., & Prakash, K. (2003). Spending time with teacher: Characteristics of preschoolers who frequently elicit versus initiate interactions with teachers. *Early Childhood Research Quarterly, 18,* 143–158.

Copley, J. V. (Ed.). (2004). *Showcasing mathematics for the young child: Activities for three-, four-, and five-year-olds.* Reston, VA: National Council of Teachers of Mathematics.

Council for Exceptional Children. (2002). *Addressing overrepresentation of African American students in special education: The prereferral process.* Arlington, VA: Author.

Council for Exceptional Children. (2009). *What every special educator must know: Ethics, standards, and guidelines.* Arlington, VA: Author.

Council for Professional Recognition. (2010). *Child Development Associate: Assessment system and competency standards.* Retrieved from http://www.cdacouncil.org/

Council Oak Montessori School. (2010). *Montessori method.* Retrieved from http://www.counciloakmontessori.org/philosophy.html

Council of Chief State School Officers & National Governors Association. (2010). *Common Core State Standards Initiative.* Retrieved from http://www.corestandards.org/

Council on Physical Education for Children. (1992). *Guidelines for elementary physical education.* Reston, VA: National Association for Sport and Physical Education.

Couse, L. J., & Chen, D. W. (2010). A tablet computer for young children? Exploring its viability for early childhood education. *Journal of Research on Technology in Education, 43*(1), 75–98.

Cratty, B. J. (1986). *Perceptual and motor development in infants and children.* Englewood Cliffs, NJ: Prentice-Hall.

Cremin, L. A. (1961). *The transformation of the school: Progressivism in American education, 1876–1957.* New York: Knopf Books.

Crick, N. R., Casas, J. F., & Ku, H. C. (1999). Relational and physical forms of peer victimization in preschool. *Developmental Psychology, 35*(2), 376–385.

Crystal, D. (1987). *The Cambridge encyclopedia of language.* Cambridge, UK: Cambridge University Press.

Cummins, J. (1981). The role of primary language development in promoting educational success for language minority children. In California Department of Education (Ed.), *Schooling and language minority children: A theoretical framework* (pp. 3–50). Los Angeles: California State University, Los Angeles, Evaluation, Dissemination, and Assessment Center.

Cunningham, B., & Watson, L. W. (2002). Recruiting male teachers. *Young Children, 57*(6), 10–15.

Daniel R. v. State Board of Education, No. 88-1279 (1989).

Darling-Hammond, L., & Snyder, J. (1992). Reframing accountability: Creating learner-centered schools. In A. Lieberman (Ed.), *The changing contexts of teaching: Ninety-first yearbook of the National Society for the Study of Education* (Part I, pp. 11–36). Chicago, IL: University of Chicago Press.

Datar, A., & Strum, R. (2004). Childhood overweight and parent- and teacher-reported behavior problems. *Archives of Pediatric and Adolescent Medicine, 158,* 804–810.

Davey, G., & Cullen, C. (1988). *Human operant conditioning and behavior modification.* Chichester, UK: Wiley.

Davis Holbrook, M. (2007). *Standards-based individualized education program examples.* Alexandria, VA: National Association of State Directors of Special Education.

Davy, J. (2006). *Rudolf Steiner: A sketch of his life and work.* Retrieved from http://www.rsarchive.org/RelAuthors/DavyJohn/

De Groot, A. M. B., & Van Hell, J. G. (2005). The learning of foreign language vocabulary. In *Handbook of bilingualism: Psycholinguistic approaches.* New York: Oxford University Press.

De Houwer, A. (1995). Bilingual language acquisition. In P. Fletcher & B. MacWhinney (Eds.), *Handbook of child language* (pp. 219–250). Oxford: Blackwell.

Deiner, P. L. (2004). *Resources for educating children with diverse abilities: Birth through eight* (3rd ed.). Clifton Park, NY: Thomson Delmar Learning.

DeKaban, A. (1970). *Neurology of early childhood.* Baltimore: Williams & Walkins.

DeKeyser, R. (2000). The robustness of critical period effects in second language acquisition. *Studies in Second Language Acquisition, 22,* 499–533.

Delaney, P. A. (1971). Asthma. *Grade Teacher, 89*(3), 16–20.

Derman-Sparks, L. (1989). *The antibias curriculum: Tools for empowering young children.* Washington, DC: National Association for the Education of Young Children.

Derman-Sparks, L., Gutierrez, M., & Phillips, C. B. (1989). *Teaching young children to resist bias: What parents can do to promote parental multicultural education?* Washington, DC: National Association for the Education of Young Children.

Derman-Sparks, L., Ramsey, P. G., & Edwards, J. O. (2011). *What if all the kids are White? Anti-bias multicultural education with young children and families.* New York: Teachers College Press.

DeVore, S., Miolo, G., & Hader, J. (2011). Individualizing instruction for preschool children using collaborative consultation. *Young Exceptional Children, 14*(4). doi:10.1177/1096250611428424

DeVries, R., & Kohlberg, L. (1987). *Constructivist early education: Overview and comparison with other programs.* Washington, DC: National Association for the Education of Young Children.

Dewey, J. (1916). *Democracy and education.* New York: Macmillan.

Dewsbury, D., Benjamin, L. T., & Wertheimer, M. (2006). *Portraits of a pioneer in psychology.* American Psychological Association and Lawrence Erlbaum Associates, Inc. Hillsdale.

De Wolff, M. S., & van Ijzendoorn, M. H. (1997). Sensitivity and attachment: A meta-analysis on parental antecedents of infant attachment. *Child Development, 68,* 571–591.

Diana v. California State Board of Education, No. C-70-37, U.S. District Court of Northern California (1970).

Dickinson, D., Wolf, M., & Stotsky, S. (1993). Words move: The interwoven development of oral and written language. In J. B. Gleason (Ed.), *The development of language* (3rd ed., pp. 369–420). Boston: Allyn & Bacon.

DiFranza, J. R., Aligne, C. A., & Weitzman, M. (2004). Prenatal and postnatal environmental tobacco smoke exposure and children's health. *Pediatrics, 113,* 1007–1015.

Dodge, D. T., & Bikart, T. S. (2000). *How curriculum frameworks respond to developmental stages: Birth through age 8.* ERIC Document ED470874.

Dodge, D. T., Heroman, C., Charles, J., & Maiorca, J. (2004). Beyond outcomes: How ongoing assessment supports children's learning and leads to meaningful curriculum. *Young Children, 59*(1), 20–28.

Dreikurs, R., & Cassel, P. (1972). *Discipline without tears.* New York: Hawthorne Books.

Dreikurs, R., & Soltz, V. (1964). *Children: The challenge.* New York: Duell, Sloan, & Pearce.

Dunn, L. M. (1968). Special education for the mildly retarded: Is much of it justifiable? *Exceptional Children, 35,* 5–22.

Dunn, L. M., & Dunn, L. M. (2004). *Peabody picture vocabulary test* (3rd ed.). San Antonio, TX: Pearson.

Dupont, H. (1994). *Emotional development, theory and applications: A neo-Piagetian perspective.* Westport, CT: Praeger.

Durand, T. M. (2010). Celebrating diversity in early care and educational settings: Moving beyond the margins. *Early Child Development and Care, 180*(7), 835–845.

Easton, F. (1997). Educating the whole child, "Head, Heart, and Hands": Learning from the Waldorf experience. *Theory Into Practice, 36*(2), 87–94.

Eckerman, K., & Whatley, J. (1977). Toys and social interaction between infant peers. *Child Development, 48,* 1146–1156.

Eckstein, A. (1986). Effect of the bilingual program on English language and cognitive development. In M. Clyne (Ed.), *An early start: Second language at primary school* (pp. 82–89). Melbourne: River Seine.

Edelen-Smith, P. (1995). Eight elements to guide goal determination for IEPs. *Intervention in School and Clinic, 30,* 297–301.

Education and the Workforce Committee. (2012). *Kline: K–12 legislation marks the next chapter in education reform.* Retrieved from http://edworkforce.house.gov

Education for All Handicapped Children Act, Pub. L. No. 94-142, 20 U.S.C. § 1400 *et seq.* (1975).

Edwards, C., Gandini, L., & Forman, G. (1993). *The hundred languages of children: The Reggio Emilia approach to early childhood education.* Norwood, NJ: Ablex.

Edwards, C. P., & Willis, L. M. (2000). Integrating visual and verbal literacies in the early childhood classroom. *Early Childhood Education Journal, 27*(4), 259–265.

Eisenberg, N., & Fabes, R. A. (1998). Prosocial development. In W. Damon (Series Ed.) & N. Eisenberg (Vol. Ed.), *Handbook of child psychology: Social, emotional, and personality development* (5th ed., Vol. 3., pp. 701–778). New York: Wiley.

Elardo, R., Bradley, R., & Caldwell, B. M. (1977). A longitudinal study of the relation of infants' home environments to language development at age three. *Child Development, 48,* 595–603.

Elementary and Secondary Education Act, Pub. L. No. 89-10, 79 Stat. 27 (1965).

Eliot, L. (1999). *What's going on in there? How the brain and mind develop in the first five years of life.* New York: Bantam.

Elksnin, L. K., & Elksnin, N. (2000). Teaching parents to teach their children to be prosocial. *Intervention in School and Clinic, 36*(1), 27–35.

Ellis, M. (1973). *Why people play.* Upper Saddle River, NJ: Prentice Hall.

Epstein, A. S. (2007). *The intentional teacher: Choosing the best strategies for young children's learning.* Washington, DC: National Association for the Education of Young Children.

Epstein, A. S. (2009). Think before you (inter)act: What it means to be an intentional teacher. *Exchange, 184*(January–February), 66–69.

Erikson, E. H. (1963). *Childhood and society* (2nd ed.). New York: Norton.

Erikson, E. H. (1982). *The life cycle completed: A review.* New York: Norton.

Espinosa, L. (2010). Classroom teachers and instruction "best practices" for young English language learners. In E. E. Garcia & E. C. Frede (Eds.), *Young English language learners: Current research and emerging directions for practice and policy* (pp. 143–164). New York: Teachers College Press.

Fang, F. (1985). An experiment on the use of classifiers by 4 to 6 years olds. *Acta Psychologica Sinica, 17,* 384–392.

Fantuzzo, J. W., McDermott, P. A., Manz, P. H., Hampton, V. R., & Burdick, N. A. (1996). The Pictorial Scale of Perceived Competence and Social Acceptance: Does it work with low-income urban children? *Child Development, 67*(3), 1071–1084.

Farmer-Dougan, V., & Kaszuba, T. (1999). Reliability and validity of play-based observations: Relationship between the PLAY behaviours observation system and standardized measures of cognitive and social skills. *Educational Psychology, 19,* 429–440.

Farrell, M. (2009). *The special education handbook: An A–Z guide* (4th ed.). New York: Routledge.

Farver, J. A. M., Kim, Y. K., & Lee-Shin, Y. (2000). Within cultural differences: Examining individual differences in Korean American and European American preschoolers' social pretend play. *Journal of Cross-Cultural Psychology, 31,* 583–602.

Federal Interagency Forum on Child and Family Statistics. (2008). *America's children: Key national indicators of well-being.* Retrieved from www.childstats.gov/americaschildren/tables.asp

Fein, G. G. (1975). A transformational analysis of pretending. *Developmental Psychology, 11,* 291–296.

Fein, G. G. (1981). Pretend play: An integrative review. *Child Development, 52,* 1095–1118.

Fein, G. G. (1984). The self-building potential of preschool play or "I got a fish all by myself." In T. D. Yawkey & A. D. Pellegrini (Eds.), *Child's play: Developmental and applied* (pp. 125–170). Hillsdale, NJ: Erlbaum.

Fein, G. G., & Schwartz, P. M. (1982). Developmental theories in early education. In B. Spodek (Ed.), *Handbook of research in early childhood education* (pp. 82–104). New York: Free Press.

Feinstein, L. (2003). *How early can we predict future educational achievement?* Centre for Economic Performance. Retrieved from http://cep.lse.ac.uk/centrepiece/v08i2/feinstein.pdf

Feuerstein, R. (1980). *Learning Potential Assessment Device (LPAD).* New York: Guilford Press.

Field, T. (1990). *Infancy.* Cambridge, MA: Harvard University Press.

Field, T. (1995). Massage therapy for infants and children. *Developmental and Behavioral Pediatrics, 16,* 105–111.

Fink, R. S. (1976). Role of dramatic play in cognitive development. *Psychological Reports, 39,* 895–906.

Fisher, K. W., & Bidell, T. (1998). Dynamic development of psychological structures in action and thought. In W. Damon (Gen. Ed.) & R. M. Lerner (Vol. Ed.), *Handbook of child psychology: Theoretical models of human development* (5th ed., Vol. 1, pp. 467–561). New York: Wiley.

Flavell, J. (1963). *The developmental psychology of Jean Piaget.* New York: D. Van Nostrand.

Flavell, J. H. (1992). Cognitive development: Past, present, and future. *Developmental Psychology, 28,* 998–1005.

Flicker, E. S., & Hoffman, J. A. (2002). Developmental discipline in the early childhood classroom. *Young Children, 57*(3), 20–26.

Florida Department of Education. (2011). *Early learning and developmental standards for four-year-olds.* Tallahassee: Author.

Ford, K. (2010). *8 strategies for preschool ELLs' language and literacy development.* Retrieved from http://www.colorincolorado.org/article/36679/

Foster, E. (1994, April 7). Baby truants at record high in St. Paul. *Minneapolis Star-Tribune,* pp. 1, 8.

Foster, J. (2007). Assistive technology. In A. M. Bursztyn (Ed.), *The Praeger handbook of special education* (pp. 78–80). Westport, CT: Greenwood Publishing Group.

Frank, L. S. (2001). *The caring classroom: Using adventure to create community in the classroom and beyond.* Portland, OR: Project Adventure.

Frankenburg, W. K., & Dodd, J. B. (1990). *Denver II screening manual.* Denver, CO: Denver Developmental Materials.

Frankenberg, W., Doods, J., Archer, P., Bresnick, B., Mashka, P., Edelman, N., & Shapiro, H. (1992). *DENVER II.* Denver, CO: Denver Developmental Materials.

Freud, S. (1973). *An outline of psychoanalysis.* London: Hogarth. (Original work published 1923)

Frost, J. L. (2010). *A history of children's play and play environments: Toward a contemporary child-saving movement.* New York: Routledge.

Frost, J. L., Bowers, L., & Wortham, S. (1990). The state of American preschool playgrounds. *Journal of Physical Education, Recreation, and Dance, 61*(8), 18–23.

Frost, J. L., & Wortham, S. (1988). The evolution of American playgrounds. *Young Children, 43*(5), 19–28.

Fuller-Thompson, E., & Minkler, M. (2005). Native American grandparents raising grandchildren: Findings from the Census 2000 Supplementary Survey and implications for social work practice. *Social Work, 50,* 131–139.

Fuller-Thompson, E., & Minkler, M. (2007). Mexican American grandparents raising grandchildren: Findings from the Census 2000 Supplementary Survey and implications for social work practice. *Families in Society, 88,* 567–574.

Furman, W., & Bierman, K. L. (1983). Developmental changes in young children's conception of friendship. *Child Development, 54,* 549–556.

Fuson, K. C. (1988). *Children's counting and concepts of number.* New York: Springer-Verlag.

Galinsky, E. (1987). *The six stages of parenthood.* Reading, MA: Addison-Wesley.

Galinsky, E., Aumann, K., & Bond, J. T. (2009). *Times are changing: Gender and generation at work and at home.* New York: Families and Work Institute.

Gallagher, A., & Lipsky, D. K. (2001). Neutrality as a moral standpoint, conceptual confusion and the full inclusion debate. *Disability and Society, 16*(5), 637–654.

Gallagher, J. J. (2002). *Society's role in educating gifted students: The role of public policy.* Storrs, CT: National Research Center on the Gifted and Talented.

Gallahue, D. (1982). *Understanding motor development in children.* New York: Wiley.

Gallahue, D., & Ozmun, J. (1998). *Understanding motor development: Infants, children, adolescents, adults.* Boston: McGraw-Hill.

Gandara, P. (2010). The Latino education crisis. *Educational Leadership, 67*(5), 24–30.

Gandara, P., Rumberger, R., Maxwell-Jolly, J., & Callahan, R. (2003). English learners in California schools: Unequal resources, unequal outcomes. *Education Policy Analysis Archives, 11*(36), 1–54.

Gander, M. J., & Gardiner, H. W. (1981). *Child and adolescent development.* Boston: Little, Brown.

Garces, E., Thomas, D., & Currie, J. (2000). *Longer term effects of Head Start.* National Bureau of Economic Research. Retrieved from http://www.nber.org/papers/w8054

Garcia, E. E., & Frede, E. C. (Eds.). (2010). *Young English language learners: Current research and emerging directions for practice and policy.* New York: Teachers College Press.

Gardiner, H. W., & Kosmitzki, C. (2005). *Lives across cultures: Cross-cultural human development.* Boston: Allyn & Bacon.

Gardner, H. (2001). *"Jerome S. Bruner" in. fifty modern thinkers on education: From Piaget to the present.* J. A. Palmer, ed. London: Routledge.

Gardner, H. (2006). *Multiple intelligences: New horizons in theory and practice.* New York: Basic Books.

Gardner, H. (2008). Who owns intelligence? In *The Jossey-Bass reader on the brain and learning* (pp. 120–132). San Francisco: Jossey-Bass.

Gargiulo, R. M., & Kilgo, J. L. (2004). *Young children with special needs.* Belmont: Wadsworth, Cengage Learning.

Garner, P. W., & Estep, K. M. (2001). Emotional competence, emotion socialization, and young children's peer-related social competence. *Early Education & Development, 12,* 29–48.

Garney, C. (1990). *Play.* Cambridge, MA: Harvard University Press.

Gartrell, D. (2001). Replacing time-out: Part one—using guidance to build an encouraging classroom. *Young Children, 56*(6), 8–16.

Gartrell, D. (2005). Guidance matters. *Young Children, 60*(6), 84–85.

Gay, G. (1979). On behalf of children: A curriculum design for multicultural education in the elementary school. *Journal of Negro Education, 48*(3), 324–340.

Geller, L. G. (1985). *Word play and language learning for children.* Urbana, IL: NCTE.

Gelman, R., & Gallistel, C. R. (1978). *The child's understanding of number.* Cambridge, MA: Harvard University Press.

Genesee, F. (2010). Dual language development in preschool children. In E. E. Garcia & E. C. Frede (Eds.), *Young English language learners: Current research and emerging directions for practice and policy* (pp. 59–79). New York: Teachers College Press.

Gentry, M., Hu, S., & Thomas, A. (2008). Ethnically diverse students. In J. A. Plucker & C. M. Callahan (Eds.), *Critical issues and practices in gifted education* (pp. 195–212). Waco, TX: Prufrock Press.

George, T. P., & Hartmann, D. P. (1996). Friendship networks of unpopular, average, and popular children. *Child Development, 67,* 2301–2316.

Gessell, A., & Ilg, F. (1937). *Feeding behavior of infants.* Philadelphia: Lippincott.

Gestwicki, C. (1992). *Home school and community relations* (2nd ed.). Albany, NY: Delmar.

Gestwicki, C. (2000). *Home, school and community relations: A guide to working with parents* (4th ed.). Clifton Park, NY: Delmar Learning.

Ghazvini, A., & Mullis, R. L. (2002). Center-based care for young children: Examining predictors of quality. *The Journal of Genetic Psychology, 163*(1), 112–125.

Gilkerson, L., & Klein, R. (Eds.). (2008). *Early development and the brain: Teaching resources for educators.* Washington, DC: Zero to Three.

Gillmore, J. B. (1971). Play: A special behavior. In R. E. Herron & B. Sutton-Smith (Eds.), *Child's play* (pp. 343–355). New York: Wiley.

Ginsberg, G. S., & Bronstein, P. (1993). Family factors related to children's intrinsic/extrinsic motivational orientation and academic performance. *Child Development, 64,* 1461–1474.

Glantz, M. D., & Johnson, J. L. (1999). *Resilience and development: Positive life adaptions.* New York: Kluwer Academic/Plenum.

Goencue, A., Mistry, J., & Mosier, C. (2000). Cultural variations in the play of toddlers. *International Journal of Behavioral Development, 24,* 321–329.

Goldenberg, C. (2008). Teaching English language learners: What the research does and does not say. *American Educator, 32*(2), 8–44.

Goldstein, J. H. (1994). *Toys, play, and child development.* New York: Cambridge University Press.

Gollnick, D. M., & Chinn, P. C. (2006). *Multicultural education in a pluralistic society.* Upper Saddle River, NJ: Pearson Prentice Hall.

Gomby, D. S., Larner, M. B., Stevenson, C. S., Lewit, E. M., & Behrman, R. E. (1995). Long-term outcomes of early childhood programs: Analysis and recommendations. *The Future of Children, 5*(3), 6–24.

Gomez, S., Garcia-Nevarez, A., Knutson Miller, K., & Strage, A. (2006, April). *Service learning impacts on career goals and commitment to service: Results from a multi-campus collaboration.* Paper presented at the Annual Conference of the American Educational Research Association, San Diego, CA.

Gonzalez-Mena, J., & Shareef, I. (2005). Discussing diverse perspectives on guidance. *Young Children, 60*(6), 34–38.

Good, T. L., & Brophy, J. E. (1990). *Educational psychology: A realistic approach* (4th ed.). Reading, MA: Addison Wesley.

Goodman, J. F. (1994). "Work" versus "play" and early childhood care. *Child and Youth Care Forum, 23*(3), 177–196.

Goodman, K. S., Smith, E. B., Meredith, R., & Goodman, Y. M. (1987). *Language and thinking in school: A whole language curriculum.* New York: Richard C. Owen.

Goodman, M. E. (1964). *Race awareness in young children.* Cambridge, MA: Addison-Wesley.

Goodnow, J. J. (2010). Culture. In M. H. Bornstein (Ed.), *Handbook of cultural developmental science* (pp. 3–20). New York: Psychology Press.

Goodwin, W. R., & Driscoll, L. A. (1980). *Handbook for measurement and evaluation in early childhood education.* San Francisco: Jossey-Bass.

Goodwin, W. R., & Driscoll, L. A. (1982). *Handbook for measurement and evaluation in early childhood education.* San Francisco: Jossey-Bass.

Gopnik, A. (2001). Theories, language, and culture: Whorf without wincing. In M. Bowerman & S. C. Levinson (Eds.), *Language acquisition and conceptual development* (pp. 45–69). Cambridge, UK: Cambridge University Press.

Gordon, I. J. (1971). *A home learning center approach to early stimulation. Research Report.* University of Florida, Gainesville. Institute for Development of Human Resources. National Institute of Mental Health (DHEW), 1–66.

Gordon, K. A. (1993). *Resilient African-American high school students' self-concept and motivational patterns: Sources of strength.* Unpublished doctoral dissertation, Stanford University, Palo Alto, CA.

Gordon, K. A. (1995). Self-concept and motivational patterns of resilient African American high school students. *Journal of Black Psychology, 21*(3), 239–255.

Gordon, T. (1974). *T.E.T.: Teacher effectiveness training.* New York: Peter H. Wyden.

Gordon, T. (1976). *P.E.T. in action.* New York: Peter H. Wyden.

Gordon Rouse, K. (1998). Resilience in infants and toddlers. *Early Childhood Education Journal, 26*(1), 47–52.

Gordon Rouse, K. (2001). Resilient students' goals and motivation. *Journal of Adolescence, 24*(4), 461–472.

Gormley, W. (2008). The effects of Oklahoma's pre-K program on Hispanic children. *Social Science Quarterly, 89,* 916–936.

Graham, P. A. (1967). *Progressive education: From Arcady to Academe.* New York: Teachers College Press.

Grave, E. M. (1993). *Ready for what/constructing meanings of readiness for kindergarten.* Albany: State University of New York Press.

Greenfield, P. M., Keller, H., Fuligni, A., & Maynard, A. (2003). Cultural pathways through universal development. *Annual Review of Psychology, 54,* 461–490.

Greenspan, S. I. (2004). Meeting learning challenges: Working with children who learn at a different pace. *Early Childhood Today, 19*(3), 23–24.

Greenwald, H. J., & Oppenheim, D. B. (1968). Reported magnitude of self-misidentification among Negro children: Artifact? *Journal of Personality and Social Psychology, 8,* 49–52.

Greenwood, C. R., Luze, G. J., Cline, G., Kuntz, S., & Leitschuh, C. (2002). Developing a general outcome measure of growth in movement for infants and toddlers. *Topics in Early Childhood Special Education, 22*(3), 143–157.

Grey, S. (1971). Home visiting programs for parents of young children. *Demonstration and Research Center for Early Education Papers and Reports, 5*(4). Nashville, TN: George Peabody College for Teachers.

Groos, K. (1901). *The play of man.* New York: Appleton.

Grosjean, F. (1982). *Life with two languages.* Cambridge, MA: Harvard University Press.

Gross, M. (1999). Small poppies: Highly gifted children in the early years. *Roeper Review, 21*(3), 207–214.

Guillory, A., Self, P., & Paden, L. (1980, April). *Odor sensitivity in one month infants.* Paper presented at the International Conference on Infant Studies, New Haven, CT.

Hakuta, K. (2011). Educating language minority students and affirming their equal rights: Research and practical perspectives. *Educational Researcher, 40*(4), 163–174. doi:10.3102/0013189X11404943

Hale, J. E. (1991). The transmission of cultural values to young African American children. *Young Children, 46*(6), 7–15.

Hale-Benson, J. (1990). Visions for children: African-American early childhood education program. *Early Childhood Research Quarterly, 5*(2), 199–213.

Hall, E. (2009). Mixed messages: The role and value of drawing in early education. *International Journal of Early Years Education, 17*(3), 179–190.

Hall, G. S. (1906). *Youth: Its education, regimen, and hygiene.* New York: Appleton.

Hall, M. (2008, March). Boost literacy with a dad and kid reading night. *Our Children,* p. 6.

Halpern, R. (1987). Major social and demographic trends affecting young families: Implications for early childhood care and education. *Young Children, 42*(6), 34–40.

Hamilton, C. E. (2000). Continuity and discontinuity of attachment from infancy through adolescence. *Child Development, 71*(3), 690–694.

Hammer, P. (1998). Young children's speech development. *Dimensions of Early Childhood, 26*(2), 3–7.

Hand, H., & Nourot, P. M. (1999). *First class: Guide to early primary education.* Sacramento: California Department of Education.

Hanna, J. (2011). *The Elementary and Secondary Education Act.* Cambridge MA: Harvard School of Education. Retrieved from http://www.gse.harvard.edu/news_events/features/2005/08/esea0819.html

Harackiewicz, J. M., Sansone, C., & Manderlink, G. (1985). Competence, achievement orientation, and intrinsic motivation: A process analysis. *Journal of Personality and Social Psychology, 48,* 493–508.

Harms, T., Clifford, R. M., & Cryer, D. (2005). *Early childhood environment rating scale (ECERS-R).* New York: Teachers College Press.

Harper, C. C., & Mclanahan, S. S. (1998, August). *Father absence and youth incarceration.* Paper presented at the 1998 annual meetings of the American Sociological Association, San Francisco.

Harrington, R. G. (1985). Batelle Developmental Inventory. In D. J. Keyser & R. C. Sweetlands (Eds.), *Test critiques*

(Vol. II, pp. 244–259). Kansas City, MO: Test Corporation of America.

Harris, J. R. (1998). *The nurture assumption: Why children turn out the way they do.* New York: Free Press.

Harris, J. R. (2002). Beyond the nurture assumption: Testing hypotheses about the child's environment. In J. G. Borkowski, S. Landesman Ramey, & M. Bristol-Power (Eds.), *Parenting and the child's world: Influences on academic, intellectual, and social-emotional development* (pp. 3–20). Mahwah, NJ: Erlbaum.

Hart, C. H., Newell, L. D., & Olsen, S. F. (2003). Parenting skills and social-communicative competence in childhood. In J. D. Greene & B. R. Burleson (Eds.), *Handbook of communication and social interaction skills* (pp. 753–800). Mahwah, NJ: Erlbaum.

Hart, J. E., & Whalon, K. (2011). Creating social opportunities for students with autism spectrum disorder in inclusive settings. *Intervention in School and Clinic, 46*(5), 273–279.

Harter, S. (1986). Cognitive developmental processes in the integration of concepts about emotions and self. *Social Cognition, 4,* 119–151.

Harter, S., & Pike, R. (1984). The Pictorial Scale of Perceived Competence and Social Acceptance for Young Children. *Child Development, 55,* 1969–1982.

Hartmann, D. P., & Pelzel, K. E. (2005). Design, measurement, and analysis in developmental research. In M. H. Bornstein & M. E. Lamb (Eds.), *Developmental science: An advanced textbook* (5th ed., pp. 103–184). Mahwah, NJ: Erlbaum.

Hartup, W. (1983). Peer relations. In P. Mussen (Ed.), *Handbook of child psychology: Socialization, personality, and development* (4th ed., Vol. 4, pp. 103–196). New York: Wiley.

Hartup, W. W. (1992). Peer relations in early and middle childhood. In V. B. van Hasselt & M. Hersen (Eds.), *Handbook of social development: A lifespan perspective* (pp. 257–281). New York: Plenum.

Hartup, W. W. (1996a). The company they keep: Friendships and their developmental significance. *Child Development, 67,* 1–13.

Hartup, W. W. (1996b). Cooperation, close relationships, and cognitive development. In W. M. Bukowski, A. F. Newcomb, & W. W. Hartup (Eds.), *The company they keep: Friendship in childhood and adolescence* (pp. 213–237). New York: Cambridge University Press.

Haugland, S. W. (2012). *Selecting developmentally appropriate software.* Presentation at the International Society for Technology in Education, June.

Haviland, J. M., & Lelwica, M. (1987). The induced affect response: 10-week-old infants' response to three emotion expressions. *Developmental Psychology, 23,* 97–104.

Hayes, B. K., & Younger, K. (2004). Category-use effects in children. *Child Development, 75,* 1719–1732.

Haywood, K. (1993). *Lifespan motor development.* Champaign, IL: Human Kinetics.

Hazen, N. (1982). *Social acceptance: How children achieve it and how teachers can help.* Elementary and Early Childhood Education Clearinghouse.

Head Start Bureau. (2003). *The Head Start path to positive child outcomes: Head Start child outcomes framework.* Washington, DC: U.S. Department of Health and Human Services, Administration for Children and Families.

Heath, S. (1983). *Ways with words: Language, life and work in communities and classrooms.* Cambridge, UK: Cambridge University Press.

Hedley, A. A., Ogden, C. L., Johnson, C. L., Carroll, M. D., Curtin, L. R., & Flegal, K. M. (2004). Prevalence of overweight and obesity among U.S. children, adolescents, and adults, 1999–2002. *Journal of the American Medical Association, 291,* 2847–2850.

Heller, K., Mezei, P. J., & Avant, M. (2009). Meeting the assistive technology needs of students with Duchenne muscular dystrophy. *Journal of Special Education Technology, 23*(4), 15–30.

Hendrickson, B. (1979). Teacher burnout: How to recognize it; what to do about it. *Learning, 7*(5), 37–39.

Henninger, M. L. (2005). *Teaching young children: An introduction.* Upper Saddle River, NJ: Pearson Prentice Hall.

Henninger, M. L. (2008). *Teaching young children: An introduction.* Upper Saddle River, NJ: Pearson Education.

Henning, M., Peterson, B. R., & King, K. (2011). Infusing science, technology, and society into an elementary teacher education program: The impact on preservice teachers. *Teacher Education and Practice, 24*(1), 46–65.

Henrich, C., & Blackman-Jones, R. (2006). Parent involvement in preschool. In E. Zigler, W. Gilliam, & S. M. Jones, *A vision for universal preschool education* (pp. 149–168). New York: Cambridge University Press.

Henry, G. T., Gordon, C. S., & Rickman, D. K. (2006). Early education policy alternatives: Comparing quality and outcomes of Head Start and state prekindergarten. *Educational Evaluation and Policy Analysis, 28*(1), 77–99.

Hernandez, H. (1989). *Multicultural education: A teacher's guide to content and process.* Columbus, OH: Merrill.

Hernandez-Sheets, R. (1998). *Ethnic identity behavioral displays and competence in an urban kindergarten: Implications for practice.* Unpublished manuscript.

Hernandez-Sheets, R. (2005). *Diversity pedagogy: Examining the role of culture in the teaching-learning process.* Boston: Pearson Education.

Hetherington, E. M. (2003). Social support and the adjustment of children in divorced and remarried families. *Childhood, 10,* 237–254.

Hewett, V. M. (2001). Examining the Reggio Emilia approach to early childhood education. *Early Childhood Education Journal, 29*(2), 95–100.

HighScope. (2003). *Preschool Child Observation Record (COR)* (2nd ed.). Clifton Park, NY: Thomson Delmar Learning.

Halford, G. S., & Andrews, G. (2006). Reasoning and problem solving. In D. Kuhn & R. Siegler (Eds.), *Handbook of child psychology: Cognition, perception, and language* (6th ed., Vol. 2, pp. 557–608). Hoboken, NJ: Wiley.

Hill, C. B. (1989). *Creating a learning climate for the early childhood years* [Fastback No. 292]. Bloomington, IN: Phi Delta Kappa Educational Foundation.

Hill, N. E., Bush, K. R., & Roosa, M. W. (2003). Parenting and family socialization strategies and children's mental health: Low-income Mexican American and Euro American mothers and children. *Child Development, 74,* 189–204.

Hillman, M., & Marshall, J. (2009). Evaluation of digital media for emergent literacy. *Computers in the Schools, 26*(4), 256–270.

Hohmann, C. (1996). *Foundations in elementary education: Overview.* Ypsilanti, MI: HighScope Press.

Hohmann, M., & Weikart, D. (1995). *Educating young children: Active learning practices for preschool and child care programs.* Ypsilanti, MI: HighScope Press.

Holochwost, S. J., DeMott, K., Buell, M., Yannetta, K., & Amsden, D. (2009). Retention of staff in the early childhood education workforce. *Child Youth Care Forum, 38,* 227–237. doi:10.10007/s10566-009-9078-6

Honig, A. (1982). *Playtime learning games for young children.* Syracuse, NY: Syracuse University Press.

Honig, A. S. (2002, November 20–23). *Everything you want to know about attachment.* Paper presented at the NAEYC conference, New York.

Honig, A. S. (2005). Comforting a quiet baby. *Scholastic Early Childhood Today, 20*(2), 18–19.

Horm-Wingerd, D., & Hyson, M. (2000). *New teachers for a new century: The future of early childhood professional preparation.* Washington, DC: National Institute on Early Childhood Development and Education.

Horsch, P., Chen, J. Q., & Wagner, S. L. (2002). The responsive classroom approach: A caring, respectful school environment as a context for development. *Education and Urban Society, 34*(3), 365–383.

Horwitz, A. R., Uro, G., Price-Baugh, R., Simon, C., Uzzell, R., Lewis, S., & Casserly, M. (2009). *Succeeding with English language learners: Lesson learned from the Great City Schools.* Washington, DC: The Council of the Great City Schools. Retrieved from http://cgcs.org/cms/lib/dc00001581/centricity/domain/4/ell_report09.pdf

Howes, C. (1987). Peer interaction of young children. *Monographs of the Society for Research in Child Development, 53*(1), Serial No. 217.

Howes, C., & Hamilton, C. E. (1992). Children's relationships with child care teachers: Stability and concordance with parental attachments. *Child Development, 63,* 867–878.

Hubbard, R. S. (1998). Creating a classroom where children can think. *Young Children, 53,* 26–31.

Hudson, R. F., Lane, H. B., & Pullen, P. C. (2005). Reading fluency assessment and instruction: What, why and how? *Reading Teacher, 58*(8), 702–714.

Huerta-Macias, A. (1981). Codeswitching: All in the family. In R. Duran (Ed.), *Latino language and communicative behavior* (pp. 153–168). Norwood, NJ: Ablex.

Hundt, T. A. (2002). Videotaping young children in the classroom. *Parents as Partners: Teaching Exceptional Children, 34*(3), 38–43.

Iervolino, A. C., Hines, M., Golombok, S. E., Rust, J., & Plomin, R. (2005). Genetic and environmental influences on sex-typed behavior during the preschool years. *Child Development, 76,* 826–840.

Ihmeidah, F. (2010). The role of computer technology in teaching reading and writing: Preschool teachers' beliefs and practices. *Journal of Research in Childhood Education, 24*(1), 60–79.

Illingworth, R. (1991). *Normal child: Some problems of the early years and their treatment.* London: Churchill-Livingstone.

Improving America's Schools Act of 1994, Pub. L. No. 103-382 Stat. 3518 (1994).

Individuals with Disabilities Education Act, 20 U.S.C. § 1400, as amended by Pub. L. No. 102-119 (1991).

Individuals with Disabilities Education Act, Pub. L. No. 101-476 (1990). Washington, DC: U.S. Government Printing Office.

Individuals with Disabilities Education Act of 1990, Pub. L. No. 108-446 Stat. 1248 (1990).

Individuals with Disabilities Education Act Amendments, 20 U.S.C. § 1400 (1997).

Individuals with Disabilities Education Improvement Act, Pub. L. No. 108-446 (2004). Washington, DC: U.S. Government Printing Office.

Inhelder, B., & Piaget, J. (1958). *The growth of logical thinking from childhood to adolescence: An essay on the construction of formal operational structures.* New York: Basic Books.

Institute of Medicine. (2004). *Preventing childhood obesity: Health in the balance.* Washington, DC: Author.

International Reading Association. (1998). Learning to read and write: Developmentally appropriate practices for young children. A joint statement of the International Reading Association (IRA) and the National Association for the Education of Young Children (NAEYC). *Young Children, 53*(4), 30–46.

International Reading Association. (2010). *Standards for reading professionals–revised 2010.* Newark, DE: Author. Retrieved from http://www.reading.org/General/CurrentResearch/Standards/Professional Standards2010.aspx

Irwin, D. M., & Bushnell, M. M. (1980). *Observational strategies for child study.* New York: Holt, Rinehart, Winston.

Izard, C. E. (1993). Four systems for emotion activation: Cognitive and noncognitive processes. *Psychological Review, 100,* 68–90.

Izard, C. E., Fantauzzo, C. A., Castle, J. M., Haynes, O. M., Rayias, M. F., & Putnam, P. H. (1995). The ontogeny and significance of infants' facial expressions in the first 9 months of life. *Developmental Psychology, 31,* 997–1013.

Jackson, N. E., & Klein, E. J. (1997). Gifted performance in young children. In N. Colangelo & G. A. Davis (Eds.), *Handbook of gifted education* (pp. 460–474). Needham Heights, MA: Allyn & Bacon.

Jacob K. Javits Gifted and Talented Students Education Act. (1988). Washington, DC: U.S. Government Printing Office.

Jacobs, R. A. (1995). *English syntax: A grammar for English language professionals.* Oxford, UK: Oxford University Press.

Jamison, K. R., Forston, L. D., & Stanton-Chapman, T. L. (2012). Encouraging social skills development through play in early childhood special education classrooms. *Young Exceptional Children, 15*(3), 2–19. doi:10.1177/1096250611435422

Janowsky, J. R., & Carper, R. (1996). Is there a neural basis for cognitive shifts in school age children? In A. J. Sameroff & M. M. Haith (Eds.), *The five to seven year shift: The age of reason and responsibility* (pp. 33–56). Chicago: University of Chicago Press.

Jeske, D. (2010). So you think you are a great teacher, but are you an intentional teacher? Presentation at the Association of Christian Schools International Northern California conference in October.

Jeske, D. L. (2011). *So you are a great teacher, but are you an intentional teacher.* Workshop presented at the Northern California region Association of Christian Schools International Conference, Sacramento.

Johnson, D. W., & Johnson, R. T. (1989). *Cooperation and competition: Theory and research.* Edina, MN: Interaction.

Johnson, H. M. (1928). *Children in the nursery school.* New York: Day.

Johnson, J., Christie, J., & Yawkey, T. (1999). *Play and early childhood development* (2nd ed.). New York: Longman.

Jolivette, K., Gallagher, P. A., Morrier, M. J., & Lambert, R. (2008). Preventing problem behaviors in young children with disabilities. *Exceptionality, 16,* 78–92.

Jordan, P. E., & Hernandez-Reif, M. (2009). Re-examination of young children's racial attitudes and skin tone preferences. *Journal of Black Psychology, 35*(3), 388–403.

Jusczyk, P. W., & Hohne, D. (1997). Infants' memory for the spoken word. *Science, 277,* 1984–1986.

Kagan, J., Kearsley, R. B., & Zelaxo, P. R. (1978). *Infancy: Its place in human development.* Cambridge, MA: Harvard University Press.

Kagan, S. L., & Reid, J. L. (2008). *Advancing ECE policy: Early childhood education (ECE) and its quest for excellence, coherence, and equity.* Washington, DC: Center on Education Policy.

Kagan, S. L., Rosenkoetter, S., & Cohen, N. E. (1997). *Considering child-based results for young children: Definitions, desirability, feasibility, and next steps.* New Haven, CT: Yale Bush Center in Child Development and Social Policy.

Kalbfleisch, M. L., & Iguchi, C. M. (2008). Twice exceptional learners. In J. A. Plucker & C. M. Callahan (Eds.), *Critical issues and practices in gifted education* (pp. 707–719). Waco, TX: Prufrock Press.

Kamens, M. W. (2004). Learning to write IEPs: A personalized, reflective approach for preservice teachers. *Intervention in School and Clinic, 40*(2), 76–80.

Kamerman, S. B., & Kahn, A. J. (2001). Child and family policies in the United States at the opening of the twenty-first century. *Social Policy & Administration, 35*(1), 69–84.

Kamii, C., & DeVries, R. (1978). *Physical knowledge in preschool education.* Englewood Cliffs, NJ: Prentice Hall.

Karmiloff-Smith, A. (1991). Beyond modularity: Innate constraints and developmental change. In S. Carey & R. Gelman (Eds.), *The epigenesis of mind: Essays on biology and cognition* (pp. 171–197). Hillsdale, NJ: Erlbaum.

Karnes, M. B., Hodgins, A. S., Teska, J. A., & Kirk, S. A. (1969). *Investigations of classroom and at-home interventions: Final report.* Washington, DC: Bureau of Research, Office of Education, U.S. Department of Health, Education, and Welfare.

Karpf, M. K., & Shatz, I. M. (2005, Spring). The divorce is over—what about the kids? *American Journal of Family Law, 19*(1), 7–11.

Katz, L. G. (1999). *Talks with teachers of young children.* Norwood, NJ: Ablex Books.

Kaufman, A. S., & Kaufman, N. L. (2008). *Kaufman Assessment Battery for Children* (2nd ed.). Circle Pines, MN: American Guidance Service.

Kawabata, Y., & Crick, N. R. (2011). The significance of cross-racial/ethnic friendship: Association with peer victimization, peer support, sociometric status, and classroom diversity. *Developmental Psychology, 47*(6), 1763–1775.

Kearsley, G. (2006). *Operant conditioning.* Retrieved from http://tip.psychology.org/skinner.html

Kelemen, D., Callanan, M. A., Casler, K., & Perez-Granados, D. R. (2005). Why things happen: Teleological explanation in parent-child conversation. *Developmental Psychology, 41,* 251–264.

Kelley, M. L., Smith, T. S., Green, A. P., Berndt, A. E., & Rodgers, M. C. (1998). Importance of father's parenting to African-American toddlers' social and cognitive development. *Infant Behavior and Development, 21*(4), 733–744.

Kellogg, R. (1969). *Analyzing children's art.* Palo Alto, CA: National Press Books.

Kenney, M. J., & Bezuszka, S. J. (2007). Just five does it: Using five numbers to make patterned squares. *Mathematics Teaching in the Middle School, 12*(8), 436–441.

Keogh, J., & Sugden, D. (1985). *Movement skill development.* New York: Macmillan.

Kilgore, K., Snyder, J., & Lentz, C. (2000). The contribution of parental discipline, parental monitoring, and school risk to early-onset conduct problems in African American boys and girls. *Developmental Psychology, 36,* 835–845.

Klahr, D., & MacWhinney, B. (1998). Information processing. In D. Kuhn & R. S. Siegler (Eds.), *Handbook of child psychology: Cognition, perception, and language* (5th ed., Vol. 2, pp. 631–678). New York: Wiley.

Klar, A. J. S. (1996). A single locus, RGHT, specifies preference for hand utilization in humans. In *Cold Spring Harbor Symposia on Quantitative Biology* (Vol. 61, pp. 59–65). Cold Spring Harbor, NY: Cold Spring Harbor Laboratory Press.

Klaus, M., & Kennell, J. (1982). *Parent-infant bonding* (2nd ed.). St. Louis, MO: Mosby.

Klein, A., & Starkey, P. J. (2004). Fostering preschool children's mathematical knowledge: Findings from the Berkeley Math Readiness Project. In D. H. Clements, J. Samara, & D. Chazen (Eds.), *Engaging young children in mathematics: Standards for early childhood mathematics* (pp. 343–360). Mahwah, NJ: Erlbaum.

Klein, M. D., Cook, R. E., & Richardson-Gibbs, A. M. (2001). *Strategies for including children with special needs in early childhood settings*. Albany, NY: Delmar.

Kliebard, H. M. (1995). *The struggle for the American curriculum*. New York: Routledge.

Klieger, A., & Yakobovitch, A. (2011). Perception of science standards' effectiveness and their implementation by science teachers. *Journal of Science Education and Technology, 20*(3), 286–299.

Kochanek, K. D., & Smith, B. L. (2004). Deaths: Preliminary data for 2002. *National Vital Statistics Reports, 52*(13). Hyattsville, MD: National Center for Health Statistics.

Kochanska, G. (1995). Children's temperament, mother's discipline, and security of attachment: Multiple pathways to emerging internalization. *Child Development, 66*(3), 597–615.

Kolb, B. (1999). Neuroanatomy and development overview. In N. Fox, L. Leavitt, & J. Warhol (Eds.), *The role of early experience in development* (pp. 5–14). Skillman, NJ: Johnson & Johnson.

Kolb, B., & Whishaw, I. (1990). *Fundamentals of human neuropsychology*. New York: Freeman.

Koren-Karie, N., Oppenheim, D., Doley, S., Sher, E., & Etzion-Carasso, A. (2002). Mothers' insightfulness regarding their infants' internal experience: Relations with maternal sensitivity and infant attachment. *Developmental Psychology, 38*, 534–542.

Kramer, R. (1976). *Maria Montessori*. New York: G.P. Putman's Sons.

Krashen, S. D., Long, M., & Scarcella, R. (1979). Age, rate, and eventual attainment in second language acquisition. *TESOL Quarterly, 13*, 573–582.

Kritchevsky, L., Prescott, E., & Walling, L. (1977). *Planning environments for young children: Physical space*. Washington, DC: National Association for the Education of Young Children.

Kroth, R. L., & Edge, D. (2007). *Communicating with parents and families of exceptional children*. Denver, CO: Love Publishing.

Kuczmarski, R. J., Ogden, C. L., Grummer-Strawn, L. M., Flegal, K. M., Guo, S. S., Wei, R., . . . Johnson, C. L. (2000). CDC growth charts: United States. *Advance Data*, No. 314. Washington, DC: Centers for Disease Control and Prevention, U.S. Department of Health and Human Services.

Kuhn, D., Nash, S. C., & Brucken, L. (1978). Sex-role concepts of two- and three-year-olds. *Child Development, 49*, 445–451.

Kuklinski, M. R., & Weinstein, R. S. (2000). The stability of teacher expectations and perceived differential teacher statement. *Learning Environments Research, 3*(1), 1–34.

Kuklinski, M. R., & Weinstein, R. S. (2001). Classroom and developmental differences in a path model of teacher expectancy effects. *Child Development, 72*, 1554–1578.

Kupetz, B., & Green, E. (1997). Sharing books with infants and toddlers: Facing the challenges. *Young Children, 52*(2), 22–27.

Labov, W. (1970). The logic of nonstandard English. In F. Williams (Ed.), *Language and poverty: Perspectives on a theme* (pp. 153–190). Chicago: Markham.

Ladd, G. W., & Golter, B. S. (1988). Parents' management of preschoolers' peer relations: Is it related to children's social competence? *Developmental Psychology, 24*, 109–117.

Laird, R. D., Pettit, G. S., Bates, J. E., & Dodge, K. A. (2003). Parents' monitoring relevant knowledge and adolescents' delinquent behavior: Evidence of correlated developmental changes and reciprocal influences. *Developmental Psychology, 74*, 752–768.

Lalonde, C. E., & Werker, J. F. (1995). Cognitive influences on cross-language speech perception. *Infant Behavior and Development, 18*, 459–475.

Lamb, M., & Bornstein, M. (1987). *Development in infancy: An introduction* (2nd ed.). New York: Random House.

Lambie, D. Z., Bond, J. T., & Weikart, D. P. (1974). *Home teaching with mothers and infants*. Ypsilanti, MI: HighScope Educational Research Foundation.

Lamy, C., Barnett, W. S., & Jung, K. (2005). *The effects of Oklahoma's early childhood four-year-old program on young children's school readiness*. New Brunswick: Rutgers, The State University of New Jersey, National Institute of Early Education Research.

Landy, J. M., & Burridge, K. R. (2000). *Motor skills and movement station lesson plans for young children: Teaching, remediation, and assessment*. Charlottesville, VA: Center for Applied Research in Education.

Lane, M. (1981). *The squirrel*. New York: Dial.

Lanza, E. (1992). Can bilingual two-year-olds code-switch? *Journal of Child Language, 19*, 633–658.

Larry P. v. Riles, No. C-70-2270, RFP (1986).

Lawhon, T., & Lawhon, D. C. (2000). Promoting social skills in young children. *Early Childhood Education Journal, 28*, 105–110.

Lawrence, E. M. (1969). *Froebel and English education: Perspectives on the founder of Kindergarten*. New York: Shoken Books.

Lay-Dopyera, M., & Dopyera, J. E. (1982). *Becoming a teacher of young children* (2nd ed.). Lexington, KY: D. C. Heath.

Lay-Dopyera, M., & Dopyera, J. E. (1993). *Becoming a teacher of young children* (5th ed.). Lexington, KY: D. C. Heath.

Learning Point Associates. (2004). *A closer look at the five essential components of effective reading instruction: A review of scientifically based reading for teachers*. Naperville, IL: Author.

Lecaunet, J. (1998). Foetal responses to auditory and speech stimuli. In A. Slater (Ed.), *Perceptual development: Visual, auditory, and speech development in infancy* (pp. 317–355). East Sussex, England: Psychology Press.

Legerstee, M. (1997). Contingency effects of people and objects on subsequent cognitive functioning in three-month-old infants. *Social Development, 6*(3), 307–321.

Lenneberg, E. (1967). *Biological foundations of language*. New York: Wilcy.

Lerner, R. M. (1989). Individual development and the family system: A lifespan perspective. In K. Krepper & R. M. Lerner

(Eds.), *Family systems and life-span development*. Hillsdale, NJ: Erlbaum.

Lessow-Hurley, J. (2000). *The foundations of dual language instruction* (3rd ed.). New York: Longman.

Lester, B., & Boukydis, C. (1992). No language, but a cry. In H. Papousek, U. Jurgens, & M. Papousek (Eds.), *Nonverbal vocal communication* (pp. 45–173). New York: Cambridge University Press.

Levenstein, P. (1970). Cognitive growth in preschoolers through verbal interactions with mothers. *American Journal of Orthopsychiatry, 40*, 426–432.

Levin, D. E. (1994). Building a peaceable classroom: Helping young children feel safe in violent times. *Childhood Education, 70*(5), 267–270.

LeVine, R. (1984). Properties of culture: An ethnographic view. In R. Schweder & R. LeVine (Eds.), *Culture theory: Essays on mind, self, and emotion*. Cambridge, UK: Cambridge University Press.

Lewin, K. (1943). Defining the field at a given time. *Psychological Review, 50*, 292–310.

Lewis, C., & Biber, B. (1951). Reactions of Negro children toward Negro and White teachers. *Experiential Educator, 20*, 97–104.

Lewis, M. (1998). Emotional competence and development. In D. Pushkar, W. M. Bukowski, A. E. Schwartzman, D. M. Stack, & D. R. White (Eds.), *Improving competence across the lifespan* (pp. 27–36). New York: Plenum.

Lewis, M., Alessandri, S. M., & Sullivan, M. W. (1990). Violation of expectancy, loss of control and anger expressions in young infants. *Developmental Psychology, 26*, 745–751.

Lewis, M., Alessandri, S. M., & Sullivan, M. W. (1992). Differences in shame and pride as a function of children's gender and task difficulty. *Child Development, 63*, 630–638.

Lewis, M., Feiring, C., & Rosenthal, S. (2000). Attachment over time. *Child Development, 71*(3), 707–720.

Lewis, M., & Ramsay, D. (2002). Cortisol response to embarrassment and shame. *Child Development, 73*, 1034–1045.

Lewkowicz, D. (1996). Infant's responses to the audible and visual responses of the human face. *Developmental Psychology, 32*, 347–366.

Lieberman, A. (1992). Introduction: The changing context of education. In A. Lieberman (Ed.), *The changing contexts of teaching: Ninety-first yearbook of the National Society for the Study of Education* (Part I, pp. 1–10). Chicago: University of Chicago Press.

Ligon, E. M., Barber, L. W., & Williams, H. J. (1971). *Let me introduce myself: A guide for parents of infant children*. Schenectady, NY: Union College Research Project.

Lilley, I. M. (1967). *Friedrich Froebel: A selection from his writings*. Cambridge, UK: Cambridge University Press.

Lindberg, L., & Swedlow, R. (1980). *Early childhood education: A guide for observation & participation*. Boston: Allyn & Bacon.

Little, J. W. (1992). Opening the black box of professional community. In A. Lieberman (Ed.), *The changing contexts of teaching: Ninety-first yearbook of the National Society for the Study of Education* (Part I, pp. 157–178). Chicago: University of Chicago Press.

Liu, E., Kardos, S. M., Kauffman, D., Peske, H. G., & Johnson, S. M. (2000). *Barely breaking even: Incentives, rewards, and the high costs of choosing to teach*. Cambridge, MA: The Project on the Next Generation of Teachers.

Liu, F. (2011). Pre-service teachers' perceptions of departmentalization of elementary schools. *International Journal of Whole Schooling, 7*(1), 40–52.

Loeber, R., & Stouthamer-Loeber, M. (1998). Development of juvenile aggression and violence: Some common misconceptions and controversies. *American Psychologist, 53*, 242–259.

Losen, D. J., & Orfield, G. (Eds.). *Racial inequality in special education*. Cambridge, MA: Harvard Education Publishing Group.

Loughling, C. E., & Suina, J. H. (1982). *The learning environment: An instructional strategy*. New York: Teachers College Press.

LoveToKnow Corp. (2012). Policymaking. In *Your Dictionary*. Retrieved from http://www.yourdictionary.com/policymaking

Lykken D. T. (2000, June). Reconstucting fathers. *American Psychologist, 55*, 681–682.

Lynch, S. A., & Simpson, C. G. (2010). Social skills: Laying the foundation for success. *Dimensions of Early Childhood, 38*(2), 3–12.

Ma, L. (2003a). *Knowing mathematics* (Vols. I & II). Boston, MA: Houghton Mifflin.

Ma, L. (2003b). *Knowing mathematics: Teachers' resources*. Boston, MA: Houghton Mifflin.

Maccoby, E. (1980). *Social development: Psychological growth and the parent-child relationship*. New York: Harcourt, Brace, Jovanovich.

Maccoby, E. E., & Martin, J. A. (1983). Socialization in the context of the family: Parent-child interaction. In E. M. Hetherington (Ed.) & P. H. Mussen (Gen. Ed.), *Handbook of child psychology: Socialization, personality, and social development* (4th ed., Vol. 4). New York: Wiley.

Machado, J. M. (1999). *Early childhood experiences in language arts: Emerging literacy*. Albany, NY: Delmar.

Machado, J. M. (2012). *Early childhood experiences in language arts: Early literacy*. Belmont, CA: Wadsworth, Cengage Learning.

MacPhee, D., Fritz, J., & Miller-Heyl, J. (1996). Ethnic variations in personal social networks and parenting. *Child Development, 67*, 3278–3295.

MacWhinney, B. (1997). Implicit and explicit processes. *Studies in Second Language Acquisition, 19*, 277–281.

Magoon, M. A., & Critchfield, T. C. (2008). Concurrent schedules of positive and negative reinforcement: Differential impact and differential-outcomes hypotheses. *Journal for the Experimental Analysis of Behavior, 90*(1), 1–22.

Main, M., & Cassidy, J. (1988). Categories of response to reunion with the parent at age 6: Predictable from infant attachment classifications and stable over a 1-month period. *Developmental Psychology, 24*(3), 415–426.

Malatesta, C. Z., & Haviland, J. M. (1982). Learning display rules: The socialization of emotion expression in infancy. *Child Development, 53*, 991–1003.

Malone, D., Jones, B. D., & Stallings, D. T. (2002). Perspective transformation: Effects of a service-learning tutoring experience on prospective teachers. *Teacher Education Quarterly, 29*(1), 61–81.

Mambretti, C. (1999). *Internet technology for schools*. Jefferson, NC: McFarland.

Mandler, J. M. (2004). *The foundations of mind: Origins of conceptional thought*. Oxford, England: Oxford University Press.

Manning, M. L., & Baruth, L. G. (2000). *Multicultural education of children and adolescents*. Needham Heights, MA: Allyn & Bacon.

Manross, M. A. (1994). *What children think, feel, and know about the overhand throw*. Master's thesis, Virginia Tech University.

Manross, M. A. (2000). Learning to throw in physical education class: Part 3. *Teaching Elementary Physical Education, 11*(3), 26–29.

Mardell-Czudnowski, C. D., & Goldenberg, D. S. (1998). *Developmental Indicators for the Assessment of Learning (DIAL-III)*. Circle Pines, MN: American Guidance Service.

Marjanovic-Umek, L., Kranjc, S., & Fekonja, U. (2002). *Developmental levels of the child's storytelling*. Eric Document (ED468907).

Markle, S. (1969). *Good frames and bad* (2nd ed.). New York: Wiley.

Markwardt, F. C., Jr. (2008). *Peabody Individual Achievement Test–Revised*. San Antonio, TX: Pearson.

Marshall, T. A., Levy, S. M., Broffitt, B., Warren, J. J., Eichenberger-Gilmore, J. M., Burnes, T. L., & Stumbo, P. J. (2003). Dental caries and beverage consumption in young children. *Pediatrics, 112*, e184–e191.

Martinez, J., & Perez, M. (2008, February/March). Latino men answer the call to get involved. *Our Children* (National PTA), *33*, 18–19.

Maryland State Department of Education. (2007). *Preschool for all in Maryland: Recommendations of the Task Force on Universal Preschool Education Report to the governor and the general assembly as required by HB 1466*. Retrieved from http://www.marylandpublicschools.org/MSDE/divisions/child_care/pubs

Mason, C. A., Cauce, A. M., Gonzales, N., & Hiraga, Y. (1996). Neither too sweet nor too sour: Problem peers, maternal control, and problem behavior in African-American adolescents. *Child Development, 67*, 2115–2130.

Mavrogenes, N. A. (1990). Helping parents help their children become literate. *Young Children, 45*(4), 4–9.

Mayer, R. E. (2003). *Learning and instruction*. Upper Saddle River, NJ: Merrill Prentice Hall.

McCarthy, D. (1983). *McCarthy scales of children's abilities*. New York: Psychological Corp.

McClure, F. (1981). Formal and functional aspects of the code-switched discourse of bilingual children. In R. Duran (Ed.), *Latino language and communicative behavior* (pp. 69–94). Norwood, NJ: Ablex.

McCullough, J. (1992). Evaluating grants programs for basic scientific research: Difficult measurement problems, few techniques and slow progress. *Evaluation Practice, 13*(2), 95–101.

McCune, L. (1985). Play-language relationships and symbolic development. In L. C. Brown & A. Gottfried (Eds.), *Play interactions* (pp. 38–45). Skillman, NY: Johnson & Johnson.

McCune, L. (1986). Play-language relationships: Implications for a theory of symbolic development. In A. W. Gottfried & C. C. Brown (Eds.), *Play interactions: The contribution of play materials and parental involvement to children's development* (pp. 67–80). Lexington, MA: Heath.

McCune-Nicolich, L. (1981). Toward symbolic functioning: Structure of early pretend games and potential parallels. *Child Development, 52*, 785–797.

McDaniel, T. R., & Davis, A. P. (1999). You've come a long way, baby—or have you? Research evaluating gender portrayal in recent Caldecott-winning books. *Reading Teacher, 52*(5), 532–536.

McDowell, D. J., Parke, R. D., & Spitzer, S. (2002). Parent and child cognitive representations of social situations and children's social competence. *Social Development, 11*(4), 469–486.

McFarland, L., Saunders, R., & Allen, S. (2009). Reflective practice and self-evaluation in learning positive guidance: Experiences of early childhood practicum students. *Early Childhood Education Journal, 36*, 505–511.

McGee-Cooper, A., Trammel, D., & Lau, B. (1990). *You don't have to go home from work exhausted! The energy engineering approach*. Dallas, TX: Bowen & Rogers.

McKown, C., & Weinstein, R. S. (2003). The development and consequences of stereotype consciousness in middle childhood. *Child Development, 74*, 498–515.

McLeod, B. D., Wood, J. J., & Weisz, J. R. (2007). Examining the association between parenting and childhood anxiety: A meta-analysis. *Clinical Psychology Review, 27*, 155–172.

McLoyd, V. C., & Smith, J. (2002). Physical discipline and behavior problems in African American, European American, and Hispanic children: Emotional support as a moderator. *Journal of Marriage and the Family, 64*, 40–53.

McNeill, D. (1966). Developmental psycholinguistics. In F. Smith & G. Miller (Eds.), *The genesis of language: A psycholinguistic approach* (pp. 15–82). Cambridge, MA: MIT Press.

Mead, G. H. (1934). *Mind, self, and society*. Chicago: University of Chicago Press.

Meece, J., & Daniels, D. H. (2008). *Child and adolescent development for educators* (3rd ed.). New York: McGraw-Hill.

Meisel, J. M. (1993). Simultaneous first language acquisition: A window on early grammatical development. *D.E.L.T.A., 9*, 353–385.

Mellon, E. (1994). Play theories: A contemporary view. *Early Child Development and Care, 102,* 91–100.

Meltzoff, A., & Moore, M. (1994). Imitation, memory, and representation of persons. *Infant Behavior and Development, 17,* 83–99.

Mendelson, H., & Haith, H. (1976). The relation between audition and vision in the human newborn. *SRCD Monograph, 41*(Whole No. 167).

Merrell, K. W. (2001). Assessment of children's social skills: Recent developments, best practices, and new directions. *Exceptionality, 9*(1–2), 3–18.

Midco. (1972). *Perspectives on parent participation in Head Start: An analysis and critique* [Prepared under Contract No. HEW-05-72-45]. Washington, DC: Project Head Start, Office of Child Development, U.S. Department of Health Education and Welfare.

Midjass, C. L. (1984). Use of space. In J. W. Keefe & J. M. Jenkins (Eds.), *Instructional leadership handbook.* Reston, VA: National Association of Secondary School Principals.

Miller, D. (2002). *Reading with meaning.* Portland, ME: Stenhouse Publishers.

Mills v. Board of Education of the District of Columbia, No. 1939-71 (1972).

Minkler, M., & Fuller-Thompson, E. (2005). African American grandparents raising grandchildren: A national study using the Census 2000 American Community Survey. *Journal of Gerontology, 60B,* S82–S92.

Miranda, N. (2006). *Study shows pre-school teacher shortage.* Retrieved from http://abclocal.go.com/kgo/story?section=politics&id=4443344

Mitchell, A., & David, J. (Eds.). (1992). *Explorations with young children.* Mt. Rainier, MD: Gryphon House.

Mitka, M. (2004). Improvement seen in U.S. immunization rates. *Journal of the American Medical Association, 292,* 1167.

Moats, L. (2000). *Whole language lives on: The illusion of "balanced" reading instruction.* Washington, DC: Thomas B. Fordham Foundation. ERIC Document (ED449465).

Mocan, H. N. (1995). *Quality adjusted cost functions for child care centers.* National Bureau of Economic Research. Cambridge, MA: Carnegie Foundation.

Monighan, P. (1985). The development of symbolic expression in preschool play and language. In P. Monighan-Nourot, B. Scales, J. Van Hoorn, & M. Almy, *Looking at children's play: A bridge between theory and practice* (pp. 14–35). New York: Teachers College Press.

Monighan-Nourot, P., Scales, B., Van Hoorn, J., & Almy, M. (1987). *Looking at children's play: A bridge between theory and practice.* New York: Teachers College Press.

Montagu, A. (1971). *Touching: The human significance of skin.* New York: Columbia University Press.

Montague, D. P. F., & Walker-Andrews, A. S. (2001). Peekaboo: A new look at infants' perception of emotion expressions. *Developmental Psychology, 37,* 826–838.

Montanaro, S. (2002). The development of co-ordinated movement. *The NAMTA Journal, 27*(1), 91–117.

Mook, D. G. (2004). *Classic experiments in psychology.* Westport, CT: Greenwood Press.

Moomaw, S., & Davis, J. A. (2010). STEM comes to preschool. *Young Children, 65*(5), 12–14.

Morland, J. (1962). Racial acceptance and preference of nursery school children in a Southern city. *Merrill-Palmer Quarterly Behavior and Development, 8,* 271–280.

Morland, J. K. (1966). A comparison of race awareness in Northern and Southern children. *American Journal of Orthopsychiatry, 26,* 22–31.

Morrow, L. (1989). *Literacy development in the early years.* Upper Saddler River, NJ: Prentice Hall.

Moses, L. J., Coon, J. A., & Wusinich, N. (2000). Young children's understanding of desire information. *Developmental Psychology, 36,* 77–90.

Mouratidis, A. A., & Sideridis, G. D. (2009). On social achievement goals: Their relations with peer acceptance, classroom belongingness, and perceptions of loneliness. *The Journal of Experimental Education, 77*(3), 285–307.

Munakata, Y. (2006). Information processing approaches to development. In W. Damon & R. M. Lerner (Series Eds.) & Deanna Khun & Robert S. Siegler (Vol. Eds.), *Handbook of child psychology: Cognition, perception and language* (6th ed., Vol. 2, pp. 426–463). Hoboken, NJ: Wiley.

Muntner, P., He, J., Cutler, J. A., Wildman, R. P., & Whelton, P. K. (2004). Trends in blood pressure among children and adolescents. *Journal of the American Medical Association, 291,* 2017–2113.

Murray-Close, D., & Crick, N. R. (2006). Mutual antipathy involvement: Gender and associations with aggression and victimization. *School Psychology Review, 35*(3), 472–492.

Mustillo, S., Worthman, C., Erkanli, A., Keeler, G., Angold, A., & Costello, E. J. (2003). Obesity psychiatric disorder: Developmental trajectories. *Pediatrics, 111,* 851–859.

Myers, D. (1998). *Psychology.* Michigan: Worth Publishers.

Myers, M., Fifer, W., Grose-Fifer, J., Sahni, R., Stark, R., & Schultze, K. (1997). A novel quantitative measure of trace-alternate EEG activity and its association with sleep states of preterm infants. *Developmental Psychobiology, 31,* 167–174.

Nash, J. M. (1997). Fertile minds. *Time, 149*(5), 48–56.

National Academy of Sciences. (2011). *A framework for K–12 science education: Practices, crosscutting concepts, and core ideas* [Report brief]. Washington, DC: Author.

National Academy of Sciences. (2012). *A framework for K–12 science education: Practices, crosscutting concepts, and core ideas* [Summary]. Washington, DC: Author.

National Academy of Sciences & Worth, K. (2009). *A framework for K–12 science education.* Washington, DC: National Academy of Sciences.

National Association for Gifted Children. (2008). *Redefining giftedness for a new century: Shifting the paradigm* [Position statement]. Washington, DC: Author. Retrieved from http://www.nagc.org/index2.aspx?id=6404

National Association for Sport and Physical Education. (2004). *Moving into the future: National standards for physical education* (2nd ed.). Reston, VA: Author.

National Association for Sport and Physical Education. (2009). *National standards & guidelines for physical education teacher education* (3rd ed.). Reston, VA: Author.

National Association for the Education of Young Children. (1996a). Celebrating holidays in early childhood programs. In *Early years are learning years* (Release No. 18). Washington, DC: Author.

National Association for the Education of Young Children. (1996b). *Guidelines for preparation of early childhood professionals*. Washington, DC: Author.

National Association for the Education of Young Children. (2001). *NAEYC standards for early childhood professional preparation: Initial licensure programs*. Washington, DC: Author.

National Association for the Education of Young Children. (2003). *Preparing early childhood professionals: NAEYC's standards for programs*. Washington, DC: Author.

National Association for the Education of Young Children. (2005, April). *Code of Ethical Conduct and Statement of Commitment*. Retrieved from http://www.naeyc.org/files/naeyc/file/positions/PSETH05.pdf

National Association for the Education of Young Children. (2009a). *The core of developmentally appropriate practice*. Washington, DC: Author. Retrieved from http://www.naeyc.org/dap/core

National Association for the Education of Young Children. (2009b). *Developmentally appropriate practice in early childhood programs serving children from birth through age 8*. Washington, DC: Author.

National Association for the Education of Young Children. (2009c). *Where we stand: On responding to linguistic and cultural diversity: Recommendations for effective early childhood education*. Washington, DC: Author. (Original work published 1995)

National Association for the Education of Young Children. (2012). *Technology and interactive media as tools in early childhood programs serving children from birth through age 8*. Position statement adopted with Fred Rodgers Center for Early Learning and Children's Media. Washington, DC: Author. Retrieved from http://www.naeyc.org/positionstatements

National Association for the Education of Young Children & National Association of Early Childhood Specialists in the State Departments of Education. (2002). *Early learning standards: Creating the conditions for success*. Retrieved from www.naeyc.org

National Association for the Education of Young Children, National Child Care Information and Technical Assistance Center & National Association for Regulatory Administration. (2010). *Child care licensing in summary*. Retrieved from www.naeyc.org

National Association of Child Care Resource and Referral Service Agencies. (2009). *Unequal opportunities for preschoolers: Differing standards for licensed child care centers and state-funded prekindergarten programs*. Retrieved from http://www.naccrra.org/node/1805

National Board for Professional Teaching Standards. (2012). Retrieved from http://www.nbpts.org/

National Center for Children in Poverty. (2010). *Percentage of children in low income and poor families by race/ethnicity, 2010*. Retrieved from http://www.nccp.org/publications/pdf/text_1049.pdf

National Center for Family Literacy. (2011). *Family literacy facts*. Retrieved on February 17, 2012 from http://www.famlit.org/

National Center for Health Statistics. (2004). *Health, United States, 2004 with chart-book trends in the health of Americans* (DHHS Publication No. 2004-1232). Hyattsville, MD: Author.

National Center for Public Policy and Higher Education. (2005). *Income of U.S. workforce projected to decline if education doesn't improve*. Retrieved from www.highereducation.org

National Center on Response to Intervention. (n.d.). *What is RTI?* Retrieved from http://www.rti4success.org/

National Coalition for Literacy. (2011). *Public policy advocacy updates*. Retrieved from http//blog.ncladvocacy.org

National Council of Teachers of English. (1954). *Language arts for today's children*. New York: Appleton-Century-Crofts.

National Council of Teachers of Mathematics. (2000). *Principles and standards for school mathematics*. Reston, VA: Author.

National Governors Association Center for Best Practices & Council of Chief State School Officers. (2010). *Common core state standards for mathematics*. Washington, DC: Author.

National Head Start Association. (2012). *Research*. Retrieved from www.nhsa.org/research/

National Institute of Child Health and Human Development. (2000). *Report of the National Reading Panel: Teaching children to read: An evidence-based assessment of the scientific research literature on reading and its implications for reading instruction*. Washington, DC: U.S. Government Printing Office.

National Institute of Child Health and Human Development. (2001). Child-care and family predictors of preschool attachment and stability from infancy. *Developmental Psychology, 37*(6), 847–862.

National Research Council. (1996). *National science education standards*. Washington, DC: National Academies Press.

National Research Council. (2001a). *Eager to learn: Educating our preschoolers*. Washington, DC: National Academies Press.

National Research Council. (2001b). *Early childhood development and learning: New knowledge for policy*. Washington, DC: National Academies Press.

National Research Council. (2011). *A framework for K–12 science education: Practices, crosscutting concepts, and core ideas*. Washington, DC: National Academies Press.

Neisworth, J. T., & Bagnato, S. J. (2000). Recommended practices in assessment. In S. Sandall, M. E. McLean, & B. J. Smith (Eds.), *DEC recommended practices in early intervention/ early childhood special education* (pp. 17–28). Longmont, CO: Sopris West.

Nelson, B. G. (2002). *The importance of men teachers: And reasons why there are so few.* Minneapolis, MN: MenTeach.

Neugebauer, B. (1992). *Alike and different: Exploring our humanity with young children.* Washington, DC: National Association for the Education of Young Children.

Neuman, S., & Roskos, K. (1993). *Language and literacy learning in the early years.* Ft. Worth, TX: Harcourt Brace Jovanovich.

New, R. (2000). The Reggio Emilia approach: It's not an approach—it's an attitude. In J. Roopnarine & J. Johnson (Eds.), *Approaches to early childhood education.* Columbus, OH: Merrill.

Newborg, J. (2003). *Battelle Developmental Inventory (BDI-2).* Rolling Meadows, IL: Riverside Publishing.

Newcomb, A. F., & Bagwell, C. L. (1995). Children's friendships and relations: A meta analytic review. *Psychological Bulletin, 117*(2), 306–347.

New York Times. (2012, February 9). No Child Left Behind Act. Retrieved from http://topics.nytimes.com/

New York University. (2007, August 3). Phonics, whole-word and whole-language processes add up to determine reading speed, study shows. *Science Daily.* Retrieved from http://www.sciencedaily.com/

Nieto, S., & Bode, P. (2011). *Affirming diversity: The sociopolitical context of multicultural education.* Boston: Pearson Education.

Nimnicht, G. P., Brown, E., Addison, B., & Johnson, S. (1971). *Parent guide: How to play learning games with a preschool child.* Morristown, NJ: General Learning Corporation.

No Child Left Behind Act of 2001, Pub. L. No. 107-110, 115 Stat. 1425 (2002).

Nodelman, P. (1999). The boys in children's books. *Riverbank Review*, 5–7.

Novak, J. R., Herman, J. L., & Gearhart, M. (1996). Establishing validity for performance-based assessments: An illustration for collections of student writing. *Journal of Education Research, 89*(4), 220–233.

Nutbrown, C. (2006). *Key concepts in early childhood education and care.* Thousand Oaks, CA: Sage.

O'Brien, S. (2010). Characterization of a unique undergraduate multidisciplinary STEM K–5 teacher preparation program. *Journal of Technology Education, 21*(2), 35–51.

Ogbu, J. U. (1994). From cultural differences to differences in cultural frames of reference. In P. M. Greenfield & R. R. Cocking (Eds.), *Cross-cultural roots of minority child development* (pp. 365–391). Hillsdale, NJ: Erlbaum.

Ogden, C. L., Flegal, K. M., Carroll, M. D., & Johnson, C. L. (2002). Mean body weight, height, and body mass index, United States 1960–2002. Advance data from *Vital and Health Statistics*, No. 247. Hyattsville, MD: National Center for Health Studies.

Olsen, L. (2010). *Reparable harm: Fulfilling the unkept promise of educational opportunity for California's long-term English learners.* Long Beach, CA: Californians Together. Retrieved from www.californianstogether.org

Olson, D. H., & Defrain, J. (1994). *Marriage and the family: Diversity and strengths.* Mountain View, CA: Mayfield.

Olson, D. H., & Gorall, D. M. (2003). Circumplex model of marital and family systems. In F. Walsh (Ed.), *Normal family processes* (3rd ed., pp. 514–547). New York: Guilford.

Olson, G., & Fuller, M. L. (2003). *Home-school relations: Working successfully with parents and families* (2nd ed.). Boston: Allyn & Bacon.

Osborn, D. K. (1980). *Early childhood education in historical perspective.* Athens GA: Education Associates.

Osher, D., Woodruff, D., & Sims, A. E. (2005). Schools make a difference: Overrepresentation of African American youth in special education and the juvenile justice system. In D. J. Losen & G. Orfield (Eds.), *Racial inequity in special education* (pp. 93–116). Cambridge, MA: Harvard Education Publishing.

Oswald, D., Coutinho, M., & Best, A. (2000). Community and school predictors of overrepresentation of minority children in special education. In D. J. Losen & G. Orfield (Eds.), *Racial inequity in special education* (pp. 93–116). Cambridge, MA: Harvard Education Publishing.

Otto, B. (2009). *Language development in early childhood.* Upper Saddle River, NJ: Pearson Prentice Hall.

Owens, R. E. (1996). *Language development.* Boston: Allyn & Bacon.

Owens, R. E. (2001). *Language development: An introduction* (5th ed.). Needham Heights, MA: Allyn & Bacon.

Pai, Y., Adler, S. A., & Shadiow, L. K. (2006). *Cultural foundations of education.* Upper Saddle River, NJ: Pearson Prentice Hall.

Pajares, M. (1992). Teachers' beliefs and educational research: Cleaning up a messy construct. *Review of Educational Research, 62*(3), 307–332.

Palmer, D., & Snodgrass Rangel, V. (2011). High stakes accountability and policy implementation: Teacher decision making in bilingual classrooms in Texas. *Educational Policy, 25*(4), 614–647.

Papillia, D. E., Olds, S. W., & Feldman R. D. (2007). *Human Development.* NY: McGraw-Hill,

Paradis, M. (2004). *A neurolinguistic theory of bilingualsim.* Amsterdam: John Benjamins.

Parke, R. D., Coltrane, S., Fabricius, W., Powers, J., & Adams, M. (2004). Assessing father involvement in Mexican American families. In R. Day & M. E. Lamb (Eds.), *Conceptualizing and measuring paternal involvement* (pp. 17–38). Mahwah, NJ: Erlbaum.

Parke, R. D., Simpkins, S. D., McDowell, D. J., Kim, M., Killian, C., Dennis, J., . . . Rah, Y. (2004). Relative contributions of families and peers to children's social development. In P. K. Smith & C. H. Hart (Eds.), *Blackwell handbook of childhood social development* (pp. 156–177). Malden, MA: Blackwell.

Parker, S. K., Schwartz, B., Todd, J., & Pickering, L. K. (2004). Thimerosal-containing vaccines and autistic spectrum disorder: A critical review of published original data. *Pediatrics, 114*, 793–804.

Parlapiano, E. H. (2006). Sounding out phonics: Get the lowdown on why this teaching method is key to reading success. *Scholastic Parents*. Retrieved from http://www2.scholastic.com/

Parten, M. (1933). Social play among preschool children. *Journal of Abnormal and Social Psychology, 28,* 136–147.

Patrick, G. T. W. (1916). *The psychology of relaxation*. Boston: Houghton Mifflin.

Payne, J. N., Towsley, A. E., & Huinker, D. M. (1990). Implications of NCTM's standards for teaching fractions and decimals. *Arithmetic Teacher, 37*(8), 23.

Peltzman, B. R. (1998). *Pioneers of early childhood education: A bio-bibliographical guide*. Westport, CT: Greenwood Press.

Penalosa, F. (1981). *Introduction to the sociology of language*. Rowley, MA: Newbury House.

Pence, A. R. (1988). *Ecological research with children and families*. New York: Teachers College Press.

Pence, A. R., & Goelman, H. (1991). The relationship of regulation, training, and motivation to quality of care in family day care. *Child & Youth Care Forum, 20*(2), 83–101.

Pennsylvania Association for Retarded Children (PARC) v. Commonwealth of Pennsylvania, No. 71-42 (1972).

Perry, B. (1990). How the brain learns best. *Instructor*, 34.

Perry, B. (2007a). Attunement: Reading the rhythms of the child. *Scholastic*. Retrieved from http://www.scholastic.com/

Perry, B. (2007b). Creating an emotionally safe classroom. *Scholastic*. Retrieved from http://www.scholastic.com/

Perry, B. (2007c). Using technology in the early childhood classroom. *Scholastic*. Retrieved from http://www.scholastic.com/

Peterson, R. (1971). Imitation: A basic behavioral mechanism. *Journal of Applied Behavioral Analysis, 4,* 1–9.

Pettit, G. S., Brown, E. G., Mize, J., & Lindsey, E. (1998). Mothers' and fathers' socializing behaviors in three contexts: Links with children's peer competence. *Merrill-Palmer Quarterly, 44*(2), 173–193.

Pettygrove, W., & Greenman, J. T. (1984). The adult world of day care. In J. T. Greenman & R. W. Fuqua (Eds.), *Making day care better: Training, evaluation and the process of change*. New York: Teachers College Press.

Pew Research Center for the People and the Press. (1998, June 8). *Internet news takes off*. Retrieved from http://www.people-press.org

Pew Research Center for the People and the Press. (2010, November 18). *The decline of marriage and rise of new families: VI. New family types*. Washington, DC: Author.

Philippou, G. N., & Christou, C. (1998). The effects of a preparatory mathematics program in changing prospective teachers' attitudes toward mathematics. *Educational Studies in Mathematics, 35,* 189–206.

Phillips, C. B. (1994). What every early childhood professional should know. In J. Johnson & J. B. McCracken (Eds.), *The early childhood career lattice: Perspectives on professional development*. Washington, DC: National Association for the Education of Young Children.

Phillips, D. A. (1996). *Reconsidering quality in early care and education*. New Haven, CT: Yale University Press.

Piaget, J. (1950). *The psychology of intelligence*. San Diego, CA: Harcourt Brace Jovanovich.

Piaget, J. (1952). *The origins of intelligence*. New York: International Universities Press.

Piaget, J. (1954). *The construction of reality in the child*. New York: Basic Books.

Piaget, J. (1955). *The language and thought of the child*. New York: Routledge & Kegan Paul.

Pianta, R. C. (2012). *Handbook of early childhood education*. New York: Guilford Press.

Plato. *Republic*. (trans. Paul Shorey), Loeb Classical Library 1930–1935. In Robert Ulich, *Three thousand years of educational wisdom*. Cambridge, MA: Harvard University Press.

Pleck, J. H., & Masciadrelli, B. P. (2004). Paternal involvement by U.S. residential fathers: Levels, sources and consequences. In M. E. Lamb (Ed.), *The role of the father in child development* (4th ed., pp. 222–271). Hoboken, NJ: Wiley.

Plucker, J. A., and Callahan, C. M. (Eds.). (2008). *Critical issues and practices in gifted education: What the research says*. Waco, TX: Prufrock Press.

Poehlmann, J. (2003). An attachment perspective on grandparents raising their very young grandchildren: Implications for intervention and research. *Infant Mental Health Journal, 24,* 149–173.

Poel, E. (2010). Engaging students with disabilities in the learning process through handheld technology. *Learning Disabilities: A Multidisciplinary Journal, 16*(3), 149–156.

Poplack, S. (1981). Syntactic structure and social function of code switching. In R. Duran (Ed.), *Latino language and communicative behavior* (pp. 169–184). Norwood, NJ: Ablex.

Powell, D. R. (2003). Relations between families and early childhood programs. *Kaufman Early Education Exchange*.

Preschott, E., Jones, E., & Kritchevsky, S. (1967). *Group day care as a child-rearing environment*. Washington, DC: Children's Bureau, Social Security Administration, Department of Health, Education and Welfare.

Pretti-Frontczak, K., Kowalksi, K., & Brown, R. D. (2002). Preschool teachers' use of assessments and curricula: A statewide examination. *Exceptional Children, 69*(1), 109–123.

Prizant, B. M., Wetherby, A. M., Rubin, E., & Laurent, A. C. (2003). The SCERTS model: A transactional, family-centered approach to enhancing communication and socioemotional abilities of children with autism spectrum disorder. *Infants and Young Children, 16,* 296–316.

Proctor, B. D., & Dalaker, J. (2003). *Poverty in the United States: 2002* (Current Population Reports, Series P60-222). Washington, DC: U.S. Government Printing Office.

Quattrin, T., Liu, E., Shaw, N., Shine, B., & Chiang, E. (2005). Obese children who are referred to the pediatric oncologist: Characteristics and outcome. *Pediatrics, 115,* 348–351.

Quinn, P. C. (2004). Development of subordinate-level categorization in 3–7-month-old infants. *Child Development, 75*, 886–899.

Ramsey, P. G. (1986). Racial and cultural categories. In C. P. Edwards (Ed.), *Promoting social and moral development in young children: Creative approaches for the classroom* (pp. 78–101). New York: Teachers College Press.

Raver, C. C. (2003). Does work pay psychologically as well as economically? The role of employment in predicting depressive systems and parenting among low-income families. *Child Development, 74*, 1720–1736.

Read, K. H. (1987). *Early childhood programs: Human relationships and learning.* New York: Holt, Rinehart & Winston.

Ricciardelli, L. A. (1992). Bilingualism and cognitive development in relation to threshold theory. *Journal of Psycholinguistic Research, 21*, 301–316.

Rice, M. (1995). Children's language acquisition. In B. Power & R. Hubbard (Eds.), *Language development: A reader for teachers* (pp. 3–16). Upper Saddle River, NJ: Merrill/Prentice Hall.

Rigby, K. (2001). *Stop the bullying.* Markham, ON, Canada: Pembroke.

Rinaldi, C., & Samson, J. (2008). English language learners and response to intervention: Referral considerations. *Teaching Exceptional Children, 40*(5), 6–14.

Robinson, N. M. (1993). Identifying and nurturing gifted, very young children. In K. A. Heller, F. J. Monks, & A. H. Passow (Eds.), *International handbook of research and development of giftedness and talent* (pp. 507–524). Oxford: Pergamon.

Robinson, V. B., Ross, G., & Neal, H. C. (2000). *Emergent literacy in kindergarten: A review of the research and related suggested activities and learning strategies.* San Mateo, CA: California Kindergarten Association.

Rogoff, B. (1990). *Apprenticeship in thinking: Cognitive development in social context.* New York: Oxford University Press.

Rogoff, B. (1998). Cognition as a collaborative process. In W. Damon (Series Ed.) & D. Kuhn & R. S. Seigler (Vol. Eds.), *Handbook of child psychology: Cognition, perception, and language* (5th ed., Vol. 2, pp. 679–744). New York: Wiley.

Rogoff, B. (2003). *The cultural nature of human development.* New York: Oxford University Press.

Rogoff, B., Mistry, J., Concu, C., & Mosier, C. (1993). Guided participation in cultural activity by toddlers and caregivers. *Monographs of Society for Research in Child Development, 58* (Serial No. 236, No. 8.). The Society for Research in Child Development, Inc. Reprinted with permission.

Roid, G. H. (2003). *Stanford-Binet Intelligence Scales for Early Childhood.* Rolling Meadows, IL: Riverside Publishing.

Roopnarine, J., & Johnson, J. (Eds.). (2000). *Approaches to early childhood education* (3rd ed.). Upper Saddle River, NJ: Merrill/Prentice Hall.

Root, S., Callahan, J., & Sepanski, J. (2002). Building teaching dispositions and service-learning practice: A multi-site study. *Michigan Journal of Community Service Learning, 8*(2), 50–60.

Rosberg, M. (1995). *Young children and literacy development.* Paper presented at the Study conference on cued speech, Malaysia.

Roschelle, J., Rafanan, K., Bhanot, R., Estrella, G., Penuel, B., Nussbaum, M., & Claro, S. (2009). Scaffolding group explanation and feedback with handheld technology: Impact on students' mathematics learning. *Educational Technology Research and Development, 58*(4), 399–419.

Ross, H., & Lollis, S. (1987). Communication with infant social games. *Developmental Psychology, 23*, 241–248.

Rothbart, M. K., & Bates, J. E. (1998). Temperament. In W. Damon (Series Ed.) & N. Eisenberg (Vol. Ed.), *Handbook of child psychology: Social, emotional, and personality development* (5th ed., Vol. 3, pp. 105–176). New York: Wiley.

Roth-Hanania, R., Busch-Rossnagel, N., & Higgins-D'Alessandro, A. (2000). Development of self and empathy in early infancy: Implications for atypical development. *Infants and Young Children, 13*, 1–14.

Roundtree, W. J. (2000). *A case study analysis of parental scaffolding among three mother-child dyads participating in the Home Instruction Program for Preschool Youngsters.* Submitted in partial fulfillment of the requirements for degree of doctor of education in Teachers College, Columbia University.

Rouse, P. (2009). *Inclusion in physical education: Fitness, motor, and social skills for students of all abilities.* Champaign, IL: Human Kinetics.

Rubin, K. H. (1982). Non-social play in preschoolers: Necessary evil? *Child Development, 53*, 651–657.

Rubin, K. H., Bukowski, W. M., & Parker, J. G. (1998). Peer interactions, relationships, and groups. In W. Damon (Series Ed.) & N. Eisenberg (Vol. Ed.), *Handbook of child psychology: Social, emotional, and personality development* (5th ed., Vol. 3, pp. 619–700). New York: Wiley.

Rubin, K. H., Cheah, C. S. L., & Fox, N. (2001). Emotion regulation, parenting and display of social reticence in preschoolers. *Early Education & Development, 12*, 97–115.

Rubin, K. H., Fein, G., & Vandenberg, B. (1983). Play. In E. M. Hetherington (Ed.) & P. H. Mussen (Series Ed.), *Handbook of child psychology: Socialization, personality, and social development* (Vol. 4, pp. 698–774). New York: Wiley.

Ruiz, N. T., Figueroa, R., & Garcia, E. (1996). *The OLE curriculum guide: Creating optimal learning environments for students from diverse backgrounds in special and general education.* Sacramento: California Department of Education Press.

Russell, D. (1956). *Children's thinking.* Boston: Ginn.

Ryan, S., Whitebrook, M., Kipnis, F., & Sakai, L. (2011). Professional development needs of directors leading in a mixed services delivery preschool system. *Early Childhood Research & Practice, 13*(1). Retrieved from http://ecrp.uiuc.edu/v13n1/ryan.html

Salkind, N. J. (2004). *An introduction to theories of human development.* Thousand Oaks, CA: Sage.

Saluja, G., Early, D. M., & Clifford, R. M. (2002). Demographic characteristics of early childhood teachers and structural elements of early care and education in the United States. *Early Childhood Research & Practice*. Retrieved from ecrp.uiuc.edu/v4n1/saluja.html

Sameroff, A., & McDonough, S. C. (1994). Educational implications of developmental transitions: Revisiting the 5 to 7 year shift. *Phi Delta Kappan, 76*(3), 188–193.

Sanchez, R. (1983). *Chicano discourse*. Rowley, MA: Newbury House.

Santos, R. M. (2004). Ensuring culturally and linguistically appropriate assessment of young children. *Young Children, 54*(6), 14–15.

Sappon-Shevin, M. (2007). *Widening the circle: The power of inclusive classrooms*. Boston: Beacon Press.

Saracho, O. N., & Spodek, B. (2007). Early childhood teachers' preparation and the quality of program outcomes. *Early Child Development and Care, 177*(1), 71–91.

Saracho, O., & Spodek, B. (2009). Educating the young mathematician: A historical perspective through the nineteenth century. *Early Childhood Education Journal, 36*(4), 297–303.

Saxe, G. B. (1981). Body parts as numerals: A developmental analysis of numeration among the Oksapmin in Papua New Guinea. *Child Development, 52*(1), 306–316.

Saxe, G. B. (1991). *Culture and cognitive development: Studies in mathematical understanding*. Hillsdale, NJ: Erlbaum.

Schaffer, H. R., & Emerson, P. E. (1964). The development of social attachments in infancy. *Monographs of the Society for Research in Child Development, 29*(3), Serial No. 94.

Schiller, F. (2003). *Contemporary perspective on play in early childhood education* (O. N. Saracho & B. Spodek, Eds.). Greenwich, CT: Information Age. (Original work published 1878)

Schiller, J. (1980). *Child care alternatives and emotional well-being*. New York: Pregena.

Schiller, P. (1997). Brain development: Research, support, and challenges. *Child Care Information Exchange, 117,* 6–10.

Schiller, P. (2001). Brain research and its implications for early childhood programs. *Child Care Information Exchange, 140,* 14–18.

Schmitz, M. F. (2005). Cultural and acculturation differences in trajectories of home environment inventory scores for Latino children and families. *Journal of Family Issues, 26,* 568–583.

Schmoker, M., & Marzano, R. J. (1999). Realizing the promise of standards-based education. *Educational Leadership, 56*(6), 17–21.

Schroeder Yu, G. (2008). Documentation: Ideas and applications from the Reggio Emilia approach. *Teaching Artist Journal, 6*(2), 126–134.

Schweinhart, L. (1993). Observing young children in action: The key to early childhood assessment. *Young Children, 48*(5), 29–33.

Sears, C. J. (1994). Recognizing and coping with tactile defensiveness in young children. *Infants and Young Children, 6,* 47–53.

Section 504 of the Rehabilitation Act, 29 U.S.C. § 794 (1973).

Seefeldt, C. (2001). *Social studies for the preschool: Primary child* (6th ed.). Upper Saddle River, NJ: Merrill/Prentice Hall.

Seifert, K. (1988). Men in early childhood education. In B. Spodek, O. N. Saracho, & D. L. Peters (Eds.), *Professionalism and the early childhood practitioner* (pp. 105–116). New York: Teachers College Press.

Selman, R. L. (1980). *The growth of interpersonal understanding: Developmental and clinical analyses*. New York: Academic.

Serbin, L. A., Powlishta, K. K., & Gulko, J. (1993). The development of sex typing in the middle childhood. *Monographs of the Society for Research in Child Development, 58*(2, Serial No. 232).

Shade, D. D. (1994). Computers and young children: New frontiers in computer hardware and software or what computer should I buy? *Day Care and Early Education, 21,* 38–39.

Shaffer, D. R. (2009). *Social and personality development*. Belmont, CA. Wadsworth Publishing Co., Inc.

Shaywitz, S. (2008). Why smart people can't read. In *The Jossey-Bass reader on the brain and learning* (pp. 242–250). San Francisco: Jossey-Bass.

Sheldon, A. (1990). Pickle fights: Gendered talk in preschool disputes. *Discourse Processes, 13*(1), 5.

Sheldon, K. M., Elliot, A. J., Kim, Y., & Kasser, T. (2001). What is satisfying about events? Testing 10 candidate psychological needs. *Journal of Personality and Social Psychology, 80,* 325–339.

Shelov, S. (1998). *American Academy of Pediatrics: Caring for your baby and young child*. New York: Bantam.

Shipley, D. (2007). *Empowering children: Play-based curriculum for lifelong learning*. Nelson, Canada: Delmar.

Shonkoff, J. P., & Phillips, D. A. (Eds.). (2000). *From neurons to neighborhoods: The science of early childhood development*. Washington, DC: National Academies Press.

Short, C. B. (2007). *4C's for peace: A curriculum for a culture of caring children*. Master's thesis, Sacramento State University.

Siegler, R. S. (1996). Emerging Minds: The process of change in children's thinking. Oxford University Press (New York).

Siegler, R. (1998). *Children's thinking*. Upper Saddle River, NJ: Prentice Hall.

Silverstein, L. B., & Auerbach, C. F. (1999). Deconstructing the essential father. *American Psychologist, 54,* 397–407.

Simpkins, S. D., Fredricks, J. A., Davis-Kean, P. E., & Eccles, J. S. (2006). Healthy mind, healthy habits: The influence of activity involvement in middle childhood. In A. C. Huston & M. N. Ripke (Eds.), *Developmental contexts in middle childhood: Bridges to adolescence and adulthood* (pp. 283–302). New York: Cambridge University Press.

Sinclair, H. (1994). Early cognitive development and the contribution of peer integration: A Piagetian view. In S. Friedman & H. Haywood (Eds.), *Developmental follow-up* (pp. 129–138). San Diego, CA: Academic.

Singer, J. L. (1973). *The child's world of make-believe: Experimental studies of imaginative play.* New York: Academic Press.

Singer, L. M., Brodzinsky, D. M., Ramsay, D., Steir, M., & Waters, E. (1985). Mother-infant attachment in adoptive families. *Child Development, 56,* 1543–1551.

Skiba, R. J., Poloni-Staudinger, L., Gallini, S., Simmons, A. B., & Feggins-Azziz, R. (2006). Disparate access: The disproportionality of African American students with disabilities across educational environments. *Council for Exceptional Children, 72*(4), 411–424.

Skinner, B. F. (1953). *Science and human behavior.* New York: Macmillan.

Skinner, B. F. (1968). *The technology of teaching.* New York: Appleton-Century-Crofts.

Skinner, B. F. (1976). *About behaviorism.* New York: Vintage Books.

Skinner, B. F. (1986). Programmed instruction revisited. *Phi Delta Kappan, 68*(2), 103–110.

Skinner, B. F. (2005). *Walden two.* Indianapolis, IN: Hackett. (Originally published in 1948)

Skinner, C. H., Neddenriep, C. E., Robinson, S. L., Ervin, R., & Jones, K. (2002). Altering educational environments through positive peer reporting: Prevention and remediation of social problems associated with behavior disorders. *Psychology in the Schools, 39*(2), 191–202.

Slaughter, J. (1993). *Beyond storybooks: Young children and the shared book experience.* Newark, DE: International Reading Association.

Slavoff, G. R., & Johnson, J. S. (1995). The effects of age on the rate of learning a second language. *Studies in Second Language Acquisition, 17,* 1–16.

Slee, P. T. (2002). *Child, adolescent, and family development.* Cambridge, UK: Cambridge University Press.

Slentz, K. L., & Krogh, S. L. (2001). *Teaching young children: Contexts for learning.* Mahwah, NJ: Erlbaum.

Smelser, N. J., Wilson, W. J., & Mitchell, F. (2001). *America becoming: Racial trends and their consequences* (Vol. 1). Washington, DC: National Academy Press.

Smilansky, S. (1990). Sociodramatic play: Its relevance to behavior and achievement in school. In E. Klugman & S. Smilansky (Eds.), *Children's play and learning: Perspectives and policy implications* (pp. 18–42). New York: Teachers College Press.

Smith, F. (1988). *Joining the literacy club: Further essays into education.* Portsmouth, NH: Heinemann Educational Books.

Smith, M. (2001). Social and emotional competencies: Contributions to young African-American children's peer acceptance. *Early Education & Development, 12,* 49–72.

Smith, P. K., & Connolly, K. J. (1980). *The ecology of preschool behavior.* Cambridge, UK: Cambridge University Press.

Smither, R. D. (1998). *The psychology of work and human performance* (3rd ed.). New York: Longman.

Snoddon, K. (2010). Technology as a learning tool for ASL literacy. *Sign Language Studies, 10*(2), 197–213.

Snow, C. E., Burns, S. M., & Griffin, P. (Eds.). (1998). *Preventing reading difficulties in young children.* Washington, DC: National Academies Press.

Snyder, J., West, L., Stockemer, V., Gibbons, S., & Almquist-Parks, L. (1996). A social learning model of peer choice in the natural environment. *Journal of Applied Developmental Psychology, 17,* 215–237.

Soderman, A. K. (1985). Dealing with difficult young children. *Young Children, 40*(5), 15–20.

Soken, A., & Pick, J. (1992). Intermodal perception of happy and angry expressive behaviors by seven-month-old infants. *Child Development, 63,* 787–795.

Soken, N. H., & Pick, A. D. (1999). Infants' perception of dynamic affective expressions: Do infants distinguish specific emotions? *Child Development, 70,* 1275–1282.

Somerville, D. E., & Leach, D. J. (1988). Direct or indirect instruction? An evaluation of three types of intervention programme for assisting students with specific reading difficulties. *Educational Research, 30*(1), 46–53.

Sonenstein, F. L., Gates, G. J., Schmidt, S., & Bolshun, N. (2002). *Primary child care arrangements of employed parents: Findings from the 1999 National Survey of America's Families.* Washington, DC: The Urban Institute.

Soundy, C. (1997). Nurturing literacy with infants and toddlers in group settings. *Childhood Education, 73,* 149–153.

Spelke, E. S., & Newport, E. L. (1998). Nativism, empiricism, and the development of knowledge. In W. Damon (Gen. Ed.) & R. Learner (Vol. Ed.), *Handbook of child psychology: Theoretical models of human development* (Vol. 1). New York: Wiley.

Spencer, M. B. (1985). Cultural cognition and social cognition as identity factors in Black children's personal growth. In M. Spencer, B. Brookins, & W. Allen (Eds.), *Beginnings: The social and affective development of Black children* (pp. 215–230). Hillsdale, NJ: Erlbaum.

Spodek, B. (1985). *Teaching in the early years* (3rd ed.). Englewood Cliffs, NJ: Prentice-Hall.

Spodek, B. (1986). Development, values, and knowledge in the kindergarten curriculum. In B. Spodek (Ed.), *Today's kindergarten: Exploring the knowledge base, extending the curriculum.* New York: Teachers College Press.

Spodek, B., & Saracho, O. N. (1994). *Right from the start: Teaching children ages three to eight.* Boston: Allyn & Bacon.

Spradley, J. P., & McCurdy, D. W. (1975). *Anthropology: The cultural perspective.* Glenview, IL: Scott, Foresman.

Spreen, O., Risser, A., & Edgell, D. (1995). *Developmental neurology.* New York: Oxford University Press.

Squires, J. K. (2000). Identifying social/emotional and behavioral problems in infants and toddlers. *Infant-Toddler Intervention, 10,* 107–119.

Sroufe, L. A. (1977). Wariness of strangers and the study of infant development. *Child Development, 48,* 1184–1199.

Stainthrop, R., & Hughes, D. (2004). An illustrative case study of precocious reading ability. *Gifted Child Quarterly, 48*(2), 107–120. doi:10.1037/02786133.24.2.225

Standing, E. M. (1984). *Maria Montessori, her life and work.* New York: New American Library.

Starkey, P., & Cooper, R. (1980). Perception of numbers by human infants. *Science, 210*(4473), 1033–1035.

Starkey, P., Klein, A., & Wakeley, A. (2004). Enhancing young children's mathematical knowledge through a pre-kindergarten mathematics intervention. *Early Childhood Research Quarterly, 19,* 99–120.

Starkey, P., Spelke, E. S., & Gelman, R. (1990). Numerical abstraction by human infants. *Cognition, 36*(2), 97–127.

Steele, C. M. (1997). A threat in the air: How stereotypes shape intellectual identity and performance. *American Psychologist, 52,* 613–629.

Steiner, J. (1977). Facial expressions of the neonate indicating the hedonics of food related chemical stimuli. In J. Weiffenbach (Ed.), *Taste and development: The genesis of sweet preference* (pp. 173–204). Bethesda, MD: National Institute of Health.

Steiner, R. (1965). *The education of the child.* London: Rudolf Steiner Press.

Stern, R. (2006). *Social and emotional learning: What is it? How can we use it to help our children?* Retrieved January 4, 2006, from http://www.aboutourkids.org/aboutour/articles/socialemotional.html

Stipek, D., Recchia, S., & McClintic, S. (1992). Self-evaluation in young children. *Monographs of the Society for Research in Child Development, 57*(1, Serial No. 226).

St. Pierre, R. G., Ricciuti, A. E., & Rimdzius, T. A. (2005). Effects of a family literacy program on low-literate children and their parents: Findings from an evaluation of the Even Start Family Literacy Program. *Developmental Psychology, 41*(6), 953–970.

St. Pierre, R. G., Ricciuti, A. E., Tao, F., Creps, C., Swartz, J., Lee, W., . . . Rimdzius, T. (2003). *Third national Even Start evaluation: Program impact and implications for improvement.* Washington, DC: U.S. Department of Education. Retrieved from http://www2.ed.gov/rschstat/eval/disadv/evenstartthird/toc.pdf

Strain, P. S., & Odom, S. L. (1986). Peer social initiations: Effective intervention for social skills development of exceptional children. *Exceptional Children, 52,* 543–551.

Strazdins, L., Clements, M. S., Korda, R. J., Broom, D. H., & D'Souza, R. M. (2006). Unsociable work? Nonstandard work schedules, family relationships, and children's well-being. *Journal of Marriage and the Family, 68,* 394–410.

Suh, J. M. (2010). Tech-knowledge & diverse learners. *Mathematics Teaching in the Middle School, 15*(8), 440–447.

Sullivan, M. W., Lewis, M., & Alessandri, S. M. (1992). Cross-age stability in emotional expressions during learning and extinction. *Developmental Psychology, 28,* 58–63.

Sulzby, E., & Teale, W. (1991). Emergent literacy. In R. Barr, M. Kamil, P. Mosenthal, & P. Pearson (Eds.), *Handbook of reading research* (Vol. 2, pp. 82–97). New York: Longman.

Sun, K., Lin, Y., & Yu, C. (2008). A study on learning effect among different learning styles in a web-based lab of science for elementary school students. *Computers & Education, 50*(4), 1411–1422.

Swartz, E. (1996). *Playing and thinking: How the kindergarten provides the basis for scientific understanding.* Retrieved from http//www.bobnancy.com/ (link to Waldorf Resources, then to In the Classroom).

Swick, K. (1991). *Perspectives on understanding and working with families.* Champaign, IL: Stipes.

Swick, K. J., Boutte, G., & Van Scoy, I. (1994). Multicultural learning through family involvement. *Dimensions of Early Childhood, 22*(4), 17–21.

Swiniarski, L. (1991). Toys: Universals for teaching global education. *Childhood Education, 67*(3), 161–163.

Talley, P. C. (1979). Evaluating the effects of implementing the system of multicultural pluristic assessment. *School Psychology Digest, 8*(1), 71–80.

Tao, L., & Healy, A. F. (1996). Cognitive strategies in discourse processing: A comparison of Chinese and English speakers. *Journal of Psycholinguistic Research, 25,* 597–616.

Tao, L., & Healy, A. F. (2002). The unitization effect in reading Chinese and English text. *Scientific Studies of Reading, 6*(2), 167–197.

Tasker, F. (2005). Lesbian mothers, gay fathers, and their children: A review. *Developmental and Behavioral Pediatrics, 26,* 224–240.

Taylor, A. S., Peterson, C. A., McMurray-Schwarz, P., & Guillou, T. S. (2002). Social skills interventions: Not just for children with special needs. *Young Exceptional Children, 5,* 19–26.

Teglasi, H. (1995). *Assessment of temperament* (Report No. EDO-CG-95-15). Washington, DC: Office of Educational Research and Improvement (ERIC Document Reproduction Service No. EDD00036).

Teplin, S. (1995). Visual impairment in infants and young children. *Infants and Young Children, 8,* 18–51.

Tesman, J. R., & Hills, A. (1994). Developmental effects of lead exposure in children. *Social Policy Report of the Society for Research in Child Development, 8*(3), 1–16.

Texas Child Care. (2002, Fall). Making marks: Art development in young children. *Texas Child Care, 26*(2), 24–32.

Thelen, E. (1995). Motor development: A new synthesis. *American Psychologist, 50,* 79–95.

Thomas, A., & Chess, S. (1969). *Temperament and development.* New York: New York University Press.

Thomas, A., & Chess, S. (1977). *Temperament and development.* New York: Brunner/Mazel.

Thomas, M. K., Barab, S. A., & Tuzun, H. (2009). Developing critical implementations of technology-rich innovations: A cross-case study of the implementation of Quest Atlantis. *Journal of Educational Computing Research, 41*(2), 125–153.

Thomas, R. M. (2000). *Comparing theories of child development, 5th edition.* Belmont, CA: Wadsworth.

Thompson, A. B. (1984). The relationships of thecher's conceptions of mathematics and mathematics teaching to instructional practice. Educational Studies in Mathematics. Vol. 15(2) p. 105–127.

Thompson, R. A., & Raikes, H. A. (2003). Toward the next quarter-century: Conceptual and methodological challenges for attachment theory. *Development & Psychopathology, 15,* 691–718.

Thompson, R. W., & Hixson, P. K. (1984). Teaching parents to encourage independent problem solving in preschool-age children. *Language, Speech, and Hearing Services in Schools, 15*(3), 175–181.

Thompson, S. K. (1975). Gender labels and early sex-role development. *Child Development, 46,* 339–347.

Tizard, B. (1981). Language at home and at school. In C. B. Cazden (Ed.), *Language in early childhood education* (pp. 17–28). Washington, DC: National Association for the Education of Young Children.

Tizard, B., & Hughes, M. (1984). *Young children learning.* Cambridge, MA: Harvard University Press.

Tolan, P. H., Gorman-Smith, D., & Henry, D. B. (2003). The developmental ecology of urban males' youth violence. *Developmental Psychology, 39,* 274–291.

Torquati, J. C., Raikes, H., & Huddleston-Casas, C. A. (2007). Teacher education, motivation, compensation, workplace support, and links to quality of center-based child care and teachers' intention to stay in the early childhood profession. *Early Childhood Research Quarterly, 22,* 261–275.

Trawick-Smith, J. (2006). *Early childhood development: A multicultural perspective.* Upper Saddle River, NJ: Merrill/Prentice Hall.

Twardosz, S., Cataldo, M. F., & Risley, T. R. (1974). An open environment design for infants and toddler day care. *Journal of Applied Behavior Analysis, 7*(4), 529–546.

U.S. Access Board. (2008). *The Americans with Disabilities Act of 2008.* Retrieved from http://access-board.gov/about/laws/ada-amendments.htm

U.S. Bureau of Labor Statistics. (2000). *Career guide to industries: Child care services.* Retrieved from stats.bls.gov/

U.S. Census Bureau. (2010). *Statistical abstract of the United States* (129th ed.). Washington, DC: U.S. Government Printing Office.

U.S. Census Bureau. (2011). *Statistical abstract of the United States* (130th ed.). Washington, DC: U.S. Government Printing Office.

U.S. Department of Agriculture & U.S. Department of Health and Human Services. (2000). *Dietary guidelines for Americans* (5th ed.). USDA Home and Garden Bulletin No. 232. Washington, DC: U.S. Department of Agriculture.

U.S. Department of Education. (2000). *Twenty-second annual report to Congress on implementation of the Individuals with Disabilities Education Act.* Washington, DC: Author.

U.S. Department of Education. (2001). *Fact sheet on the major provisions of the conference report to H.R.I., the No Child Left Behind Act.* Retrieved from http://www.ed.gov/nclb/overview/intro/factsheet.html

U.S. Department of Education. (2002). *Good start, grow smart: The Bush administration's early childhood initiative.* Washington, DC: Government Printing Office.

U.S. Department of Education. (2005). *Thirty years of progress in educating children with disabilities through IDEA.* Retrieved from http://www2.ed.gov/policy/speced/leg/idea/history30.html

U.S. Department of Education. (2006). *Assistive Technology Act: Annual report to Congress: Fiscal years 2004–2005.* Retrieved from http://ed.gov/about/reports/annuals/rsa/atsg/2004/index.html

U.S. Department of Education. (2007). *A 25 year history of the IDEA.* Retrieved from http://www2.ed.gov/policy/speced/leg/idea/history.html

U.S. Department of Education. (2010a). *Meeting the needs of English learners and other diverse learners.* Retrieved from http://www2.ed.gov/policy/elsec/leg/blueprint/english-learners-diverse-learners.pdf

U.S. Department of Education. (2010b). *Report of children and students served under IDEA, Part B, in the U.S. and outlying areas, by age and disability category.* Data file, Office of Special Education Programs, Data Analysis System. Retrieved from http://www.ideadata.org/populationdata.asp

U.S. Department of Education. (2011). *Race to the Top fund.* Retrieved from http://www2.ed.gov/programs/racetothetop/index.htm

U.S. Department of Education. (2012a). *ESEA flexibility.* Retrieved from http://www.ed.gov/esea/flexibility

U.S. Department of Education. (2012b). *History of Indian education.* Retrieved from http://www2.ed.gov/about/offices/list/oese/oie/history.html

U.S. Department of Health and Human Services. (2006). *Good Start, Grow Smart: A guide to Good Start, Grow Smart and other federal early learning initiatives.* Retrieved from http://www.acf.hhs.gov/programs/occ/initiatives/gsgs/fedpubs/GSGSBooklet.pdf

U.S. Department of Health and Human Services. (2008). *The Head Start Act.* Retrieved from http://eclkc.ohs.acf.hhs.gov/hslc/standards/Head%20Start%20Act

U.S. Department of Health and Human Services. (2012). *Child care and development fund.* Retrieved from http://www.hhs.gov/

U.S. Department of Health and Human Services Head Start Bureau. (2003). *National reporting system.* Washington, DC: Author.

U.S. Department of Health and Human Services Office of Head Start. (2010). *Head Start program fact sheet.* Retrieved from http://www.acf.hhs.gov/

U.S. Department of Health, Education, and Welfare Office of Education. (1969). *History of Title I ESEA.* Retrieved from http://www.eric.ed.gov/

U.S. Senate Committee on Health Education Labor and Pensions. (2011). HELP committee approves bipartisan bill to fix No Child Left Behind. Retrieved from http://www.help.senate.gov/newsroom/press/release/?id=9b968366-140f-4b60-a568-2f6efa48877c&groups=Chair

Valero, A. (2002). *Emergent literacy development among Latino students in a rural preschool classroom.* Unpublished doctoral dissertation, University of California, Davis.

Vance, M., & Boals, B. (1989). *The discrepancy between elementary principals and kindergarten teachers' view @ the content and procedures which constitute a kindergarten program* (ERIC Document Reproduction Service No. ED314166).

Vandell, D., & Mueller, E. (1980). Peer play and friendships during the first two years. In H. Foot, A. Chapman, & J. Smith (Eds.), *Friendship and social relations in children* (pp. 181–208). New York: Wiley.

Van Hoorn, J., Nourot, P. M., Scales, B., & Alward, K. R. (2007). *Play at the center of the curriculum.* Upper Saddle River, NJ: Pearson Education.

Varendi, H., Porter, R. H., & Weinberg, J. (1997). Natural odor preferences of newborns change over time. *Acta Pediatrica, 86,* 985–990.

Vartuli, S. (1987). *Family day care provider training and assessment.* Paper presented at the biennial meeting of the Society for Research in Child Development, Kansas City, MO.

Vaughn, B. E., Lefever, G. B., Seifer, R., & Barglow, P. (1989). Attachment behavior, attachment security, and temperament during infancy. *Child Development, 60,* 728–737.

Vaughn, B. E., Stevenson-Hinde, J., Waters, E., Kotsaftis, A., Lefever, G. B., Shouldice, A., . . . Belsky J. (1992). Attachment security and temperament in infancy and early childhood: Some conceptual clarifications. *Developmental Psychology, 28,* 463–473.

Vickerius, M., & Sandberg, A. (2006). The significance of play and the environment around play. *Early Child Development and Care, 176*(2), 207–217.

Vinovskis, M. A. (2005). *The birth of Head Start: Preschool education in the Kennedy and Johnson administrations.* Chicago: University of Chicago Press.

Von Hofsten, C. (1984). Developmental changes in the organization of prereaching movements. Developmental Psychology Vol. 20, p. 378–388.

Von Hofsten, C. (1982). Eye-hand co-ordination in the newborn. *Developmental Psychology, 18,* 450–461.

Vosniadu, S. (1987). Children and metaphors. *Child Development, 58,* 870–895.

Vosniadou, S. and Brewer, W. F. (1987). Theories of knowledge restructuring in development. Review of Educational Research 57(1), 51–67.

Vygotsky, L. S. (1962). *Thought and language* (E. Haufmann & G. Vakar, Eds. & Trans.). Cambridge, MA: MIT Press. (Original work published 1934)

Vygotsky, L. S. (1967). Play and its role in the mental development of the child. *Soviet Psychology, 12,* 62–76.

Vygotsky, L. S. (1978). *Mind in society: The development of higher mental processes* (M. Cole, V. John-Steiner, S. Scribner, & E. Souberman, Eds.). Cambridge, MA: Harvard University Press. (Original work published 1930, 1933, 1935)

Vygotsky, L. S. (1994). *Thought and language* (Rev. ed., Trans. Alex Kozulin). Cambridge, MA: MIT Press.

Wade, C., & Travis, C. (1990). *Psychology* (2nd ed.). New York: Harper & Row.

Wade, C., & Travis, C. (2008). *Psychology* (9th ed.). Upper Saddle River, NJ: Prentice Hall.

Wallach, F. (1999). A playground safety update. *Parks & Recreation, 33,* 95–99.

Wartner, U. G., Grossman, K., Fremmer-Bombik, E., & Suess, G. (1994). Attachment patterns at age six in South Germany: Predictability from infancy and implications for preschool behavior. *Child Development, 65,* 1014–1027.

Wasserman, S. (1992). Serious play in the classroom- How messing around can win you the Nobel Prize. *Childhood Education, 68,*(3), 133–139.

Wasserman, S. (2000). *Serious players in the primary classroom: Empowering children through active learning experiences* (2nd ed.). New York: Teachers College Press.

Watson, J. B. (1913). Psychology as the behaviorist views it. *Psychological Review, 20,* 158–177.

Watts, H. (2000). *What is special about the kindergarten in Auroville? A comparative study of childhood education in Montessori, Waldorf, Progressive Schools and Auroville.* The Sri Aurobindo International Institute for Educational Research. Retrieved from www.auroville.org/education/avschools/kindergarten/kindergarten_ch2.htm

Weber, E. (1984). *Ideas influencing early childhood education.* New York: Teachers College Press.

Webster-Stratton, C. (2000, June). The incredible years training series. *Juvenile Justice Bulletin,* pp. 1–23.

Wechsler, D. (2002). *Wechsler Preschool and Primary Scale of Intelligence (WPPSI).* New York: Psychological Corporation.

Wechsler, D. (2003). *Wechsler Intelligence Scale for Children* (4th ed.). New York: Psychological Corporation.

Wehman, P., & Abramson, M. (1976). Three theoretical approaches to play. *The American Journal of Occupational Therapy, 30*(9), 551–559.

Weikart, D., Rogers, L., Adcock, C., & McClelland, D. (1971). *The cognitively oriented curriculum.* Washington, DC: National Association for the Education of Young Children.

Weinraub, M., & Lewis, M. (1977). The determinants of children's responses to separation. *Monographs of the Society for Research in Child Development, 42*(4, Serial No. 172).

Weinstein, C. S. (1979). The physical environment of the school: A review of the research. *Review of Educational Research, 49,* 557–610.

Weishaar, M. K. (2001). The regular educator's role in the Individual Education Plan. *Clearing House, 75*(2), 96–98.

Weiss, H., & Stephen, N. (2009). *From periphery to center: A new vision for family, school, and community partnerships.* Cambridge, MA: Harvard Family Research Project. Retrieved from http://www.hfrp.org/family-involvement/informing-family-engagement-policy#policybriefs

Welch-Ross, M. K., & Schmidt, C. R. (1996). Gender-schema development and children's constructive story memory: Evidence for a developmental method. *Child Development, 67,* 820–835.

Wellhousen, K. (2002). *Outdoor play every day: Innovative play concepts for early childhood.* Albany, NY: Delmar.

Wellman, H. M., Phillips, A. T., & Rodriguez, T. (2000). Young children's understanding of perception, desire, and emotion. *Child Development, 67,* 768–788.

Werner, E. E., & Johnson, J. L. (1999). Can we apply resilience? In M. D. Glantz, J. L. Johnson, & L. Huffman (Eds.), *Resilience and development: Positive life adaptations* (pp. 259–268). New York: Plenum Press.

Werner, E. E., & Smith, R. S. (2001). *Journeys from childhood to midlife: Risk, resilience, and recovery.* New York: Cornell University Press.

Werner, J., & Van Den Bos, G. (1993). Developmental psychoacoustics: What infants and children hear. *Hospital and Community Psychology, 44,* 624–626.

Wesley, P. W., & Buysse, V. (2003). Making meanings of school readiness in schools and communities. *Early Childhood Research Quarterly, 18,* 351–375.

Westby, C. E., Dominguez, M. S., & Oetter, P. (1996). A performance/competence model of observational assessment. *Language, Speech, and Hearing Services in Schools, 27*(2), 144–156.

Westman, J. (1994). *Licensing parents: Can we prevent parental abuse and neglect?* New York: Plenum.

Westmoreland, H., Rosenberg, M., Lopez, M. E., & Weiss, H. (2009). *Seeing is believing: Promising practices for how school districts promote family engagement.* Cambridge, MA: Harvard Family Research Project. Retrieved from http://www.hfrp.org/family-involvement/informing-family-engagement-policy#policybriefs

Whaley, K. (1990). The emergence of social play in infancy: A proposed developmental sequence of infant-adult play. *Early Childhood Research Quarterly, 5,* 347–358.

Whaley, K., & Rubenstein, T. (1994). How toddlers "do" friendship: A descriptive analysis of naturally occurring friendships in a group child care setting. *Journal of Social and Personal Relationships, 11,* 383–400.

White, B. (1975). *The first three years of life.* Englewood Cliffs, NJ: Prentice Hall.

White, L. A., & Dillingham, B. (1973). *The concept of culture.* Minneapolis: Burgess.

Whitebook, M., Sakai, L., Gerber, E., & Howes, C. (2001). *Then & now: Changes in child care staffing, 1994–2000.* Washington, DC: Center for the Child Care Workforce.

Whiting, B. B., & Edwards, C. P. (1988). *Children of different worlds: The formation of social behavior.* Cambridge, MA: Harvard University Press.

Willatts, P. (1999). Development of means-end behavior in young infants: Pulling a support to retrieve a distant object. *Developmental Psychology, 35,* 651–667.

Williams, J., & Best, D. (1990). *Sex and psych: Gender and self viewed cross-culturally.* Newbury Park, CA: Sage.

Williams, K. (2001). Understanding the student with Asperger syndrome: Guidelines for teachers. *Intervention in School and Clinic, 36,* 287–292.

Williams, M. (1983). *Perceptual and motor development.* Englewood Cliffs, NJ: Prentice Hall.

Williams, R. (1972, September). *Black intelligence test of cultural homogeneity.* American Psychological Association Convention, Honolulu, Hawaii.

Willis, E. A., & Ricciuti, H. N. (1974). *Longitudinal observations of infants' daily arrivals at a day care center.* Tech. report: Cornell research program in early development and education. Ithaca, NY: Cornell University.

Winzer, M. A. (1986). Early development in special education: Some aspects of enlightenment thought. *Remedial and Special Education, 7,* 42–49.

Winzer, M. A. (1993). *The history of special education: From isolation to integration.* Washington, DC: Gallaudet University Press.

Witherington, D. C., Campos, J. J., & Herenstein, M. J. (2001). Principles of emotion and its development in infancy. In G. Bremner & A. Fogel (Eds.), *Blackwell handbook of infant development* (pp. 427–464). Malden, MA: Blackwell.

Wolery, M., & Wilbers, J. (1994). *Including children with special needs in early childhood programs.* Washington, DC: National Association for the Education of Young Children.

Wolfe, L. (2002) *Learning for the past: Historical voices in early childhood education,* 2nd ed. Mayerthorpe, Alberta, Canada: Piney Branch Press.

Wolff, M., Rutten, P., & Bayer, A. F., III. (1992). *Where we stand: Can Americans make it in the race for health, wealth, and happiness?* New York: Bantam Books.

Wolff, P. (1966). The causes, controls, and organization of behavior in the neonate. *Psychological Issues, 5*(1, Whole No. 17), 7–11.

Wolfinger, D. (1994). *Science and mathematics in early childhood education.* New York: HarperCollins.

Wong-Fillmore, L., & Snow, C. (2000). *What teachers need to know about language: Research report.* Washington, DC: Center for Applied Linguistics.

Wood, B. S. (1976). *Children and communication: Verbal and nonverbal language development.* Englewood Cliffs, NJ: Prentice-Hall.

Wood, D. J., Bruner, J. S., & Ross, G. (1976). The role of tutoring in problem solving. *Journal of Child Psychology and Psychiatry, 17,* 89–100.

Working Group on ELL Policy. (2010). *Improving educational outcomes for English language learners: Recommendations for the reauthorization of the Elementary and Secondary Education Act.* Retrieved from http://www.cal.org/topics/ell/ELL-Working-Group-ESEA.pdf

Wortham, S. C. (2005). *Tests and measurement in early childhood education* (4th ed.). Columbus, OH: Merrill.

Yaden, D., Rowe, D., & MacGillivray, L. (2000). Emergent literacy: A polyphony of perspectives. In M. Kamil, P. Mosenthal, P. Pearson, & R. Barr (Eds.), *Handbook of reading research* (Vol. III, pp. 425–454). Mahwah, NJ: Erlbaum.

York, S. (2003). *Roots and wings: Affirming culture in early childhood programs.* St. Paul, MN: Redleaf Press.

Yu, A., & Bain, B. (1980). *Language, class and cultural implications on the first and second language acquisition: A cross-cultural* study of cognitive consequences. Paper presented at the Los Angeles Second Language Research Forum.

Yugar, J. M., & Shapiro, E. S. (1996). *Friendship and friendship quality in preschool: Development of a measure.* Unpublished manuscript. Bethlehem, PA: Lehigh University.

Yugar, J. M., & Shapiro, E. S. (2001). Elementary children's school friendship: A comparison of peer assessment methodologies. *School Psychology Review, 30*(4), 568–585.

Zacharos, K., Koliopoulos, D., Dokimaki, M., & Kassoumi, H. (2007). Views of prospective early childhood education teachers, towards mathematics and its instruction. *European Journal of Teacher Education, 30*(3), 305–318.

Zeanah, P., Nagle, G., Stafford, B., Rice, T., & Farrer, J. (2005). *Addressing socio-emotional development and infant mental health in early childhood systems: Executive summary.* Los Angeles, CA: UCLA Center for Healthier Children, Families, and Communities.

Zero to Three. (2010). *Parenting infants and toddlers today: Tuning in to Dad: Key findings from a 2009 parent study, 30.* Retrieved from http://www.zerotothree.org/about-us/funded-projects/parenting-resources/keyfindings_hr.pdf

Zero to Three National Center for Infants, Toddlers, and Families. (2008). *Early learning guidelines for infants and toddlers.* Retrieved from http://zerotothree.org/

Zhou, Q., Eisenberg, N., Losoya, S. H., Fabes, R. A., Reiser, M., Guthrie, I. K., . . . Shepard, S. A. (2002). The relations of parental warmth and positive expressiveness to children's empathy-related responding and social functioning: A longitudinal study. *Child Development, 73,* 893–915.

Zigler, G., Gilliam, W. S., & Barnett, W. S. (2011). *The pre-k debates: Current controversies and issues.* Baltimore, MD; Paul H. Brookes Publishing Co.

Zigler, E., & Styfco, S. J. (2004). *The Head Start debates.* Baltimore: Paul H. Brookes.

Zimmerman, B. J. & Schunk, D. H. (2003). *Educational psychology: A century of contributions.* (2003). New York, NY: Routledge.

Zucker, T. A., Moody, A. K., & McKenna, M. C. (2009). The effects of electronic books on pre-kindergarten-to-grade 5 students: A research synthesis. *Journal of Educational Computing Research, 40*(1), 47–87.

Photo Credits

Chapter 1

Photo, chapter opener, page 2. © istockphotos.com/ Rich Legg.
Photo, page 5. © istockphotos.com/ meshaphoto.
Photo, page 8. © istockphotos.com/fatihhoca.
Photo, page 12. © istockphotos.com/jo unruh.
Photo, page 14. ©
Photo, page 16. © Digital vision/ thinkstock.
Photo, page 22. © istockphotos.com/ Dean Mitchell.

Chapter 2

Photo, chapter opener, page 28. © Getty Images.
Photo, page 32. Wikimedia.
Photo, page 33. Wikimedia.
Photo, page 36. © istockphotos.com/ Ralf Hettler.
Photos, Figure 2.1, page 39. © Courtesy of Red Hen LLC.
Photo, page 40. © Getty Images.
Photo, page 44. © Photo by Eva Watson-Schutze.

Chapter 3

Photo, chapter opener, page 56. © istockphotos
.com/ Christopher Futcher
Photos, page 58, top. © istockphotos.com/ Elena Schweitzer
Photos, page 58, bottom. © istockphotos.com/ Elena Schweitzer
Photo, page 59. © istockphotos.com/Jeffrey Hochstrasser
Photo, page 61. © istockphotos.com/Catherine Yuelet
Photo, page 63. © istockphotos.com/matka_Wariatka
Photo, page 64. © istockphotos.com/ omgimages
Photo, page 66. © istockphotos.com/ Piotr Kwiatkowski

Chapter 4

Photo, chapter opener, page 80. © istockphotos
.com/ Christopher Futcher.
Photo, page 83. © Wikipedia.
Photo, page 85. © Thinkstock/Comstock/thinkstock.
Photo, page 87. © Jupiterimages/creates/thinkstock.
Photo, page 88. © Bettmann/CORBIS.
Photo, page 92, left. © Altrendo images/ stockbyte/ thinkstock.
Photos, page 92, middle. © Jupiter images/ photos
.com/ thinkstock.
Photos, page 92, right. © Comstock Images/ Comstock/
Thinkstock.
Photo, page 94. © istockphotos.com/ Kris Hanke.
Photo, page 95. © Getty images/ liquid library/ thinkstock.
Photo, page 98. © Wikipedia.
Photo, page 100. © Steve Mason/ Photo Disc/ Thinkstock.
Photo, page 101. © AP Photo/ Urie Bronfenbrenner.
Photo, page 103. © Ted Streshinsky/ CORBIS.
Photo, page 104. © Ann Kaplan/ CORBIS .

Photo, page 105. © Photodisc/ Thinkstock.
Photo, page 107. © Bettmann/CORBIS.

Chapter 5

Photo, chapter opener, page 112. © Comstock Images/
Comstock/Thinkstock.
Photo, page 119. © istockphotos.com/xefstock.
Photo, page 123. © istockphotos.com/ Christopher Futcher.
Photo, page 124. © Jupiterimages/liquidlibrary/Thinkstock.
Photo, page 130, top. © istockphotos.com/ Nicky Gordon.
Photo, page 130, bottom. © istockphotos.com/ Mark Bowden.
Photo, page 131. © istockphotos.com/ Derek Latta.
Photo, page 134. © © Jupiterimages/Brand X Pictures/ Thinkstock.
Photo, page 136. © istockphotos.com / Andres Balcazar.

Chapter 6

Photo, chapter opener, page 140. © istockphotos
.com/ fatihhoca.
Photo, page 142. © istockphotos.com/Moddboardimages.
Photo, page 148. © istockphotos.com/jo unruh.
Photo, page 151. © istockphotos.com/MBI Images.
Photo, page 154. © Stockbyte/stockbyte/thinkstock.
Photo, page 160. © Comstock Images/Comstock/Thinkstock.

Chapter 7

Photo, chapter opener, page 168. © istockphotos
.com/ Kim Gunkel.
Photo, page 171. © Stockbyte/stockbyte/ thinkstock.
Photo, page 174. © istockphotos.com/Kim Gunkel.
Photo, page 181. © istockphotos.com/Catherine Yuelet.
Photo, page 183. © istockphotos.com/ Christopher Futcher.
Photo, page 187. © istockphotos.com/Rich Legg.
Photo, page 188. © Tony Kurdzuk/Star Ledger/Corbis.
Photo, page 189. © Author.
Photo, page 191, top. © Author.
Photo, page 191, bottom. © Author.

Chapter 8

Photo, chapter opener, page 204. © istockphotos
.com/blend_images.
Photo, page 206. © istockphotos.com/Kim Gunkel.
Photo, page 210. © Creatas/thinkstock.
Image, page 211. © Courtesy of Barefoot Books.
Photo, page 215. © Courtesy of Karen Arrington, Lower School Technology Specialist, Trinity Valley School TX.
Photo, page 221. © istockphotos.com/Erna Vader.

Chapter 9

Photo, chapter opener, page 230. © istockphotos
.com/ jo unruh.

Photo, page 233. © istockphotos.com / Kai Chiang.

Photo, page 234. © Jupiterimages/Comstock/thinkstock.

Photo, page 235. © istockphotos.com/ SciencePhotoLibrary.

Photo, page 236. © istockphotos.com/ Charles Mann.

Photo, page 237. © stockcredits.com/ strods.

Photo, page 241. © stockcredits.com/ Olga Usikova.

Photo, page 244. © Zedcor Wholly Owned/ photoobjects.net/ thinkstock.

Photo, page 246. © istockcredits.com/ Blend_Images.

Photo, page 248. © istockcredits.com/Stephanie Horrocks.

Photo, page 249. © Comstock images/ thinkstock.

Chapter 10

Photo, chapter opener, page 256. © istockphotos
.com/SergiyN.

Photo, page 267. ©

Photo, page 269. © iStockphoto.com/Ana Blazic.

Photo, page 270. © istockphoto.com/xefstock.

Photo, page 272. © istockphoto.com/xefstock.

Photo, page 274. © istockphoto.com/Gary Sludden.

Photo, page 277. © istockphotos.com/Moodboard_Images.

Chapter 11

Photo, chapter opener, page 286. © istockphotos
.com/ kali9.

Photo, page 289. © istockphotos.com/ arthor carlo fraco.

Photo, page 291. © Bananastock/thinkstock

Photo, page 291. © Bananastock/thinkstock.

Photo, page 291. © George Doyle/ stockbyte/ thinkstock.

Photo, page 292. © Digital Vision/ Thinkstock.

Photo, page 293. © istockphotos.com/ Hongqi Zhang.

Photo, page 296. © Bananastock/thinkstock.

Photo, page 305 © istockphotos.com/ Kim Gunkel

Photo, left, page 306. © Comstock/thinkstock.

Photo, right, page 306. © istock photos.com/ Monique Heydenrych.

Photo, page 307. © istockphotos.com/ Nataliia Sdobnikova.

Photo, page 310. ©

Chapter 12

Photo, chapter opener, page 318. © istockphotos
.com/ Catherine Yuelet.

Photo, page 320. © Comstock/thinkstock.

Photo, page 325. © istockphotos.com/ Marcela Barsse.

Photo, page 328. © istockphotos.com.

Photo, page 331. © istockphotos.com/ LifesizeImages.

Photo, page 332. © istockphotos.com/ Zsolt Biczo.

Photo, page 335. © istockphotos.com/ Ferran Traite Soler.

Chapter 13

Photo, chapter opener, page 344. © Istockphotos
.com/ xefstock.

Photo, page 349. Istockphotos.com/ fatihhoca.

Photo, page 350. Thinkstock/ Ryan Mcvay/ Lifesize.

Photo, page 351. Istockphotos.com/ Robert Dant.

Photo, page 353. istockphotos.com/ Maartje Van Caspel.

Photo, page 358. istockphotos.com/Sean Locke.

Chapter 14

Photo, chapter opener, page 368. © istockphotos
.com/Pavel Losevsky.

Photo, page 371, top. © istockphotos.com/fauk74.

Photo, page 371, bottom. © Jupiterinages/polka dot/ thinkstock.

Photo, page 372© Jupiterinages/polka dot/thinkstock.

Photo, page 377. © istockphotos.com/ sean locke.

Photo, page 378. © istockphotos.com/bradley mason.

Photo, page 382. © Comstock/thinkstock.

Photo, page 383. © Creates images/thinkstock.

Photo, page 385. © Ryan Mcvay/
photodisc/thinkstock.

Chapter 15

Photo, chapter opener, page 392. © altrendo images/
Stockbyte/Thinkstock.

Photo, page 395, left. © Creates/thinkstock.

Photo, page 395, right, top. © istockphotos.com/ Dean Mitchell.

Photo, page 395, right, bottom. © Jupiterimages/ Brand X Pictures/ Thinkstock.

Photo, page 397. © istockphotos.com/ Petro Feketa.

Photo, page 399. © istockphotos.com/
Nathan Gleave.

Photo, page 404. © Bananastock/thinkstock.

Photo, page 406. © istockphotos.com/Catherine Yeulet.

Photo, page 407. © istockphotos.com/ Tatiana Gladskikh.

Photo, page 409. © Jupiterimages/Comstock/ thinkstock.

Photo, page 410. ©stockphotos.com/ HultonArchive.

Photo, page 413. © istockphotos.com/
Juanmonino.

Chapter 16

Photo, chapter opener, page 322. © istockphotos
.com/ Mark Bowden.

Photo, page 426. © Jupiterimages/ creates/ thinkstock.

Photo, page 428. © Los Angeles County
Office of Education.

Photo, page 434. ©.Author.

Photo, page 435. © thinkstock/ Ryan Mcvay.

Photo, page 437. © istockphotos.com/ Blend_Images.

Photo, page 443. © istockphotos.com/ jo unruh.

Author Index

Aber, J. L., 299
Aboud, F., 215
Abraham, C., 240
Abramson, M., 276
Ackerman, D., 437
Adams, E. J., 290
Adams, M., 407
Adcock, C., 62
Adesso, V. J., 151, 154
Adkinson, C., 116
Adler, S. A., 207
Akhtar, N., 321
Alessandri, S. M., 290
Aligne, C. A., 381
Allen, J., 258, 267–268, 272
Allen, K. E., 371–372
Allen, S., 232
Almquist-Parks, L., 134
Almy, M., 273–274
Alward, K. R., 267–268
Amsden, D., 9, 434
Anderson, A. H., 128
Angold, A., 385
Antler, J., 44–45
Archer, P., 117–119
Aries, Phillippe, 31
Arterberry, M. E., 97
Artiles, A., 174–175
Asher, S., 134
Aubrey, C., 358
Auer, J. C. P., 326
Auerbach, C. F., 408
August, D., 430
Aumann, K., 406
Aunio, P., 358
Avant, M., 357
Azmitia, M., 296

Bacon, M. K., 218
Bagdi, A., 371
Bagnato, S. J., 153
Bagwell, C. L., 134
Bahrick, L., 122
Bain, B., 98
Baker, C., 326
Bakhurst, D., 50
Baldwin Dancy, R., 14
Bandura, A., 235, 305
Banks, J. A., 209, 212
Banks, M., 121
Barab, S. A., 357

Barber, L. W., 219
Barbour, A. C., 337
Barker, L. E., 373, 379
Barnett, W. S., 431, 437–439
Barnett, W. S., 31
Baroody, A. J., 348
Barrera, M. E., 348
Barry, H., 218
Barton, E. E., 183
Baruth, L. G., 213
Bates, J. E., 297, 303
Bateson, G., 276
Baumrind, D., 294, 400, 416
Beck, J., 185
Behne, T., 93
Behrman, R. E., 69
Bellinger, D., 381
Benjamin, L. T., 47
Bennet, C., 207, 222
Bennett, K., 118
Bentzen, W. R., 144, 146–147
Berenson, G. S., 381
Berg, W., 116
Bergen, D., 271
Berger, K. S., 97, 400, 404–406
Bergin, D. A., 296
Berk, L., 404
Berk, L. E., 96, 100
Berlyne, D. E., 276
Berndt, A. E., 131
Bernstein, B., 324
Bertenthal, B., 118, 121
Best, D., 307
Bezuszka, S. J., 351
Bhanot, R., 357
Bhatia, T., 326
Bialystok, E., 325
Biber, B., 215
Biel, L., 332
Bierman, K. L., 134
Bikart, T. S., 135
Billman, J., 143
Bjorklund, D., 84–88, 96
Blackman-Jones, R., 414
Blair, K. A., 293
Blanchett, W. J., 174
Bloom, L., 290
Boals, B., 258
Bobys, A., 328
Bode, P., 14–15
Boerwinkle, E., 381

Clifford, R. M., 16, 378
Cline, G., 156
Cloud, N., 326–327
Cohen, A. J., 72
Cohen, D.H., 53
Cohen, N. E., 24, 69
Cole, P. M., 296
Coley, R. J., 358
Coltrane, S., 406–407
Conger, R., 407
Connolly, K. J., 259
Conroy, M. A., 246
Conway, J., 68
Cook, N. R., 381
Cook, R. E., 266
Coon, J. A., 291
Cooper, R., 348
Coplan, R. J., 298
Copley, J. V., 355
Copple, C., 153, 332, 413
Corwyn, R. F., 162, 378
Cory-Slechta, D. A., 381
Costello, E. J., 385
Couchenor, D., 398
Couse, L. J., 357
Cox, C., 381
Cratty, B. J., 373
Cremin, L.A., 44
Creps, C., 443
Crick, N. R., 299, 310–311
Critchfield, T. C., 67
Crouter, A. C., 406
Cryer, D., 378
Crystal, D., 325
Cullen, C., 68
Cummins, J., 435
Currie, J., 70
Curtin, L. R., 383
Cutler, J. A., 384

Dalaker, J., 379
Daniels, D. H., 90
Darling-Hammond, L., 206
Datar A., 385
Davey, G., 68
David, J., 64
Davis, A. P., 307
Davis, C. A., 246
Davis, J. A., 356
Davis Holbrook, M., 180
Davis-Kean, P. E., 400
Davy, J., 65
De Groot, A. M. B., 327
De Houwer, A., 325
De Wolff, M. S., 304
Defrain, J., 398
Deiner, P. L., 373
DeKaban, A., 114
DeKeyser, R., 326

Delaney, P. A., 244
DeMott, K., 9, 434
Denham, S. A., 293
Dennis, J., 407
Derman-Sparks, L., 211, 223
DeVore, S., 187
DeVries, R., 61, 87, 266
Dewey, J., 86
Dewsbury, D., 47
Dickinson, D., 328
DiFranza, J. R., 381
Dillingham, B., 207
Dodd, J. B., 152
Dodge, D. T., 135, 148
Dodge, K. A., 297
Dokimaki, M., 355
Doley, S., 304
Dominguez, M. S., 150
Doods, J., 117–119
Dopyera, J. E., 144
Doster, J. A., 151
Dreikurs, R., 235–236
Driscoll, L. A., 143, 146
D'Souza, R. M., 406
Dunn, L. M., 153, 174
Durand, T. M., 416

Early, D. M., 16
Easton, F., 65
Eccles, J. S., 400
Eckerman, K., 133
Eckstein, A., 327
Edelen-Smith, P., 180
Edelman, N., 117–119
Edge, D., 193
Edgell, D., 114
Edwards, C., 61
Edwards, C. P., 296, 331
Edwards, E., 30–34, 36–41, 45–46, 48, 52–53
Edwards, J. O., 211
Eichenberger-Gilmore, J. M., 379
Eichenofer, M., 7
Eisenberg, N., 293–294, 305
Elardo, R., 324
Eliot, L., 120
Elksnin, L. K., 240, 305
Elksnin, N., 240, 305
Elliot, A. J., 106
Ellis, M., 275
Emerson, P. E., 131, 290
Enz, B., 330
Epstein, A. S., 7, 156–158
Epstein, A. S., 5
Epstein, D. J., 437
Erdley, C., 134
Erikson, E. H., 133, 265
Erkanli, A., 385
Ervin, R., 246
Espinosa, L., 435–436

Johnson, S. M., 7
Jolivette, K., 231, 246
Jones, B. D., 8
Jones, K., 246
Jones, S. M., 299
Jordan, P. E., 215
Jung, K., 438–439
Jusczyk, P. W., 126
Jusko, T. A., 381

Kagan, J., 290
Kagan, S. L., 24, 425, 430
Kahn, A. J., 428, 444
Kalbfleisch, M. L., 188
Kamens, M. W., 180
Kamerman, S. B., 428, 444
Kamii, C., 266
Kardos, S. M., 7
Karnes, M. B., 219
Karpf, M. K., 407
Kasser, T., 106
Kassoumi, H., 355
Kaszuba, T., 154
Katz, L. G., 11
Kauffman, D., 7
Kaufman, A. S., 151
Kaufman, N. L., 151
Kawabata, Y., 311
Kearsley, R. B., 290
Keeler, G., 385
Kelemen, D., 85
Keller, H., 85
Kelley, M. L., 131
Kennell, J., 131
Kenney, M. J., 351
Keogh, J., 372–373
Kilgo, J. L., 44
Kilgore, K., 297
Killian, C., 407
Kim, M., 407
Kim, Y., 106
Kim, Y. K., 298
Kim-Cohen, J., 400
King, K., 356
Kirk, S. A., 219
Klahr, D., 97
Klaus, M., 131
Klein, A., 348, 352
Klein, E. J., 136
Klein, M. D., 266
Klein, R., 122
Kliebard, H. M., 63–64
Klieger, A., 356
Knutson Miller, K., 8
Kochanek, K. D., 373
Kochanoff, A., 293
Kochanska, G., 245
Kohlberg, L., 61, 87
Kolb, B., 115
Koliopoulos, D., 355

Koo, A., 400
Korda, R. J., 406
Koren-Karie, N., 304
Kosmitzki, C., 373
Kowalksi, K., 153
Kramer, R., 40
Kranjc, S., 130
Krashen, S. D., 326
Kritchevsky, L., 261
Krogh, S. L., 267
Kroth, R. L., 193
Ku, H. C., 299, 310–311
Kuczmarski, R. J., 372
Kuhn, D., 306
Kuklinski, M. R., 308
Kuntz, S., 156
Kupetz, B., 330, 335

Labov, W., 322
Ladd, G. W., 293
Lahey, B., 151
Laird, R. D., 297
Lalonde, C. E., 126
Lamb, M., 131
Lambert, R., 231
Lambie, D. Z., 219
Lamy, C., 438–439
Lane, H. B., 156
Lane, M., 335
Lanphear, B. P., 381
Lanza, E., 326
Larner, M. B., 69
Lau, B., 10
Laurent, A. C., 308
Lawhon, D. C., 240
Lawhon, T., 240
Lawrence, E. M., 38
Lay-Dopyera, M., 144
Leach, D. J., 12
Lecaunet, J., 121
Lee, W., 443
Lee-Shin, Y., 298
Legerstee, M., 348
Leitschuh, C., 156
Lelwica, M., 291
Lenneberg, E., 323–324
Lentz, C., 297
Lerner, R. M., 398
Lessow-Hurley, J., 327
Lester, B., 126
Levenstein, P., 219
Levin, D. E., 249
LeVine, R., 207
Levy, S. M., 379
Lewin, K., 84
Lewis, C., 215
Lewis, M., 290, 303
Lewis, S., 436
Lewit, E. M., 69
Lewkowicz, D., 122

Li, S., 381
Lickliter, R., 122
Lieberman, A., 206
Ligon, E. M., 219
Lilley, I. M., 38
Lin, Y., 357
Lindberg, L., 332
Lindsey, E., 295
Little, J. W., 206
Liu, E., 7, 356, 384
Liu, F., 356
Liu, Y., 358
Loeber, R., 297
Lollis, S., 133
Long, M., 326
Lopez, M. E., 191
Losen, D. J., 174, 176
Losoya, S. H., 293–294
Loughling, C. E., 261
Luze, G. J., 156
Lykken D. T., 408
Lynch, S. A., 296

Ma, L., 358
Maccoby, E., 131
Maccoby, E. E., 294
MacGillivray, L., 328
Machado, J. M., 320, 323, 336
MacWhinney, B., 97, 323
Magoon, M. A., 67
Main, M., 303
Maiorca, J., 148
Malatesta, C. Z., 131, 290
Malone, D., 8
Mambretti, C., 333
Manderlink, G., 5
Manning, M. L., 213
Manross, M. A., 374
Manz, P. H., 156
Mardell-Czudnowski, C. D., 152
Marjanovic-Umek, L., 130
Markle, S., 67
Markwardt, F. C., Jr., 152
Marotz, L. R., 371–372
Marshall, J., 356
Marshall, T. A., 379
Martin, J. A., 294
Martinez, J., 410, 413
Marzano, R. J., 24
Masciadrelli, B. P., 406
Mash, C., 97
Mashka, P., 117–119
Mason, C. A., 295
Maurer, D., 348
Mavrogenes, N. A., 336
Maxwell-Jolly, J., 7
Mayer, R. E., 337
Maynard, A., 85
McCarthy, D., 152
McClelland, D., 62

McClintic, S., 290
McClure, F., 326
McCullough, J., 151
McCune, L., 274
McCune-Nicolich, L., 274
McCurdy, D. W., 207
McDaniel, T. R., 307
McDermott, P. A., 156
McDonough, S. C., 125
McDowell, D. J., 295, 407
McFarland, L., 232
McGee-Cooper, A., 10
McGoldrick, M., 399–400
McHale, S. M., 406
McKenna, M. C., 356
McKown, C., 308
Mclanahan, S. S., 409
McLeod, B. D., 400
McLoyd, V., 407
McMurray-Schwarz, P., 296
McNeill, D., 323
Mead, G. H., 267–268
Meece, J., 90
Meisel, J. M., 325
Mellon, E., 274
Meltzoff, A., 134
Mendelson, H., 122
Meredith, R., 336
Merrell, K. W., 154–155
Mezei, P. J., 357
Miller, D., 41–43, 47
Minkler, M., 404
Miolo, G., 187
Miranda, N., 8
Mistry, J., 298
Mitchell, A., 64
Mitchell, F., 13
Mitka, M., 379
Mize, J., 295
Moats, L., 328
Mocan, H. N., 72
Moffitt, T. E., 400
Monighan, P., 274
Monighan-Nourot, P., 273–274
Montagu, A., 120
Montague, D. P. F., 291
Montanaro, S., 119
Moody, A. K., 356
Mook, D. G., 67
Moomaw, S., 356
Moore, M., 134
Morgan, J., 400
Morland, J., 215
Morland, J. K., 215
Morrier, M. J., 231, 246
Morrow, L., 334
Moses, L. J., 291
Mosier, C., 298
Mouratidis, A. A., 297
Muckelroy, A., 8

Uro, G., 436
Uzzell, R., 436

Vacca, J., 371
Valero, A., 193
van Balen, F., 403
van den Bloom, D. C., 403
Van Den Bos, G., 121
Van Hell, J. G., 327
Van Hoorn, J., 267–268, 273–274
van Ijzendoorn, M. H., 304
Van Scoy, I., 213
Vance, M., 258
Vandell, D., 134
Vandenberg, B., 273
Varendi, H., 120
Vartuli, S., 258
Vespo, J., 296
Vickerius, M., 258
Vinovskis, M. A., 70
Vosniadu, S., 128
Vukelich, C., 330
Vygotsky, L. S., 98, 233, 266–267,
    276–277, 324, 346

Wade, C., 5
Wagner, S. L., 249
Wakeley, A., 348
Waldfogel, J., 406
Walker-Andrews, A. S., 291
Wallace, L., 407
Wallach, F., 378
Walling, L., 261
Waninger, K. N., 371
Warren, J. J., 379
Wartner, U. G., 303
Wasserman, S., 272, 278
Watson, J. B., 234
Watts, H., 58–59
Weber, E., 31, 34–35, 37, 52, 87, 98, 108
Webster-Stratton, C., 247
Wechsler, D., 153
Wehman, P., 276
Wei, R., 372
Weikart, D., 62–63
Weikart, D. P., 219
Weinberg, J., 120
Weinraub, M., 290
Weinstein, R. S., 308
Weishaar, M. K., 180
Weiss, H., 191–192
Weisz, J. R., 400
Weitzman, M., 381
Welch-Ross, M. K., 307
Wellhousen, K., 262, 265
Wellman, H. M., 291
Werker, J. F., 126
Werner, E. E., 310
Werner, J., 121
Wertheimer, M., 47
West, L., 134

Westby, C. E., 150
Westman, J., 408
Westmoreland, H., 191
Wetherby, A. M., 308
Whaley, K., 131, 134
Whalon, K., 189
Whatley, J., 133
Whelton, P. K., 384
Whishaw, I., 115
White, B., 119
White, L. A., 207
Whitebook, M., 9–10
Whiting, B. B., 296
Wilbers, J., 220–221
Wildman, R. P., 384
Willatts, P., 93
Williams, H. J., 219
Williams, J., 307
Williams, K., 308
Williams, M., 117
Williams, R., 152
Willis, E. A., 258
Willis, L. M., 331
Wilson, W. J., 13
Winsler, A., 96, 100
Winzer, M. A., 171
Witherington, D. C., 290
Wolery, M., 183, 220–221
Wolf, M., 328
Wolfe, L., 52–53
Wolff, M., 116
Wolff, P., 116
Wolfinger, D., 347
Wong-Fillmore, L., 7
Wood, B. S., 321
Wood, D. J., 100
Wood, J. J., 400
Woodruff, D., 222
Wortham, S., 266
Wortham, S. C., 144, 146–148, 161
Worthman, C., 385
Wusinich, N., 291

Yaden, D., 328
Yakobovitch, A., 356
Yannetta, K., 9, 434
Yawkey, T., 271
York, S., 215, 416
Younger, K., 95
Yu, A., 98
Yu, C., 357
Yugar, J. M., 154

Zacharos, K., 355
Zeanah, P., 379
Zelaxo, P. R., 290
Zhou, Q., 293–294
Zigler, E., 104
Zigler, G., 31
Zimmerman, B. J., 48
Zucker, T. A., 356

Subject Index

AAC systems. *See* Augmentative and alternative communication systems

Absorbent mind, 41

Academic achievement gap, 425

Academic degrees

  associate's degree, 17, 19

  master's degree, 18–19

Acceleration, 191

Accommodation (cognitive development theory), 90–92, 276

Accommodation (health impairments), 179

Accountability, 160, 429

Accreditation, 20–21

Action books, 335

Active engagement, 273

Active learning, 62

Active listening, 232, 237, 243

Acts of creation, 4

Adaptation, 90

Adequate yearly progress, 429

Adler, Alfred, 235

Adoptive parents, 403

Advocate role, 12–13

African Americans, 295, 373

Age of Reason, 37

Ages and Stages Questionnaire, 152

Aggression

  physical, 310–311

  relational, 300, 311

  social competence and, 298–299

AIMSweb Standard Reading Assessment Passages, 157

Alert activity stage, 116

Alert inactivity stage, 116

Alternative assessments, 149

American Recovery and Reinvestment Act, 439–440, 442

Americans with Disabilities Act, 173, 179

Ancient educational theorists, 30

Anger, 290, 292

Anthroposophy, 65

Antibias curriculum, 211

Apprenticeship learning, 100

Aries, Philippe, 31

Aristotle, 30

Arithmetic, 349

Arousal modulation theory, of play, 276

Arousal states, 115–116

Art, 331

Art supplies, 260

Asian groups, 13

Assessment(s)

  age of child and, 161

  alternative methods of, 149

  best practices in, 141

  communication with parents and family about, 159–160

  concerns associated with, 158–162

  criterion-referenced, 149

  curriculum-based, 153

  definition of, 142

  description of, 148–149

  domains of, 151–152

  environment considerations, 161–162

  for ethnic minorities, 151–154

  formative, 156

  intelligence-based, 151–153

  intentional teachers' use of, 156

  norm-referenced, 149

  number sense, 156

  observation as method of, 141. *See also* Observation(s)

  performance, 149

  psychometrics of, 158–159

  reading fluency, 156–157

  reliability of, 158–159

  research, 154, 156

  rubrics, 156

  special education referral, 178

  of special-needs children, 136

  teacher's knowledge about, 160

  teaching improvements through, 156–158

  TeamS model, 150

  test bias issues, 160–161

  types of, 149–151

  validity of, 158–159

Assimilation, 90–92, 276

Assistive technologies, 170, 184–186, 192, 357, 373

Assistive Technology Act, 184–185

Associate teacher, 18

Associate's degree, 17, 19

Associative play, 270

Attachment

  assessment of, 301–302

  caregiving characteristics that affect, 302

  definition of, 299

  emotional development and, 131–133

  factors that influence, 303

  insecure-ambivalent, 299–300

  insecure-avoidant, 299

  insecure-disoriented-disorganized, 300–301

to mothers, 294
  secure, 299, 302, 304
  stability of, 303
  strange situation assessment of, 301–302
  temperament and, 302–303
  types of, 299–301
Attachment disorders, 246
Attention, 232, 235
Augmentative and alternative communication
    systems, 185
Authoritarian parenting style, 294–295
Authoritative parenting style, 294–295, 399
Autism
  description of, 170
  statistics regarding, 174–175
Autism spectrum disorders
  characteristics of, 170
  social communication skills development in
      children with, 188–189
Autonomy versus shame and doubt stage, of
    psychosocial development, 47, 103, 105, 133
Aversive stimulation, 67

Babbling stage, 320
"Baby boomer" retirement, 8
Bachelor's degree, 18–19
Balancing, 372
Bank Street College of Education, 44–45
Bank Street model, 63–64
Bank Street School for Children, 63
Basic grammar, 320
Bathroom facilities, 262
Battelle Developmental Inventory, 152, 154
BDI-2. *See* Battelle Developmental Inventory
Beginning chapter books, 335
Behavior(s)
  discussion of, 243
  evoking, 238–239
  ignoring of, 243
  modeling of, 239
  parental involvement in dealing with, 247
  positive attention given to, 242
  prosocial, 238, 240
Behavior expectations, 238
Behavioral competence, 310
Behavioral theorists, 323
Behaviorism
  early childhood programs based on, 66–68
  focus of, 289
  guidance and, 234–235
  history of, 66
  learning as viewed by, 67
  limitations of, 67
  mission of, 66–67
  motivation and, 67–68
  philosophy of, 66–67
  radical, 106
  strengths of, 67
Behaviorist model, of language development, 323

Bilingual Education Act, 427, 434
Bilingual education programs, 427
Bilingualism
  brain development and, 327
  code switching, 326–327
  cognitive development and, 327
  definition of, 325
  in early childhood teachers, 8
  sequential, 326
  simultaneous, 325–326
Binet, Alfred, 41
Binocular vision, 371
Binuclear family, 407
Bioecological systems theory, 101–103, 394–396, 398
Black Intelligence Test of Cultural Homogeneity,
    152, 154
Blocks, 260
Bloom, Benjamin
  description of, 48–49
  taxonomies of, 48–49
Blow, Susan Elizabeth, 52
Blueprint for Reform, 441
Board books, 335
Bodily/kinesthetic intelligence, 190
Books, 129, 334–335
Bowlby, John, 3, 132
Boys
  gender roles, 306–307
  motor development of, 372
  physical development of, 372
  social competence development in, 297
Brain
  information processing by, 125
  language development and, 125–126
Brain development
  bilingualism and, 327
  cognitive development and, 121–122
  emotional development and, 131
  language development and, 125–126
  physical, 114–115
Brigance Diagnostic Inventory of Early
    Development–Revised, 152
Bronfenbrenner, Urie
  bioecological theory of development, 101–103,
      394–396, 398
  Head Start program founding by, 104
  parental involvement, 218
Bruner, Jerome, 49–50, 266
Bullying, 102, 299–300, 310–311
Bureau of Educational Experiments, 44
Burnout, 9–10

California, 18–19, 433
Cambridge Nursery School, 45
Career, teaching as, 8
Case, Robbie, 124
Caste, 213
Center-based child care, 73–74
Centuries of Childhood, 31

Cephalocaudal principle, 370
Certification, Early Childhood/Generalist, 23
Chauvinism, 409
Checklist, 146
Chemistry, 353
Child Care and Development Fund, 442
Child care policies, 439–442
Child care programs
    accreditation of, 20–21
    attachment and, 133
    Child Development Associate credentialing
        requirement for working in, 16–17
    college-affiliated, 72
    demand for, 9
    financing of, 71–72
    history of, 68–69
    licensing requirements for, 19–20, 73–76
    in United States, 68–69
    university-affiliated, 72
Child care settings
    center-based, 73–74
    home-based, 73
Child Care Subsidy Program, 443
Child Development Associate credentialing,
    16–17, 19
Child Find, 176
Child observation record, 63, 152
"Child Outcomes Framework," 24
Child-centered teaching, 45
Childhood obesity, 381, 383–385
Children of color, 215
Children who are gifted and talented
    acceleration for, 191
    communication with parents of, 191
    developmental milestones in, 135–136
    enrichment for, 191
    ethnic minorities underrepresented in, 189
    methods for identifying, 135–136
    parents of, 191
    programs for, 188–191
    as twice exceptional learners, 188
Children with exceptional needs
    assistive technologies for, 184–186
    definition of, 170
    early literacy development in, 185–186
    family of, 191–193
    inclusion of, 169, 171, 187–188
    legislation, 171–174
    parents of, 191–193
Children with special needs
    assessment of, 136
    assistive technologies for, 170, 184–186, 192,
        357, 373
    augmentative and alternative communication
        systems for, 185
    challenges to inclusion of, 187–188
    characteristics of, 222
    communication with parents of, 191–193
    developmental delays in, 174, 221, 373

developmental milestones in, 136
early childhood special education for, 220–222
early interventions for, 221
early literacy development in, 185–186
emotional development in, 308–309
family of, communication with, 191–193
full inclusion of, 169, 171, 184, 187–188
guidance techniques in, 246
historical events in education of, 172
inclusion of, 169, 171, 187–188
infants, 182
language disorders, 222
learning disabilities, 222
least restrictive environment for, 172
legislation, 171–174
mainstreaming of, 183, 187–188, 220
motor development delays in, 373
parents of, 191–194
physical development delays in, 373
play for, 277–278
positive behavior support for, 246–247
preschool programs for, 187, 221–222
problematic behaviors used by, 246
resources for families with, 193–194
school-age children, 182–183
social development in, 308–309
special education services for, 182–183
technology use with, 357
toddlers, 182
Children's Defense Fund, 74
Choices, as guidance techniques, 238–239, 242
Chronosystem, 102–103, 395–396
Circumplex family systems model, 398–399
Classical conditioning, 107
Classification, 95, 348
Classroom/classroom environment. *See also*
    Environment
    arrangement of, 258
    Bank Street, 64
    in Bank Street model, 64
    design of, 263–264
    diversity in, 13
    encouraging, 249
    equipment, 259–261
    guidance facilitation through, 248–249
    HighScope, 62–63
    in HighScope curriculum, 63
    illustration of, 263–264
    for infants, 258
    layout of, 263–264
    for learning, 259–267
    learning centers in, 259
    literacy promotion in, 330–334
    materials, 259–261, 330–332
    in Montessori program, 59
    multicultural education, 223
    peaceable, 249
    for play, 258–264
    for preschool, 258–259

print materials in, 331–332
in Reggio Emilia programs, 59, 61
responsive, 249
setting up, 262
technology in, 279
in Waldorf model, 66
Clinical interview method, 42, 88
Co-constructing knowledge, 59
Code of Ethical Conduct and Statement of
Commitment, 6
Code switching, 326–327
Cognition
emotional expression and, 291
language and, 126
Cognitive development
bilingualism and, 327
games for, 279
in infants, 433
play and, 268–269
theories of. *See* Cognitive development theory
in toddlers, 433
Cognitive development theory (Bruner), 49–50
Cognitive development theory (Piaget)
accommodation, 90–92, 276
adaptation, 90
assimilation, 90–92, 276
cognitive equilibrium, 90–92
concrete operations stage, 95, 123, 321
conventional knowledge, 90
description of, 42, 87–89, 122–123
diagram of, 89
formal operations stage, 95
limitations of, 96–97, 123–124
logico-mathematical knowledge, 90
physical knowledge, 89
play in, 276
preoperational stage, 93–96, 123, 291, 321
schemes, 88–89
sensorimotor stage, 92–93, 123, 321
social knowledge, 90
Vygotsky's sociocultural theory versus, 98
weaknesses in, 123–124
Cognitive equilibrium, 90–92
Cognitive maps, 66
Cognitive milestones
brain development, 121–122
developmental theory. *See* Cognitive
development theory
memory, 124–125
perceptual organization, 122
Cognitive researchers, 124
Cohabitation without marriage, 402
Cohesion, 399
Collaborative group work, 61
Collaborative learning, 100–101
Collectivist cultures, 296–297
College-affiliated programs, 72
Columbia Teachers College, 53
Comenius, John Amos, 33–34

Common Core State Standards, 354–355,
431–432
Communication
autism spectrum disorder children, 188–189
in family, 399
language used for, 126, 131
of limits, 238
with parents, 159–160, 191–193
play and, 271
Community engagement, 418
Competence, 5, 150, 156
Computer games, 279
Computers
educational use of, 356–357
media, 333
Concept formation, 350–351
Conceptual knowledge, 321
Concrete operations stage, of Piaget's cognitive
development theory, 95, 123, 321
Concrete supports, for social communication
skills development in autism spectrum
disorder children, 189
Concurrent validity, 159
Connecticut, 75
Conservation tasks, 94, 96
Consolidation stage, of early
childhood teachers, 11
Construct validity, 158–159
Constructive play, 268
Constructivist theory of learning, 42, 86–87
Constructivists
behaviorists versus, 289
cognitive development as viewed by, 87
Jean Piaget, 41–42, 87–96, 289, 346. *See also*
Piaget, Jean
Lev Semyonovich Vygotsky. *See* Vygotsky, Lev
Semyonovich
Content validity, 158–159
Contribution approach, to multicultural
curriculum, 212
Convention on the Rights of the Child, 133
Conventional knowledge, 90
Conversational skills, 157
Cooperative learning groups, 296
Cooperative play, 269–271
Coordinated movement, 119–120
Coparenting relationships, 407
Coparents, 405
COR. *See* Child observation record
Core competency standards, of National
Association for the Education of Young
Children, 19–20, 22
Cortisol, 131
Counting ability, 349
Creativity, 271–272
Credentialing, 16–17, 19
Creeping, 118
Criterion-referenced assessments, 149
Critical thinking, 85

Cross-modal perception, 122
Cultural awareness, 208–210
Cultural diversity, 207
Cultural pluralism, 207
Cultural sensitivity, 213
Culturally diverse family, 416–418
Culturally insensitive behavior, 210
Culture
    collectivist, 296–297
    definition of, 207
    Erikson's views on, 47
    ethnic identity influenced by, 216
    individualistic, 296–297
    knowledge learned through, 289
    learning about, 14, 217
    mathematics, science, and technology skills
        affected by, 358–359
    social competence learned from, 296–297
Curriculum
    antibias, 211
    Bank Street, 64
    emergent, 60
    HighScope, 61–63
    holidays inclusion in, 211
    language arts, 329–330
    mathematics, science, and technology,
        359–361
    multicultural, 209–212
    preschool, 332–334
Curriculum-based assessments, 153

Daniel R.R. v. State Board of Education,
    172, 188
Dark Ages, 30–31
Data collection, 352
Day care centers, 12
Decision making and social action approach, to
    multicutural curriculum, 212
Deferred imitation, 92
Delay gratification, 292
Demandingness, 294
Democratic life skills, 249
Dental care, 379–380
Denver II, 152
Depth perception, 371
Development
    Bronfenbrenner's bioecological
        theory of, 101–103
    cognitive. See Cognitive development
    community engagement in, 418
    definition of, 82
    emotional. See Emotional development
    enrichment strategies for promoting, 135
    factors that influence, 83
    fathers' effect on, 410
    genetics of, 82–83
    learning and, 84
    physical. See Physical development
    play and, 267–273, 278

sensoriperceptual, 371
    social. See Social development
    socioeconomic status and, correlation
        between, 407
Developmental contextualism model, 398–399
Developmental delays, 174, 221, 373
Developmental milestones
    arousal states, 115–116
    brain development. See Brain development
    cognition. See Cognitive milestones
    coordinated movement, 119–120
    friendships, 133–134
    in gifted and talented children, 135–136
    implications of, 134–136
    language. See Language development
    motor skills, 117–119, 271
    peer relationships, 133–134
    perceptual development, 120
    physical, 114–115
    psychosocial development, 133
    reflexes, 116–117
    self-help skills, 119–120
    in special-needs children, 136
Developmental stages, of early childhood
        teachers, 10–11
Developmentalists, 84
Developmentally appropriate principle, 3
Dewey, John, 43–44, 86
DIAL III, 152
Diana v. California State Board
    of Education, 172
Diary, 143–144
DIBELS. See Dynamic Indicators of Basic Early
    Literacy Skills
Differentiated curriculum, 191
Difficult temperament, 302
Direct instruction, 12
Direct monitoring, 293
Director, 18
Disability categories, 174–175
Discipline, 232. See also Guidance
Discovery, 261
Discussion of behavior and emotions, 232, 243
Disequilibrium, 90
Distraction, 242
Diverse learners, 7
Diversity
    cultural, 207
    emotional development affected by, 307–308
    social competence and, 297
    social development affected by, 307–308
    student, 13
    teacher, 14
    teaching affected by, 206
Divorce, 402–403, 407–408
DNA, 82–83
Doctorate in education, 19
Doctorate in philosophy, 19
Domain specificity, 124

prosocial behaviors, 304–305
resilience and, 309–311
theoretical perspectives on, 288–289
in toddlers, 433
"Emotional processing" portfolio, 149
Encouragement, 236
Encouraging classroom, 249
Engagement
active, in play, 273
community, 418
parental, in child's educational
experiences, 411–416
English immersion, 427, 436
English language learners
challenges for, 435
dual-language programs for, 435
education policies for, 424, 434–437
language disorder classification of, 222
in special education classes, 174
strategies for, 438
Structured English immersion for, 435–436
teachers for, 7
Enrichment, 191
Environment. See also Classroom/classroom
environment
assessments of, 161–162
in Bank Street model, 64
definition of, 258
evaluations of, 161–162
in HighScope curriculum, 63
for learning, 259–267
literacy promotion in, 330–334
in Montessori program, 59
multicultural education, 223
physical activity, 378
in Reggio Emilia programs, 59, 61
safe, 262, 266
in Waldorf model, 66
Environmental manipulations, 238–240
Environmental science, 353–354
Erasmus, 33
Erikson, Erik
description of, 46–47
photograph of, 103
psychosocial development theory of, 46–47,
103–105, 133, 289, 416
Ethics, 4, 6
Ethnic additive approach, to multicutural
curriculum, 212
Ethnic group
definition of, 216
parenting styles based on, 295
Ethnic identity, 215–216
Ethnic minorities
assessments for, 151–154
evaluations for, 151–154
immunization rates in, 379
motor development of, 373
physical development of, 373

poverty in, 373
in special education classes, 174–175
underrepresentation of, in gifted and
talented programs, 189
Ethnicity, 213, 216
Ethnocentrism, 208
European influences
on education, 32–35
on kindergarten movement, 50–51
Evaluation(s)
age of child and, 161
communication with parents and family
about, 159–160
concerns associated with, 158–162
definition of, 142
description of, 148–149
environment considerations, 161–162
for ethnic minorities, 151–154
formative, 149
performance-based tests, 158
psychometrics of, 158–159
reliability of, 158–159
research, 154, 156
special education referral, 177–178
standardized, 149, 151
summative, 149
teacher's knowledge about, 160
test bias issues, 160–161
types of, 149–151
validity of, 158–159
Even Start, 426–427, 444
Event sampling, 144, 146
Evoking behaviors, 238–239
Exosystems, 102–103, 395–396
Expectations, as guidance technique, 238
Exploratory activities, 332
Expressive language, 222
Expressive tones, 271
Extended family, 403
External speech, 324
Extinction, 68
Eye-hand coordination, 375

Face validity, 158–159
Facilitator role, 12
Family. See also Parent(s)
binuclear, 407
Bronfenbrenner's bioecological system of
development and, 394–396
of children who are gifted and talented, 191
of children with special needs, 191–193
communication, 159–160, 399
competent, 410–411
culturally sensitive engagement of, 416–418
demographics of, 401–402
diverse structure of, 401–402
dual-earner, 406
engagement in educational experiences, 413
evolving of, 394–405

Language
  beginnings of, 126
  cognition and, 126
  communication uses of, 126, 131
  competency in, 327
  concept formation and, 350–351
  expressive, 222
  Indo-European, 325
  learning of, 322
  mathematical teaching
      through, 351
  morphology, 320–321
  phonology, 321
  pragmatics, 322
  in preoperational stage of cognitive
      development, 94
  primary, 325, 327
  receptive, 222
  rules of, 320–322
  second, 325–327
  semantics, 321
  social interactions and, 324
  syntax, 321, 325
  teaching of, 334
  thinking and, 42
  verbal, 319
Language acquisition
  simultaneous, 325–326
  social interaction's role in, 324
  storybook reading for, 334
Language acquisition device, 323
Language arts
  curriculum for, 329–330
  skills for, 336
Language development
  adults' role in, 324
  behaviorist model of, 323
  books for, 129
  brain development and, 125–126
  conversational skills and, 157
  description of, 319
  exploratory activities for, 332
  grammar affected by, 128
  in infants, 126–128, 433
  interactionist model of, 324
  literacy development affected
      by, 129–130, 327–328
  milestones in, 127–128
  nativist model of, 323–324
  parental influence on, 324
  phases or stages of, 126–128
  play and, 267, 271
  pragmatics of, 322
  speech development after, 129
  storytelling secondary to, 130–131
  theories of, 323–324
  in toddlers, 433
  Vygotsky's views on, 324
Language disorder, 222

Language Instruction for Limited English
      Proficient and Immigrant Students, 434
Lanham Act, 72
Larry P. v. Riles, 172
Lateralization, 115
Lead exposure, 380–381
Learning
  behaviorist perspective of, 67
  collaborative, 100–101
  constructivist view of, 86–87
  definition of, 84
  development and, 84
  environments for, 259–267
  observational, 235
  operant, 234
  Piaget's views on, 88
  play used for, 277–278
  student-centered, 206
  technology used in, 357
  through modeling, 235, 239
  Vygotsky's beliefs about, 277
Learning centers, 259
Learning disabilities, 222
Learning Potential Assessment
      Device, 151
Learning theory. *See* Behaviorism
Least restrictive environment, 171
Leonard and Gertrude, 36
Lesbian parenting, 402–405
Lesson plans
  early childhood, 165, 199–200, 227,
      283, 315, 341, 365, 389
  early elementary, 166, 201–202, 228, 254,
      284–285, 316, 342, 366, 390
  infants, 164, 198, 226, 252, 281–282,
      314, 340, 363–364, 388
  preschool, 253
  toddlers, 164, 198, 226, 252, 281–282, 314,
      340, 363–364, 388
Lewin, Kurt, 84
Library materials and equipment, 260
Licensing, 19–20, 73–76
Life science, 352–353
Lighting, 262
Limits and choices, as guidance techniques,
      238–239, 242
Linguistally diverse family, 416–418
Linguistic intelligence, 190
Listening
  active, 232, 237, 243
  development of, 329
  materials and equipment for, 260
  types of, 329
Literacy
  art and, 331
  assistive technology used in development of,
      185–186
  content standards in, 24
  developmental age-based skills, 333

early development of, in children with special needs, 185–186
emergent, 328–330, 334, 336
family programs for, 337
language development influences on, 129–130
No Child Left Behind Act promotion of, 430
reading fluency and, 156
teaching of, 334
Literacy development
    activities for, 332–334
    children's books for, 334–335
    curriculum to support, 332–334
    emergent literacy, 328–330, 334, 336
    environment to support, 330–334
    factors that affect, 336
    language as foundation for, 129–130, 327–328
    learning materials and activities for, 332–334
    parental involvement in, 336
Local education agency, 424
Locus of control, 394
Logical consequences, 236, 239
Logical mathematical intelligence, 190
Logico-mathematical knowledge, 90
LPAD. *See* Learning Potential Assessment Device
Luther, Martin, 32–33

Macrosystems, 102–103, 395–396
Mainstreaming, of children with special needs, 183, 187–188, 220
Make-believe, 274, 276
Malaguzzi, Loris, 59
Malnutrition, 382
Manipulatives, 261, 348–349, 374
Mann, Mary Tyler Peabody, 51
Marriage, 401–402
Marxism, 42
Maslow, Abraham
description of, 47–48
hierarchy of human needs, 47–48, 104–107
Master teacher, 17–18
Master's degree, 18–19
Maternal employment, 406–407
Mathematical reasoning, 355
Mathematics, science, and technology.
    See also Science
    age-appropriate use, 356–357
    arithmetic, 349
    classification, 348
    common core standards of, 354–355
    computers, 356–357
    content standards in, 24
    cultural differences, 358–359
    curriculum for, 359–361
    data collection, 352
    development and, 346–347
    early childhood teacher knowledge and attitudes about, 355–356
    early exposure to, 347
    earth science, 353

environmental science, 353–354
fractions, 351
geometry, 349–350
health, 354
in kindergarten, 354
knowledge areas in, 351–354
life science, 352–353
measurement, 349
National Association for the Education of Young Children recommendations for, 359–361
number concepts, 349
number sense, 348, 350
nutrition, 354
parental involvement in, 357–358
patterning, 348
physical science, 353
programs for, 352
seriation, 348
skills in, 348–351
socioeconomic differences, 358–359
space science, 353
spatial concepts, 350
teaching of, 359–361
Maturational theory, 370
Maturity stage, of early childhood teachers, 11
McCarthy Scales of Children's Abilities, 152
McKinney-Vento Homeless Assistance Act, 444
McMillan, Margaret, 38–40, 69
McMillan, Rachel, 69
Measurement, 349
Memory development, 124–125
Mental health, 378–379
Mental structures, 88
Mesosystems, 102, 395
Metacognition, 84
Metacommunicative theory, of play, 276
Metalinguistic awareness, 271
Metamemory, 125
Microsystems, 102, 395–396
Middle Ages, 30–31
Middle childhood friendships, 134
Migrant education policies, 427
Milestones. *See* Developmental milestones
Mills v. Board of Education of the District of Columbia, 172
Minorities. *See* Ethnic minorities
Mitchell, Lucy Sprague, 44–45, 63
Modeling, 235, 239
Montessori, Maria, 40–41, 58
Montessori program, 58–59
Morphology, 320–321
Mothers
    attachment to, 294
    paraprofessional role of, 411
    social competence affected by, 293–294
Motivation
    behaviorists' views on, 67–68
    intrinsic, 5

Motor development
    description of, 372–373
    in infants, 433
    physical development and, integration
        of, 375–378
    space requirements for, 377
    in toddlers, 433
Motor skills, 117–119, 271
Movement, 374–375
Movement General Outcome Measurement, 156
Multicultural curriculum, 209–210
Multicultural education
    age to begin, 213
    approaches to, 212
    community involvement in, 219–220
    curriculum to support, 209–212
    definition of, 207–208
    environment to support, 223
    family involvement in, 217–220
    goals of, 209–210
    in infants, 213
    parental involvement in, 217–220
    program models for, 219–220
    promotion of, 223
    teacher preparation for, 210–211
Multicultural perspective
    cultural awareness, 208–210
    teaching from, 208–212
Multimodality, 371
Multiple intelligences theory, 61, 189–190
Musical intelligence, 190
Myelin sheaths, 114

Narrative descriptions, 144–145
National Assessment of Educational Progress
    (NAEP) Fluency Scale, 157
National Association for Gifted
    Children, 188, 191
National Association for Sport and Physical
    Education, 265, 375, 377
National Association for the Education of Young
    Children (NAEYC)
    accreditation from, 21
    assessments used to improve teaching, 158
    assistive technology position statement by, 184
    Code of Ethical Conduct and Statement of
        Commitment, 6
    core competency standards, 19–20, 22
    diversity recommendations, 15
    early childhood program standards of, 21
    family standards, 393
    history of, 46, 53
    holidays, 211
    intentional teaching, 156
    mathematics curriculum recommendations,
        359–360
    movement recommendations, 374
    observation guidelines, 142–143
    physical activity recommendations, 374

play standards, 257
    principles of, 75, 141
    science curriculum recommendations, 360
    standards of, 3, 19–21, 29, 57, 81, 113, 141,
        169–170, 205, 231, 238, 257, 287, 319,
        345, 369, 393, 424
    teaching levels, 16–17
    technology and, 356, 360–361
National Association of Early Childhood
    Specialists in the State Departments of
    Education (NAECS-SDE), 24
National Board of Professional Teaching
    Standards early childhood/generalist
    standards, 22–24
National Center on Response to
    Intervention, 179
National Child Care Information Center, 74
National Head Start Association, 70
National Institute for Early Education
    Research, 437
National Science Education Standards, 353
Nativist model, of language
    development, 323–324
Natural consequences, 236, 239
Naturalistic intelligence, 190
Naturalistic observation, 154–155
NCLB. See No Child Left Behind Act
Need for achievement and prestige, 106
Need for belonging and love, 106
Need for security and safety, 105–106
Need for self-actualization, 47–48, 106
Needs, hierarchy of, 47–48, 104–107
Needs addressing human survival, 104
Negative reinforcement, 67–68
Negative stereotypes, 308
Negotiation, 270–271
Neoconservative view of parenting, 408
Neo-Piagetians, 124, 126
Neurological maturation, 370
Neurons, 114–115
No Child Left Behind Act
    accountability under, 429
    adequate yearly progress, 429
    Blueprint for Reform, 441
    description of, 173–174, 188, 425, 428–429
    early literacy promotion, 430
    English immersion programs, 436
    English language learners under, 434
    Head Start programs affected by, 432
    provisions of, 429
    scientifically based reading instruction, 430
    scientifically based research, 429
    updating of, 440
Nonliteral behavior, 274
Nonprofit programs, 72
Nonreinforcement, 68
Nonshared environments, 400
Norm-referenced assessments, 149
Number concepts, 349

education of, 16–19
ethics and, 4, 6
facilitator role of, 12
in HighScope curriculum, 62–63
in individual education plan team, 180
instructor role of, 12
intrinsic motivation of, 5
knowledge and skills of, 22
in Montessori programs, 58–59
nurturer role of, 11–12
parents and, 14–15, 218
parent-teacher conferences, 413–414
personality of, 4–5
qualifications of, 434–435
reasons for becoming, 4
in Reggio Emilia programs, 60–61
requirements for becoming, 16–19
researcher role of, 61
retention of, 434
rewards of being, 7–8
as role model, 5
roles of, 11–15, 61, 206, 357
salary of, 9
self-awareness of, 4–5
shortage of, 8–10
teaching philosophy of, 6–7
turnover rate for, 9–10
in Waldorf model, 65–66
Teacher competencies, 22
Teacher-child relationship, 9
Teacher-devised tests, 158
Teacher-directed instruction, 206
Teacher's assistant, 18
Teaching
assessments used to improve, 156–158
as career choice, 8
child-centered, 45
diversity effects on, 206
intentional, 5, 7, 156
observations effect on, 148
philosophy of, 6–7
Team planning, 60
TeamS assessment model, 150
Technology
age-appropriate use of, 356–357
assistive, 170, 184–186, 192, 357, 373
in classrooms, 279
curriculum. See Mathematics, science, and technology
National Association for the Education of Young Children curriculum recommendations, 360–361
software, 360
Television, 347
Temperament
attachment and, 302–303
biological basis of, 302
difficult, 302
easy, 302

guidance methods and, 244–245
slow-to-warm-up, 302–303
styles of, 302–303
Temporary Assistance for Needy Families, 412, 442
Test bias, 160–161
Theory. See also specific theory
bioecological systems, 101–103
cognitive development. See Cognitive development theory
definition of, 84–85
guidance and, 233–237
infant's use of, 85
information processing, 97–98, 124
physical development, 370
on play, 274–277
uses of, 85
Theory theorists, 85
Thinking, language and, 42
Thirty Years' War, 33
Time sampling, 144
Time-in, 232, 244
Time-out, 232, 244
Title I, Education for the Disadvantaged, 426
Toddlers
biting by, 240
classroom environment for, 258, 332
fine motor skill development in, 332
guiding the behavior of, 240
peer relationships in, 134
physical activity guidelines for, 376
physical environment for, 258
play environment for, 262
racial awareness in, 214
with special needs, early intervention services for, 182
Tooth decay, 379–380
Touch sense, 120–121, 371
Touch-and-smell books, 335
Transcendentalism, 51
Transformation approach, to multicultural curriculum, 212
Trust versus mistrust stage, of psychosocial development, 47, 103, 105, 133
Turnover rate, 9–10
Tutorial intervention, 100
Twice exceptional learners, 188
Two-word utterances, 128

Uninvolved parenting style, 294–295
United States
demographic changes in, 13
kindergarten movement in, 51–53
poverty in, 412
progressive education contributors in, 43–50
Universal preschool, 439
Universal screenings, 179
University-affiliated programs, 72

Unstructured space, 377
U.S. Department of Agriculture nutrition
    guidelines, 382
U.S. Department of Health and Human Services
    nutrition guidelines, 382
U.S. House of Representatives Education and the
    Workforce Committee, 441
Utterances, 128

Vaccines, 379
Validity
    of assessments, 158–159
    of evaluations, 158–159
    of observations, 155
    types of, 158–159
Ventilation, 262
Verbal language, 319
Videotapes
    as communication tool with parents and
        family, 159
    as observational method, 147
Vision sense, 121, 371
Visual modeling strategy, for social
    communication skills development in
    autism spectrum disorder children, 189
Visually directed reaching, 117
Vocabulary
    development of, 157–158
    whole-word, 337
Vygotsky, Lev Semyonovich
    conceptual knowledge, 321
    constructivism, 42–43, 346–347
    description of, 42–43
    language development and, 324
    learning beliefs of, 277

play as viewed by, 266–267
sociocultural development theory of,
    42–43, 98–101, 277, 397

Walden Two, 108
Waldorf education, 65–66
Waldorf model, 65–66
Walking, 118
Watson, John B., 66, 106, 289. *See also*
    Behaviorism
Wechsler Intelligence Scale for Children, Fourth
    Edition, 153
Wechsler Preschool and Primary Scale of
    Intelligence, 153
Whaley's stages of infant-adult social play, 132
Whole-language approach, 336–337
Whole-word approach, 337
WISC-IV. *See* Wechsler Intelligence Scale for
    Children, Fourth Edition
Women
    Margaret McMillan, 38–40
    Maria Montessori, 40–41
Wordless books, 335
Working model, 85
World in Pictures, The, 34
WPPSI. *See* Wechsler Preschool and Primary
    Scale of Intelligence
Writing
    development of, 330
    materials and equipment for, 260, 330

Zero to Three National Center for Infants,
    Toddlers, and Families, 432
Zone of proximal development (ZPD),
    42, 98–100, 234, 266, 277

About the Authors

Dr. Kimberly A. Gordon Biddle

Dr. Kimberly A. Gordon Biddle has a double BA in psychology and music from the University of Redlands. She also has an EdS in program evaluation and a PhD in child and adolescent development from the Stanford University School of Education. She taught in various preschools as an assistant teacher as she worked while completing her years of higher education. She has more than 20 years' experience as a college professor and has numerous accomplishments and awards, including early childhood grants from First 5 Sacramento County. In terms of awards, she was an American Psychological Association MFP Fellow in graduate school and won her college's Outstanding Teaching Award at Sacramento State. She has written more than 15 publications and presented at more than 40 conferences. Some of her publications have appeared in the *Early Childhood Education Journal* and the *eJournal of Education Policy*. Conference presentations have been at the American Educational Research Association and the Head Start National Research Conference. Currently, she is a professor of child development at California State University, Sacramento, where she prepares students to teach young children.

Dr. Ana Garcia-Nevarez

Dr. Ana Garcia-Nevarez is the chair of the undergraduate studies division in the College of Education and a professor at California State University, Sacramento. She received a BA in psychology and child development from California State University, Northridge, and an MA in school psychology and a PhD in curriculum and instruction (emphasis in elementary education) from Arizona State University. She was a Regents' graduate academic scholar at Arizona State University. She has taught at California State University, Sacramento, since 2001. She has taught courses in cross-cultural child development, language and literacy development, curriculum and instruction, and research methods. Her research interest includes evaluating preservice teachers' attitudes toward diversity, civic engagement, and career development. Her research agenda has allowed her to be an active member in the preschool and elementary school community. Dr. Garcia-Nevarez is the author of several research articles and monographs. She regularly presents at national and international conferences.

Dr. Wanda Roundtree Henderson

Dr. Wanda Roundtree Henderson has been intimately involved in the design, implementation, execution, and evaluation of early childhood and family support programs within the New York City metropolitan area, in California, and throughout the country for approximately 30 years. In her current position as interim director of child development at the Sacramento City Unified School District, Dr. Roundtree Henderson provides fiduciary and programmatic oversight for the department, which serves approximately 3,000 children, from birth to age 12 years, and their families. Dr. Roundtree Henderson is a part-time adjunct lecturer at California State University, Sacramento, in the Department of Child Development. She has also served as a consultant/trainer and has accessed many educational platforms, forums, and instititions of higher education as a speaker and lecturer in the disciplines of early childhood education, psychology, and developmental psychology. Dr. Henderson is the recipient of many awards and recognitions for her scholastic achievements and work in the fields of early childhood education and family support. Dr. Henderson holds a BA in psychology and education from Hunter College of the City University of New York. She also holds a master's degree in developmental psychology, a master's of education, and a doctorate in early childhood education/curriculum and teaching from Teachers College, Columbia University, in New York City. She is married to Dr. Darryl Henderson, clinical psychologist and director of the Center for Counseling and Diagnostic Services at California State University, Sacramento.

Dr. Alicia Valero-Kerrick

Dr. Alicia Valero-Kerrick is a lecturer of child development at California State University, Sacramento. She received her PhD in education from the University of California, Davis. She also holds a double BA in psychology and Chicano studies from the University of California, Davis. Previously, she worked as a cohort instructor in the Early Development, Care and Education program at California State University, Sacramento. She also has worked as a bilingual school psychologist, an evaluation coordinator, a training coordinator, and a private educational consultant. Dr. Valero-Kerrick has experience with staff development and training for early childhood education teachers working with infants, toddlers, preschoolers, and kindergartners.

SAGE researchmethods

The essential online tool for researchers from the world's leading methods publisher

Find exactly what you are looking for, from basic explanations to advanced discussion

More content and new features added this year!

"I have never really seen anything like this product before, and I think it is really valuable."

John Creswell, University of Nebraska–Lincoln

Discover **Methods Lists**— methods readings suggested by other users

Watch video interviews with leading methodologists

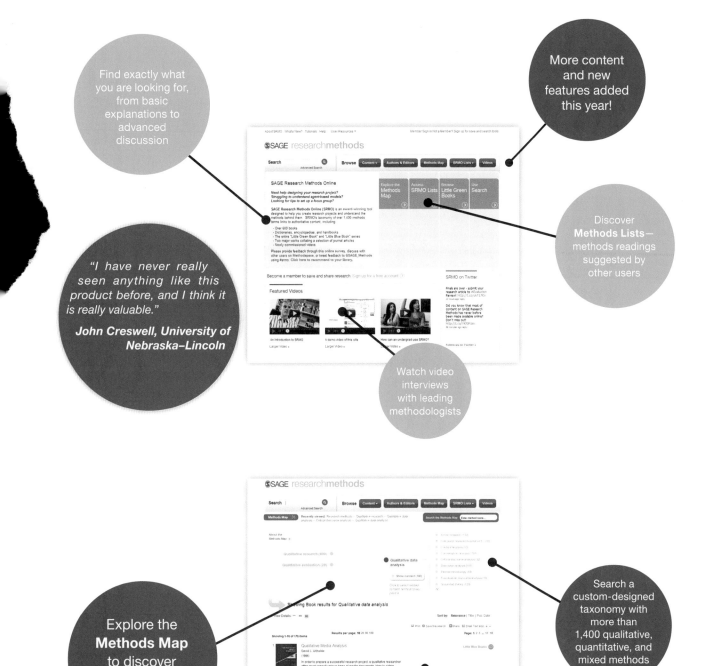

Explore the **Methods Map** to discover links between methods

Search a custom-designed taxonomy with more than 1,400 qualitative, quantitative, and mixed methods terms

Uncover more than 120,000 pages of book, journal, and reference content to support your learning

Find out more at
www.sageresearchmethods.com